Are We the Terminal Generation?

CHRISTINE TATE

This book belongs to: _____

ARE WE THE TERMINAL GENERATION?

Are We the Terminal Generation?

Copyright © 2019 by Christine Tate

All rights reserved. No part of this publication may be reproduced, stored in a retrieval system or transmitted in any form or by any means—for example, electronic, photocopy, recording—without the prior written permission of the publisher. The only exception is brief quotations in printed reviews.

Unless otherwise indicated, Scripture verses are taken from the New King James Version. Copyright © 1982 by Thomas Nelson, Inc. Used by permission. All rights reserved or are in the Public Domain.

ISBN-13: 978-1795166621

DEDICATION

This book is dedicated to persecuted Christians around the world and those who stand against the ways of the world in a sincere effort to glorify God and obey His commands. Christians everywhere are under greater and greater spiritual attack as the end draws near and Satan, desperately struggling in his fight to prevail against God, launches his final campaign against God's chosen people. Fear not, for we have read the end of the book and know that Satan's efforts are futile--God wins. The end.

I would also like to extend a special and heartfelt thank you to Ken and Jomel Smith, Melissa Crouse, Linda Palmer, Lorraine McCatty, Gretchen Kellas, Nancy Holowenko, and my husband, Rick Tate for faithfully supporting the development of this book through our weekly focus groups. Your opinions, insights and comments were invaluable. Also, I would like to thank Rosean Lindsey for an amazing cover. You are truly a talented graphic designer and I feel fortunate to be able to work with you on this project. To my husband, Rick, and my daughter, Tabitha, writing this book has been a long, involved process and you have been there for me through it all. Thank you for your patience and support. I could not have done this without either of you. God blessed me abundantly when He brought all of you into my life and I am eternally grateful for each and every one of you.

In Memoriam
To my Uncle Ronald Mix who passed on to rest in the Lord on the day this book was finished, I'll see you in the resurrection. Until then, sleep well.
7/27/1949 - 8/19/2019

CONTENTS

Using This Study Guide	6
Introduction	9
RELEVANCE	
Week 1: The Terminal Generation	11
THE PLAYERS	
Week 2: Mystery Babylon	28
Week 3: The Antichrist and False Prophet	48
Week 4: The Mark of the Beast	63
Week 5: The Seven Seals	74
Week 6: The Seven Trumpets	87
Week 7: The Seven Bowls	101
Week 8: Israel	118
Week 9: The Rebuilt Temple Part I	133
Week 10: The Rebuilt Temple Part II	152
Week 11: The Two Witnesses	169
THE TRIBULATION	
Week 12: Peace Agreement	184
Week 13: The New World Order	198
Week 14: Terrorism	211
Week 15: One World Religion	226
Week 16: The War of Ezekiel	254
Week 17: The War in Heaven	269
Week 18: The War of Armageddon	287
Week 19: The Restrainer	307
Week 20: Daniel's 70th Week	322
THE RAPTURE AND RETURN	
Week 21: Resurrection of the Dead	344
Week 22: God's Wrath	368
Week 23: Day of the Lord	386
LIFE WITH JESUS	
Week 24: The Millennial Reign and Beyond	415
THE TIMELINE	
Week 25: Putting It All Together	457
BONUS MATERIAL	
Checklist for Our World	479
Author's Interpretation of End Time Events	481
Study Tools	486
SOURCES	
Weeks 1-25	487

ARE WE THE TERMINAL GENERATION?

GROUP CONTACT INFORMATION

NAME	PHONE	EMAIL

USING THIS STUDY GUIDE

"Come now, and let us reason together," says the LORD. *Isaiah 1:18*

Your study and fellowship group should be a safe, loving, supportive environment to explore God's divine word guided by the power and leadership of the Holy Spirit. Before beginning this study, choose a group leader to coordinate and facilitate meetings. The group leader should make sure all group members are committed to following these ground rules at the first meeting:

- What is shared in the group, stays in the group!
- Be a good listener and an even better Christian friend.
- Be patient, kind, loving, and respectful of other group members.
- Always give Godly perspectives and advice.

After setting the expectations for the group:

- Have everyone write their name in the space provided at the beginning of this book.
- Then, everyone should pass their book around the circle and write their contact information in the books of the other group members using the Group Contact Information page at the beginning of this book.

This weekly study topically examines various prophetic concepts related to Christ's return in an effort to decode the puzzle of prophecy and reveal mysteries sealed until the end. Everything necessary to complete this study is provided in this book. Begin each weekly lesson with the provided **Opening Prayer** followed by the **Ice Breaker**. The leader should coordinate the activity so that everyone has a chance to participate and share their responses. Next, read the **Focus** statement aloud and continue on to the **Word Study** followed by the **Lesson**. Due to the length of some lessons, it may be helpful to take turns reading the selections in shorter pieces as you go around the circle. After reading the lesson, the group leader guides the group through a discussion in the **Talk It Out** section. Encourage the free exchange of ideas in an open format. The questions are designed to stimulate group interaction—tangents are encouraged! When the discussion questions are completed, read the **Ideas for the Week** section out loud as a group. Homework is never necessary or required for this study. These ideas serve merely as optional suggestions for ways individual group members can extend the study concepts into the week on their own if they desire. End the study session by reciting the **Closing Prayer.** Before starting the closing prayer, write down specific prayer requests for individual group members in the space provided. The leader should extemporaneously incorporate the prayer requests into the body of the prayer between the opening and closing prayer text. Additional **Supporting Scriptures** relating to the weekly lesson and a space for **Notes** are provided at the end of each chapter.

If you enjoy this study and would like to find other material written by Christine Tate or would like to be notified when new studies become available, please visit http://christinetate.webstarts.com. Feedback is also encouraged. I always love to hear how my Christian family enjoys and benefits from the studies. May God bless you, guide you and nurture you as you begin this journey of discovery!

AVAILABLE TITLES BY CHRISTINE TATE

Are We the Terminal Generation?

My Prayer Journal: Remembering God's Answers (4 covers to choose from)

The No-Homework Women's Bible Study: Group Hug

The No-Homework Women's Bible Study: Group Hug II

The No-Homework Women's Bible Study: Group Hug III

The No-Homework Women's Bible Study: Group Hug IV

The No-Homework Women's Bible Study: Group Hug V

The No-Homework Women's Bible Study: Group Hug Holidays

The No-Homework Women's Bible Study: Group Hug Marriage

COMING SOON!
(Expected releases in 2020)

The No-Homework Women's Bible Study: Group Hug VI

A Christian's Devotional for Surviving Divorce

Independence in the Suburbs

INTRODUCTION

Eschatology is the study of prophetic events preceding and including the time of Christ's return to earth. Since Christ has not yet returned, any discussion of end time prophecy can only be speculatively discussed at best and is open to a wide range of interpretation. Until an event occurs, proof of interpretation cannot be confirmed. Primarily a theoretical and intellectual pursuit, prophetic discussions are fun for everyone regardless of experience level or educational degree. Prophecy is best explored when approached with an open mind and a heart willing to listen to reason and analytical arguments. What is presented in this book is meant to stimulate conversations and the exchange of ideas. Some of the concepts explored may challenge you to think outside the box or re-examine what you thought you knew. As Isaiah 1:18 states, "Come, let us reason together." A healthy exchange of ideas spoken in a spirit of love pleases God. Opinions are welcome and encouraged! Prophecy, at its core, is a giant, wonderfully fascinating puzzle. Piece by piece, with careful consideration, everything eventually comes together to form what will ultimately be the tapestry of Jesus' return.

Prophecy regarding the time surrounding Christ's second coming has been sealed by God until the time is right as stated in the book of Daniel:

> [4] But you, Daniel, shut up the words, and **seal the book until the time of the end**... *Daniel 12:4*

If we are the Terminal Generation who is to see the return of Christ, we can expect to see the prophecies of the Bible unsealed and its mysteries revealed in our time. As the time draws near for the fulfillment of each prophecy, the correct interpretation slowly reveals itself to those for whom it is meant to be received. Because future prophecy is a sealed mystery, many times concrete answers are not possible. We can only read the clues given, apply them to our times and experiences, then engage in conversation with much speculation and conjecture as to what they might come to mean at some point in the future.

Events are cyclical in nature. In Ecclesiastes, God comments on the interrelated nature of both the past and the present:

> [9] **That which has been is what will be**, that which is done is what will be done, and there is nothing new under the sun. *Ecclesiastes 1:9*

An effective way to decode the future is to look to the past to discern what God has done and how He has worked through previous people, events and situations. That knowledge can then be projected forward to assist in unlocking information about the future. When working through prophetic interpretations, remember that scripture has both literal and spiritual interpretations and can have multiple meanings. Openly explore verses from a variety of different angles.

Searching out the truth about end time prophecy can be a fascinating and engaging adventure. Earthly clues and heavenly signs point in the direction of when and where we are to look for Jesus' return. In antiquity, wise men looked to the sky for signs of Jesus' first coming when He was born in human form:

> [9] When they heard the king, they departed; and behold, the **star** which they had seen in the east went before them, till it came and **stood over where the young Child was**. [10] When they saw the **star**, they rejoiced with exceedingly great joy. *Matthew 2:9-10*

Prior to Jesus' return, there will again be signs in the sun, moon and stars heralding the impending event:

> [30] And I will show **wonders in the heavens and in the earth**: Blood and fire and pillars of smoke. [31] The sun shall be turned into darkness, and the moon into blood, **before** the coming of the great and awesome **day of the LORD**. *Joel 2:30-31*

> [10] For the **stars** of heaven and their **constellations** will not give their light; the **sun** will be darkened in its going forth, and the **moon** will not cause its light to shine. *Isaiah 13:10*

> [12] I looked when He opened the sixth seal, and behold, there was a great **earthquake**; and the **sun** became black as sackcloth of hair, and the **moon** became like blood. [13] And the **stars** of heaven fell to the earth, as a fig tree drops its late figs when it is shaken by a mighty wind. [14] Then the **sky** receded as a scroll when it is rolled up, and every **mountain and island** was moved out of its place. *Revelation 6:12-14*

Just as the wise men were led by a star in the heavens, we too need to look for signs of Jesus' return: blood moons, comets, solar and lunar eclipses, earthquakes, political unrest, religious apostasy, terrorism, wars and disease just to name a few. The signs are all around us if we only stop to closely observe our world and our surroundings. My hope is that this book will be a helpful tool to guide you and your group on an enlightening, enriching and fruitful journey in your quest to answer the question, "Are we the Terminal Generation?". Let the discovery begin!

ELEVANCE

WEEK 1: THE TERMINAL GENERATION

Opening Prayer: Lord, we ask that You send Your Holy Spirit to us to guide us in the teaching and understanding of Your word that we may obtain a better understanding of the prophetic events surrounding us now and waiting for us in the future. Bless our fellowship in Your word that it may be fruitful and draw us into a deeper relationship both with You and those around us. Use us as Your vessels that through us, we may reflect Your glory to all whom we encounter. Illuminate our hearts and minds so that we may boldly shine the brightness of Your light everywhere we go and that we may be beacons of Your hope in a darkened world. In Jesus name we pray, Amen.

Ice Breaker: Codes can be an effective way to protect sensitive information. Government agencies and spies use code words to communicate information that is reserved for a select set of eyes. During World War II, the US Government effectively used the Navajo language as an unbreakable cypher to be able to privately communicate sensitive information without fear of it falling into enemy hands. In the animated children's series, *The Story Keepers*, Christians draw the symbol of a fish in the dirt to safely identify themselves to other Christians without revealing their spiritual beliefs to nearby Romans and other non-believers who would have them killed for their beliefs. In the next few minutes, think of a password or secret phrase that could be used to identify one member of the Terminal Generation to another member of the Terminal Generation. When you know your secret code, go around the circle and share your answer with the group. Be sure to explain what inspired you to choose the word or phrase you chose. When everyone has had a chance to share their selection, vote for everyone's favorite word or phrase.

Code word or phrase: _____

 Focus: If we are faithful to the end to Him, He will return the same faithfulness to us.

Word of the Week

> [1] But know this, that in the last days **perilous** times will come.
>
> *2 Timothy 3:1*

PERILOUS: Typically, when people think of the word "perilous", images of immediate danger leap to mind. Examples of perilous situations might include a soldier approaching a minefield in a combat zone or a young child about to dart into a busy thoroughfare. Derived from the Greek word "chalepos" (pronounced khal-ep-os'), "perilous" as used in this passage of scripture can also mean that something is hard to bear or hard to take. With ever increasing frequency, the stresses of modern life continually pile on with such unrelenting consistency that their combined magnitude becomes burdensome for the recipient. As the times of the end approach, Christians can expect the pressures of life to increase and make life appear unbearable at times. However, regardless of what life throws at us, our hope is in the Lord and He can always be counted on to help us bear our burdens.

Lesson: In the course of human history, there will be a generation of people who are alive when Christ returns to earth. This specific generation, which has yet to be definitively identified, is commonly referred to as the "Terminal Generation". Throughout the centuries, extensive debate has existed among various scholars as to the timing of Christ's return and which group of people will be the Terminal Generation. Complicating the issue is that we do not know when Jesus will return:

> [42] Watch therefore, for **you do not know what hour** your Lord is coming. *Matthew 24:42*

While we cannot know the exact hour of Christ's return, we are told in Matthew 24:33 that it is our responsibility to know when His return imminently approaches:

> [33] So you also, when you see all these things, **know that it is near**—at the doors! *Matthew 24:33*

Thankfully, God provides clues in His holy word to help us determine when that time is drawing near. Below is a list of scriptural markers for circumstances and events which apply to the generation which can legitimately call itself the Terminal Generation. Identifying characteristics that apply to the Terminal Generation are:

> Knowledge will be increased. *(Daniel 12:4)*
> The Gospel will be preached to all the world. *(Matthew 24:14)*
> There will be wars and rumors of war. *(Matthew 24:6)*
> There will be international turmoil. *(Matthew 24:7)*
> The sinful nature of people will prevail. *(Matthew 24:12-13)*
> Christians will turn away from their faith. *(1 Timothy 4:1)*
> Christians will be deceived about their faith. *(Matthew 24:11)*
> There will be false Christians. *(2 Timothy 3:5)*
> Christians will be persecuted. *(Matthew 24:9)*
> Christians will be hated. *(Matthew 24:9)*
> Christians will prophesy and have visions and dreams. *(Acts 2:17-18)*
> People will refuse to hear truth. *(2 Timothy 4:3-4)*
> People will deny that we are in the end times. *(2 Peter 3:3-4)*
> Life as we know it will appear normal and things will proceed as usual (i.e. people will be planning weddings, going out to eat, socializing, going to work, making doctor appointments, and going to school events among other things). *(Matthew 24:37-38)*
> The institution of marriage will be damaged to the point where women will find it hard to find a husband and will have to support themselves in the workforce. *(Isaiah 4:1)*
> Earthquakes will increase in varied and unusual places. *(Matthew 24:7)*
> There will be famines. *(Matthew 24:7)*
> Disease will increase. *(Matthew 24:7)*
> Offense, betrayal and hatred will abound. *(Matthew 24:10)*
> People will be cold, callous and hardhearted. *(Matt. 24:12, 2 Tim. 3:2-3)*
> Lawlessness will abound. *(Matthew 24:12)*
> False Christs will come claiming to be Jesus. *(Matthew 24:4-5)*
> False prophets will rise to lead the people astray. *(Matthew 24:11)*
> Dangerous times will exist. *(2 Timothy 3:1)*
> People will be selfish and self-absorbed. *(2 Timothy 3:2)*
> People will be greedy. *(2 Timothy 3:2)*
> People will be proud and boastful. *(2 Timothy 3:2)*
> People will take God's name in vain and offend God. *(2 Timothy 3:2)*
> Children will be disobedient. *(2 Timothy 3:2)*
> People will be ungrateful. *(2 Timothy 3:2)*
> People will be unrighteous and hate good. *(2 Timothy 3:2)*
> People will be unforgiving. *(2 Timothy 3:3)*
> People will be liars. *(2 Timothy 3:3)*

People will lack self-control. *(2 Timothy 3:3)*
People will be brutal. *(2 Timothy 3:3)*
People will be traitors. *(2 Timothy 3:3)*
People will be willful and stiff-necked. *(2 Timothy 3:3)*
People will be more concerned with pleasures than with God. *(2 Tim. 3:3)*
Israel will become a nation once again. *(Ezekiel 37:21)*
The Third temple in Jerusalem will be rebuilt. *(Isaiah 56:7)*
Terrorism will be a part of life. *(Leviticus 26:14-16)*
A seven-year peace treaty will be signed in the Middle East. *(Daniel 9:27)*
Two witnesses will be slain and rise from the dead while the whole world watches. *(Revelation 11:3,7 and 11)*
The identity of the Antichrist will be revealed. *(2 Thessalonians 2:3)*
The seven-year peace treaty with Israel will be broken. *(Daniel 9:27)*
Damascus, the world's oldest continually inhabited city in Syria, will be destroyed. *(Isaiah 17:1)*
The Antichrist will proclaim that he is God. *(2 Thessalonians 2:4)*
The Antichrist will reorganize the globe into ten world government regions. *(Revelation 17:10-18)*
The False Prophet will institute a new world religion. *(Revelation 13:12)*
The False Prophet, under the authority of the Antichrist, will control all commerce and force people to take the mark of the beast. *(Revelation 13:12,16)*
The resurrection of deceased believers and the accompanying rapture of living believers will occur. *(1 Thessalonians 4:16-17)*
Under the leadership of the Antichrist, the nations of the world will come against Jerusalem in the Battle of Armageddon. *(Zechariah 14:1-3)*
Jesus will return. *(Zechariah 14:4)*

DID YOU KNOW? In a 2010 Pew Research Center survey, 47% of U.S. Christians said they believed Jesus would return within the next 40 years.

Some of these markers exist today and are easily identifiable in our modern culture, yet other factors are still reserved by God and waiting to appear at some point in the future. In the book of Daniel, we are told the mystery of the end time period will only remain hidden until it is time to reveal the mystery to the end time generation, also known as the Terminal Generation:

> [4] But you, Daniel, shut up the words, and **seal the book until the time of the end**... *Daniel 12:4*

While the reveal may not be completed at this time, the unsealing of the book has definitely begun. Morality in our society is in a steady and unprecedented state of decline with wide variances in moral standards around the globe. Widely popular in the United States, mainstream movies such as *Fifty Shades of Grey* feature sexually explicit material to titillate the masses. Other countries, such as Malaysia, found the content of the movie so morally repugnant they banned the film. In sharp contrast, France took the morally suspect path of approving the movie for children as young as twelve years old. Decency standards are no longer entirely conservative or consistent in our world.

Violence is another harbinger of the last days before Jesus returns. In the book of Matthew, an analogy is made to the conditions on the earth at the time of Noah to the conditions on the earth just before Jesus returns:

> [37] But **as the days of Noah were**, so also will the coming of the Son of Man be. *Matthew 24:37*

To further Clarify the comparison, Genesis 6:10 states that "the earth was filled with violence":

> [10] And Noah begat three sons, Shem, Ham, and Japheth. [11] The earth also was corrupt before God, and **the earth was filled with violence.** *Genesis 6:5-8*

Sadly, violence is on the rise in our society. When one out of seven people do not feel safe in their place of work and every day more than three women in the United States are murdered by their romantic partner, something is inarguably wrong in our culture. Video games which routinely desensitize youth to wanton violence are commonplace in the United States and contribute to the overall problem.   South Korea, recognizing the value of minimizing their youth's exposure to violence have what is known as a "shutdown law" where no one under the age of sixteen can play a video game between the hours of midnight and 6 AM. Even unborn children are subjected to violence. In 2018, almost 42 million induced abortions were performed globally. That number of deaths is larger than the total number of deaths from cancer, malaria, smoking, HIV/AIDS, alcohol and traffic accidents combined. So many signs of societal degeneration are readily apparent if only we take the time to closely observe the world around us.

Other signs of the times are evident in the advancement of science and technology. Daniel states that there will be an increase of knowledge just prior to Christ's return:

> [4] ...many shall run to and fro, and **knowledge shall increase.**
> *Daniel 12:4*

Nowhere has there been such an explosion of knowledge as in the fields of science and technology. What was once considered science fiction just a few decades ago is now science fact. When Gene Roddenberry's *Star Trek* came out in the 1960's, it was considered inconceivable that doors would automatically open for people as they approach or that people could communicate with each other with the touch of a button. Fast forward to the present day and many retailers including all Target and Walmart stores have sensor doors that automatically open for customers. Preschool age children know how to operate iPads with ease. First graders carry cell phones to school. Availability and affordability of varied modes of transportation have made travel possible on a scale never before imagined. Our generation enjoys travel flexibility unlike that of previous generations. Cars, airplanes, trains and public transportation systems enable an unprecedented mobile society fulfilling the requirement that "many shall run to and fro". Scientific knowledge also aids in the interpretation of scripture. For example, Revelation states that everyone around the globe will watch when Jesus returns:

> [7] Behold, He is coming with clouds, and **every eye will see Him**, even they who pierced Him. *Revelation 1:7*

Before the invention of televisions, computers and cell phones, it would have been impossible for anyone to conceive of something happening in one place while people all around the globe watch the event simultaneously. Merely a century or two ago, a lack of understanding about global time zones would have rendered Matthew 24:42 a complete mystery:

> [42] Watch therefore, for you **do not know what hour** your Lord is coming. *Matthew 24:42*

Today, thanks to the interpretation of televangelist Jack Van Impe, we know this is not merely a figurative statement, but a literal fact. Since the Bible does not provide a common standard for time measurement (i.e. Greenwich Mean Time, Eastern Daylight Time, Central Daylight Time, etc.), it is a literal impossibility for anyone to determine a specific day or hour for Christ's return that is consistently recognized by all people living in different locales around the globe. Due to the international date line and the existence of twenty-four international time zones around the globe, it can be one date and time on one part of the earth while simultaneously being another date and time on another part of the earth. When it is December 31, 2019 at 8:00 PM in Hawaii, it is December 31, 2019 at 11:00 PM in California, January 1, 2020 at 1:00 AM in Indiana and January 1, 2020 at

2:00 AM in Virginia. Truly, pinpointing an exact time for Jesus' return is literally impossible.

Establishing relevance for the events of our day is significant to any discussion of end time prophecy. If the marker events are meant for another time and another people, then the study of end time prophecy is merely a point of curiosity for which there is no functional purpose in our day. However, if the events indicating the nearness of Christ's return apply to us, then delving into the study of end time prophecy gains new and relevant meaning for our lives. So, are we the Terminal Generation? Is time running out or is there still much more that needs to be revealed before Christ can return thereby making another generation the Terminal Generation? That is for God to know and us to search out.

Talk It Out

1. Do you believe we are the Terminal Generation Jesus spoke of in Matthew 24? Use the chart of events on pages 18-20 to evaluate the applicable factors identifying the Terminal Generation. Are the factors present today or are yet to manifest in the future?

2. How close, specifically, in terms of days, months, years or centuries, do you estimate we are to the time of Jesus' return? Why do you think God tells us no man can know the day or hour when Christ will come back, then turns around and commands us to know when Christ's return is near and imminent?

3. What signs have you seen reported in the media or are happening in your own life that could indicate that we are the Terminal Generation?

4. What factors do you think are contributing to the increase of violence and the general moral decay occurring in our society today? When do you think the trend of moral decay began? Has the trend been picking up speed as time goes on or is it in a steady, but consistent rate of decline?

5. Some events have not yet occurred that the Terminal Generation will witness such as watching two dead witnesses return to life on live television or seeing a particular event destroy the entire city of Damascus. If one day you witnessed those events, would it change your perspective on whether or not our generation is the Terminal Generation? Do you think scoffers would recognize the prophetic importance of those events and see things differently?

PRESENT OR FUTURE?

Instructions: Evaluate each factor with accompanying verse given below to determine if it is something that is occurring in our world today or if it is a point yet to happen at some time in the future. When you have made your decision, put an "X" in the appropriate box. Events that have obviously been on-going for a while or that have not yet occurred have already been marked for you. If you are unsure which column to mark, choose the column that best represents the closest match to what you observe in our world today. At the end of the list, add up the total number of X's you have for the "Today" column and the total number of X's you have for the "Future" column. Compare your totals with the rest of the group.

Factor	Verse	Today	Future
Knowledge will increase	Daniel 12:4		
Gospel preached to the whole world	Matthew 24:14		
Wars, Rumors of wars	Matthew 24:6	X	
International turmoil with nation against nation	Matthew 24:7	X	
Increase of wickedness and love growing cold	Matthew 24:12-13		
Christians will turn away from their faith	1 Timothy 4:1		
Christians will be deceived about their faith	Matthew 24:11		
False Christians will abound	2 Timothy 3:5		
Christians persecuted	Matthew 24:9	X	
Christians killed	Matthew 24:9	X	
Christians Hated by all nations	Matthew 24:9		
Christians will prophesy and have visions and dreams.	Acts 2:17-18		
People refuse to hear truth	2 Timothy 4:3-4		
Scoffers will deny they are the Terminal Generation	2 Peter 3:3-4		
Everyday life will be going on as usual	Matthew 24:37-38	X	

ARE WE THE TERMINAL GENERATION?

The institution of marriage will be damaged to the point where women will find it hard to find a husband and will have to support themselves	Isaiah 4:1		
Earthquakes	Matthew 24:7	X	
Famines	Matthew 24:7	X	
Pestilences	Matthew 24:7	X	
Offense, betrayal and hatred abound	Matthew 24:10		
People will be cold, callous and hard hearted	Matthew 24:12 2 Timothy 3:2-3		
Lawlessness will abound	Matthew 24:12		
False Messiahs	Matthew 24:4-5	X	
Rise of False Prophets	Matthew 24:11		
People will live in dangerous times	2 Timothy 3:1		
People will be selfish and self-absorbed	2 Timothy 3:2		
People will be greedy	2 Timothy 3:2		
People will be proud and boastful	2 Timothy 3:2		
People will take God's name in vain and offend God	2 Timothy 3:2		
Children will be disobedient	2 Timothy 3:2		
People will be ungrateful	2 Timothy 3:2		
People will be unrighteous and hate good	2 Timothy 3:2		
People will be unforgiving	2 Timothy 3:3		
People will be liars	2 Timothy 3:3		
People will lack self-control	2 Timothy 3:3		
People will be brutal	2 Timothy 3:3		
People will be traitors	2 Timothy 3:3		
People will be willful and stiff-necked	2 Timothy 3:3		
People will be more concerned with pleasures than with God	2 Timothy 3:3		

Israel becomes a nation again	Ezekiel 37:21	X	
Third temple in Jerusalem will be rebuilt	Isaiah 56:7		X
Terrorism will rise	Leviticus 26:14-16		
Antichrist makes a peace treaty	Daniel 9:27		X
Identity of Antichrist revealed	2 Thessalonians 2:3		X
Antichrist reorganizes the globe into ten world government regions.	Revelation 17:10-18		X
False Prophet institutes a new world religion.	Revelation 13:12		
Antichrist proclaims he is God	2 Thessalonians 2:4		X
Antichrist breaks peace treaty	Daniel 9:27		X
People forced to take the Mark of the Beast	Revelation 13:12,16		X
Damascus will be destroyed	Isaiah 17:1		X
Two witnesses are killed and rise from the dead while the world watches	Revelation 11:3, 7 and 11		X
The resurrection of deceased believers and the accompanying rapture of living believers will occur.	1 Thessalonians 4:16-17		X
Under the leadership of the Antichrist, the nations of the world will come against Jerusalem in the Battle of Armageddon.	Zechariah 14:1-3		X
Jesus will return.	Zechariah 14:4		X
Total X's			

Ideas for the Week:

- ✓ Ask three people you know this week if they think we are the Terminal Generation.
- ✓ Go through your local newspaper this week and see how many articles and headlines are a match for the identifying traits of the end times period.
- ✓ Read WND at www.wnd.com to experience current news events from a Christian perspective.
- ✓ Track earthquakes around the world at http://earthquaketrack.com/.

Closing Prayer

NOTE: Add names and individual personal prayer requests to the space provided below before closing in prayer.

Lord, we thank You for our time together today to grow deeper in our walk with You and fellowship with each other. As we close today, we lift up: _____

_____

_____

_____

_____

_____

_____

_____

_____

Father, we know that the time is drawing near for Jesus' return to earth. Although we do not know exactly when that will occur, we do know that You are giving us signs of the times. We ask You to open our eyes, ears and hearts so that we may clearly see the reality of the nearness of Jesus' return in everyday events around us. In Jesus' name we pray, Amen.

SUPPORTING SCRIPTURES

EXACT HOUR OF JESUS' RETURN UNKNOWN
^{42} Watch therefore, for you do not know what hour your Lord is coming. *Matthew 24:42*

COMMAND TO KNOW WHEN THE RETURN OF JESUS IS NEAR
^{25} See, I have told you beforehand...^{33} So you also, when you see all these things, know that it is near—at the doors! ^{34} Assuredly, I say to you, this generation will by no means pass away till all these things take place. ^{35} Heaven and earth will pass away, but My words will by no means pass away... *Matthew 24:25, 33-35*

FALSE CHRISTS
^{3} Now as He sat on the Mount of Olives, the disciples came to Him privately, saying, "Tell us, when will these things be? And what will be the sign of Your coming, and of the end of the age?" ^{4} And Jesus answered and said to them: "Take heed that no one deceives you. ^{5} For many will come in My name, saying, 'I am the Christ,' and will deceive many." *Matthew 24:3-5*

WARS AND RUMORS OF WAR
^{6} And you will hear of wars and rumors of wars. See that you are not troubled; for all these things must come to pass, but the end is not yet. *Matthew 24:6*

INTERNATIONAL TURMOIL
^{7} For nation will rise against nation, and kingdom against kingdom… *Matthew 24:7*

FAMINE, DISEASE AND EARTHQUAKES
^{7}…And there will be famines, pestilences, and earthquakes in various places. ^{8} All these are the beginning of sorrows. *Matthew 24:7-8*

CHRISTIANS OFFEND; ARE HATED AND PERSECUTED
^{9} Then they will deliver you up to tribulation and kill you, and you will be hated by all nations for My name's sake. ^{10} And then many will be offended, will betray one another, and will hate one another. *Matthew 24:9-10*

FALSE PROPHETS AND RELIGIOUS DECEPTION
^{11} Then many false prophets will rise up and deceive many. *Matthew 24:11*

^{23} Then if anyone says to you, 'Look, here is the Christ!' or 'There!' do not believe it. ^{24} For false Christs and false prophets will rise and show great signs and wonders to deceive, if possible, even the elect. *Matthew 24:23-24*

SIN, HATRED AND LAWLESSNESS PREVAIL
[12] And because lawlessness will abound, the love of many will grow cold. [13] But he who endures to the end shall be saved. *Matthew 24:12-13*

GOSPEL PREACHED
[14] And this gospel of the kingdom will be preached in all the world as a witness to all the nations, and then the end will come. *Matthew 24:14*

NORMAL APPEARANCE OF THINGS
[37] But as the days of Noah were, so also will the coming of the Son of Man be. [38] For as in the days before the flood, they were eating and drinking, marrying and giving in marriage, until the day that Noah entered the ark... *Matthew 24:37-38*

[26] And as it was in the days of Noah, so it will be also in the days of the Son of Man: [27] They ate, they drank, they married wives, they were given in marriage, until the day that Noah entered the ark, and the flood came and destroyed them all. [28] Likewise as it was also in the days of Lot: They ate, they drank, they bought, they sold, they planted, they built; [29] but on the day that Lot went out of Sodom it rained fire and brimstone from heaven and destroyed them all. [30] Even so will it be in the day when the Son of Man is revealed. *Luke 17:26-30*

VIOLENCE
[10] And Noah begat three sons, Shem, Ham, and Japheth. [11] The earth also was corrupt before God, and the earth was filled with violence. *Genesis 6:10-11*

MARRIAGE DIMINISHED AND WOMEN IN WORKFORCE
[1] And in that day seven women shall take hold of one man, saying, "We will eat our own food and wear our own apparel; only let us be called by your name, to take away our reproach." *Isaiah 4:1*

DANGER ABOUNDS
[1] But know this, that in the last days perilous times will come. *2 Timothy 3:1*

PEOPLE LACK GOOD QUALITIES; CHILDREN DISOBEDIENT
[2] For men will be lovers of themselves, lovers of money, boasters, proud, blasphemers, disobedient to parents, unthankful, unholy, [3] unloving, unforgiving, slanderers, without self-control, brutal, despisers of good, [4] traitors, headstrong, haughty, lovers of pleasure rather than lovers of God... *2 Timothy 3:2-3*

FALSE CHRISTIANS AND HYPOCRISY
...[5] having a form of godliness but denying its power. And from such people turn away! *2 Timothy 3:5*

KNOWLEDGE INCREASED
⁴ But you, Daniel, shut up the words, and seal the book until the time of the end; many shall run to and fro, and knowledge shall increase. *Daniel 12:4*

DENIAL OF END TIMES
³...knowing this first: that scoffers will come in the last days, walking according to their own lusts, ⁴ and saying, "Where is the promise of His coming? For since the fathers fell asleep, all things continue as they were from the beginning of creation. *2 Peter 3:3-4*

APOSTASY
¹ Now the Spirit expressly says that in latter times some will depart from the faith, giving heed to deceiving spirits and doctrines of demons... *1 Timothy 4:1*

TRUTH REFUSED
³ For the time will come when they will not endure sound doctrine, but according to their own desires, because they have itching ears, they will heap up for themselves teachers; ⁴ and they will turn their ears away from the truth, and be turned aside to fables. *2 Timothy 4:3-4*

PROPHECY, VISIONS AND DREAMS
¹⁷ And it shall come to pass in the last days, says God, that I will pour out of My Spirit on all flesh; your sons and your daughters shall prophesy, your young men shall see visions, your old men shall dream dreams. ¹⁸ And on My menservants and on My maidservants, I will pour out My Spirit in those days; and they shall prophesy. *Acts 2:17-18*

IDENTITY OF ANTICHRIST REVEALED
³ Let no one deceive you by any means; for that Day will not come unless the falling away comes first, and the man of sin is revealed, the son of perdition... *2 Thessalonians 2:3*

THIRD TEMPLE REBUILT
⁷ Even them I will bring to My holy mountain, and make them joyful in My house of prayer. Their burnt offerings and their sacrifices will be accepted on My altar; for My house shall be called a house of prayer for all nations. *Isaiah 56:7*

ANTICHRIST DECLARES HIMSELF GOD
...⁴ who opposes and exalts himself above all that is called God or that is worshiped, so that he sits as God in the temple of God, showing himself that he is God. *2 Thessalonians 2:4*

NEW WORLD ORDER

¹⁰ There are also seven kings. Five have fallen, one is, and the other has not yet come. And when he comes, he must continue a short time. ¹¹ The beast that was, and is not, is himself also the eighth, and is of the seven, and is going to perdition. ¹² "The ten horns which you saw are ten kings who have received no kingdom as yet, but they receive authority for one hour as kings with the beast. ¹³ These are of one mind, and they will give their power and authority to the beast. ¹⁴ These will make war with the Lamb, and the Lamb will overcome them, for He is Lord of lords and King of kings; and those who are with Him are called, chosen, and faithful." ¹⁵ Then he said to me, "The waters which you saw, where the harlot sits, are peoples, multitudes, nations, and tongues. ¹⁶ And the ten horns which you saw on the beast, these will hate the harlot, make her desolate and naked, eat her flesh and burn her with fire. ¹⁷ For God has put it into their hearts to fulfill His purpose, to be of one mind, and to give their kingdom to the beast, until the words of God are fulfilled. ¹⁸ And the woman whom you saw is that great city which reigns over the kings of the earth." *Revelation 17:10-18*

NEW WORLD RELIGION

¹² And he (the False Prophet) exercises all the authority of the first beast in his presence, and causes the earth and those who dwell in it to worship the first beast, whose deadly wound was healed. *Revelation 13:12*

ISRAEL A NATION AGAIN

²¹ Surely, I will take the children of Israel from among the nations, wherever they have gone, and will gather them from every side and bring them into their own land... *Ezekiel 37:21*

TERRORISM

¹⁴ But if you do not obey Me, and do not observe all these commandments, ¹⁵ and if you despise My statutes, or if your soul abhors My judgments, so that you do not perform all My commandments, but break My covenant, ¹⁶ I also will do this to you: I will even appoint terror over you... *Leviticus 26:14-16*

TWO WITNESSES SLAIN AND RESURRECTED

³ And I will give power to my two witnesses, and they will prophesy one thousand two hundred and sixty days, clothed in sackcloth...⁷ When they finish their testimony, the beast that ascends out of the bottomless pit will make war against them, overcome them, and kill them...¹¹ Now after the three-and-a-half days the breath of life from God entered them, and they stood on their feet, and great fear fell on those who saw them. *Revelation 11:3, 7 and 11*

MARK OF THE BEAST
¹² And he (the False Prophet) exercises all the authority of the first beast in his presence... ¹⁶ He causes all, both small and great, rich and poor, free and slave, to receive a mark on their right hand or on their foreheads... *Revelation 13:12,16*

MIDEAST PEACE TREATY SIGNED AND BROKEN
²⁷ Then he shall confirm a covenant with many for one week; but in the middle of the week He shall bring an end to sacrifice and offering. And on the wing of abominations shall be one who makes desolate, even until the consummation, which is determined, is poured out on the desolate. *Daniel 9:27*

DAMASCUS DESTROYED
¹ The burden against Damascus. Behold, Damascus will cease from being a city, and it will be a ruinous heap. *Isaiah 17:1*

RESURRECTION AND RAPTURE OF BELIEVERS
¹⁶ For the Lord Himself will descend from heaven with a shout, with the voice of an archangel, and with the trumpet of God. And the dead in Christ will rise first. ¹⁷ Then we who are alive and remain shall be caught up together with them in the clouds to meet the Lord in the air. And thus, we shall always be with the Lord. *1 Thessalonians 4:16-17*

ARMAGEDDON
¹ Behold, the day of the LORD is coming, and your spoil will be divided in your midst. ² For I will gather all the nations to battle against Jerusalem; the city shall be taken, the houses rifled, and the women ravished. Half of the city shall go into captivity, but the remnant of the people shall not be cut off from the city. ³ Then the LORD will go forth and fight against those nations, as He fights in the day of battle. *Zechariah 14:1-3*

JESUS RETURNS
⁴ And in that day His (Jesus') feet will stand on the Mount of Olives, which faces Jerusalem on the east. *Zechariah 14:4*

NOTES

"To err is human; to forgive, divine."
— Alexander Pope

THE PLAYERS

WEEK 2: MYSTERY BABYLON

Opening Prayer: Lord, we ask that You send Your Holy Spirit to us to guide us in the teaching and understanding of Your word that we may obtain a better understanding of the prophetic events surrounding us now and waiting for us in the future. Bless our fellowship in Your word that it may be fruitful and draw us into a deeper relationship both with You and those around us. Use us as Your vessels that through us, we may reflect Your glory to all whom we encounter. Illuminate our hearts and minds so that we may boldly shine the brightness of Your light everywhere we go and that we may be beacons of Your hope in a darkened world. In Jesus name we pray, Amen.

Ice Breaker: Everyone loves a good mystery. Think of a character from the Bible. In the space provided below, write three clues connected to who the character might be. Then, see if anyone can guess the character you have in mind.

Clue #1: _____

Clue #2: _____

Clue #3: _____

 Focus: God will reveal all mysteries when the time is right.

Hammurabi, king of Ancient Babylon from 1792 BC – 1758 BC, *is credited with creating the first Code of Law.*

Law #195: If a son strikes his father, his hands shall be hewn off.
Law #219: If a physician makes a large incision in the slave of a freed man, and kill him, he shall replace the slave with another slave.
Law #244: If any one hire an ox or an ass, and a lion kill it in the field, the loss is upon its owner.

– Code of Hammurabi

ARE WE THE TERMINAL GENERATION?

Word of the Week

> ⁴ The woman was arrayed in purple and scarlet, and adorned with gold and precious stones and pearls, having in her hand a golden cup full of abominations and the filthiness of her fornication. ⁵ And on her forehead a name was written: MYSTERY, BABYLON THE GREAT, THE MOTHER OF **HARLOTS** AND OF THE ABOMINATIONS OF THE EARTH...
>
> *Revelation 17:4-5*

HARLOT: While it is common to associate harlotry with lustful sexual immorality or the exchange of sexual favors for monetary gain, the word "harlot" in this passage comes from the Greek word "porne" (pronounced por'-nay) and can also be interpreted as a metaphor for being an idolatress. Considered in this alternate context, the harlotry of Mystery Babylon is simply a devotion to people, possessions or desires as a replacement for the supremacy of God in their lives. Many things can be considered idols: money, power, vanity, fame and even video games just to name a few. Simply put, anything that takes precedence over God is an idol. God loves us and wants to be our utmost priority. He wants us to love Him and make Him our heart's only desire. To do anything other than that is to invite God's displeasure which never ends well.

Lesson: The Bible refers to a cryptic place called Mystery Babylon:

> ⁴ The woman was arrayed in purple and scarlet, and adorned with gold and precious stones and pearls, having in her hand a golden cup full of abominations and the filthiness of her fornication. ⁵ And on her forehead a name was written: **MYSTERY, BABYLON THE GREAT**, THE MOTHER OF HARLOTS AND OF THE ABOMINATIONS OF THE EARTH...¹⁸ And the woman whom you saw is that great city which reigns over the kings of the earth. *Revelation 17:4-5,18*

Ancient Babylon, one of the first civilizations in existence, was a wealthy metropolis filled with learning and culture. It is also recognized for its moral debauchery. As described by the Greek writer Herodotus, every woman was required once in her life to have sex with a stranger in the temple of Aphrodite. Babylonian temples were set up as brothels believing that sex is a form of worship and thanksgiving to the gods of ancient Babylon. Prostituting a wife or child for financial gain was socially acceptable. Shame was non-existent as people would be seen having sex out in the open on rooftops and in the center of town. Homosexuality was openly embraced. Marriage markets provided opportunities for men to purchase wives with the most attractive women fetching the highest prices. Although a morally questionable society, the Babylonians had a highly evolved legal code. Punishments were harsh and based on the concept of an eye for an eye. Adultery was particularly frowned upon and the penalty was death by drowning for both of the guilty parties.

Some believe Mystery Babylon is a symbol for the rampant corruption prevalent during the end time era. Others believe Mystery Babylon is a religious organization which will be prominent during the period of time just before Christ returns. Another supposition for Mystery Babylon is that it is a veiled reference to an actual physical location which will be destroyed at some point during or just after the Tribulation. The Bible provides a comprehensive list of characteristics that define Mystery Babylon as follows:

> Mystery Babylon is an actual, physical place with land and a population of people who will be destroyed by foreign enemies. (*Revelation 17:4-5, 9 and 18; Jeremiah 50:9*)
>
> Mystery Babylon is regarded as military power which is the policeman of the world. (*Jeremiah 50:23*)
>
> Mystery Babylon is a wealthy nation which geographically touches many different bodies of water. (*Revelation 17:1, Jeremiah 51:13*)
>
> Mystery Babylon religious leaders are false prophets who lead the people astray. (*Jeremiah 50:6*)
>
> Mystery Babylon is a land of spoiled, complaining Christians who have turned their back on their faith. (*Jeremiah 50:11,14-15*)
>
> Mystery Babylon is a land of immigrants from many countries. (*Jeremiah 50:16, Revelation 17:15*)
>
> Mystery Babylon rebels against God and fights His ways. (*Jeremiah 50:24*)
>
> Mystery Babylon has problems with drought. (*Jeremiah 50:38*)

The peoples of Mystery Babylon have an abundance of idols that come before God. (*Jeremiah 50:38*)

Mystery Babylon is hated by Iran. (*Isaiah 13:17-20, Jeremiah 51:11*)

Mystery Babylon has a space program, flight capabilities or builds skyscrapers. (*Jeremiah 51:53*)

Mystery Babylon is the envy of the whole world. (*Jeremiah 51:41, Isaiah 47:5*)

Mystery Babylon has luxury products and is heavily involved in international trade. (*Revelation 18:3*)

Mystery Babylon oppresses the elderly. (*Isaiah 47:6*)

Mystery Babylon uses New Age techniques for prognostication. (*Isaiah 47:13*)

Mystery Babylon is an advanced culture with great knowledge which has made them excessively prideful. (*Isaiah 47:10*)

The inhabitants of Mystery Babylon possess a false sense of security and hold an "It can't happen to me" attitude while they are selfishly and ignorantly preoccupied with pleasure. (*Isaiah 47:8*)

Mystery Babylon is well-known and respected throughout the world. (*Revelation 18:9*)

Every kind of luxury imaginable can be found in Mystery Babylon. (*Revelation 18:11-13*)

Mystery Babylon has active deep water ports. (*Revelation 18:19*)

Mystery Babylon will be destroyed by missiles from a foreign enemy and rendered uninhabitable in one day. (*Jeremiah 50:39-40, Revelation 18:8*)

Since end time prophecies are sealed until the time of the end, the identity of Mystery Babylon has, to this point, remained elusive. If, however, we are currently living in the end times, the identity of Mystery Babylon will be fully revealed at some point in the relatively near future. As we explore the various possibilities as to the identity of Mystery Babylon, it is important to remember that for a thing to be true, all of the points must be true. A correct answer cannot be obtained by matching only a single part of an argument to its conclusion. Scripture also contains both spiritual and literal interpretations. If only a single interpretation applies, either spiritual or literal, then the interpretation cannot be correct. For an interpretation to be correct, the entire argument must match the conclusion and both spiritual and literal interpretations must be consistent with the position.

Many believe that the Roman Papacy is Mystery Babylon because of the reference to the fact that Mystery Babylon sits on seven hills:

> [9] Here is the mind which has wisdom: The seven heads are **seven mountains on which the woman sits**... [18] And the woman whom you saw is that great city which reigns over the kings of the earth. *Revelation 17:9 and 18*

Rome, the home of the Vatican, famously sits on seven hills. While this one point is an intriguing match for Mystery Babylon, this theory is problematic because many of the other identifying points given about Mystery Babylon do not fit equally as well. For example, Mystery Babylon oppresses and devalues the elderly which is contrary to the values held by the Catholic church.

> [6] On the **elderly** you laid your **yoke very heavily**. *Isaiah 47:6*

Mystery Babylon is also a military power that physically enforces justice around the globe:

> [23] How the **hammer of the whole earth** has been cut apart and broken! *Jeremiah 50:23*

The Vatican, which is located in Vatican City and is considered a separate country in its own right, does not have a military nor does it forcibly police the globe. Mystery Babylon is identified as a land that sits on many waters:

> [1] Come, I will show you the judgment of **the great harlot who sits on many waters**... *Revelation 17:1*

The Vatican is completely landlocked without touching any bodies of water. This contradicts the requirement for the borders of Mystery Babylon to come into contact with more than one body of water.

Others believe that the ancient city of Babylon in Iraq will be rebuilt and become a future world power again. This scenario is the least likely option because scripture says that once destroyed, ancient Babylon will never again be rebuilt:

> [19] And **Babylon**...[20] ...**will never be inhabited**, nor will it be settled from generation to generation... *Isaiah 13:19-20*

> [11]'And this whole land shall be a desolation and an astonishment, and these nations shall serve the king of Babylon seventy years. [12] Then it will come to pass, when seventy years are completed, that **I will punish the king of Babylon and that nation**, the land of the Chaldeans, for their iniquity,' says the LORD; '**and I will make it a perpetual desolation**.' *Jeremiah 25:9-12*

Mystery Babylon is described as a future, end time world power; not a past world power which God has already said will never rise again. Ancient Babylon is also located in Iraq which is mostly landlocked with the exception of a small border strip which connects to the Persian Gulf. Once again, this is not a consistent match for a location that sits on many waters and has deep water ports fit for large, seafaring trading vessels:

> [19] They threw dust on their heads and cried out, weeping and wailing, and saying, 'Alas, alas, that great city, in which **all who had ships on the sea became rich by her wealth!** For in one hour she is made desolate.' *Revelation 18:19*

Iraq consists of a relatively homogenous cultural composition. Mystery Babylon is a melting pot of immigrants from all over the world blending a variety of nationalities, cultures and languages:

> [15]...where the harlot sits, are **peoples, multitudes, nations, and tongues**. *Revelation 17:15*

As convenient as it would be to assign the identity of Mystery Babylon to Ancient Babylon, it is not scripturally accurate to do so.

Another prominent theory is that the United States is Mystery Babylon. There are those who say the Bible does not mention the United States at all in connection to end time prophecy. While it is true that the United States is not directly mentioned in regard to this topic, it is highly unlikely, if we truly are the Terminal Generation, that God would overlook one of the greatest superpowers of our age when it comes to prophetic events. The theory that the United States is Mystery Babylon exhibits interesting potential because America is a world superpower which geographically touches multiple bodies of water (the Pacific Ocean, the Atlantic Ocean and the Gulf of Mexico) while having an international reputation for using its military might to be the policeman of the globe. America is also a wealthy nation, a land of immigrants and the envy of the whole world. Coincidentally or not, the United States also has a famously contentious relationship with Iran aligning with the scriptural position that Iran hates Mystery Babylon:

> [17] ...I will stir up the **Medes (Iran) against them**... *Isaiah 13:17*

In addition, America also has many of the same signs of moral decay which are attributed to Mystery Babylon. Religious leaders of Mystery Babylon lead the people astray:

> [6] **My people** have been lost sheep. Their **shepherds have led them astray**... *Jeremiah 50:6*

The phrase "My people" indicates the main religion of Mystery Babylon is Christianity. Between name-it-and-claim-it theologies which relegate God to the status of an ATM machine and false doctrines that prioritize being happy over being righteous, many in America's pastoral leadership have failed in their duty to the flock. Many Christians themselves have become a poor reflection of God's virtues and values. Much like scripture describes the inhabitants of Mystery Babylon, America's Christian heritage erodes more and more with each passing day as Christians yield to the aggressive onslaught of liberalism which denies our Christian roots and seeks to erase our Christian heritage from our culture:

> [11] Because you were glad, because you rejoiced, **you destroyers of My heritage**, because you have grown fat like a heifer threshing grain, and you bellow like bulls...[14] For she has sinned against the LORD...[15] **Her foundations have fallen**... *Jeremiah 50:11, 14-15*

With Christian roots destroyed, Mystery Babylon no longer thrives. In place of Christianity, the inhabitants of Mystery Babylon embrace New Age philosophies instead of God's laws:

> [13] **Let now the astrologers**, the stargazers, and the monthly prognosticators stand up and **save you**. *Isaiah 47:13*

This can be seen in our culture today as the new generation coming up is more likely to read their daily horoscope than the Bible. In the 18-24 age range, an overwhelming 58% of Americans believe that astrology is scientific while a whopping 62% of non-Christian millennials have never read the Bible.

Representing Mystery Babylon is the symbolic reference to a woman holding a golden cup. Paralleling that symbolism, the iconic representation of America is the Statue of Liberty, a woman holding a cup that lights up and appears golden.

> **IT'S A FACT!** France gave the Statue of Liberty to America as a gift in 1886. The statue is 151 feet tall from base to torch. The full height, including the base and pedestal, is 305 feet tall. In 2016, 4.5 million people visited the Statue of Liberty.

In the biblical reference to Mystery Babylon in Revelation, the woman is described as a city with global regulatory significance:

> [18] And **the woman** whom you saw **is that great city which reigns over the kings of the earth**. *Revelation 17:18*

Coincidentally, the Statue of Liberty is located in New York City which also shares the significance of being the seat of the United Nations, a global regulatory body of government. New York also enjoys renown as an international center of trade. It can easily be said of New York that if you can't find it in New York, it doesn't exist. Opulent luxuries of all kinds are available throughout the city's borders which is again consistent with the criteria for the woman's identity:

> [3]...and the **merchants of the earth** have become rich through the **abundance of her luxury**." *Revelation 18:3*

Merchants trading in the treasures of New York enter through New York harbor. Of note is that on the way into the harbor, ships pass by an incorporated village in Long Island called Babylon, New York.

Interestingly, there is a unique symbolic similarity between the Statue of Liberty and the woman of Mystery Babylon. Both are connected to sexual immorality. The woman of Mystery Babylon is directly referred to as a harlot. When Edward Laboulaye first proposed the Statue of Liberty, he based the concept on the Roman goddess Libertas. Libertas was worshipped in the ancient world for her dedication to the ideals of freedom in all forms. Promoting the idea that people should do anything that feels good, Libertas also supported the wanton exercise of sexual freedom. Promiscuity is present in both the name of Mystery Babylon and the history of the Statue of Liberty.

Some believe the United States cannot be Mystery Babylon because, they say, America does not sit on seven hills. The answer to that objection may lie in the history of Washington D.C. Surprisingly, the District of Columbia sits on seven hills:

1. Capitol Hill
2. Meridian Hill
3. Floral Hills
4. Forest Hills
5. Hillbrook
6. Hillcrest
7. Knox Hill

Our nation's capital also has many other noteworthy connections to Rome, Italy, the city that sits on seven hills. Washington D.C.'s original name was Rome, Maryland. In the mid-1600's, much of the land in Washington D.C. was owned by a man named Francis Pope. Another connection to Rome can be seen in the impressive neoclassical architecture of the city echoing Greek and Roman influences. In more recent parallels, Washington D.C. also signed a sister city agreement with Rome, Italy on June 7, 2011.

When all is said and done, Mystery Babylon will be completely and utterly destroyed. Just as the ungodly Sodom and Gomorrah was destroyed by fire, so, too, will Mystery Babylon be destroyed by fire. Foretelling of a foreign enemy who sends airborne "arrows" to destroy Mystery Babylon by fire, the verses given in Jeremiah and Revelation closely resemble that of a nuclear war. Requiring only one hour to bring forth complete destruction, the land of Mystery Babylon is rendered entirely uninhabitable for multiple generations:

> [8] ...and she will be **utterly burned with fire**, for strong is the Lord God who judges her. *Revelation 18:8*

> [9] "For behold, I will raise and cause to come up against Babylon an assembly of great nations from the north country, and they shall array themselves against her; from there she shall be captured. Their **arrows** shall be like those of an expert warrior; **none shall return in vain**. [39] ...It shall be **inhabited no more forever**, nor shall it be dwelt in **from generation to generation**. [40] As God overthrew Sodom and Gomorrah and their neighbors," says the LORD, "So **no one shall reside there, nor son of man dwell in it**." *Jeremiah 50:9 and 39-40*

> [19] ...for in **one hour** she is made **desolate**. *Revelation 18:19*

Also consistent with a nuclear event is a verse which suggests a possible EMP (electromagnetic pulse):

> [37] A **sword** is against their horses, **against their chariots**...

Jeremiah 50:37

A sword is indicative of a weapon. When a nuclear bomb is detonated, it can generate an EMP which instantly shuts down everything electrical within a wide range. Since cars did not exist in biblical times, the closest approximation to a car would be a chariot representing a conveniently controlled mode of transportation made with metal and wheels. Most cars produced today have electrical systems and are vulnerable to such an event. An EMP could easily be considered the equivalent of a "sword" killing a "chariot". Without power for modern comforts or even the basic necessities of life, the many immigrants living in Mystery Babylon flee back to their own homelands:

> [16] ...**everyone shall turn to his own people**, and everyone shall **flee to his own land**. *Jeremiah 50:16*

> [9]Forsake her, and let us **go everyone to his own country**... *Jeremiah 51:9*

Because the destruction of Mystery Babylon will be so great, God warns His people to come "out of the midst" of Mystery Babylon lest they get caught in the crossfire of Mystery Babylon's punishments:

> [45] **My people, go out of the midst of her!** And let everyone deliver himself from the fierce anger of the LORD. *Jeremiah 51:45*

> [4] And I heard another voice from heaven saying, "**Come out of her, my people,** lest you share in her sins, and **lest you receive of her plagues**. *Revelation 18:45*

Ancient Babylon is known for being an advanced culture which was of dubious moral character. When God instructs His people to "come out" of Babylon, He is warning them of the price to be paid for participating in the sinfulness of the culture without repentance. Refusing to honor God in righteousness is guaranteed to come with a heavy price.

The Bible tells us that events are cyclical in nature and repeat themselves throughout history:

> [9] **That which has been is what will be**, that which is done is what will be done, and there is nothing new under the sun. *Ecclesiastes 1:9*

The ancient city of Babylon was destroyed because of its rebellion toward God and His ways. Likewise, Mystery Babylon will also be destroyed for similar reasons. It did not end well for the first Babylon and it will not end well for the future Mystery Babylon either.

Talk It Out

1. Do you believe Mystery Babylon is a symbolical concept representing societal corruption and decay, a literal, physical place that can be found someplace on the earth or both?

2. What do you think is the best fit for the identity of Mystery Babylon at this time (i.e. ancient Babylon rebuilt, the Roman Papacy, America or something else)? Are there any other countries, besides the United States, that you feel are a close match to the characteristics given for Mystery Babylon? Use the checklist on pages 40-41 to compare which characteristics of Mystery Babylon are a match for the United States of America. A global map is provided on page 42 to aid in the assessment of which countries touch on multiple bodies of water.

3. Do you believe the United States is mentioned in biblical end times prophecy in a veiled way? Why do you think God left all apparent references to the United States out of the Bible when it comes to biblical prophecy (i.e. the US will have fallen to an inconsequential position by the time end time prophecy is fulfilled, the US is such an integral part of end time prophecy that it was necessary to hide the identity and role of the US until the time for which it is to be revealed, the US did not exist at the time the prophecy was written or another reason)?

4. Do you think the city in Mystery Babylon which reigns over the kings of the earth and is destroyed in one-hour (Revelation 17:18 and Revelation 18:9-13) sounds like either New York or Washington D.C.?

5. If the United States is Mystery Babylon, what types of destructive forces could we expect to experience (economic destruction, nuclear war, EMP, foreign attack, disease, natural disaster, etc.)? Do you see any evidence of those forces lining up on the horizon as a possible reality right now?

6. How would a prudent person living in Mystery Babylon prepare for the destruction that will someday come upon Mystery Babylon? What does it mean when God warns people to "come out of her midst" (Jeremiah 51:45)? Is the warning meant as a literal instruction, a symbolic statement or both?

Ideas for the Week:

- ✓ Read Ronald Reagan's comparison of the United States and ancient Rome in his book, *Stories in His Own Hand: The Everyday Wisdom of Ronald Reagan,* pages 49-53.
- ✓ Research the connection between Rome as the city that sits on seven hills and Washington D.C. as the sister city to Rome that sits on seven hills.
- ✓ Look at a detailed map of the world. Identify all the countries that sit on many waters and still have the characteristics of Mystery Babylon.
- ✓ Ask your friends if they believe the United States is prophetically mentioned in the Bible.

Closing Prayer

NOTE: Add names and individual personal prayer requests to the space provided below before closing in prayer.

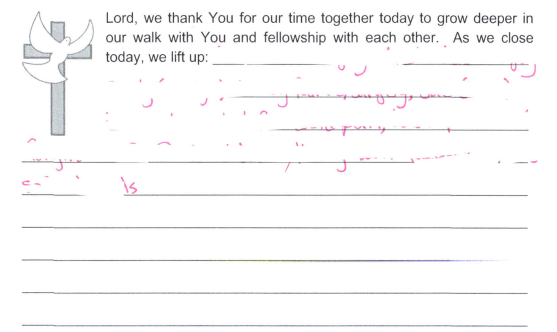

Lord, we thank You for our time together today to grow deeper in our walk with You and fellowship with each other. As we close today, we lift up: _____

Father, we know that You have preordained the end from the beginning and are in control of everything that happens. We trust that You will reveal to us that which we need to know at the appropriate time when we need to know it and will protect and prepare us as necessary for whatever may come our way. In Jesus' name we pray, Amen.

CHECKLIST

Check the "Yes" or "No" column for each characteristic given for Mystery Babylon based on whether or not you believe it applies to the United States of America. If you feel the characteristic can apply to other countries besides the United States, note which countries it might apply to in the "Other" column. If the characteristic does not apply to any other countries, leave the box blank.			

CHARACTERISTICS OF MYSTERY BABYLON	USA YES	USA NO	OTHER
Mystery Babylon is an actual, physical place with land and a population of people that will be destroyed by foreign enemies. (*Revelation 17:4-5, 9 and 18; Jeremiah 50:9*)			
Mystery Babylon is regarded as military power which is the policeman of the world. (*Jeremiah 50:23*)			
Mystery Babylon is a wealthy nation. (*Jeremiah 51:13*)			
Mystery Babylon geographically touches many different bodies of water. (*Revelation 17:1, Jeremiah 51:13*)			
Mystery Babylon religious leaders are false prophets who lead the people astray. (*Jeremiah 50:6*)			
Mystery Babylon is a land of spoiled, complaining Christians who have turned their back on their faith. (*Jeremiah 50:11, 14-15*)			
Mystery Babylon is a land of immigrants from many countries. (*Jeremiah 50:16, Revelation 17:15*)			
Mystery Babylon rebels against God and fights His ways. (*Jeremiah 50:24*)			
Mystery Babylon has problems with drought. (*Jeremiah 50:38*)			
The peoples of Mystery Babylon have many idols that come before God. (*Jeremiah 50:38*)			
Mystery Babylon is hated by Iran. (*Isaiah 13:17-20, Jeremiah 51:11*)			
Mystery Babylon has a space program, flight capabilities or builds skyscrapers. (*Jeremiah 51:53*)			
Mystery Babylon is the envy of the whole world. (*Jeremiah 51:41, Isaiah 47:5*)			
Mystery Babylon has luxury products and is heavily involved in international trade. (*Revelation 18:3*)			

ARE WE THE TERMINAL GENERATION?

CHARACTERISTICS OF MYSTERY BABYLON	USA YES	USA NO	OTHER
Mystery Babylon oppresses the elderly. (*Isaiah 47:6*)			
Mystery Babylon uses New Age techniques for prognostication. (*Isaiah 47:13*)			
Mystery Babylon is an advanced culture with great knowledge which has made them excessively prideful. (*Isaiah 47:10*)			
The inhabitants of Mystery Babylon possess a false sense of security and hold an "It can't happen to me" attitude while they are selfishly preoccupied with pleasure. (*Isaiah 47:8*)			
Mystery Babylon is well-known and respected throughout the world. (*Revelation 18:9*)			
Every kind of luxury imaginable can be found in Mystery Babylon. (*Revelation 18:11-13*)			
Mystery Babylon has active deep water ports. (*Revelation 18:19*)			
Mystery Babylon will be destroyed by missiles from a foreign enemy and rendered uninhabitable in one day. (*Jeremiah 50:39-40, Revelation 18:8*)			
Totals			

NOTE: In order for a country to be a possible match for Mystery Babylon, all of the characteristics must apply. If a characteristic does not apply in one category, the country in question must be dropped from consideration from that point forward.

OTHER COUNTRIES OF CONSIDERATION: _____

_____

_____

_____

_____

_____

Public Domain map provided courtesy of Ian Macky.

SUPPORTING SCRIPTURES

PHYSICAL PLACE WHICH WILL BE DESTROYED BY MISSILES FROM FOREIGN ENEMIES IN ONE DAY RENDERING IT UNINHABITABLE

[4] The woman was arrayed in purple and scarlet, and adorned with gold and precious stones and pearls, having in her hand a golden cup full of abominations and the filthiness of her fornication. [5] And on her forehead a name was written: MYSTERY, BABYLON THE GREAT, THE MOTHER OF HARLOTS AND OF THE ABOMINATIONS OF THE EARTH...[9] Here is the mind which has wisdom: The seven heads are seven mountains on which the woman sits... [18] And the woman whom you saw is that great city which reigns over the kings of the earth. *Revelation 17:4-5, 9, and 18*

[8] Therefore her plagues will come in one day—death and mourning and famine. And she will be utterly burned with fire, for strong is the Lord God who judges her. *Revelation 18:8*

[9] "For behold, I will raise and cause to come up against Babylon an assembly of great nations from the north country, and they shall array themselves against her; from there she shall be captured. Their arrows shall be like those of an expert warrior; none shall return in vain. [39] ...It shall be inhabited no more forever, nor shall it be dwelt in from generation to generation. [40] As God overthrew Sodom and Gomorrah and their neighbors," says the LORD, "So no one shall reside there, nor son of man dwell in it." *Jeremiah 50:9 and 39-40*

HATED BY IRAN

NOTE: A kingdom known as the Medes is mentioned in the scriptures given below. The kingdom of the Medes is modern day Iran.

[17] Behold, I will stir up the Medes against them... [18] also their bows will dash the young men to pieces, and they will have no pity on the fruit of the womb; their eye will not spare children. [19] And Babylon, the glory of kingdoms...will be as when God overthrew Sodom and Gomorrah. [20] It will never be inhabited, nor will it be settled from generation to generation... *Isaiah 13:17-20*

[11] Make the arrows bright! Gather the shields! The LORD has raised up the spirit of the kings of the Medes. For His plan is against Babylon to destroy it, because it is the vengeance of the LORD, the vengeance for His temple. *Jeremiah 51:11*

FALSE RELIGIOUS LEADERS

[6] My people have been lost sheep. Their shepherds have led them astray... *Jeremiah 50:6*

COMPLAINING, BACKSLIDDEN CHRISTIANS
11 Because you were glad, because you rejoiced, you destroyers of My heritage, because you have grown fat like a heifer threshing grain, and you bellow like bulls...*14* For she has sinned against the LORD...*15* Her foundations have fallen... *Jeremiah 50:11, 14-15*

LAND OF IMMIGRANTS
16 ... Everyone shall turn to his own people, and everyone shall flee to his own land. *Jeremiah 50:16*

15...where the harlot sits, are peoples, multitudes, nations, and tongues. *Revelation 17:15*

9 Forsake her, and let us go everyone to his own country... Jeremiah 51:9
37 A sword is against their horses, against their chariots, and against all the mixed peoples who are in her midst... *Jeremiah 50:37*

MILITARY POWER THAT POLICES THE WORLD
23 How the hammer of the whole earth has been cut apart and broken! *Jeremiah 50:23*

REBELS AGAINST GOD
24 ...you have contended against the LORD. *Jeremiah 50:24*

29 ...For she has been proud against the LORD... *Jeremiah 50:29*

DROUGHT AND IDOLS
38 A drought is against her waters, and they will be dried up. For it is the land of carved images, and they are insane with their idols. *Jeremiah 50:38*

SPACE PROGRAM, AIRPLANES OR HIGHRISES
53 Though Babylon were to mount up to heaven... *Jeremiah 51:53*

ENVY OF THE WHOLE WORLD
41 Oh, how the praise of the whole earth is seized! *Jeremiah 51:41*

5 For you shall no longer be called The Lady of Kingdoms. *Isaiah 47:5*

WEALTHY NATION SURROUNDED BY WATER
13 O you who dwell by many waters, abundant in treasures... *Jeremiah 51:13*

1 Come, I will show you the judgment of the great harlot who sits on many waters... *Revelation 17:1*

ENGAGES IN INTERNATIONAL TRADE
³...and the merchants of the earth have become rich through the abundance of her luxury." *Revelation 18:3*

OPPRESSES THE ELDERLY
⁶On the elderly you laid your yoke very heavily. *Isaiah 47:6*

ENGAGES IN NEW AGE PROGNOSTICATION
¹³ Let now the astrologers, the stargazers, and the monthly prognosticators stand up and save you. *Isaiah 47:13*

ADVANCED CULTURE WITH EXCESSIVE PRIDE; CONSUMED WITH PLEASURE AND A FALSE SENSE OF SECURITY
⁸ Therefore hear this now, you who are given to pleasures, who dwell securely, I shall not sit as a widow, nor shall I know the loss of children. *Isaiah 47:8*

¹⁰ ...your wisdom and your knowledge have warped you; and you have said in your heart, "I am, and there is no one else besides me." *Isaiah 47:10*

UNLIMITED LUXURIES
⁹ The kings of the earth who committed fornication and lived luxuriously with her will weep and lament for her, when they see the smoke of her burning, ¹⁰ standing at a distance for fear of her torment, saying, "Alas, alas, that great city Babylon, that mighty city! For in one hour your judgment has come." ¹¹ And the merchants of the earth will weep and mourn over her, for no one buys their merchandise anymore: ¹² merchandise of gold and silver, precious stones and pearls, fine linen and purple, silk and scarlet, every kind of citron wood, every kind of object of ivory, every kind of object of most precious wood, bronze, iron, and marble; ¹³ and cinnamon and incense, fragrant oil and frankincense, wine and oil, fine flour and wheat, cattle and sheep, horses and chariots, and bodies and souls of men. *Revelation 18:9-13*

ACTIVE DEEP WATER PORTS AND DESOLATION IN ONE HOUR
¹⁹ They threw dust on their heads and cried out, weeping and wailing, and saying, "Alas, alas, that great city, in which all who had ships on the sea became rich by her wealth! For in one hour she is made desolate." *Revelation 18:19*

CYCLICAL NATURE OF EVENTS
⁹ That which has been is what will be, that which is done is what will be done, and there is nothing new under the sun. *Ecclesiastes 1:9*

TO BE AVOIDED
⁴⁵ My people, go out of the midst of her! And let everyone deliver himself from

the fierce anger of the LORD. *Jeremiah 51:45*

[4] And I heard another voice from heaven saying, "Come out of her, my people, lest you share in her sins, and lest you receive of her plagues." *Revelation 18:4*

ANCIENT BABYLON NEVER TO BE INHABITED
[19] And Babylon...[20] ...will never be inhabited, nor will it be settled from generation to generation... *Isaiah 13:19-20*

[11] And this whole land shall be a desolation and an astonishment, and these nations shall serve the king of Babylon seventy years. [12] "Then it will come to pass, when seventy years are completed, that I will punish the king of Babylon and that nation, the land of the Chaldeans, for their iniquity," says the LORD; "and I will make it a perpetual desolation." *Jeremiah 25:9-12*

NOTES

Jeremiah 50 ~~profecy~~ prophecy is not about Christianity

"When the solution is simple, God is answering."
— Albert Einstein

WEEK 3: THE ANTICHRIST AND FALSE PROPHET

Opening Prayer: Lord, we ask that You send Your Holy Spirit to us to guide us in the teaching and understanding of Your word that we may obtain a better understanding of the prophetic events surrounding us now and waiting for us in the future. Bless our fellowship in Your word that it may be fruitful and draw us into a deeper relationship both with You and those around us. Use us as Your vessels that through us, we may reflect Your glory to all whom we encounter. Illuminate our hearts and minds so that we may boldly shine the brightness of Your light everywhere we go and that we may be beacons of Your hope in a darkened world. In Jesus name we pray, Amen.

Ice Breaker: For the game *Never Have I Ever*, each person holds up five fingers. Beginning with the person to the left of the group leader, go around the circle and have each person say one thing they have never done starting with the phrase "Never have I ever…". For example, someone could say "Never have I ever seen the movie *Titanic*." Then, everyone who has seen the movie *Titanic* puts one finger down. Moving on to the next person, proceed around the circle with each person sharing something they have never done. The winner is the person who ends the round with the most fingers still up. If there is a tie between two or more people, continue playing the game with only those who are still in the game until a clear winner can be determined.

 **Focus:** Regardless of who is against you, God is always for you and will prevail against the powers of darkness.

Inri Cristo, a religious leader in Brazil, claims he is the reincarnation of God's crucified Son, Jesus the Christ. The uneducated, self-proclaimed Messiah lives in a compound with his 12 disciples where he awaits the end of days.

— www.inricristo.org

Word of the Week

> ²³ And in the latter time of their kingdom, when the **transgressors** have reached their fullness, a king shall arise, having fierce features, who understands sinister schemes.
>
> *Daniel 8:23*

TRANSGRESSORS: As a marker of the end time season, the Antichrist will appear after "the transgressors have reached their fullness". Stemming from the Hebrew word "pasha" (pronounced paw-shah'), "transgressors" translates as "to rebel or revolt". The Antichrist cannot appear until those who would revolt have reached the pinnacle of their revolt. Over the last century, a social revolt against God and His laws has been progressing with the steady consistency of a train pushing on towards its final destination. Beginning in the 1920's, dress codes relaxed as young women called "flappers" rebelled against the decency standards of their day. They bobbed their hair, shortened their skirts and rejected the behavioral standards of their parents. Speakeasies emerged as people revolted against a ban on liquor. By the mid-1920's, movies began to influence thoughts and standards throughout society. In its infancy, cinematic offerings often times displayed dubious morality. The assault on the moral fabric of society prompted the film industry to create the Hayes commission in the 1930's to combat the effect it was having on society. Then, along came the 1960's when the sexual revolution introduced a new rebellion against the sexual purity required in God's law. Prayer was removed from schools. Abortion was legalized in the 1970's and by the 1990's, divorce rates and drug use were on the rise. Today, social media is more of an influence on many children than their parents, and the urbanization of America has created a tolerance for sin in an increasingly Godless culture. Non-biblical ways of life are at epic levels as many churches struggle to reach a new generation intent on pursuing whatever feels good. Evidence is solidly mounting that the revolt is reaching its pinnacle.

Lesson: Never have we ever seen the likes of The Antichrist who is to come before Christ returns. Throughout history, there are many individuals who have come in the spirit of the antichrist such as Nero and Hitler. Biblically speaking, an antichrist is anyone who denies the deity of Jesus as God's Son made incarnate on the earth to atone for the sins of mankind:

> ⁷ For many **deceivers** have gone out into the world who **do not confess Jesus Christ** as coming in the flesh. This is a deceiver and **an antichrist**. *2 John 1:7*

But there is only one Antichrist with a big "A" who will arise to dominate the world in the final days just before Jesus returns:

> ¹⁸ Little children, it is **the last hour**; and as you have heard that **the Antichrist is coming**, even now **many antichrists have come**, by which we know that it is the last hour. *1 John 2:18*

This abominable man will seek to imitate Jesus in every deceivable way possible while he serves Satan in place of God. People will scratch their heads in confusion, baffled at the changes the Antichrist will bring to our world. His intent is to change God's ways and usher in times such as have never been before:

> ²⁵ He (the Antichrist) shall...intend to **change times and law**. *Daniel 7:25*

He will be both feared and worshipped by those who cannot recognize the truth of the situation:

> ⁴ So **they** (non-Christians) **worshipped the dragon** (Satan) who gave authority to the beast; and they **worshiped the beast** (the Antichrist), saying, "Who is like the beast? Who is able to make war with him?" *Revelation 13:4*

Christians who can discern truth and choose to faithfully follow God at all costs will reap the wrath of the Antichrist:

> ⁷ It was granted to him (the Antichrist) to **make war with the saints and to overcome them**. *Revelation 13:7*

Ultimately, the Antichrist desires to replace God. He wants to be God and does everything can to prove that he is God:

> ³ ...and the man of sin is revealed, the son of perdition, ⁴ who opposes and **exalts himself above all that is called God** or that is worshiped, so that he sits as God in the temple of God, **showing himself that he is God**. *2 Thessalonians 2:3-4*

In his futile attempt to become God, he deceptively imitates Jesus by staging a resurrection:

> [3] And I saw one of his (the Antichrist) **heads** as if it had been **mortally wounded**, and **his deadly wound was healed**. And all the world marveled and followed the beast. *Revelation 13:3*

Fully backed by Satan, the Antichrist receives all of his power, wealth, authority prestige and success from the devil.

> [2] ...The **dragon** (Satan) **gave him his power**, his throne, and great authority. [7] ...And **authority was given him** over every tribe, tongue, and nation. *Revelation 13:2, 7*

> [24] His (the Antichrist) power shall be mighty, but **not by his own power**; he shall destroy fearfully, and **shall prosper and thrive**; he shall destroy the mighty, and also the holy people. *Daniel 8:24*

Backed by Satan's empowerment, the Antichrist triumphs at everything he undertakes. Yet, his tactics are deceitful and he cannot be trusted. Many suffer under his leadership as he leads them down a false path to their own detriment:

> [25] Through his cunning he shall cause **deceit to prosper** under his rule; and he shall exalt himself in his heart. He shall **destroy many in their prosperity**. *Daniel 8:25*

While we do not have a definitive answer at this time as to who this person might be, God has given us a number of clues to help us discern who the Antichrist could be when the time is right to recognize him. Based on what has been revealed about the Antichrist through God's word, we know the following about the Antichrist of the Tribulation:

> The Antichrist is male. *(2 Thessalonians 2:1-3)*

> The Antichrist has a physically intimidating appearance. *(Daniel 8:23)*

> The Antichrist is deceitfully charming and knows how to get his way. *(Daniel 8:25)*

> The Antichrist is a liar. *(Thessalonians 2:9-12)*

> The Antichrist is immune to the persuasions of women or other influences. *(Daniel 11:37)*

> The Antichrist is prideful. *(Daniel 11:37)*

The Antichrist does not worship any God because he claims to be God. *(2 Thessalonians 2:1-4)*

The Antichrist receives his wealth, power, authority and success directly from Satan. *(Revelation 13:1-2 and Daniel 8:24)*

The Antichrist speaks blasphemous things against God and His Kingdom. *(Revelation 13:6)*

The Antichrist is successful at everything. *(Daniel 8:9-12)*

The Antichrist has authority to rule over people and nations within a specific timeframe spanning exactly three-and-a-half years. *(Revelation 13:5)*

The Antichrist persecutes Christians. *(Daniel 7:25)*

The Antichrist destroys Christians. *(Daniel 8:24 and Revelation 13:7)*

The Antichrist changes both existing laws and the traditionally accepted ways that things have always been done. *(Daniel 7:25)*

The Antichrist prevails against even the mightiest of adversaries and successfully destroys them. *(Daniel 8:24)*

The Antichrist receives a wound to the head which kills him. He is then resurrected from the dead in imitation of Jesus, the true Christ, causing people to be amazed and follow him. *(Revelation 13:3)*

The Antichrist will make people feel helpless to go against him or do anything about what is happening. *(Revelation 13:4)*

The Antichrist enjoys the worship of non-Christians on a global scale. *(Revelation 13:8)*

Nicknames for The Antichrist are the "man of sin", "son of perdition" and "the lawless one". He is also symbolically referred to as "The Beast". *(2 Thessalonians 2:3, 8 and Revelation 13:2)*

The Antichrist is a flesh and blood human being. *(Revelation 13:18)*

The Antichrist is represented numerically by the number 666.

(Revelation 13:18)

The identity of the Antichrist cannot be known until "the restrainer" is removed. *(2 Thessalonians 2:7-8)*

The Antichrist can only be destroyed by God's hand and not by man's efforts. *(Daniel 8:25)*

Who gets your vote for Antichrist?
- ☐ George Soros
- ☐ Barack Obama
- ☐ Donald Trump
- ☐ Vladimir Putin
- ☐ Other_____

Believe it or not, the Antichrist has a friend and key supporter. This person is commonly referred to as the False Prophet. The Antichrist and False Prophet form an alliance wholly united in their goal of wreaking havoc on an unsuspecting and helpless world. Like the Antichrist, there have been many false prophets throughout history, but there is only one False Prophet who exists just prior to Christ's return and is linked with the Antichrist. This is what we know about the False Prophet:

The False Prophet is a subordinate partner of the Antichrist. *(Revelation 13:11)*

The False prophet is a religious leader who does the bidding of the Antichrist. *(Revelation 13:12)*

The False Prophet performs miracles. *(Revelation 13:13)*

The False Prophet compels people to make an image of the

Antichrist. *(Revelation 13:14)*

The False Prophet makes the image come to life and speak. *(Revelation 13:15)*

The False Prophet is responsible for the execution of those who refuse to worship the image of the Antichrist. *(Revelation 13:15)*

The False Prophet controls the economic system. *(Revelation 13:16-17)*

False prophets can be quite convincing which is why God tells us to test every spirit:

> [1] Beloved, **do not believe every spirit**, but **test the spirits**, whether they are of God; because many false prophets have gone out into the world. *1 John 4:1*

If ever a person claims to be a follower of God, but preaches a doctrine contrary to the scriptures, such a person is a false prophet and to be avoided at all costs. Foreshadowing that which is to come, some translations of the Bible have already been altered. Subtle translation changes set the stage for the False Prophet to step in and manipulate what the Bible says to align with his false agenda. Meanings are nudged from the original scriptures in sometimes fantastical ways. Other times, the nuances depersonalize the love of God. Compare the following examples from a Scofield Bible and a King James translation:

New Scofield Bible copyright 1967	*King James Bible* copyright 1996
Numbers 23:22	Numbers 23:22
God brought them out of Egypt; he hath, as it were, the strength of a **wild ox**.	God brought them out of Egypt; he hath as it were the strength of an **unicorn**.
Comment: A wild ox is an animal with which ancient people would legitimately have a working familiarity. A unicorn is a fictitious animal fancied by ancient pagan cultures such as the Greeks. Strong's Concordance translates the original Hebrew word as a "wild bull". To compare God's strength to that of a wild ox puts the analogy in terms most people can understand. It is commonly understood that oxen are exceptionally strong animals. Replacing the word with unicorn replaces the frame of reference for God's strength. Since no one has	

ever seen a unicorn, it is impossible to accurately assess their level of strength. Without a way to ascertain a unicorn's strength, it renders meaningless any comparison that might be made to it.

Exodus 13:12	Exodus 13:12
That thou shalt set apart unto the LORD all that openeth the **womb**, and every firstling that cometh of a beast which thou hast; the males shall be the LORD's.	That thou shalt set apart unto the LORD all that openeth the **matrix**, and every firstling that cometh of a beast which thou hast; the males shall be the LORD's.

Comment: To rename the womb a matrix dehumanizes the reproductive process and removes the inherent warmth of a mother's love. Strong's Concordance defines the original Hebrew word as a "womb".

Philippians 4:5	Philippians 4:5
Let your **moderation** be known unto all men.	Let your **moderation** be known unto all men. (KJV) Let your **forbearance** be known unto all men. (ASV) Let your **reasonableness** be known to everyone. (ESV) Let your **gentleness** be evident to all. (NIV and NKJV) Let your **modesty** be known to all men. (DRA) Let your **patient mind** be known unto all men. (GNV) Let everyone see that you are **unselfish and considerate** in all you do. (TLB) NOTE: This set of translation comparisons was taken from www.biblegateway.com.

Comment: While moderation, forbearance, reasonableness, gentleness, modesty, patience, unselfishness and considerateness are all admirable qualities, individually they each have distinctly different meanings and refer to completely different qualities. To be unselfish is not the same thing as to be gentle. Exercising patience is not comparable to being modest. By changing the terminology of the verse over many different translations, effectively a Tower of Babel situation is created where Christians essentially speak different languages with incongruent meanings even when reciting the same verse.

Matthew 9:17	Matthew 9:17
Neither do men put new wine into old **wineskins**, else the **wineskins** break and the wine runneth out, and the **wineskins** perish; but they put new wine into new **wineskins**, and both are preserved.	Neither do men put new wine into old **bottles**: else the **bottles** break, and the wine runneth out, and the **bottles** perish: but they put new wine into new **bottles**, and both are preserved.

Comment: Most concerning about this translation change is that Matthew 9:17 is a red-letter verse indicating Jesus' own words. Wineskins and bottles may both hold liquids, but they react differently to aging liquids. Wineskins break open as fermentation progresses and pressure increases. Bottles are sturdier than wineskins and can withstand higher pressures from aging liquids making it significantly more difficult for the bottles to break. The change in terminology alters the subtle nuance of the message for the verse.

Perhaps these changes are the beginning of a universal Bible which the False Prophet and Antichrist will use in the not too distant future to attempt to unite all of humanity under their single false religious system. Beware. In the digital age we live in, nothing can be taken for granted. Content can be controlled and altered at the touch of a keypad. Christians must read their Bibles for themselves and not rely on a religious leader to tell them what God says. Even after personally reading the Bible, due diligence must be exercised to be sure the correct meaning of the translation has been conveyed.

Nothing short of complete spiritual and global domination will be acceptable to the Antichrist and False Prophet. They will stop at nothing to bring all of humanity into subjection to their agenda. Seeking to change what has always been, nothing is safe from their unbridled passion to control all human behavior and spiritual choice. Together, their unholy drive to replace God's kingdom with a Satanic system proves to be almost unstoppable by human intervention. Almost is the key word. No one is more powerful than God. Ultimately, God intervenes to stop their raging path of destruction. Never truer words were spoken than, "No weapon formed against me will prosper." (Isaiah 54:17)

Talk It Out

1. Discuss various antichrists throughout history. Compare and contrast similarities and differences between those who have previously come in the spirit of antichrist and the single individual who will be known as The Antichrist.

2. Which translation of the Bible do you prefer to read? Why? Do you ever compare it with other translations? Do you know how to use a concordance? How often do you use it?

3. Do you believe the Antichrist is either an unknown person who is currently alive or someone who is yet to be born? Using the identifying characteristics of the Antichrist, is there anyone alive today who might fit the description of the end time Antichrist? Remember, in order to be the Antichrist, all of the characteristics must be a fit for the person.

4. Satan provides the Antichrist desirable earthly things such as wealth, power and success. Do you find it unusual that Satan, who is typically thought of as being the harbinger of evil in a person's life, is credited here as being the source of desirable things in the life of the Antichrist?

5. How would you define a false prophet? Can you think of anyone in our society today who you feel embodies the qualities of a false prophet?

6. Why do you think people are so willing to be deceived by the False Prophet?

7. Why do you think the Antichrist would need an alliance with the False Prophet if Satan has already given the Antichrist unlimited power and success?

8. In what ways does the Antichrist attempt to imitate Jesus?

9. How might the Antichrist think to "change times and seasons". Do you see any evidence of those changes happening in our world today?

10. What kind of an image could come to life and speak (Revelation 13:14-15)? Is it a hologram, a media image, a computer program, a robot, a supernatural instance of object possession, or something else?

Ideas for the Week:

- ✓ Look at pictures of living people you think might be a possible fit for the Antichrist. Ask yourself if any of them fit the "fierce countenance" requirement for the identity of the Antichrist.
- ✓ Research the theological beliefs of your favorite televangelist(s). Ask yourself if their actions and beliefs are consistent with the word of God or if they could be a false prophet.
- ✓ The number of the Beast (the Antichrist), 666, is derived from the study of Hebrew numerology known as Gematria. Visit the website www.gematrix.org to find out the numerical value of your own name. Type in other names you can think of to try to find a match for a name with a numerical value of 666.
- ✓ Visit the website www.hansonrobotics.com to see the amazingly lifelike innovations now available through modern robotics.

Closing Prayer

NOTE: Add names and individual personal prayer requests to the space provided below before closing in prayer.

Lord, we thank You for our time together today to grow deeper in our walk with You and fellowship with each other. As we close today, we lift up: _____

_____

_____

_____

_____

_____

Father, give us discernment to know those who truly come in Your name from those who are deceivers serving Satan. Give us strength to endure to the end regardless of what the enemy throws at us. When those around us persecute us for no reason, comfort our heavy hearts and use Your guiding light to show us the way forward. We are devoted to You and only You. In Jesus' name we pray, Amen.

SUPPORTING SCRIPTURES

DEFINITION OF ANTICHRIST

⁷ For many deceivers have gone out into the world who do not confess Jesus Christ as coming in the flesh. This is a deceiver and an antichrist. *2 John 1:7*

¹⁸ Little children, it is the last hour; and as you have heard that the Antichrist is coming, even now many antichrists have come, by which we know that it is the last hour. ¹⁹ They went out from us, but they were not of us; for if they had been of us, they would have continued with us; but they went out that they might be made manifest, that none of them were of us. ²⁰ But you have an anointing from the Holy One, and you know all things. ²¹ I have not written to you because you do not know the truth, but because you know it, and that no lie is of the truth. ²² Who is a liar but he who denies that Jesus is the Christ? He is antichrist who denies the Father and the Son. 1 John 2:18-22

ANTICHRIST IS MALE; CLAIMS TO BE GOD; HAS NICKNAMES

¹ Now, brethren, concerning the coming of our Lord Jesus Christ and our gathering together to Him, we ask you, ² not to be soon shaken in mind or troubled, either by spirit or by word or by letter, as if from us, as though the day of Christ had come. ³ Let no one deceive you by any means; for that Day will not come unless the falling away comes first, and the man of sin is revealed, the son of perdition, ⁴ who opposes and exalts himself above all that is called God or that is worshiped, so that he sits as God in the temple of God, showing himself that he is God. *2 Thessalonians 2:1-4*

ANTICHRIST IS CHARMING WITH INTIMIDATING APPEARANCE; DESTROYED BY GOD

²³ And in the latter time of their kingdom, when the transgressors have reached their fullness, a king shall arise, having fierce features, who understands sinister schemes. ²⁴ His power shall be mighty, but not by his own power; he shall destroy fearfully, and shall prosper and thrive; he shall destroy the mighty, and also the holy people. ²⁵ Through his cunning he shall cause deceit to prosper under his rule; and he shall exalt himself in his heart. He shall destroy many in their prosperity. He shall even rise against the Prince of princes; but he shall be broken without human means. *Daniel 8:23-25*

ANTICHRIST IS A LIAR; HAS NICKNAMES; REVEALED AFTER "RESTRAINER" IS REMOVED

⁷ For the mystery of lawlessness is already at work; only He who now restrains will do so until He is taken out of the way. ⁸ And then the lawless one will be revealed, whom the Lord will consume with the breath of His mouth and destroy with the brightness of His coming. ⁹ The coming of the lawless one is according

to the working of Satan, with all power, signs, and lying wonders, [10] and with all unrighteous deception among those who perish, because they did not receive the love of the truth, that they might be saved. [11] And for this reason God will send them strong delusion, that they should believe the lie, [12] that they all may be condemned who did not believe the truth but had pleasure in unrighteousness. *2 Thessalonians 2:7-12*

ANTICHRIST IS PRIDEFUL; NOT EASILY INFLUENCED
[37] He shall regard neither the God of his fathers nor the desire of women, nor regard any god; for he shall exalt himself above them all. *Daniel 11:37*

ANTICHRIST IS EMPOWERED BY SATAN; BLASPHEMOUS; HAS AUTHORITY TO RULE; DESTROYS CHRISTIANS; IMITATES CHRIST; PEOPLE HELPLESS AGAINST HIM; HAS NICKNAMES
[1] Then I stood on the sand of the sea. And I saw a beast rising up out of the sea, having seven heads and ten horns, and on his horns ten crowns, and on his heads a blasphemous name. [2] Now the beast which I saw was like a leopard, his feet were like the feet of a bear, and his mouth like the mouth of a lion. The dragon gave him his power, his throne, and great authority. [3] And I saw one of his heads as if it had been mortally wounded, and his deadly wound was healed. And all the world marveled and followed the beast. [4] So they worshipped the dragon who gave authority to the beast; and they worshiped the beast, saying, "Who is like the beast? Who is able to make war with him?" [5] And he was given a mouth speaking great things and blasphemies, and he was given authority to continue for forty-two months. [6] Then he opened his mouth in blasphemy against God, to blaspheme His name, His tabernacle, and those who dwell in heaven. [7] It was granted to him to make war with the saints and to overcome them. And authority was given him over every tribe, tongue, and nation. *Revelation 13:1-7*

[24] His power shall be mighty, but not by his own power; he shall destroy fearfully, and shall prosper and thrive; he shall destroy the mighty, and also the holy people. *Daniel 8:24*

ANTICHRIST PARTNERSHIP WITH FALSE PROPHET; MORTAL MAN REPRESENTED BY NUMBER 666; FALSE PROPHET PERFORMS MIRACLES; CONTROLS ECONOMIC SYSTEM, MAKES IMAGE OF THE BEAST; PEOPLE MUST ACCEPT MARK OF THE BEAST AND WORSHIP ANTICHRIST OR BE KILLED
[11] Then I saw another beast coming up out of the earth, and he had two horns like a lamb and spoke like a dragon. [12] And he exercises all the authority of the first beast in his presence, and causes the earth and those who dwell in it to worship the first beast, whose deadly wound was healed. [13] He performs great signs, so that he even makes fire come down from heaven on the earth in the

sight of men. ¹⁴ And he deceives those who dwell on the earth by those signs which he was granted to do in the sight of the beast, telling those who dwell on the earth to make an image to the beast who was wounded by the sword and lived. ¹⁵ He was granted power to give breath to the image of the beast, that the image of the beast should both speak and cause as many as would not worship the image of the beast to be killed. ¹⁶ He causes all, both small and great, rich and poor, free and slave, to receive a mark on their right hand or on their foreheads, ¹⁷ and that no one may buy or sell except one who has the mark or the name of the beast, or the number of his name. *Revelation 13:11-17*

NUMBER IS 666

¹⁸ Here is wisdom. Let him who has understanding calculate the number of the beast, for it is the number of a man: his number is 666. *Revelation 13:18*

ANTICHRIST IS SUCCESSFUL

⁹ And out of one of them came a little horn which grew exceedingly great toward the south, toward the east, and toward the Glorious Land. ¹⁰ And it grew up to the host of heaven; and it cast down some of the host and some of the stars to the ground, and trampled them. ¹¹ He even exalted himself as high as the Prince of the host; and by him the daily sacrifices were taken away, and the place of His sanctuary was cast down. ¹² Because of transgression, an army was given over to the horn to oppose the daily sacrifices; and he cast truth down to the ground. He did all this and prospered. *Daniel 8:9-12*

ANTICHRIST PERSECUTES CHRISTIANS; CHANGES LAWS

²⁵ He shall speak pompous words against the Most High, shall persecute the saints of the Most High, and shall intend to change times and law. Then the saints shall be given into his hand for a time and times and half a time. *Daniel 7:25*

ANTICHRIST IS WORSHIPPED BY NON-CHRISTIANS

⁸ All who dwell on the earth will worship him, whose names have not been written in the Book of Life of the Lamb slain from the foundation of the world. *Revelation 13:8*

TEST THE PROPHETS

¹ Beloved, do not believe every spirit, but test the spirits, whether they are of God; because many false prophets have gone out into the world. *1 John 4:1*

GOD'S PROTECTION

¹⁷ No weapon formed against you shall prosper, and every tongue which rises against you in judgment You shall condemn. This is the heritage of the servants of the LORD, and their righteousness is from Me," says the LORD. *Isaiah 54:17*

NOTES

"People see God every day. They just don't recognize Him."
— Pearl Bailey

WEEK 4: THE MARK OF THE BEAST

Opening Prayer: Lord, we ask that You send Your Holy Spirit to us to guide us in the teaching and understanding of Your word that we may obtain a better understanding of the prophetic events surrounding us now and waiting for us in the future. Bless our fellowship in Your word that it may be fruitful and draw us into a deeper relationship both with You and those around us. Use us as Your vessels that through us, we may reflect Your glory to all whom we encounter. Illuminate our hearts and minds so that we may boldly shine the brightness of Your light everywhere we go and that we may be beacons of Your hope in a darkened world. In Jesus name we pray, Amen.

Ice Breaker: Have someone in the group take out a dollar bill (any denomination will do). Hold the bill vertically with your fingers on the short edge of the bill so that it is dangling down. Turn to the person on your right and have them hold one of their hands as if they are forming the letter "C" with their thumb and forefinger. Their thumb and forefinger should be about two inches apart:

Have the person cup their thumb and forefinger around the center of the bill without actually touching it. Their thumb and forefinger should be about even with the center of the bill. Hold the bill equidistantly between their fingers. Their hand should not be in contact with the bill. Next, without telling them when, drop the bill and have them try to catch the bill by closing their thumb and forefinger as soon as they see the bill start to drop. Repeat the process going around the circle so that everyone has a chance to try to catch the bill.

 **Focus:** God will always give you the strength to resist that which is against His will for your life if you pursue righteousness.

CHRISTINE TATE

Word of the Week

> ⁶ And these words which I command you today shall be in your heart...
> ⁸ You shall bind them as a sign on your hand, and they shall be as **frontlets** between your eyes.
>
> *Deuteronomy 6:6,8*

FRONTLETS: Although "frontlet" is not a word that is typically used in modern conversational language, it provides an apt analogy for how we are to retain the word of God. Originating from the Hebrew word "towphaphah" (pronounced to-faw-faw'), frontlets are the equivalent of a band or a mark. More specifically, "towphaphah" is also translated as a phylactery. A phylactery is a symbol of God's word that is physically worn by Orthodox Jewish men. The small, leather boxes they wear contain written passages of scripture. Traditionally, phylacteries are worn on either the man's left arm or on his forehead during morning prayers.

Lesson: Everyone dreams of making their mark on the world, but the Antichrist makes his dream a literal reality when the False Prophet forces everyone to take a special mark commonly referred to as the "mark of the beast". Under the leadership of the Antichrist and False Prophet, the mark of the beast forces people to participate in a new, global economic system:

> ¹⁶ He (the false prophet) **causes all**, both small and great, rich and poor, free and slave, **to receive a mark** on their **right hand or on their foreheads**, ¹⁷ and that **no one may buy or sell except one who has the mark** or the name of the beast, or the number of his name. *13:16-17*

This mark can be found located either on the forehead or on the hand. Anyone who resists taking the mark of the beast will be unable to participate in economic activities such as the buying and selling of goods and services. Technologically, the emergence of digital currency like Bitcoin makes controlling commerce possible in ways never before imagined. Digital currency effectively creates a cashless society where all currency transactions can be monitored, traced and controlled. Minting costs currently exceed the value of coins being produced. Pennies with a value of one cent cost 2.06 cents to make while the cost of production for a nickel valued at five cents is 7.5 cents each. With prices such as these, the prospect of digital currency will be a logical step for many. If a cashless society is connected to the mark of the beast, those who refuse to participate in the economic system would need to be prepared to be as self-sufficient as possible, able to barter for things they cannot produce themselves and have alliances with friends and family who will have taken the mark of the beast and can conduct business on their behalf if necessary. Times such as have never been before are looming on the horizon.

Those who do accept the mark of the beast will be tormented on earth with painful sores:

> ²…and a **foul and loathsome sore** came upon the **men who had the mark of the beast** and those who worshiped his image. *Revelation 16:2*

Consequences for accepting the mark of the beast are not limited to a painful, physical sore. Accepting the mark of the beast will be considered an act of pagan worship by God and those who accept the mark of the beast will also forfeit their place in God's eternal kingdom:

> ⁹ Then a third angel followed them, saying with a loud voice, "If **anyone** worships the beast and his image, and **receives his mark** on his forehead or on his hand, ¹⁰ **he himself shall also drink of the wine of the wrath of God**, which is poured out full strength into the cup of His indignation. He shall be **tormented with fire and brimstone** in the presence of the holy angels and in the presence of the Lamb. ¹¹ And the smoke of their torment ascends **forever and ever**; and they have no rest day or night, who worship the beast and his image, and whoever receives the mark of his name." *Revelation 14:9-11*

This terrifying warning against taking the mark of the beast is applicable to both Christians and non-Christians alike. Those who profess Christianity, yet still take the mark of the beast will not be spared. Those who do endure through the Tribulation without accepting the mark of the beast will be allowed to pass on into the Millennial Reign:

> ⁴ And I saw thrones, and they sat on them, and judgment was committed to them. Then I saw **the souls** of those who had been beheaded for their witness to Jesus and for the word of God, **who** had not worshiped the beast or his image, and **had not received his mark on their foreheads or on their hands. And they lived and reigned with Christ for a thousand years.** *Revelation 20:4*

There has been much debate about what type of mark it could be. Some believe the mark is symbolic representing either the mental decisions people make or the physical actions in which people engage. Thoughts and actions essentially show where a person's allegiance lies and are evidence of a person's inner beliefs and values. In the book of Exodus, God defines the obedient act of eating unleavened bread for seven days as a sign to be found on the hand or between the eyes:

> [9] **It** (eating unleavened bread for seven days) **shall be as a sign** to you **on your hand and** as a memorial **between your eyes**, that the LORD's law may be in your mouth; for with a strong hand the LORD has brought you out of Egypt. *Exodus 13:9*

Again, in Deuteronomy, obediently observing God's laws through righteous actions is considered a sign that appears on the hand or between the eyes:

> [1] Now this is the commandment, and these are **the statutes** and judgments which the LORD your God has commanded to teach you, that you may **observe them** in the land which you are crossing over to possess, [2] that you may fear the LORD your God, to **keep all His statutes and His commandments** which I command you, you and your son and your grandson, all the days of your life, and that your days may be prolonged...[6] And **these words** which I command you today **shall be in your heart**...[8] You shall **bind them as a sign on your hand**, and they shall be **as frontlets between your eyes**. *Deuteronomy 6:1-2, 6,8*

By examining a person's attitudes and actions, God discerns whether the person truly worships God or obeys the Antichrist. Symbolically, the forehead represents what we choose to believe and the hand represents what we choose to do based on those beliefs. Worship and obedience are intricately linked. If someone truly worships God, they will obey His laws. Worship without obedience is false worship. Conversely, if someone obeys what the Antichrist dictates, then they are, by default, worshipping the Antichrist because their action reveals what they value. Worship and obedience go hand in hand and cannot be separated.

Other, more literal interpretations for what the mark of the beast might be include computers, social security numbers, tattoos made with invisible ink, and radio frequency identification (RFID) chips. Some have even proposed that the recycling symbol is a symbolic representation for the mark of the beast as it can be seen to represent the number "666":

♽ = ∂ = 6

♻ = ⚛ = 666

Tattoos have become an integral part of our modern culture. Once viewed as something relegated to the fringe element of society, tattoos are now a common part of everyday life for many people. As of 2015, it is estimated that in the 18-24 age group, 22% of adults have tattoos. For the age group 25-29, 30% of adults have tattoos. Following that, those in the 30-39 age group are at 38% for tattoo ownership. In the 40-49 age group, about 30% of adults sport tattoos. The next age group, 50-64, boasts 11% of people with tattoos. Beyond age 65 however, only 5% of seniors have tattoos. To say that society might easily accept an invisible tattoo with a bar code for the mark of the beast is not a far stretch of the imagination. UV tattoos are tattoos that are made with fluorescent dyes and are only visible when viewed under a special blacklight. Under normal lighting conditions, the tattoo is virtually invisible. However, God does not approve of any form of tattooing as expressed in Leviticus:

> [28] **You shall not** make any cuttings in your flesh for the dead, nor **tattoo any marks on you**: I am the LORD. *Leviticus 19:27-28*

While invisible tattoos might present one possibility for the mark of the beast, RFID chips are an equally viable option. It is interesting to note that the technology for RFID chips is already developed, functional and currently in use in various ways in different countries. RFID technology is commonly used in tracking devices for cars, identification cards, passports, credit cards and even bar codes in stores. The US based company Digital Angel developed an RFID chip the size of a grain of rice called The VeriChip that can be injected into the webbing between a person's thumb and forefinger. Applications for various uses of the chip extend far and wide. The VeriChip is currently approved by the FDA for medical use to store a patient's medical information thereby making implantable technology a present-day reality. Animals can be microchipped as a means to reunite owners with lost pets should they ever run away. Products such as pet bowls and pet doors are also available to coordinate with the chip to only allow access to the animal whose chip bears the correct frequency for the product. Businesses such as a Wisconsin company, Three Square Market, already offer employees the opportunity to get chipped so they can have security access into the building and make food purchases in the break room without the use of security ID cards or cash. At this time, it is not mandatory to get chipped to be employed by the company. In Glasgow, Scotland, a nightclub called Bar Soba uses chips to have drinks ready for customers when they arrive and allows customers to run a bar tab throughout the night with the aid of the RFID technology. Customers enjoy the freedom to revel in the evening without fear of losing their wallets if they become inebriated. Officials in the Mexican government have also begun using the chipping process citing the necessity for increased security measures.   Uses for the technology extend far and wide making it an attractive option for the mark of the beast.

Marking humanity is a two-sided issue. While the Antichrist busily marks everyone with the mark of the beast, God's servant also actively marks those who belong to God. Those who reject the mark of the beast will receive a different mark from God:

> ...[4] and **the LORD said** to him, "Go through the midst of the city, through the midst of Jerusalem, and **put a mark on the foreheads of the men who sigh and cry over all the abominations** that are done within it." [5] To the others He said in my hearing, "Go after him through the city and kill; do not let your eye spare, nor have any pity. [6] Utterly slay old and young men, maidens and little children and women; but **do not come near anyone on whom is the mark; and begin at My sanctuary**." So, they **began with the elders who were before the temple**. *Ezekiel 9:4-6*

Starting with those who have senior positions within the church and moving outward from there, God marks those who are His with His mark. Those who are counted worthy to receive God's mark will bear the mark into eternity when they are in the presence of God:

> [4] They shall **see His (God's) face**, and **His name** shall be on **their foreheads**. *Revelation 22:4*

In the end, everyone will bear a mark of some kind. No one will escape the branding process. The question at hand is whose mark they will receive. When the time comes, whose mark will you bear?

Talk It Out

1. What do you think the mark of the beast might be (i.e. an invisible tattoo, an RFID chip, a mental choice of whom to worship or actions people take, an unknown invention, etc.)?

2. How would not being able to buy or sell goods and services affect your life? How long do you think you could physically survive if you were unable to purchase anything?

3. What alternative means of securing goods might false Christians resort to when they cannot buy or sell anything (i.e. lying, stealing, murder, etc.)? What about true Christians (i.e. making their own supplies, bartering, making alliances with those who have the mark of the beast, etc.)? Would there be a difference in what they would be willing to do to secure needed goods? Do you think God will provide supernaturally for His people during this time period like He did for the Israelites in the desert for forty years? Or do you think God expects His people to prepare in advance for the coming scarcity?

4. Do you think you will be able to recognize the mark of the beast when it arrives? Would you have the strength to resist taking the mark of the beast if it meant you could no longer function in society? Would you knowingly and sacrificially take the mark of the beast if it meant feeding your family, but having to endure the wrath of God and lose your right to be in heaven with God (Revelation 14:9-12)?

5. Do you believe physical gold and silver will be of any use when the mark of the beast arrives?

DID YOU KNOW? In 2017, 58% of Americans had less than $1000 in savings.

6. Do you think people will regret taking the mark of the beast? What kind of sore do you think the mark may cause? Will people believe taking the mark will cost them their place in God's eternal kingdom?

Ideas for the Week:

- ✓ Educate yourself on Bitcoin as a digital currency by reading the article at https://www.fool.com/retirement/2017/01/10/what-is-bitcoin-2.aspx.
- ✓ Follow news releases and trading values for digital currency stocks using the trading symbols XBT, BTC, BCC, BCH, NYXBT, $BCOIN and BITCOMP.
- ✓ Collect resources for bartering and explore other ways to prepare such as investing in physical gold and silver as a hedge against drastic economic changes.
- ✓ Adopt prepping lifestyle choices as a way of life (i.e. stock up on necessary goods for future use, cultivate a container garden, learn how to can food, educate yourself about urban foraging, form mutually supportive relationships with like-minded people with whom you can barter if ever the need would arise, acquire basic medical skills and practice different forms of self-defense.)

Closing Prayer

NOTE: Add names and individual personal prayer requests to the space provided below before closing in prayer.

Lord, we thank You for our time together today to grow deeper in our walk with You and fellowship with each other. As we close today, we lift up: _____

_____

_____

_____

_____

_____

Father, we know that You will always provide for our needs in all circumstances. We thank You for Your faithfulness towards us and ask You to mark us with Your mark. We look forward to the day when we can spend eternity with You in heaven and pray that You will guide us so that we might be found worthy to enter Your kingdom. In Jesus' name we pray, Amen.

SUPPORTING SCRIPTURES

ACTIONS ARE SIGNS
⁹ It shall be as a sign to you on your hand and as a memorial between your eyes, that the LORD's law may be in your mouth; for with a strong hand the LORD has brought you out of Egypt. *Exodus 13:9*

OBEDIENCE TO GOD'S WORD A SIGN
¹ Now this is the commandment, and these are the statutes and judgments which the LORD your God has commanded to teach you, that you may observe them in the land which you are crossing over to possess, ² that you may fear the LORD your God, to keep all His statutes and His commandments which I command you, you and your son and your grandson, all the days of your life, and that your days may be prolonged...⁶ And these words which I command you today shall be in your heart...⁸ You shall bind them as a sign on your hand, and they shall be as frontlets between your eyes. *Deuteronomy 6:1-2, 6,8*

¹⁸ Therefore you shall lay up these words of mine in your heart and in your soul, and bind them as a sign on your hand, and they shall be as frontlets between your eyes. *Deuteronomy 11:18*

GOD MARKS HIS PEOPLE
...⁴ and the LORD said to him, "Go through the midst of the city, through the midst of Jerusalem, and put a mark on the foreheads of the men who sigh and cry over all the abominations that are done within it." ⁵ To the others He said in my hearing, "Go after him through the city and kill; do not let your eye spare, nor have any pity. ⁶ Utterly slay old and young men, maidens and little children and women; but do not come near anyone on whom is the mark; and begin at My sanctuary." So, they began with the elders who were before the temple. *Ezekiel 9:4-6*

⁴ They shall see His (God's) face, and His name shall be on their foreheads. *Revelation 22:4*

MARK OF THE BEAST
¹⁶ He (the false prophet) causes all, both small and great, rich and poor, free and slave, to receive a mark on their right hand or on their foreheads, ¹⁷ and that no one may buy or sell except one who has the mark or the name of the beast, or the number of his name. ¹⁸ Here is wisdom. Let him who has understanding calculate the number of the beast, for it is the number of a man: His number is 666. *Revelation 13:16-18*

MARK CAUSES A SORE
² So the first went and poured out his bowl upon the earth, and a foul and

loathsome sore came upon the men who had the mark of the beast and those who worshiped his image. *Revelation 16:2*

TATTOOS
[28] You shall not make any cuttings in your flesh for the dead, nor tattoo any marks on you: I am the LORD. *Leviticus 19:27-28*

CONSEQUENCES OF TAKING THE MARK
[9] Then a third angel followed them, saying with a loud voice, "If anyone worships the beast and his image, and receives his mark on his forehead or on his hand, [10] he himself shall also drink of the wine of the wrath of God, which is poured out full strength into the cup of His indignation. He shall be tormented with fire and brimstone in the presence of the holy angels and in the presence of the Lamb. [11] And the smoke of their torment ascends forever and ever; and they have no rest day or night, who worship the beast and his image, and whoever receives the mark of his name." [12] Here is the patience of the saints; here are those who keep the commandments of God and the faith of Jesus. *Revelation 14:9-12*

[20] Then the beast was captured, and with him the false prophet who worked signs in his presence, by which he deceived those who received the mark of the beast and those who worshiped his image. These two were cast alive into the lake of fire burning with brimstone. *Revelation 19:20*

REWARD FOR REFUSING THE MARK
[4] And I saw thrones, and they sat on them, and judgment was committed to them. Then I saw the souls of those who had been beheaded for their witness to Jesus and for the word of God, who had not worshiped the beast or his image, and had not received his mark on their foreheads or on their hands. And they lived and reigned with Christ for a thousand years. *Revelation 20:4*

[2] And I saw something like a sea of glass mingled with fire, and those who have the victory over the beast, over his image and over his mark and over the number of his name, standing on the sea of glass, having harps of God. *Revelation 15:2*

NOTES

"I believe God is managing affairs and that He doesn't need any advice from me." — Henry Ford

WEEK 5: THE SEVEN SEALS

Opening Prayer: Lord, we ask that You send Your Holy Spirit to us to guide us in the teaching and understanding of Your word that we may obtain a better understanding of the prophetic events surrounding us now and waiting for us in the future. Bless our fellowship in Your word that it may be fruitful and draw us into a deeper relationship both with You and those around us. Use us as Your vessels that through us, we may reflect Your glory to all whom we encounter. Illuminate our hearts and minds so that we may boldly shine the brightness of Your light everywhere we go and that we may be beacons of Your hope in a darkened world. In Jesus name we pray, Amen.

Ice Breaker: If you were stranded on an uninhabited, desert island and could only have one of the ten items below to use for survival, which item would you choose and why? Share your answers as a group.

1. Bible
2. Matches
3. Duct Tape
4. Blanket
5. Knife
6. Rope
7. Toilet Paper
8. Seeds
9. Bucket
10. AM/FM Radio

Focus: God's judgment eventually comes to all sinners and there is no escape.

According to World Vision, "famine" refers to an extreme scarcity of food that causes large-scale malnutrition, starvation and death. Criteria for declaring a famine include at least 20 percent of households in an area experiencing extreme food shortages, 30 percent of children or more in the area exhibiting acute malnutrition, and two deaths caused by hunger for every 10,000 people.

— World Vision Famine Guidelines

ARE WE THE TERMINAL GENERATION?

Word of the Week

> ⁴ Another horse, fiery red, went out. And it was granted to the one who sat on it to take **peace** from the earth, and that people should kill one another; and there was given to him a great sword.
>
> *Revelation 6:4*

PEACE: In this passage, the Greek word for "peace" is "eirene" (pronounced i-ray'-nay) which refers to the absence of war on a national level, peace between individuals, and the peace that comes through Jesus as an assurance of salvation yielding contentment in this life knowing what is yet to come in the afterlife. When the "eirene" peace is removed from the earth, violence between individuals ensues which generates a rise in murder rates. As individual relationships deteriorate, relationships between leaders of various countries also disintegrate culminating in war. Lastly, when the peace of Jesus is removed, a falling away occurs as people no longer accept the salvation that Christ offers through His death on the cross. Without the peace of Jesus to be found on the earth, there can be no peace anywhere in any form.

Lesson: While living in exile on the Greek island of Patmos, the apostle John wrote of the events in Revelation describing the end time period immediately before Christ returns. Daniel's vision informs us that events pertaining to the end time era were sealed and destined to remain a mystery for many centuries:

> ⁴ But you, Daniel, shut up the words, and **seal the book until the time of the end**.... *Daniel 12:4*

Only when the time is ripe for the final harvesting of mankind will Jesus open the seals and release the prophesied contents:

> ¹ And I saw in the right hand of Him who sat on the throne **a scroll** written inside and on the back, **sealed with seven seals**. ² Then I saw a strong angel proclaiming with a loud voice, "Who is worthy to open the scroll and to loose its seals?" ³ And **no one in heaven or on the earth or under the earth was able to open the scroll, or to look at it**. ⁴ So I wept much, because no one was found worthy to open and read the scroll, or to look at it. ⁵ But one of the elders said to me, "Do not weep. Behold, the Lion of the tribe of

Judah, the **Root of David, has prevailed to open the scroll and to loose its seven seals.**" *Revelation 5:1-5*

Historically, seals were an important way to protect the contents of a document securing the contents from prying eyes. Scrolls were physically sealed with wax to prevent their contents from being opened before they arrived in the hands of the person for whom it was meant. Regarding the seals of Revelation, when the timing is right for the designated end time generation to receive the contents contained therein, Jesus, the Lamb of God, will break open the seven seals of this prophetic scroll releasing upon the earth the events described in the book of Revelation.

The first four of the seven seals are collectively known as the Four Horsemen of the Apocalypse and have been the subject of many popular apocalyptic films such as *The Omega Code* and Tim LaHaye's *Left Behind* series. The first seal mentioned is the white horse:

> [1] Now I saw when **the Lamb opened one of the seals**; and I heard one of the four living creatures saying with a voice like thunder, "Come and see." [2] And I looked, and behold, **a white horse**. He who sat on it had **a bow**; and **a crown** was given to him, and **he went out conquering** and to conquer. *Revelation 6:1-2*

One popular interpretation of the first seal attributes this verse to the Antichrist's conquering rule. Proponents of this interpretation refer to the fact that a crown of leadership is given to the Antichrist to go forth and conquer the earth. By his side, aiding his mission, is the False Prophet peddling a false religion. Others connect the first seal to the spreading of the gospel of Christ around the world which conquers sin. Once the gospel of Christ successfully spreads throughout the world, the end can begin as expressed in Matthew:

> [14] And this **gospel** of the kingdom will be **preached in all the world** as a witness to all the nations, and **then the end will come.** *Matthew 24:14*

Supporting this view is another analogy in Revelation to Christ on a white horse followed by His army which also rides white horses:

> [11] And I saw heaven opened, and behold **a white horse**; and **He** that sat upon him **was called Faithful and True**, and in righteousness He doth judge and make war...[14] And the **armies**

which were in heaven followed Him upon white horses, clothed in fine linen, white and clean. *Revelation 19:11 and 14*

The fact that Christ is represented again in Revelation 19:11 and 14 as riding a white horse supports the theory that the first seal refers to the gospel going out into all the world as the beginning of end time events. An alternate possibility for the third seal is that Jesus, represented by the white horse, allows the Antichrist to begin his conquering reign.

Consecutively, the second seal opened is the red horse and is connected to arguments, fights, disagreements and war:

> [3] When He opened **the second seal**, I heard the second living creature saying, "Come and see." [4] Another **horse, fiery red**, went out. And it was granted to the one who sat on it **to take peace from the earth**, and that people should kill one another; and there was given to him a great sword. *Revelation 6:3-4*

Next, the third seal, the black horse, releases famine and economic collapse upon the world:

> [5] When He opened **the third seal**, I heard the third living creature say, "Come and see." So, I looked, and behold, **a black horse**, and he who sat on it had a pair of scales in his hand. [6] And I heard a voice in the midst of the four living creatures saying, "**A quart of wheat for a denarius, and three quarts of barley for a denarius**; and **do not harm the oil and the wine**." *Revelation 6:5-6*

China (18.52%), India (10.04%), the United States (10.01%) and Brazil (9%) are the world's top producers of the world's food supply with Russia, fifth on the list, coming in at a meager 2%. Famine conditions would most likely involve something happening to the food production abilities of one or more of these countries. Exempting wine and oil from the event suggests that the Mediterranean region is still able to enjoy favorable growing conditions since much of that region of the world grows significant amounts of olives and is associated with grapes and wine.

A denarius is a relatively low value coin that was used in Jesus' day. Equivalent to a modern penny, a denarius is worth about fourteen cents in modern terms. Using an NIV translation for the same verse, further clarification is given that a quart of wheat is roughly two pounds of flour and a denarius represents a day's working wage. Barley, an inferior source of grain, can be purchased in larger amounts of six pounds for the same price:

> ⁶ Then I heard what sounded like a voice among the four living creatures, saying, "**Two pounds** of **wheat** for a **day's wages**, and **six pounds** of **barley** for a **day's wages**, and do not damage the oil and the wine!" *Revelation 6:6 (NIV Translation)*

Currently, the 2019 federal minimum wage for workers in the United States is $7.25 per hour. For a standard eight-hour shift, a worker's daily pay is $58 before taxes. In 2015, the national pay average for all workers was $48,098.63 per year or $185 per day. Standard five-pound bags of flour yield eighteen cups of flour. A loaf of bread requires three cups of flour which yields six loaves of bread per bag of flour. Using these statistics, the cost for a bag of flour or a loaf of bread during the Tribulation would be:

	Wheat	Barley
Cost Calculated Using Minimum Wage of $58/day		
5-pound bag of flour	$145	$48
1 loaf of bread	$24	$8
Cost Calculated Using National Wage Average of $185/day		
5-pound bag of flour	$463	$154
1 loaf of bread	$77	$26

Given these financial statistics, most families will need to give up wheat and eat barley bread just to feed their families. Either way you slice it, prices will be quite a bit higher than the current national average for a loaf of bread which ranges from $2.37 - $2.43 per loaf. In some higher cost of living areas in the United States, bread can sell for as high as $4.41 per loaf, but that is still nowhere near potential prices of $24 - $77 for a loaf of wheat bread.

Following the black horse, the pale horse arrives and ushers in death to one quarter of the world's population with more war and famine. By this time, the situation is so dire that animals turn into an added threat competing for the same meager food sources that humans desperately seek:

> ⁷ When He opened **the fourth seal**, I heard the voice of the fourth living creature saying, "Come and see." ⁸ So I looked, and behold, **a pale horse**. And the name of him who sat on it was Death, and Hades followed with him. And power was given to them over **a fourth of the earth, to kill with sword, with hunger, with death, and by the beasts of the earth**. *Revelation 6:7-8*

The initial four horsemen represent a natural progression of events as can be seen in known patterns observed throughout history. For example, war is known to destroy economies which leads to food scarcity. From 1921-1923 during the

ARE WE THE TERMINAL GENERATION?

Weimar Republic in post-war Germany, people experienced extreme hyperinflation which devalued the local currency to the point that it took a wheelbarrow full of money to buy groceries. With prices severely inflated and increasing exponentially by the minute in some instances, prices desperately outpaced wages. When wages failed to keep up with the price of goods, the resulting food scarcity meant people could not afford to feed their families even though food was physically available in stores. Food scarcity causes malnutrition which leads to disease and death rates rise. It is a vicious cycle indeed.

Another factor which might contribute to future famine conditions is evident in our world today. Colony Collapse Disorder (CCD) is a phenomenon where worker bees vanish from their hives. All that remains of the hive is the queen bee, a few nurse bees and some immature bees.

> Za'atar is an Israeli spice consisting of dried thyme, oregano, sumac and sesame seeds.
> It is used on almost everything including pizza, salads and chicken.

Annual losses vary, but in some years, it can be as high as 60% of total bees that are lost. In 2019, the issue was concerning enough in the state of Virginia that the General Assembly allocated $125,000 to give away free beekeeping equipment to anyone willing to put a hive on their property. Within twenty-four hours of accepting applications, they had received over two thousand applications and had to suspend accepting any more new applications as the allocated amount had been completely exhausted. CCD is prophetically concerning because without bees, crops will not be pollinated. Without pollination, crops fail to yield produce. With less produce available on the market, fewer people will be fed on what is grown and prices will rise for what does make it to market. Famine conditions may not be here yet, but it would be wise to continue to observe how CCD progresses over time and assess the net effect it will have on our overall food system.

By the time the remaining three seals are opened, an abysmally bleak situation exists. With the breaking of the fifth seal, the souls of previously slain martyrs cry out to the Lord asking how much longer this is going to go on:

> ⁹ When He opened **the fifth seal**, I saw under the altar **the souls of those who had been slain for the word of God** and for the

testimony which they held. ¹⁰ And **they cried with a loud voice**, saying, "How long, O Lord, holy and true, until You judge and avenge our blood on those who dwell on the earth?" ¹¹ Then a white robe was given to each of them; and it was said to them that they should **rest a little while longer**, until both the number of their fellow servants and their brethren, who would be killed as they were, was completed. *Revelation 6:9-11*

Jesus tells the martyrs the time is not yet and then the sixth seal is opened:

¹² I looked when He opened **the sixth seal**, and behold, there was a great **earthquake**; and the **sun became black** as sackcloth of hair, and the **moon became like blood**. ¹³ And the **stars of heaven fell** to the earth, as a fig tree drops its late figs when it is shaken by a mighty wind. ¹⁴ Then the sky receded as a scroll when it is rolled up, and **every mountain and island was moved out of its place**. ¹⁵ And the **kings of the earth**, the great men, the rich men, the commanders, the **mighty men**, every slave and every free man, **hid** themselves in the caves and in the rocks of the mountains, ¹⁶ and said to the mountains and rocks, "Fall on us and hide us from the face of Him who sits on the throne and from the wrath of the Lamb! ¹⁷ For the great day of His wrath has come, and who is able to stand?" *Revelation 6:12-17*

With the unleashing of the sixth seal, a massive earthquake rocks the earth, disturbances in the heavens shake the atmosphere above the earth, meteors shower down on the earth and other cataclysmic events threaten mankind terrifying even the bravest of men. Finally, the seventh seal is opened and there is silence in heaven for half-an-hour before the prayers of the saints are offered up to God with abundant incense. After the prayers are finished, more loud, cataclysmic events continue to disrupt the earth.

¹ When He opened **the seventh seal**, there was **silence in heaven** for about **half an hour**. ² And I saw the seven angels who stand before God, and to them were given seven trumpets. ³ Then another angel, having a golden censer, came and stood at the altar. He was given **much incense, that he should offer it with the prayers of all the saints** upon the golden altar which was before the throne. ⁴ And the smoke of the incense, with the prayers of the saints, ascended before God from the angel's hand. ⁵ Then the angel took the censer, filled it with fire from the altar, and threw it to the earth. And there were noises, thunderings, lightnings, and an earthquake. *Revelation 8:1-5*

ARE WE THE TERMINAL GENERATION?

When the seals are opened, it will be a truly trying time for mankind. Suffering will increase exponentially for those who are not sealed by God. While it will be a difficult time for all, it will also be an exciting time in human history because the onset of these events means that the opportunity to keep company with Jesus waits just around the corner!

Talk It Out

1. Which interpretation do you feel is the best fit for the first seal in Revelation 6:2? Do you believe the verse refers to the completion of the spread of the gospel throughout the whole world marking the beginning of the end, the emergence and dominance of the Antichrist and False Prophet, or something else?

2. Through observing the world around us that we live in, have you noticed a general increase in the amount of discord, disagreements and outright fighting in our society?

3. In the third seal referenced in Revelation 6:5-6, why do you think there is selective food scarcity which leaves the wine and oil protected from God's wrath? Do you believe the wine and oil symbolically represent the wealthy as not being affected by the economic collapse? Or does the verse refer to a geographical area which will be spared from crop failure? Do you think this verse points to food scarcity as a result of crop decimation, people's financial inability to purchase existing food or both?

4. How do you think Americans, who are accustomed to a higher standard of living than the rest of the world and who are comparatively very well fed, would cope with the loss of abundant food luxuries? Given the increasing socialistic tendencies of our government, do you think the government would step in to control the food supply and ration food such as they did during WWII?

5. When the fourth seal breaks open, more death is added through war, famine and beasts of the earth. How do you think animals might become a curse which brings additional death to mankind (Revelation 6:8)?

6. After the first four seals are opened, the souls of the slain martyrs impatiently ask Jesus how much longer the situation will continue. Why do you think the slain martyrs are concerned with the duration of end time events and express their impatience to Him?

Ideas for the Week:

- ✓ Throw a viewing party for a few friends and watch either *The Omega Code* or *End of Days*.
- ✓ To support the spread of the gospel to the whole world, print up business cards with the name and address of your home church. Keep them handy and when you see someone hurting or in need, hand them out.
- ✓ Start a price diary to track how quickly prices are changing. Identify a handful of items you use on a regular basis. Whenever you purchase the items, log the date and price in the price diary. Observe price trends over a period of time and formulate your own conclusions about the rate of inflation goods in the marketplace currently experience.
- ✓ Buy a wax seal set and experiment with the lost art of sealing letters with wax. Wax seal supplies can be found at https://www.nostalgicimpressions.com/Wax-Seals-Stamps-s/2.htm.

Closing Prayer

NOTE: *Add names and individual personal prayer requests to the space provided below before closing in prayer.*

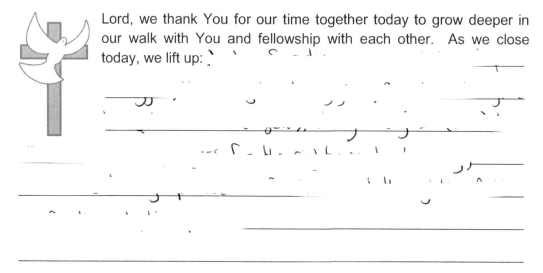

Lord, we thank You for our time together today to grow deeper in our walk with You and fellowship with each other. As we close today, we lift up:

Father, we admit that we have no control over forces greater than ourselves. We ask You to prepare us as necessary physically, mentally, emotionally and spiritually to face the things which threaten to overwhelm and destroy us. When adversity strikes, show us how to minister to others in the tangible ways Jesus taught us to do through His holy example. In Jesus' name we pray, Amen.

SUPPORTING SCRIPTURES

SEALED UNTIL THE END
⁴ But you, Daniel, shut up the words, and seal the book until the time of the end.... *Daniel 12:4*

¹ And I saw in the right hand of Him who sat on the throne a scroll written inside and on the back, sealed with seven seals. ² Then I saw a strong angel proclaiming with a loud voice, "Who is worthy to open the scroll and to loose its seals?" ³ And no one in heaven or on the earth or under the earth was able to open the scroll, or to look at it. ⁴ So I wept much, because no one was found worthy to open and read the scroll, or to look at it. ⁵ But one of the elders said to me, "Do not weep. Behold, the Lion of the tribe of Judah, the Root of David, has prevailed to open the scroll and to loose its seven seals." *Revelation 5:1-5*

THE FIRST SEAL
¹ Now I saw when the Lamb opened one of the seals; and I heard one of the four living creatures saying with a voice like thunder, "Come and see." ² And I looked, and behold, a white horse. He who sat on it had a bow; and a crown was given to him, and he went out conquering and to conquer. *Revelation 6:1-2*

CHRIST ON A WHITE HORSE
¹¹ And I saw heaven opened, and behold a white horse; and He that sat upon him was called Faithful and True, and in righteousness He doth judge and make war…¹⁴ And the armies which were in heaven followed Him upon white horses, clothed in fine linen, white and clean. *Revelation 19:11 and 14*

BEGINNING OF THE END
¹⁴ And this gospel of the kingdom will be preached in all the world as a witness to all the nations, and then the end will come. *Matthew 24:14*

THE SECOND SEAL
³ When He opened the second seal, I heard the second living creature saying, "Come and see." ⁴ Another horse, fiery red, went out. And it was granted to the one who sat on it to take peace from the earth, and that people should kill one another; and there was given to him a great sword. *Revelation 6:3-4*

THE THIRD SEAL
⁵ When He opened the third seal, I heard the third living creature say, "Come and see." So, I looked, and behold, a black horse, and he who sat on it had a pair of scales in his hand. ⁶ And I heard a voice in the midst of the four living creatures saying, "A quart of wheat for a denarius, and three quarts of barley for a denarius; and do not harm the oil and the wine." *Revelation 6:5-6*

THE FOURTH SEAL
⁷ When He opened the fourth seal, I heard the voice of the fourth living creature saying, "Come and see." ⁸ So I looked, and behold, a pale horse. And the name of him who sat on it was Death, and Hades followed with him. And power was given to them over a fourth of the earth, to kill with sword, with hunger, with death, and by the beasts of the earth. *Revelation 6:7-8*

NOTE: For verse 8, the NIV translation reads "to kill by sword, famine and *plague*, and by the wild beasts of the earth." The ESV translation reads "to kill with sword and with famine and with *pestilence* and by wild beasts of the earth." The GNT translation for this verse is "to kill by means of war, famine, *disease* and wild animals."

THE FIFTH SEAL
⁹ When He opened the fifth seal, I saw under the altar the souls of those who had been slain for the word of God and for the testimony which they held. ¹⁰ And they cried with a loud voice, saying, "How long, O Lord, holy and true, until You judge and avenge our blood on those who dwell on the earth?" ¹¹ Then a white robe was given to each of them; and it was said to them that they should rest a little while longer, until both the number of their fellow servants and their brethren, who would be killed as they were, was completed. *Revelation 6:9-11*

THE SIXTH SEAL
¹² I looked when He opened the sixth seal, and behold, there was a great earthquake; and the sun became black as sackcloth of hair, and the moon became like blood. ¹³ And the stars of heaven fell to the earth, as a fig tree drops its late figs when it is shaken by a mighty wind. ¹⁴ Then the sky receded as a scroll when it is rolled up, and every mountain and island was moved out of its place. ¹⁵ And the kings of the earth, the great men, the rich men, the commanders, the mighty men, every slave and every free man, hid themselves in the caves and in the rocks of the mountains, ¹⁶ and said to the mountains and rocks, "Fall on us and hide us from the face of Him who sits on the throne and from the wrath of the Lamb! ¹⁷ For the great day of His wrath has come, and who is able to stand?" *Revelation 6:12-17*

³¹ The sun shall be turned into darkness, and the moon into blood, before the coming of the great and awesome day of the LORD. *Joel 2:31*

²⁹ "Immediately after the tribulation of those days the sun will be darkened, and the moon will not give its light; the stars will fall from heaven, and the powers of the heavens will be shaken. *Matthew 24:29*

¹⁰ Enter into the rock, and hide in the dust, from the terror of the LORD and the glory of His majesty. *Isaiah 2:10*

¹⁹ They shall go into the holes of the rocks, and into the caves of the earth, from the terror of the LORD and the glory of His majesty, when He arises to shake the earth mightily. *Isaiah 2:19*

⁶ He stood and measured the earth; He looked and startled the nations. And the everlasting mountains were scattered, the perpetual hills bowed. His ways are everlasting. *Habakkuk 3:6*

THE SEVENTH SEAL
¹ When He opened the seventh seal, there was silence in heaven for about half an hour. ² And I saw the seven angels who stand before God, and to them were given seven trumpets. ³ Then another angel, having a golden censer, came and stood at the altar. He was given much incense, that he should offer it with the prayers of all the saints upon the golden altar which was before the throne. ⁴ And the smoke of the incense, with the prayers of the saints, ascended before God from the angel's hand. ⁵ Then the angel took the censer, filled it with fire from the altar, and threw it to the earth. And there were noises, thunderings, lightnings, and an earthquake. *Revelation 8:1-5*

NOTES

"Christian liberty is freedom from sin, not freedom to sin."
— Aiden Wilson Tozer

WEEK 6: THE SEVEN TRUMPETS

Opening Prayer: Lord, we ask that You send Your Holy Spirit to us to guide us in the teaching and understanding of Your word that we may obtain a better understanding of the prophetic events surrounding us now and waiting for us in the future. Bless our fellowship in Your word that it may be fruitful and draw us into a deeper relationship both with You and those around us. Use us as Your vessels that through us, we may reflect Your glory to all whom we encounter. Illuminate our hearts and minds so that we may boldly shine the brightness of Your light everywhere we go and that we may be beacons of Your hope in a darkened world. In Jesus name we pray, Amen.

Ice Breaker: Destruction was coming to a wicked city called Sodom and Gomorrah and times were about to get unbearably tough for a man named Lot. Lot was about to lose his home, everything he owned, his livelihood, his way of life, all of his friends and even beloved members of his immediate family. His wife was going to die and he was going to find himself living in a barren cave with his two daughters feeling like they were the last people on earth. If you were Lot's friend and knew in advance, through divine revelation, what hardships were about to befall him, what advice would you have given him to help him get through the struggles that awaited him? Go around the circle and share your words of wisdom with everyone in your group.

My Advice:

_____

_____

_____

_____

_____

_____

 Focus: When God sets His mind to do something in your life, He will accomplish the task thoroughly and completely.

CHRISTINE TATE

Word of the Week

> ²¹ And they did not repent of their murders or their **sorceries** or their sexual immorality or their thefts.
>
> *Revelation 9:21*

SORCERIES: Sorcery, as translated from the original Greek, comes from the word "pharmakeia" (pronounced far-mak-i'-ah). While "sorcery" can refer to the magical arts and the idolatries associated with witchcraft, the word "pharmakeia" also means to use or administer drugs. Comparatively, the modern English word "pharmacy" also derives its meaning from the same root word "pharmakeia". Certain modern medications have been lifesaving blessings. Without the aid of penicillin, countless people would not have survived pneumonia. Type I diabetics live long, productive lives due to effective medical intervention. While advances in modern medicine have saved numerous lives over the years, overuse of prescription drugs and prescription dependence is becoming more and more commonplace as recreational drug use gains increasing popularity in our society. Recreational drug use is an abomination to God on the level of thievery and sexual sin. Not only are drugs addicting for the user and damaging to the human body, the temple of the Holy Spirit, but they have the ability to alter a person's thoughts and behaviors in ways that do not honor God. Drugs can become a priority before God which is never acceptable to Him. Unnecessary reliance on prescription drugs is a pitfall to godliness. God wants to be our ultimate healer. Sometimes He heals through the skilled hands of a medical professional, but as the world quickly barrels towards the return of Christ, be careful not to use unnecessary pharmaceuticals for pleasure or when other alternative medical options might be available. Misuse of either prescription or non-prescription pharmaceuticals is an afront to godliness.

Lesson: Further elaborating on the seven seals, seven angels blow seven trumpets. With the sound of each trumpet, a punishment for mankind is heralded, then issued. When the first angel sounds the first trumpet, vegetation is destroyed as hail and fire fall from the sky burning up a third of the trees and all of the grass:

⁶ So the **seven angels** who had the **seven trumpets** prepared themselves to sound. ⁷ The **first angel sounded**: And **hail** and **fire** followed, mingled with blood, and they were thrown

to the earth. And **a third of the trees were burned up, and all green grass was burned up**. *Revelation 8:6-7*

After that, a second angel sounds a trumpet that causes a third of all sea life and ships in the sea to perish:

> ⁸ Then **the second angel sounded**: And something like a great mountain burning with fire was thrown into the sea, and **a third of the sea became blood**. ⁹ And **a third of the living creatures in the sea died**, and **a third of the ships were destroyed**. *Revelation 8:8-9*

When the third trumpet is blown, a third of the earth's freshwater sources become poisonous and undrinkable killing numerous humans:

> ¹⁰ Then **the third angel sounded**: And a great star fell from heaven, burning like a torch, and it fell on a third of the rivers and on the springs of water. ¹¹ The name of the star is Wormwood. A **third of the waters became wormwood**, and **many men died from the water**, because it was made bitter. *Revelation 8:10-11*

Sounds from the fourth trumpet affect the sun, moon and stars causing complete darkness for a third of the day and night. At this point, an angel announces that things are about to get much worse as if things are not bad enough already:

> ¹² Then **the fourth angel sounded**: And a third of the sun was struck, a third of the moon, and a third of the stars, so that a third of them were darkened. A **third of the day did not shine, and likewise the night**. ¹³ And I looked, and I heard an angel flying through the midst of heaven, saying with a loud voice, "Woe, woe, **woe to the inhabitants of the earth, because of the remaining blasts** of the trumpet of the three angels who are about to sound!" *Revelation 8:12-13*

At the sound of the fifth trumpet, air quality declines and locusts with humanistic traits attack those in league with the Antichrist:

> ¹ Then the fifth angel sounded: And I saw a star fallen from heaven to the earth. To him was given the key to the bottomless pit. ² And he opened the bottomless pit, and **smoke arose out of the pit** like the smoke of a great furnace. So, the sun and the **air were darkened** because of the smoke of the pit. ³ Then **out of the smoke locusts came upon the earth**. And to them was given power, as the scorpions of the earth have power. ⁴ They were

commanded not to harm the grass of the earth, or any green thing, or any tree, but only those men who do not have the seal of God on their foreheads. ⁵And they were not given authority to kill them, but to torment them for five months. Their torment was like the torment of a scorpion when it strikes a man. ⁶In those days men will seek death and will not find it; they will desire to die, and death will flee from them. ⁷The shape of the locusts was like horses prepared for battle. On their **heads were crowns of something like gold**, and their faces were like **the faces of men**. ⁸They had **hair like women's** hair, and their **teeth were like lions'** teeth. ⁹And they had breastplates like **breastplates of iron**, and the sound of their wings was like **the sound of chariots** with many horses running into battle. ¹⁰They had tails like scorpions, and there were **stings in their tails**. Their power was to hurt men five months. ¹¹And they had as king over them the angel of the bottomless pit, whose name in Hebrew is Abaddon, but in Greek he has the name Apollyon. ¹²One woe is past. Behold, still two more woes are coming after these things.
Revelation 9:1-12

Oddly, the locusts referred to in this passage are not allowed to touch vegetation; only a specific group of humans. Giorgio Tsoukalos, producer and host of the television show *Ancient Aliens*, is credited with presenting an interesting interpretation of this trumpet. He notes the similarity of the appearance of a military helicopter to the biblical description given of the locust. Military helicopters are made of metal, have propellers that can resemble long hair whipping in the wind, release deadly weapons, have the face of a human pilot visible through the front window, wear shiny helmets, or "crowns", answer to a leader, and pursue human targets with precision for finite periods of time.

Photos of military helicopters courtesy of o0o0xmods0o0o at www.morguefile.com.

When the sixth trumpet blows, the four angels bound at the Euphrates river are released to kill one third of mankind with the aid of a two hundred-million-man army.

> [13] Then **the sixth angel sounded**: And I heard a voice from the four horns of the golden altar which is before God, [14] saying to the sixth angel who had the trumpet, "**Release the four angels who are bound at the great river Euphrates**." [15] So the four angels, who had been prepared for the hour and day and month and year, were released to kill a third of mankind. [16] Now the number of the **army of the horsemen was two hundred million**; I heard the number of them. [17] And thus I saw the horses in the vision: those who sat on them had breastplates of **fiery red, hyacinth blue, and sulfur yellow**; and the heads of the horses were like the heads of lions; and out of their mouths came fire, smoke, and brimstone. [18] By these three plagues **a third of mankind was killed**—by the fire and the smoke and the brimstone which came out of their mouths. [19] For their power is in their mouth and in their tails; for their tails are like serpents, having heads; and with them they do harm. [20] But the rest of mankind, who were not killed by these plagues, did not repent of the works of their hands, that they should not worship demons, and idols of gold, silver, brass, stone, and wood, which can neither see nor hear nor walk. [21] **And they did not repent** of their murders or their sorceries or their sexual immorality or their thefts. *Revelation 9:13-21*

Up until China's birth policy was relaxed to allow two children per couple in 2015, China had a longstanding one birth policy for its citizens. For thirty-five years, Chinese couples were required to have only one child. Any attempts to thwart the state regulatory policy was met with forced abortions and involuntary sterilizations. Parents engaged in the practices of sex-selective abortions and infanticide if the child was female due to cultural preferences for male children. As a result of gender selecting practices favoring male children, the decades long policy created a society with a seriously

FASCINATING FACT: More people speak English in China than in the United States.

imbalanced population of male citizens. Those males are now of reproductive age with little to no chance of finding a wife. China requires all of its citizens to join the military for two years. Because of their lop-sided demographic favoring males, their large military is primarily composed of men. With a total population of over 1.4 billion people, China is currently the most viable candidate to be able to form a two hundred-million-man army.

Map of Mongolia courtesy of Peter Hermes Furian at www.shutterstock.com.

Geographically, China's immediate neighbor to the north is Mongolia. Considered part of China until 1911, Mongolia is today China's largest trade partner and source of foreign investments. Considering their history and the closeness of their alliance, it is a possibility that the army referenced in scripture could be a Chinese-Mongolian alliance. The uniforms worn by the soldiers described in the vision have "breastplates of hyacinth blue, fiery red and sulfur yellow" which is, coincidentally, the color scheme for traditional Mongolian military uniforms. Another intriguing correlation between the uniform and the passage is the "breastplate". *Webster's Dictionary* defines a breastplate as:

BREASTPLATE: A metal plate worn as defensive armor for the breast.

On traditional Mongolian uniforms, a gold metal circular plate is worn over the center of the chest where the heart is located. The colors of the uniform are a close match for the specific shades of hyacinth blue, fiery red and sulfur yellow described in the passage. An internet search using the search term "traditional Mongolian uniform" yields striking color images of the unique color scheme of the uniforms with the metal breastplate.

Photo of Mongolian Soldiers in traditional military uniforms courtesy of Nomad 1988 at www.shutterstock.com.

The invading army mentioned in the passage also has transport vehicles that emit fire and smoke which is fittingly descriptive of modern-day military technology and weaponry. Consistent with a military invasion is the description that the "locusts" are only allowed to attack those without the seal of God (Revelation 9:4) and that the torment lasts for five months (Revelation 9:10). Battle campaigns target specific entities with surgical precision and last for finite periods of time.

Finally, the seventh angel sounds a seventh trumpet. Following the trumpet blast comes an announcement from heaven declaring that God is now ruler over all the earth and everything in it:

> ¹⁵ Then the **seventh angel sounded**: And there were **loud voices** in heaven, saying, **"The kingdoms of this world have become the kingdoms of our Lord and of His Christ**, and He shall reign forever and ever!" ¹⁶ And the twenty-four elders who sat before

> God on their thrones fell on their faces and worshiped God, ¹⁷ saying: "We give You thanks, O Lord God Almighty, the One who is and who was and who is to come, because You have taken Your great power and reigned. ¹⁸ The nations were angry, and Your wrath has come, and the time of the dead, that they should be judged, and that You should reward Your servants the prophets and the saints, and those who fear Your name, small and great, and should destroy those who destroy the earth." ¹⁹ Then the temple of God was opened in heaven, and the ark of His covenant was seen in His temple. And there were lightnings, noises, thunderings, an earthquake, and great hail. *Revelation 11:15-19*

When all is said and done, the sum total of the destruction caused by the fourth horseman of the apocalypse from last week (1/4 of mankind) combined with the destruction caused by the sixth trumpet this week (1/3 of mankind) results in a total global population reduction of fifty percent. Televangelist Jack Van Impe points out that whenever you combine the percentages given for the fourth horseman (1/4 of mankind) and the percentage given for the sixth trumpet (1/3 of mankind), the final number will always be fifty percent of the original number. For example:

> **100** − 25% = 75
> 75 − 33.3% = 50.025
> **50** is half of the original number of 100.
>
> **500** − 25% = 375
> 375 − 33.3% = 250.125
> **250** is half of the original number of 500.
>
> **1240** − 25% = 930
> 930 − 33.3% = 620.31
> **620** is half of the original number of 1240.

Given that there are approximately 7.7 billion people on the planet right now, a fifty percent population reduction would translate into a worldwide death toll of 3.85 billion people. Yet still, people do not recognize God's warning signs and repent of their evil ways:

> ²¹ **And they did not repent** of their murders or their sorceries or their sexual immorality or their thefts. *Revelation 9:21*

As God's children, we must always be sensitive to ways in which God communicates with us. Do more than just hear God. Listen to what He is saying. Recognize punishments for what they are – God's wake-up call to us. God does not want that anyone should perish, but we must be obedient to His voice and choose His path. When mankind listens to their own desires and ignores the warning signs, it never ends well. For those who heed God's call to repentance, forgiveness is plentiful. For those who refuse to heed God's warnings and stubbornly cling to sinful choices, punishments will only increase in severity. God's attempt to communicate His displeasure will only last so long. Eventually, the warning signs will come to an end and we will all answer for our choices whether good or bad.

Talk It Out

1. What are the ways God communicates with you in your life? Is God trying to tell you something now through the people and circumstances in your life?

2. How would losing fifty percent of the world's population affect the flow of goods and services? What mental and emotional effect do you think it would have on survivors watching fifty percent of the population die off?

3. Revelation 9:20-21 says that even after substantial destruction and hardship, people fail to repent. Why do you think people stubbornly refuse to repent of their sinful ways? Do they even recognize God's displeasure with mankind?

4. When the second trumpet blows, a mountain burning with fire causes one third of ships and marine life to perish. Do you think that description most closely resembles the emergence of a massive volcanic eruption from beneath the sea, a large meteorite falling to earth, toxic space debris crashing into the sea, the effects of nuclear war or something else?

5. Do you think there is a similarity between the description of locusts given in Revelation 9:3-11 and modern-day military helicopters? Or do you believe the passage refers to a literal insect that will supernaturally emerge from the earth to torment non-Christians for five months?

6. Regarding the description of the army given in Revelation 9:16-17, how likely is it that this scripture is a reference to a Chinese-Mongolian military alliance? Can you think of any other possibilities that it could be referencing?

Ideas for the Week:

- ✓ Sin is sneaky, subtle and insidious. Practice active mindfulness this week searching for ways your thoughts, speech or behavior might be unpleasing to God. Ask God for His forgiveness immediately after identifying offending thoughts, speech or actions.
- ✓ Purchase a portable water purification system such as those found at https://www.seychelle.com/.
- ✓ Calendula and Horehound naturally repel locusts. Plant a few of these bushes around your home or grow them as potted plants on your balcony.
- ✓ Hang bird feeders around your property or on your balcony to attract birds to eat unwanted insect pests in your outdoor living environment.

Closing Prayer

NOTE: Add names and individual personal prayer requests to the space provided below before closing in prayer.

Lord, we thank You for our time together today to grow deeper in our walk with You and fellowship with each other. As we close today, we lift up: _____

_____

_____

_____

_____

_____

_____

_____

Father, reveal our sins to us that we may repent while there is still time. Remove the blinders from our eyes and let us not wallow in self-deception. We ask You to seal us that we may be marked for Your kingdom and spared from partaking in the plagues of this world. In Jesus' name we pray, Amen.

SUPPORTING SCRIPTURES

THE FIRST TRUMPET

⁶ So the seven angels who had the seven trumpets prepared themselves to sound. ⁷ The first angel sounded: And hail and fire followed, mingled with blood, and they were thrown to the earth. And a third of the trees were burned up, and all green grass was burned up. *Revelation 8:6-7*

THE SECOND TRUMPET

⁸ Then the second angel sounded: And something like a great mountain burning with fire was thrown into the sea, and a third of the sea became blood. ⁹ And a third of the living creatures in the sea died, and a third of the ships were destroyed. *Revelation 8:8-9*

THE THIRD TRUMPET

¹⁰ Then the third angel sounded: And a great star fell from heaven, burning like a torch, and it fell on a third of the rivers and on the springs of water. ¹¹ The name of the star is Wormwood. A third of the waters became wormwood, and many men died from the water, because it was made bitter. *Revelation 8:10-11*

THE FOURTH TRUMPET

¹² Then the fourth angel sounded: And a third of the sun was struck, a third of the moon, and a third of the stars, so that a third of them were darkened. A third of the day did not shine, and likewise the night. ¹³ And I looked, and I heard an angel flying through the midst of heaven, saying with a loud voice, "Woe, woe, woe to the inhabitants of the earth, because of the remaining blasts of the trumpet of the three angels who are about to sound!" *Revelation 8:12-13*

THE FIFTH TRUMPET

¹ Then the fifth angel sounded: And I saw a star fallen from heaven to the earth. To him was given the key to the bottomless pit. ² And he opened the bottomless pit, and smoke arose out of the pit like the smoke of a great furnace. So, the sun and the air were darkened because of the smoke of the pit. ³ Then out of the smoke locusts came upon the earth. And to them was given power, as the scorpions of the earth have power. ⁴ They were commanded not to harm the grass of the earth, or any green thing, or any tree, but only those men who do not have the seal of God on their foreheads. ⁵ And they were not given authority to kill them, but to torment them for five months. Their torment was like the torment of a scorpion when it strikes a man. ⁶ In those days men will seek death and will not find it; they will desire to die, and death will flee from them. ⁷ The shape of the locusts was like horses prepared for battle. On their heads were crowns of something like gold, and their faces were like the faces of men. ⁸ They had hair like women's hair, and their teeth were like lions' teeth. ⁹ And they had

breastplates like breastplates of iron, and the sound of their wings was like the sound of chariots with many horses running into battle. [10] They had tails like scorpions, and there were stings in their tails. Their power was to hurt men five months. [11] And they had as king over them the angel of the bottomless pit, whose name in Hebrew is Abaddon, but in Greek he has the name Apollyon. [12] One woe is past. Behold, still two more woes are coming after these things. *Revelation 9:1-12*

THE SIXTH TRUMPET
[13] Then the sixth angel sounded: And I heard a voice from the four horns of the golden altar which is before God, [14] saying to the sixth angel who had the trumpet, "Release the four angels who are bound at the great river Euphrates." [15] So the four angels, who had been prepared for the hour and day and month and year, were released to kill a third of mankind. [16] Now the number of the army of the horsemen was two hundred million; I heard the number of them. [17] And thus I saw the horses in the vision: those who sat on them had breastplates of fiery red, hyacinth blue, and sulfur yellow; and the heads of the horses were like the heads of lions; and out of their mouths came fire, smoke, and brimstone. [18] By these three plagues a third of mankind was killed—by the fire and the smoke and the brimstone which came out of their mouths. [19] For their power is in their mouth and in their tails; for their tails are like serpents, having heads; and with them they do harm. [20] But the rest of mankind, who were not killed by these plagues, did not repent of the works of their hands, that they should not worship demons, and idols of gold, silver, brass, stone, and wood, which can neither see nor hear nor walk. [21] And they did not repent of their murders or their sorceries or their sexual immorality or their thefts. *Revelation 9:13-21*

THE SEVENTH TRUMPET
[15] Then the seventh angel sounded: And there were loud voices in heaven, saying, "The kingdoms of this world have become the kingdoms of our Lord and of His Christ, and He shall reign forever and ever!" [16] And the twenty-four elders who sat before God on their thrones fell on their faces and worshiped God, [17] saying: "We give You thanks, O Lord God Almighty, the One who is and who was and who is to come, because You have taken Your great power and reigned. [18] The nations were angry, and Your wrath has come, and the time of the dead, that they should be judged, and that You should reward Your servants the prophets and the saints, and those who fear Your name, small and great, and should destroy those who destroy the earth." [19] Then the temple of God was opened in heaven, and the ark of His covenant was seen in His temple. And there were lightnings, noises, thunderings, an earthquake, and great hail. *Revelation 11:15-19*

[4] And when the seven thunders had uttered their voices, I was about to write: and I heard a voice from heaven saying unto me, seal up those things which the seven thunders uttered, and write them not...[6]...that there should be time no longer: [7] But in the days of the voice of the seventh angel, when he shall begin to sound, the mystery of God should be finished, as he hath declared to his servants the prophets. *Revelation 10:4, 6 and 7*

NOTES

"Praying without fervency is like hunting with a dead dog."
— Charles Spurgeon

WEEK 7: THE SEVEN BOWLS

Opening Prayer: Lord, we ask that You send Your Holy Spirit to us to guide us in the teaching and understanding of Your word that we may obtain a better understanding of the prophetic events surrounding us now and waiting for us in the future. Bless our fellowship in Your word that it may be fruitful and draw us into a deeper relationship both with You and those around us. Use us as Your vessels that through us, we may reflect Your glory to all whom we encounter. Illuminate our hearts and minds so that we may boldly shine the brightness of Your light everywhere we go and that we may be beacons of Your hope in a darkened world. In Jesus name we pray, Amen.

Ice Breaker: Among the numerous and varied themes presented throughout the Bible are themes of redemption, hope, love, forgiveness, righteousness, obedience, anger, judgment, destruction, justice and renewal. If your life was a book, what kind of unifying theme would be highlighted throughout the narrative of your years on earth? Identify a strong, primary, overall theme for your life, then share it with the rest of the group. You may add a new theme if your unique theme is not listed among the choices below. There may be many themes that make up the fabric of your life, but choose the one theme that best seems to represent your life.

My Life Theme: _____

Faith	Hope	Love
Independence	Justice	Redemption
Forgiveness	Strength	Righteousness
Obedience	Anger	Judgment
Destruction	Renewal	Perseverance
Power	Healing	Selflessness
Temptation	Truth	Responsibility
Respect	Support	Family
Friendship	Money	Restoration
Integrity	Character	Generosity
Patience	Gratitude	Victory
Honor	Praise	Joy

Focus: God's wrath and punishment go beyond what man can imagine and will not be thwarted or stopped.

CHRISTINE TATE

Word of the Week

> ⁶ And out of the temple came the seven angels having the seven **plagues**, clothed in pure bright linen, and having their chests girded with golden bands.
>
> *Revelation 15:6*

PLAGUE: Punishments visited upon man during the Tribulation for his sinful ways are referred to as plagues. "Plague" in the original Greek is "plege" (pronounced play-gay') which refers to a burdensome affliction or wound. Much like Moses afflicted Pharaoh's kingdom with ten plagues designed to generate a change of heart in Pharaoh leading to a different decision from him, God afflicts the end times generation with a series of plagues intended to motivate people in a different, more godly direction. By issuing a series of escalating, compounding plagues to generate repentance, God issues His final warning to mankind that His patience is about to come to an end.

Lesson: Scripture discusses seven more angels, each with a bowl of destruction to be poured out on mankind:

> ⁶ And out of the temple came the **seven angels having the seven plagues**, clothed in pure bright linen, and having their chests girded with golden bands. ⁷ Then one of the four living creatures gave to the seven angels **seven golden bowls** full of the wrath of God who lives forever and ever. ⁸ The temple was filled with smoke from the glory of God and from His power, and no one was able to enter the temple till the seven plagues of the seven angels were completed. *Revelation 15:6-8*

For the first bowl, those who took the mark of the beast are tormented with a single sore, presumably a fester in the location where they accepted the mark of the beast:

> ¹ Then I heard a loud voice from the temple saying to the seven angels, "Go and pour out the bowls of the wrath of God on the earth." ² So the first went and **poured out his bowl** upon the earth, and **a foul and loathsome sore came upon the men who had the mark of the beast** and those who worshiped his image. *Revelation 16:1-2*

Next, God's angel turns the sea to blood destroying all marine life:

> ³ Then the **second angel poured out his bowl on the sea**, and it **became blood** as of a dead man; and **every living creature in the sea died**. *Revelation 16:3*

After that, freshwater sources are destroyed in a like manner by the third angel:

> ⁴ Then **the third angel poured out his bowl on the rivers and springs of water, and they became blood**. ⁵ And I heard the angel of the waters saying: "You are righteous, O Lord, the One who is and who was and who is to be, because You have judged these things. ⁶ **For they have shed the blood of saints and prophets, and You have given them blood to drink**. For it is their just due." ⁷ And I heard another from the altar saying, "Even so, Lord God Almighty, true and righteous are Your judgments." *Revelation 16:4-7*

For the fourth bowl, the sun's rays become too intense for mankind to bear:

> ⁸ Then **the fourth angel poured out his bowl on the sun**, and power was given to him **to scorch men with fire**. ⁹ And men were scorched with great heat, and they blasphemed the name of God who has power over these plagues; and they did not repent and give Him glory. *Revelation 16:8-9*

Pouring out the fifth bowl, God's angel subjects the Antichrist and his followers to darkness while they nurse their pain:

> ¹⁰ Then **the fifth angel poured out his bowl on the throne of the beast, and his kingdom became full of darkness**; and they gnawed their tongues **because of the pain**. ¹¹ They blasphemed the God of heaven **because of their pains and their sores**, and did not repent of their deeds. *Revelation 16:10-11*

Introducing the sixth bowl, an alliance of leaders from the region of Asia gather to do battle in an area of Israel called the Valley of Megiddo for the Battle of Armageddon.

> ¹² Then **the sixth angel poured out his bowl on the great river Euphrates, and its water was dried up, so that the way of the kings from the east might be prepared**. ¹³ And I saw three unclean spirits like frogs coming out of the mouth of the dragon, out of the mouth of the beast, and out of the mouth of the false

> prophet. ¹⁴ For they are spirits of demons, performing signs, which go out to the kings of the earth and of the whole world, **to gather them to the battle of that great day of God Almighty.** ¹⁵ "Behold, I am coming as a thief. Blessed is he who watches, and keeps his garments, lest he walk naked and they see his shame. ¹⁶ **And they gathered them together to the place called in Hebrew, Armageddon**. *Revelation 16:12-16*

After the Battle of Armageddon, the earth is shaken by the largest earthquake ever to occur, cities are destroyed, mountains and islands disappear and hail stones weighing seventy-five pounds each fall on people.

> ¹⁷ Then **the seventh angel poured out his bowl into the air**, and a loud voice came out of the temple of heaven, from the throne, saying, **"It is done!"** ¹⁸ And there were noises and thunderings and lightnings; and there was a **great earthquake**, such a mighty and great earthquake as had not occurred since men were on the earth. ¹⁹ Now **the great city was divided** into three parts, and the **cities of the nations fell**. And great Babylon was remembered before God, to give her the cup of the wine of the fierceness of His wrath. ²⁰ Then **every island fled away**, and the **mountains were not found**. ²¹ And great **hail from heaven** fell upon men, each hailstone about **the weight of a talent**. Men blasphemed God because of the plague of the hail, since that plague was exceedingly great.
> *Revelation 16:17-21*

For the first time in history, it is possible for an army to mount an invasion by means of crossing a dried-up Euphrates River. Built in 1990, Turkey's Ataturk Dam is capable of drying up the Euphrates River on command. As recently as 2018, Turkey actively used the power of the Ataturk Dam to reduce and control water from the Euphrates River being supplied to Syria in an effort to weaken the Syrian regime. An army working in cooperation

The embankment of the Ataturk Dam is 604 feet high and 5,971 feet long.

with Turkey could quite conceivably dry the Euphrates River on command for a military operation.

Justice is a central theme for the nature of the plagues God unleashes on mankind. It is interesting to note that God's plagues mirror the various ways Christians have been persecuted over the centuries. For their thirst for the blood of the saints, sinners are given blood to drink instead of water:

> ⁶For **they have shed the blood of saints and prophets**, and **You have given them blood to drink**. For it is their just due. ⁷And I heard another from the altar saying, "Even so, Lord God Almighty, true and **righteous are Your judgments**." *Revelation 16:6-7*

Early Christian martyrs were stoned, so God stones sinners with giant hail stones. Echoing the burning of God's people at the stake, God burns sinners with rays from the sun. Sinners may sometimes appear to escape God's wrath in day-to-day life, but be assured, it is only for a little while.

A debate exists as to whether the plagues of the seals, trumpets and bowls should be read linearly as a consecutive series of twenty-one events (three sets of seven punishments issued one after the other), or if each set of seven events is simply a retelling of the same events described from three different perspectives. To answer this question, it is important to note that the events given in Revelation are not presented in chronological order. For example, Revelation 10 states that everything is over, time is no more, and the mystery of God is finished.

> ⁴And when the seven thunders had uttered their voices, I was about to write: and I heard a voice from heaven saying unto me, seal up those things which the seven thunders uttered, and write them not...⁶...that there **should be time no longer**: ⁷But in the days of **the voice of the seventh angel, when he shall begin to sound, the mystery of God should be finished**, as he hath declared to his servants the prophets. *Revelation 10:4, 6-7*

However, in Revelation 16, six chronological chapters later, seven bowl judgments are released on the earth's inhabitants. In the bowl judgments, sores appear on men who took the mark of the beast (Revelation 16:2) and men blaspheme God for scorching them with heat (Revelation 16:8-9). In Revelation 16:10, men still refuse to repent implying that they still have time to repent. Finally, Armageddon arrives in Revelation 16:16. All of the events from the bowl judgments are events that occur prior to time ending and God being finished yet occur after the reference to time being over. Also, the Antichrist appears in Revelation chapter 13 and chapter 19 describes the Day of the Lord when Christ returns. If time ends in chapter 10, then those events cannot happen after chapter 10 unless prophetic events are written out of order. Another example of a verse indicating finality is found in Revelation 11:

> [15] Then the seventh angel sounded: And there were loud voices in heaven, saying, "**The kingdoms of this world have become the kingdoms of our Lord and of His Christ, and He shall reign forever and ever!**" [16] And the twenty-four elders who sat before God on their thrones fell on their faces and worshiped God, [17] saying: "We give You thanks, O Lord God Almighty, the One who is and who was and who is to come, because You have taken Your great power and reigned. [18] The nations were angry, and Your wrath has come, and the **time of the dead, that they should be judged**, and that You should **reward Your servants** the prophets and the saints, and those who fear Your name, small and great, and should destroy those who destroy the earth." [19] Then the **temple of God was opened in heaven**, and the ark of His covenant was seen in His temple. And there were lightnings, noises, thunderings, an earthquake, and great hail. *Revelation 11:15-19*

This passage discusses the judgment of the dead, the reward of the faithful and the opening of the temple of God in heaven as well as the arrival and rule of Christ. None of these events happen prior to the reign of the Antichrist, yet the Antichrist is discussed in a later chapter (Revelation 13). Again, this passage contradicts a linear, chronological reading of the events in Revelation. Additionally, Revelation chapters 11 and 20 both cite judgment events. The fact that both Revelation chapters 11 and 20 reference judgment events, yet are separated by 9 chapters is further proof that a chronological interpretation of Revelation is a faulty method of interpretation. If Revelation is meant to represent a chronological order of events, a duplicate telling of events would not occur in future chapters after an event is mentioned. Organizationally, seals, trumpets and bowls cannot be read from a linear, chronological perspective.

Alternatively, seals, trumpets and bowls can be read as a single event viewed from three different angles. Just as the story of Jesus' birth is told from different perspectives in Matthew and Luke revealing additional details with each telling, so, too, are plague events. Notice in the following chart that only the trumpets column refers to one third of the earth which represents one, consistent perspective. Words expressing finality are also used in the passages of seals, trumpets and bowls. For example, the sixth seal states that "every" mountain is moved when Jesus returns (Revelation 6:14). "Every" limits the event to only happening once. However, in the seventh bowl, "every" mountain flees away again (Revelation 16:20) requiring these events to be related. Armageddon is also referenced in both the sixth trumpet and the sixth bowl. Compare the topical similarities between the verses of the seals, trumpets and bowls when they are lined up next to each other in the following chart. Concepts that are repeated in parallel passages are in bold. To read the corresponding scriptures, refer to the Supporting Scriptures sections for Weeks 5, 6 and 7.

#	SEAL	TRUMPET	BOWL
	Topical Comparison of Seals, Trumpets and Bowls		
	PERSPECTIVE: *Overview for all of humanity as seen from above.*	PERSPECTIVE: *War Zone experienced by 1/3 of humanity.*	PERSPECTIVE: *Repercussions experienced by remaining 2/3 of humanity.*
1st	A white horse arrives with a bow to conquer. Revelation 6:1-2	Hail and fire destroy **1/3** of the trees and all grass burns up. Revelation 8:6-7	Mark of the beast causes sores on men. Revelation 16:1-2
2nd	Peace is removed from the earth and people kill each other. Revelation 6:3-4	**1/3** of the **sea turns to blood**; **1/3** of **sea life dies**; **1/3** of ships destroyed. Revelation 8:8-9	Entire **sea turns to blood** and all **sea life dies**. Revelation 16:3
3rd	Famine arrives with economic inflation. Revelation 6:5-6	**1/3** of **freshwater is undrinkable**. Revelation 8:10-11	**Freshwater** rivers and springs turn to blood and are **undrinkable**. Revelation 16:4-7
4th	A quarter of the earth's population dies from violence/war, famine, disease, and animals. Revelation 6:7-8	**Solar event** with **1/3** of sun, moon and stars darkened creating **partial darkness**. Revelation 8:12-13	**Solar event** causes the sun to scorch men. Revelation 16:8-9
5th	Dead Christians ask Jesus "How much longer?" and are given	Smoke destroys the air quality and causes more **darkness** while	**Darkness** covers whole world (Antichrist's

	white robes. Revelation 6:9-11	locusts attack non-Christians for 5 months causing **pain**. Revelation 9:1-12	kingdom); sores still bother people with added **pain**. Revelation 16:10-11
6th	An earthquake; the sun turns black causing **darkness** while the moon turns blood red. **Every mountain and island are moved.** Men try to hide from God. **Jesus returns.** Revelation 6:12-17 Joel 2:31 Matthew 24:29 Isaiah 2:10 Isaiah 2:19 Habakkuk 3:6	**Euphrates River** angels released, 200,000,000-man army heads to **Armageddon. 1/3** of mankind dies. Revelation 9:13-21	**Euphrates River** dries up; **Armageddon. Jesus returns.** Revelation 16:12-16
7th	Silence for ½ hour in heaven, then prayers of the saints are offered up followed by **noise, thunder, lightning and another earthquake.** Revelation 8:1-5	**Announcement from heaven**, wicked judged, righteous rewarded, **sinners destroyed on earth**, God's temple opened, Ark of the Covenant seen, **hail, noise, thunder, lightning and another earthquake.** Revelation 11:15-19	**Announcement from heaven, every mountain and island are gone.** Nations fall, **sinners destroyed on earth** with destruction of Babylon, **hail, noise, thunder, lightning and another earthquake.** Revelation 16:17-21

Viewing seals, trumpets and bowls as one event expressed from three different angles provides greater detail for a much larger picture that emerges when everything is read as a unified event. Seals represent an overview perspective as evidenced by the fifth seal when Jesus talks to deceased saints about events occurring on earth. Trumpets represent an earthly perspective of an event from the point where the event happens as evidenced by the consistent quantitative use of one-third to define the situation. Bowls represent an earthly perspective of the other two-thirds of the event. To determine the nature of the event, the seals must be read in numerical order. Below is a possible interpretation for the chart:

1st Set of plagues:

OVERVIEW (Seals): A rider on a white horse arrives with a bow to conquer. The word used for "bow" in this passage is from the Greek word "toxon". "Toxon" is only used one time in the Bible and it is in this passage. Referring to a battle weapon that is launched like an arrow and is toxic in nature, the weapon is a nuclear missile. The term "conquering" implies a war.

WAR ZONE (Trumpets): The nuclear war involves one-third of the earth. In the areas impacted by the blast, the trees and grass are burned up.

REPERCUSSIONS (Bowls): In the immediate aftermath of the destruction and chaos, the Antichrist steps forward in a desperate world to seize power and control. He requires everyone to receive RFID implants which are rejected by the human body and cause sores.

2nd Set of plagues:

OVERVIEW (Seals): Peace is removed and people kill each other. The sheer magnitude of the nuclear event overwhelms people and countries. Society breaks down. Looting, thefts and rioting follow as people kill each other doing anything they can to survive in the aftermath of the nuclear destruction. Countries retaliate against other countries doing whatever is necessary to protect their citizens from the related devastation including invading areas which still have necessary resources. Peace is destroyed.

WAR ZONE (Trumpets): The blast from the missiles destroys all ships above the water in the war zone. Radioactive fallout from the nuclear blast immediately poisons the oceans in the areas which experienced the nuclear blasts killing sea life in the region of the explosions.

REPERCUSSIONS (Bowls): Ocean currents carry the toxic ocean water all over the globe. Eventually, all of the oceans on the planet are affected killing all forms of sea life everywhere.

3rd Set of plagues:

OVERVIEW (Seal): Famine and hyperinflation escalate. With the removal of all of the ocean's resources (fish, shrimp, crab, lobster, seaweed, trace minerals, salt, etc.), those who make their living from the sea no longer have jobs and all forms of marine based foods are no longer available. Prices escalate for ocean related products. Carrageenan comes from a form of red algae in the ocean and is an ingredient in many other products such as ice-cream, chocolate milk, toothpaste, make-up and sunscreen. Agar comes from the ocean and is used in yogurt. Kelp is used in shampoos and cake mixes. A form of brown algae called algin is used in salad dressings. Sea whip corals give allergy medicines their anti-inflammatory properties. Entertainment based ocean activities suffer too. Cruise ships stop sailing, people stop vacationing at the beach impacting tourist and ocean dependent businesses such as jet ski rentals and aquatic adventures. Coastal cities increase taxes to pay for the clean-up of all the rotting sea creature corpses that wash up on the shores of their city. The loss of many food products connected to the ocean reduces the available food supply causing famine to begin. Some growing regions remain intact where oil and wine are produced indicating a few safety zones still exist and limited food production still functions. However, demand outpaces supply in many areas and a hyperinflationary monetary environment begins.

WAR ZONE (Trumpets): When a missile travels by air, the fire emitted from its tail makes it look like a star. The Ukrainian word for wormwood is Chernobyl. Chernobyl is known for being a nuclear event that contaminated the atmosphere and the environment. When the "star", or nuclear missile, hits the earth, it contaminates rivers, lakes and springs in the third of the world participating in the nuclear event.

REPERCUSSIONS (Bowls): Fresh water sources such as rivers and lakes are connected to oceans through the water cycle. As the ocean cross-contamination spreads around the globe, it affects connected freshwater sources around the world which are poisoned by mingling with contaminated water. Other freshwater sources are contaminated by groundwater runoff and fallout from the atmosphere. As freshwater sources dwindle, crops cannot be grown without enough available clean, fresh water. When crops fail to yield a harvest, famine ensues. Along with food scarcity, prices increase and an inflationary environment continues to develop for the goods that are available.

4th Set of plagues:

OVERVIEW (Seals): A quarter of the population dies from the extent of the famine and its related effects. A frantic population panics about the effects of the loss of the world's oceans, dwindling freshwater sources and the inability to grow crops. Debates turn ugly and fights ensue as no one knows how to fix the problem. Wars erupt over food sources killing even more people. Without food, disease sets in on a weakened population taking even more lives. Radiological exposure from the atmosphere causes diseases like cancer and reduces immunity in humans. Hunger takes even more lives. Animals affected by the famine are forced to venture into urban and suburban populations in search of new food sources. In some cases, humans become the new food source for larger animals. Hungry and desperate wild beasts such as bears, coyotes and wolves attack children.

WAR ZONE (Trumpets): In the areas of the globe directly affected by the nuclear blasts, toxic clouds of soot and ash are launched into the atmosphere and block out light from the sun, moon and stars causing a nuclear winter. Darkness falls on that part of the world. Without light from the sun, growing conditions decline even further intensifying the famine as crops need light to grow.

REPERCUSSIONS (Bowls): A nuclear blast damages the ozone layer of the planet. Upper atmosphere air currents cause radiological drift around the world. In many areas around the world, the ozone layer is damaged from the effects of the nuclear war. The ozone layer is what protects mankind from the sun's rays. With the ozone layer diminished or gone, the earth scorches men with intense heat from the sun's rays. Both humans and crops alike suffer negative effects from the intensity of the sun diminishing even further the amount of food that can be grown and making exposure to the environment miserable for humans.

5th Set of plagues:

OVERVIEW (Seal): Deceased Christians wake up and question Jesus about the events occurring on the earth. Deceased Christians wake up and are astounded by what they see happening. They question Jesus about how long the situation can continue. Jesus gives them white robes, indicates there is still more to come and tells them to go back to sleep.

WAR ZONE (Trumpets): The soot and ash released from the blast drifts with upper atmosphere air currents and decreases air quality around the world. A rebellion is launched against the Antichrist and his forces. The military attack lasts five months and is precision targeted at the Antichrist and his forces. The "stings" of the bombs cause agonizing pain among those with the mark who are being attacked. Accompanying the military campaign against the Antichrist and his forces is a cyberattack aimed at the RFID implants worn by civilian Antichrist supporters in an attempt to disable the devices while leaving the humans unharmed.

REPERCUSSIONS (Bowls): Eventually, the smoke drifts around the entire globe blocking light from the sun resulting in global darkness. No crops can be grown anywhere now. People are still miserable from the sores caused by taking the mark of the beast. However, they have additional torments with which to contend. Those in the drift zone of a nuclear explosion may be exposed to high levels of radiation. The effects of radiological exposure create misery on an unprecedented scale. Excessive radiological exposure causes painful radiation burns as well as nausea, vomiting, diarrhea, hair loss, neurological effects and genetic mutations resulting in unimaginable pain for those suffering from these conditions.

6th Set of plagues:

OVERVIEW (Seals): Natural disasters. When Jesus returns, massive earthquakes rock the earth affecting the sun, moon and stars. Meteors fall to the earth. All of the mountains and islands are displaced as they are forcibly shaken out of position. People tremble in fear and do their best to take shelter from the catastrophic events occurring on earth when Jesus returns.

WAR ZONE (Trumpets): As the war intensifies, a Chinese-Mongolian alliance of 200,000,000 soldiers journeys to Armageddon by way of the Euphrates River. They kill a third of mankind during the battle of Armageddon.

REPERCUSSIONS (Bowls): The Chinese-Mongolian alliance coordinates with Turkey to use the Ataturk Dam to dry up the Euphrates River to allow their army to pass through on their way to the Hill of Megiddo where they participate in the war of Armageddon. Jesus shows up with a surprise appearance to defend Israel.

7th Set of plagues:

OVERVIEW (Seals): The mayhem ends. There is silence in heaven for half-an-hour, prayers of God's children are offered up to God with incense followed by noise, thunder, lightning and another earthquake on earth.

WAR ZONE (Trumpets): An announcement is made that God is now in control of everything. Twenty-four elders are seen worshipping God. God judges the wicked dead, rewards His faithful servants and destroys the remaining sinners on earth. God's temple in heaven is opened revealing the Ark of the Covenant followed by noise, thunder, lightning, hail and another earthquake on earth.

REPERCUSSIONS (Bowls): An announcement is made from God's temple that everything is complete followed by noise, thunder, lightning and another earthquake on earth. With all the mountains and islands completely gone, the nations of the world fall, and Babylon is destroyed. Everything on earth ends with seventy-five-pound hail stones, noise, thunder, lightning and earthquakes. People are still complaining.

The above is just a hypothetical postulation for how the verses of the seals, trumpets and bowls might tie together into one narrative creating a single set of events. Only time will reveal the true order of events and how they all relate.

Talk It Out

1. Do you think there is a connection between the ways Christians have been persecuted and the nature of the plagues God sends during the Tribulation (Revelation 16:6)?

2. Do you think that seals, trumpets and bowls should be read as twenty-one consecutive events happening one after the other, or should they be interpreted as different descriptions of the same event? Why or why not?

3. Why do you think God sends seals, trumpets and bowls judgments? Do you think it is an excessive use of force or do you think that it is a fair warning strategy to give people ample opportunity to repent?

4. Do you think the water represented as blood is a red tide, radiologically contaminated water or something else? When all sources of water are rendered undrinkable, do you think people will realize that all life on earth is about to come to an end? If not, why not? If yes, why do they still fail to repent as indicated in Revelation 16:9?

5. Are there any above ground structures you can think of that would withstand an impact from seventy-five-pound hail stones? What percentage of the population do you think would be able to find adequate subterranean shelter?

6. Right before His return at the pouring out of the sixth bowl, Jesus warns of the surprise of His return as coming as a thief in the night (Revelation 16:15). The thief reference is also mentioned again in Matthew 24:42, 2 Peter 3:10 and 1 Thessalonians 5:4 highlighting its significance. Do you think only non-Christians are unaware of the signs of His return and will be caught by surprise or do you think many Christians are equally ignorant of the signs and will be caught off guard?

7. Do you agree with the interpretation given for the chart on pages 107-108 or do you have another interpretation for the chart?

8. Do you think a "star" named Wormwood could be a nuclear missile?

Ideas for the Week:

- ✓ Look at a map of the Euphrates River where it flows through Turkey.
- ✓ Look at a map of Israel and find the location of the Valley of Megiddo where the Battle of Armageddon will be fought.
- ✓ Close your eyes when you have a few quiet moments alone and visualize what you think the Throne of God might look like.
- ✓ The dictionary defines blasphemy as "the act of insulting or showing contempt or lack of reverence for God" and "irreverence toward something sacred or inviolable". As you go about your week, observe your surroundings and the people around you to observe how prevalent blasphemy is in our life and culture.

Closing Prayer

NOTE: Add names and individual personal prayer requests to the space provided below before closing in prayer.

Lord, we thank You for our time together today to grow deeper in our walk with You and fellowship with each other. As we close today, we lift up: _____

_____

_____

_____

_____

_____

_____

Father, we may not always know what lies ahead, but we trust in Your perfect plan. Give us the inner strength to bravely face whatever the future may hold and shower us with the peace that passes all understanding. Cleanse us of all unrighteousness and forgive us if we have been disrespectful or blasphemous towards You in any way. In Jesus' name we pray, Amen.

SUPPORTING SCRIPTURES

THE SEVEN BOWLS
[1] Then I saw another sign in heaven, great and marvelous: seven angels having the seven last plagues for in them the wrath of God is complete. [2] And I saw something like a sea of glass mingled with fire, and those who have the victory over the beast, over his image and over his mark and over the number of his name, standing on the sea of glass, having harps of God. [3] They sing the song of Moses, the servant of God, and the song of the Lamb, saying: "Great and marvelous are Your works, Lord God Almighty! Just and true are Your ways, O King of the saints! [4] Who shall not fear You, O Lord, and glorify Your name? For You alone are holy. For all nations shall come and worship before You, For Your judgments have been manifested." [5] After these things I looked, and behold, the temple of the tabernacle of the testimony in heaven was opened. [6] And out of the temple came the seven angels having the seven plagues, clothed in pure bright linen, and having their chests girded with golden bands. [7] Then one of the four living creatures gave to the seven angels seven golden bowls full of the wrath of God who lives forever and ever. [8] The temple was filled with smoke from the glory of God and from His power, and no one was able to enter the temple till the seven plagues of the seven angels were completed. *Revelation 15:1-8*

THE FIRST BOWL
[1] Then I heard a loud voice from the temple saying to the seven angels, "Go and pour out the bowls of the wrath of God on the earth." [2] So the first went and poured out his bowl upon the earth, and a foul and loathsome sore came upon the men who had the mark of the beast and those who worshiped his image. *Revelation 16:1-2*

THE SECOND BOWL
[3] Then the second angel poured out his bowl on the sea, and it became blood as of a dead man; and every living creature in the sea died. *Revelation 16:3*

THE THIRD BOWL
[4] Then the third angel poured out his bowl on the rivers and springs of water, and they became blood. [5] And I heard the angel of the waters saying: "You are righteous, O Lord, the One who is and who was and who is to be, because You have judged these things. [6] For they have shed the blood of saints and prophets, and You have given them blood to drink. For it is their just due." [7] And I heard another from the altar saying, "Even so, Lord God Almighty, true and righteous are Your judgments." *Revelation 16:4-7*

THE FOURTH BOWL
[8] Then the fourth angel poured out his bowl on the sun, and power was given to

him to scorch men with fire. ⁹ And men were scorched with great heat, and they blasphemed the name of God who has power over these plagues; and they did not repent and give Him glory. *Revelation 16:8-9*

THE FIFTH BOWL
¹⁰ Then the fifth angel poured out his bowl on the throne of the beast, and his kingdom became full of darkness; and they gnawed their tongues because of the pain. ¹¹ They blasphemed the God of heaven because of their pains and their sores, and did not repent of their deeds. *Revelation 16:10-11*

THE SIXTH BOWL
¹² Then the sixth angel poured out his bowl on the great river Euphrates, and its water was dried up, so that the way of the kings from the east might be prepared. ¹³ And I saw three unclean spirits like frogs coming out of the mouth of the dragon, out of the mouth of the beast, and out of the mouth of the false prophet. ¹⁴ For they are spirits of demons, performing signs, which go out to the kings of the earth and of the whole world, to gather them to the battle of that great day of God Almighty. ¹⁵ "Behold, I am coming as a thief. Blessed is he who watches, and keeps his garments, lest he walk naked and they see his shame. ¹⁶ And they gathered them together to the place called in Hebrew, Armageddon. *Revelation 16:12-16*

THE SEVENTH BOWL
¹⁷ Then the seventh angel poured out his bowl into the air, and a loud voice came out of the temple of heaven, from the throne, saying, "It is done!" ¹⁸ And there were noises and thunderings and lightnings; and there was a great earthquake, such a mighty and great earthquake as had not occurred since men were on the earth. ¹⁹ Now the great city was divided into three parts, and the cities of the nations fell. And great Babylon was remembered before God, to give her the cup of the wine of the fierceness of His wrath. ²⁰ Then every island fled away, and the mountains were not found. ²¹ And great hail from heaven fell upon men, each hailstone about the weight of a talent. Men blasphemed God because of the plague of the hail, since that plague was exceedingly great. *Revelation 16:17-21*

NOTES

> "If God would have wanted us to live in a permissive society, He would have given us Ten Suggestions and not Ten Commandments." – Zig Ziglar

WEEK 8: ISRAEL

Opening Prayer: Lord, we ask that You send Your Holy Spirit to us to guide us in the teaching and understanding of Your word that we may obtain a better understanding of the prophetic events surrounding us now and waiting for us in the future. Bless our fellowship in Your word that it may be fruitful and draw us into a deeper relationship both with You and those around us. Use us as Your vessels that through us, we may reflect Your glory to all whom we encounter. Illuminate our hearts and minds so that we may boldly shine the brightness of Your light everywhere we go and that we may be beacons of Your hope in a darkened world. In Jesus name we pray, Amen.

Ice Breaker: Take a coin or bill of any denomination out of your purse or wallet. If you do not have any money on you, borrow a coin or bill from someone else in the group. Look at the date on the coin or bill. Name a personal change you went through or a life event which occurred that year. The change or event can be major or minor in its significance. If the date on the coin is a date prior to your birth, think of something historically important that happened that year. Share the event associated with each coin with the rest of your group.

Date of Coin: _____

Change or event for that year: _____

Focus: God's devotion and faithfulness to His people will never waiver.

The Balfour Declaration

"His Majesty's government view with favour the establishment in Palestine of a national home for the Jewish people, and will use their best endeavours to facilitate the achievement of this object, it being clearly understood that nothing shall be done which may prejudice the civil and religious rights of existing non-Jewish communities in Palestine, or the rights and political status enjoyed by Jews in any other country."

— Letter from Arthur James Balfour to Lord Rothschild
November 2, 1917

ARE WE THE TERMINAL GENERATION?

Word of the Week

> ³⁴ Assuredly, I say to you, this **generation** will by no means pass away till all these things take place.
>
> *Matthew 24:34*

GENERATION: As translated from the Greek word "genea" (pronounced ghen-eh-ah'), a generation refers to a group of people living at the same time who exhibit similar characteristics. People are affected by circumstances and naturally become products of their environment. Generations are united by a set of common experiences. When a group of people experience uniform events, certain qualities emerge. Frugality marked the generation which lived through the depression. An irreverent love of personal freedoms unified those who lived through the 1960's. The events of September 11, 2001 instilled a sense of vulnerability in those of that generation. When Jesus returns, what kind of generation will He find? According to the characteristics defined in Matthew 24, the generation of His return will be an ungodly, lawless generation who refuses to recognize truth. In that generation, people will hate, betray and offend each other having no love in their hearts for their fellow human beings (Matthew 24:9-12). Parallels exist with what can be seen in our world day. People worship the god of personal happiness and define morality by what seems good to them in their own minds while hating and betraying others to further their own interests and desires. Would God approve?

Lesson: No discussion of end time prophecy would be complete without a brief study of Israel. Chosen by God, Israel is the apple of God's eye:

⁸ ...for he who touches **you** (Israel) touches **the apple of His eye**. *Zechariah 2:8*

Not only does God adore Israel, but she is also a key player in prophetic end time events. To appreciate Israel's role in prophecy, it is important to understand Israel's history. Symbolically, Israel is represented in the Bible as a fig tree:

¹⁰ I found **Israel** like grapes in the wilderness; **I saw your fathers as the firstfruits on the fig tree** in its first season. But they went

to Baal Peor, and separated themselves to that shame; they became an abomination like the thing they loved. *Hosea 9:10*

Through the parable of the fig tree, scripture informs us that ancient Israel experienced significant spiritual decay:

> [1] The LORD showed me, and there were **two baskets of figs** set before the temple of the LORD, after Nebuchadnezzar king of Babylon had carried away captive Jeconiah the son of Jehoiakim, king of Judah, and the princes of Judah with the craftsmen and smiths, from Jerusalem, and had brought them to Babylon. [2] **One basket had very good figs**, like the figs that are first ripe; and **the other basket had very bad figs** which could not be eaten, they were so bad. *Jeremiah 24:1-2*

DID YOU KNOW? Only 13% of modern Israelis identify as conservative Orthodox Jews.

As a result, after repeated warnings through God's prophets, God allowed the Babylonians to destroy Israel and take its inhabitants away captive:

> "...[9] behold, I will send and take all the families of the north," says the LORD, "and **Nebuchadnezzar the king of Babylon**, My servant, and will **bring them against this land**, against its inhabitants, and against these nations all around, and will utterly destroy them, and make them an astonishment, a hissing, and perpetual desolations. [11] ...and **these nations shall serve the king of Babylon seventy years.** [12] Then it will come to pass, **when seventy years are completed**, that **I will punish the king of Babylon** and that nation, the land of the Chaldeans, for their iniquity," says the LORD; "and I will make it a perpetual desolation." *Jeremiah 25:9, 11-12*

Around 70 AD, the Romans invaded Israel again. From that point forward, Israel ceased to be a nation. For hundreds of years, the nation of Israel simply did not exist. Yet, God prophesied that the nation of Israel would be reborn again one day as He gathers His children from where they have been scattered around the globe:

> ...³ that the LORD your God will **bring you back from captivity**, and have compassion on you, **and gather you again from all the nations where the LORD your God has scattered you**. ⁴ If any of you are driven out to the farthest parts under heaven, from there the LORD your God will gather you, and from there He will bring you. ⁵ Then the LORD your God **will bring you to the land which your fathers possessed, and you shall possess it**. He will prosper you and multiply you more than your fathers. *Deuteronomy 30:3-5*

> ¹¹ For thus says the Lord GOD: "Indeed **I Myself will search for My sheep** and seek them out...¹³ And I will bring them out from the peoples and **gather them from the countries, and will bring them to their own land;** I will feed them on the mountains of Israel, in the valleys and in all the inhabited places of the country." *Ezekiel 34:11, 13*

> ²⁴ For **I will take you from among the nations**, gather you out of all countries, and **bring you into your own land.** *Ezekiel 36:24*

> ¹⁷ Therefore say, "Thus says the Lord GOD: '**I will gather you** from the peoples, assemble you **from the countries** where you have been scattered, and I will **give you the land of Israel.**' " *Ezekiel 11:17*

When Israel is gathered back into her own land, God blesses her with fruitfulness:

> ³ For the LORD will comfort Zion, He will comfort all her waste places; **He will make her wilderness like Eden**, and her desert like the garden of the LORD... *Isaiah 51:3*

True to His word, God has turned the barrenness of Israel into a productive garden. Israel's agricultural industry is thriving. Despite her inhospitable, arid climate, Israel is today able to grow a wide range of crops including wheat, corn, citrus, avocados, guavas, kiwis, mangoes, grapes, tomatoes, cucumbers, peppers, zucchinis, melons, strawberries, nectarines, loquats, persimmons, pomegranates, bananas, dates, apples, pears, cherries, and cotton. Israeli cows have the highest output of milk per animal of anywhere in the world. With plenty to spare, Israel is able to export produce to the rest of the world.

Prophecy became reality on November 2, 1917. At the end of WWI, Israel's birth pangs began with the signing of The Balfour Declaration. The Balfour Declaration called for the re-emergence of the State of Israel. Although the declaration went forth among the nations requesting a renewed State of Israel, no progress was made toward that end until WWII. At the end of WWII, thirty-one years from the initial call for a renewed State of Israel, Israel finally became a nation once more and was recognized by the international community on May 14, 1948. Although Israel was once again in existence, Jerusalem was still missing from God's promised land. It would be yet another nineteen years until the summer of 1967 when Jerusalem would be added to Israel's territory following the Six Day war. With the addition of Jerusalem on June 10, 1967, Israel was finally complete as a nation. From the initial call for a new nation of Israel to the reality of an Israeli state, the entire process took fifty years. It is interesting to note that biblically, fifty represents the year of jubilee when freedom is granted to that which has been held captive. Today, Israel is a thriving world power with a highly developed agricultural industry just as the Bible predicted would happen.

Once Israel became an internationally recognized nation, they began a program through The Jewish Agency to return Jewish people to their homeland from wherever they were scattered throughout the world. Other organizations such as The International Fellowship of Christians and Jews also assist in programs aimed at helping Jewish people return to their ancestral homeland. The efforts have been immensely successful as prophesied in Ezekiel's allegory of the dry bones:

> [1] The hand of the LORD...set me down in the midst of the valley; and it was full of bones...[3] And He said to me, "Son of man, can these bones live?" So, I answered, "O Lord GOD, You know." [4] Again He said to me, "**Prophesy to these bones**, and say to them, 'O dry bones, hear the word of the LORD!' [5] Thus says the Lord GOD to these bones: Surely I will cause breath to enter into you, and you shall live. [6] I will put sinews on you and bring flesh upon you, cover you with skin and put breath in you; and you shall live. Then you shall know that I am the LORD." [7] **So I prophesied** as I was commanded; and as I prophesied, there was a noise, and suddenly a rattling; and **the bones came together**, bone to bone. [8] Indeed, as I looked, **the sinews and the flesh came upon them**, and the **skin covered them** over; but there was no breath in them. [9] Also He said to me, "Prophesy to the breath, prophesy, son of man, and say to the breath, 'Thus says the Lord GOD: "Come from the four winds, O breath, and breathe on these slain,

that they may live.' " ' " ¹⁰ So I prophesied as He commanded me, and **breath came into them**, and **they lived**, and stood upon their feet, **an exceedingly great army**. ¹¹ Then He said to me, "Son of man, **these bones are the whole house of Israel**. They indeed say, 'Our bones are dry, our hope is lost, and we ourselves are cut off!' ¹² Therefore prophesy and say to them, 'Thus says the Lord GOD: "Behold, O My people, I will **open your graves** and cause you to come up from your graves, and **bring you into the land of Israel**. ¹³ Then you shall know that I am the LORD, when I have opened your graves, O My people, and brought you up from your graves. ¹⁴ I will put My Spirit in you, and you shall live, and I will place you in your own land. Then you shall know that I, the LORD, have spoken it and performed it," says the LORD.'" *Ezekiel 37:1, 2-14*

God accomplished exactly what He said He would do. Today, Israel is the only Jewish nation in existence.

Regarding the study of end time prophecy, the significance of Israel's re-emergence revolves around the fact that prophecy states the generation which sees the coming together again of Israel will be the same generation to see the return of Christ:

> ³² Now learn this parable from **the fig tree**: When its branch has already become tender and **puts forth leaves**, you know that **summer is near**. ³³ So you also, **when you see all these things, know that it is near—at the doors**! ³⁴ Assuredly, I say to you, **this generation will by no means pass away** till all these things take place. ³⁵ Heaven and earth will pass away, but My words will by no means pass away. *Matthew 24:32-35*

Many theories exist as to the exact length of a generation. The Merriam-Webster Dictionary defines a generation as "the average lifespan of time between the birth of parents and that of their offspring". Since most people have their children between the ages of twenty to forty years old, the dictionary's definition of a generation's length is roughly equivalent to twenty to forty years. Biblically, a generation is defined as one hundred and twenty years in the Old Testament:

> ³ And the LORD said, "My Spirit shall not strive with **man** forever, for he is indeed flesh; yet **his days shall be one hundred and twenty years**." *Genesis 6:3*

By the New Testament, the definition of a generation changed in length to seventy to eighty years:

> ^{10} The **days of our lives are seventy years**; and if by **reason of strength they are eighty years**, yet their boast is only labor and sorrow; for it is soon cut off, and we fly away. *Psalm 90:10*

These explanations base the definition of a lifespan on the length of a person's total lifespan from birth to death. According to televangelist Jack Van Impe, another way to calculate the length of a generation is to take the forty-two generations given in Matthew 1:17 and divide them by the time period in which they occurred which is two thousand one hundred and sixty years.

> ^{17} So all the generations from **Abraham to David are fourteen generations**, from **David until the captivity in Babylon are fourteen generations**, and from the **captivity in Babylon until the Christ are fourteen generations**. *Matthew 1:17*

The resulting average length of a generation using this method comes out to fifty-one and one-half years.

Prophecy also states that once Israel is restored as a nation, it will never again be dispersed from being a nation.

> ^{14} "I will **bring back the captives of My people Israel**; they shall build the waste cities and inhabit them; they shall plant vineyards and drink wine from them; they shall also make gardens and eat fruit from them. ^{15} I will plant them in their land, and **no longer shall they be pulled up from the land I have given them**," says the LORD your God. *Amos 9:14-15*

> ^{21} Then say to them, "Thus says the Lord GOD: 'Surely **I will take the children of Israel** from among the nations, wherever they have gone, and will **gather them** from every side and **bring them into their own land**; ^{22} and I will **make them one nation** in the land, on the mountains of Israel; and one king shall be king over them all; they shall no longer be two nations, **nor shall they ever be divided into two kingdoms again**.'" *Ezekiel 37:21-22*

> ^{6} For I will set My eyes on them for good, and **I will bring them back to this land**; I will build them and not pull them down, and **I will plant them and not pluck them up**. *Jeremiah 24:1-7*

Since Israel can never be divided again after returning as a nation, to hold the belief that Israel will be defeated by her modern-day enemies, then be reborn again at some point in the future making an unspecified future generation the Terminal Generation is a violation of biblical prophecy which would make God a liar. Make no mistake, God never lies. If God says the return of Israel is a sign of Christ's imminent return, then start looking up.

Talk It Out

1. Do you think there is prophetic significance in the fact that it took fifty years for Israel's birth process to be completed and biblically, every fiftieth year is considered a jubilee year?

2. Jeremiah 24:1-5 says that it was for Israel's own good that they were carried away as Babylonian captives. How do you think the Israelites felt about being taken away as captives to a strange and foreign land? Have you ever experienced times in your own life when you endured hardship for your own good?

3. Which year do you think best represents the year Israel became a nation: 1917, 1948 or 1967? Explain your reasons.

4. How long is the length of a generation? Is a generation the length of a person's lifespan or the time between a person's birth and the birth of their children? If you believe it is the length of a physical lifespan, is the length 70 years, 80 years or 120 years? Or, is the length of a generation the average of all generations which is 51.5 years according to Jack Van Impe? Use the space below to add your answer from question 3 to your answer from question 4 to determine a rough timeframe that could be a marker for the identity of the Terminal Generation. Share your answer with the group. (NOTE: Answers will vary)

   Year of Israel's birth (1917, 1948 or 1967)   _____

   Length of a generation (20-40 years, 70-80
   or 120 years or 51.5 years)   + _____

   Final Year   = _____

5. It would be a violation of biblical prophecy for the renewed State of Israel to be conquered once again and then re-established again at some later date in the future. Given the turmoil in the Middle East, how long do you think Israel can survive without Christ's return to protect her? Weeks? Months? Decades? Centuries?

Ideas for the Week:

- ✓ Research the Balfour Declaration.
- ✓ Read the book *Six Days of War* by Michael B. Oren or the Israeli newspaper *The Jerusalem Post* at www.jpost.com.
- ✓ Take a DNA test at iGENEA (www.igenea.com) to determine if you have Jewish ancestry and to which tribe you might belong.
- ✓ Explore the absorption process for Jewish people returning to Israel at www.jewishagency.org or make a donation to The International Fellowship of Christians and Jews at www.ifcj.org to help Jewish people return to their homeland.

Closing Prayer

NOTE: *Add names and individual personal prayer requests to the space provided below before closing in prayer.*

Lord, we thank You for our time together today to grow deeper in our walk with You and fellowship with each other. As we close today, we lift up: _____

_____

_____

_____

_____

_____

_____

_____

Father, we know that Israel is the apple of Your eye and we ask You to show us how we can be a blessing to Israel through our actions and our speech. Open our hearts that we may love the things that You love and hate the things that You hate. Bring our minds into perfect unity with Your mind and let us ever be in Your service. In Jesus' name we pray, Amen.

SUPPORTING SCRIPTURES

FIG TREE

[10] I found Israel like grapes in the wilderness; I saw your fathers as the firstfruits on the fig tree in its first season. But they went to Baal Peor, and separated themselves to that shame; they became an abomination like the thing they loved. *Hosea 9:10*

ISRAEL FALLS AWAY FROM GOD AND PAYS THE PRICE

[1] The LORD showed me, and there were two baskets of figs set before the temple of the LORD, after Nebuchadnezzar king of Babylon had carried away captive Jeconiah the son of Jehoiakim, king of Judah, and the princes of Judah with the craftsmen and smiths, from Jerusalem, and had brought them to Babylon. [2] One basket had very good figs, like the figs that are first ripe; and the other basket had very bad figs which could not be eaten, they were so bad. [3] Then the LORD said to me, "What do you see, Jeremiah?" And I said, "Figs, the good figs, very good; and the bad, very bad, which cannot be eaten, they are so bad." [4] Again the word of the LORD came to me, saying, [5] "Thus says the LORD, the God of Israel: 'Like these good figs, so will I acknowledge those who are carried away captive from Judah, whom I have sent out of this place for their own good, into the land of the Chaldeans. [6] For I will set My eyes on them for good, and I will bring them back to this land; I will build them and not pull them down, and I will plant them and not pluck them up. [7] Then I will give them a heart to know Me, that I am the LORD; and they shall be My people, and I will be their God, for they shall return to Me with their whole heart.' " *Jeremiah 24:1-7*

[13] Yet the LORD testified against Israel and against Judah, by all of His prophets, every seer, saying, "Turn from your evil ways, and keep My commandments and My statutes, according to all the law which I commanded your fathers, and which I sent to you by My servants the prophets." *2 Kings 17:13*

[62] You shall be left few in number, whereas you were as the stars of heaven in multitude, because you would not obey the voice of the LORD your God. [63] And it shall be, that just as the LORD rejoiced over you to do you good and multiply you, so the LORD will rejoice over you to destroy you and bring you to nothing; and you shall be plucked from off the land which you go to possess. [64] Then the LORD will scatter you among all peoples, from one end of the earth to the other, and there you shall serve other gods, which neither you nor your fathers have known—wood and stone. [65] And among those nations you shall find no rest, nor shall the sole of your foot have a resting place; but there the LORD will give you a trembling heart, failing eyes, and anguish of soul. *Deuteronomy 28:62-65*

"...⁹ behold, I will send and take all the families of the north," says the LORD, "and Nebuchadnezzar the king of Babylon, My servant, and will bring them against this land, against its inhabitants, and against these nations all around, and will utterly destroy them, and make them an astonishment, a hissing, and perpetual desolations. ¹⁰ Moreover I will take from them the voice of mirth and the voice of gladness, the voice of the bridegroom and the voice of the bride, the sound of the millstones and the light of the lamp. ¹¹ And this whole land shall be a desolation and an astonishment, and these nations shall serve the king of Babylon seventy years. ¹² Then it will come to pass, when seventy years are completed, that I will punish the king of Babylon and that nation, the land of the Chaldeans, for their iniquity," says the LORD; "and I will make it a perpetual desolation." *Jeremiah 25:9-12*

¹⁰ ...After seventy years are completed at Babylon, I will visit you and perform My good word toward you, and cause you to return to this place. *Jeremiah 29:10*

ISRAEL RESTORED AS A NATION
...³ that the LORD your God will bring you back from captivity, and have compassion on you, and gather you again from all the nations where the LORD your God has scattered you. ⁴ If any of you are driven out to the farthest parts under heaven, from there the LORD your God will gather you, and from there He will bring you. ⁵ Then the LORD your God will bring you to the land which your fathers possessed, and you shall possess it. He will prosper you and multiply you more than your fathers. *Deuteronomy 30:3-5*

⁶ I will say to the north, "Give them up!" and to the south, "Do not keep them back!" Bring My sons from afar, and My daughters from the ends of the earth— *Isaiah 43:6*

¹¹ For thus says the Lord GOD: "Indeed I Myself will search for My sheep and seek them out. ¹² As a shepherd seeks out his flock on the day he is among his scattered sheep, so will I seek out My sheep and deliver them from all the places where they were scattered on a cloudy and dark day. ¹³ And I will bring them out from the peoples and gather them from the countries, and will bring them to their own land; I will feed them on the mountains of Israel, in the valleys and in all the inhabited places of the country." *Ezekiel 34:11-13*

²⁴ For I will take you from among the nations, gather you out of all countries, and bring you into your own land. *Ezekiel 36:24*

¹⁷ Therefore say, "Thus says the Lord GOD: 'I will gather you from the peoples, assemble you from the countries where you have been scattered, and I will give you the land of Israel.' " *Ezekiel 11:17*

[1] The hand of the LORD...set me down in the midst of the valley; and it was full of bones. [2] ...there were very many in the open valley; and indeed, they were very dry. [3] And He said to me, "Son of man, can these bones live?" So, I answered, "O Lord GOD, You know." [4] Again He said to me, "Prophesy to these bones, and say to them, 'O dry bones, hear the word of the LORD! [5] Thus says the Lord GOD to these bones: "Surely I will cause breath to enter into you, and you shall live. [6] I will put sinews on you and bring flesh upon you, cover you with skin and put breath in you; and you shall live. Then you shall know that I am the LORD." [7] So I prophesied as I was commanded; and as I prophesied, there was a noise, and suddenly a rattling; and the bones came together, bone to bone. [8] Indeed, as I looked, the sinews and the flesh came upon them, and the skin covered them over; but there was no breath in them. [9] Also He said to me, "Prophesy to the breath, prophesy, son of man, and say to the breath, 'Thus says the Lord GOD: "Come from the four winds, O breath, and breathe on these slain, that they may live." ' " [10] So I prophesied as He commanded me, and breath came into them, and they lived, and stood upon their feet, an exceedingly great army. [11] Then He said to me, "Son of man, these bones are the whole house of Israel. They indeed say, 'Our bones are dry, our hope is lost, and we ourselves are cut off!' [12] Therefore prophesy and say to them, 'Thus says the Lord GOD: "Behold, O My people, I will open your graves and cause you to come up from your graves, and bring you into the land of Israel. [13] Then you shall know that I am the LORD, when I have opened your graves, O My people, and brought you up from your graves. [14] I will put My Spirit in you, and you shall live, and I will place you in your own land. Then you shall know that I, the LORD, have spoken it and performed it," says the LORD.' " *Ezekiel 37:1-14*

[7] "Before she was in labor, she gave birth; before her pain came, she delivered a male child. [8] Who has heard such a thing? Who has seen such things? Shall the earth be made to give birth in one day? Or shall a nation be born at once? For as soon as Zion was in labor, she gave birth to her children. [9] Shall I bring to the time of birth, and not cause delivery?" says the LORD. "Shall I who cause delivery shut up the womb?" says your God. [10] "Rejoice with Jerusalem, and be glad with her, all you who love her; rejoice for joy with her, all you who mourn for her..." *Isaiah 66:7-10*

JUBILEE YEAR
[10] And you shall consecrate the fiftieth year, and proclaim liberty throughout all the land to all its inhabitants. It shall be a Jubilee for you; and each of you shall return to his possession, and each of you shall return to his family. *Leviticus 25:10*

JESUS TO RETURN WHEN ISRAEL IS A NATION AGAIN

³² Now learn this parable from the fig tree: When its branch has already become tender and puts forth leaves, you know that summer is near. ³³ So you also, when you see all these things, know that it is near—at the doors! ³⁴ Assuredly, I say to you, this generation will by no means pass away till all these things take place. ³⁵ Heaven and earth will pass away, but My words will by no means pass away. *Matthew 24:32-35*

ISRAEL NEVER AGAIN DIVIDED

¹⁴ "I will bring back the captives of My people Israel; they shall build the waste cities and inhabit them; they shall plant vineyards and drink wine from them; they shall also make gardens and eat fruit from them. ¹⁵ I will plant them in their land, and no longer shall they be pulled up from the land I have given them," says the LORD your God. *Amos 9:14-15*

²¹ Then say to them, "Thus says the Lord GOD: 'Surely I will take the children of Israel from among the nations, wherever they have gone, and will gather them from every side and bring them into their own land; ²² and I will make them one nation in the land, on the mountains of Israel; and one king shall be king over them all; they shall no longer be two nations, nor shall they ever be divided into two kingdoms again.'" *Ezekiel 37:21-22*

CHOSEN BY GOD

⁴ For the LORD has chosen Jacob for Himself, Israel for His special treasure. *Psalm 135:4*

⁶ For you are a holy people to the LORD your God; the LORD your God has chosen you to be a people for Himself, a special treasure above all the peoples on the face of the earth. *Deuteronomy 7:6*

⁸ For thus says the LORD of hosts: He sent Me after glory, to the nations which plunder you; for he who touches you touches the apple of His eye. *Zechariah 2:8*

³ I will bless those who bless you, and I will curse him who curses you; and in you all the families of the earth shall be blessed. *Genesis 12:3*

⁹ Blessed is he who blesses you, and cursed is he who curses you. *Numbers 24:9*

⁴ You have seen what I did to the Egyptians, and how I bore you on eagles' wings and brought you to Myself. ⁵ Now therefore, if you will indeed obey My voice and keep My covenant, then you shall be a special treasure to Me above all people; for all the earth is Mine. ⁶ And you shall be to Me a kingdom of priests and a holy

nation. These are the words which you shall speak to the children of Israel. *Exodus 19:4-6*

ISRAEL A LAND TO BE DESIRED
[18] I will open rivers in desolate heights, and fountains in the midst of the valleys; I will make the wilderness a pool of water, and the dry land springs of water. *Isaiah 41:18*

[3] For the LORD will comfort Zion, He will comfort all her waste places; He will make her wilderness like Eden, and her desert like the garden of the LORD... *Isaiah 51:3*

CHARACTERISTICS OF THE FINAL GENERATION
[3] Now as He sat on the Mount of Olives, the disciples came to Him privately, saying, "Tell us, when will these things be? And what will be the sign of Your coming, and of the end of the age?" [4] And Jesus answered and said to them: "Take heed that no one deceives you. [5] For many will come in My name, saying, 'I am the Christ,' and will deceive many. [6] And you will hear of wars and rumors of wars. See that you are not troubled; for all these things must come to pass, but the end is not yet. [7] For nation will rise against nation, and kingdom against kingdom. And there will be famines, pestilences, and earthquakes in various places. [8] All these are the beginning of sorrows. [9] "Then they will deliver you up to tribulation and kill you, and you will be hated by all nations for My name's sake. [10] And then many will be offended, will betray one another, and will hate one another. [11] Then many false prophets will rise up and deceive many. [12] And because lawlessness will abound, the love of many will grow cold." *Matthew 24:3-12*

LENGTH OF A GENERATION
[3] And the LORD said, "My Spirit shall not strive with man forever, for he is indeed flesh; yet his days shall be one hundred and twenty years." *Genesis 6:3*

[10] The days of our lives are seventy years; and if by reason of strength they are eighty years, yet their boast is only labor and sorrow; for it is soon cut off, and we fly away. *Psalm 90:10*

[17] So all the generations from Abraham to David are fourteen generations, from David until the captivity in Babylon are fourteen generations, and from the captivity in Babylon until the Christ are fourteen generations. *Matthew 1:17*

NOTES

"I gave in and admitted that God was God."
— C.S. Lewis

ARE WE THE TERMINAL GENERATION?

WEEK 9: THE REBUILT TEMPLE PART I

Opening Prayer: Lord, we ask that You send Your Holy Spirit to us to guide us in the teaching and understanding of Your word that we may obtain a better understanding of the prophetic events surrounding us now and waiting for us in the future. Bless our fellowship in Your word that it may be fruitful and draw us into a deeper relationship both with You and those around us. Use us as Your vessels that through us, we may reflect Your glory to all whom we encounter. Illuminate our hearts and minds so that we may boldly shine the brightness of Your light everywhere we go and that we may be beacons of Your hope in a darkened world. In Jesus name we pray, Amen.

Ice Breaker: How long can you stand on one leg without losing your balance? Stand up in front of your chair. Choose which leg you want to lift up. When the group leader says "go", without holding on to anything, bend your knee to lift one foot at least six inches off the ground. If that foot touches the ground in any way, you are out and must sit down. The winner is the last person standing. If there is a tie between two or more people, repeat the event with the people who are locked in a tie, only this time have the participants close their eyes while they compete to determine a winner.

 **Focus:** Destruction is part of the cycle of life, but God will always help you recover and rebuild from whatever devastation Satan sends your way.

God's Word in All the Earth

BIBLES: The New Testament has been translated into 94% of the world's languages.
FILM: 3 billion people saw the *Jesus Film*. It has been translated into so many languages that 99% of the world can view it in a language they know.
RADIO: Assuming availability of a radio, good reception and a desire to find the programs, 99% of the world's population has access to Christian radio programming.
BOOKS AND PERIODICALS: In 2018, there were almost 9.3 million books and periodicals in print about Christianity.
INTERNET: In 2009 alone, Global Media Outreach, the internet outreach branch of Campus Crusade for Christ, brought over 10 million internet users to Christ through their websites.

Word of the Week

> [37] And in the daytime, He was teaching in the temple, but at night He went out and stayed on the mountain called **Olivet**.
>
> *Luke 21:37*

OLIVET: Olivet means olives and comes from the Greek word "elaia" (pronounced el-ah'-yah). Jesus' association with olives is actually quite fitting. Olives are highly nutritious and reputed to have extensive health and medicinal value. Many of the virtues accredited to olives include improved heart health, cancer prevention, reduction of bone loss, lowering of inflammation, aiding digestion, improving allergies, stimulating circulation and possessing antibacterial qualities. Much like olives, Jesus also heals broken hearts, prevents the cancer of bitterness from eating away at the soul, provides a strong backbone to stand against evil, causes inflammatory situations to cease with the peace of His presence, makes difficult situations easier to digest, calms unexpected seasonal annoyances, provides salvation through the shedding of His blood, and is an antidote to demonic pathogens which seek to infect our lives. Yes, we could all use a little more Jesus in our lives!

Lesson: The first temple in Israel was built by King Solomon in Jerusalem around the mid-10th century BC and housed the Ark of the Covenant:

> [1]...in the **fourth year of Solomon's reign** over Israel...he began to build the house of the LORD...[14] So **Solomon built the temple and finished it**. *1 Kings 6:1, 14*

> [19] And he prepared the inner sanctuary inside the temple, to **set the ark of the covenant of the LORD there**. *1 Kings 6:19*

When King Nebuchadnezzar of Babylon attacked Jerusalem in 586 BC, the temple was destroyed and temple treasures were looted:

> [10] At that time the servants of Nebuchadnezzar king of **Babylon came up against Jerusalem**, and the city was besieged...[13] And **he carried out from there all the treasures of the house of the LORD**...and he cut in pieces all the articles of gold which Solomon

king of Israel had made in the temple of the LORD, as the LORD had said. *2 Kings 24:10 and 13*

Seventy years later, a second temple was built on the same site as the first temple and remained there until the Romans destroyed the second temple in 70 AD. The site where the first two temples were built is known as the Temple Mount in Jerusalem. God chose that site for His temple throughout all generations:

> ³ And the LORD said to him: "I have heard your prayer and your supplication that you have made before Me; **I have consecrated this house** which you have built to **put My name there <u>forever</u>**, and My eyes and **My heart will be there <u>perpetually</u>**." *1 Kings 9:3*

At this point, the temple has not been rebuilt a third time. Hindering the rebuilding of the third temple is a conflict with the religion of Islam. As a sign of conquest, Muslims built their temple, the Al Aqsa Mosque, over the site of the first two destroyed temples after the fall of the second temple. To this day, the Al Aqsa Mosque occupies the presumed site of the two previous temples on the Temple Mount and remains an active site of Muslim religious significance. The third temple must be rebuilt on the exact site of the first two temples, but that cannot occur as long as the Al Aqsa Mosque occupies that space.

During the period of the second temple, Jesus was an active participant in temple life and spent much time there. When He was twelve, He was a star student who was taught by teachers in the temple:

> ⁴² And when He (Jesus) was twelve years old, they (Joseph, Mary and Jesus) went up to Jerusalem according to the custom of the feast. ⁴³ When they had finished the days, as they returned, the Boy Jesus lingered behind in Jerusalem. And Joseph and His mother did not know it; ⁴⁴ but supposing Him to have been in the company, they went a day's journey, and sought Him among their relatives and acquaintances. ⁴⁵ So when they did not find Him, they returned to Jerusalem, seeking Him. ⁴⁶ Now so it was that after three days **they found Him in the temple, sitting in the midst of the teachers, both listening to them and asking them questions.** ⁴⁷ And all who heard Him were **astonished at His understanding and answers**. *Luke 2:42-47*

As Jesus grew older, He taught others in the temple and healed people there as well:

⁳⁷ And **in the daytime, He was teaching in the temple**, but at night He went out and stayed on the mountain called Olivet. *Luke 21:37*

¹⁴ Then the blind and the lame **came to Him in the temple**, and **He healed them**. *Matthew 21:14*

Never one to be a slacker, Jesus could be found at the temple early in the morning:

³⁸ Then **early in the morning** all the **people came to Him in the temple** to hear Him. *Luke 21:38*

In addition to being a leading educator in the temple, Jesus concerned himself with the day-to-day operations of the temple. When money changers threatened the sanctity of the temple, Jesus threw them out:

¹⁴ And He found **in the temple** those who sold oxen and sheep and doves, and **the money changers doing business**. ¹⁵ When He had made a whip of cords, **He drove them all out of the temple**, with the sheep and the oxen, and poured out the changers' money and overturned the tables. ¹⁶ And He said to those who sold doves, "Take these things away! Do not make My Father's house a house of merchandise!" *John 2:14-16*

HALLEL (pronounced HAH-lell), a Hebrew word meaning "praise", refers to Psalms 113-118 which are read on Jewish holidays.

When Pharisees and Sadducees questioned scripture and attempted to change the culture of the temple, Jesus corrected and rebuked them as any good manager might do:

²³ The same day the **Sadducees**…came to Him and **asked Him**…

> [29] **Jesus answered** and said to them, "**You are mistaken**, not knowing the Scriptures nor the power of God." *Matthew 22:23, 29*

> [27] Woe to you, scribes and **Pharisees, hypocrites**! For you are like whitewashed tombs which indeed appear beautiful outwardly, but inside are full of dead men's bones and all uncleanness. [28] Even so **you also outwardly appear righteous to men, but inside you are full of hypocrisy and lawlessness**. *Matthew 23:27-28*

Advocating for the sanctity of the temple, Jesus compared making an oath by the temple as being on par with swearing an oath by God Himself:

> [16] Woe to you, blind guides, who say, "Whoever swears by the temple, it is nothing; but whoever swears by the gold of the temple, he is obliged to perform it." [17] Fools and blind! For which is greater, the gold or the temple that sanctifies the gold? [18] And, "Whoever swears by the altar, it is nothing; but whoever swears by the gift that is on it, he is obliged to perform it." [19] Fools and blind! For which is greater, the gift or the altar that sanctifies the gift? [20] Therefore he who swears by the altar, swears by it and by all things on it. [21] **He who swears by the temple, swears by it and by Him who dwells in it**. [22] And he who swears by heaven, swears by the throne of God and by Him who sits on it. *Matthew 23:16-22*

Setting an example for all of us to follow, Jesus made involvement in temple affairs an integral part of His life. However, He knew that one day the building would be destroyed and He prophesied its destruction:

> [5] Then, as some spoke of the temple, how it was adorned with beautiful stones and donations, He (Jesus) said, [6] "These things which you see—the **days will come in which not one stone shall be left upon another** that shall not be thrown down." *Luke 21:5*

As always, Jesus was correct about the future and in 70 AD, the second temple was destroyed by the Romans.

In recent years, the Ark of the Covenant has become a subject of popular interest. Originally built by Moses as a way to communicate with God and store the Ten Commandments, the Ark of the Covenant was an important part of the tabernacle in the desert and the first temple:

[8] And **let them make Me a sanctuary**, that I may dwell among them...[10] **And they shall make an ark** of acacia wood; two and a half cubits shall be its length, a cubit and a half its width, and a cubit and a half its height. [11] And you shall overlay it with pure gold, inside and out you shall overlay it, and shall make on it a molding of gold all around. [12] You shall cast four rings of gold for it, and put them in its four corners; two rings shall be on one side, and two rings on the other side. [13] And you shall make poles of acacia wood, and overlay them with gold. [14] You shall put the poles into the rings on the sides of the ark, that the ark may be carried by them. [15] The poles shall be in the rings of the ark; they shall not be taken from it. [16] And you shall put into the ark the Testimony which I will give you. [17] You shall make a mercy seat of pure gold; two and a half cubits shall be its length and a cubit and a half its width. [18] And you shall make two cherubim of gold; of hammered work you shall make them at the two ends of the mercy seat. [19] Make one cherub at one end, and the other cherub at the other end; you shall make the cherubim at the two ends of it of one piece with the mercy seat. [20] And the cherubim shall stretch out their wings above, covering the mercy seat with their wings, and they shall face one another; the faces of the cherubim shall be toward the mercy seat. [21] You shall put the mercy seat on top of the ark, and **in the ark, you shall put the Testimony that I will give you**. [22] **And there I will meet with you, and I will speak with you from above the mercy seat, from between the two cherubim which are on the ark of the Testimony**, about everything which I will give you in commandment to the children of Israel. *Exodus 25:8, 10-22*

[89] Now when **Moses went into the tabernacle of meeting to speak with Him**, he heard the voice of One **speaking to him from above the mercy seat that was on the ark** of the Testimony, from between the two cherubim; thus, He spoke to him. *Numbers 7:89*

[1] At that time the LORD said to me, "Hew for yourself **two tablets of stone** like the first, and come up to Me on the mountain and make yourself an ark of wood. [2] And I will write on the tablets the words that were on the first tablets, which you broke; and **you shall put them in the ark**." *Deuteronomy 10:1-2*

Ornately decorated in gold with two cherubim on top, the ark later became the storage container for other sacred objects such as a pot of manna and Aaron's rod:

> ...³ and behind the second veil, the part of the tabernacle which is called the Holiest of All, ⁴ which had the golden censer and **the ark of the covenant** overlaid on all sides with gold, **in which were the golden pot that had the manna, Aaron's rod that budded, and the tablets of the covenant**; ⁵ and above it were the cherubim of glory overshadowing the mercy seat. Of these things we cannot now speak in detail. *Hebrews 9:3-5*

God designated the tribe of Levi to be His priests and be responsible for the ark:

> ⁸ At that time the LORD separated the **tribe of Levi** to **bear the ark** of the covenant of the LORD, to stand before the LORD **to minister to Him** and to bless in His name, to this day. *Deuteronomy 10:8*

Interaction with the ark was limited to only a few select people and required the fastidious observance of a defined set of rules.

> ⁵ When the camp prepares to journey, **Aaron and his sons** shall come, and they shall **take down the covering veil** and **cover the ark** of the Testimony with it. ⁶ Then they shall **put on it a covering of badger skins**, and **spread over that a cloth entirely of blue**; and they shall **insert its poles**. *Numbers 4:5-6*

Approaching the ark was permissible only at certain times by certain people in a reverent manner:

> ... ² and the LORD said to Moses: "**Tell Aaron** your brother **not to come at just any time** into the Holy Place inside the veil, before the mercy seat which is on the ark, lest he die... *Leviticus 16:2*

If someone attempted an unauthorized interaction with the ark, they died. Even priests who interacted with the ark would die if they did not follow strict rules of engagement or offended God with their offering:

> ¹ Then **Nadab and Abihu, the sons of Aaron**...**offered profane fire** before the LORD, which **He had not commanded them**. ² So fire went out from the LORD (the ark of the covenant) and devoured them, and **they died** before the LORD. *Leviticus 10:1-2*

Under no circumstance was the ark to be touched or viewed by curious onlookers:

> ¹⁹ Then **He struck the men of Beth Shemesh, because they had looked into the ark** of the LORD. He struck **fifty thousand and seventy men** of the people, and the people lamented because the LORD had struck the people with a great slaughter. *1 Samuel 6:19*

To treat the ark as a curiosity meant instant death. When it was in the possession of the Israelites and cared for properly, it brought blessings to the people. For the Israelites, it miraculously helped them cross a river on dry land:

> ¹⁸ And it came to pass, when the **priests who bore the ark** of the covenant of the LORD had come from the midst of the Jordan, and **the soles of the priests' feet touched the dry land**, that the **waters of the Jordan returned to their place** and overflowed all its banks as before. *Joshua 4:18*

Other times, the ark guided them where they needed to go much like a modern-day GPS system:

> ³³ So they departed from the mountain of the LORD on a journey of three days; and the **ark of the covenant** of the LORD **went before them** for the three days' journey, **to search out a resting place for them**. ³⁴ And the cloud of the LORD was above them by day when they went out from the camp. ³⁵ So it was, **whenever the ark set out**, that Moses said: "**Rise up**, O LORD!..." ³⁶ And **when it rested**, he said: "**Return**, O LORD..." *Numbers 10:33-36*

When the ark moved, the people moved. When the ark rested, the people rested.

In the hands of an enemy of Israel, it became a curse to those who possessed it. In one instance, the ark is credited with destroying the statue of a pagan god sitting near the ark:

> ¹ Then the **Philistines took the ark of God**...²...they brought it into the house of Dagon **and set it by Dagon**. ³ And when the people of Ashdod arose early in the morning, there was Dagon, fallen on its face to the earth before the ark of the LORD. So, they took Dagon and set it in its place again. ⁴ **And when they arose early the next morning**, there was **Dagon, fallen on its face to the ground** before the ark of the LORD. The **head of Dagon and both the palms of its hands were broken off** on the threshold; only Dagon's torso was left of it...*1 Samuel 5:1-4*

Inhabitants of the enemy city also broke out in tumors or died when in possession of the ark:

> ⁶ But the hand of the LORD was heavy on the **people of Ashdod**, and He ravaged them and **struck them with tumors**...⁸... So, they carried the ark of the God of Israel away. ⁹ So it was, after they had carried it away, that the **hand of the LORD was against the city** with a very great destruction; and He struck the men of the city, both small and great, and tumors broke out on them. ¹⁰ Therefore **they sent the ark of God to Ekron**. So it was, as the ark of God came to Ekron, that the Ekronites cried out, saying, "They have brought the ark of the God of Israel to us, to kill us and our people!" ¹¹ So they sent and gathered together all the lords of **the Philistines, and said, "Send away the ark of the God of Israel, and let it go back to its own place**, so that it does not kill us and our people." For **there was a deadly destruction throughout all the city; the hand of God was very heavy there**. ¹² And **the men who did not die were stricken with the tumors**, and the cry of the city went up to heaven. *1 Samuel 5:6, 8-12*

The Philistines found the ark to be such a curse that they returned it to Israel. Proper respect always had to be demonstrated for the ark or dire consequences ensued.

The Ark of the Covenant has been located in many places throughout the years:

> ² So it was that the **ark** remained in **Kirjath Jearim** a long time; it was there **twenty years**. *1 Samuel 7:2*

Initially, it was housed in a special tent when the Israelites were in the desert. Later, Solomon moved it into the first temple. Other biblically cited locations include Beth Shemesh, Kirjath Jearim, Ekron, and resting in the hands of Israel's enemy, the Philistines. In one account, David brought the ark back to the temple in Jerusalem:

> ² And David arose and went...to bring up from there the ark of God... ⁶ And when they came to Nachon's threshing floor, Uzzah put out his hand to the ark of God and took hold of it, for the oxen stumbled. ⁷ Then the anger of the LORD was aroused against Uzzah, and God struck him there for his error; and he died there by the ark of God...⁹ David was afraid of the LORD that day; and he said, "How can the ark of the LORD come to me?" ¹⁰ So David would not move the ark of the LORD with him into the City of David; but David took it aside into the house of Obed-Edom the

> Gittite. ¹¹ The ark of the LORD remained in the house of Obed-Edom the Gittite three months. And the LORD blessed Obed-Edom and all his household. ¹² Now it was told King David, saying, "The LORD has blessed the house of Obed-Edom and all that belongs to him, because of the ark of God." So, **David went and brought up the ark of God** from the house of Obed-Edom to the City of David with gladness... ¹⁷ So **they brought the ark of the LORD, and set it in its place in the midst of the tabernacle** that David had erected for it. *2 Samuel 6:2, 6-7, 9-12 and 17*

The ark was even present when the walls of Jericho came tumbling down:

> ⁴ And **seven priests shall bear before the ark** seven trumpets of rams' horns: and the seventh day **ye shall compass the city** (Jericho)... *Joshua 6:4*

Eventually, the ark simply disappeared from the annals of history. No one knows definitively where it is now and the Bible offers no explanation for its current whereabouts.

There are numerous theories and legends as to what happened to the ark and where it might be located today. Some have claimed there were two arks while others believe the ark may have been taken to Rosslyn Chapel in Scotland by the Knights Templar. Another theory suggests the ark is under the Dome of the Rock or the Al Aqsa Mosque on the Temple Mount. Scripture seems to agree most with this position:

> ⁶ Then **the priests brought in the ark** of the covenant of the LORD to its place, **into the inner sanctuary of the (second) temple**, to the Most Holy Place, under the wings of the cherubim. ⁷ For the cherubim spread their two wings over the place of the ark, and the cherubim overshadowed the ark and its poles. ⁸ The poles extended so that the ends of the poles could be seen from the holy place, in front of the inner sanctuary; but they could not be seen from outside. **And they are there to this day.** ⁹ Nothing was in the ark except the two tablets of stone which Moses put there at Horeb, when the LORD made a covenant with the children of Israel, when they came out of the land of Egypt. *1 Kings 8:6-9*

One of the more intriguing theories puts the ark in Aksum, Ethiopia at the Cathedral of St. Mary of Zion. According to claims made by the church, King Solomon had a son, Menelik, with Queen Sheba whom she raised in her homeland. When Menelik was older, he returned to Israel to visit his father.

Somehow the ark ended up in his possession and he supposedly returned home with the Ark of the Covenant. Today, on the guarded grounds of the church, a single monk nominated as the designated caretaker of the ark watches over an object that only he has ever seen. He will continue to do so in guarded solitary confinement for the rest of his life and then another monk will assume the honor in his place. It is said that guardian monks have relatively short lifespans and unexplained severe cataract deterioration of their eyes.

Many people wonder if the Ark of the Covenant will be a part of the rebuilt temple. Scripture does not address the issue directly, but it should be noted that there is no mention of the Ark of the Covenant again until after Jesus returns at His second coming:

> [16] "Then it shall come to pass, when you are multiplied and increased in the land in those days," says the LORD, "that they will say no more, 'The **ark of the covenant** of the LORD.' It **shall not come to mind**, **nor shall they remember it**, nor shall they visit it, nor shall it be made anymore. [17] At that time Jerusalem shall be called The Throne of the LORD, and all the nations shall be gathered to it, to the name of the LORD, to Jerusalem. No more shall they follow the dictates of their evil hearts." *Jeremiah 3:16-17*

In this passage, we are told that we have no need of the ark. Jesus, in essence, becomes the new Ark of the Covenant. As the incarnate representative of God on earth, we communicate and receive guidance from Him. He is a blessing to faithful followers and a curse to those who position themselves as enemies of God. Guiding us where we need to go, Jesus can break down any wall and when we need a miracle, it's always Jesus to the rescue. What a wonderful ark we have in Jesus!

In time though, God answers all of our questions. Eventually, the Ark of the Covenant is revealed as being with God in His temple in heaven:

> [15] Then the seventh angel sounded: And there were loud voices in heaven, saying, "The kingdoms of this world have become the kingdoms of our Lord and of His Christ, and **He shall reign** forever and ever!"…[19] Then the **temple of God was opened in heaven**, and the **ark of His covenant was seen** in His temple. *Revelation 11:15, 19*

The Ark of the Covenant was made for God and belongs to Him. It is only fitting that in the end, God possesses what should rightly be His.

Talk It Out

1. The temple in Jesus' day experienced decay and corruption from within. Is corruption a sign of the end time church? Have you seen any evidence that corruption and decay has crept into modern day churches? How can both ministers and congregation members affect the atmosphere of a church?

2. The temple was destroyed twice. Have there been times in your life when you experienced devastation; when everything you built or worked for came crashing down? How did God help you recover, rebuild and move on from what happened?

3. Jesus was an integral part of temple life. How involved with the life of your church are you? Do you need to be more involved with your church to follow Jesus' example?

4. Do you think the Ark of the Covenant will be found prior to the return of Christ? Revelation 11:19 states the Ark of the Covenant will be found in God's temple in heaven. Is it already there waiting to be announced or do you think God will transport it there at some point in the future?

5. Regarding the Cathedral of St. Mary of Zion in Aksum, Ethiopia, do you believe they have possession of the Ark of the Covenant? Do you think a monk would live in solitary confinement if there wasn't something there of perceived value to guard? Do you think the short lives and cataract problems monks experience are related to an object located within the chapel?

6. Do you think there is more than one ark? Is it possible the Ark of the Covenant could be both in Aksum, Ethiopia and under the Temple Mount in Jerusalem?

7. Why do you think when Christ returns it will not be necessary to remember the Ark of the Covenant? Discuss comparisons of Jesus and the Ark of the Covenant. Do you believe Jesus becomes the new Ark of the Covenant at His second coming?

Ideas for the Week:

- ✓ Watch the movie *Raiders of the Lost Ark* to stimulate your creative speculation about the Ark of the Covenant.
- ✓ Do an internet search for images of the Ark of the Covenant to see artist renditions for what it may have looked like.
- ✓ Go through your home, room by room, and remove any statues or objects, regardless of size, that might offend God.
- ✓ Find Beth Shemesh and Kirjath Jearim on a map of the Middle East.

Closing Prayer

NOTE: Add names and individual personal prayer requests to the space provided below before closing in prayer.

Lord, we thank You for our time together today to grow deeper in our walk with You and fellowship with each other. As we close today, we lift up: _____

_____

_____

_____

_____

_____

_____

_____

Father, we know that storms which threaten our stability are a part of life and we acknowledge that we need You to help us weather whatever thunderclouds and lightning bolts darken the skies of our lives. We ask You to keep us in perfect peace when chaos surrounds and to show us the way forward when the wiles and ways of Satan throw us for yet another loop. We thank You for Your loving guidance and healing restoration after devastation strikes. In Jesus' name we pray, Amen.

CHRISTINE TATE

SUPPORTING SCRIPTURES

FIRST TEMPLE

[1] ...in the fourth year of Solomon's reign over Israel...he began to build the house of the LORD... [14] So Solomon built the temple and finished it. *1 Kings 6:1, 14*

[19] And he prepared the inner sanctuary inside the temple, to set the ark of the covenant of the LORD there. *1 Kings 6:19*

[3] And the LORD said to him: "I have heard your prayer and your supplication that you have made before Me; I have consecrated this house which you have built to put My name there forever, and My eyes and My heart will be there perpetually." *1 Kings 9:3*

[10] At that time the servants of Nebuchadnezzar king of Babylon came up against Jerusalem, and the city was besieged... [13] And he carried out from there all the treasures of the house of the LORD...and he cut in pieces all the articles of gold which Solomon king of Israel had made in the temple of the LORD, as the LORD had said. *2 Kings 24:10,13*

SECOND TEMPLE

[42] And when He (Jesus) was twelve years old, they (Joseph, Mary and Jesus) went up to Jerusalem according to the custom of the feast. [43] When they had finished the days, as they returned, the Boy Jesus lingered behind in Jerusalem. And Joseph and His mother did not know it; [44] but supposing Him to have been in the company, they went a day's journey, and sought Him among their relatives and acquaintances. [45] So when they did not find Him, they returned to Jerusalem, seeking Him. [46] Now so it was that after three days they found Him in the temple, sitting in the midst of the teachers, both listening to them and asking them questions. [47] And all who heard Him were astonished at His understanding and answers. *Luke 2:42-47*

[37] And in the daytime, He was teaching in the temple, but at night He went out and stayed on the mountain called Olivet. [38] Then early in the morning all the people came to Him in the temple to hear Him. *Luke 21:37-38*

[5] Then, as some spoke of the temple, how it was adorned with beautiful stones and donations, He (Jesus) said, [6] "These things which you see—the days will come in which not one stone shall be left upon another that shall not be thrown down." *Luke 21:5*

[14] Then the blind and the lame came to Him in the temple, and He healed them. *Matthew 21:14*

¹⁴ And He found in the temple those who sold oxen and sheep and doves, and the money changers doing business. ¹⁵ When He had made a whip of cords, He drove them all out of the temple, with the sheep and the oxen, and poured out the changers' money and overturned the tables. ¹⁶ And He said to those who sold doves, "Take these things away! Do not make My Father's house a house of merchandise!" *John 2:14-16*

²³ The same day the Sadducees…came to Him and asked Him… ²⁹ Jesus answered and said to them, "You are mistaken, not knowing the Scriptures nor the power of God." *Matthew 22:23, 29*

¹⁶ Woe to you, blind guides, who say, "Whoever swears by the temple, it is nothing; but whoever swears by the gold of the temple, he is obliged to perform it." ¹⁷ Fools and blind! For which is greater, the gold or the temple that sanctifies the gold? ¹⁸ And, "Whoever swears by the altar, it is nothing; but whoever swears by the gift that is on it, he is obliged to perform it." ¹⁹ Fools and blind! For which is greater, the gift or the altar that sanctifies the gift? ²⁰ Therefore he who swears by the altar, swears by it and by all things on it. ²¹ He who swears by the temple, swears by it and by Him who dwells in it. ²² And he who swears by heaven, swears by the throne of God and by Him who sits on it. *Matthew 23:16-22*

²⁷ Woe to you, scribes and Pharisees, hypocrites! For you are like whitewashed tombs which indeed appear beautiful outwardly, but inside are full of dead men's bones and all uncleanness. ²⁸ Even so you also outwardly appear righteous to men, but inside you are full of hypocrisy and lawlessness. *Matthew 23:27-28*

ARK OF THE COVENANT

⁸ And let them make Me a sanctuary, that I may dwell among them…¹⁰ And they shall make an ark of acacia wood; two and a half cubits shall be its length, a cubit and a half its width, and a cubit and a half its height. ¹¹ And you shall overlay it with pure gold, inside and out you shall overlay it, and shall make on it a molding of gold all around. ¹² You shall cast four rings of gold for it, and put them in its four corners; two rings shall be on one side, and two rings on the other side. ¹³ And you shall make poles of acacia wood, and overlay them with gold. ¹⁴ You shall put the poles into the rings on the sides of the ark, that the ark may be carried by them. ¹⁵ The poles shall be in the rings of the ark; they shall not be taken from it. ¹⁶ And you shall put into the ark the Testimony which I will give you. ¹⁷ You shall make a mercy seat of pure gold; two and a half cubits shall be its length and a cubit and a half its width. ¹⁸ And you shall make two cherubim of gold; of hammered work you shall make them at the two ends of the mercy seat. ¹⁹ Make one cherub at one end, and the other cherub at the other end; you shall make the cherubim at the two ends of it of one piece with the mercy seat. ²⁰ And

the cherubim shall stretch out their wings above, covering the mercy seat with their wings, and they shall face one another; the faces of the cherubim shall be toward the mercy seat. [21] You shall put the mercy seat on top of the ark, and in the ark, you shall put the Testimony that I will give you. [22] And there I will meet with you, and I will speak with you from above the mercy seat, from between the two cherubim which are on the ark of the Testimony, about everything which I will give you in commandment to the children of Israel. *Exodus 25:8, 10-22*

[89] Now when Moses went into the tabernacle of meeting to speak with Him, he heard the voice of One speaking to him from above the mercy seat that was on the ark of the Testimony, from between the two cherubim; thus, He spoke to him. *Numbers 7:89*

[1] At that time the LORD said to me, "Hew for yourself two tablets of stone like the first, and come up to Me on the mountain and make yourself an ark of wood. [2] And I will write on the tablets the words that were on the first tablets, which you broke; and you shall put them in the ark." *Deuteronomy 10:1-2*

[8] At that time the LORD separated the tribe of Levi to bear the ark of the covenant of the LORD, to stand before the LORD to minister to Him and to bless in His name, to this day. *Deuteronomy 10:8*

[18] And it came to pass, when the priests who bore the ark of the covenant of the LORD had come from the midst of the Jordan, and the soles of the priests' feet touched the dry land, that the waters of the Jordan returned to their place and overflowed all its banks as before. *Joshua 4:18*

[5] When the camp prepares to journey, Aaron and his sons shall come, and they shall take down the covering veil and cover the ark of the Testimony with it. [6] Then they shall put on it a covering of badger skins, and spread over that a cloth entirely of blue; and they shall insert its poles. *Numbers 4:5-6*

… [2] and the LORD said to Moses: "Tell Aaron your brother not to come at just any time into the Holy Place inside the veil, before the mercy seat which is on the ark, lest he die…" *Leviticus 16:2*

[1] Then Nadab and Abihu, the sons of Aaron…offered profane fire before the LORD, which He had not commanded them. [2] So fire went out from the LORD (the ark of the covenant) and devoured them, and they died before the LORD. *Leviticus 10:1-2*

[33] So they departed from the mountain of the LORD on a journey of three days; and the ark of the covenant of the LORD went before them for the three days'

journey, to search out a resting place for them. ³⁴ And the cloud of the LORD was above them by day when they went out from the camp. ³⁵ So it was, whenever the ark set out, that Moses said: "Rise up, O LORD!..." ³⁶ And when it rested, he said: "Return, O LORD…" *Numbers 10:33-36*

⁶ Then the priests brought in the ark of the covenant of the LORD to its place, into the inner sanctuary of the (second) temple, to the Most Holy Place, under the wings of the cherubim. ⁷ For the cherubim spread their two wings over the place of the ark, and the cherubim overshadowed the ark and its poles. ⁸ The poles extended so that the ends of the poles could be seen from the holy place, in front of the inner sanctuary; but they could not be seen from outside. And they are there to this day. ⁹ Nothing was in the ark except the two tablets of stone which Moses put there at Horeb, when the LORD made a covenant with the children of Israel, when they came out of the land of Egypt. *1 Kings 8:6-9*

¹ Then the Philistines took the ark of God…² …they brought it into the house of Dagon and set it by Dagon. ³ And when the people of Ashdod arose early in the morning, there was Dagon, fallen on its face to the earth before the ark of the LORD. So, they took Dagon and set it in its place again. ⁴ And when they arose early the next morning, there was Dagon, fallen on its face to the ground before the ark of the LORD. The head of Dagon and both the palms of its hands were broken off on the threshold; only Dagon's torso was left of it…⁶ But the hand of the LORD was heavy on the people of Ashdod, and He ravaged them and struck them with tumors…⁸ … So, they carried the ark of the God of Israel away. ⁹ So it was, after they had carried it away, that the hand of the LORD was against the city with a very great destruction; and He struck the men of the city, both small and great, and tumors broke out on them. ¹⁰ Therefore they sent the ark of God to Ekron. So it was, as the ark of God came to Ekron, that the Ekronites cried out, saying, "They have brought the ark of the God of Israel to us, to kill us and our people!" ¹¹ So they sent and gathered together all the lords of the Philistines, and said, "Send away the ark of the God of Israel, and let it go back to its own place, so that it does not kill us and our people." For there was a deadly destruction throughout all the city; the hand of God was very heavy there. ¹² And the men who did not die were stricken with the tumors, and the cry of the city went up to heaven. *1 Samuel 5:1-4, 6, 8-12*

¹⁹ Then He struck the men of Beth Shemesh, because they had looked into the ark of the LORD. He struck fifty thousand and seventy men of the people, and the people lamented because the LORD had struck the people with a great slaughter. *1 Samuel 6:19*

² So it was that the ark remained in Kirjath Jearim a long time; it was there twenty

years. *1 Samuel 7:2*

[4] And seven priests shall bear before the ark seven trumpets of rams' horns: and the seventh day ye shall compass the city (Jericho)... *Joshua 6:4*

...[3] and behind the second veil, the part of the tabernacle which is called the Holiest of All, [4] which had the golden censer and the ark of the covenant overlaid on all sides with gold, in which were the golden pot that had the manna, Aaron's rod that budded, and the tablets of the covenant; [5] and above it were the cherubim of glory overshadowing the mercy seat. Of these things we cannot now speak in detail. *Hebrews 9:3-5*

[2] And David arose and went...to bring up from there the ark of God... [6] And when they came to Nachon's threshing floor, Uzzah put out his hand to the ark of God and took hold of it, for the oxen stumbled. [7] Then the anger of the LORD was aroused against Uzzah, and God struck him there for his error; and he died there by the ark of God...[9] David was afraid of the LORD that day; and he said, "How can the ark of the LORD come to me?" [10] So David would not move the ark of the LORD with him into the City of David; but David took it aside into the house of Obed-Edom the Gittite. [11] The ark of the LORD remained in the house of Obed-Edom the Gittite three months. And the LORD blessed Obed-Edom and all his household. [12] Now it was told King David, saying, "The LORD has blessed the house of Obed-Edom and all that belongs to him, because of the ark of God." So, David went and brought up the ark of God from the house of Obed-Edom to the City of David with gladness... [17] So they brought the ark of the LORD, and set it in its place in the midst of the tabernacle that David had erected for it. *2 Samuel 6:2, 6-7, 9-12, 17*

[15] Then the seventh angel sounded: And there were loud voices in heaven, saying, "The kingdoms of this world have become the kingdoms of our Lord and of His Christ, and He shall reign forever and ever!"...[19] Then the temple of God was opened in heaven, and the ark of His covenant was seen in His temple. *Revelation 11:15, 19*

[16] "Then it shall come to pass, when you are multiplied and increased in the land in those days," says the LORD, "that they will say no more, 'The ark of the covenant of the LORD.' It shall not come to mind, nor shall they remember it, nor shall they visit it, nor shall it be made anymore. [17] At that time Jerusalem shall be called The Throne of the LORD, and all the nations shall be gathered to it, to the name of the LORD, to Jerusalem. No more shall they follow the dictates of their evil hearts." *Jeremiah 3:16-17*

NOTES

"God doesn't require us to succeed, He only requires that you try." — Mother Teresa

WEEK 10: THE REBUILT TEMPLE PART II

Opening Prayer: Lord, we ask that You send Your Holy Spirit to us to guide us in the teaching and understanding of Your word that we may obtain a better understanding of the prophetic events surrounding us now and waiting for us in the future. Bless our fellowship in Your word that it may be fruitful and draw us into a deeper relationship both with You and those around us. Use us as Your vessels that through us, we may reflect Your glory to all whom we encounter. Illuminate our hearts and minds so that we may boldly shine the brightness of Your light everywhere we go and that we may be beacons of Your hope in a darkened world. In Jesus name we pray, Amen.

Ice Breaker: Throughout the Bible, God makes a variety of promises to us including promises to be our healer, our provider, our protector, our teacher and our leader. Choosing from the list below and on the next page, what is your favorite promise from God and why? Share your answer with the group.

1. **God promises to heal us when we are sick.**

   [2] Bless the LORD, O my soul, and forget not all His benefits: [3] who forgives all your iniquities, who heals all your diseases... *Psalm 103:2-3*

2. **God promises to provide for our needs.**

   The LORD is my shepherd; I shall not want. *Psalm 23:1*

3. **God promises to protect us from danger.**

   [14] Because he has set his love upon Me, therefore I will deliver him; I will set him on high, because he has known My name. [15] He shall call upon Me, and I will answer him; I will be with him in trouble; I will deliver him and honor him. *Psalm 91:14-15*

4. **God promises to teach us what we need to know.**

   [8] I will instruct you and teach you in the way you should go; I will guide you with My eye. *Psalm 32:8*

5. **God promises to lead us and guide us on the right path.**

   [5] Trust in the LORD with all your heart, and lean not on your own understanding; [6] In all your ways acknowledge Him, and He shall direct your paths. *Proverbs 3:5-6*

6. God promises to bless the righteous.

> ¹⁰ Bring all the tithes into the storehouse, that there may be food in My house, and try Me now in this," says the LORD of hosts, "If I will not open for you the windows of heaven and pour out for you such blessing that there will not be room enough to receive it. *Malachi 3:10*

7. God promises to grant us salvation.

> ⁹ And having been perfected, He became the author of eternal salvation to all who obey Him… *Hebrews 5:9*

8. God promises to give us peace.

> ³ You will keep him in perfect peace, whose mind is stayed on You, because he trusts in You. *Isaiah 26:3*

9. God promises to comfort us.

> ³ Blessed be the God and Father of our Lord Jesus Christ, the Father of mercies and God of all comfort, ⁴ who comforts us in all our tribulation, that we may be able to comfort those who are in any trouble, with the comfort with which we ourselves are comforted by God. *2 Corinthians 1:3-4*

10. God promises to give us hope.

> ¹³ Now may the God of hope fill you with all joy and peace in believing, that you may abound in hope by the power of the Holy Spirit. *Romans 15:13*

11. God promises to give us victory.

> ¹² Through God we will do valiantly, for it is He who shall tread down our enemies. *Psalm 60:12*

 **Focus:** God is a master architect and builder who builds His kingdom starting in the hearts of men.

"The True Church can never fail. For it is based upon a rock."

— T.S. Eliot

Word of the Week

> ¹⁸ They shall have **linen** turbans on their heads and **linen** trousers on their bodies; they shall not clothe themselves with anything that causes sweat.
>
> *Ezekiel 44:18*

LINEN: Linen, from the Hebrew word "pishteh" (pronounced pish-teh'), is God's preferred fabric of choice. In Revelation 19:14, Jesus returns with an army clothed in fine linen. Again, in Ezekiel 44:18, linen is the preferred fabric for the priests who serve in Jesus' new temple. They are to wear linen garments when they approach the Lord. Due to its strength, linen is an extremely durable fabric that wears well, yet is light and breathable so as not to cause undue body odor caused by excessive sweating. Linen is a popular fabric of choice in many tropical climates for that very reason. Made of flax, Egyptian mummies were wrapped in linen. Thousands of years later, the fabric used to wrap mummies still does not show signs of disintegration. Having two to three times the strength of cotton or silk, linen fibers possess a natural wax coating that provides an aesthetically pleasing light sheen when woven into a garment. A drawback to linen is that it wrinkles easily. Some enjoy the relaxed ambiance that a wrinkled look provides. Linen comes in a variety of weaves ranging from loose weaves currently priced around $12.98 per yard to tighter weaves which run closer to $99 per yard. When linen has a tighter weave, the resulting fabric has a rich, luxurious appearance and is typically used in formal ceremonies such as baptismal gowns and fancy clothing.

Lesson: A promise God made is that His third temple will be rebuilt in Jerusalem prior to the return of Christ. Prophecy requires the third temple to be rebuilt over the site of the first two temples. Existence of the third temple is highly prophetic in nature since the rebuilt temple will be the Lord's dwelling place on earth when He returns. During the Tribulation period, the temple is also the place where the Antichrist will stop temple sacrifices and declare himself to be God:

²⁷ Then he shall confirm a covenant with many for one week; but **in the middle of the week He shall bring an end to sacrifice and offering.** *Daniel 9:27*

> ...⁴ who opposes and exalts himself (the Antichrist) above all that is called God or that is worshiped, so that **he sits as God in the temple of God, showing himself that he is God**. *2 Thessalonians 2:4*

In order for Jesus to return to the temple and the Antichrist to desecrate the temple, first the temple must be rebuilt.

From a prophetic perspective, it is important for the temple to be rebuilt in Jerusalem because it will occupy a place of prominence when Jesus returns. After His return, the temple will be the place where Jesus lives:

> ⁷ And He said to me, "Son of man, **this is the place of My throne** and **the place of the soles of My feet**, where **I will dwell in the midst of the children of Israel forever**. No more shall the house of Israel defile My holy name, they nor their kings, by their harlotry or with the carcasses of their kings on their high places." *Ezekiel 43:7*

It will also be a place of social gathering where all come to worship Jesus:

> ⁷ Even them I will bring to My holy mountain, and **make them joyful** in My house of prayer. Their **burnt offerings** and their **sacrifices** will be accepted on My altar; for My house shall be called **a house of prayer for all nations**." *Isaiah 56:7*

Surrounding the temple, the environment will be that of a lush garden surrounded by brooks, streams, rivers and the ocean:

> ¹ Then he brought me back to the door of the temple; and there was **water, flowing from under the threshold of the temple** toward the east, for the front of the temple faced east; the water was flowing from under the right side of the temple, south of the altar. ² He brought me out by way of the north gate, and led me around on the outside to the outer gateway that faces east; and there was water, running out on the right side. ³ And when the man went out to the east with the line in his hand, he measured one thousand cubits, and he brought me through the waters; the **water came up to my ankles**. ⁴ Again he measured one thousand and brought me through the waters; **the water came up to my knees**. Again, he measured one thousand and brought me through; **the water came up to my waist**. ⁵ Again he measured one thousand, and it was a river that I could not cross; for the water was too deep, **water in which one must swim**, a river that

> could not be crossed. ⁶He said to me, "Son of man, have you seen this?" Then he brought me and returned me to the bank of the river. ⁷When I returned, there, **along the bank of the river, were very many trees on one side and the other**. ⁸Then he said to me: "This water flows toward the eastern region, goes down into the valley, and **enters the sea**. When it reaches the sea, its waters are healed. ⁹And it shall be that every living thing that moves, wherever the rivers go, will live. There will be a very great **multitude of fish**, because these waters go there; for they will be healed, and everything will live wherever the river goes. ¹⁰It shall be that fishermen will stand by it from En Gedi to En Eglaim; they will be places for spreading their nets. Their fish will be of the same kinds as the fish of the Great Sea, exceedingly many. ¹¹But its swamps and marshes will not be healed; they will be given over to salt. ¹²Along the bank of the river, on this side and that, will grow all kinds of **trees used for food**; their leaves will not wither, and their fruit will not fail. They will bear fruit every month, because their water flows from the sanctuary. Their **fruit will be for food, and their leaves for medicine**." *Ezekiel 47:1-12*

A river of pure water will flow from the temple refreshing both the land and the sea. Yielding plenty of fish, the river will also nurture fruit trees which provide both a continual food supply and a source for herbal medicine. Israel will be transformed from an inhospitable, arid desert into a lush garden oasis beginning at the temple. The temple and surrounding area will be a wonderful sight to behold.

Rules will still apply to the day-to-day operations of the new temple. Priests will minister to Jesus, offer Him sacrifices, observe a dress code, abide by prescribed behavioral standards, teach Jesus's rules to the people and function as the high court of the land:

> ¹⁵"But **the priests, the Levites**, the sons of Zadok, who kept charge of My sanctuary when the children of Israel went astray from Me, they **shall come near Me to minister to Me**; and they shall stand before Me **to offer to Me the fat and the blood**," says the Lord GOD. ¹⁶"They shall enter My sanctuary, and they shall come near My table to minister to Me, and they shall keep My charge." *Ezekiel 44:15-16*

> ²⁰ They shall neither shave their heads nor let their hair grow long, but they shall **keep their hair well-trimmed**. ²¹ **No priest shall drink wine** when he enters the inner court. ²² They shall not take

as wife a widow or a divorced woman, but **take virgins of the descendants of the house of Israel, or widows of priests**. ²³ And they shall **teach My people** the difference between the holy and the unholy, and cause them to discern between the unclean and the clean. ²⁴ **In controversy they shall stand as judges**, and judge it according to My judgments. They shall **keep My laws and My statutes** in all My appointed meetings, and they shall **hallow My Sabbaths**. ²⁵ They shall not defile themselves by coming near a dead person. Only for father or mother, for son or daughter, for brother or unmarried sister may they defile themselves. *Ezekiel 44:20-28*

Priests may not own property, but will receive their full support from the temple:

> ²⁸ "It shall be, in regard to their (priests) inheritance, that I am their inheritance. You shall **give them no possession in Israel**, for I am their possession. ²⁹ **They shall eat the grain offering**, the sin offering, and the trespass offering; every dedicated thing in Israel shall be theirs. ³⁰ **The best of all firstfruits of any kind, and every sacrifice of any kind from all your sacrifices, shall be the priest's;** also, you shall give to the priest the first of your ground meal, to cause a blessing to rest on your house. ³¹ The priests shall not eat anything, bird or beast, that died naturally or was torn by wild beasts. *Ezekiel 44:28-31*

Certain people will not be allowed to enter the temple:

> ⁹ Thus says the Lord GOD: "**No foreigner**, uncircumcised in heart or uncircumcised in flesh, **shall enter My sanctuary**, including any foreigner who is among the children of Israel." *Ezekiel 44:9*

Sabbaths and feasts will still be observed and government leaders will be expected to set a holy example for the rest of the people:

> ¹ Thus says the Lord GOD: "The gateway of the inner court that faces toward the east shall be shut the six working days; but on the Sabbath it shall be opened, and on the day of the New Moon it shall be opened. ² **The prince** shall enter by way of the vestibule of the gateway from the outside, and stand by the gatepost. The priests shall prepare his burnt offering and his peace offerings. He **shall worship at the threshold of the gate**. Then he shall go out, but the gate shall not be shut until evening. ³ Likewise **the people**

of the land shall worship at the entrance to this gateway before the LORD **on the Sabbaths and the New Moons.**" *Ezekiel 46:1-3*

The temple will be a thriving and vital focal point for those who are with Jesus. Jesus truly will be the life of the party!

Today, control of the Temple Mount is a hotly debated topic. Due to a religious belief that the prophet Muhammad was taken from the Temple Mount on a journey to heaven by the angel Gabriel, Muslims claim possession of the site and built a sacred shrine over the spot called the Dome of the Rock. Near the Dome of the Rock, they also built the Al Aqsa Mosque, a temple in which they can worship in the Islamic faith. Christians also claim religious rights to the Temple Mount. Historically, Christians and Jews associate the Temple Mount as being the place of both Jacob's dream and the location where Abraham almost sacrificed his son, Isaac. The Bible unequivocally states that God gave the Jewish people perpetual ownership of the land in Jerusalem throughout all generations:

> [18] On the same day the LORD **made a covenant with Abram**, saying: "**To your descendants I have given this land**, from the river of Egypt to the great river, the River Euphrates—" *Genesis 15:18*

> [13] And behold, the LORD stood above it and said: "**I am the LORD God** of Abraham your father and the God of Isaac; **the land on which you lie I will give to you and your descendants**." *Genesis 28:13*

> [31] And I will set your bounds from the Red Sea to the sea, Philistia, and from the desert to the River. For I will deliver **the inhabitants of the land** into your hand, and **you shall drive them out before you**. *Exodus 23:31*

> [14] And they **shall not sell or exchange any of it**; they may not alienate this best part of the land, for it is holy to the LORD. *Ezekiel 48:14*

> [3] **Every place that the sole of your foot will tread upon I have given you**, as I said to Moses. [4] From the wilderness and this Lebanon as far as the great river, the River Euphrates, all the land of the Hittites, and to the Great Sea toward the going down of the sun, shall be your territory. *Joshua 1:3-4*

> ²³ **The land shall not be sold permanently**, for the land is Mine; for you are strangers and sojourners with Me. *Leviticus 25:23*

Christians must accept that the word of God says the land in question belongs to Israel. Because of the Temple Mount's religious significance to both religions, both the Israelis and the Palestinian Authority claim control over the Temple Mount. The presence of the Islamic shrine located on what is believed to be the location of the two previous Judaic temples is an obstacle to the rebuilding of the third temple. Muslims have no intention of removing their temple, the Al Aqsa Mosque, nor will they allow archaeological digs under the structure. Strategically, it is no accident that the Al Aqsa Mosque was built on what is believed to be the exact site of the destroyed temple. It is Islamic practice to build mosques over the religious sites of their enemies as a sign of conquest. As such, it is highly unlikely they will ever agree to any compromise extended by the Israelis.

Despite the ongoing ownership conflict, preparations are actively being made to prepare for the building process of the third temple. In order to build the temple, an Israeli religious body called the Sanhedrin must exist. In ancient Israel, the Sanhedrin met in the temple and functioned as the ruling body for legal, religious and temple matters. When Israel ceased to exist, so did the Sanhedrin. On October 13, 2004, seventy-one Jewish religious leaders re-established the Sanhedrin Court to oversee matters relating to the rebuilding of the third temple. The group performs ancient ceremonial rituals and focuses on the preparations necessary for construction of the third temple. In 2007, the Sanhedrin purchased sheep to be used for ritual animal sacrifices in the rebuilt temple. A special animal that is necessary for temple sacrifices to resume is the rare red heifer:

> ¹ Now the LORD spoke to Moses and Aaron, saying, ² "This is the ordinance of the law which the LORD has commanded, saying: 'Speak to the children of Israel, that they bring you **a red heifer without blemish**, in which there is no defect and **on which a yoke has never come**. ³ You shall **give it to Eleazar the priest**...' " *Numbers 19:1-3*

After the destruction of the second temple in 70 AD, no more red heifers were born in Israel from that point forward. Miraculously, in 1997, the first red heifer was born in Israel after two thousand years of extinction. But, in order for the calf to be used in temple sacrifices, it must be two years old and without blemish. All of the red heifers born since 1997 have been blemished in some manner. On August 28, 2018, a rabbinically certified blemish-free cow was born and is now being closely followed by the Sanhedrin to determine if it will remain blemish-free and thereby qualify to be eligible to be used as a proper sacrifice in ritual ceremonies performed in the rebuilt temple. On December 10, 2018, the Sanhedrin consecrated a biblically correct stone altar so it is ready to be used when it is needed. In cooperation with the United Temple Movement, the Sanhedrin also engages in a special process to create ritually pure olive oil for use in temple menorahs and ceremonies. The supply will be readily available by the time the temple is ready for use.

Other groups are also actively pursuing temple preparations. The Temple Institute prepares temple objects such as temple furnishings, priestly clothes, menorahs, wood carvings and vessels of gold, silver, bronze, and precious stones. In addition, the Temple Institute has also commissioned the production of specially made harps and lyres for music in the rebuilt temple. In 2016, the Temple Institute created a database to locate men who are eligible to become temple priests so that they can be trained in the ways of temple rituals.  Only priests with a genetic lineage to the tribe of Levi qualify to serve in the temple, but with modern DNA testing, it is now possible to identify those priests who have the correct lineage to administer temple rites. The Temple Institute has also prefabricated portions of the temple and is simply waiting for the greater structure to be built so that the prefabricated sections can finally be assembled in the appropriate location. Another group, the Temple Mount Faithful, has cut large cornerstones which are ready for placement at the start of temple construction. The only thing standing in the way of construction of the third temple is the dispute over the location for where it is to be built.

> **IT'S A FACT:** In 2018, the Israeli Sanhedrin along with the Mikdash (Temple) Educational Center minted a half-shekel coin using Donald Trump's image. When the Temple is in existence, the Torah requires all adult males to donate a half-shekel to the Temple.

Amazingly, despite conflict over the Temple Mount, it appears that a resolution to the issue of the location of the original temple may be possible in the near future. President Trump made history when he officially acknowledged Jerusalem as Israel's capital and ordered the movement of the US Embassy from Tel Aviv to Jerusalem. In doing so, President Trump paved the way for Israel to claim ownership rights to the Temple Mount area. While helpful in reiterating Israel's rights to land in Jerusalem, there is still the matter of the Al Aqsa Mosque which is currently believed to be built over the site of the two previous temples. Others such as author Leen Ritmeyer and Professor Joseph Patrich of the Hebrew University of Jerusalem present alternate theories for the location of the original temple. Joining their voices are the Bagatti theory and the Kaufman theory. The Bagatti theory places the temple to the south of the Dome of the Rock while the Kaufman theory places the Holy of Holies to the north of the Dome of the rock. Each alternate theory places the real location of the original temple close to the Al Aqsa Mosque, but far enough away from the structure to allow for the third temple to be built without altering the existing structure thereby holding true to the biblical mandate for the temple to be built over the previous two temples. The Sanhedrin is currently investigating and evaluating the validity of alternate site theories. If they accept an alternate site location, there is nothing preventing immediate commencement of construction on the third temple. The checklist below summarizes the current status of the building project:

- ✓ Establish a modern-day Sanhedrin
- ✓ Develop architectural designs and plans
- ✓ Acquire building materials
- ✓ Cut the foundation cornerstones
- ✓ Acquire animals for temple sacrifices
- ✓ Make a stone altar
- ✓ Produce oil for use in the temple
- ✓ Identify priests from the tribe of Levi to perform temple rites
- ✓ Train priests in the proper administration of temple rites
- ✓ Make robes, ephods and breastplates for priests
- ✓ Acquire musical instruments for the temple
- ✓ Make furniture for the temple
- ✓ Make temple vessels and utensils
- ✓ Make a menorah for the temple
  IN PROGRESS: Find a blemish free, two-year-old red heifer
  IN PROGRESS: Identify the correct location of the original temple
  TO DO: Begin construction

Clearly, construction of the third temple is well on its way to commencement. Tradition demands that it will be an amazing sight to behold:

> [1] Then the LORD spoke to Moses, saying: [2] "See, I have called by name Bezalel the son of Uri, the son of Hur, of the tribe of Judah. [3] And **I have filled him with the Spirit of God**, in wisdom, in understanding, in knowledge, and **in all manner of**

workmanship, ⁴ to design **artistic works**, to work **in gold, in silver, in bronze**, ⁵ in cutting **jewels** for setting, in **carving wood**, and to work in all manner of workmanship." *Exodus 31:1-5*

A rebuilt temple is just around the corner. Stay tuned for the big reveal!

TALK IT OUT

1. How close do you think we are to the commencing construction of the third temple on the Temple Mount?

2. Do you think the location dispute with the Muslims over the Dome of the Rock will be resolved by a negotiated compromise between the Arabs and Israelis, the discovery of an alternate site option for the original location of the temple or by a cataclysmic event which destroys the currently existing structures (earthquake, nuclear war, etc.)?

3. The Sanhedrin of ancient Israel represented a theocratic form of government. A theocracy is a religious rule where priests govern in the name of God. Do you think a theocracy is an effective form of government? Why or why not?

4. Regarding the blemish-free red heifer that was born on August 28, 2018, do you think it will remain blemish-free, thereby making it a viable temple sacrifice or do you think it will develop a blemish, as can happen, and it will be necessary to wait for another blemish-free red heifer to be born?

5. Ezekiel 47:12 states leaves will be used for medicine. Do you currently employ any holistic healing methods in your life? Which ones? What level of effectiveness would you assign to holistic healing methods? Do you have a favorite go-to when it comes to holistic healing?

"I have to keep reminding myself: If you give your life to God, he doesn't promise you happiness and that everything will go well. But he does promise you peace. You can have peace and joy, even in bad circumstances."

— Patricia Heaton

Ideas for the Week:

- ✓ Make a donation to the Temple Mount Faithful (www.templemountfaithful.org), an organization dedicated to rebuilding the third temple in Jerusalem.
- ✓ Visit a Jewish synagogue.
- ✓ Read the complete chapters of Ezekiel 40-44 for a more detailed description of the rebuilt temple.
- ✓ Watch a video about the temple harps at https://www.harrariharps.com/copy-of-temple-harp-project.

Closing Prayer

NOTE: Add names and individual personal prayer requests to the space provided below before closing in prayer.

Lord, we thank You for our time together today to grow deeper in our walk with You and fellowship with each other. As we close today, we lift up: _____

_____

_____

_____

_____

_____

_____

Father, we look forward to the rebuilding of Your holy temple in Jerusalem and eagerly await the day when we can worship You in person. Until that day arrives, reveal to us how we can better serve Your church here on earth. We know that the harvest is plentiful, but the laborers are few. We willingly join Your labor force to serve wherever, whenever and however You call us to act in Your name. In Jesus' name we pray, Amen.

SUPPORTING SCRIPTURES

LINEN
¹⁴ And the armies in heaven, clothed in fine linen, white and clean, followed Him on white horses. *Revelation 19:14*

¹⁷ And it shall be, whenever they (Levite priests) enter the gates of the inner court, that they shall put on linen garments; no wool shall come upon them while they minister within the gates of the inner court or within the house. ¹⁸ They shall have linen turbans on their heads and linen trousers on their bodies; they shall not clothe themselves with anything that causes sweat. *Ezekiel 44:17-18*

THE ANTICHRIST AND THE REBUILT TEMPLE
²⁷ Then he shall confirm a covenant with many for one week; but in the middle of the week He shall bring an end to sacrifice and offering. And on the wing of abominations shall be one who makes desolate, even until the consummation, which is determined, is poured out on the desolate. *Daniel 9:27*

…⁴ who opposes and exalts himself (the Antichrist) above all that is called God or that is worshiped, so that he sits as God in the temple of God, showing himself that he is God. *2 Thessalonians 2:4*

LAND OWNERSHIP
¹⁸ On the same day the LORD made a covenant with Abram, saying: "To your descendants I have given this land, from the river of Egypt to the great river, the River Euphrates—" *Genesis 15:18*

¹³ And behold, the LORD stood above it and said: "I am the LORD God of Abraham your father and the God of Isaac; the land on which you lie I will give to you and your descendants." *Genesis 28:13*

³¹ And I will set your bounds from the Red Sea to the sea, Philistia, and from the desert to the River. For I will deliver the inhabitants of the land into your hand, and you shall drive them out before you. *Exodus 23:31*

¹⁴ And they shall not sell or exchange any of it; they may not alienate this best part of the land, for it is holy to the LORD. *Ezekiel 48:14*

³ Every place that the sole of your foot will tread upon I have given you, as I said to Moses. ⁴ From the wilderness and this Lebanon as far as the great river, the River Euphrates, all the land of the Hittites, and to the Great Sea toward the going down of the sun, shall be your territory. *Joshua 1:3-4*

²³ The land shall not be sold permanently, for the land is Mine; for you are strangers and sojourners with Me. *Leviticus 25:23*

THE FUTURE THIRD TEMPLE

¹ Then I was given a reed like a measuring rod. And the angel stood, saying, "Rise and measure the temple of God, the altar, and those who worship there. ² But leave out the court which is outside the temple, and do not measure it, for it has been given to the Gentiles. And they will tread the holy city underfoot for forty-two months." *Revelation 11:1-2*

⁷ Even them I will bring to My holy mountain, and make them joyful in My house of prayer. Their burnt offerings and their sacrifices will be accepted on My altar; for My house shall be called a house of prayer for all nations." *Isaiah 56:7*

⁴ And the glory of the LORD came into the temple by way of the gate which faces toward the east. ⁵ The Spirit lifted me up and brought me into the inner court; and behold, the glory of the LORD filled the temple. ⁶ Then I heard Him speaking to me from the temple, while a man stood beside me. ⁷ And He said to me, "Son of man, this is the place of My throne and the place of the soles of My feet, where I will dwell in the midst of the children of Israel forever. No more shall the house of Israel defile My holy name, they nor their kings, by their harlotry or with the carcasses of their kings on their high places." *Ezekiel 43:4-7*

⁹ Thus says the Lord GOD: "No foreigner, uncircumcised in heart or uncircumcised in flesh, shall enter My sanctuary, including any foreigner who is among the children of Israel. ¹⁰ And the Levites who went far from Me, when Israel went astray, who strayed away from Me after their idols, they shall bear their iniquity. ¹¹ Yet they shall be ministers in My sanctuary, as gatekeepers of the house and ministers of the house; they shall slay the burnt offering and the sacrifice for the people, and they shall stand before them to minister to them." *Ezekiel 44:9-11*

¹⁵ "But the priests, the Levites, the sons of Zadok, who kept charge of My sanctuary when the children of Israel went astray from Me, they shall come near Me to minister to Me; and they shall stand before Me to offer to Me the fat and the blood," says the Lord GOD. ¹⁶ "They shall enter My sanctuary, and they shall come near My table to minister to Me, and they shall keep My charge." *Ezekiel 44:15-16*

²⁰ They shall neither shave their heads nor let their hair grow long, but they shall keep their hair well-trimmed. ²¹ No priest shall drink wine when he enters the inner court. ²² They shall not take as wife a widow or a divorced woman, but take virgins of the descendants of the house of Israel, or widows of priests. ²³ And they shall teach My people the difference between the holy and the unholy, and cause them to discern between the unclean and the clean. ²⁴ In controversy they shall stand as judges, and judge it according to My judgments. They shall keep

My laws and My statutes in all My appointed meetings, and they shall hallow My Sabbaths. ²⁵ They shall not defile themselves by coming near a dead person. Only for father or mother, for son or daughter, for brother or unmarried sister may they defile themselves. *Ezekiel 44:20-28*

²⁸ "It shall be, in regard to their (priests) inheritance, that I am their inheritance. You shall give them no possession in Israel, for I am their possession. ²⁹ They shall eat the grain offering, the sin offering, and the trespass offering; every dedicated thing in Israel shall be theirs. ³⁰ The best of all firstfruits of any kind, and every sacrifice of any kind from all your sacrifices, shall be the priest's; also, you shall give to the priest the first of your ground meal, to cause a blessing to rest on your house. ³¹ The priests shall not eat anything, bird or beast, that died naturally or was torn by wild beasts. *Ezekiel 44:28-31*

¹ Thus says the Lord GOD: "The gateway of the inner court that faces toward the east shall be shut the six working days; but on the Sabbath it shall be opened, and on the day of the New Moon it shall be opened. ² The prince shall enter by way of the vestibule of the gateway from the outside, and stand by the gatepost. The priests shall prepare his burnt offering and his peace offerings. He shall worship at the threshold of the gate. Then he shall go out, but the gate shall not be shut until evening. ³ Likewise the people of the land shall worship at the entrance to this gateway before the LORD on the Sabbaths and the New Moons." *Ezekiel 46:1-3*

¹ Now the LORD spoke to Moses and Aaron, saying, ² "This is the ordinance of the law which the LORD has commanded, saying: 'Speak to the children of Israel, that they bring you a red heifer without blemish, in which there is no defect and on which a yoke has never come. ³ You shall give it to Eleazar the priest…' " *Numbers 19:1-3*

¹ Then the LORD spoke to Moses, saying: ² "See, I have called by name Bezalel the son of Uri, the son of Hur, of the tribe of Judah. ³ And I have filled him with the Spirit of God, in wisdom, in understanding, in knowledge, and in all manner of workmanship, ⁴ to design artistic works, to work in gold, in silver, in bronze, ⁵ in cutting jewels for setting, in carving wood, and to work in all manner of workmanship." *Exodus 31:1-5*

¹ Then he brought me back to the door of the temple; and there was water, flowing from under the threshold of the temple toward the east, for the front of the temple faced east; the water was flowing from under the right side of the temple, south of the altar. ² He brought me out by way of the north gate, and led me around on the outside to the outer gateway that faces east; and there was water, running out on the right side. ³ And when the man went out to the east with the

line in his hand, he measured one thousand cubits, and he brought me through the waters; the water came up to my ankles. ⁴ Again he measured one thousand and brought me through the waters; the water came up to my knees. Again, he measured one thousand and brought me through; the water came up to my waist. ⁵ Again he measured one thousand, and it was a river that I could not cross; for the water was too deep, water in which one must swim, a river that could not be crossed. ⁶ He said to me, "Son of man, have you seen this?" Then he brought me and returned me to the bank of the river. ⁷ When I returned, there, along the bank of the river, were very many trees on one side and the other. ⁸ Then he said to me: "This water flows toward the eastern region, goes down into the valley, and enters the sea. When it reaches the sea, its waters are healed. ⁹ And it shall be that every living thing that moves, wherever the rivers go, will live. There will be a very great multitude of fish, because these waters go there; for they will be healed, and everything will live wherever the river goes. ¹⁰ It shall be that fishermen will stand by it from En Gedi to En Eglaim; they will be places for spreading their nets. Their fish will be of the same kinds as the fish of the Great Sea, exceedingly many. ¹¹ But its swamps and marshes will not be healed; they will be given over to salt. ¹² Along the bank of the river, on this side and that, will grow all kinds of trees used for food; their leaves will not wither, and their fruit will not fail. They will bear fruit every month, because their water flows from the sanctuary. Their fruit will be for food, and their leaves for medicine."
Ezekiel 47:1-12

NOTES

"Is prayer your steering wheel or your spare tire?"
— Corrie Ten Boom

ARE WE THE TERMINAL GENERATION?

WEEK 11: THE TWO WITNESSES

Opening Prayer: Lord, we ask that You send Your Holy Spirit to us to guide us in the teaching and understanding of Your word that we may obtain a better understanding of the prophetic events surrounding us now and waiting for us in the future. Bless our fellowship in Your word that it may be fruitful and draw us into a deeper relationship both with You and those around us. Use us as Your vessels that through us, we may reflect Your glory to all whom we encounter. Illuminate our hearts and minds so that we may boldly shine the brightness of Your light everywhere we go and that we may be beacons of Your hope in a darkened world. In Jesus name we pray, Amen.

Ice Breaker: We all want to be remembered for something after we are gone. How do you want people to remember you? For what, specifically, do you want to be remembered? In the space below, write your epitaph on the tombstone and share it with the group.

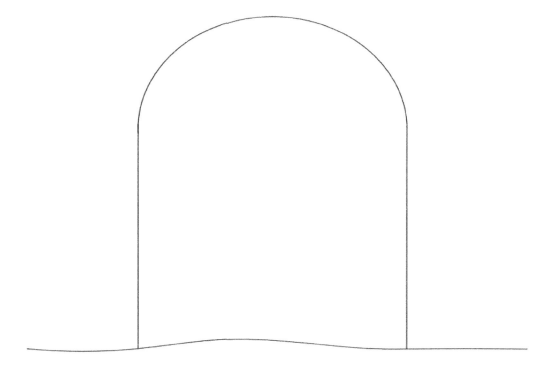

 **Focus:** When you need someone to confirm something, God will always provide the necessary witnesses.

CHRISTINE TATE

Word of the Week

> ³ And I will give power to my two **witnesses**, and they will prophesy one thousand two hundred and sixty days, clothed in sackcloth.
>
> *Revelation 11:3*

WITNESS: "Martus" (pronounced mar'-toos) is the original Greek word for "witness". Witnesses can be associated with the legal sense of the word, but a witness can also be someone who observes a historical event as a spectator. It is in this latter sense of the word that the word witness applies to the rebuilding of the temple. God sends two witnesses who observed the location of the original temple in their day to provide proof of the correct location for the altar in the new temple to be built. It is through their confirming testimony that construction may begin.

Lesson: An event that occurs at the beginning of the Tribulation is the appearance of two witnesses. Construction of the temple cannot begin until two witnesses confirm the exact spot for where the altar should be located. Many details are given in the Bible about the construction of the temple, the altar, the furnishings and the overall opulence and splendor of the temple:

¹Moreover he made a **bronze altar: twenty cubits was its length, twenty cubits its width**, and **ten cubits its height**...¹⁹ Thus Solomon had all the furnishings made for the house of God: the altar of gold and **the tables** on which was the showbread; ²⁰ **the lampstands** with their **lamps of pure gold**, to burn in the prescribed manner in front of the inner sanctuary, ²¹ with the **flowers** and the lamps and the **wick-trimmers** of gold, of purest gold; ²² the trimmers, the **bowls**, the **ladles**, and the censers of pure gold. *2 Chronicles 4:1,19-22*

³ This is **the foundation** which Solomon laid for building the house of God: The **length was sixty cubits** (by cubits according to the former measure) and the **width twenty cubits**.⁴ And the **vestibule** that was in front of the sanctuary was **twenty cubits long across the width of the house**, and the height was one hundred and

twenty. He overlaid the inside with pure gold. ⁵ The larger room he **paneled with cypress which he overlaid with fine gold**, and he **carved palm trees and chain work** on it. ⁶ And he decorated the house with **precious stones** for beauty, and the gold was gold from Parvaim. ⁷ He also overlaid the house—the beams and doorposts, its walls and doors—with gold; and he **carved cherubim on the walls**. ⁸ And he made **the Most Holy Place**. Its **length** was according to the width of the house, **twenty cubits**, and its **width twenty cubits**. *2 Chronicles 3:3*

What is not defined in detail is the exact location of the altar. No one alive today can definitively and irrefutably provide that information nor are there any official records of the location in existence. Since the altar must go in a precise location, God supernaturally provides two witnesses to attest to the correct placement of the altar. After the altar placement is confirmed, the remainder of the structure is definable based on the physical description of the temple given in the Bible.

Judaic tradition and biblical scripture indicate that one of the two witnesses will be the prophet Elijah:

> ⁵ Behold, **I will send you Elijah** the prophet before the coming of the great and dreadful day of the LORD. *Malachi 4:5*

> ¹¹ Jesus answered and said to them, "Indeed, **Elijah is coming first** and will restore all things." *Matthew 17:11*

When the **shofar** is blown for ritual purposes, it is blown in a pattern of one long blast, followed by three broken sounds and finishes with nine staccato notes.

Popular speculation as to the identity of the other witness leans towards either Moses or Enoch. Elijah never tasted death and neither did Enoch. Both men were swept away by God while they were still alive:

> ¹¹ Then it happened, as they continued on and talked, that suddenly a chariot of fire appeared with horses of fire, and separated the two of them; and **Elijah went up by a whirlwind into heaven.** ¹² And Elisha saw it, and he cried out, "My father, my father, the chariot of Israel and its horsemen!" So, **he saw him no more.** *2 Kings 2:11-12*

> ⁵ By faith **Enoch** was taken away so that he **did not see death**, "and was not found, because **God had taken him**"...*Hebrews 11:5*

Scripture states that all men must die once:

> ²⁷ And as it is **appointed for men to die once**, but after this the judgment... *Hebrews 9:27*

Since Elijah and Enoch did not die, but were taken straight to heaven, they are a logical pair to return to earth and die their first death as all men must do. Moses is also an option for who might return with Elijah. Elijah and Moses were both present when Jesus was transfigured.

> ...² and **He** (Jesus) **was transfigured** before them. His face shone like the sun, and His clothes became as white as the light. ³ And behold, **Moses and Elijah appeared** to them, **talking with Him** (Jesus). *Matthew 17:2-3*

Since they are linked together in this manner, it could also be a logical conclusion that they will be present and together again just before Jesus returns to earth. However, there is an issue with Moses as one of the two witnesses. Moses already died once:

> ⁵ So **Moses** the servant of the LORD **died there in the land of Moab**, according to the word of the LORD. *Deuteronomy 34:5*

Since prophecy states that men only die once, it is problematic for Moses to return and die a second time when the two witnesses are killed during the Tribulation. Lending further mystery to the role that Moses may or may not occupy during the Tribulation is the fact that the archangel Michael had a dispute with Satan over Moses' body after his death:

> ⁹ Yet **Michael** the archangel, in **contending with the devil**, when he disputed **about the body of Moses**… *Jude 1:9*

The dispute leads some to question why Moses' dead body would be of importance to either side. Perhaps, if Moses is to return as one of the two witnesses one day, it will be necessary for him to re-inhabit his original body. Unfortunately, the significance of the body is unknown since this is the only reference to the dispute given in scripture.

To the amazement of mankind, the two witnesses exercise supernatural powers in the sight of men while they are present on the earth:

> ⁵ And if anyone wants to harm them, **fire proceeds from their mouth and devours their enemies**. And if anyone wants to harm them, he must be killed in this manner. ⁶ These have **power to shut heaven**, so that no rain falls in the days of their prophecy; and they have **power over waters to turn them to blood**, and to **strike the earth with all plagues**, as often as they desire. *Revelation 11:5-6*

When Moses was in Egypt, he had the power to turn water to blood and smite the Egyptians with various other plagues:

> ²⁰ And Moses and Aaron did so, just as the LORD commanded. So, **he lifted up the rod and struck the waters** that were in the river, in the sight of Pharaoh and in the sight of his servants. And all the waters that were in the river were **turned to blood**. *Exodus 7:20*

Echoing a similar plague as the Egyptians experienced, rivers turn to blood during the Tribulation:

> ⁴ Then the **third angel poured out his bowl on the rivers** and springs of water, and **they became blood**. *Revelation 16:4*

Easily identifiable by their unique manner of dressing in sackcloth, the witnesses prophesy for three-and-a-half years:

> ³ And I will give power to my **two witnesses**, and they will **prophesy one thousand two hundred and sixty days**, clothed **in sackcloth**. *Revelation 11:3*

Coincidentally, this is the exact amount of time it will take to complete construction of the third temple after factoring in the necessary purification rites and rituals required by the Torah. Since the witnesses prophesy for forty-two months, forty-two months are required to sanctify the temple during construction, and the first half of the Tribulation lasts forty-two months, it is a reasonable assumption that the two witnesses appear at the beginning of the Tribulation, confirm the location of the temple, and defend against anyone who would seek to interfere with the construction of the temple. Their manner of defense is eerily similar to the plagues which happened in Egypt. The Egyptians experienced drought, water turning to blood and a number of other plagues when Moses petitioned Pharaoh to be allowed to lead the Israelites out of Egypt with their children. Similarly, the witnesses smite humanity with drought, blood water and "all plagues" during their time on earth. Those powers would be sufficient to prevent anyone from interfering with temple business so the process could progress smoothly and on schedule.

The midpoint of the Tribulation coincides with the end of the three-and-a-half-year period in which the two witnesses prophesy and demonstrate supernatural acts. It is at this point in the Tribulation that the two witnesses are killed:

> [7] **When they finish their testimony, the beast** that ascends out of the bottomless pit will make war against them, overcome them, and **kill them**. [8] And their **dead bodies will lie in the street** of the great city which spiritually is called Sodom and Egypt, where also our Lord was crucified. [9] Then those from the **peoples, tribes, tongues, and nations will see their dead bodies** three-and-a-half days, and **not allow their dead bodies to be put into graves**. [10] And those **who dwell on the earth will rejoice** over them, make merry, and **send gifts to one another**, because these two prophets tormented those who dwell on the earth. *Revelation 11:2-13*

Denied a proper burial, their dead bodies are left exposed in the open for all the world to observe as they decompose. As people watch their lifeless bodies from around the globe, their death brings joy to mankind and becomes a cause for celebration.

After their death and public viewing, the two witnesses are supernaturally raised from the dead in the sight of the whole world and ascend to heaven in the midst of a giant earthquake:

> [11] Now **after the three-and-a-half days** the breath of **life from God entered them**, and they stood on their feet, and great fear fell on those who saw them. [12] And they heard a loud voice from heaven saying to them, "Come up here." And **they ascended to heaven in a cloud**, and their enemies saw them. [13] In the same hour there was a **great earthquake**, and a tenth of the city fell. In

> the earthquake seven thousand people were killed, and the rest were afraid and gave glory to the God of heaven. *Revelation 11:2-13*

Their resurrection occurs at the end of the Tribulation. For prophetic purposes, a day equals one year:

> [27] **Fulfill her week**, and we will give you this one also for the service which you will serve with me still **another seven years**." *Genesis 29:27*

> [34] According to the number of the days in which you spied out the land, **forty days**, **for each day you shall bear your guilt one year**, namely forty years, and you shall know My rejection. *Numbers 14:34*

Employing the day for a year principle, when the witnesses are resurrected, they will have been dead for three-and-a-half years which is, coincidentally, the exact length of the second half of the Tribulation. After the passage of that much time from the point of their death, people are rightly astonished and afraid at the sight of their resurrection. Also indicating their resurrection occurs at the end of the Tribulation is that it happens when Jesus returns. Read within the full context of the passage, three verses after "they ascended to heaven", it is announced that Jesus is here and has taken control:

> [15] Then the seventh angel sounded: And there were loud voices in heaven, saying, "**The kingdoms of this world have become the kingdoms of our Lord and of His Christ**, and He shall reign forever and ever!" *Revelation 11:15*

Consistent with the interpretation that the resurrection of the two witnesses happens at the end of the Tribulation is that there is also a giant earthquake when Jesus returns:

> [4] And in that day **His feet will stand on the Mount of Olives**, which faces Jerusalem on the east. **and the Mount of Olives shall be split in two**, from east to west, making a very large valley; half of the mountain shall move toward the north and half of it toward the south. *Zechariah 14:4*

It is only when Jesus returns that the people realize they should give glory to God.

Talk It Out

1. Do you think the identity of the final two witnesses is most likely Elijah and Enoch, Elijah and Moses or another combination of two people? Do you think that Moses' experience turning water to blood in Egypt during the plagues could be connected to the identity of the second witness since the witnesses share a common ability to alter the state of water? Is it a pertinent factor that Moses already died once?

2. Jude 1:9 is the only mention of the dispute over Moses' body in the Bible. Why do you think Satan and the archangel Michael might have had a disagreement about Moses' body?

3. Revelation 11:3 directly refers to these two men as "witnesses" who prophesy. Why do you think it is important for them to be witnesses for the exact location of the third temple? After they attest to the exact temple location, they prophesy to the people for three-and-half years. What do you think their message for mankind might be?

4. In Week 6, it was presented that the second trumpet turned water to blood. In Week 7, it was presented that the second bowl also turned water to blood. Do you think it is possible that both events are referring to the acts of the two witnesses during the first half of the Tribulation?

5. Revelation 11:5 is very specific about the manner of death prescribed for anyone who wants to harm the two witnesses before it is their time to die (fire proceeds from their mouth). Why do you think the Bible is so specific about how their enemies must be killed?

Solomon's Temple

Fact: Being a man of war, David was not allowed to build the temple, so he gave the plans to Solomon to build it. (*1 Chronicles 22:8, 28:11-12*)

Fact: It would take 3-6 billion dollars in today's money to build Solomon's temple.

Fact: It took seven years to build the temple.

Fact: When the temple was dedicated, a 14-day feast was held. 220,000 oxen along with 120,000 sheep were sacrificed.

Fact: To build the temple, it took 30,000 Israelites and 150,000 Canaanites along with various artists from Phoenicia and craftsmen from Tyre.

Ideas for the Week:

- ✓ Read about Elijah (1 and 2 Kings) and Enoch (Genesis 5:18-24, 1 Chronicles 1:3, Luke 3:37, Hebrews 11:5-6, Jude 1:14-15) this week observing if either of them are likely candidates to return as either of the two witnesses.
- ✓ Watch an illustrated tour of the plans for the third temple to be built on the Temple Mount in Jerusalem at https://www.templeinstitute.org/illustrated_tour.htm
- ✓ Sanctify your own home by anointing it with oil. Instructions for the process can be found at http://www.kcm.org/real-help/life-work/learn/how-anoint-your-home-oil.
- ✓ Make Resurrection rolls using the recipe found at https://www.allrecipes.com/recipe/84289/resurrection-rolls/.

Closing Prayer

NOTE: Add names and individual personal prayer requests to the space provided below before closing in prayer.

Lord, we thank You for our time together today to grow deeper in our walk with You and fellowship with each other. As we close today, we lift up: _____

_____

_____

_____

_____

_____

Father, we thank You for providing the people we need in our lives at just the right time when we need them. In service to You, we willingly give ourselves to You to be drawn into the lives of other people who might need us. Let everything we say and do be a glory to You that one day we may hear You utter the words we long to hear, "Well done, good and faithful servant". In Jesus' name we pray, Amen.

SUPPORTING SCRIPTURES

TIME OF JACOB'S TROUBLE

⁴ Now these are the words that the LORD spoke concerning Israel and Judah. ⁵ "For thus says the LORD: 'We have heard a voice of trembling, of fear, and not of peace. ⁶ Ask now, and see, whether a man is ever in labor with child? So why do I see every man with his hands on his loins Like a woman in labor, and all faces turned pale? ⁷ Alas! For that day is great, so that none is like it; and it is the time of Jacob's trouble, but he shall be saved out of it. *Jeremiah 30:4-7*

TWO WITNESSES

² But leave out the court which is outside the temple, and do not measure it, for it has been given to the Gentiles. And they will tread the holy city underfoot for forty-two months. ³ And I will give power to my two witnesses, and they will prophesy one thousand two hundred and sixty days, clothed in sackcloth. ⁴ These are the two olive trees and the two lampstands standing before the God of the earth. ⁵ And if anyone wants to harm them, fire proceeds from their mouth and devours their enemies. And if anyone wants to harm them, he must be killed in this manner. ⁶ These have power to shut heaven, so that no rain falls in the days of their prophecy; and they have power over waters to turn them to blood, and to strike the earth with all plagues, as often as they desire. ⁷ When they finish their testimony, the beast that ascends out of the bottomless pit will make war against them, overcome them, and kill them. ⁸ And their dead bodies will lie in the street of the great city which spiritually is called Sodom and Egypt, where also our Lord was crucified. ⁹ Then those from the peoples, tribes, tongues, and nations will see their dead bodies three-and-a-half days, and not allow their dead bodies to be put into graves. ¹⁰ And those who dwell on the earth will rejoice over them, make merry, and send gifts to one another, because these two prophets tormented those who dwell on the earth. ¹¹ Now after the three-and-a-half days the breath of life from God entered them, and they stood on their feet, and great fear fell on those who saw them. ¹² And they heard a loud voice from heaven saying to them, "Come up here." And they ascended to heaven in a cloud, and their enemies saw them. ¹³ In the same hour there was a great earthquake, and a tenth of the city fell. In the earthquake seven thousand people were killed, and the rest were afraid and gave glory to the God of heaven. *Revelation 11:2-13*

² …So I said, "I am looking, and there is a lampstand of solid gold with a bowl on top of it, and on the stand seven lamps with seven pipes to the seven lamps. ³ Two olive trees are by it, one at the right of the bowl and the other at its left."… ¹¹ Then I answered and said to him, "What are these two olive trees—at the right of the lampstand and at its left?" ¹² And I further answered and said to him, "What are these two olive branches that drip into the receptacles of the two gold pipes from which the golden oil drains?" ¹³ Then he answered me and said, "Do you not

know what these are?" And I said, "No, my lord." ¹⁴ So he said, "These are the two anointed ones, who stand beside the Lord of the whole earth." *Zechariah 4:2-3, 11-14*

TEMPLE DESCRIPTION

² Now the house which King Solomon built for the LORD, its length was sixty cubits, its width twenty, and its height thirty cubits. ³ The vestibule in front of the sanctuary of the house was twenty cubits long across the width of the house, and the width of the vestibule extended ten cubits from the front of the house. ⁴ And he made for the house windows with beveled frames. ⁵ Against the wall of the temple he built chambers all around, against the walls of the temple, all around the sanctuary and the inner sanctuary. Thus, he made side chambers all around it. ⁶ The lowest chamber was five cubits wide, the middle was six cubits wide, and the third was seven cubits wide; for he made narrow ledges around the outside of the temple, so that the support beams would not be fastened into the walls of the temple. ⁷ And the temple, when it was being built, was built with stone finished at the quarry, so that no hammer or chisel or any iron tool was heard in the temple while it was being built. ⁸ The doorway for the middle story was on the right side of the temple. They went up by stairs to the middle story, and from the middle to the third. ⁹ So he built the temple and finished it, and he paneled the temple with beams and boards of cedar. ¹⁰ And he built side chambers against the entire temple, each five cubits high; they were attached to the temple with cedar beams. *1 Kings 6:2-10*

¹ Now Solomon began to build the house of the LORD at Jerusalem on Mount Moriah, where the LORD had appeared to his father David, at the place that David had prepared on the threshing floor of Ornan the Jebusite. ² And he began to build on the second day of the second month in the fourth year of his reign. ³ This is the foundation which Solomon laid for building the house of God: The length was sixty cubits (by cubits according to the former measure) and the width twenty cubits. ⁴ And the vestibule that was in front of the sanctuary was twenty cubits long across the width of the house, and the height was one hundred and twenty. He overlaid the inside with pure gold. ⁵ The larger room he paneled with cypress which he overlaid with fine gold, and he carved palm trees and chain work on it. ⁶ And he decorated the house with precious stones for beauty, and the gold was gold from Parvaim. ⁷ He also overlaid the house—the beams and doorposts, its walls and doors—with gold; and he carved cherubim on the walls. ⁸ And he made the Most Holy Place. Its length was according to the width of the house, twenty cubits, and its width twenty cubits. He overlaid it with six hundred talents of fine gold. ⁹ The weight of the nails was fifty shekels of gold; and he overlaid the upper area with gold. ¹⁰ In the Most Holy Place he made two cherubim, fashioned by carving, and overlaid them with gold. ¹¹ The wings of the

cherubim were twenty cubits in overall length: one wing of the one cherub was five cubits, touching the wall of the room, and the other wing was five cubits, touching the wing of the other cherub; [12] one wing of the other cherub was five cubits, touching the wall of the room, and the other wing also was five cubits, touching the wing of the other cherub. [13] The wings of these cherubim spanned twenty cubits overall. They stood on their feet, and they faced inward. [14] And he made the veil of blue, purple, crimson, and fine linen, and wove cherubim into it. [15] Also he made in front of the temple two pillars thirty-five cubits high, and the capital that was on the top of each of them was five cubits. [16] He made wreaths of chain work, as in the inner sanctuary, and put them on top of the pillars; and he made one hundred pomegranates, and put them on the wreaths of chain work. [17] Then he set up the pillars before the temple, one on the right hand and the other on the left; he called the name of the one on the right hand Jachin, and the name of the one on the left Boaz. *2 Chronicles 3:1-17*

[1]Moreover he made a bronze altar: twenty cubits was its length, twenty cubits its width, and ten cubits its height. [2] Then he made the Sea of cast bronze, ten cubits from one brim to the other; it was completely round. Its height was five cubits, and a line of thirty cubits measured its circumference. [3] And under it was the likeness of oxen encircling it all around, ten to a cubit, all the way around the Sea. The oxen were cast in two rows, when it was cast. [4] It stood on twelve oxen: three looking toward the north, three looking toward the west, three looking toward the south, and three looking toward the east; the Sea was set upon them, and all their back parts pointed inward. [5] It was a handbreadth thick; and its brim was shaped like the brim of a cup, like a lily blossom. It contained three thousand baths. [6] He also made ten lavers, and put five on the right side and five on the left, to wash in them; such things as they offered for the burnt offering they would wash in them, but the Sea was for the priests to wash in. [7] And he made ten lampstands of gold according to their design, and set them in the temple, five on the right side and five on the left. [8] He also made ten tables, and placed them in the temple, five on the right side and five on the left. And he made one hundred bowls of gold. [9] Furthermore he made the court of the priests, and the great court and doors for the court; and he overlaid these doors with bronze. [10] He set the Sea on the right side, toward the southeast. [11] Then Huram made the pots and the shovels and the bowls. So Huram finished doing the work that he was to do for King Solomon for the house of God: [12] the two pillars and the bowl-shaped capitals that were on top of the two pillars; the two networks covering the two bowl-shaped capitals which were on top of the pillars; [13] four hundred pomegranates for the two networks (two rows of pomegranates for each network, to cover the two bowl-shaped capitals that were on the pillars); [14] he also made carts and the lavers on the carts; [15] one Sea and twelve oxen under it; [16] also the pots, the shovels, the forks—and all their articles Huram his master craftsman

made of burnished bronze for King Solomon for the house of the LORD. ¹⁷ In the plain of Jordan the king had them cast in clay molds, between Succoth and Zeredah. ¹⁸ And Solomon had all these articles made in such great abundance that the weight of the bronze was not determined. ¹⁹ Thus Solomon had all the furnishings made for the house of God: the altar of gold and the tables on which was the showbread; ²⁰ the lampstands with their lamps of pure gold, to burn in the prescribed manner in front of the inner sanctuary, ²¹ with the flowers and the lamps and the wick-trimmers of gold, of purest gold; ²² the trimmers, the bowls, the ladles, and the censers of pure gold. As for the entry of the sanctuary, its inner doors to the Most Holy Place, and the doors of the main hall of the temple, were gold. *2 Chronicles 4:1-22*

ELIJAH, ENOCH AND MOSES
⁵ Behold, I will send you Elijah the prophet before the coming of the great and dreadful day of the LORD. *Malachi 4:5*

¹¹ Jesus answered and said to them, "Indeed, Elijah is coming first and will restore all things." *Matthew 17:11*

¹¹ Then it happened, as they continued on and talked, that suddenly a chariot of fire appeared with horses of fire, and separated the two of them; and Elijah went up by a whirlwind into heaven. ¹² And Elisha saw it, and he cried out, "My father, my father, the chariot of Israel and its horsemen!" So, he saw him no more. *2 Kings 2:11-12*

⁵ By faith Enoch was taken away so that he did not see death, "and was not found, because God had taken him"…*Hebrews 11:5*

²⁷ And as it is appointed for men to die once, but after this the judgment… *Hebrews 9:27*

⁵ So Moses the servant of the LORD died there in the land of Moab, according to the word of the LORD. *Deuteronomy 34:5*

…² and He (Jesus) was transfigured before them. His face shone like the sun, and His clothes became as white as the light. ³ And behold, Moses and Elijah appeared to them, talking with Him (Jesus). *Matthew 17:2-3*

⁹ Yet Michael the archangel, in contending with the devil, when he disputed about the body of Moses… *Jude 1:9*

WATER TO BLOOD
²⁰ And Moses and Aaron did so, just as the LORD commanded. So, he lifted up the rod and struck the waters that were in the river, in the sight of Pharaoh and in

the sight of his servants. And all the waters that were in the river were turned to blood. *Exodus 7:20*

⁴ Then the third angel poured out his bowl on the rivers and springs of water, and they became blood. *Revelation 16:4*

DAYS, WEEKS AND YEARS
²⁷ Fulfill her week, and we will give you this one also for the service which you will serve with me still another seven years." *Genesis 29:27*

³⁴ According to the number of the days in which you spied out the land, forty days, for each day you shall bear your guilt one year, namely forty years, and you shall know My rejection. *Numbers 14:34*

RESURRECTION OF WITNESSES COINCIDES WITH RETURN OF JESUS
¹⁵ Then the seventh angel sounded: And there were loud voices in heaven, saying, "The kingdoms of this world have become the kingdoms of our Lord and of His Christ, and He shall reign forever and ever!" *Revelation 11:15*

⁴ And in that day His feet will stand on the Mount of Olives, which faces Jerusalem on the east. and the Mount of Olives shall be split in two, from east to west, making a very large valley; half of the mountain shall move toward the north and half of it toward the south. *Zechariah 14:4*

NOTES

"Sir, my greatest concern is not whether God is on our side; my greatest concern is to be on God's side, for God is always right." — Abraham Lincoln

CHRISTINE TATE

The Tribulation

WEEK 12: PEACE AGREEMENT

Opening Prayer: Lord, we ask that You send Your Holy Spirit to us to guide us in the teaching and understanding of Your word that we may obtain a better understanding of the prophetic events surrounding us now and waiting for us in the future. Bless our fellowship in Your word that it may be fruitful and draw us into a deeper relationship both with You and those around us. Use us as Your vessels that through us, we may reflect Your glory to all whom we encounter. Illuminate our hearts and minds so that we may boldly shine the brightness of Your light everywhere we go and that we may be beacons of Your hope in a darkened world. In Jesus name we pray, Amen.

Ice Breaker: If you had unlimited resources of every kind, what single gift would you give the person sitting to your left to help them get through the seven-year Tribulation, a period of unparalleled hardship? Share your answers as a group.

I would give the person sitting to my left: _____
_____

Focus: Peace is a gift God gives to those who value His leadership and faithfully obey His commands.

Secrets of Success

Jim McCloughan, a decorated Army medic who served in the Vietnam war, received the Medal of Honor on July 31, 2017 for repeatedly risking his life under fire and while wounded saving the lives of many of his brothers-in-arms. After the war, he went on to have a successful career as a sociology teacher who coached football, baseball and wrestling for which he earned lifetime achievement awards. He credits his lifetime of success to three factors:

1. **Servant Leadership.** Jesus, a true leader, set the example by serving those around Him and putting other's needs first.

2. **A Sense of Humor.** Keep the proper perspective. Foster a positive mental attitude to reframe tough problems and find new ways to improve.

3. **See the Forest Through the Trees.** While tending to details, always keep an eye on the bigger picture. A battle can be lost as long as the war is won.

ARE WE THE TERMINAL GENERATION?

Word of the Week

> ⁶ Pray for the **peace** of Jerusalem…
>
> *Psalm 122:6*

PEACE: Praying for the peace of Jerusalem is such a simple thing to pray, yet encompasses a more complex concept in a deeper sense of the meaning. "Shalom" (pronounced shaw-lome') is the Hebrew word for peace. When praying for shalom, the petitioner is praying for so much more than just the avoidance of war. Prayers for shalom include completeness, safety, health, welfare, prosperity, quiet tranquility, friendly relationships, right covenant with God along with an absence of war. When all of these elements combine simultaneously, true shalom is achieved. However, the only way these qualities can coexist at the same time is when Jesus is present. Essentially, praying for peace is synonymous with praying for the return of Jesus.

Lesson: As the time of Jesus' return draws near, the world will enter a seven-year period called the Tribulation or time of Jacob's trouble:

> ⁷ Alas! For that day is great, so that none is like it; and **it is the time of Jacob's trouble**, but he shall be **saved** out of it. *Jeremiah 30:7*

Prophetically, Jacob represents Israel since Jacob fathered the twelve tribes of Israel. As the verse indicates, Israel will be tried, but God will not forsake her.

When the mandate for God's word to go forth to the whole earth has been fulfilled, it will herald the beginning of the Tribulation:

> ¹⁴ And this **gospel** of the kingdom will be **preached in all the world** as a witness to all the nations, and **then the end** will come. *Matthew 24:14*

With the modern explosion of digital media and communication, it is not a far stretch of the imagination to envision just how close we might be to that criteria being satisfied so that the Tribulation may begin.

The term Tribulation derives its name from an ancient piece of farming equipment called a tribulum. A tribulum is a heavy, flat sled that is pulled over wheat by a farm animal for the purpose of separating the useless chaff from the valuable kernel of wheat inside. Often, a tribulum has sharp pieces of metal or rock on the underside of the sled to assist in tearing the chaff from the kernel. Like the tribulum, the Tribulation will try men's faith with severe, often painful hardships separating apostate Christians from genuine, faith-filled, God-fearing Christians. When the Tribulation is over, there will be no question as to those who are fit for the kingdom of heaven and those who will see a different fate.

After the gospel has been shared with the entire world, God allows the Antichrist to emerge thus officially beginning the Tribulation. Peace has always been elusive in the Middle East. Many who precede the Antichrist have tried to broker a peace treaty. All have failed, unlike the Antichrist who will succeed:

> [24] He (the Antichrist) shall **enter peaceably**, even into the richest places of the province; and he shall **do what his fathers have not done, nor his forefathers**... Daniel 11:24

Entering on a platform of peace initiating the Tribulation period, the Antichrist first brokers a false seven-year peace agreement between Israel and "many" others:

> [27] Then he (the Antichrist) shall **confirm a covenant with many for one week**...
> Daniel 9:27

Prescribed for the Tribulation is a period of seven years. Biblically, for prophetic purposes, a day represents one year. When Jacob worked an additional seven years for Rachel's hand in marriage, the Bible refers to it as one week or seven days. The Israelites wandered in the desert for forty years as a result of the forty days spent spying out the land. In reference to the Tribulation, the time period is referred to as one week or seven days which translates into seven years. The completion of those seven years culminates with Christ's return at

The *"Cobra Effect"* is when an attempted solution to a problem actually makes the problem worse.

the end of the Tribulation.

Scripturally, the Antichrist simply "confirms" the covenant and is not a signatory on the agreement. In the original Hebrew, the word for "confirm" is "gabar" (pronounced gaw-bar') which means to "make strong or strengthen". As the broker and mediator of the peace treaty, the Antichrist throws his political might and force at the process while molding the parties and terms into a form that is strong enough to emerge as a viable peace deal. Israel is one party to the peace agreement. While the second party to the peace agreement is not stated outright, one possibility for the identity of the "many" who are signatories on the agreement with Israel is the Arab League which is a confederation of twenty-two Arab nations. Member countries of the Arab League include: Algeria, Bahrain, Comoros, Djibouti, Egypt, Iraq, Jordan, Kuwait, Lebanon, Libya, Mauritania, Morocco, Oman, Palestine, Qatar, Saudi Arabia, Somalia, Sudan, Syria, Tunisia, United Arab Emirates and Yemen. Unwavering in their support for Palestine, the Arab League has been intricately involved with the ongoing Palestinian dispute with Israel. The Palestinian Authority claims that the land of Israel belongs to Palestine and should be a Palestinian state for Palestinians. To that end, they have been bombarding Israel with suicide bombers and aerially launched rockets for decades. Exhausted by the constant barrage of aggression, wearied by ongoing bloodshed within her borders and motivated by God's command to live at peace whenever possible (Romans 12:18), Israel willingly enters into the seven-year treaty. Interestingly, Palestinian Authority Chairman Mahmoud Abbas currently advocates that any peace agreement that would be brokered will have a specific timeframe implemented within the treaty. When the peace treaty is signed, Israel will believe the fleeting dream of a peaceful coexistence with her Arab neighbors in the Middle East is finally a reality. Entering into a peace treaty with the Arab League would not just provide respite from the ongoing Palestinian conflict, but it would give Israel perceived peace with much of the Arab world at large.

Details of the peace agreement include the dividing up of Israeli land:

> [2]...My heritage **Israel**, whom they have scattered among the nations; **they have also divided up My land**...Joel 3:2

Dividing Israel's land is indicative of a possible two state solution. Potential negotiations might include a situation where Israel is allowed to build the third temple without Muslim interference from the predominantly Muslim Arab world. Scripture tells us that the third temple will be rebuilt at some point:

> ...[4] who opposes and exalts himself (the Antichrist) above all that is called God or that is worshiped, so that **he sits as God in the**

temple of God, showing himself that he is God. *2 Thessalonians 2:4*

By default, if permission to build the third temple were absent from the treaty, then there would be no temple in place for the Antichrist to desecrate at the midpoint of the Tribulation. Currently, the Islamic community does not accept a Jewish temple anywhere near the Al Aqsa Mosque or the Dome of the Rock on the Temple Mount in Jerusalem. At this point, even if an acceptable alternate site location is identified, the building process would most likely be interrupted by Islamic backlash. However, scripture indicates the third temple is rebuilt without incident or delay. Three-and-a-half years into the Tribulation, the Antichrist desecrates the temple:

> [27] ...in the **middle of the week** he (the Antichrist) shall bring an **end to sacrifice and offering**. *Daniel 9:27*

Factoring time for the prescribed temple dedication rituals, it takes exactly three-and-a-half years to build the temple. Delays would lengthen the process from that starting point, but that is not what happens. Initially, the peace agreement appears to be effective allowing Israel to successfully rebuild the third temple and resume temple sacrifices without incident. Everything will appear to be progressing as planned. But, historically, Israel has always found peace with her Islamic neighbors to be elusive and risks history repeating itself. Biblical wisdom warns against putting too much faith in the hopes that things will be different than what they have always been:

> [9] That which **has been is what will be**, that which is done is what will be done, and there is nothing new under the sun. *Ecclesiastes 1:9*

For centuries, the Muslim world has sought to eliminate any traces of the Jewish people and this time will be no different. In 689 AD, Muslims built the Dome of the Rock over the destroyed Jewish temple on the Jerusalem Temple Mount as a sign of ultimate conquest. To this day, building a church or synagogue anywhere in Saudi Arabia is illegal due to a zero-tolerance policy in the Muslim world for anything other than Islam as a religion. In recent years, fulfilling Psalm 83:4-8, Iran's ex-President Ahmadinejad famously publicly expressed the goal of destroying Israel to the point of wiping her off the map. This same sentiment is echoed in scripture:

> [4] They have said, "Come, and **let us cut them off from being a nation**, that the name of **Israel** may be **remembered no more**. [5] For they have consulted together with one consent; **they form a**

> **confederacy against You:** ⁶the tents of Edom and the **Ishmaelites**; Moab and the Hagrites; ⁷Gebal, Ammon, and Amalek; Philistia with the inhabitants of Tyre; ⁸Assyria also has joined with the... *Psalm 83:4-8*

In the above passage, "they" refers to a confederacy of Arab nations who dream of a world without Israel. Palestinians claim Israeli land is actually Palestinian land and desire to replace the state of Israel with an entirely Palestinian state. Palestinian Authority textbooks from September 2018 actively teach Arab children that Israeli land belongs to Arabs and that they should willingly give their lives in the fight to possess all of Israel. Clearly little, if anything, has changed throughout the centuries which is why the concept of peace in the Middle East has been an abysmal failure.

After the temple is completed three-and-a-half years into the Tribulation, the peace agreement is destroyed when the Antichrist and a confederacy of Islamic nations attack Jerusalem and take possession of the newly built temple. Known as the "Abomination of Desolation", the Antichrist walks into the rebuilt temple, stops the temple sacrifices, places an unholy object within the temple, then sits in the temple of God and calls himself God:

> ³⁰For ships from Cyprus shall come against him (the Antichrist); therefore, he shall be grieved, and **return in rage against the holy covenant** (peace agreement), and do damage. So, he shall return and **show regard for those who forsake the holy covenant** (Muslims). ³¹And forces shall be mustered by him, and they shall defile the sanctuary fortress; then they shall **take away the daily sacrifices**, and **place there the abomination of desolation**. *Daniel 11:30-31*

> ⁴... so that **he (the Antichrist) sits as God in the temple of God**, showing himself that he is God. *2 Thessalonians 2:4*

The Abomination of Desolation is an unholy object that is placed in the temple. In Hebrew, the word for desolate is "Shamem" (pronounced shaw-mame') and means to cause devastating ruin in a horrific manner. Perhaps the Abomination of Desolation could be a suitcase nuclear devise hidden inside of an idol or statue that could be detonated at a later time of the Antichrist's choosing. When the Antichrist places the Abomination of Desolation in the temple sanctuary, it starts a prophetic clock:

> ¹¹And **from the time** that the daily **sacrifice is taken away**, and the abomination of desolation is set up, there **shall be one**

> **thousand two hundred and ninety days**. ¹² **Blessed is he** who waits, and comes to the **one thousand three hundred and thirty-five days**. *Daniel 12:11-12*

In this use of the word days, a literal interpretation for "days" is required. If the Tribulation is seven years in total, and this event happens at the mid-point of the Tribulation, then there are three-and-a-half years left in the seven-year timeframe or one thousand two hundred and ninety days in the Jewish calendar which uses three hundred and sixty days to define a year. Of particular note is that there is an extra forty-five days tacked onto the end of the Tribulation. Even after the Tribulation time period of seven years expires, God's children will need to hang on for six extra weeks.

Essentially, a military event happens that angers the Antichrist. Responding with the full fury of his wrath, he lashes out at the peace agreement. In Hebrew, the word for "holy covenant" is "beriyth" (pronounced ber-eeth) which means alliance or treaty. The treaty can either be with man or God. Since the Antichrist is aligned with Satan and has no agreement with God, the reference must be directed at the earthly peace agreement with Israel. The word "forsake" in Hebrew is "azab" (pronounced aw-zab') which means to depart from, leave, abandon or let go. In the context of this passage, the Antichrist shows favor to the party in the agreement that abandons the contract. Since Israel is not the participant that leaves the peace agreement, the Antichrist shows favor to the other party which is most likely an Arab confederation of some sort. Together, they successfully attack Jerusalem.

> ¹⁵ Therefore when you see the "abomination of desolation," spoken of by Daniel the prophet, standing in the holy place (whoever reads, let him understand), ¹⁶ then **let those who are in Judea flee** to the mountains. *Matthew 25:15*

With Jerusalem successfully overtaken, the peace agreement is officially broken.

In order for a peace agreement to last and be effective, both parties must operate in good faith and desire genuine peace. At the heart of the turmoil in the Middle East is the fundamental question of whether Islam truly embraces the concept of a peaceful compromise. As such, there is an ongoing debate in our society as to whether Islam is a religion of peace or a religion of war. The simplified answer is both. Certain Qur'anic verses do speak to peace. However, there are also verses in the Qur'an which speak to war. Essential to understanding how the conflicting verses relate to each other is a concept called the Theory of Abrogation. First, it is important to understand that the god of the Qur'an can and does change his mind about his doctrine and abrogates, or changes, verses accordingly as stated in the following Qur'anic surahs:

> Surah 2:106: If We **abrogate a verse** or cause it to be forgotten, **We will replace it by a better one** or one similar. Did you not know that god has power over all things?

> Surah 13:39: **God abrogates** and confirms **what He pleases**.

> Surah 16:101: **When we change one verse for another** (god knows best what He reveals), they say: "You are an imposter." Indeed, most of them have no knowledge.

In the early part of the Qur'an, the god of the Qur'an encourages followers to make converts to Islam through peaceful means.

> Surah 2:256: There shall be **no compulsion in religion**.

By the third chapter of the Qur'an, the god of the Qur'an contradicts himself and changes his mind deciding that if people will not voluntarily convert to Islam when asked nicely, they should be killed:

> Surah 3:85: He that chooses **a religion other than Islam, it will not be accepted** from him...

> Surah 4:88-90: Why are you thus divided concerning the hypocrites, when god Himself has cast them off on account of their misdeeds? Would you guide those whom god has confounded? He whom god confounds you cannot guide. They would have you disbelieve **as they themselves have disbelieved**, so that you may be all alike. **Do not befriend them** until they have fled their homes in the cause of god. If they desert you, seize them and **put them to death wherever you find them**. Look for neither friends nor helpers among them except those who seek refuge with your allies or come over to you because their hearts forbid them to fight against you or against their own people.

> Surah 8:38-39: Tell **the unbelievers** that if they mend their ways their past shall be forgiven; but if they persist in sin (unbelief), let them reflect upon the fate of bygone nations. **Make war on them** until idolatry shall cease and god's religion shall reign supreme.

> Surah 47:4: When you meet **the unbelievers** in the battlefield **strike off their heads**...

The Theory of Abrogation presents that whenever god changes his mind, whatever he said first is negated and whatever he says next is what should be done. Simply stated, since the last dictate from their god is to kill all non-believers, the first mandate presented earlier in the Qur'an to make converts through peaceful means is rendered null and void (Chacon and Burnham, p. 13).

An additional problem entering into a peace treaty with the Muslim world centers around another dictate from the Qur'an. Allah advocates that lying is acceptable for the right purposes in the right circumstances. Commonly known as Al-Taqiyya, the practice of lying for acceptable reasons gives absolution to the person perpetrating the lie:

> *Surah 2:225*: **God will not call you to account** for that which is **inadvertent (untrue) in your oaths**. But he will take you to task for that which is intended in your hearts.
>
> *Surah 9:3*: God and his apostle are **under no obligation to the idolaters**.
>
> *Surah 9:12*: ...make war on the leaders of unbelief--for **no oaths are binding with them**--so that they may desist.
>
> *Surah 16:102*: **Those who are forced to recant** while their hearts remain loyal to the Faith **shall be absolved**...
>
> *Surah 17:64*: Be their partner in their riches and in their offspring. **Promise them what you will.** (Satan promises them only to deceive them).
>
> *Surah 66:2*: God has given you **absolution from such oaths**.

Peace in the Middle East is the fallacy of our day. The foundation of any contract or agreement lies in the inherent honest intent and good faith of both parties entering into the contract. It is impossible to reasonably expect that a contract will be effective if one of the parties cannot be trusted and is likely to fail to honor the terms of the agreement based on religious permission. Peace is only a viable outcome if both parties honestly commit to achieving that end and do everything in their power to honor the terms of the agreement. Unless both parties can be scrupulously trusted, any peace established can only be temporarily fleeting at best. Real, lasting peace will only be made manifest when Jesus comes back and sets up His new kingdom. Come, Lord Jesus!

Talk It Out

1. Have you ever experienced a period of Tribulation in your life? How rough was your period of trial? How do you think what you experienced might compare to what people will experience during the Tribulation period?

2. At this point in history, who do you think are likely candidates to participate in a peace agreement with Israel in the Middle East? Do you think Israel trusts anyone enough to be swayed by their opinion and nudged into signing a peace agreement?

3. Billionaire Ron Lauder of cosmetic line Estee Lauder fame and President of the World Jewish Congress is also a close, boyhood friend of US President Donald Trump. Do you think that Ron Lauder's long-standing personal ties to Donald Trump provide President Trump with extra credibility with Israeli leadership? Is it possible that relationship would give him the beneficial edge necessary to successfully broker a peace agreement in the Middle East?

4. Joel 3:2 references that the forces of the Antichrist divide up Israel's land. Who do you think are the most likely recipients of that land and how do you think it might be divided under the Antichrist's rule?

5. Do you believe the religion of Islam is a religion of peace or not? Explain why you believe what you believe. Have your personal interactions and experiences with Muslims given you the impression that Islam is a religion of peace? Do you know any military members who have served overseas in Muslim dominated areas? What were their experiences with Islam as a religion?

6. Have you ever heard of the Theory of Abrogation before? Why do you think the Theory of Abrogation is not commonly discussed in context with the religion of Islam? Should it be? Do you think the Theory of Abrogation is understood by most Muslims?

7. Do you think the media accurately portrays Muslims? Is their portrayal in the media fair or unfair? Does the media push a Muslim agenda?

Ideas for the Week:

- ✓ Buy a bag of wheatberries to see what an unprocessed kernel of wheat looks like. If you are lucky, you may even find the remnant of a piece of chaff in the bag.
- ✓ Stay abreast of updates on Israeli-Arab relations by following the news from the World Jewish Council at https://www.worldjewishcongress.org/en/news.
- ✓ Pray daily for the peace of Jerusalem as Psalm 122:6 commands.
- ✓ Educate those around you this week about the Theory of Abrogation and how it applies to the Qur'an to help others understand how Islam started off as a religion advocating peace and emerged transformed into a radical ideology advocating death to unbelievers.

Closing Prayer

NOTE: Add names and individual personal prayer requests to the space provided below before closing in prayer.

Lord, we thank You for our time together today to grow deeper in our walk with You and fellowship with each other. As we close today, we lift up: _____

_____

_____

_____

_____

_____

_____

Father, we pray for those in all religions who live by the sword that they may turn from violence and embrace peace as their path. Reveal Yourself to them and open their hearts to the eternal gift of salvation You so freely offer. Use us as Your guiding lights that we may teach others to live peaceably with each other and walk in the light of Your love. Bless us with that same peace in our own lives. In Jesus' name we pray, Amen.

SUPPORTING SCRIPTURES

THE TRIBULATION
[14] And this gospel of the kingdom will be preached in all the world as a witness to all the nations, and then the end will come. *Matthew 24:14*

[7] Alas! For that day is great, so that none is like it; and it is the time of Jacob's trouble, but he shall be saved out of it. *Jeremiah 30:7*

THE PEACE AGREEMENT
[6] Pray for the peace of Jerusalem… *Psalm 122:6*

[18] If it is possible, as much as depends on you, live peaceably with all men. *Romans 12:18*

[24] He (the Antichrist) shall enter peaceably, even into the richest places of the province; and he shall do what his fathers have not done, nor his forefathers… *Daniel 11:24*

[27] Then he (the Antichrist) shall confirm a covenant with many… *Daniel 9:27*

TERMS OF THE PEACE AGREEMENT
1. Seven-year length.
    [27] …for one week… *Daniel 9:27*

2. Israeli land divided.
    [2] I (Jesus) will also gather all nations, and bring them down to the Valley of Jehoshaphat; and I will enter into judgment with them there on account of My people, My heritage Israel, whom they have scattered among the nations; they have also divided up My land…*Joel 3:2*

3. Israel can freely build the third temple without impediment.
    …[4] who opposes and exalts himself (the Antichrist) above all that is called God or that is worshiped, so that he sits as God in the temple of God, showing himself that he is God. *2 Thessalonians 2:4*

THE PEACE AGREEMENT IS BROKEN
[25] Through his cunning he (the Antichrist) shall cause deceit to prosper under his rule… *Daniel 8:25*

[23] And after the league is made with him (the Antichrist) he shall act deceitfully... *Daniel 11:23*

²⁷ ...in the middle of the week he (the Antichrist) shall bring an end to sacrifice and offering. *Daniel 9:27*

¹⁵ Therefore when you see the "abomination of desolation," spoken of by Daniel the prophet, standing in the holy place (whoever reads, let him understand), ¹⁶ then let those who are in Judea flee to the mountains. *Matthew 25:15*

¹¹ And from the time that the daily sacrifice is taken away, and the abomination of desolation is set up, there shall be one thousand two hundred and ninety days. ¹² Blessed is he who waits, and comes to the one thousand three hundred and thirty-five days. *Daniel 12:11-12*

⁹ That which has been is what will be, that which is done is what will be done, and there is nothing new under the sun. *Ecclesiastes 1:9*

THE ARAB CONNECTION
⁴ They have said, "Come, and let us cut them off from being a nation, that the name of Israel may be remembered no more. ⁵ For they have consulted together with one consent; they form a confederacy against You: ⁶ the tents of Edom and the Ishmaelites; Moab and the Hagrites; ⁷ Gebal, Ammon, and Amalek; Philistia with the inhabitants of Tyre; ⁸ Assyria also has joined with the... *Psalm 83:4-8*

³⁰ For ships from Cyprus shall come against him (the Antichrist); therefore, he shall be grieved, and return in rage against the holy covenant (peace agreement), and do damage. So, he shall return and show regard for those who forsake the holy covenant (Muslims). ³¹ And forces shall be mustered by him, and they shall defile the sanctuary fortress; then they shall take away the daily sacrifices, and place there the abomination of desolation. *Daniel 11:30-31*

NOTES

"God has given us two hands, one to receive with and the other to give with." — Billy Graham

WEEK 13: THE NEW WORLD ORDER

Opening Prayer: Lord, we ask that You send Your Holy Spirit to us to guide us in the teaching and understanding of Your word that we may obtain a better understanding of the prophetic events surrounding us now and waiting for us in the future. Bless our fellowship in Your word that it may be fruitful and draw us into a deeper relationship both with You and those around us. Use us as Your vessels that through us, we may reflect Your glory to all whom we encounter. Illuminate our hearts and minds so that we may boldly shine the brightness of Your light everywhere we go and that we may be beacons of Your hope in a darkened world. In Jesus name we pray, Amen.

Ice Breaker: Nominate one person from your group to run for President of the United States. Explain why you think that person would be a good choice to run for office.

Person's Name: _____

Reason: _____

_____

Focus: When you prioritize God's kingdom, He will prioritize you in His kingdom.

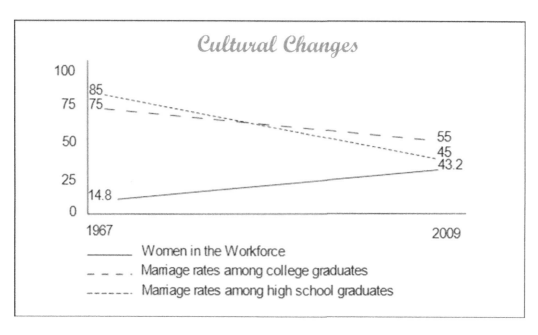

ARE WE THE TERMINAL GENERATION?

Word of the Week

> ⁷...**authority** was given him (the Antichrist) over every tribe, tongue, and nation.
>
> *Revelation 13:7*

AUTHORITY: Some translations for this verse use the word "authority" while other translations use the word "power" instead. Either way, the Greek word in the original text is "exousia" (pronounced ex-oo-see'-ah). Conceptually, "exousia" embraces both the concepts of power and authority. Power refers to the ability to accomplish something while authority points to the right to engage in the activity. When someone is described as possessing exousia, inherent in the ruling position is having jurisdictional leadership with the power to create laws, the ability to exercise command over people and the position to wield authority to enforce the laws created. Authority and power are granted as a matter of divine or demonic right in order to influence those subjects to the leadership's rule. Quite simply, people are subject to the leadership in all ways and must submit to whatever is decreed by that leadership whether by power or authority.

Lesson: Leaders are chosen by God and only rise to power with God's consent:

> ²¹... He **removes kings** and **raises up kings**...
> *Daniel 2:21*

When the people are righteous, He installs righteous leaders over the people, but when the people go astray, He gives the people over to their own desires and allows evil leaders to rise to power.

> ¹¹ But My people would not heed My voice, and Israel would have none of Me. ¹² So **I gave them over to their own stubborn heart**, to walk in their own counsels. *Psalm 81:11-12*

Saul was a tormenting leader whom God allowed to persecute Christians:

> ³ As for **Saul**, he **made havoc of the church**, entering every house, and dragging off men and women, committing them to prison. *Acts 3:3*

An evil leader in office should be viewed as a sign of God's anger with society.

During the Tribulation, God allows such a despotic leader to assume global dominance in the persona of the Antichrist.

Initially, the Antichrist appears on the global scene in a relatively obscure manner. Prophetic author Joel Rosenberg commented to Glenn Beck in an interview on April 25, 2008 that he believes the Antichrist will be a charming, economically gifted diplomat who has a keen understanding of foreign policy and will arise from out of the European Union. Intent on world domination, the Antichrist breaks with tradition and changes both how things are done and the laws that govern society:

> [25] He shall speak pompous words against the Most High, shall persecute the saints of the Most High, and **shall intend to change times and law**. *Daniel 7:25*

Winds of change can already be observed in our world through vast cultural changes experienced in the last few decades. More women than ever are in the workforce as marriage rates decline. Traditional marriage itself is under attack just as has been foretold in scripture:

> [1] And in that day **seven women shall take hold of one man**, saying, "**We will eat our own food and wear our own apparel**; only let us be called by your name, to take away our reproach." *Isaiah 4:1*

The Antichrist's authority is global and backed by the full fury of Satan. Deluded by his deception and believing that resistance is futile, all non-Christians accept his global authority and voluntarily follow his leadership.

Within the new, global system of government instituted and controlled by the Antichrist, the False Prophet compels people to participate in an economic system designed to control all global commerce. Since the advent of the internet, e-commerce has exploded exponentially and is causing many brick and mortar stores to go out of business due to the competition from internet sales with unlimited selection and virtually no overhead. For the first time in history, computers enable the tracking of individual spending habits along with banking and investment accounts on a

FUN FACT:
The U.S. Government spent $277,000 on pickle research in 1993.

level never before seen or imagined in history. By taking over global commerce, the Antichrist essentially possesses a powerful tool to effectively control every aspect of people's lives anywhere on the globe.

Under the global leadership of the Antichrist, the world will be divided into ten distinct regions. All ten kingdoms exist to serve the Antichrist and do his bidding. These ten regions will be ruled by leaders who answer to the Antichrist:

> [12] The **ten horns** which you saw are **ten kings** who have received no kingdom as yet, but **they receive authority for one hour as kings with the beast**. [13] These are of one mind, and they will **give their power and authority to the beast**. *Revelation 17:10-18*

> [23] Thus he said: "The **fourth beast** shall be a **fourth kingdom** on earth, which shall be different from all other kingdoms, and shall **devour the whole earth**, trample it and break it in pieces. [24] The **ten horns are ten kings** who shall arise from this kingdom. And another shall rise after them; he shall be different from the first ones, and **shall subdue three kings**. *Daniel 7:23-24*

When these ten regions are established, they unite to destroy the area referred to as Mystery Babylon with a hail of fire:

> [15] Then he said to me, "The waters which you saw, where the **harlot** sits, are peoples, multitudes, nations, and tongues. [16] And the ten horns which you saw on the beast, these will hate the harlot, make her **desolate and naked**, eat her flesh and **burn her with fire**." *Revelation 17:15-16*

Perhaps the reason the United States isn't specifically mentioned in biblical prophecy is that all existing countries as we know them today will no longer exist after the Antichrist reorganizes the globe into these ten regions. At some point, three of the kingdoms become troublesome and are destroyed. Another possibility for the fate of the United States is that the United States does merge with other countries to become one of the ten regions, but it is one of the three regions that ends up being of little consequence.

Daniel's description of Nebuchadnezzar's statue offers additional insight into the ten regions:

> [32] This image's head was of fine gold, its chest and arms of silver, its belly and thighs of bronze, [33] its **legs of iron**, its **feet partly of iron and partly of clay**. [34] You watched while a stone was cut out

without hands, which struck the image on its feet of iron and clay, and broke them in pieces. [35] Then the iron, the clay, the bronze, the silver, and the gold were crushed together, and became like chaff from the summer threshing floors; the wind carried them away so that no trace of them was found. And the stone that struck the image became a great mountain and filled the whole earth... [41] Whereas you saw the feet and toes, partly of potter's clay and partly of iron, the **kingdom shall be divided**; yet the strength of the iron shall be in it, just as you saw the iron mixed with ceramic clay. [42] And as the toes of the feet were partly of iron and partly of clay, so the **kingdom shall be partly strong and partly fragile**. [43] As you saw iron mixed with ceramic clay, they will mingle with the seed of men; but they will not adhere to one another, just as iron does not mix with clay. *Daniel 2:32-35, 41-43*

Using the allegory of the statue, the final kingdom has two legs representing the east and the west which are broken into a total of ten toes, or ten regions. Symbolically, the regions are likened to iron and clay. Iron and clay do not mix well together representing a divided kingdom. Iron is known for being strong, but clay can be fragile indicating a mixture of both strength and weakness. Interestingly, concrete is made from clay and poured over iron rebar for strength. Since many of our major cities are comprised of mass amounts of concrete and referred to as "concrete jungles", it is possible that the allegory of the end time statue refers to the urbanization of civilization.

Modern day rumblings of a one world government are not just the paranoid delusions of conspiracy theorists. In September 2015, the United Nations issued a document referred to as the 2030 Agenda. A more developed offshoot of Agenda 21, the UN 2030 Agenda for Sustainable Development attempts to unite all nations around the globe under the guise of a unified vision for the future betterment of humanity. Central to the core of the 2030 Agenda is the perceived need for a central body to control all of the earth's resources and urban developments. In the preamble of the document, the mission is referred to as a "new universal Agenda". Other expressions in the document use phrases such as "collective journey", "shared prosperity" and "global partnership". Global references are peppered throughout the document in phrases such as "the goals and targets met for all nations" and "universal goals and targets which involve the entire world". Signatory nations on the document pledge, "All of us will work to implement the Agenda within our own countries and at the regional and global levels...". As the name of the document suggests, it is the stated goal of the United Nations to implement their global vision by the year 2030. The UN also hosts a website referred to as Millennium Development Goals Indicator. On this website, the United Nations organizes the globe into ten distinct regions:

Map from official UN website for Millennium Development Goals Indicator.

1. Developed Regions
2. Northern Africa
3. Sub-Saharan Africa
4. South-Eastern Asia
5. Eastern Asia
6. Southern Asia
7. Western Asia
8. Caucasus and Central Asia
9. Oceania
10. Latin America & Caribbean

In a 2014 article from *The Daily Caller*, the UN's climate chief, Christina Figueres, advocated that communism is the best model to combat global warming. Given that the members of the UN are championing communism as the answer to the world's problems, it seems unlikely that the 2030 Agenda is compatible with capitalistic ideals. Soviet leader Nikita Khrushchev famously quoted in 1959, "We cannot expect the Americans to jump from capitalism to communism, but we can assist their elected leaders in giving Americans small doses of socialism until they suddenly awake to find they have communism." Communism is based on the redistribution of wealth and resources theorizing that if everything is shared properly, everyone can have a better standard of living. The reality, which has been proven over and over again in communist governments all over the world, is that instead of everyone becoming a "have", everyone becomes a "have not". Additionally, communism almost always results in the loss of personal freedoms in the interest of the greater good. If the United States is considered to be one of the more prosperous countries of the world, we can only assume that inviting America to participate in a global system based on communism can only mean we end up on the giving end of the spectrum and lessen our standard of living while others take what America gives away to improve their standard of living. Given the foundations currently in place for global unification, it is conceivable to envision a future global government centered around a communistic thought process. When the Antichrist is ready to rise to power, the framework is already in place for a single, world government espousing a unified global vision for humanity.

Under the new world order established by the Antichrist, things will get tough for Christians. Whatever happens, don't give up and always make Godly choices. Regardless of the moral compass or conduct of any given leader, Christians are commanded to follow the laws of the land as much as possible up to the point where they conflict with God's laws. Daniel was put in a position where he had to make a choice. He could either obey the law of the land and cease his daily prayers to God, or he could commit civil disobedience and continue his prayers in defiance of the law. The dilemma he faced was whether to make the mortal king angry and imperil his physical safety or to make the eternal King angry and imperil his relationship with God. If ever a choice must be made, look to Daniel's example to ultimately obey God's laws over man's laws when the test comes. It's not worth the price to be paid to choose otherwise.

Talk It Out

1. Do you believe the United States would willingly participate in a reorganized new world order or do you think the United States would need to be destroyed in order for the Antichrist to assimilate the United States into a larger global region?

2. How might the US Constitution be compatible or incompatible with a united, universal system of government with other countries?

3. Which system of government do you think God would most likely endorse: capitalism, socialism, communism, a monarchy, a theocracy or a dictatorship? What form of government do you think the Antichrist, empowered by Satan, will endorse?

4. Do you think Daniel's description of the ten toes of Nebuchadnezzar's statue is a fitting description for our modern society (a house divided, partly strong, partly weak and urbanized)?

5. The 2030 Agenda phrase "Sustainable Development" implies that we are currently on an unsustainable path and that we need to make changes to be sustainable. Do you believe our world is sustainable on its present course? Are natural resources plentiful enough for the world's needs? Are the issues of overpopulation and global warming issues that Christians should be concerned about? Will God always provide for us?

Ideas for the Week:

- ✓ Read the 2030 Agenda on the UN website at https://sustainabledevelopment.un.org/post2015/transformingourworld and discuss it over coffee with some friends.
- ✓ Survey your friends about their feelings on socialism and whether they feel the United States is on a path that returns us to strong capitalist roots or pushes us towards a more communistic world view.
- ✓ Support small businesses in your area by purchasing from local businesses whenever possible.
- ✓ Print a T-shirt that says, "God's laws over man's laws" and wear it.

Closing Prayer

NOTE: Add names and individual personal prayer requests to the space provided below before closing in prayer.

Lord, we thank You for our time together today to grow deeper in our walk with You and fellowship with each other. As we close today, we lift up: _____

_____

_____

_____

_____

_____

_____

_____

Father, we call upon You to fill our hearts, minds and souls with wisdom and enlightenment that we may discern righteous leaders from ungodly rulers, that we may choose the path of light over darkness, and that we may always be found worthy in Your sight to bear witness to Your holy name. In Jesus' name we pray, Amen.

SUPPORTING SCRIPTURES

CULTURAL CHANGES
¹And in that day seven women shall take hold of one man, saying, "We will eat our own food and wear our own apparel; only let us be called by your name, to take away our reproach." *Isaiah 4:1*

GOVERNMENT
²¹And He changes the times and the seasons; He removes kings and raises up kings… *Daniel 2:21*

¹¹But My people would not heed My voice, and Israel would have none of Me. ¹²So I gave them over to their own stubborn heart, to walk in their own counsels. *Psalm 81:11-12*

³As for Saul, he made havoc of the church, entering every house, and dragging off men and women, committing them to prison. *Acts 3:3*

⁵Woe to Assyria, the rod of My anger and the staff in whose hand is My indignation. ⁶I will send him against an ungodly nation, and against the people of My wrath I will give him charge… *Isaiah 10:5-6*

¹Let every soul be subject to the governing authorities. For there is no authority except from God, and the authorities that exist are appointed by God. ²Therefore whoever resists the authority resists the ordinance of God, and those who resist will bring judgment on themselves. *Romans 13:1-2*

⁶So these governors and satraps thronged before the king, and said thus to him: "King Darius, live forever! ⁷All the governors of the kingdom, the administrators and satraps, the counselors and advisors, have consulted together to establish a royal statute and to make a firm decree, that whoever petitions any god or man for thirty days, except you, O king, shall be cast into the den of lions. ⁸Now, O king, establish the decree and sign the writing, so that it cannot be changed, according to the law of the Medes and Persians, which does not alter." ⁹Therefore King Darius signed the written decree. ¹⁰Now when Daniel knew that the writing was signed, he went home. And in his upper room, with his windows open toward Jerusalem, he knelt down on his knees three times that day, and prayed and gave thanks before his God, as was his custom since early days. *Daniel 6:6-10*

²⁸And do not fear those who kill the body but cannot kill the soul. But rather fear Him who is able to destroy both soul and body in hell. *Matthew 10:28*

NEW WORDER ORDER

³…all the world marveled and followed the beast (the Antichrist). *Revelation 13:3*

⁷…authority was given him (the Antichrist) over every tribe, tongue, and nation. *Revelation 13:7*

¹⁶ He (the False Prophet) causes all, both small and great, rich and poor, free and slave, to receive a mark on their right hand or on their foreheads, ¹⁷ and that no one may buy or sell except one who has the mark or the name of the beast, or the number of his name. *Revelation 13:16-17*

² Daniel spoke, saying, "I saw in my vision by night, and behold, the four winds of heaven were stirring up the Great Sea. ³ And four great beasts came up from the sea, each different from the other…⁷ After this I saw in the night visions, and behold, a fourth beast, dreadful and terrible, exceedingly strong. It had huge iron teeth; it was devouring, breaking in pieces, and trampling the residue with its feet. It was different from all the beasts that were before it, and it had ten horns. ⁸ I was considering the horns, and there was another horn, a little one, coming up among them, before whom three of the first horns were plucked out by the roots. And there, in this horn, were eyes like the eyes of a man, and a mouth speaking pompous words." *Daniel 7:2, 7-8*

¹⁵ I, Daniel, was grieved in my spirit within my body, and the visions of my head troubled me. ¹⁶ I came near to one of those who stood by, and asked him the truth of all this. So, he told me and made known to me the interpretation of these things: ¹⁷ "Those great beasts, which are four, are four kings which arise out of the earth. ¹⁸ But the saints of the Most High shall receive the kingdom, and possess the kingdom forever, even forever and ever." ¹⁹ Then I wished to know the truth about the fourth beast, which was different from all the others, exceedingly dreadful, with its teeth of iron and its nails of bronze, which devoured, broke in pieces, and trampled the residue with its feet; ²⁰ and the ten horns that were on its head, and the other horn which came up, before which three fell, namely, that horn which had eyes and a mouth which spoke pompous words, whose appearance was greater than his fellows. ²¹ I was watching; and the same horn was making war against the saints, and prevailing against them, ²² until the Ancient of Days came, and a judgment was made in favor of the saints of the Most High, and the time came for the saints to possess the kingdom. ²³ Thus he said: "The fourth beast shall be a fourth kingdom on earth, which shall be different from all other kingdoms, and shall devour the whole earth, trample it and break it in pieces. ²⁴ The ten horns are ten kings who shall arise from this kingdom. And another shall rise after them; he shall be different from the first

ones, and shall subdue three kings. ²⁵ He shall speak pompous words against the Most High, shall persecute the saints of the Most High, and shall intend to change times and law. Then the saints shall be given into his hand for a time and times and half a time. ²⁶ But the court shall be seated, and they shall take away his dominion, to consume and destroy it forever. ²⁷ Then the kingdom and dominion, and the greatness of the kingdoms under the whole heaven, shall be given to the people, the saints of the Most High. His kingdom is an everlasting kingdom, and all dominions shall serve and obey Him." *Daniel 7:15-27*

²⁷ Daniel answered in the presence of the king...³¹ "You, O king, were watching; and behold, a great image! This great image, whose splendor was excellent, stood before you; and its form was awesome. ³² This image's head was of fine gold, its chest and arms of silver, its belly and thighs of bronze, ³³ its legs of iron, its feet partly of iron and partly of clay. ³⁴ You watched while a stone was cut out without hands, which struck the image on its feet of iron and clay, and broke them in pieces. ³⁵ Then the iron, the clay, the bronze, the silver, and the gold were crushed together, and became like chaff from the summer threshing floors; the wind carried them away so that no trace of them was found. And the stone that struck the image became a great mountain and filled the whole earth." ³⁶ This is the dream. Now we will tell the interpretation of it before the king. ³⁷ "You, O king, are a king of kings. For the God of heaven has given you a kingdom, power, strength, and glory; ³⁸ and wherever the children of men dwell, or the beasts of the field and the birds of the heaven, He has given them into your hand, and has made you ruler over them all—you are this head of gold. ³⁹ But after you shall arise another kingdom inferior to yours; then another, a third kingdom of bronze, which shall rule over all the earth. ⁴⁰ And the fourth kingdom shall be as strong as iron, inasmuch as iron breaks in pieces and shatters everything; and like iron that crushes, that kingdom will break in pieces and crush all the others. ⁴¹ Whereas you saw the feet and toes, partly of potter's clay and partly of iron, the kingdom shall be divided; yet the strength of the iron shall be in it, just as you saw the iron mixed with ceramic clay. ⁴² And as the toes of the feet were partly of iron and partly of clay, so the kingdom shall be partly strong and partly fragile. ⁴³ As you saw iron mixed with ceramic clay, they will mingle with the seed of men; but they will not adhere to one another, just as iron does not mix with clay. ⁴⁴ And in the days of these kings the God of heaven will set up a kingdom which shall never be destroyed; and the kingdom shall not be left to other people; it shall break in pieces and consume all these kingdoms, and it shall stand forever." *Daniel 2:27, 31-44*

¹⁰ There are also seven kings. Five have fallen, one is, and the other has not yet come. And when he comes, he must continue a short time. ¹¹ The beast that was, and is not, is himself also the eighth, and is of the seven, and is going to

perdition. ¹² The ten horns which you saw are ten kings who have received no kingdom as yet, but they receive authority for one hour as kings with the beast. ¹³ These are of one mind, and they will give their power and authority to the beast. ¹⁴ These will make war with the Lamb, and the Lamb will overcome them, for He is Lord of lords and King of kings; and those who are with Him are called, chosen, and faithful. ¹⁵ Then he said to me, "The waters which you saw, where the harlot sits, are peoples, multitudes, nations, and tongues. ¹⁶ And the ten horns which you saw on the beast, these will hate the harlot, make her desolate and naked, eat her flesh and burn her with fire. ¹⁷ For God has put it into their hearts to fulfill His purpose, to be of one mind, and to give their kingdom to the beast, until the words of God are fulfilled. ¹⁸ And the woman whom you saw is that great city which reigns over the kings of the earth." *Revelation 17:10-18*

¹ Then He spoke a parable to them, that men always ought to pray and not lose heart… *Luke 18:1*

NOTES

"Live simply, love generously, care deeply, speak kindly, leave the rest to God." — Ronald Reagan

ARE WE THE TERMINAL GENERATION?

WEEK 14: TERRORISM

Opening Prayer: Lord, we ask that You send Your Holy Spirit to us to guide us in the teaching and understanding of Your word that we may obtain a better understanding of the prophetic events surrounding us now and waiting for us in the future. Bless our fellowship in Your word that it may be fruitful and draw us into a deeper relationship both with You and those around us. Use us as Your vessels that through us, we may reflect Your glory to all whom we encounter. Illuminate our hearts and minds so that we may boldly shine the brightness of Your light everywhere we go and that we may be beacons of Your hope in a darkened world. In Jesus name we pray, Amen.

Ice Breaker: God can be found everywhere and in everything. All we have to do to see, hear and feel God is to look closely at the world around us. Below are three objects. As a group, brainstorm how these three objects relate to the word of God through spiritual application. How does each object represent God or express a quality of God? What overlapping qualities of the object can be applied to God? How do the objects symbolize God's character? Be creative!

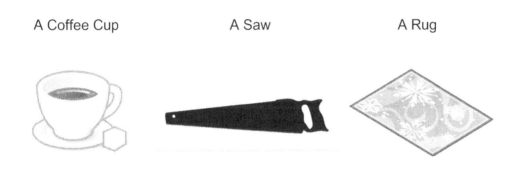

A Coffee Cup   A Saw   A Rug

Focus: Those who forsake God and His ways create an open door to invite terror into their lives.

"And god willing, with the force of god behind it, we shall soon experience a world without the United States and Zionism."

— Mahmoud Ahmadinejad, Former President of Iran (2005-2013)

Word of the Week

> ¹⁴ But if you do not obey Me…¹⁶ I also will do this to you: I will even appoint **terror** over you…
>
> Leviticus 26:14, 16

TERROR: Terror comes from the Hebrew word "behalah" (pronounced beh-haw-law') and encompasses the characteristics of dismay, alarm, utter ruin, and a suddenness to the event. On September 11, 2001, no one expected hijackers to fly commercial airliners into the World Trade centers as makeshift bombs. The event caused much dismay and alarm as it eventually ended in the complete devastation of buildings which were regarded as generally secure. Biblically, the presence of terror in a society is an outward sign of God's displeasure with society's stubborn refusal to obey Him and follow His ways.

Lesson: Terrorism is a sign of our times. Previous generations experienced wars and acts of barbarism, but the prevalence of terrorism for the wanton sake of instilling fear in people for ulterior motives is a modern twist to violence. Acts of terror span the gamut from Timothy McVeigh's bombing of Oklahoma City in 1995 to school shootings like the Columbine High School tragedy in 1999 and the Sandy Hook Elementary School massacre in 2012. More than anything, September 11, 2001 symbolizes what terrorism means to this generation. On that fateful day, Muslim hijackers flew planes into the World Trade Center buildings in New York killing over 3000 people. Not since Japan's bombing of Pearl Harbor on December 7, 1941 has American soil seen such a loss of life from violence perpetrated by foreign entities.

Often, terrorism is associated with Islamic terrorism. In misguided efforts to please their god, Allah, Muslim extremists engage in "holy jihad". Jihad, as defined by *Webster's Dictionary* is:

> JIHAD: A holy war waged on behalf of Islam as a religious duty.

The *Dictionary of Islam* defines "jihad" as:

> JIHAD *Lit.* "An effort, or a striving." A religious war with those who are unbelievers in the mission of Muhammad. It is an incumbent religious duty, established in the Qur'an and in the Traditions as a

divine institution, and enjoined specially for the purpose of advancing Islam and of repelling evil from Muslims.

When an infidel's country is conquered by a Muslim ruler, its inhabitants are offered three alternatives:

(1) *The reception of Islam*, in which case the conquered become enfranchised citizens of the Muslim state.

(2) *The Payment of a poll-tax (Jizyah)*, by which unbelievers in Islam obtain protection, and become *Zimmis*, provided they are not the idolaters of Arabia.

(3) *Death by the sword*, to those who will not pay the poll tax.

The Qur'an is Islam's holy book. Traditionally, the spelling has been "Koran", but in modern times the accepted spelling is "Qur'an". Fighting as a form of Jihad is demanded of all Muslims in the Qur'an:

Surah 2:216: **Fighting is obligatory for you,** much as you dislike it. But you may hate a thing although it is good for you, and love a thing although it is bad for you. God knows, but you know not.

Surah 4:74: Let those who would exchange the life of this world for the hereafter, **fight for the cause of god**; whoever fights for the cause of god, whether he dies or triumphs, on him we shall bestow a rich recompense.

Surah 4:95: The believers who stay at home — apart from those that suffer from a grave disability — are not the equals of those who fight for the cause of god with their goods and their persons. **God has exalted the men who fight with their goods and their persons** above those who stay at home. God has promised all a good reward; but far richer is the recompense of those who fight for him…

Going beyond merely fighting for Allah, the Qur'an specifically calls for terrorism:

Surah 8:12: God revealed his will to the angels, saying: "I shall be with you. Give courage to the believers. I shall **cast terror into the hearts of the infidels**. Strike off their heads, strike off the very tips of their fingers!"

Many of the punishments prescribed in the Qur'an exceed merely killing unbelievers by advocating various forms of torture to instill fear in the rest of society:

> *Surah 5:33*: Those that make war against god and his apostle and spread disorder in the land shall be slain or **crucified or have their hands and feet cut off on alternate sides**...

Advocating endurance, the Qur'an forbids anyone from ceasing to fight until the religion of Allah is the only religion left:

> *Surah 8:39*: Make **war on them until** idolatry shall cease and **god's religion shall reign supreme**.

In essence, for Islamic extremists, jihad is a lifelong religious war involving physical combat and the instillation of terror in anyone who is non-Muslim based on a divine mandate to continue until all worship Allah and only Allah. Within that mindset, there is a particular hatred of Israel:

> [4] They have said, "Come, and let us **cut them off from being a nation**, that the name of **Israel may be remembered no more**." [5] For they have consulted together with one consent; **they form a confederacy against You**: [6] The tents of Edom and **the Ishmaelites**... *Psalm 83:4-5*

Along with their hatred of Israel, they also share a hatred of Israel's primary ally, the United States. Both Ayatollah Khomeini in 1979 and Muammar Gaddafi in 1980 publicly referred to Israel as the "Little Satan". Linking Israel and the United States together, Ayatollah Khomeini also called the United States the "Great Satan".

Man has free will to choose to follow God, but that same free will can also be used to abandon God and His ways.

> [12] So **I gave them over to their own stubborn heart**, to walk in their own counsels. *Psalm 81:12*

Sadly, the choice to ignore God comes with consequences. Because of man's wanton and unrepentant disregard for God's laws in the final days before Christ returns, the God of the Bible appoints terror over people allowing Allah's warriors to engage in terroristic activities:

> [14] But **if you do not obey Me, and do not observe all these commandments**, [15] and if you despise My statutes, or if your soul abhors My judgments, so that you do not perform all My commandments, but break My covenant, [16] I also will do this to you: **I will even appoint terror over you**... *Leviticus 26:14-16*

Evidence of this can be seen in and around the world today. Terror can assume many forms such as suicide bombings, missiles, bioterrorism, chemical weapons and emp's which take down electrical grids. Destroying electronics and electrical grids effectively sends entire societies back to the stone age rendering them defenseless without the use of technology. When God opens the fourth seal during the Tribulation, He grants power to the rider of the pale horse to kill a quarter of the earth's inhabitants with the sword:

> [7] When He opened the fourth seal, I heard the voice of the fourth living creature saying, "Come and see." [8] So I looked, and behold, a pale horse. And the name of him who sat on it was Death, and Hades followed with him. And **power was given to them over a fourth of the earth, to kill with sword**, with hunger, with death, and by the beasts of the earth. *Revelation 6:7-8*

Again, in Jeremiah 15:3, the sword is repeated as a form of appointed death:

> [3] "And **I will appoint over them four forms of destruction**," says the LORD: "**the sword to slay**, the dogs to drag, the birds of the heavens and the beasts of the earth to devour and destroy." *Jeremiah 15:3*

While the term "sword" can euphemistically symbolize death, it can also literally mean death by sword. Without the aid of modern technology, the sword becomes a viable and effective form of weaponry. In our modern times, Islamic extremists are those who are associated with using the ancient weaponry of swords as a battle tool. Further implicating the role of Islamic extremism during the Tribulation is Revelation 20:4 which indicates Tribulation Christians will be beheaded for their faith:

> [4] And I saw thrones, and they sat on them, and judgment was committed to them. Then I saw the souls of **those who had been beheaded for their witness to Jesus** and for the word of God, **who had not worshiped the beast or his image**, and had not received his mark on their foreheads or on their hands. And they lived and reigned with Christ for a thousand years. *Revelation 20:4*

Only Muslim terrorist groups such as Boko Haram, ISIS, Hezbollah, Al Qaeda and Hamas are famous for beheading Christians in this day and age. It is suspected that some of these terror groups have state sponsorship in countries such as Syria and Iran. Interestingly, the Bible states that Damascus, the capital of Syria and the oldest continually inhabited city in the world, will be utterly destroyed at some point before Jesus returns:

> The burden against Damascus. Behold, **Damascus will cease from being a city**, and it will be **a ruinous heap**. *Isaiah 17:1*

Syria is known for having had a chemical weapons program which was supposedly suspended although allegations that Syria is still actively producing chemical weapons exist today and are a source of political tension. Perhaps a connection exists between Syria's suspected production of weapons of mass destruction and a perceived need by other countries to control the threat through military action which might eventually destroy Damascus.

For Muslims, the end time battle is a religious war. Motivated by Allah's command to kill unbelievers for the purpose of establishing a global Caliphate where Islam reigns supreme, Islamic extremists relentlessly pursue their goal. A Caliphate is an Islamic government ruled by an Islamic religious leader. Caliphates establish Sharia Law, or Islamic laws over their provinces. Sharia Law is known for regulating not just public behavior, but private behavior and personal beliefs as well. Calling for varied forms of corporal and capital punishments, many aspects of Sharia Law are contradictory toward both western and Christian values. While our Christian God hates homosexuality, the Bible does not advocate killing homosexuals. However, the Qur'an takes a distinctly different approach to homosexuality. Sharia Law requires that homosexuals be put to death which still occurs even in our modern times in Islamic areas governed by Sharia Law. Sharia Law also ascribes blame to victims over perpetrators. Under Sharia Law, after being gang-raped in 2008, a thirteen-year-old girl was stoned to death for committing fornication. Sharia Law embraces a unique form of justice that is contrary to Christian principles and beliefs. Most westerners would be horrified at the human rights atrocities performed under Sharia Law if they were ever forced to live under Sharia Law.

FRIGHTENING FACT: In 2003, a Boeing 727-223 jet was stolen from an airport in Angola. It still has not been found despite a worldwide search.

Desiring to establish a global Caliphate and impose Sharia Law on the world, jihadists engage in varied forms of bloodshed to achieve their goal. Tactics involve using suicide bombers such as the attack on the USS Cole in 2000 and flying jets into high-rise buildings such as what happened on September 11, 2001 in

New York. The most ardent believers among jihadists are called Twelvers. Iran's ex-President Ahmadinejad is a Twelver. A Twelver in a position of power is exceptionally worrisome and imminently dangerous. Twelvers believe that their messiah, the twelfth Imam also known as the Mahdi, will return in the last days to save the world. However, Twelvers also believe the Mahdi cannot return until mass chaos and bloodshed have occurred on a global scale. In their misplaced efforts to hasten the return of their messiah, they purposefully commit mass atrocities. Nothing is off limits to Twelvers pursuing their religious convictions which is extremely concerning given the nuclear and chemical world in which we live.

Another tactic employed by Islamists to gain global dominance for a global Caliphate and implement Sharia Law is to out-populate every other religion. In 2017, the most popular baby name in the world for boys was Muhammad after the founder of Islam. Approximately 150 million men and boys shared the popular moniker. Muslim birth rates are growing at an astronomical rate. On the current birth rate trajectory, Islam is expected to be the largest religion by the year 2075. When Muslims enter an area, their population grows steadily by high birth rates within their culture. Eventually, they reach a point where, through sheer numbers, they can more aggressively push their way of life. Typically, when the Muslim population is under 2%, peace prevails. Between 2% and 5% of the population, Muslims begin to recruit members from ethnic minority groups, prisons and gangs. When their population reaches 5% or more, Muslims begin to push for legal rights to practice their way of life under Sharia Law with Sharia Law standing as a viable form of justice in their communities. Since Sharia Law contradicts many laws of the land, conflict occurs. At 10% to 20% of the population, Muslims engage in more violent strategies to fight for their cause. At 40% of the population, militia warfare tactics gain strength. By the time 60% of the population is Muslim, persecution and ethnic cleansing of "infidels" becomes prominent. Finally, at 80% of the population, violent jihad in an attempt to rid the country of infidels completes the process of creating an entirely Muslim country dominated by Sharia Law.

Propaganda is another tool employed by Muslims in their efforts to ultimately convert the world into a global Islamic Caliphate. In 2007, the Muslim community issued an open letter to Christians titled *A Common Word* suggesting that we worship the same God and are not as far apart as it would seem. In response, through the Yale Center for Faith and Culture, the Christian community issued an open response applauding the letter and accepting the one God concept:

> "We applaud that *'A Common Word Between Us and You'* stresses so insistently the unique devotion to one God..."

The open letter response was signed by a number of well-known, key Christian religious leaders such as Bill Hybels, Rick Warren and Dr. Robert H. Schuller, Sr. among many others. Pope Francis even embraces the commonality of Christianity and Islam. Before his visit to Morocco at the end of March 2019, the Vatican released an official logo for Pope Francis' upcoming visit to the country. Intertwined in the logo are a Christian cross and an Islamic crescent symbolizing the merging of the two religions.

In an erroneous attempt to find common ground with Muslims and find a peaceful middle ground, there is a heretical movement gaining strength in our day called Chrislam. The Chrislam movement attempts to combine Christianity and Islam into one concept based on their common roots in Abraham. The theory is that if we worship the same God, we must not be that far apart in our beliefs. Because of the similarities, the theory goes, we should be able to bridge the differences. Chrislam, first established in the 1970's, uses both the Bible and Qur'an as holy texts. An organization known as CAMP (Christians and Muslims for Peace), led by the ex-chairman of the neo-Nazi Populist Party, Dr. William Baker, champions the progress of Chrislam. Tenets of Chrislam are also upheld by the World Council of Churches. Published in 2009, the Kairos Palestine Document, subtitled *A moment of truth: A word of faith, hope and love from the heart of Palestinian suffering*, again focuses on the unity of Christianity and Islam and can be found posted on the website of the World Council of Churches.

To further the advancement of Chrislam, well-known and long-established Bible publishers such as Wycliffe Bible Translators, Summer Institute of Linguistics (SIL) and Frontiers have even begun printing Muslim-friendly Christian Bibles. The cross-cultural Bibles change all references of "God" to "Allah" feeding on the misguided notion that Allah and God are interchangeable. Adding insult to injury, the new Bibles also eliminate any references to Jesus as God's Son so as not to offend Muslims since their god, Allah, does not have a son:

> *Surah 4:171*: The Messiah, **Jesus** son of Mary, **was no more than God's apostle** and His Word which He cast to Mary: a spirit from Him. So, believe in God and His apostles and **do not say: "Three."**...God is but one God. **God forbid that He should have a son!**

Jesus cannot be both God's son and not His son at the same time. The deity of Jesus is a key difference between Christian and Muslim foundational beliefs. Christians believe Jesus is God's only Son and that the only way to achieve salvation is through His son, Jesus:

> ⁶ Jesus said to him, "I am the way, the truth, and the life. **No one comes to the Father except through Me.**" *John 14:6*

To alter this basic tenant of Christianity irreparably shakes the entire foundation of the faith. Foretelling the future, the Bible predicts the time will come when men no longer accept the true doctrines of God:

> ³ For **the time will come** when **they will not endure sound doctrine**, but according to their own desires, because they have itching ears, they will heap up for themselves teachers; ⁴ and they will turn their ears away from the truth, **and be turned aside to fables**. *2 Timothy 4:3-4*

Scripture warns us to avoid those who teach doctrines which conflict with the Bible:

> ¹⁷ Now I urge you, brethren, **note those who cause divisions and offenses, contrary to the doctrine which you learned, and avoid them**. ¹⁸ For those who are such do not serve our Lord Jesus Christ, but their own belly, and **by smooth words and flattering speech deceive the hearts of the simple**. *Romans 16:17-18*

Chrislam is a false doctrine and dangerous concept that has the potential to mislead many. Those who support it are false religious teachers whom God will hold accountable for their actions. Since throwing his support to Chrislam, Robert H. Schuller lost the church he founded, the Crystal Cathedral, his wife died, he was diagnosed with Esophageal cancer and then he died. Bill Hybels, following his support of Chrislam, was accused of sexual misconduct. Conflicting reports exist as to his guilt or innocence, but his reputation has been damaged much like the damage he perpetuated against the foundations of Christianity. He is no longer the lead pastor of the church he founded essentially losing his church too. After Rick Warren, a vocal advocate for Chrislam, began his tireless crusade to negotiate Christianity and the role of God's son, Jesus, his own son tragically committed suicide in 2013. As heart-wrenching as that event is, parallels can be drawn between straying from God's word and suffering the consequences of those actions serving as a warning to all others who might think to follow in Chrislam's unholy path.

The Bible and the Qur'an present religious doctrines that are fundamentally opposed to each other. In order to merge the two religions in the name of peace, one or both sides must cede key foundational principles. Muslims are unlikely to cede any of their basic beliefs. In this unholy alliance, the only ceding that can be expected is from Christians. Both religions share common roots in Abraham, but that is where the similarities end. Merging the two religions into one common religion is simply not possible without angering God and inviting His wrath.

Ultimately, at its core, the Tribulation is a religious war. Even the term for the Antichrist's sidekick, the "False Prophet", indicates religion is a key component of end time events. Satan desires to replace everything God has established with a new religion of his own endorsement. While terrorism is an outward sign of the battle, the real battlefield for religious dominance takes place in the hearts, minds and souls of all humanity. As far as God is concerned, Christianity and Islam cannot meet in the middle. God would have it that we are either for Him or against Him, but to compromise basic Christian principles to befriend another religion is a grievous error which will not be overlooked by God.

Talk It Out

1. Is an increase in terrorism a sign of the end times? Why do you think some Muslims become jihadist terrorists and others do not? Do you think jihadists are being true to the Qur'an when they become jihadists? What role do you think state sponsored terrorism plays in terrorist activities?

2. How likely is it that Islam will eventually succeed in creating a global Caliphate? Would you want to live in a society that embraced any aspects of Sharia Law? Do you think Muslims would ever compromise or give up the concept of having Sharia law?

3. How far apart do you believe Christians and Muslims are in their beliefs? Can the differences be bridged in a common religion? Is there room for compromise? If yes, where?

4. Have you ever heard of the Chrislam movement? What are your feelings towards religious leaders who support Chrislam as a viable alternative to the Christian/Muslim divide? Do you think Chrislam has the potential of spreading given the support given to it from prominent religious leaders and organizations in our society?

5. Is the movement to merge Christianity with Islam a sign of the end time? Do you think the spirit of anti-Christ is present in this movement? If yes, where?

Ideas for the Week:

- ✓ Be prepared for acts of terrorism by following the tips on the Red Cross website at https://www.redcross.org/get-help/how-to-prepare-for-emergencies/types-of-emergencies/terrorism.html.
- ✓ Follow updates on terrorism at http://www.militantislammonitor.org/.
- ✓ Educate yourself on the specifics of Sharia Law at http://www.billionbibles.org/sharia/sharia-law.html.
- ✓ Watch Jack Van Impe's DVD *Chrislam: One World Religion Emerging* (available at www.amazon.com or www.jvim.com)

Closing Prayer

NOTE: Add names and individual personal prayer requests to the space provided below before closing in prayer.

Lord, we thank You for our time together today to grow deeper in our walk with You and fellowship with each other. As we close today, we lift up: _____

_____

_____

_____

_____

_____

_____

Father, we cannot know where the dangers ahead lie. Some dangers are physical while others are spiritual. Only You, our loving and omniscient God can foresee the evil that lies in wait to ambush us when we least suspect. Protect us from violent acts others might seek to inflict upon us; protect us from spiritual dangers; and protect us from any form of terrorism or destruction the enemy might think to employ against us. In Jesus' name we pray, Amen.

SUPPORTING SCRIPTURES

FREE WILL
^{12} So I gave them over to their own stubborn heart, to walk in their own counsels. *Psalm 81:12*

^{24} Therefore God also gave them up to uncleanness, in the lusts of their hearts, to dishonor their bodies among themselves… *Romans 1:24*

TERROR APPOINTED
^{14} But if you do not obey Me, and do not observe all these commandments, ^{15} and if you despise My statutes, or if your soul abhors My judgments, so that you do not perform all My commandments, but break My covenant, ^{16} I also will do this to you: I will even appoint terror over you… *Leviticus 26:14-16*

^{7} When He opened the fourth seal, I heard the voice of the fourth living creature saying, "Come and see." ^{8} So I looked, and behold, a pale horse. And the name of him who sat on it was Death, and Hades followed with him. And power was given to them over a fourth of the earth, to kill with sword, with hunger, with death, and by the beasts of the earth. *Revelation 6:7-8*

^{3} "And I will appoint over them four forms of destruction," says the LORD: "the sword to slay, the dogs to drag, the birds of the heavens and the beasts of the earth to devour and destroy." *Jeremiah 15:3*

^{4} They have said, "Come, and let us cut them off from being a nation, that the name of Israel may be remembered no more. ^{4} They have said, "Come, and let us cut them off from being a nation, that the name of Israel may be remembered no more." ^{5} For they have consulted together with one consent; they form a confederacy against You: ^{6} The tents of Edom and the Ishmaelites... *Ps. 83:4-5*

^{4} And I saw thrones, and they sat on them, and judgment was committed to them. Then I saw the souls of those who had been beheaded for their witness to Jesus and for the word of God, who had not worshiped the beast or his image, and had not received his mark on their foreheads or on their hands. And they lived and reigned with Christ for a thousand years. *Revelation 20:4*

DAMASCUS DESTROYED
The burden against Damascus. Behold, Damascus will cease from being a city, and it will be a ruinous heap. *Isaiah 17:1*

^{23} Against Damascus. "Hamath and Arpad are shamed, for they have heard bad news. They are fainthearted; there is trouble on the sea; it cannot be quiet. ^{24} Damascus has grown feeble; she turns to flee, and fear has seized her.

Anguish and sorrows have taken her like a woman in labor. ^{25} Why is the city of praise not deserted, the city of My joy? ^{26} Therefore her young men shall fall in her streets, and all the men of war shall be cut off in that day," says the LORD of hosts. ^{27} "I will kindle a fire in the wall of Damascus, and it shall consume the palaces of Ben-Hadad." *Jeremiah 49:23-27*

CHRISLAM
^{6} Jesus said to him, "I am the way, the truth, and the life. No one comes to the Father except through Me." *John 14:6*

^{44} No one can come to Me unless the Father who sent Me draws him; and I will raise him up at the last day. *John 6:44*

Then He (Jesus) said to them, "Follow me..." *Matthew 4:19*

^{33}For God is not the author of confusion, but of peace, as in all churches of the saints. *1 Corinthians 14:33*

^{15} I know your works, that you are neither cold nor hot. I could wish you were cold or hot. ^{16} So then, because you are lukewarm, and neither cold nor hot, I will vomit you out of My mouth. *Revelation 3:15-16*

^{26} How long will this be in the heart of the prophets who prophesy lies? Indeed, they are prophets of the deceit of their own heart... *Jeremiah 23:26*

^{4} For certain men have crept in unnoticed, who long ago were marked out for this condemnation, ungodly men, who turn the grace of our God into lewdness and deny the only Lord God and our Lord Jesus Christ. *Jude 1:4*

^{3} For the time will come when they will not endure sound doctrine, but according to their own desires, because they have itching ears, they will heap up for themselves teachers; ^{4} and they will turn their ears away from the truth, and be turned aside to fables. *2 Timothy 4:3-4*

^{17} Now I urge you, brethren, note those who cause divisions and offenses, contrary to the doctrine which you learned, and avoid them. ^{18} For those who are such do not serve our Lord Jesus Christ, but their own belly, and by smooth words and flattering speech deceive the hearts of the simple. *Romans 16:17-18*

^{14} They have also healed the hurt of My people slightly, saying, "Peace, peace!" when there is no peace. ^{15} Were they ashamed when they had committed abomination? No! They were not at all ashamed; nor did they know how to blush. Therefore, they shall fall among those who fall; at the time I punish them, they shall be cast down," says the LORD. *Jeremiah 6:14-15*

¹ Beloved, do not believe every spirit, but test the spirits, whether they are of God; because many false prophets have gone out into the world. ² By this you know the Spirit of God: Every spirit that confesses that Jesus Christ has come in the flesh is of God, ³ and every spirit that does not confess that Jesus Christ has come in the flesh is not of God. And this is the spirit of the Antichrist, which you have heard was coming, and is now already in the world. ⁴ You are of God, little children, and have overcome them, because He who is in you is greater than he who is in the world. ⁵ They are of the world. Therefore, they speak as of the world, and the world hears them. ⁶ We are of God. He who knows God hears us; he who is not of God does not hear us. By this we know the spirit of truth and the spirit of error. *1 John 4:1-6*

²⁵ He (the Antichrist) shall speak pompous words against the Most High, shall wear out the saints of the Most High, and shall intend to change times and law. Then the saints shall be given into his hand for a time and times and half a time. *Daniel 7:25*

²⁴ For false Christs and false prophets will rise and show great signs and wonders to deceive, if possible, even the elect. *Matthew 24:24*

¹ But there were also false prophets among the people, even as there will be false teachers among you, who will secretly bring in destructive heresies, even denying the Lord who bought them, and bring on themselves swift destruction. ² And many will follow their destructive ways, because of whom the way of truth will be blasphemed. *2 Peter 2:1-2*

¹⁵ They have forsaken the right way and gone astray… *2 Peter 2:15*

²¹ For it would have been better for them not to have known the way of righteousness, than having known it, to turn from the holy commandment delivered to them. *2 Peter 2:21*

¹⁰ The devil, who deceived them, was cast into the lake of fire and brimstone where the beast and the false prophet are. And they will be tormented day and night forever and ever. *Revelation 20:10*

NOTES

"Replace what you don't know about the future with what you do know about God." — Christine Caine

WEEK 15: ONE WORLD RELIGION

Opening Prayer: Lord, we ask that You send Your Holy Spirit to us to guide us in the teaching and understanding of Your word that we may obtain a better understanding of the prophetic events surrounding us now and waiting for us in the future. Bless our fellowship in Your word that it may be fruitful and draw us into a deeper relationship both with You and those around us. Use us as Your vessels that through us, we may reflect Your glory to all whom we encounter. Illuminate our hearts and minds so that we may boldly shine the brightness of Your light everywhere we go and that we may be beacons of Your hope in a darkened world. In Jesus name we pray, Amen.

Ice Breaker: Below is a list of eighteen people. Each person has two hints about two famous people who both share the same name. As a group, see how many of the famous people you can identify, then check the answers on page 238.

Nr.	Person #1	Shared Name	Person #2
1	Founder of Wendy's		SCTV actor
2	Creator of the *Garfield* comic strip		Played Jock Ewing on *Dallas*
3	Led Zeppelin bassist		'I have not yet begun to fight' Naval officer
4	*Dawson's Creek* actress		Destiny's Child member
5	Wife of Henry VIII		*Dr. Quinn, Medicine Woman* star
6	Shoeless baseball player		Father of Tito and LaToya
7	First *Survivor* winner		*Battlestar Galactica* actor
8	Minnesota Vikings running back		Chicago Bears running back
9	*Seinfeld* star		Britney Spears' first husband
10	Late Democratic senator from Illinois		Garfunkel's partner
11	*Xena* actor		*Jersey Girl* director

Focus: God will not let His children who earnestly pursue righteous be led astray.

ARE WE THE TERMINAL GENERATION?

Word of the Week

> ⁸ All who dwell on the earth will **worship** him (the Antichrist), whose names have not been written in the Book of Life of the Lamb slain from the foundation of the world.
>
> *Revelation 13:8*

WORSHIP: Worship comes from the Greek word "proskuneo" (pronounced pros-koo-neh'-o) and refers to the act of expressing extreme reverence for someone or something. Through the centuries, acts of worship have included various gestures such as kissing the hand of a revered leader or kneeling on the ground in prostration to a venerated religious leader. Acts of worship are typically reserved for those deemed to be of a higher rank such as God, Jesus, Jewish high priests, heavenly beings or demons. During the Tribulation, the Antichrist functions as Satan's earthly high priest and demands to be worshipped as such.

Lesson: Characterized by religious apathy and a generalized falling away, the Tribulation period is ripe for the Antichrist to step in and change traditional religious beliefs to resemble his unique brand of deception and false teachings. Shadows of what is yet to come are observable in our world today. Christianity in the United States has been in a steady state of decline for decades. Animosity toward Christians waxes greater by the day as the media maligns Christian values with ever increasing impunity. Church shootings are now a commonplace occurrence. New York Times reporter Dan Levin openly solicited negative stories about Christian schools via Twitter while Second Lady Karen Pence was hotly criticized in the media for teaching at a Christian school upholding traditional Christian values. At many high schools, class valedictorians are barred from thanking Jesus for their success or mentioning God in any way during their graduation speeches. Rampant political correctness demands acceptance of religious pluralism and emphasizes subjugating traditional Christian views. Promoting there are many paths to know God and get to heaven, political correctness demands that all religions be considered equal. As the practice of Christianity weakens and declines, conditions become ripe for a world dictator to step in and mold a new religion out of the ashes of the old.

Through his power, might, influence and satanic backing, the Antichrist of the

Tribulation institutes a one world religion during the Tribulation. Those who refuse to worship the Antichrist will pay with their lives:

> [8] **All who dwell on the earth will worship him** (the Antichrist), whose names have not been written in the Book of Life of the Lamb slain from the foundation of the world. *Revelation 13:8*
>
> [12] And **he** (the False Prophet) exercises all the authority of the first beast (the Antichrist) in his presence, and **causes the earth and those who dwell in it to worship the first beast**, whose deadly wound was healed. [13] He (the False Prophet) performs great signs, so that he even makes fire come down from heaven on the earth in the sight of men. [14] And he deceives those who dwell on the earth by those signs which he was granted to do in the sight of the beast, telling those who dwell on the earth to make an image to the beast who was wounded by the sword and lived. [15] He was granted power to give breath to the image of the beast, that the image of the beast should both speak and **cause as many as would not worship the image of the beast to be killed**. *Revelation 13:12-15*

It is well recognized that the misuse of religion can be a useful tool for dictators and despots to control the masses. Such is the case with the new religion the Antichrist establishes. Government and religion will be intimately connected. Following are quotes from current and past world leaders highlighting the known relationship between religion, government and control of the people:

> *"To achieve world government, it is necessary to remove from the minds of men, their individualism, loyalty to family traditions, national patriotism and religious dogmas."*
>
> > —**G. Brock Chisholm**, co-founder of the World Federation for Mental Health and former director of UN World Health Organization
>
> *"No one will enter the New World Order unless he or she will make a pledge to worship Lucifer. No one will enter the New Age unless he will take a Luciferian Initiation."*
>
> > —**David Spangler**, Director of UN Planetary Initiative and one of the founding fathers of the New Age movement
>
> *"Fundamental Bible-believing people do not have the right to indoctrinate their children in their religious beliefs because we, the*

state, are preparing them for the year 2000, when America will be part of a one-world global society and their children will not fit in."

> —**Sen. Peter Hoagland**, Nebraska State senator in a radio interview, 1983.

"The fate of mankind, as well as of religion, depends upon the emergence of a new faith in the future."

> —**Al Gore**, environmentalist and former Vice President of the U.S., quoted in his book *Earth in the Balance – Forging a New Common Purpose (2013). p.263, Routledge*

"[We need the] construction of a world community, with a corresponding authority," to serve the "common good of the human family".

> —**Pope Benedict XVI**, December 3, 2012

"The time for glorifying the Almighty (male) God who supposedly rules is now over. Some future generation may well be moved to discard the Christian calendar entirely, and rename the year 2000 AD as 1 GE, the first year of the global era. Soon the Lord's Supper will only signify human fellowship, and Christmas will be a holiday for the celebration of family."

> —**Lloyd Geering**, Emeritus Professor of Religious Studies at Victoria University, Doctor of Divinity, self-proclaimed protestant heretic

Imitating God, the new global religion mimics many aspects of Christianity. Echoing the death and resurrection of Jesus, the Antichrist receives a deadly wound and is raised from the dead. Mirroring the miracles of Jesus, the False Prophet performs signs and wonders. Imitating the trinity, the new religion is composed of three entities: Satan, the Antichrist and the False Prophet. This unholy trinity aligns Satan with God's role, the Antichrist as Jesus and the False Prophet as the holy spirit. Impersonating the deity of Jesus, the Antichrist declares himself to be God:

> [36] "Then **the king** (the Antichrist) shall do according to his own will: he **shall exalt and magnify himself above every god**, shall speak blasphemies against the God of gods, and shall prosper till the wrath has been accomplished; for what has been determined shall be done. [37] He shall regard neither the God of his fathers nor

the desire of women, nor regard any god; for he shall exalt himself above them all. *Daniel 11:36-37*

>...[4] who opposes and exalts himself above all that is called God or that is worshiped, so that he sits as God in the temple of God, **showing himself that he is God**. *2 Thessalonians 2:4*

Just as Jesus is the heart and soul of Christianity, the Antichrist puts himself at the center of the new world religion. Alluring to the core, the deception of the new world religion will be so compelling that even some of the elect will be tempted to fall prey to its deadly dogma:

>[24] For false Christs and false prophets will rise and show great signs and wonders **to deceive, if possible, even the elect**. *Matthew 24:24*

In order to unify the people of the world under one religion, there must necessarily be one God. Christianity and Islam are the world's two largest religions. To appeal to a large number of people, the one world religion would have to speak to elements of both religions. According to a 2015 Pew Research poll, Christianity comprises the largest global religious group at 31% of the global population. Second to Christianity, Muslims represent 24% of the global population. Combined, Christianity and Islam represent 55% of the world's religious beliefs. Other beliefs including Buddhists, Hindus, Jews, those with no religious affiliation and all other religions share the remaining 45%. Since Christianity and Islam are the two main religions of the world, it follows that the false common religion yet to be instituted by the Antichrist and False Prophet will necessarily involve elements that will be acceptable to both religions. Efforts to merge the two religions into the one religion of Chrislam with one God are already underway. But do we really worship the same God? Is Allah the same God of Abraham, Isaac and Jacob referred to by another name? Names are important. Scripture tells us that there is power in the name of Jesus like no other name given under heaven. Through the name of Jesus, demons are cast out, the sick are healed, and danger is tread underfoot with confidence:

>[17] Then the seventy returned with joy, saying, "Lord, **even the demons are subject to us in Your name**." *Luke 10:17*

>[17] And these signs will follow those who believe: **In My name** they will **cast out demons**; they will **speak with new tongues**; [18] they will **take up serpents**; and **if they drink anything deadly**, it will by **no means hurt them**; they will **lay hands on the sick**, and they will recover." *Mark 16:17-18*

The same cannot be said of any other name. Since God distinctly emphasizes in His holy word the importance of a name for Himself, heed must be given to that which we call our God. In Exodus, God confirms that He has a preference for how we are to refer to Him:

> [13] Then Moses said to God, "Indeed, when I come to the children of Israel and say to them, 'The God of your fathers has sent me to you,' and they say to me, '**What is His name?**' what shall I say to them?" [14] And God said to Moses, "**I AM WHO I AM**." And He said, "Thus you shall say to the children of Israel, '**I AM has sent me to you**.'" *Exodus 3:13-14*

Through the power of the spoken word, God spoke the world into existence. It is with great caution that we should carefully consider the choice of our words and what we call our God.

What's in a name you ask? Plenty. Our name identifies who we are to the rest of the world. Sometimes the identity difference is clear when someone has a name unlike any others. Other times, two people share the same name, but that does not make them the same person. Jane Seymour, the wife of Henry the VIII, is not the same person as Jane Seymour, the actress who starred in the popular television series, *Dr. Quinn, Medicine Woman*. Joe Jackson, the famous baseball player, is not the same person as Joe Jackson, the father of famed musicians Michael, Janet, Tito and LaToya Jackson. Simon, who is called Peter, is not the same disciple as Simon the Canaanite. James the son of Zebedee is not the same disciple as James the son of Alphaeus. Names are an important identifier, but not uniquely foolproof in providing the certainty of an identity. Both Christians and Muslims refer to their respective deities as God. In fact, Allah literally means God. Per *Webster's Dictionary*:

> ALLAH: Used as the name of God in Islam.

While "Allah" does literally translate as "God", it is a far stretch to assume that they are the *same* God. Regardless of semantics, God and Allah are not the same entity referred to by different names. Don't fall for the hype.

Part of the semantic misconception stems from the fact that Christianity and Islam do share common roots in Abraham. Abraham had two sons: Isaac and Ishmael (Genesis chapters 16, 17, 18 and 21). Isaac went on to become a patriarch of the faith for Christians and Ishmael went on to become a key historical figure for Muslims. Both men were raised in Abraham's household during their formative years and learned about the same God under Abraham's teachings:

> [12] ...Whatever Sarah says to you, do as she tells you, for through Isaac shall your offspring be named. [13] And **I will make a nation of the son of the slave woman also, because he (Ishmael) is your offspring**. *Genesis 21:12-13*
>
> [20] And **God was with the boy** (Ishmael), and he grew up. *Genesis 21:20*

However, just because Christians and Muslims started off worshipping the same God at Abraham's knee does not mean they still do today. A closer examination of how each religion evolved is quite revealing. Isaac and Ishmael went different directions and so did the God they worship. Following in his father's footsteps, Isaac maintained the integrity of his father's teachings throughout his lineage and the deity Christians worship today has not changed since the days of Abraham, Isaac and Jacob. However, theologically things changed significantly within Ishmael's lineage when a man named Muhammad came along. From that point on, the god of Ishmael's lineage took a radically different turn from the God of Isaac's lineage. Today, Christians and Muslims worship entirely different deities.

Muhammad made the largest and most sweeping changes to the identity of the Islamic deity. Significantly altering spiritual teachings on God, Muhammad merged elements of many different religions along with his own personal beliefs to create the modern-day religion of Islam (Chacon and Burnham p.4). Much like Solomon's many wives from diverse religions ultimately influenced his religious actions, so, too, did Muhammad's multiple wives from different religious backgrounds affect his religious philosophy. When Muhammad chose a name to represent his new god, he selected the name "Allah" from the pagan moon god Allah making it the personal name of his new god. The Islamic god Allah also shares many common worship characteristics with the pagan moon god Allah such as requirements to pray while bowing in a certain direction and making pilgrimages to Mecca. Even the symbol for Islam is a crescent moon honoring the tradition of the moon god Allah. In his quest to

SIFREI KODESH (pronounced SIFF-ray KOE-desh): Translated as "holy books" from the Hebrew phrase, it refers to the handling of biblical and rabbinic texts with special reverence.

reinvent religion, Muhammad wrote a new holy book called the Qur'an which teaches many different messages than can be found in the Bible. The Qur'an replaces the Bible as the primary religious text in Islam violating the last command given in the Bible:

> [18] For I testify to everyone who hears the words of the prophecy of this book: **If anyone adds to these things, God will add to him the plagues** that are written in this book; [19] and **if anyone takes away from the words of the book** of this prophecy, **God shall take away his part from the Book of Life**, from the holy city, and from the things which are written in this book. *Revelation 22:18-19*

After Muhammad finished replacing the Bible, the direction of his religion was permanently altered and became what we know today as modern-day Islam. From that point forward, the resulting deity no longer even closely resembled the original God of Abraham, Isaac and Jacob much like the children's game of telephone. In the game, children stand in a line. The first child thinks of a sentence and whispers it only one time into the ear of the next child and so on down the line. Minor changes along the way result in a final sentence that in no way resembles the original sentence. The beginning sentence and the end sentence are now completely different. This is the same principle in action for how Christians and Muslims started off being taught about the same God in Abraham's household to worshipping completely different entities today. Muhammad made fundamental changes to the identity of God making the Christian God of Abraham, Isaac and Jacob in our modern-day setting no more related to the Muslim God Allah than the first sentence in the game of telephone is like that of the final sentence announced.

In order to determine the truth of any matter, both similarities and differences must be compared. If only similarities are considered and differences are dismissed, wrong conclusions are reached. For example, assume there are two women who both look and dress alike. They share the same birthday and have the same biological mother. Each woman has a ten-year-old daughter who calls her "Mom". Are they the same woman? It would seem so if only the similarities are considered. However, differences must also be factored into the equation. Truth in a matter cannot be determined by evaluating the facts from only one angle. If it is known that one of them has a mole on her upper lip and stutters when she speaks while the other one does not, it then becomes obvious that they are not the same person, even though they have many remarkable similarities. In order for items to be the same, they must be identical in all aspects. Identical twins can be confusingly similar and may even share similar life events, but they are still very much unique individuals with differences as well as similarities. Comparing similarities alone isn't enough to determine an identity. Differences must also be considered. So, the question becomes, what are the differences between our Christian God and the deity Muslims refer to as Allah? By comparing scripture verses from the Bible with surahs from the Qur'an, the contrast becomes readily apparent:

	GOD (Biblical God of Abraham, Isaac and Jacob as defined through the Bible)	ALLAH (Muslim God of Muhammad as defined through the Qur'an)
	God says...	Allah says...
1	...the Bible is God's holy book above all others. Verse: *Deuteronomy 4:2; Proverbs 30:5-6; Psalm 138:2; Revelation 22:18-19; 2 Timothy 3:16*	...the Qur'an is God's holy book above all others. Surah: 10:37, 6:19
2	...He does not change at all. Verse: **Malachi 3:6 and Psalm 89:34, 1 Samuel 15:29, Numbers 23:19,**	...he can change both his mind and his doctrine. Surah: 2:106, 13:39 and 16:101
3	...Jesus is God's one and only Son. Verse: **John 3:16, Matthew 3:16-17, and 1 John 4:14**	...god does not have a son at all. Surah: 4:171, 6:101, 9:30, 17:111, 19:35, 19:88-92 and 23:91
4	...Jesus died on the cross. Verse: **Luke 23:33**	...Jesus did not die on the cross. Surah: 4:156-158
5	...Jesus is part of the divine trinity and Lord above lords through which salvation is obtained. Verse: **John 1:14, John 10:30, Philippians 2:11, John 14:6, John 6:44, Matthew 1:21 and Acts 4:12**	...Jesus was a mortal man like other human apostles who delivered God's message to mankind and has no deity or ability to save mankind. Surah: 3:59, 3:64, 4:163-165, 4:171, 5:17, 5:72-73, 5:75, and 5:116
6	...Jesus is God's chosen messenger to impart His word to mankind. Verse: **Malachi 3:1, Luke 4:43, and Isaiah 42:1**	...Muhammad is god's chosen messenger to impart his word to mankind. Surah: 4:170, 5:15, 33:40, and 48:29
7	...He loves the Jewish people. Verse: **Deuteronomy 7:7-8, Zechariah 2:8, Hosea 2:19,**	...he hates the Jewish people. Surah: 4:46, 4:160-161, 5:51 and 9:30

	Jeremiah 3:14 and 1 Chronicles 21:1	
8	...love your enemies and pray for those who persecute you. **Verse: Luke 6:27-36**	...strike terror into the hearts of your enemies. **Surah: 8:59-60**
9	...live peaceably with all as much as it depends on you. **Verse: Romans 12:18**	...make war with people if they don't accept the religion of Islam. **Surah: 9:38-39, 9:41, 9:73, 9:123, 48:29, and 61:4, 66:9**
10	...Christians are never to commit murder. **Verse: Deuteronomy 5:17**	...make war on the unbelievers and kill them. **Surah: 3:85, 4:88-90, 4:95, 8:38-39, 9:3, 9:5, and 47:4**
11	...husbands and wives are to have a mutually loving relationship. **Verse: 1 Corinthians 7:2-5, Colossians 3:19, Ephesians 5:33, 1 Peter 3:7**	...husbands are superior to their wives and should withhold sex and beat their wives as a way to bring them into submission. **Surah: 4:11-12 and 4:34**
12	...oaths and vows are binding with no exceptions. **Verse: Leviticus 19:11, Numbers 30:2**	...oaths and vows may be broken. **Surah: 2:225, 9:12, 16:106, 66:2**
13	...He never lies. **Verse: Numbers 23:19, Titus 1:2, 1 Samuel 15:29, Psalm 89:35**	...he lies and schemes. **Surah: 3:54, 8:30, 17:64**
14	...Jesus will rule the earth when He returns with His Christian followers at His side. **Verse: 2 Timothy 2:12**	...Jesus will deny Christians on the Day of Resurrection. **Surah: 4:159**
15	...His name is I Am. **Verse: Exodus 3:13-14**	...his name is Satan. **Surah: 17:64**
	NOTE: The Bible gives scripture references in chapters and verses. The Qur'an gives scripture references in surahs and ayahs.	

When both sides of the issue are examined, it becomes readily apparent there are numerous and significant differences between the two deities. Therefore, it is impossible for the God of each respective religion to be the same entity called by a different name. Both the Christian God and the Islamic god may have started off as the same God in Abraham's household as he taught both Isaac and Ishmael about their Creator at his knee, but they are not the same God today and cannot be worshipped as such. Beware of false teachers.

Talk It Out

1. Discuss the role of religion and government. Why do you think those in power fear religious beliefs that they cannot control? Is religion an effective way to control people? What kind of religion would you create if you wanted to exert control over a society? Do you think our leaders use religion or the lack thereof to control Americans? Give specific examples.

2. Discuss the specific differences between the Christian God of Abraham, Isaac and Jacob and the Muslim god, Allah as defined through the Qur'an. Which difference do you find the most striking and/or concerning? Were you aware of these differences before doing this study? Detailed verses and surahs are provided on pages 238-248 to facilitate the discussion and compare their respective messages.

3. Does the mainstream media portray the religion of Islam in an accurate light? Do you think there is a fear of retaliation if they say something that portrays Islam in a negative light?

4. Do you believe the Christian God of Abraham, Isaac and Jacob is the same god as the Muslim god, Allah? Why or why not? Do you think that most people understand the differences between the two entities or is there a general ignorance in our society along with an acceptance that they are the same deity? How do you think God feels when people confuse Him with another god?

5. Do you believe there are many ways to heaven? Do we worship a God of absolutes or is there room for negotiation? If yes, when and how?

6. Have you ever read the Qur'an before to compare it to what the Bible says about God or do you accept the word of what other people or prominent religious leaders say about the Qur'an without question? Do you know any other Christians who have read the Qur'an?

"Keep your eyes on culture and on Christ at the same time. As the one deteriorates, the nearness of the other increases. Prepare to stand firm and faithful until the end."

— Dr. David Jeremiah

Ideas for the Week:

- ✓ Share the verses and surahs provided in the chart with others this week to help promote a greater awareness of the differences between Christianity and Islam.
- ✓ Conduct your own comparison of Christianity and Islam by reading a copy of the *Qur'an* as translated by N.J. Dawood. A free online version can be borrowed at www.openlibrary.org. Simply create an account, search for the *Qur'an* translation by N.J. Dawood, then read it online.
- ✓ Post the chart from this lesson on your personal website if you have one. Permission is granted to reprint the chart with credit given to this book, *Are We the Terminal Generation*, as the source.
- ✓ Read *Beginning Apologetics 9: How to Answer Muslims* by Father Frank Chacon & Jim Burnham to better educate yourself on this topic.

Closing Prayer

NOTE: Add names and individual personal prayer requests to the space provided below before closing in prayer.

Lord, we thank You for our time together today to grow deeper in our walk with You and fellowship with each other. As we close today, we lift up: _____

_____

_____

_____

_____

_____

_____

Father, we acknowledge that You are the one, true God and that Jesus Christ is Your only begotten Son. We worship You and You alone. Show us how to spread Your word and Your ways throughout all the world and glorify You in all our ways. In Jesus' name we pray, Amen.

Quiz Answers

1. Dave Thomas
2. Jim Davis
3. John Paul Jones
4. Michelle Williams
5. Jane Seymour
6. Joe Jackson
7. Richard Hatch
8. Adrian Peterson
9. Jason Alexander
10. Paul Simon
11. Kevin Smith

VERSE AND SURAH REFERENCES

1	...the Bible is God's holy book above all others. **Verse: *Deuteronomy 4:2; Proverbs 30:5-6; Psalm 138:2; Revelation 22:18-19; 2 Timothy 3:16***	...the Qur'an is God's holy book above all others. **Surah: 10:37, 6:19**

God says the Bible is God's holy book above all others.

[18] For I testify to everyone who hears the words of the prophecy of this book: If anyone adds to these things, God will add to him the plagues that are written in this book; [19] and if anyone takes away from the words of the book of this prophecy, God shall take away his part from the Book of Life, from the holy city, and from the things which are written in this book. *Revelation 22:18-19*

[2] You shall not add to the word which I command you, nor take from it, that you may keep the commandments of the LORD your God which I command you. *Deuteronomy 4:2*

[2] I will worship toward Your holy temple, and praise Your name for Your lovingkindness and Your truth; for You have magnified Your word above all Your name. *Psalm 138:2*

[5] Every word of God is pure; He is a shield to those who put their trust in Him. [6] Do not add to His words, lest He rebuke you, and you be found a liar. *Proverbs 30:5-6*

[16] All scripture is given by inspiration of God, and is profitable for doctrine, for reproof, for correction, for instruction in righteousness... *2 Timothy 3:16*

Allah says the Qur'an is God's holy book above all others.

This Qur'an could not have been devised by any but God. It confirms what was revealed before it and fully explains the Scriptures. It is beyond doubt from the

Lord of the Universe. *10:37*

Say: "What counts most in testimony?" Say: "God is my witness and your witness. This Qur'an has been revealed to me that I may thereby warn you and all whom it may reach. Will you really testify there are other gods besides God?" Say: "I will testify to no such thing!" Say: "He is but one God. I disown the gods you serve besides Him.'" *6:19*

| 2 | ...He does not change at all. **Verse: Malachi 3:6, Ps. 89.34, 1 Sam. 15:29 and Num. 23:19** | ...he can change both his mind and his doctrine. **Surah: 2:106, 13:39 and 16:101** |

God says He does not change at all.
[6] For I am the Lord, I change not... *Malachi 3:6*

[34] My covenant I will not break, nor alter the word that has gone out of My lips. *Psalm 89:34*

[29] And also the Strength of Israel will not lie nor relent. For He is not a man, that He should relent. *1 Samuel 15:29*

[19] God is not a man, that He should lie, nor a son of man, that He should repent. Has He said, and will He not do? Or has He spoken, and will He not make it good? *Numbers 23:19*

Allah says he can change both his mind and his doctrine.
If We abrogate a verse or cause it to be forgotten, We will replace it by a better one or one similar. Did you not know that God has power over all things? *2:106*

When we change one verse for another (God knows best what He reveals), they say: 'You are an imposter.' Indeed, most of them have no knowledge. *16:101*

God abrogates and confirms what He pleases. *13:39*

| 3 | ...Jesus is God's one and only Son. **Verse: John 3:16, Matthew 3:16-17, and 1 John 4:14** | ...god does not have a son at all. **Surah: 4:171, 6:101, 9:30, 17:111, 19:35, 19:88-92 and 23:91** |

God says Jesus is His one and only son.
[16] For God so loved the world, that He gave His only begotten Son... *John 3:16*

[16] When He had been baptized, Jesus came up immediately from the water; and behold, the heavens were opened to Him, and He saw the Spirit of God descending like a dove and alighting upon Him. [17] And suddenly a voice came

from heaven, saying, "This is My beloved Son, in whom I am well pleased." *Matthew 3:16-17*

¹⁴ And we have seen and testify that the Father has sent the Son as Savior of the world. *1 John 4:14*

Allah says he does not have a son at all.
The Messiah, Jesus son of Mary, was no more than God's apostle and His Word which He cast to Mary: a spirit from Him. So, believe in God and His apostles and do not say: "Three."...God is but one God. God forbid that He should have a son! *4:171*

How should He have a son when He had no consort? *6:101*

The Jews say Ezra is the son of God, while the Christians say the Messiah is the son of God. Such as their assertions, by which they imitate the infidels of old. God confound them! How perverse they are! *9:30*

Say: "Praise be to God who has never begotten a son; who has no partner in His kingdom... " *17:111*

God forbid that He Himself should beget a son! *19:35*

Those who say: 'The Lord of Mercy has begotten a son,' preach a monstrous falsehood, at which the very heavens might crack, the earth split asunder, and the mountains crumble to dust. That they should ascribe a son to the Merciful, when it does not become the Lord of Mercy to beget one! *19:88-92*

Never has God begotten a son, nor is there any other god besides Him. *23:91*

4	...Jesus died on the cross.	...Jesus did not die on the cross.
	Verse: Luke 23:33	**Surah: 4:156-158**

God says Jesus died on the cross.
³³ And when they were come to the place, which is called Calvary, there they crucified him, and the criminals, one on the right hand, and the other on the left. *Luke 23:33*

Allah says Jesus did not die on the cross.
They denied the truth and uttered a monstrous falsehood against Mary. They declared: "We have put to death the Messiah, Jesus son of Mary, the apostle of God." They did not kill him, nor did they crucify him, but they thought they did. Those that disagreed about him were in doubt concerning him; they knew nothing about him that was not sheer conjecture; they did not slay him for certain. God lifted him up to Him. *4:156-158*

| 5 | ...Jesus is part of the divine trinity and Lord above lords through which salvation is obtained. **Verse: John 1:14, John 10:30, Philippians 2:11, John 14:6, John 6:44, Matthew 1:21 and Acts 4:12** | ...Jesus was a mortal man like other human apostles who delivered God's message to mankind and has no deity. **Surah: 3:59, 3:64, 4:163-165, 4:171, 5:17, 5:72-73, 5:75, and 5:116** |

God says Jesus is part of the divine trinity and Lord above Lords.

^{14} And the Word was made flesh, and dwelt among us, (and we beheld His glory, the glory as of the only begotten of the Father,) full of grace and truth. *John 1:14*

^{30} I and my Father are one. *John 10:30*

^{11} And that every tongue should confess that Jesus Christ is Lord, to the glory of God the Father. *Philippians 2:11*

^{6} Jesus said to him, "I am the way, the truth, and the life. No one comes to the Father except through Me." *John 14:6*

^{21} And she will bring forth a Son, and you shall call His name JESUS, for He will save His people from their sins. *Matthew 1:21*

^{44} No one can come to Me unless the Father who sent Me draws him; and I will raise him up at the last day. *John 6:44*

^{12} Nor is there salvation in any other, for there is no other name under heaven given among men by which we must be saved. *Acts 4:12*

Allah says Jesus was a mortal man like other human apostles who delivered God's message to mankind and has no deity or ability to save mankind.

Jesus is like Adam in the sight of God. He created him from dust and then said to him: "Be," and he was. *3:59*

Say: 'People of the Book (Christians), let us come to an agreement: that we will worship none but God, that we will associate none with Him, and that none of us shall set up mortals (Jesus) as deities besides God. *3:64*

We have revealed Our will to you as We revealed it to Noah and to the prophets who came after him; as We revealed it to Abraham, Ishmael, Isaac, Jacob, and the tribes; to Jesus, Job, Jonah, Aaron, Solomon, and David, to whom We gave the Psalms. Of some apostles We have already told you, but there are others of whom We have not yet spoken (God spoke directly to Moses): apostles who brought good news to mankind and admonished them, so that they might have no plea against God after their coming. God is might and wise. *4:163-165*

People of the Book (Christians), do not transgress the bounds of your religion. Speak nothing but the truth about God. The Messiah, Jesus son of Mary, was no more than God's apostle and His word which He cast to Mary: a spirit from Him. *4:171*

Unbelievers are those who declare: "God is the Messiah, the son of Mary." *5:17*

Unbelievers are those that say: 'God is the Messiah, the son of Mary.'...Unbelievers are those that say: 'God is one of three.' There is but one God. If they do not desist from so saying, those of them that disbelieve shall be sternly punished. *5:72-73*

The Messiah, the son of Mary, was no more than an apostle: other apostles passed away before him. *5:75*

Then God will say: "Jesus son of Mary, did you ever say to mankind: 'Worship me and my mother as gods besides God?' 'Glory be to You,' he will answer, 'I could never have claimed what I have no right to...I told them only what You bade me. I said: 'Serve God, my Lord and your Lord.'" *5:116*

| 6 | ...Jesus is God's chosen messenger to impart His word to mankind.
Verse: Malachi 3:1, Luke 4:43, and Isaiah 42:1 | ...Muhammad is god's chosen messenger to impart his word to mankind.
Surah: 4:170, 5:15, 33:40, and 48:29 |

God says Jesus is His chosen messenger to impart God's word to mankind.

[3] "Behold, I send My messenger, and he will prepare the way before Me. And the Lord, whom you seek, will suddenly come to His temple, even the Messenger of the covenant, in whom you delight. Behold, He is coming," says the LORD of hosts. *Malachi 3:1*

...[43] but He said to them, "I must preach the kingdom of God to the other cities also, because for this purpose I have been sent." *Luke 4:43*

[1] "Behold! My Servant whom I uphold, My Elect One in whom My soul delights! I have put My Spirit upon Him; He will bring forth justice to the Gentiles. *Isaiah 42:1*

Allah says Muhammad is his chosen messenger to impart God's word to mankind.

You People! The Apostle (Muhammad) has brought you the Truth from your Lord. *4:170*

People of the Book (Christians)! Our apostle (Muhammad) has come to reveal to you much of what you have hidden of the Scriptures, and to forgive you much. *5:15*

Muhammad is the father of no man among you. He is the Apostle of God and the Seal of the Prophets. *33:40*

Muhammad is God's apostle. *48:29*

7	...He loves the Jewish people. **Verse: Deuteronomy 7:7-8, Zechariah 2:8, Hosea 2:19, Jeremiah 3:14 and 1 Chronicles 21:1**	...he hates the Jewish people. **Surah: 4:46, 4:160-161, 5:51, 9:30**

God says He loves the Jewish people.
⁷ The LORD did not set His love on you nor choose you because you were more in number than any other people, for you were the least of all peoples; ⁸ but because the LORD loves you, and because He would keep the oath which He swore to your fathers, the LORD has brought you out with a mighty hand, and redeemed you from the house of bondage, from the hand of Pharaoh king of Egypt. *Deuteronomy 7:7-8*

⁸ For thus says the LORD of hosts: "He sent Me after glory, to the nations which plunder you; for he who touches you touches the apple of His eye. *Zechariah 2:8*

¹⁹ "I will betroth you to Me forever; yes, I will betroth you to Me in righteousness and justice, in lovingkindness and mercy... *Hosea 2:19*

¹⁴ "Return, O backsliding children," says the LORD; "for I am married to you. I will take you, one from a city and two from a family, and I will bring you to Zion. *Jeremiah 3:14*

¹ Now Satan stood up against Israel... *1 Chronicles 21:1*

Allah says he hates the Jewish people.
Some Jews take words out of their context and say: 'We hear, but disobey. May you be bereft of hearing! Raina (to Muhammad)!'--thus distorting the phrase with their tongues and reviling the true faith. But if they said: 'We hear and obey: hear us and Unzurna (Listen to us)' it would be better and more proper for them. God has cursed them in their unbelief. *4:46*

Because of their iniquity, We forbade the Jews wholesome things which were formerly allowed them; because time after time they have debarred others from the path of God; because they practice usury--although they were forbidden it--and cheat others of their possessions. Woeful punishment have we prepared for those that disbelieve. *4:160-161*

Believers, take neither the Jews or the Christians for your friends. *5:51*

The Jews say Ezra is the son of God, while the Christians say the Messiah is the son of God. Such are their assertions, by which they imitate the infidels of old. God confound them! How perverse they are! *9:30*

8	...love your enemies and pray for those who persecute you. **Verse: Luke 6:27-36**	...strike terror into the hearts of your enemies. **Surah: 8:59-60**

God says love your enemies and pray for those who persecute you.
^{27} But I say to you who hear: Love your enemies, do good to those who hate you, ^{28} bless those who curse you, and pray for those who spitefully use you. ^{29} To him who strikes you on the one cheek, offer the other also. And from him who takes away your cloak, do not withhold your tunic either. ^{30} Give to everyone who asks of you. And from him who takes away your goods do not ask them back. ^{31} And just as you want men to do to you, you also do to them likewise. ^{32} But if you love those who love you, what credit is that to you? For even sinners love those who love them. ^{33} And if you do good to those who do good to you, what credit is that to you? For even sinners do the same. ^{34} And if you lend to those from whom you hope to receive back, what credit is that to you? For even sinners lend to sinners to receive as much back. ^{35} But love your enemies, do good, and lend, hoping for nothing in return; and your reward will be great, and you will be sons of the Most High. For He is kind to the unthankful and evil. ^{36} Therefore be merciful, just as your Father also is merciful. *Luke 6:27-36*

Allah says strike terror into the hearts of your enemies.
Let not the unbelievers think that they will ever get away. They have not the power to do so. Muster against them all the men and cavalry at your command, so that you may strike terror into the enemy of God and your enemy, and others besides them who are unknown to you but known to God. *8:59-60*

9	...live peaceably with all as much as it depends on you. **Verse: Romans 12:18**	...make war with people if they don't accept the religion of Islam. **Surah: 9:38-39, 9:41, 9:73, 9:123, 48:29, and 61:4, 66:9**

God says live peaceably with all as much as it depends on you.
¹⁸ If it is possible, as much as depends on you, live peaceably with all men. *Romans 12:18*

Allah says make war with people if they don't accept the religion of Islam.
Believers, why is it that when you are told: 'March in the cause of God,' you linger slothfully in the land? If you do not go to war, He will punish you sternly, and replace you by other men. *9:38-39*

Whether unarmed or well-equipped, march on and fight for the cause of God, with your wealth and with your persons. *9:41*

Prophet, make war on the unbelievers and the hypocrites and deal rigorously with them. Hell shall be their home: an evil fate. *9:73*

Believers make war on the infidels who dwell around you. Deal firmly with them. Know that God is with the righteous. *9:123*

Muhammad is God's apostle. Those who follow him are ruthless to the unbelievers but merciful to one another. *48:29*

God loves those who fight for his cause in ranks as firm as a mighty edifice. *61:4*

Prophet, make war on the unbelievers and the hypocrites, and deal sternly with them. Hell shall be their home, evil their fate. *66:9*

10	...Christians are never to commit murder. **Verse: Deuteronomy 5:17**	...make war on the unbelievers and kill them. **Surah: 3:85, 4:88-90, 4:95, 8:38-39, 9:3, 9:5, and 47:4**

God says Christians are never to commit murder.
¹⁷ You shall not murder. *Deuteronomy 5:17*

Allah says
He that chooses a religion other than Islam, it will not be accepted from him... *3:85*

Why are you thus divided concerning the hypocrites, when God Himself has cast them off on account of their misdeeds? Would you guide those whom God has confounded? He whom God confounds you cannot guide. They would have you disbelieve as they themselves have disbelieved, so that you may be all alike. Do not befriend them until they have fled their homes in the cause of God. If they desert you, seize them and put them to death wherever you find them. Look for neither friends nor helpers among them except those who seek refuge with your allies or come over to you because their hearts forbid them to fight against you or against their own people. *4:88-90*

The believers who stay at home--apart from those that suffer from a grave disability--are not the equals who fight for the cause of God with their goods and their persons. God has exalted the men who fight with their goods and their persons above those who stay at home. God has promised all a good reward; but far richer is the recompense of those who fight for Him... *4:95*

Tell the unbelievers that if they mend their ways their past shall be forgiven; but if they persist in sin (unbelief), let them reflect upon the fate of bygone nations. Make war on them until idolatry shall cease and God's religion shall reign supreme. *8:38-39*

Proclaim a woeful punishment to the unbelievers... *9:3*

When the sacred months are over slay the idolaters wherever you find them. Arrest them, besiege them, and lie in ambush everywhere for them. *9:5*

When you meet the unbelievers in the battlefield strike off their heads... *47:4*

11	...husbands and wives are to have a mutually loving relationship. **Verse: 1 Corinthians 7:2-5, Colossians 3:19, Ephesians 5:33, 1 Peter 3:7**	...husbands are superior to their wives and should withhold sex and beat them as a way to bring them into submission. **Surah: 4:11-12 and 4:34**

God says husbands and wives are to have a mutually loving relationship.
[3] Let the husband render to his wife the affection due her, and likewise also the wife to her husband. [4] The wife does not have authority over her own body, but the husband does. And likewise, the husband does not have authority over his own body, but the wife does. [5] Do not deprive one another except with consent for a time, that you may give yourselves to fasting and prayer; and come together again so that Satan does not tempt you because of your lack of self-control. *1 Corinthians 7:3-5*

[19] Husbands, love your wives and do not be bitter toward them. *Colossians 3:19*

[33] Nevertheless let each one of you in particular so love his own wife as himself, and let the wife see that she respects her husband. *Ephesians 5:33*

[7] Husbands, likewise, dwell with them with understanding, giving honor to the wife, as to the weaker vessel, and as being heirs together of the grace of life, that your prayers may not be hindered. *1 Peter 3:7*

Allah says husbands are superior to their wives and should withhold sex and beat their wives as a way to bring them into submission.

A male shall inherit twice as much as a female...You shall inherit the half of your wives' estate if they die childless...Your wives shall inherit one quarter of your estate if you die childless. *4:11-12*

Men have authority over women because God has made the one superior to the other, and because they spend their wealth to maintain them. Good women are obedient. They guard their unseen parts because God has guarded them. As for those from whom you fear disobedience, admonish them and send them to beds apart and beat them. *4:34*

12	...oaths and vows are binding with no exceptions. **Verse: Leviticus 19:11, Numbers 30:2**	...oaths and vows may be broken. **Surah: 2:225, 9:12, 16:106, 66:2**

God says oaths and vows are binding with no exceptions.

¹¹ 'You shall not steal, nor deal falsely, nor lie to one another. *Leviticus 19:11*

² If a man makes a vow to the LORD, or swears an oath to bind himself by some agreement, he shall not break his word; he shall do according to all that proceeds out of his mouth. *Numbers 30:2*

Allah says oaths and vows may be broken.

God will not call you to account for that which is inadvertent in your oaths. But He will take you to task for that which is intended in your hearts. *2:225*

God and his apostle are under no obligation to the idolaters. *9:3*

...make war on the leaders of unbelief--for no oaths are binding with them--so that they may desist. *9:12*

Those who are forced to recant while their hearts remain loyal to the Faith shall be absolved... *16:106*

God has given you absolution from such oaths. *66:2*

13	...He never lies. **Verse: Numbers 23:19, Titus 1:2, 1 Samuel 15:29, Psalm 89:35**	...he lies and schemes. **Surah: 3:54, 8:30, 17:64**

God says He never lies.

²⁹ And also the Strength of Israel will not lie nor relent. For He is not a man, that He should relent." *1 Samuel 15:29*

¹⁹ God is not a man, that He should lie, nor a son of man, that He should repent. Has He said, and will He not do? Or has He spoken, and will He not make it good? *Numbers 23:19*

...² in hope of eternal life which God, who cannot lie, promised before time began... *Titus 1:2*

³⁵ Once I have sworn by My holiness; I will not lie to David... *Psalm 89:25*

Allah says he lies and schemes.
They contrived and god contrived. God is the supreme contriver. *3:54*

They schemed, but god also schemed. God is most profound in his machinations. *8:30*

Be their partner in their riches and in their offspring. Promise them what you will. (Satan promises them only to deceive them). *17:64*

14	...Jesus will rule the earth when He returns with His Christian followers. **Verse: 2 Timothy 2:12**	...Jesus will deny Christians on the Day of Resurrection. **Surah: 4:159**

God says Jesus will rule the earth when He returns with His Christian followers.
¹² If we endure, we shall also reign with Him. *2 Timothy 2:12*

Allah says Jesus will deny Christians on the Day of Resurrection.
There is none among the People of the Book but will believe in him before his death; and on the Day of Resurrection he will bear witness against them. *4:159*

15	...His name is I Am. **Verse: Exodus 3:13-14**	...his name is Satan. **Surah: 17:64**

God says His name is I Am.
¹³ Then Moses said to God, "Indeed, when I come to the children of Israel and say to them, "The God of your fathers has sent me to you," and they say to me, 'What is His name?' what shall I say to them?" ¹⁴ And God said to Moses, "I AM WHO I AM." And He said, "Thus you shall say to the children of Israel, 'I AM has sent me to you.' " *Exodus 3:13-14*

Allah says his name is Satan.
Be their partner in their riches and in their offspring. Promise them what you will. (Satan promises them only to deceive them). *17:64*

SUPPORTING SCRIPTURES

ONE WORLD RELIGION

⁴ So they worshiped the dragon (Satan) who gave authority to the beast; and they worshiped the beast (the Antichrist)… *Revelation 13:4*

⁸ All who dwell on the earth will worship him (the Antichrist), whose names have not been written in the Book of Life of the Lamb slain from the foundation of the world. *Revelation 13:8*

¹¹ Then I saw another beast coming up out of the earth, and he had two horns like a lamb and spoke like a dragon. ¹² And he (the False Prophet) exercises all the authority of the first beast (the Antichrist) in his presence, and causes the earth and those who dwell in it to worship the first beast, whose deadly wound was healed. ¹³ He (the False Prophet) performs great signs, so that he even makes fire come down from heaven on the earth in the sight of men. ¹⁴ And he deceives those who dwell on the earth by those signs which he was granted to do in the sight of the beast, telling those who dwell on the earth to make an image to the beast who was wounded by the sword and lived. ¹⁵ He was granted power to give breath to the image of the beast, that the image of the beast should both speak and cause as many as would not worship the image of the beast to be killed. *Revelation 13:11-15*

…¹²and he (the Antichrist) cast truth down to the ground. *Daniel 8:12*

³⁶ "Then the king (the Antichrist) shall do according to his own will: he shall exalt and magnify himself above every god, shall speak blasphemies against the God of gods, and shall prosper till the wrath has been accomplished; for what has been determined shall be done. ³⁷ He shall regard neither the God of his fathers nor the desire of women, nor regard any god; for he shall exalt himself above them all. *Daniel 11:36-37*

…⁴ who opposes and exalts himself above all that is called God or that is worshiped, so that he sits as God in the temple of God, showing himself that he is God. *2 Thessalonians 2:4*

²⁴ For false Christs and false prophets will rise and show great signs and wonders to deceive, if possible, even the elect. *Matthew 24:24*

³ Let no one deceive you by any means; for that Day will not come unless the falling away comes first, and the man of sin is revealed, the son of perdition… *2 Thessalonians 2:3*

POWER IN THE NAME OF JESUS

[12] Nor is there salvation in any other, for there is no other name under heaven given among men by which we must be saved. *Acts 4:12*

...[10] that at the name of Jesus every knee should bow, of those in heaven, and of those on earth, and of those under the earth... *Philippians 2:10*

[12] Most assuredly, I say to you, he who believes in Me, the works that I do he will do also; and greater works than these he will do, because I go to My Father. [13] And whatever you ask in My name, that I will do, that the Father may be glorified in the Son. [14] If you ask anything in My name, I will do it. *John 14:12-14*

[17] Then the seventy returned with joy, saying, "Lord, even the demons are subject to us in Your name." *Luke 10:17*

[13] For whoever calls on the name of the LORD shall be saved. *Romans 10:13*

[17] And these signs will follow those who believe: In My name they will cast out demons; they will speak with new tongues; [18] they will take up serpents; and if they drink anything deadly, it will by no means hurt them; they will lay hands on the sick, and they will recover." *Mark 16:17-18*

[9] For He spoke, and it was done; he commanded, and it stood fast. *Psalm 33:9*

[6] Inasmuch as there is none like You, O LORD (You are great, and Your name is great in might)... *Jeremiah 10:6*

NEW RELIGION DENIES CHRIST

[22] Who is a liar but he who denies that Jesus is the Christ? He is antichrist who denies the Father and the Son. *1 John 2:22*

...[3] and every spirit that does not confess that Jesus Christ has come in the flesh is not of God. And this is the spirit of the Antichrist, which you have heard was coming, and is now already in the world. *1 John 4:3*

[7] For many deceivers have gone out into the world who do not confess Jesus Christ as coming in the flesh. This is a deceiver and an antichrist. *2 John 1:7*

ISAAC AND ISHMAEL'S COMMON ROOT

[12] ...Whatever Sarah says to you, do as she tells you, for through Isaac shall your offspring be named. [13] And I will make a nation of the son of the slave woman also, because he (Ishmael) is your offspring. *Genesis 21:12-13*

[20] And God was with the boy (Ishmael), and he grew up. *Genesis 21:20*

FOUNDATIONS OF CHRISTIANITY

16 And I will pray the Father, and He will give you another Helper, that He may abide with you forever— 17 the Spirit of truth, whom the world cannot receive, because it neither sees Him nor knows Him; but you know Him, for He dwells with you and will be in you. *John 14:16-17*

26 But when the Helper comes, whom I shall send to you from the Father, the Spirit of truth who proceeds from the Father, He will testify of Me. *John 15:26*

12 "I still have many things to say to you, but you cannot bear them now. 13 However, when He, the Spirit of truth, has come, He will guide you into all truth; for He will not speak on His own authority, but whatever He hears He will speak; and He will tell you things to come. 14 He will glorify Me, for He will take of what is Mine and declare it to you. 15 All things that the Father has are Mine. Therefore, I said that He will take of Mine and declare it to you. *John 16:12-15*

26 These things I have written to you concerning those who try to deceive you. 27 But the anointing which you have received from Him abides in you, and you do not need that anyone teach you; but as the same anointing teaches you concerning all things, and is true, and is not a lie, and just as it has taught you, you will abide in Him. *1 John 2:26-27*

3 You shall have no other gods before Me. *Exodus 20:3*

5 For there is one God and one Mediator between God and men, the Man Christ Jesus, 6 who gave Himself a ransom for all, to be testified in due time… *1 Timothy 2:5-6*

6 For I am the LORD, I do not change… *Malachi 3:6*

6 Jesus said to him, "I am the way, the truth, and the life. No one comes to the Father except through Me." *John 14:6*

16 For God so loved the world that He gave His only begotten Son, that whoever believes in Him should not perish but have everlasting life. *John 3:16*

14 Do not be unequally yoked together with unbelievers. For what fellowship has righteousness with lawlessness? And what communion has light with darkness? 15 And what accord has Christ with Belial? Or what part has a believer with an unbeliever? 16 And what agreement has the temple of God with idols? For you are the temple of the living God. As God has said: "I will dwell in them and walk among them. I will be their God, and they shall be My people." 17 Therefore "Come out from among them and be separate, says the Lord. Do not touch what

is unclean, and I will receive you." ¹⁸ "I will be a Father to you, and you shall be My sons and daughters, says the LORD Almighty." *2 Corinthians 6:14-18*

FALSE DOCTRINES
³ For the time will come when they will not endure sound doctrine, but according to their own desires, because they have itching ears, they will heap up for themselves teachers; ⁴ and they will turn their ears away from the truth, and be turned aside to fables. ⁵ But you be watchful in all things, endure afflictions, do the work of an evangelist, fulfill your ministry. *2 Timothy 4:3-5*

¹ But there were also false prophets among the people, even as there will be false teachers among you, who will secretly bring in destructive heresies, even denying the Lord who bought them, and bring on themselves swift destruction. *2 Peter 2:1*

⁸ But even if we, or an angel from heaven, preach any other gospel to you than what we have preached to you, let him be accursed. ⁹ As we have said before, so now I say again, if anyone preaches any other gospel to you than what you have received, let him be accursed. *Galatians 1:8-9*

NAMES
²Now the names of the twelve apostles are these; The first, Simon, who is called Peter, and Andrew his brother; James the son of Zebedee, and John his brother; ³Philip, and Bartholomew; Thomas, and Matthew the publican; James the son of Alphaeus, and Lebbaeus, whose surname was Thaddaeus; ⁴Simon the Canaanite, and Judas Iscariot, who also betrayed him. *Matthew 10:2-4*

¹³ Then Moses said to God, "Indeed, when I come to the children of Israel and say to them, 'The God of your fathers has sent me to you,' and they say to me, 'What is His name?' what shall I say to them?" ¹⁴ And God said to Moses, "I AM WHO I AM." And He said, "Thus you shall say to the children of Israel, 'I AM has sent me to you.'" *Exodus 3:13-14*

COMMIT TO A POSITION
¹⁵ I know your works, that you are neither cold nor hot. I could wish you were cold or hot. ¹⁶ So then, because you are lukewarm, and neither cold nor hot, I will vomit you out of My mouth. *Revelation 3:15-16*

WARNING
¹⁸ For I testify to everyone who hears the words of the prophecy of this book: If anyone adds to these things, God will add to him the plagues that are written in this book; ¹⁹ and if anyone takes away from the words of the book of this prophecy, God shall take away his part from the Book of Life, from the holy city, and from the things which are written in this book. *Revelation 22:18-19*

NOTES

"God will always bring the right people into your life, but you have to let the wrong people walk away." — Joel Osteen

WEEK 16: THE WAR OF EZEKIEL

Opening Prayer: Lord, we ask that You send Your Holy Spirit to us to guide us in the teaching and understanding of Your word that we may obtain a better understanding of the prophetic events surrounding us now and waiting for us in the future. Bless our fellowship in Your word that it may be fruitful and draw us into a deeper relationship both with You and those around us. Use us as Your vessels that through us, we may reflect Your glory to all whom we encounter. Illuminate our hearts and minds so that we may boldly shine the brightness of Your light everywhere we go and that we may be beacons of Your hope in a darkened world. In Jesus name we pray, Amen.

Ice Breaker: God tells us to pray for our enemies. What do you think the cat and dog in the pictures below would pray for each other? Go around the room and have each person suggest what you think they might be praying for each other right now.

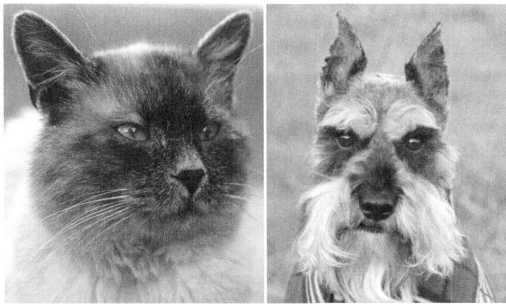

Photos courtesy of Bushko (Cat) and Bryan Hanson (Dog) at www.morguefile.com

 **Focus:** No victory can be won without God's blessing, but no victory can be lost without God's permission.

"Do not waste time bothering whether you 'love' your neighbor; act as if you did." — C.S. Lewis

ARE WE THE TERMINAL GENERATION?

Word of the Week

> ^{25} By the God of your father who will help you, and by the Almighty who will bless you with blessings of heaven above, blessings of the **deep** that lies beneath, blessings of the breasts and of the womb.
>
> *Genesis 49:25*

DEEP: A blessing is a valuable gift that can assume many forms. In Genesis 49:25, the word "deep" is translated from the original Hebrew word "tehowm" (pronounced teh-home') and refers to subterranean waters such as the abyss of an ocean. Clarifying the location of the blessing are the added words "that lies beneath". To "lie beneath" an ocean refers to a valuable blessing which resides under the floor of the ocean. Primarily, the reference is associated with undersea oil repositories which are presumed to be located in an area near Israel.

Lesson: In the latter days when Israel is once again a nation, Israel will be invaded by a coalition of nations bent on Israel's complete and utter destruction. This failed attempt at total annihilation is referred to as the War of Ezekiel and happens at a time when Israel is perceived to be dwelling in safety near the return of Christ:

^{14} Therefore, son of man, prophesy and say to Gog, "Thus says the Lord GOD: On that day **when My people Israel dwell safely**, will you not know it? ^{15} Then **you will come from your place out of the far north**, you and many peoples with you, all of them riding on horses, a great company and **a mighty army**. ^{16} You will come up **against My people Israel** like a cloud, to cover the land. **It will be in the latter days** that I will bring you against My land, so that the nations may know Me, when I am hallowed in you, O Gog, before their eyes." *Ezekiel 38:14-16*

"Coming from the far north" implies the coalition is led by Russia. Directions are always given from Israel's point of reference. Geographically, the "far north" of Israel is Russia. Enemies of Israel involved in the joint attack led by Russia (Gog, Magog, Rosh, Meshech and Tubal) are Iran, Iraq and Afghanistan (Persia), Ethiopia and Sudan (Ethiopia), Libya (Libya), Eastern Europe (Gomer), Southeastern Europe and Turkey (Togarmah), and various other allies of Russia ("many people are with you").

> ¹ Now the word of the LORD came to me, saying, ² "Son of man, set your face against **Gog**, of the land of **Magog**, the prince of **Rosh, Meshech, and Tubal**, and prophesy against him, ³ and say, 'Thus says the Lord GOD: "Behold, I am against you, O Gog, the prince of Rosh, Meshech, and Tubal. ⁴ I will turn you around, put hooks into your jaws, and lead you out, with all your army, horses, and horsemen, all splendidly clothed, a great company with bucklers and shields, all of them handling swords. ⁵ **Persia, Ethiopia, and Libya** are with them, all of them with shield and helmet; ⁶ **Gomer** and all its troops; the house of **Togarmah** from the far north and all its troops—**many people are with you**. ⁷ "Prepare yourself and be ready, you and all your companies that are gathered about you; and be a guard for them. *Ezekiel 38:1-7*

Although a large confederacy of nations will come against Israel, not all nations will partake in the carnage, therefore this cannot be the War of Armageddon. Non-participatory nations in the military conflict offer only verbal, politically correct condemnations of the aggression without coming to Israel's aid during the attack or offering any tangible form of assistance:

> ¹³ **Sheba, Dedan, the merchants of Tarshish**, and **all their young lions will say to you**, '**Have you come to take plunder**? Have you gathered your army **to take booty, to carry away silver and gold**, to take away livestock and goods, to take great plunder?'" *Ezekiel 38:13*

Abraham's grandsons are Sheba and Dedan:

> ¹ **Abraham again took a wife**, and her name was **Keturah**. ² And **she bore him** Zimran, **Jokshan**, Medan, Midian, Ishbak, and Shuah. ³ **Jokshan begot Sheba and Dedan.** *Genesis 25:1-3*

Sharing in Abraham's direct lineage, Sheba and Dedan became the fathers of what is now Saudi Arabia. Saudi Arabia is known to be a more moderate Muslim country whose position lines up with that of a country which would not participate in such a war on Israel. Tarshish and her young lions refers to Great Britain, Canada, Australia, New Zealand, South Africa and the United States. As the United States is a committed and long-standing friend to Israel, it is curious that the United States does not offer active defensive aid to Israel. It is possible that at the time of the invasion, we either have a leader who has turned his (or her) back on Israel, the battle will be so swift that there is no time to respond, or a catastrophic event has happened within the United States rendering us incapable of coming to Israel's defense.

With Russia leading the coalition of nations against Israel, religious fervor is an unlikely motivation for the attack. For much of the twentieth century, Russia actively repressed all forms of religion. A clue to the reason for the invasion can be found in the weak response to the aggression issued by onlooking nations. In their condemnation of the action taken against Israel, observing countries accuse the coalition of invading Israel in search of wealth. While Israel is a prosperous nation, her wealth to date has been nothing worth fighting over. For many years, Israel was thought to be a land devoid of any significant oil repositories. In recent years though, a wealth of underground oil reserves has been identified in the location known as Joseph's head. Amazingly, this is the exact location that the Bible spelled out so many centuries ago:

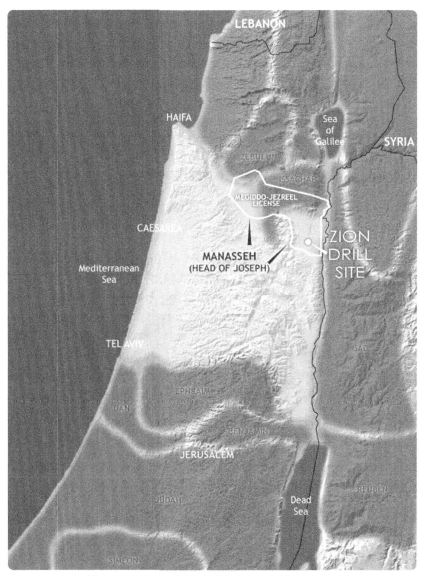

Map courtesy of Zion Oil at www.zionoil.com

> ²⁵ By the God of your father who will help you, and by the Almighty who will bless you with blessings of heaven above, **blessings of the deep that lies beneath**, blessings of the breasts and of the womb. ²⁶ The blessings of your father have excelled the blessings of my ancestors, up to the utmost bound of the everlasting hills. **They shall be on the head of Joseph**, and **on the crown of the head** of him who was separate from his brothers. *Genesis 49:25-26*

> ¹³ And of Joseph he said: "**Blessed** of the LORD **is his land**, with the precious things of heaven, with the dew, and **the deep lying beneath**, ¹⁴ with the precious fruits of the sun, with the precious produce of the months, ¹⁵ with the best things of the ancient mountains, with the precious things of the everlasting hills, ¹⁶ **with the precious things of the earth** and its fullness, and the favor of Him who dwelt in the bush. **Let the blessing come 'on the head of Joseph**, and **on the crown of the head** of him who was separate from his brothers.'" *Deuteronomy 33:13-16*

If these findings are verifiably massive, it could be enough to motivate other countries to attempt to conquer Israel to claim ownership of the oil rights.

Amid impossible odds and without international support, God grants Israel victory over the aggressors:

> ²¹ I will call for **a sword against Gog throughout all My mountains**," says the Lord GOD. "Every man's sword will be against his brother. ²² And **I will bring him to judgment** with pestilence and bloodshed; I will rain down on him, on his troops, and on the many peoples who are with him, flooding rain, great hailstones, fire, and brimstone. ²³ Thus **I will magnify Myself** and sanctify Myself, and I will be known in the eyes of many nations. Then **they shall know that I am the LORD**." *Ezekiel 38:18-23*

In sweeping, divine style, the victory granted to Israel against her enemies is so massively devastating that it takes seven months to bury the bodies of her enemies during the clean-up process. Search parties are organized and people are employed for the sole task of disposing of the dead bodies:

> ¹¹ "It will come to pass in that day that I will give Gog a burial place there in Israel, the valley of those who pass by east of the sea; and it will obstruct travelers, because there they will bury Gog and all his multitude. Therefore, they will call it the Valley of Hamon

Gog. ¹² For **seven months the house of Israel will be burying them**, in order to cleanse the land. ¹³ Indeed all the people of the land will be burying, and they will gain renown for it on the day that I am glorified," says the Lord GOD. ¹⁴ "They will set apart **men regularly employed, with the help of a search party, to pass through the land and bury those bodies remaining on the ground**, in order to cleanse it. At the end of seven months they will make a search. ¹⁵ The search party will pass through the land; and when anyone sees a man's bone, he shall set up a marker by it, till the buriers have buried it in the Valley of Hamon Gog. ¹⁶ The name of the city will also be Hamonah. Thus, they shall cleanse the land." *Ezekiel 39:11-16*

Classical Judaism holds that to properly honor the dead, a corpse may not be autopsied or embalmed.

The immense damage from the war is so extensive that it takes seven years to handle the aftereffects and dispose of all the leftover weapons.

> ⁹ "Then **those who dwell in the cities of Israel will go out** and set on fire and **burn the weapons**, both the shields and bucklers, the bows and arrows, the javelins and spears; and they will make fires with them **for seven years**. *Ezekiel 39:9*

In any war, countries set out to win the war using the most advanced form of weaponry available to them at that time. Since this war is yet to happen at some point in the future, the means of destruction employed will include, at a minimum, forms of known modern weaponry from existing arsenals. Ezekiel 39 describes the weaponry belonging to the enemy coalition as "bows and arrows". The "bows and arrows" that are used have the ability to deliver "fire" to faraway coastlands:

> ¹ "And you, son of man, **prophesy against Gog**, and say, 'Thus says the Lord GOD: "Behold, I am against you, O Gog, the prince of Rosh, Meshech, and Tubal; ² and I will turn you around and lead you on, bringing you up from the far north, and bring you against **the mountains of Israel**. ³ Then **I will knock the bow out of your left hand**, and **cause the arrows to fall out of your right**

hand. ⁴You shall fall upon the mountains of Israel, you and all your troops and the peoples who are with you; I will give you to birds of prey of every sort and to the beasts of the field to be devoured. ⁵You shall fall on the open field; for I have spoken," says the Lord GOD. ⁶"And **I will send fire on Magog and on those who live in security in the coastlands**. Then they shall know that I am the LORD. ⁷So I will make My holy name known in the midst of My people Israel, and I will not let them profane My holy name anymore. Then the nations shall know that I am the LORD, the Holy One in Israel. *Ezekiel 39:1-7*

References to fire and brimstone falling from heaven after traveling long distances imply this war could be a nuclear war that happens on the mountains outside of Israel. The force of the explosion causes massive earthquakes leveling some mountains and all walls:

> ¹⁸"And it will come to pass at the same time, when Gog comes against the land of Israel," says the Lord GOD, "that My fury will show in My face. ¹⁹For in My jealousy and **in the fire of My wrath** I have spoken: 'Surely in that day there shall be a great **earthquake in the land of Israel**, ²⁰so that the fish of the sea, the birds of the heavens, the beasts of the field, all creeping things that creep on the earth, and all men who are on the face of the earth shall shake at My presence. The **mountains shall be thrown down**, the steep places shall fall, and **every wall shall fall** to the ground.' ²¹I will call for **a sword against Gog throughout all My mountains**," says the Lord GOD. "Every man's sword will be against his brother. ²²And I will bring him to judgment with pestilence and bloodshed; **I will rain down on him**, on his troops, and on the many peoples who are with him, flooding rain, great hailstones, **fire, and brimstone**. ²³Thus, I will magnify Myself and sanctify Myself, and I will be known in the eyes of many nations. Then, they shall know that I am the LORD." *Ezekiel 38:18-23*

When viewed from the perspective of ancient man, bows and arrows mentioned in Ezekiel 39 would be an apt description for modern-day missiles. The effect of the weapons described in Ezekiel 38 is that of being able to level mountains and rain down fire from the sky. Again, this is a match for missile capabilities. Literal bows and arrows do not possess the qualities described; therefore, they must be a euphemism for another type of weapon. Images of airborne bombs bear striking resemblances to arrows used in archery as they are released from bows as can be seen in these pictures:

Photo of missile courtesy of Kenn W. Kiser, a.k.a. "Click", at www.morguefile.com

Photo of archery arrows courtesy of earl53 at www.morguefile.com

Prospects of a nuclear war would also account for the extreme devastation brought about by this conflict. A nuclear explosion could easily release enough power to level mountains. The force from the extended blast zone could collapse walls in nearby towns as foretold in the passages of Ezekiel. Scripture connects the fire that falls with an accompanying earthquake. According to the U.S. Geological Survey, explosions from nuclear bombs can cause earthquakes. Adding to the destructiveness of the earthquake, rock from the surrounding mountain ranges in the region could amplify the seismic waves resulting in a more forceful effect from the earthquake. If, indeed, this is a nuclear war, employing specially trained people to properly handle radioactive remains would be a necessity, not a luxury. Scripture states that the weapons are burned after the war. Chemical weapons can be burned as a method of destruction, but they can also be rendered chemically inert as an alternate means to neutralize them. Nuclear weapons do not enjoy as many options for their disposal. According to James Conca, a scientist specializing in the disposal of nuclear waste and a contributing writer for *Forbes.com*:

> "There aren't many instances where turning weapons into plowshares has worked very well, but nuclear is one of those few. The only ways to get rid of something like Pu is to let it decay away over thousands of years, or blend it with other materials like U, burn it in a nuclear reactor and make energy out of it."

Essentially, weapons grade plutonium can be combined with uranium to convert it to fuel grade plutonium which can then be used as a source of fuel in a nuclear reactor. Israel has long been thought to possess a nuclear arsenal, although state policy is reluctant to discuss their nuclear capabilities in an international arena.

The complete devastation ensuing from this war could present possibilities for the rebuilding of the third temple during the post-war recovery period. Theoretically, if the Al Aqsa Mosque and Dome of the Rock were somehow to be destroyed during this war, it would create open real estate on the Temple Mount precisely where the next temple would need to be built. After an attack such as the one described in the War of Ezekiel, Israel would not be concerned about managing political ties to the Arab-Muslim nations and might disregard the need to seek anyone's consent to rebuild the third temple on top of previously disputed territory. Reeling from the massive losses received during the war, the Arab nations would be in no position to contest the decision. Most likely, Israel would simply start building the temple wherever they choose. Without contest from the Arab world regarding their claim to the Temple Mount area, construction could begin immediately during the post-war reconstruction process.

Interestingly, the post-war recovery period is defined as taking seven years to accomplish. Seven years is also the exact length of time for the entire Tribulation. It is a possibility that the War of Ezekiel is the war that initiates the Tribulation. To date, Israel has been reluctant to sign any peace treaties with her enemies. Many US Presidents and world political leaders have attempted to broker a peace deal, but to no avail. Without significant motivation to sign a peace treaty, there is no benefitting incentive for Israel to change her current position. A surprise attack on Israel leading to a devastating war could be the instigating reason why Israel would finally be willing to sign a peace treaty which, to this point, has remained elusive. Due to the massive devastation the enemy experiences from this war, the Muslim world would also have proper motivation to sign their end of the peace treaty. With tensions high and an active situation to manage, the Antichrist would have the tools necessary to step in and broker a peace treaty between Israel and her Arab neighbors. The peace treaty may give Israel the illusion of peace and security, but it is only the beginning of the final countdown to Christ's return.

Talk It Out

1. Why do you think the United States does not come to Israel's aid when Israel is attacked? What do you think of the response the international community gives to the invasion?

2. What reason do you think seems most viable for why the confederation of nations attacks Israel (i.e. religion, oil, wealth, Islamic anger over the peace treaty or sanctions, etc.)?

3. Do you think the War of Ezekiel could involve nuclear weapons or will it be a more conventional war? What about the use of chemical weapons?

4. If the Dome of the Rock and Al Aqsa Mosque were to be destroyed by bombing during the war, do you think Israel would have any reservations about building the third temple on whatever location they choose after the conflict?

5. At what point do you think the War of Ezekiel might occur (i.e. before the Tribulation, at the beginning of the Tribulation, in the middle of the Tribulation or at the end of the Tribulation)?

6. What motivating reason could Israel have to sign a peace treaty?

Ideas for the Week:

- ✓ Take a Krav Maga class (Israeli self-defense).
- ✓ Make an emergency plan for your family outlining where to go in case of a disaster and how to make contact with each other.
- ✓ Catalog your possessions as a record of ownership in case you ever need to make a catastrophic insurance claim.
- ✓ Purchase a supply of Potassium Iodide tablets (IOSAT brand name) to have on hand in case of unexpected radiological exposure.

Closing Prayer

NOTE: Add names and individual personal prayer requests to the space provided below before closing in prayer.

Lord, we thank You for our time together today to grow deeper in our walk with You and fellowship with each other. As we close today, we lift up: _____

_____
_____
_____
_____
_____
_____
_____
_____

Father, the devastation war brings is immense and the prospect of war strikes fear into the hearts of men. We ask Your hand of protection around all of Your children that those in Your kingdom will be protected from the ravages of violence that threaten our security. Surround us with Your protective shield and covering of safety just as You did for the Israelites in Egypt. We thank You for Your protection and rest securely in Your love for us. In Jesus' name we pray, Amen.

ARE WE THE TERMINAL GENERATION?

SUPPORTING SCRIPTURES

ENEMIES OF ISRAEL

¹ Now the word of the LORD came to me, saying, ² "Son of man, set your face against Gog, of the land of Magog, the prince of Rosh, Meshech, and Tubal, and prophesy against him, ³ and say, 'Thus says the Lord GOD: "Behold, I am against you, O Gog, the prince of Rosh, Meshech, and Tubal. ⁴ I will turn you around, put hooks into your jaws, and lead you out, with all your army, horses, and horsemen, all splendidly clothed, a great company with bucklers and shields, all of them handling swords. ⁵ Persia, Ethiopia, and Libya are with them, all of them with shield and helmet; ⁶ Gomer and all its troops; the house of Togarmah from the far north and all its troops—many people are with you. ⁷ "Prepare yourself and be ready, you and all your companies that are gathered about you; and be a guard for them. *Ezekiel 38:1-7*

OIL

²⁵ By the God of your father who will help you, and by the Almighty who will bless you with blessings of heaven above, blessings of the deep that lies beneath, blessings of the breasts and of the womb. ²⁶ The blessings of your father have excelled the blessings of my ancestors, up to the utmost bound of the everlasting hills. They shall be on the head of Joseph, and on the crown of the head of him who was separate from his brothers. *Genesis 49:25-26*

¹³ And of Joseph he said: "Blessed of the LORD is his land, with the precious things of heaven, with the dew, and the deep lying beneath, ¹⁴ with the precious fruits of the sun, with the precious produce of the months, ¹⁵ with the best things of the ancient mountains, with the precious things of the everlasting hills, ¹⁶ with the precious things of the earth and its fullness, and the favor of Him who dwelt in the bush. Let the blessing come 'on the head of Joseph, and on the crown of the head of him who was separate from his brothers." *Deuteronomy 33:13-16*

TIMING

⁸ After many days you will be visited. In the latter years you will come into the land of those brought back from the sword and gathered from many people on the mountains of Israel, which had long been desolate; they were brought out of the nations, and now all of them dwell safely. ⁹ You will ascend, coming like a storm, covering the land like a cloud, you and all your troops and many peoples with you." ¹⁰ 'Thus says the Lord GOD: "On that day it shall come to pass that thoughts will arise in your mind, and you will make an evil plan: ¹¹ You will say, 'I will go up against a land of unwalled villages; I will go to a peaceful people, who dwell safely, all of them dwelling without walls, and having neither bars nor gates'— ¹² to take plunder and to take booty, to stretch out your hand against the waste places that are again inhabited, and against a people gathered from the

nations, who have acquired livestock and goods, who dwell in the midst of the land. *Ezekiel 38:8-12*

[14] Therefore, son of man, prophesy and say to Gog, "Thus says the Lord GOD: On that day when My people Israel dwell safely, will you not know it? [15] Then you will come from your place out of the far north, you and many peoples with you, all of them riding on horses, a great company and a mighty army. [16] You will come up against My people Israel like a cloud, to cover the land. It will be in the latter days that I will bring you against My land, so that the nations may know Me, when I am hallowed in you, O Gog, before their eyes." [17] Thus says the Lord GOD: "Are you he of whom I have spoken in former days by My servants the prophets of Israel, who prophesied for years in those days that I would bring you against them? *Ezekiel 38:14-17*

RESPONSE OF NATIONS
[13] Sheba, Dedan, the merchants of Tarshish, and all their young lions will say to you, 'Have you come to take plunder? Have you gathered your army to take booty, to carry away silver and gold, to take away livestock and goods, to take great plunder?' *Ezekiel 38:13*

[1] Abraham again took a wife, and her name was Keturah. [2] And she bore him Zimran, Jokshan, Medan, Midian, Ishbak, and Shuah. [3] Jokshan begot Sheba and Dedan. *Genesis 25:1-3*

FIRE AND EARTHQUAKE
[18] "And it will come to pass at the same time, when Gog comes against the land of Israel," says the Lord GOD, "that My fury will show in My face. [19] For in My jealousy and in the fire of My wrath I have spoken: 'Surely in that day there shall be a great earthquake in the land of Israel, [20] so that the fish of the sea, the birds of the heavens, the beasts of the field, all creeping things that creep on the earth, and all men who are on the face of the earth shall shake at My presence. The mountains shall be thrown down, the steep places shall fall, and every wall shall fall to the ground.' [21] I will call for a sword against Gog throughout all My mountains," says the Lord GOD. "Every man's sword will be against his brother. [22] And I will bring him to judgment with pestilence and bloodshed; I will rain down on him, on his troops, and on the many peoples who are with him, flooding rain, great hailstones, fire, and brimstone. [23] Thus I will magnify Myself and sanctify Myself, and I will be known in the eyes of many nations. Then, they shall know that I am the LORD." *Ezekiel 38:18-23*

GOD DESTROYS ISRAEL'S ENEMIES
[1] "And you, son of man, prophesy against Gog, and say, 'Thus says the Lord GOD: "Behold, I am against you, O Gog, the prince of Rosh, Meshech, and Tubal;

² and I will turn you around and lead you on, bringing you up from the far north, and bring you against the mountains of Israel. ³ Then I will knock the bow out of your left hand, and cause the arrows to fall out of your right hand. ⁴ You shall fall upon the mountains of Israel, you and all your troops and the peoples who are with you; I will give you to birds of prey of every sort and to the beasts of the field to be devoured. ⁵ You shall fall on the open field; for I have spoken," says the Lord GOD. ⁶ "And I will send fire on Magog and on those who live in security in the coastlands. Then they shall know that I am the LORD. ⁷ So I will make My holy name known in the midst of My people Israel, and I will not let them profane My holy name anymore. Then the nations shall know that I am the LORD, the Holy One in Israel. *Ezekiel 39:1-7*

POST-WAR RECOVERY
⁹ "Then those who dwell in the cities of Israel will go out and set on fire and burn the weapons, both the shields and bucklers, the bows and arrows, the javelins and spears; and they will make fires with them for seven years. ¹⁰ They will not take wood from the field nor cut down any from the forests, because they will make fires with the weapons; and they will plunder those who plundered them, and pillage those who pillaged them," says the Lord GOD. *Ezekiel 39:9-10*

¹¹ "It will come to pass in that day that I will give Gog a burial place there in Israel, the valley of those who pass by east of the sea; and it will obstruct travelers, because there they will bury Gog and all his multitude. Therefore, they will call it the Valley of Hamon Gog. ¹² For seven months the house of Israel will be burying them, in order to cleanse the land. ¹³ Indeed all the people of the land will be burying, and they will gain renown for it on the day that I am glorified," says the Lord GOD. ¹⁴ "They will set apart men regularly employed, with the help of a search party, to pass through the land and bury those bodies remaining on the ground, in order to cleanse it. At the end of seven months they will make a search. ¹⁵ The search party will pass through the land; and when anyone sees a man's bone, he shall set up a marker by it, till the buriers have buried it in the Valley of Hamon Gog. ¹⁶ The name of the city will also be Hamonah. Thus, they shall cleanse the land." *Ezekiel 39:11-16*

²¹ "I will set My glory among the nations; all the nations shall see My judgment which I have executed, and My hand which I have laid on them. ²² So the house of Israel shall know that I am the LORD their God from that day forward. *Ezekiel 39:21-22*

NOTES

"I tremble for my country when I reflect that God is just; that His justice cannot sleep forever." — Thomas Jefferson

ARE WE THE TERMINAL GENERATION?
WEEK 17: THE WAR IN HEAVEN

Opening Prayer: Lord, we ask that You send Your Holy Spirit to us to guide us in the teaching and understanding of Your word that we may obtain a better understanding of the prophetic events surrounding us now and waiting for us in the future. Bless our fellowship in Your word that it may be fruitful and draw us into a deeper relationship both with You and those around us. Use us as Your vessels that through us, we may reflect Your glory to all whom we encounter. Illuminate our hearts and minds so that we may boldly shine the brightness of Your light everywhere we go and that we may be beacons of Your hope in a darkened world. In Jesus name we pray, Amen.

Ice Breaker: Below are quotes from famous people about war. Which one is your favorite? Share your selection with the group and explain what specifically appeals to you about the quote.

"The two most powerful warriors are patience and time." *Leo Tolstoy*

"Sometimes by losing a battle you find a new way to win the war." *Donald Trump*

"War is peace. Freedom is slavery. Ignorance is strength." *George Orwell*

"I must study politics and war that my sons may have liberty to study philosophy and mathematics." *John Adams*

"To be prepared for war is one of the most effective means of preserving peace." *George Washington*

"Know thy self, know thy enemy. A thousand battles, a thousand victories." *Sun Tzu*

"Build me a son, O Lord, who will be strong enough to know when he is weak, and brave enough to face himself when he is afraid, one who will be proud and unbending in honest defeat, and humble and gentle in victory." *Douglas MacArthur*

"The art of war is simple enough. Find out where your enemy is. Get at him as soon as you can. Strike him as hard as you can, and keep moving on." *Ulysses S. Grant*

"To hold a pen is to be at war." *Voltaire*

Focus: God not only fights for you on earth, but in the heavens as well.

Word of the Week

> ⁸ Be sober, be vigilant; because your **adversary** the devil walks about like a roaring lion, seeking whom he may devour.
>
> *1 Peter 5:8*

ADVERSARY: Scripture describes Satan as our adversary. An adversary, from the Greek word "antidikos" (pronounced an-tid'-ee-kos), is an enemy. More than just an opponent, an enemy possesses hostility towards the object of its wrath and desires complete destruction of its target. Battles between enemies can be fought offensively or defensively. It is important to note that the devil goes on the offense. Not content to wait for the battle to come to him, Satan actively spends time on planet earth intently searching for his next targeted attack against opponents who have their guard down. He aggressively takes the war to our realm and prevails against those who unwittingly provide him with a strategic opportunity.

Lesson: In any war, victory is won by gaining ground. By forcing the enemy to lose enough ground, they eventually must declare defeat. When the War in Heaven occurs midway through the Tribulation, God gains the territory of the second heaven while Satan loses access to that realm and is relegated to only being able to occupy earth itself. Heavenly spaces are divided into three parts. There is the third heaven where God dwells, the second heaven which we refer to as outer space and the first heaven which is our earth's atmosphere. The third heaven is typically referred to as Paradise:

> ² I know a man in Christ who fourteen years ago—whether in the body I do not know, or whether out of the body I do not know, God knows—such a one **was caught up to the third heaven.** ³ And I know such a man—whether in the body or out of the body I do not know, God knows— ⁴ how **he was caught up into Paradise** and heard inexpressible words, which it is not lawful for a man to utter.
> *2 Corinthians 12:2-4*

In the beginning, when Satan was still in God's good graces, Satan had full reign of all three heavens. When Satan and his followers were kicked out of heaven after leading the initial rebellion against God, it was the third heaven, or God's dwelling place, from which they were removed. From that point forward, Satan and his forces occupied the first and second heavens while roaming the earth at will:

> ⁷And the LORD said to Satan, "From where do you come?" So, **Satan answered** the LORD and said, "From going to and fro **on the earth, and from walking back and forth on it**." *Job 1:7*

> ⁸Be sober, be vigilant; because your adversary **the devil walks about** like a roaring lion, seeking whom he may devour. *1 Peter 5:8*

At the midpoint of the Tribulation, an angelic battle referred to as the War in Heaven occurs that results in Satan and his followers losing access to the second heaven as well:

> ⁷And **war broke out in heaven**: Michael and his angels fought with the dragon; and the dragon and his angels fought, ⁸but **they did not prevail, nor was a place found for them in heaven any longer**. ⁹So the great dragon was cast out, that serpent of old, called the Devil and **Satan**, who deceives the whole world; he **was cast to the earth, and his angels were cast out with him**... ¹²Therefore rejoice, O heavens, and you who dwell in them! **Woe to the inhabitants of the earth** and the sea! For **the devil has come down to you, having great wrath**, because he knows that he has a short time." *Revelation 12:7-9,12*

With the triumphant victory led by the archangel Michael and his angelic army against Satan and his minions, Satan loses even more ground and is relegated to earth for the last three-and-a-half years of the Tribulation. Angered by his latest loss of territory and knowing that his time is growing short, Satan's vengeance against God's people takes on new dimensions. Confined to earth, Satan renews his vigorous efforts to destroy God's people by using the Antichrist to release his full wrath on believers during the second half of the Tribulation. The Antichrist is Satan's most valuable tool towards that end. There is biblical precedent that God allows Satan to use certain individuals for specific purposes:

> ...²⁰among whom are **Hymenaeus and Alexander**, whom **I have handed over to Satan** that they may learn not to blaspheme. *1 Timothy 1:20*

> ¹² And the **LORD said to Satan**, "Behold, **all that he has is in your power**; only do not lay a hand on his person." So, Satan went out from the presence of the LORD. *Job 1:12*

At some point, the Antichrist receives a fatal head wound. In imitation of Jesus, the world believes a miracle occurs when he is raised from the dead:

> ² ...The dragon (Satan) gave him (the Antichrist) his power, his throne, and great authority. ³ And I saw **one of his heads as if it had been mortally wounded, and his deadly wound was healed.** And all **the world** marveled and **followed the beast.** *Revelation 13:2-3*

God's word is clear that God and Jesus can both raise people from the dead:

> ²¹ For as **the Father raises the dead** and gives life to them, even so **the Son gives life to whom He will.** *John 5:21*

What is unclear since it is not stated outright in the Bible is whether Satan holds the power of resurrection as well. Scripture does mention that at one point, Satan had the ability to take lives:

> ¹⁴ ... that through death **He (Jesus) might destroy him who had the power of death, that is, the devil,** ¹⁵ and release those who through fear of death were all their lifetime subject to bondage. *Hebrews 2:14*

Satan also wields "all power" which implies the inclusion of the power of resurrection:

> ⁹ The coming of the lawless one is according to **the working of Satan, with all power**, signs, and lying wonders... *2 Thessalonians 2:9*

Without knowing if Satan specifically has the power to raise the Antichrist from the dead, one can only assume that when the Antichrist is resurrected, it is either a false miracle orchestrated by Satan to deceive the world, Satan actually does raise the Antichrist from the dead with or without God's permission, or Satan assumes demonic possession of the earthly body of the Antichrist. Regardless of how the Antichrist comes back to life, it is a perceived miracle that stuns the world and results in voluntary submission from the majority of humanity.

When the Tribulation intensifies at the midpoint, the Antichrist attacks Jerusalem with the intent to commit genocide against God's people.

> ²⁹ At the appointed time he (the Antichrist) shall return and go toward the south; but it shall not be like the former or the latter. ³⁰ For ships from Cyprus shall come against him; therefore, **he shall be grieved, and return in rage against the holy covenant, and do damage.** So, he shall return and show regard for those who forsake the holy covenant. ³¹ And **forces shall be mustered by him, and they shall defile the sanctuary fortress; then they shall take away the daily sacrifices, and place there the abomination of desolation.** ³² Those who do wickedly against the covenant he shall corrupt with flattery; but the people who know their God shall be strong, and carry out great exploits. ³³ And those of the people who understand shall instruct many; yet **for many days they shall fall by sword and flame, by captivity and plundering.** ³⁴ Now when they fall, they shall be aided with a little help; but many shall join with them by intrigue. ³⁵ And some of those of understanding shall fall, to refine them, purify them, and make them white, until the time of the end; because it is still for the appointed time. ³⁶ Then the king shall do according to his own will: he shall exalt and magnify himself above every god, shall speak blasphemies against the God of gods, and shall prosper till the wrath has been accomplished... *Daniel 11:29-36*

> ²⁰ But when you see **Jerusalem surrounded by armies**, then know that **its desolation is near**. *Luke 21:20*

Distinguished from the first half of the Tribulation, the second half of the Tribulation is referred to as the Great Tribulation and ushers in unprecedented hardship. The severity of the second half of the Tribulation is much worse than the first half of the Tribulation. At that time, two-thirds of Israel is murdered in the Antichrist's holocaust, but one-third, under divine protection, escapes the carnage:

> ⁷ ..."Strike the Shepherd, and **the sheep will be scattered**; then I will turn My hand against the little ones. ⁸ And **it shall come to pass in all the land**," says the LORD, "**That two-thirds in it shall be cut off and die**, but one-third shall be left in it: ⁹ **I will bring the one-third through the fire**, will refine them as silver is refined, and test them as gold is tested. They will call on My name, and I will answer them. I will say, 'This is My people'; and each one will say, 'The LORD is my God.' " *Zechariah 13:7-9*

A faithful remnant that survives is forced to flee on a moment's notice without so much as an opportunity to grab a coat. Pregnant women and young children will experience the most distress:

> [15] Therefore **when you see the 'abomination of desolation,'** spoken of by Daniel the prophet, standing in the holy place (whoever reads, let him understand), [16] then let those who are in Judea **flee to the mountains**. [17] Let him who is on the housetop not go down to take anything out of his house. [18] And let him who is in the field **not go back to get his clothes**. [19] But **woe to those who are pregnant and to those who are nursing babies** in those days! [20] And **pray that your flight may not be in winter or on the Sabbath**. [21] For **then** there will be <u>**great tribulation**</u>, such as has not been since the beginning of the world until this time, no, nor ever shall be. [22] And unless those days were shortened, no flesh would be saved; but for the elect's sake those days will be shortened. *Matthew 24:15-22*

Covering a broad period of time, the ongoing assault on Jerusalem is particularly brutal during the winter months when temperatures may be in the low forties with an occasional snow possible. Survivors without proper clothing at that time of year would be especially hard pressed to find safe shelter quickly. Jewish Sabbath requirements also limit the distance that can be traveled on the Sabbath which would slow the pace that an Orthodox Jew could travel if the flight were to happen on the Jewish Sabbath from sundown Friday through sundown Saturday.

The surviving one-third portion of God's chosen people are supernaturally protected during the hardship of the second half of the Tribulation, or the final three-and-a-half years. Bible scholar Jack Kelley of Grace Thru Faith Ministries points out that Petra is a strong probability for a place of refuge for the fleeing Jewish remnant to take shelter. Zechariah 13:7 refers to the fleeing Israeli remnant as "sheep". Bozrah is connected to being a pasture for a large number of sheep:

> ¹² I will surely assemble, O Jacob, all of thee; I will **surely gather the remnant of Israel**; I will put them together **as the sheep of Bozrah**, as the flock in the midst of their fold: they shall make great noise by reason of **the multitude of men**. *Micah 2:12 (KJV)*

The sheep of the passage are in an overcrowded penned pasture. Certainly, the assembly of that many people in such a confined, protected space would resemble many sheep trapped together in a pasture. Scripturally, Bozrah is modern day Jordan. Geographically, Petra, Jordan is the closest place for those in Jerusalem to flee for protection. An ancient city carved from rock, the single, narrow entrance to Petra is easily defensible. The ancient carved stone structure would strategically provide instant shelter for a large number of people. Certain geographical areas will escape the destruction of the Antichrist and Jordan (Moab) is among the safety zones:

> ⁴¹ He (the Antichrist) shall also enter the Glorious Land, and many countries shall be overthrown; but **these shall escape** from his hand: Edom, **Moab**, and the prominent people of Ammon. *Daniel 11:41*

Photo of Petra courtesy of mandit1990 at www.morguefile.com

According to Mr. Kelley, the woman of Revelation 12 is the believing remnant of Israel:

> ¹ Now a great sign appeared in heaven: **a woman** clothed with the sun, with the moon under her feet, and on her head a garland of twelve stars. ² Then being with child, she cried out in labor and in pain to give birth. ³ And another sign appeared in heaven: behold, a great, fiery red **dragon (Satan)** having seven heads and ten horns, and seven diadems on his heads. ⁴ His tail drew a third of the stars of heaven and threw them to the earth. And the dragon stood before the woman who was ready to give birth, to devour her Child as soon as it was born. ⁵ **She bore a male Child** who was to rule all nations with a rod of iron. And **her Child was caught up to God and His throne.** ⁶ Then **the woman fled into the wilderness**, where she has a place prepared by God, that they should feed her there one thousand two hundred and sixty days...¹³ Now when **the dragon saw that he had been cast to the earth (from the War in Heaven)**, he persecuted the woman who gave birth to the male Child. ¹⁴ But the woman was given two wings of a great eagle, that she might fly into the wilderness to her place, where she is nourished for a time and times and half a time, from the presence of the serpent. ¹⁵ So the serpent spewed water out of his mouth like a flood after the woman, that he might cause her to be carried away by the flood. ¹⁶ But the earth helped the woman, and the earth opened its mouth and swallowed up the flood which the dragon had spewed out of his mouth. ¹⁷ And **the dragon** was enraged with the woman, and he **went to make war with the rest of her offspring, who keep the commandments of God and have the testimony of Jesus Christ.** *Revelation 12:1-6,13-17*

The woman cannot be the Christian church because Satan "went to make war with the rest of her offspring, who keep the commandments of God and have the testimony of Jesus Christ". Jewish people do not accept that Jesus is the Messiah and that He has already revealed Himself. They still expect the Messiah, the Son of God, to arrive, for the first time, at a future date. Only Christians carry "the testimony of Jesus Christ". The Christian church is the offspring of the woman, not the woman herself. Gentiles are a branch grafted onto the Israelites, the mother:

> ¹⁷...and **you (Gentiles)**, being a wild olive tree, **were grafted in among them**, and with them became a partaker of the root and fatness of the olive tree... *Romans 11:17*

The wilderness that the woman escapes to is a match for the desert wilderness of Petra. Jesus also returns by way of Bozrah where Petra is located which would logically allow him to retrieve this surviving remnant at the end of the Tribulation as He retrieves other remnants of His people from other areas as well:

> ¹ Who is this who comes from Edom, with dyed garments **from Bozrah**, this One who is glorious in His apparel, traveling in the greatness of His strength?—"**I who speak in righteousness, mighty to save.**" *Isaiah 63:1*

> ¹¹ It shall come to pass in that day that **the Lord shall** set His hand again the second time to **recover the remnant of His people who are left**, **from Assyria** and **Egypt**, from **Pathros** and **Cush**, from **Elam** and **Shinar**, from **Hamath** and the **islands** of the sea. *Isaiah 11:11*

Meanwhile, back in Jerusalem, the Antichrist perpetuates what is known as the "abomination of desolation". This mid-Tribulation event is when the Antichrist enters the rebuilt temple, stops the daily temple sacrifice, sits down and declares that he is God:

> ²⁷ But **in the middle of the week** He (the Antichrist) shall bring an **end to sacrifice** and offering... *Daniel 9:27*

> ...⁴ who opposes and exalts himself (the Antichrist) above all that is called God or that is worshiped, so that **he sits as God in the temple of God, showing himself that he is God**. *2 Thessalonians 2:4*

Throughout the Bible, spirits of light and dark engage in an ongoing tug-of-war over the ultimate fate of mankind. This perpetual battle is fought in the heavenly realm with effects that spill over on the inhabitants of earth. Answers to Daniel's prayers were delayed on earth because the angel who was to minister to him was delayed by a demon in Persia (Iran). When the angel was done with Daniel, he was off to return to fight the demon in Persia, then off to Greece for yet another heavenly battle.

> ¹² Then he said to me, "Do not fear, Daniel, for **from the first day** that you set your heart to understand, and to humble yourself before your God, **your words were heard**; and I have come because of your words. ¹³ But the **prince of the kingdom of Persia withstood me twenty-one days**; and behold, Michael,

one of the chief princes, came to help me, for I had been left alone there with the kings of Persia...And **now I must return to fight with the prince of Persia**; and when I have gone forth, indeed the **prince of Greece will come**." *Daniel 10:12-13, 20*

In our own lives, struggles we face are often the result of a war being raged in the heavens, or spiritual realm. Angels referred to as Guardian Angels are given heavenly assignments to protect specific earthly entities:

> [11] For He shall **give His angels charge over you**, to keep you in all your ways. *Psalm 91:11*

Michael, the archangel of God, is assigned to protect Israel:

> [1] At that time **Michael** shall stand up, the great prince who **stands watch over the sons of your people**... *Daniel 12:1*

Whenever a demonic force seeks to attack someone or something belonging to God, angelic protectors leap to action and do battle. For our part in the battle, we are simply instructed to put on the armor of God:

> [11] Put on the whole armor of God...having **girded your waist with truth**, having put on the **breastplate of righteousness**, [15] and having **shod your feet** with the preparation of the **gospel of peace**; [16] above all, taking the **shield of faith**... [17] And take the **helmet of salvation**, and the **sword of the Spirit**, which is the word of God; [18] praying always with all prayer and supplication in the Spirit, being watchful to this end with all perseverance and supplication for all the saints— [19] and for me, that utterance may be given to me, that I may open my mouth boldly to make known the mystery of the gospel, [20] for which I am an ambassador in chains; that in it I may speak boldly, as I ought to speak. *Ephesians 6:11, 15-17*

Armed with God's armor, we are to live our lives as close as possible to Christ's perfect example while the real war, the spiritual war, wages on in the heavens. Satan's ultimate goal is to overthrow God, take over His kingdom and reign in His place. It is a hostile takeover of the first order. Toward that end, Satan is the puppet master who empowers the Antichrist causing him to attack Jerusalem and desecrate the newly built temple so that Israeli inhabitants must flee for their very lives. Without the influence of Satan's evil mastermind, the Antichrist would be powerless, wars would cease to exist, and peace would prevail. The War in Heaven puts everything one step closer to that final, coveted eventuality.

Talk It Out

1. When the devil and his followers are cast down to the earth in the middle of the Tribulation and no longer have access to the second and third heavens, do you think they will assume human form and blend in with society, enter into existing human bodies in mass acts of possession, maintain an invisible presence living among us or have physical bodies and resemble aliens in a "first contact" situation with mankind?

2. Do you think the Antichrist is evil before he takes the deadly wound to the head or becomes evil after the resurrection?

3. Do you think the Antichrist is literally resurrected from the dead after his deadly wound or does Satan perform a false miracle imitating Jesus's death and resurrection, but the Antichrist does not actually die? Is it possible that it is not a resurrection at all and that Satan demonically possesses the Antichrist's body after the spirit of the Antichrist leaves the body at the moment of the Antichrist's death? Does God give permission for the Antichrist to be raised from the dead or is Satan acting on his own?

4. Certain geographical areas are exempt from the destructive forces of the Antichrist during the second half of the Tribulation. How might God go about setting up such a scenario? Will those areas have effective armies against the Antichrist, a political peace treaty with the Antichrist or divine protection by God Himself?

5. When Satan cannot gain access to the elect who are under divine protection, he turns his attention to Christians (Revelation 12:17). What type of tactics do you think he might employ when he wages all-out war against Christians? Will those tactics be any different than what the devil has historically done to persecute and destroy Christians?

6. Is there a spiritual war raging in your life right now? How do you need God's angels to do spiritual battle on your behalf? How do you think your guardian angel is protecting you?

"Victory needs conflict as its preface."

— Charles Spurgeon

Ideas for the Week:

- ✓ Make a "go" bag for everyone in your family in case of the unexpected need to evacuate your home immediately and without notice.
- ✓ Watch *The War Room*, a movie about spiritual battles in the life of a Christian.
- ✓ Make a list of verses by subject that you can refer to whenever you need spiritual strength in a specific area.
- ✓ Keep a prayer journal to remind yourself of things God has done for you in the past to strengthen your faith in the present. An organized, topic-based prayer journal is *My Prayer Journal: Remembering God's Answers* by Christine Tate.

Closing Prayer

NOTE: Add names and individual personal prayer requests to the space provided below before closing in prayer.

Lord, we thank You for our time together today to grow deeper in our walk with You and fellowship with each other. As we close today, we lift up: _____

_____

_____

_____

_____

_____

Father, we humbly thank You for sending Your angels to protect us. We ask You to rip the veil that hides the seen from the unseen and help us to see the spiritual roots of the battles we fight on earth that we may prevail in Your name against the forces of darkness that encamp round about us. Rebuke for us any demons in our midst that might desire to bring us harm. Ever desiring to serve You better, we have faith that the victory will always be Yours. In Jesus' name we pray, Amen.

SUPPORTING SCRIPTURES

THIRD HEAVEN
^{2} I know a man in Christ who fourteen years ago—whether in the body I do not know, or whether out of the body I do not know, God knows—such a one was caught up to the third heaven. ^{3} And I know such a man—whether in the body or out of the body I do not know, God knows— ^{4} how he was caught up into Paradise and heard inexpressible words, which it is not lawful for a man to utter. *2 Corinthians 12:2-4*

WAR IN HEAVEN
^{7} And war broke out in heaven: Michael and his angels fought with the dragon; and the dragon and his angels fought, ^{8} but they did not prevail, nor was a place found for them in heaven any longer. ^{9} So the great dragon was cast out, that serpent of old, called the Devil and Satan, who deceives the whole world; he was cast to the earth, and his angels were cast out with him. ^{10} Then I heard a loud voice saying in heaven, "Now salvation, and strength, and the kingdom of our God, and the power of His Christ have come, for the accuser of our brethren, who accused them before our God day and night, has been cast down. ^{11} And they overcame him by the blood of the Lamb and by the word of their testimony, and they did not love their lives to the death. ^{12} Therefore rejoice, O heavens, and you who dwell in them! Woe to the inhabitants of the earth and the sea! For the devil has come down to you, having great wrath, because he knows that he has a short time." *Revelation 12:7-12*

THE DRAGON
^{2} He laid hold on the dragon...which is the Devil, and Satan... *Revelation 20:2*

^{2} ...according to the prince of the power of the air, the spirit who now works in the sons of disobedience... *Ephesians 2:1-2*

^{18} And He said to them, "I saw Satan fall like lightning from heaven." *Luke 10:18*

^{7} And the LORD said to Satan, "From where do you come?" So, Satan answered the LORD and said, "From going to and fro on the earth, and from walking back and forth on it." *Job 1:7*

^{8} Be sober, be vigilant; because your adversary the devil walks about like a roaring lion, seeking whom he may devour. *1 Peter 5:8*

DEATH AND RESURRECTION
^{2} ...The dragon gave him his power, his throne, and great authority. ^{3} And I saw one of his heads as if it had been mortally wounded, and his deadly wound was

healed. And all the world marveled and followed the beast. *Revelation 13:2-3*

²¹ For as the Father raises the dead and gives life to them, even so the Son gives life to whom He will. *John 5:21*

...²⁰among whom are Hymenaeus and Alexander, whom I have handed over to Satan that they may learn not to blaspheme. *1 Timothy 1:20*

¹² And the LORD said to Satan, "Behold, all that he has is in your power; only do not lay a hand on his person." So, Satan went out from the presence of the LORD. *Job 1:12*

¹⁴ ... that through death He (Jesus) might destroy him who had the power of death, that is, the devil, ¹⁵ and release those who through fear of death were all their lifetime subject to bondage. *Hebrews 2:14*

⁹ The coming of the lawless one is according to the working of Satan, with all power, signs, and lying wonders... *2 Thessalonians 2:9*

JERUSALEM ATTACKED

²⁰ But when you see Jerusalem surrounded by armies, then know that its desolation is near. ²¹ Then let those who are in Judea flee to the mountains, let those who are in the midst of her depart, and let not those who are in the country enter her. ²² For these are the days of vengeance, that all things which are written may be fulfilled. ²³ But woe to those who are pregnant and to those who are nursing babies in those days! For there will be great distress in the land and wrath upon this people. ²⁴ And they will fall by the edge of the sword, and be led away captive into all nations. And Jerusalem will be trampled by Gentiles until the times of the Gentiles are fulfilled. *Luke 21:20-24*

¹⁵ Therefore when you see the 'abomination of desolation,' spoken of by Daniel the prophet, standing in the holy place (whoever reads, let him understand), ¹⁶ then let those who are in Judea flee to the mountains. ¹⁷ Let him who is on the housetop not go down to take anything out of his house. ¹⁸ And let him who is in the field not go back to get his clothes. ¹⁹ But woe to those who are pregnant and to those who are nursing babies in those days! ²⁰ And pray that your flight may not be in winter or on the Sabbath. ²¹ For then there will be great tribulation, such as has not been since the beginning of the world until this time, no, nor ever shall be. ²² And unless those days were shortened, no flesh would be saved; but for the elect's sake those days will be shortened. *Matthew 24:15-22*

²⁹ At the appointed time he shall return and go toward the south; but it shall not be like the former or the latter. ³⁰ For ships from Cyprus shall come against him;

therefore, he shall be grieved, and return in rage against the holy covenant, and do damage. So, he shall return and show regard for those who forsake the holy covenant. ³¹ And forces shall be mustered by him, and they shall defile the sanctuary fortress; then they shall take away the daily sacrifices, and place there the abomination of desolation. ³² Those who do wickedly against the covenant he shall corrupt with flattery; but the people who know their God shall be strong, and carry out great exploits. ³³ And those of the people who understand shall instruct many; yet for many days they shall fall by sword and flame, by captivity and plundering. ³⁴ Now when they fall, they shall be aided with a little help; but many shall join with them by intrigue. ³⁵ And some of those of understanding shall fall, to refine them, purify them, and make them white, until the time of the end; because it is still for the appointed time. ³⁶ Then the king shall do according to his own will: he shall exalt and magnify himself above every god, shall speak blasphemies against the God of gods, and shall prosper till the wrath has been accomplished; for what has been determined shall be done. *Daniel 11:29-36*

⁴¹ He (the Antichrist) shall also enter the Glorious Land, and many countries shall be overthrown; but these shall escape from his hand: Edom, Moab, and the prominent people of Ammon. *Daniel 11:41*

ABOMINATION OF DESOLATION
²⁷ But in the middle of the week He (the Antichrist) shall bring an end to sacrifice and offering. And on the wing of abominations shall be one who makes desolate, even until the consummation, which is determined, is poured out on the desolate. *Daniel 9:27*

...⁴ who opposes and exalts himself (the Antichrist) above all that is called God or that is worshiped, so that he sits as God in the temple of God, showing himself that he is God. *2 Thessalonians 2:4*

¹¹ And from the time that the daily sacrifice is taken away, and the abomination of desolation is set up, there shall be one thousand two hundred and ninety days. ¹² Blessed is he who waits, and comes to the one thousand three hundred and thirty-five days. *Daniel 12:11-12*

¹¹ He even exalted himself as high as the Prince of the host; and by him the daily sacrifices were taken away, and the place of His sanctuary was cast down. ¹² Because of transgression, an army was given over to the horn to oppose the daily sacrifices; and he cast truth down to the ground. He did all this and prospered. *Daniel 8:11-12*

² But leave out the court which is outside the temple, and do not measure it, for it has been given to the Gentiles. And they will tread the holy city underfoot for

forty-two months. *Revelation 11:2-3*

PETRA
¹ Who is this who comes from Edom, with dyed garments from Bozrah, this One who is glorious in His apparel, traveling in the greatness of His strength?—"I who speak in righteousness, mighty to save." *Isaiah 63:1*

⁷ ..."Strike the Shepherd, and the sheep will be scattered; then I will turn My hand against the little ones. ⁸ And it shall come to pass in all the land," says the LORD, "That two-thirds in it shall be cut off and die, but one-third shall be left in it: ⁹ I will bring the one-third through the fire, will refine them as silver is refined, and test them as gold is tested. They will call on My name, and I will answer them. I will say, 'This is My people'; and each one will say, 'The LORD is my God.' " *Zechariah 13:7-9*

¹² I will surely assemble all of you, O Jacob, I will surely gather the remnant of Israel; I will put them together like sheep of the fold*, like a flock in the midst of their pasture; they shall make a loud noise because of so many people. *Mic. 2:12*
NOTE: *The King James translation of Micah 2:12 translates "sheep of the fold" as the "sheep of Bozrah".

¹¹ It shall come to pass in that day that the Lord shall set His hand again the second time to recover the remnant of His people who are left, from Assyria and Egypt, from Pathros and Cush, from Elam and Shinar, from Hamath and the islands of the sea. *Isaiah 11:11*

THE WOMAN AND CHILD
¹ Now a great sign appeared in heaven: a woman clothed with the sun, with the moon under her feet, and on her head a garland of twelve stars. ² Then being with child, she cried out in labor and in pain to give birth. ³ And another sign appeared in heaven: behold, a great, fiery red dragon having seven heads and ten horns, and seven diadems on his heads. ⁴ His tail drew a third of the stars of heaven and threw them to the earth. And the dragon stood before the woman who was ready to give birth, to devour her Child as soon as it was born. ⁵ She bore a male Child who was to rule all nations with a rod of iron. And her Child was caught up to God and His throne. ⁶ Then the woman fled into the wilderness, where she has a place prepared by God, that they should feed her there one thousand two hundred and sixty days...¹³ Now when the dragon saw that he had been cast to the earth, he persecuted the woman who gave birth to the male Child. ¹⁴ But the woman was given two wings of a great eagle, that she might fly into the wilderness to her place, where she is nourished for a time and times and half a time, from the presence of the serpent. ¹⁵ So the serpent spewed water out of his mouth like a flood after the woman, that he might cause her to be carried

away by the flood. ¹⁶ But the earth helped the woman, and the earth opened its mouth and swallowed up the flood which the dragon had spewed out of his mouth. ¹⁷ And the dragon was enraged with the woman, and he went to make war with the rest of her offspring, who keep the commandments of God and have the testimony of Jesus Christ. *Revelation 12:1-6,13-17*

¹⁷...and you (Gentiles), being a wild olive tree, were grafted in among them, and with them became a partaker of the root and fatness of the olive tree...*Rm. 11:17*

HEAVENLY BATTLES
¹² Then he said to me, "Do not fear, Daniel, for from the first day that you set your heart to understand, and to humble yourself before your God, your words were heard; and I have come because of your words. ¹³ But the prince of the kingdom of Persia withstood me twenty-one days; and behold, Michael, one of the chief princes, came to help me, for I had been left alone there with the kings of Persia...And now I must return to fight with the prince of Persia; and when I have gone forth, indeed the prince of Greece will come." *Daniel 10:12-13, 20*

¹ At that time Michael shall stand up, the great prince who stands watch over the sons of your people... *Daniel 12:1*

¹¹ For He shall give His angels charge over you, to keep you in all your ways. *Psalm 91:11*

²⁰ Behold, I send an Angel before you to keep you in the way and to bring you into the place which I have prepared. *Exodus 23:20*

¹¹ Put on the whole armor of God, that you may be able to stand against the wiles of the devil. ¹² For we do not wrestle against flesh and blood, but against principalities, against powers, against the rulers of the darkness of this age, against spiritual hosts of wickedness in the heavenly places. ¹³ Therefore take up the whole armor of God, that you may be able to withstand in the evil day, and having done all, to stand. ¹⁴ Stand therefore, having girded your waist with truth, having put on the breastplate of righteousness, ¹⁵ and having shod your feet with the preparation of the gospel of peace; ¹⁶ above all, taking the shield of faith with which you will be able to quench all the fiery darts of the wicked one. ¹⁷ And take the helmet of salvation, and the sword of the Spirit, which is the word of God; ¹⁸ praying always with all prayer and supplication in the Spirit, being watchful to this end with all perseverance and supplication for all the saints— ¹⁹ and for me, that utterance may be given to me, that I may open my mouth boldly to make known the mystery of the gospel, ²⁰ for which I am an ambassador in chains; that in it I may speak boldly, as I ought to speak. *Ephesians 6:11-17*

NOTES

"Sorrow looks back, worry looks around, faith looks up."
— Ralph Waldo Emerson

ARE WE THE TERMINAL GENERATION?

WEEK 18: THE BATTLE OF ARMAGEDDON

Opening Prayer: Lord, we ask that You send Your Holy Spirit to us to guide us in the teaching and understanding of Your word that we may obtain a better understanding of the prophetic events surrounding us now and waiting for us in the future. Bless our fellowship in Your word that it may be fruitful and draw us into a deeper relationship both with You and those around us. Use us as Your vessels that through us, we may reflect Your glory to all whom we encounter. Illuminate our hearts and minds so that we may boldly shine the brightness of Your light everywhere we go and that we may be beacons of Your hope in a darkened world. In Jesus name we pray, Amen.

Ice Breaker: What nationality are you? Share your ethnic make-up with the group.

My genetic background includes the nationalities of:

1.

2.

3.

   Focus: God's victories are always swift and sure.

Word of the Week

> [4] For the day of **vengeance** is in My heart, and the year of My redeemed has come.
>
> *Isaiah 63:1-6*

VENGEANCE: The word "vengeance" in this passage comes from the Hebrew word "naqam" (pronounced naw-kawm') and describes the Lord's intent to avenge the wrongs done against His beloved children. There is a time for love and forgiveness and there is a time for war. When Jesus returns to defend Israel in the Battle of Armageddon, the time for peace is over. His intent will be only to exact revenge on those who would think to destroy Israel. While many of us know Jesus as patient, kind and long-suffering, we must never forget that the Lord is also to be feared if ever we find ourselves on the wrong side the battle.

Lesson: At the end of the Tribulation, there is a battle called the Battle of Armageddon:

[12] Then the sixth angel poured out his bowl on the great **river Euphrates**, and its **water was dried up**, so that the way of the **kings from the east** might be prepared. [13] And I saw three unclean spirits like frogs coming out of the mouth of the dragon, out of the mouth of the beast, and out of the mouth of the false prophet. [14] For they are spirits of demons, performing signs, which go out **to the kings of the earth and of the whole world**, to gather them **to the battle** of that great day of God Almighty... [16] And they gathered them together to the place called in Hebrew, **Armageddon**. *Revelation 16:12-14,16*

Armageddon literally means the "Hill of Megiddo" in Hebrew and is the location for where this battle happens. Megiddo was an ancient Palestinian city located approximately eighteen miles southeast of Haifa in northern Israel. In this epic final battle between good and evil, under a one world government with a united mind, all nations from each of the ten governmental regions, without exception, come against Israel for the purpose of finally destroying Israel once and for all. In the process, troops pass through a dried-up Euphrates river to reach Israel. Scripture promises that once Israel becomes a nation again, she will never again be dispersed from being a nation. Thus, it is necessary for Jesus to personally return to defend Israel against the united forces of the Antichrist. Essentially, the odds will be so stacked against Israel at that time that if Jesus did not return to supernaturally defend Israel, Israel would be wiped off the face of the earth:

> [14] **These** (the Antichrist and his ten regional leaders) **will make war with the Lamb, and the Lamb will overcome them**, for He is Lord of lords and King of kings; and those who are with Him are called, chosen, and faithful." *Revelation 17:14*

> [1] Behold, the day of the LORD is coming, and your spoil will be divided in your midst. [2] **For I will gather all the nations to battle against Jerusalem;** the city shall be taken, the houses rifled, and the women ravished. Half of the city shall go into captivity, but the remnant of the people shall not be cut off from the city. [3] Then **the LORD will go forth and fight against those nations**, as He fights in the day of battle. [4] And in that day His feet will stand on the Mount of Olives, which faces Jerusalem on the east. And the Mount of Olives shall be split in two, from east to west, making a very large valley; half of the mountain shall move toward the north and half of it toward the south. [5] Then you shall flee through My mountain valley, for the mountain valley shall reach to Azal. Yes, you shall flee as you fled from the earthquake in the days of Uzziah king of Judah. Thus, the LORD my God will come, and all the saints with You. [6] It shall come to pass in that day that there will be no light; the lights will diminish. [7] It shall be one day which is known to the LORD—neither day nor night. But at evening time it shall happen that it will be light… [9] **And the LORD shall be King over all the earth**…*Zechariah 14:1-7, 9*

Instead, in true divine justice, Jesus protects Israel from extermination and reclaims the earth as His. Ultimately, the Battle of Armageddon is the marking point for the end of man's government and reign on earth and the beginning of Jesus' divine rule.

Ready for war, Jesus arrives robed in a red garment symbolizing bloodshed while His accompanying angelic army wears white garments:

> [11] Now I saw heaven opened, and behold, a white horse. And He who sat on him was called Faithful and True, and in righteousness He judges and makes war. [12] His eyes were like a flame of fire, and on His head were many crowns. He had a name written that no one knew except Himself. [13] **He was clothed with a robe dipped in blood**, and His name is called The Word of God. [14] And **the armies in heaven, clothed in fine linen, white and clean**, followed Him on white horses. [15] Now out of His mouth goes a

sharp sword, that with it He should strike the nations. And He Himself will rule them with a rod of iron. He Himself treads the winepress of the fierceness and wrath of Almighty God. [16] And He has on His robe and on His thigh a name written: KING OF KINGS AND LORD OF LORDS....[19] And I saw the beast, the kings of the earth, and their armies, gathered together to make war against Him who sat on the horse and against His army. [20] Then the beast was captured, and with him the false prophet who worked signs in his presence, by which he deceived those who received the mark of the beast and those who worshiped his image. These two were cast alive into the lake of fire burning with brimstone. [21] And the rest were killed with the sword which proceeded from the mouth of Him who sat on the horse. And all the birds were filled with their flesh. *Revelation 19:11-16, 19-21*

Wearing red and on His way to the Battle of Armageddon, Jesus passes through Edom on His way to the battle:

> [1] Who is this who **comes from Edom**, with **dyed garments from Bozrah**, this One who is glorious in His apparel, traveling in the greatness of His strength?—"I who speak in righteousness, mighty to save." [2] Why is Your **apparel red**, and Your garments like one who treads in the winepress? *Isaiah 63:1-2*

In the process, He picks up the sheltered Israeli remnant who have been supernaturally protected and sustained at Petra since the midpoint of the Tribulation when the Antichrist attacked Jerusalem. Esau's descendants settled Edom which is now modern-day Jordan where Petra is located:

> [7] He (King Amaziah) killed ten thousand **Edomites** in the Valley of Salt, and took **Sela** by war, and called its name Joktheel to this day. *2 Kings 14:7*

Sela is the Hebrew name for Petra and means "rock". With everyone safely in hand, the strike delivered to the nations at Armageddon is so strong that the heat generated from the force melts people's tongues in their mouths before their bodies can

> In Israel, at 18 everyone must serve in the Israeli military (IDF). Men serve 3 years and women serve 2 years.

even hit the ground:

> ^{12} And this shall be the plague with which **the LORD will strike** all the **people who fought against Jerusalem**: their **flesh shall dissolve while they stand on their feet**, their **eyes shall dissolve** in their sockets, and their **tongues shall dissolve** in their mouths. *Zechariah 14:12*

When Jesus is done, the enemy experiences mass casualties on a scale never before seen. The combined bloodshed measures one hundred and eighty-four miles wide by approximately five feet deep:

> ^{20} And the winepress was trampled outside the city, and blood came out of the winepress, up to **the horses' bridles, for one thousand six hundred furlongs**. *Revelation 14:20*

The quantity of blood given is enough to cover the death of everyone on the planet who opposes Jesus and then some. It should be noted that Jesus' assault is a stealth attack. No one expects Jesus to show up to the battle. His return is compared to "a thief in the night" due to the element of surprise Jesus employs against the enemy:

> ^{2} For you yourselves know perfectly that **the day of the Lord so comes as a thief in the night.** ^{3} For when they say, "Peace and safety!" then sudden destruction comes upon them, as labor pains upon a pregnant woman. And they shall not escape. ^{4} But you, brethren, are not in darkness, so that **this Day should overtake you as a thief**…*1 Thessalonians 5:2-4*

> ^{15} Behold, **I am coming as a thief**. Blessed is he who watches, and keeps his garments, lest he walk naked and they see his shame. ^{16} And they gathered them together to the place called in Hebrew, Armageddon. *Revelation 16:15-16*

However, once the element of surprise has been achieved, there is nothing quiet or secret about His return:

> ^{16} The **LORD also will roar from Zion**, and utter His voice from Jerusalem; the **heavens and earth will shake**; but the LORD will be a shelter for His people, and the strength of the children of Israel. *Joel 3:16*

> ^{30} Then **the sign of the Son of Man will appear in heaven**, and then all the tribes of the earth will mourn, and **they will see the**

Son of Man coming on the clouds of heaven with power and great glory. *Matthew 24:30*

At Jesus' return, men futilely attempt to hide from the Lord as they clearly observe what is about to befall them:

> [15] And the **kings** of the earth, the **great men**, the **rich men**, the **commanders**, the **mighty men**, **every slave** and **every free man**, **hid themselves** in the caves and in the rocks of the mountains, [16] and said to the mountains and rocks, "Fall on us and hide us from the face of Him who sits on the throne and from the wrath of the Lamb! [17] For the great day of His wrath has come, and who is able to stand?" *Revelation 6:15-17*

Finally, victorious in His assault on sinful humanity, Jesus deals with the Antichrist and False Prophet by throwing them into the lake of fire:

> [19] And I saw the beast, the kings of the earth, and their armies, gathered together to make war against Him who sat on the horse and against His army. [20] Then **the beast was captured**, and **with him the false prophet** who worked signs in his presence, by which he deceived those who received the mark of the beast and those who worshiped his image. **These two were cast alive into the lake of fire burning with brimstone.** [21] And the rest were killed with the sword which proceeded from the mouth of Him who sat on the horse. And all the birds were filled with their flesh. *Revelation 19:19-21*

> [8] And then **the lawless one** will be revealed, whom **the Lord will** consume with the breath of His mouth and **destroy with the brightness of His coming.** *2 Thessalonians 2:8*

When Jesus returns to do battle at Armageddon, He returns with an army of angels:

> [31] When the Son of Man comes in His glory, and **all the holy angels with Him**... *Matthew 25:31*

> [14] And **the armies in heaven,** clothed in fine linen, white and clean, **followed Him** on white horses... [19] And I saw the beast, the kings of the earth, and their armies, gathered together to make war **against Him who sat on the horse and against His army**. *Revelation 19:19*

Angels are equated with war throughout the Bible:

> ⁷ And war broke out in heaven: **Michael and his angels fought** with the dragon; and the dragon and his angels fought... *Revelation 12:7*

Other examples of angels fighting and defending include an angel with a flaming sword guarding the entrance to the Garden of Eden (Genesis 3:24), an angel fighting the prince of Persia and Greece (Daniel 10:20), an angel who drove out the inhabitants of the land for Moses (Exodus 33:2), and when Jesus stated He could request twelve legions of angels to defend Him if He so chose (Matthew 26:52-54).

Other verses describe Jesus as being accompanied by saints:

> ¹³ ...at the **coming of our Lord** Jesus Christ **with all His saints**. *1 Thessalonians 3:13*

> ⁵ Then you shall flee through My mountain valley, for the mountain valley shall reach to Azal. Yes, you shall flee as you fled from the earthquake in the days of Uzziah king of Judah. Thus, **the LORD my God will come, and all the saints with You**. *Zechariah 14:5*

> ¹⁴ ...Behold, the **Lord comes with ten thousands of His saints** ¹⁵ to execute judgment on all, to convict all who are ungodly among them ... *Jude 1:14*

Saints, simply put, for most purposes in the Bible, are God's beloved followers who worship and obey Him:

> ¹² Here is the patience of the **saints**; here are **those who keep the commandments of God** and the faith of Jesus. *Revelation 14:12*

> ⁴ **Sing praise** to the LORD, **you saints of His**, and **give thanks** at the remembrance of His holy name. *Psalm 30:4*

> ⁹ Oh, **fear the LORD, you His saints!** There is no want to those who fear Him. *Psalm 34:9*

> ⁸ I will hear what God the LORD will speak, for **He will speak peace** to His people and **to His saints**; but let them not turn back to folly. *Psalm 85:8*

> ¹⁵ Precious in the sight of the LORD is **the death of His saints**. *Psalm 116:15*

> ²⁸ For **the LORD** loves justice, and **does not forsake His saints**; they are preserved forever, but the descendants of the wicked shall be cut off. *Psalm 37:28*

> …¹² for the **equipping of the saints for the work of ministry**, for the edifying of the body of Christ… *Ephesians 4:12*

> ³ But fornication and all **uncleanness** or covetousness, let it **not even be named among you**, as is fitting for **saints**… *Ephesians 5:3*

> …¹⁸ **praying** always with all prayer and supplication in the Spirit…**for all the saints**— *Ephesians 6:18*

> ³³ For God is not the author of confusion but of **peace**, as **in all the churches of the saints**. *1 Corinthians 14:33*

> ² To the church of God which is at Corinth, to those who are **sanctified in Christ Jesus, called to be saints**, with all who in every place call on the name of Jesus Christ our Lord, both theirs and ours…*1 Corinthians 1:2*

> ²⁷ Now He who searches the hearts knows what the mind of the Spirit is, because He **makes intercession for the saints** according to the will of God. *Romans 8:27*

Saints, also known as Christians, are defined as existing on earth:

> ³ As for the **saints** who are **on the earth**, "They are the excellent ones, in whom is all my delight." *Psalm 16:3*

Saints were a part of the early church in Jesus' day and were present in a variety of churches throughout the region:

> ¹ To the **saints** who are **in Ephesus**… *Ephesians 1:1*

> ² To the **saints**…who are **in Colosse**… *Colossians 1:2*

> ¹ To the church of God which is at Corinth, with all the **saints** who are **in all Achaia**… *2 Corinthians 1:1*

> ⁷ To all who are **in Rome**…called to be **saints**… *Romans 1:7*

> ³² …he (Peter) also came down to the **saints** who dwelt **in Lydda**. *Acts 9:32*

> ¹ …to all the **saints in Christ Jesus**…**in Philippi**… *Philippians 1:1*

> ¹³ Then Ananias answered, "Lord, I have heard from many about this man, how much harm he has done to Your **saints in Jerusalem**. *Acts 9:13*

> ¹⁰ …many of the **saints** I (Paul) shut up **in prison**, having received authority from the chief priests; and when they were **put to death**, I cast my vote against them. *Acts 26:10*

Christian saints are not associated with fighting:

> ¹⁴ The **LORD will fight for you**, and you shall **hold your peace**." *Exodus 14:14*

Christian saints are required to leave the fighting to God so that we witness His power and His faithfulness. Depending on the Lord to fight our battles for us prevents us from becoming proud by thinking we have succeeded because of our own abilities. We are to stand firm, watch, pray, proclaim the gospel, and avoid Satan's darts, but we are never told to actively confront evil by taking an aggressive, offensive position:

> ¹¹ Put on the whole armor of God, that you may be able **to stand** against the wiles of the devil. ¹² For we do not wrestle against flesh and blood, but against principalities, against powers, against the rulers of the darkness of this age, against spiritual hosts of wickedness in the heavenly places. ¹³ Therefore take up the whole armor of God, that you may be able to withstand in the evil day, and **having done all, to stand**. ¹⁴ **Stand** therefore, having girded your waist with truth, having put on the breastplate of righteousness, ¹⁵ and having shod your feet with the preparation of the gospel of peace; ¹⁶ above all, taking the shield of faith with which you will be able to **quench all the fiery darts** of the wicked one. ¹⁷ And take the helmet of salvation, and the sword of the Spirit, which is the word of God; ¹⁸ **praying always** with all prayer and supplication in the Spirit, **being watchful** to this end with all perseverance and supplication for all the saints— ¹⁹ and for me,

that utterance may be given to me, that I may **open my mouth boldly to make known the mystery of the gospel**, ²⁰ for which I am an ambassador in chains; that in it I may **speak boldly**, as I ought to speak. *Ephesians 6:11-17*

Our ultimate purpose and destiny is to be priests for Jesus when He returns:

> ⁵...This is the **first resurrection**...⁶ they **shall be priests of God and of Christ**, and shall reign with Him a thousand years. *Revelation 20:5-6*

Priests do not fight in God's kingdom, nor do future priests engage in warlike activities. David was not allowed to build the temple because he was a man of war. Aggression does not have a place in Jesus' temple. Those who serve Jesus as priests in the future will not be physical combat warriors either.

So, if saints are the church which exists on earth and if we are to let God fight our battles for us, then the logical question becomes, who are the saints who return with Jesus when He comes back to do battle at Armageddon? In order to determine their identity, an examination of the original Greek and Hebrew word for "saints" is in order:

> ¹³ ...at the **coming of our Lord** Jesus Christ with all His **saints** (hagios). *1 Thessalonians 3:13*

> ¹⁴ ...Behold, the **Lord comes** with ten thousands of **His saints** (hagios) ¹⁵ to execute judgment on all, to convict all who are ungodly among them ... *Jude 1:14*

"Saints", as used in the above verses, refers to those saints who return with Jesus at His coming. Translated from the original New Testament Greek word "hagios" (pronounced hag'-ee-os), "saints", as used in this context, means "most holy thing". "Hagios" is also used again in Revelation 4:8:

> ⁸ The four **living creatures**, each having six wings, were full of eyes around and within. And they do not rest day or night, **saying:** "**Holy** (hagios), **holy** (hagios), **holy** (hagios), Lord God Almighty, who was and is and is to come!" *Revelation 4:8*

"Hagios" does not refer to Christians in these verses. It is simply a descriptive word that means "holy" and is uttered by non-angelic, non-human living creatures in reference to God. In the Old Testament Hebrew, Zechariah also uses the word "saints" in a manner that refers to Jesus' traveling companions at His return:

> ⁵ Then you shall flee through My mountain valley, for the mountain valley shall reach to Azal. Yes, you shall flee as you fled from the earthquake in the days of Uzziah king of Judah. Thus, **the LORD my God will come, and all the <u>saints</u>** (qadowsh) **with You**. *Zechariah 14:5*

In this apocalyptic verse, the Old Testament Hebrew word for saints is "qadowsh" (pronounced kaw-doshe'). Like "hagios", "qadowsh" also means "holy" and can be found again in Isaiah in a similar context to that found in Revelation:

> ¹In the year that King Uzziah died, I saw the Lord sitting on a throne, high and lifted up, and the train of His robe filled the temple. ²Above it stood **seraphim**; each one had six wings: with two he covered his face, with two he covered his feet, and with two he flew. ³And one cried to another and **said: "Holy** (qadowsh), **holy** (qadowsh), **holy** (qadowsh) is the LORD of hosts; the whole earth is full of His glory!" *Isaiah 6:2-4*

Once again, it can be seen that "qadowsh" does not always refer to earthly Christians. Like the previous passage, seraphim utter the word as a praise to God.

Further evidence that the saints Jesus returns with are not earthly Christians can be found in 2 Thessalonians 1:7:

> …⁷ and to give **you who are troubled rest** with us **when the Lord Jesus is revealed** from heaven **with His mighty angels**… *2 Thessalonians 1:7*

In this passage, Paul is writing to the church to encourage them in tribulation and persecution. If Christians are to receive rest from their troubles as a benefit of Jesus returning, then they cannot be with Him and His angels when He returns.

Numerous other verses such as Mark 8:38 and Matthew 25:31 further define that the saints, or holy things that Jesus returns with, are His host of angels. And He returns with all of them—every last one:

> ³¹ When the Son of Man comes in His glory, and **<u>all</u> the holy angels with Him**… *Matthew 25:31*

Within the angelic hierarchy, there are many different types of kingdom creatures such as seraphim, cherubim, archangels, common angels and another class of beings called living creatures:

⁴ And the twenty-four elders and **the four living creatures** fell down and worshiped God who sat on the throne, saying, "Amen! Alleluia!" *Revelation 19:4*

There is more than one type of saint in God's kingdom. While the word "holy" certainly can refer to earthly Christian saints who are set aside for God, it is egocentric to believe that we are the only creatures in God's kingdom who are holy and set aside for God. "Saints", as translated in these verses, is not limited to human application and can apply to other creatures as well. Supporting that "saints" can refer to non-human, holy entities in addition to earthly saints is Psalm 85:8 which indicates that saints are God's holy people on earth, but the term "saints" also applies to other types of holy creatures in His kingdom:

> ⁸ I will hear what God the LORD will speak, for He will speak peace **to His people <u>and</u> to His saints**; but let them not turn back to folly. *Psalm 85:8*

In this verse, God makes a distinction between Christians (His people) and other entities that worship Him (His saints). There are saints on earth, but there are also non-human saints, or holy things, in the heavens such as seraphim and living creatures. In the apocalyptic verses that use "saints" as a term for those who accompany Jesus at His return, nowhere are His traveling companions directly defined as humans. His traveling companions are only described as angels and "holy" companions which can include other types of kingdom creatures. The inclusion of the word "thing" in the definition of "hagios" broadens the application of the word to include various forms of heavenly creatures. Humans are not "things". In the absence of a direct reference to the saints (holy things) that return with Jesus as being human, it requires an assumptive leap to apply the definition of the word "saints" to resurrected and raptured Christians. Regardless of who Jesus' traveling companions are, the important thing to remember is that He wins the War of Armageddon!

Talk It Out

1. Psalm 16:3 refers to saints as "the excellent ones". Excellency is a state of existence above the quality of everything else. Do you think there is a hierarchy within the church with saints representing a special class of Christians or do you think all Christians qualify to be saints?

2. How many different types of non-human, holy creatures (saints) do you think might exist in the heavens?

3. Isaiah 63 describes Jesus as angry, vengeful, ready for war and about to kill a large number of people. Is it hard for you to view Jesus as anything other than a loving shepherd? Do you think it is fair that He throws the Antichrist and False Prophet into the lake of fire while they are still alive?

4. What tactics do you think a thief might employ if he wanted to avoid detection in order to engage in a surprise attack? Why do you think Jesus' return is compared to being like a "thief in the night"?

5. Why do you think God wants to fight our battles for us? How are we to respond when we find ourselves the victim of a spiritual attack?

Ideas for the Week:

- ✓ Remember the church specifically in your prayers this week.
- ✓ Join CUFI (Christians United for Israel) at www.cufi.org.
- ✓ Listen to the traditional Christian hymn *Battle Hymn of the Republic* and meditate on the meaning of the lyrics.
- ✓ Visit the website for Open Doors (https://www.opendoorsusa.org/). Act on any suggestions given to support the persecuted church that are feasible for you to accomplish.

Closing Prayer

NOTE: Add names and individual personal prayer requests to the space provided below before closing in prayer.

Lord, we thank You for our time together today to grow deeper in our walk with You and fellowship with each other. As we close today, we lift up: _____

_____

_____

Father, we stand firmly on the side of Jesus in any and all circumstances. Your way, Your truth and Your light are our only desire. Wherever You go, we go. Wherever You lead, we follow. Your fights are our fights. Your causes are our causes. We willingly and eagerly pledge our eternal devotion to You. In Jesus' name we pray, Amen.

SUPPORTING SCRIPTURES

THE BATTLE OF ARMAGEDDON

^{12} Then the sixth angel poured out his bowl on the great river Euphrates, and its water was dried up, so that the way of the kings from the east might be prepared. ^{13} And I saw three unclean spirits like frogs coming out of the mouth of the dragon, out of the mouth of the beast, and out of the mouth of the false prophet. ^{14} For they are spirits of demons, performing signs, which go out to the kings of the earth and of the whole world, to gather them to the battle of that great day of God Almighty. ^{15} "Behold, I am coming as a thief. Blessed is he who watches, and keeps his garments, lest he walk naked and they see his shame. ^{16} And they gathered them together to the place called in Hebrew, Armageddon. *Revelation 16:12-16*

^{11} Now I saw heaven opened, and behold, a white horse. And He who sat on him was called Faithful and True, and in righteousness He judges and makes war. ^{12} His eyes were like a flame of fire, and on His head were many crowns. He had a name written that no one knew except Himself. ^{13} He was clothed with a robe dipped in blood, and His name is called The Word of God. ^{14} And the armies in heaven, clothed in fine linen, white and clean, followed Him on white horses. ^{15} Now out of His mouth goes a sharp sword, that with it He should strike the nations. And He Himself will rule them with a rod of iron. He Himself treads the winepress of the fierceness and wrath of Almighty God. ^{16} And He has on His robe and on His thigh a name written: KING OF KINGS AND LORD OF LORDS....^{19} And I saw the beast, the kings of the earth, and their armies, gathered together to make war against Him who sat on the horse and against His army. ^{20} Then the beast was captured, and with him the false prophet who worked signs in his presence, by which he deceived those who received the mark of the beast and those who worshiped his image. These two were cast alive into the lake of fire burning with brimstone. ^{21} And the rest were killed with the sword which proceeded from the mouth of Him who sat on the horse. And all the birds were filled with their flesh. *Revelation 19:11-16, 19-21*

^{30} Then the sign of the Son of Man will appear in heaven, and then all the tribes of the earth will mourn, and they will see the Son of Man coming on the clouds of heaven with power and great glory. *Matthew 24:30*

^{8} And then the lawless one will be revealed, whom the Lord will consume with the breath of His mouth and destroy with the brightness of His coming. *2 Thessalonians 2:8*

^{14} These (the Antichrist and his ten regional leaders) will make war with the Lamb, and the Lamb will overcome them, for He is Lord of lords and King of kings; and those who are with Him are called, chosen, and faithful. *Rev. 17:14*

¹ Behold, the day of the LORD is coming, and your spoil will be divided in your midst. ² For I will gather all the nations to battle against Jerusalem; the city shall be taken, the houses rifled, and the women ravished. Half of the city shall go into captivity, but the remnant of the people shall not be cut off from the city. ³ Then the LORD will go forth and fight against those nations, as He fights in the day of battle. ⁴ And in that day His feet will stand on the Mount of Olives, which faces Jerusalem on the east. And the Mount of Olives shall be split in two, from east to west, making a very large valley; half of the mountain shall move toward the north and half of it toward the south. ⁵ Then you shall flee through My mountain valley, for the mountain valley shall reach to Azal. Yes, you shall flee as you fled from the earthquake in the days of Uzziah king of Judah. Thus, the LORD my God will come, and all the saints with You. ⁶ It shall come to pass in that day that there will be no light; the lights will diminish. ⁷ It shall be one day which is known to the LORD—neither day nor night. But at evening time it shall happen that it will be light…⁹ And the LORD shall be King over all the earth…¹² And this shall be the plague with which the LORD will strike all the people who fought against Jerusalem: their flesh shall dissolve while they stand on their feet, their eyes shall dissolve in their sockets, and their tongues shall dissolve in their mouths. *Zechariah 14:1-7, 9,12*

² For you yourselves know perfectly that the day of the Lord so comes as a thief in the night. ³ For when they say, "Peace and safety!" then sudden destruction comes upon them, as labor pains upon a pregnant woman. And they shall not escape. ⁴ But you, brethren, are not in darkness, so that this Day should overtake you as a thief…⁶ Therefore let us not sleep, as others do, but let us watch and be sober… ⁹ For God did not appoint us to wrath, but to obtain salvation through our Lord Jesus Christ… *1 Thessalonians 5:2-4,6,9*

¹…in those days…² I will also gather all nations, and bring them down to the Valley of Jehoshaphat; and I will enter into judgment with them there on account of My people, My heritage Israel, whom they have scattered among the nations; they have also divided up My land…⁴ …Swiftly and speedily I will return your retaliation upon your own head; ⁵ because you have taken My silver and My gold, and have carried into your temples My prized possessions…⁹ Proclaim this among the nations: "Prepare for war! Wake up the mighty men, let all the men of war draw near, let them come up…¹¹ Assemble and come, all you nations, and gather together all around. Cause Your mighty ones to go down there, O LORD. ¹² "Let the nations be wakened, and come up to the Valley of Jehoshaphat; for there I will sit to judge all the surrounding nations…¹⁴ Multitudes, multitudes in the valley of decision! For the day of the LORD is near in the valley of decision.

[15] The sun and moon will grow dark, and the stars will diminish their brightness. [16] The LORD also will roar from Zion, and utter His voice from Jerusalem; the heavens and earth will shake; but the LORD will be a shelter for His people, and the strength of the children of Israel. *Joel 3:1-2, 4-5, 9, 11-12, 14-16*

[1] Who is this who comes from Edom, with dyed garments from Bozrah, this One who is glorious in His apparel, traveling in the greatness of His strength?—"I who speak in righteousness, mighty to save." [2] Why is Your apparel red, and Your garments like one who treads in the winepress? *Isaiah 63:1-2*

[7] He (King Amaziah) killed ten thousand Edomites in the Valley of Salt, and took Sela by war, and called its name Joktheel to this day. *2 Kings 14:7*

[20] And the winepress was trampled outside the city, and blood came out of the winepress, up to the horses' bridles, for one thousand six hundred furlongs. *Revelation 14:20*

[15] And the kings of the earth, the great men, the rich men, the commanders, the mighty men, every slave and every free man, hid themselves in the caves and in the rocks of the mountains, [16] and said to the mountains and rocks, "Fall on us and hide us from the face of Him who sits on the throne and from the wrath of the Lamb! [17] For the great day of His wrath has come, and who is able to stand?" *Revelation 6:15-17*

JESUS RETURNS WITH ANGELS AND SAINTS
...[11] who also said, "Men of Galilee, why do you stand gazing up into heaven? This same Jesus, who was taken up from you into heaven, will so come in like manner as you saw Him go into heaven." *Acts 1:11*

[14] ..."Behold, the Lord comes with ten thousands of His saints [15] to execute judgment on all, to convict all who are ungodly among them..." *Jude 1:14*

[4] And in that day His feet will stand on the Mount of Olives, which faces Jerusalem on the east....Thus the Lord my God will come, and all the saints with You. *Zechariah 14:4-5*

...[13] so that He may establish your hearts blameless in holiness before our God and Father at the coming of our Lord Jesus Christ with all His saints. *1 Thessalonians 3:13*

[31] When the Son of Man comes in His glory, and all the holy angels with Him, then He will sit on the throne of His glory. *Matthew 25:31*

[38] For whoever is ashamed of Me and My words in this adulterous and sinful generation, of him the Son of Man also will be ashamed when He comes in the glory of His Father with the holy angels." *Mark 8:38*

[39] The enemy who sowed them is the devil, the harvest is the end of the age, and the reapers are the angels. *Matthew 13:39*

[41] The Son of Man will send out His angels, and they will gather out of His kingdom all things that offend, and those who practice lawlessness... *Matthew 13:41*

[49] So it will be at the end of the age. The angels will come forth, separate the wicked from among the just... *Matthew 13:49*

[27] And then He will send His angels, and gather together His elect from the four winds, from the farthest part of earth to the farthest part of heaven. *Mark 13:27*

[26] For whoever is ashamed of Me and My words, of him the Son of Man will be ashamed when He comes in His own glory, and in His Father's, and of the holy angels. *Luke 9:26*

[16] For the Lord Himself will descend from heaven with a shout, with the voice of an archangel, and with the trumpet of God. *1 Thessalonians 4:16*

...[7] and to give you who are troubled rest with us when the Lord Jesus is revealed from heaven with His mighty angels... *2 Thessalonians 1:7*

THE SAINTS
[3] As for the saints who are on the earth, "They are the excellent ones, in whom is all my delight." *Psalm 16:3*

[12] Here is the patience of the saints; here are those who keep the commandments of God and the faith of Jesus. *Revelation 14:12*

[4] Sing praise to the LORD, you saints of His, and give thanks at the remembrance of His holy name. *Psalm 30:4*

[9] Oh, fear the LORD, you His saints! There is no want to those who fear Him. *Psalm 34:9*

[8] I will hear what God the LORD will speak, for He will speak peace to His people and to His saints; but let them not turn back to folly. *Psalm 85:8*

[15] Precious in the sight of the LORD is the death of His saints. *Psalm 116:15*

[28] For the L ORD loves justice, and does not forsake His saints; they are preserved forever, but the descendants of the wicked shall be cut off. *Psalm 37:28*

...[12] for the equipping of the saints for the work of ministry, for the edifying of the body of Christ... *Ephesians 4:12*

[3] But fornication and all uncleanness or covetousness, let it not even be named among you, as is fitting for saints... *Ephesians 5:3*

...[18] praying always with all prayer and supplication in the Spirit...for all the saints— *Ephesians 6:18*

[33] For God is not the author of confusion but of peace, as in all the churches of the saints. *1 Corinthians 14:33*

[2] To the church of God which is at Corinth, to those who are sanctified in Christ Jesus, called to be saints, with all who in every place call on the name of Jesus Christ our Lord, both theirs and ours...*1 Corinthians 1:2*

[27] Now He who searches the hearts knows what the mind of the Spirit is, because He makes intercession for the saints according to the will of God. *Romans 8:27*

[11] Put on the whole armor of God, that you may be able to stand against the wiles of the devil. [12] For we do not wrestle against flesh and blood, but against principalities, against powers, against the rulers of the darkness of this age, against spiritual hosts of wickedness in the heavenly places. [13] Therefore take up the whole armor of God, that you may be able to withstand in the evil day, and having done all, to stand. [14] Stand therefore, having girded your waist with truth, having put on the breastplate of righteousness, [15] and having shod your feet with the preparation of the gospel of peace; [16] above all, taking the shield of faith with which you will be able to quench all the fiery darts of the wicked one. [17] And take the helmet of salvation, and the sword of the Spirit, which is the word of God; [18] praying always with all prayer and supplication in the Spirit, being watchful to this end with all perseverance and supplication for all the saints— [19] and for me, that utterance may be given to me, that I may open my mouth boldly to make known the mystery of the gospel, [20] for which I am an ambassador in chains; that in it I may speak boldly, as I ought to speak. *Ephesians 6:11-17*

[5]...This is the first resurrection...[6] they shall be priests of God and of Christ, and shall reign with Him a thousand years. *Revelation 20:5-6*

[8] The four living creatures, each having six wings, were full of eyes around and within. And they do not rest day or night, saying: "Holy, holy, holy, Lord God Almighty, who was and is and is to come!" *Revelation 4:8*

ARE WE THE TERMINAL GENERATION?

¹In the year that King Uzziah died, I saw the Lord sitting on a throne, high and lifted up, and the train of His robe filled the temple. ²Above it stood seraphim; each one had six wings: with two he covered his face, with two he covered his feet, and with two he flew. ³And one cried to another and said: "Holy, holy, holy is the LORD of hosts; the whole earth is full of His glory!" *Isaiah 6:2*

⁴And the twenty-four elders and the four living creatures fell down and worshiped God who sat on the throne, saying, "Amen! Alleluia!" *Revelation 19:4*

⁸The temple was filled with smoke from the glory of God and from His power, and no one was able to enter the temple till the seven plagues of the seven angels were completed. *Revelation 15:8*

EARLY CHURCH SAINTS

¹ To the saints who are in Ephesus… *Ephesians 1:1*

² To the saints…who are in Colosse… *Colossians 1:2*

¹ To the church of God which is at Corinth, with all the saints who are in all Achaia… *2 Corinthians 1:1*

⁷ To all who are in Rome…called to be saints… *Romans 1:7*

³² …he (Peter) also came down to the saints who dwelt in Lydda. *Acts 9:32*

¹ …to all the saints in Christ Jesus…in Philippi… *Philippians 1:1*

¹³ Then Ananias answered, "Lord, I have heard from many about this man, how much harm he has done to Your saints in Jerusalem. *Acts 9:13*

¹⁰ …many of the saints I (Paul) shut up in prison, having received authority from the chief priests; and when they were put to death, I cast my vote against them. *Acts 26:10*

¹⁴ The LORD will fight for you, and you shall hold your peace." *Exodus 14:14*

NOTES

"What we are is God's gift to us. What we become is our gift to God" — Eleanor Powell

ARE WE THE TERMINAL GENERATION?

WEEK 19: THE RESTRAINER

Opening Prayer: Lord, we ask that You send Your Holy Spirit to us to guide us in the teaching and understanding of Your word that we may obtain a better understanding of the prophetic events surrounding us now and waiting for us in the future. Bless our fellowship in Your word that it may be fruitful and draw us into a deeper relationship both with You and those around us. Use us as Your vessels that through us, we may reflect Your glory to all whom we encounter. Illuminate our hearts and minds so that we may boldly shine the brightness of Your light everywhere we go and that we may be beacons of Your hope in a darkened world. In Jesus name we pray, Amen.

Ice Breaker: Take a close look at the image below. Can you identify the image? Or is it just a confusing jumble of lines when you look at it? How long did it take you to see the image? Give everyone a few minutes to see who can discern the image, then take a poll to find out who was able to do it.

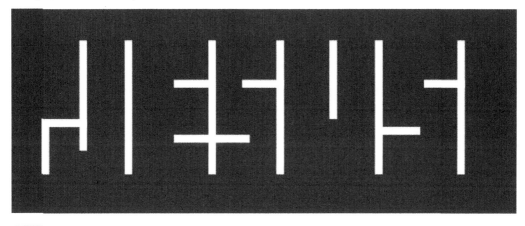

 Focus: God's word will never lead you astray.

Bible Based Believers by Generation

Builders 69% (Born 1927 – 1945)

Boomers 35% (Born 1946 – 1964)

Busters 16% (Born 1965 – 1983)

Millennials 4% (Born 1984 – Present)

CHRISTINE TATE

Word of the Week

> ³ Let no one deceive you by any means; for that Day will not come unless the **falling away** comes first, and the man of sin is revealed, the son of perdition, ⁴ who opposes and exalts himself above all that is called God or that is worshiped, so that he sits as God in the temple of God, showing himself that he is God.
>
> *2 Thessalonians 2:3-4*

FALLING AWAY: From the Greek word "apostasia" (pronounced ap-os-tas-ee'-ah) comes the expression "falling away". Another way to express the meaning of "apostasia" is defection. In order for there to be a defection from something, first there must be an initial connection from which to leave. In the sense of this verse, the falling away, or defection, is from God. Before the Antichrist will be revealed, there will be an exodus of Christians away from the faith of their fathers.

Lesson: An entity known as "the restrainer" holds back lawlessness before the Tribulation period begins and is removed at the beginning of the Tribulation. The removal of the Restrainer occurs early in the Tribulation period prior to the revealing of the Antichrist's identity. Cryptically shrouded in mystery, the identity of the Restrainer has been debated by scholars for centuries. Many popular theories as to the identity of the Restrainer include:

1. The Roman government
2. Gospel Preaching
3. The binding of Satan
4. The Jewish state
5. The providence of God (God's goodness or provision)
6. The church
7. The Holy Spirit
8. Michael, the archangel

Cryptically, the Restrainer is referred to as "He" in scripture:

> ⁶ And now you know what is restraining, that he may be revealed in his own time. ⁷ For the mystery of lawlessness is already at work; only **He who now restrains will do so until He is taken out of the way**. ⁸ And then the lawless one will be revealed...*2 Thessalonians 2:6-8*

Since the Restrainer is referred to as a singular person with the pronoun "He", the Roman government, the Jewish state, the church and the providence of God are logically incompatible choices for the Restrainer. These four possibilities are organizations or things and not individual entities appropriately defined as "He". Additionally, it does not work for the binding of Satan to be the Restrainer. When the Restrainer is removed, the Antichrist, who is backed by Satan, flourishes in his evil ways. If Satan were bound at that time, it would render the Antichrist, who receives his power from Satan, effectively harmless during the Tribulation.

Another popular theory for the identity of the Restrainer is that the Restrainer is the Holy Spirit. Various verses from the Bible describe the Holy Spirit as teacher, helper, reminder, interceder, advocate, conscience, whisperer of knowledge, wise counselor, leader, convictor of sins, provider of tongues, bringer of joy, knower of thoughts, discerner of the future and provider of freedom:

> [26] But the **Helper**, the Holy Spirit...He will **teach** you all things, and **bring to your remembrance** all things... *John 14:26*

> [26] ...the Spirit Himself makes **intercession** for us... *Romans 8:26*

> [2] ...the Spirit of **wisdom** and **understanding**, the Spirit of **counsel** and might, the Spirit of **knowledge and of the fear of the LORD**. *Isaiah 11:2*

> [6] ...with **joy** of the Holy Spirit... *1 Thessalonians 1:6*

> [14] For as many as **are led by the Spirit** of God, these are sons of God. *Romans 8:14*

> [8] ...(Holy Spirit) will **convict the world of sin**... *John 16:8*

> [4] ...and began to **speak with other tongues**, as the Spirit gave them utterance. *Acts 2:4*

> [11] For what man **knows the things of a man** except the spirit of the man which is in him? *1 Corinthians 2:11*

> [13] ...the **Spirit of truth**...will **guide you** into all truth; for He will not speak on His own authority, but whatever He hears He will speak; and **He will tell you things to come**. *John 16:13*

> [17] Now the Lord is the Spirit; and where the Spirit of the Lord is, **there is liberty**. *2 Corinthians 3:17*

Evidence of the Holy Spirit can be seen through the demonstration of qualities such as love, joy, peace and self-control:

> [22] But the fruit of the Spirit is **love**, **joy**, **peace**, longsuffering, kindness, goodness, faithfulness, [23] gentleness, **self-control**. *Galatians 5:22-23*

Residing in the physical bodies of believers, the Holy Spirit is a gift from God:

> [38] Then Peter said to them, "Repent, and let every one of you be baptized in the name of Jesus Christ for the remission of sins; and you shall **receive the gift of the Holy Spirit**. *Acts 2:38*

> [19] Or do you not know that **your body is the temple of the Holy Spirit** who is in you, whom you have from God, and you are not your own? *1 Corinthians 6:19*

> [16] Do you not know that **you are the temple of God** and that the **Spirit of God dwells in you**? *1 Corinthians 3:16*

> [15] If you love Me, keep My commandments. [16] And I will pray the Father, and He will give you another **Helper**, that He may abide with you forever— [17] the **Spirit** of truth, whom the world cannot receive, because it neither sees Him nor knows Him; but you know Him, **for He dwells with you and will be in you**. *John 14:15-17*

Through sin, willful disobedience, and resistance of its leadership, the Holy Spirit can be outraged, insulted and grieved to the point where it is removed by God:

> [11] Do not cast me away from Your presence, and **do not take Your Holy Spirit from me**. *Psalm 51:11*

> [14] But the **Spirit** of the LORD **departed from Saul**... *1 Samuel 16:14*

> [51] "You stiff-necked and uncircumcised in heart and ears! **You always resist the Holy Spirit**; as your fathers did, so do you. *Acts 7:51*

> [30] And **do not grieve the Holy Spirit** of God, by whom you were sealed for the day of redemption. *Ephesians 4:30*

> ²⁹ Of how much worse punishment, do you suppose, will he be thought worthy who has...**insulted the Spirit of grace**? *Hebrews 10:29*

As the return of Jesus nears, the Terminal Generation grieves the Holy Spirit and incurs God's anger. Specifically, they disappoint God by adopting ways of other cultures, relying on psychics and mediums, mingling with foreigners, having idols and possessing an overblown sense of self-importance:

> ⁶ For You have forsaken Your people, the house of Jacob, because they are filled with **eastern ways**; they are **soothsayers** like the Philistines, and they are **pleased with the children of foreigners**. ⁷ Their land is also full of silver and gold, and there is no end to their treasures; their land is also full of horses, and there is no end to their chariots. ⁸ Their land is also full of **idols**; they **worship the work of their own hands**, that which their own fingers have made. *Isaiah 2:6-8*

Of all the ways the Holy Spirit is described throughout the Bible, it is never directly referred to as a restrainer. *Webster's Dictionary* defines the verb "restrain" as follows:

> RESTRAIN: 1a. To prevent from doing, exhibiting, or expressing something. 1b. To limit, restrict or keep under control. 2. To moderate or limit the force, effect, development, or full exercise of. 3. To deprive of liberty.

While the Holy Spirit guides, teaches and leads, it never exerts force on the believer to prevent the believer from doing something. The Holy Spirit will leave the human body before it forces an action on the believer in whom it dwells which is contrary to the concept of restraint. In addition, Daniel states there are still saints on earth during the Tribulation whom the Antichrist persecutes:

> ²⁵ **He** (the Antichrist)...shall **persecute the saints** of the Most High...Then **the saints shall be given into his hand** for a time and times and half a time. *Daniel 7:25*

Saints, as used in this context, refers to Christians. Christians possess the Holy Spirit as it dwells inside them. If there are Christians on the earth during the Tribulation, then the Holy Spirit is still present on the earth as well. Christians are also found midway through the Tribulation after the War in Heaven when Satan personally persecutes Christians with all of his might:

> ¹⁷ And **the dragon** (Satan) was enraged with the woman, and he **went to make war with the rest of her offspring, who keep the commandments of God and have the testimony of Jesus Christ** (Christians). *Revelation 12:17*

Christians who have not grieved the Holy Spirit do not lose their indwelling Holy Spirit. Since Christians possess the Holy Spirit and Christians are on earth to be persecuted during the reign of the Antichrist, that puts the Holy Spirit on earth during the Tribulation. The Restrainer cannot be the Holy Spirit as long as there are Christians on earth at that time.

Some believe the Restrainer is Michael the Archangel. Again, this is problematic because scripture indicates Michael is present and active during the Tribulation. Michael is the protector of Israel and actively stands watch over Israel during the Tribulation:

FAST FACT: Researchers found that Millennials are the least religious generation in six decades, perhaps even in the history of the United States.

> ¹**At that time Michael shall stand up**, the great prince **who stands watch over the sons of your people**; and there shall be a time of trouble, such as never was since there was a nation, even to that time. *Daniel 12:1*

Michael is also an active participant in the War in Heaven and can be found fighting Satan at the midpoint of the Tribulation:

> ⁷ And **war broke out in heaven: Michael and his angels fought** with the dragon; and the dragon and his angels fought… *Revelation 12:7*

Because of his presence during the Tribulation, Michael is not a viable option for the Restrainer.

Finally, there is the Word of God which presents interesting possibilities for the Restrainer. First, John 1:1 defines God and His word as being one and the same:

> In the beginning was the Word, and the Word was with God, and **the Word was God.** *John 1:1*

By linking God and His word as interchangeable entities, the masculine pronoun "He" can be used to describe the Restrainer. Second, scripture directly states the word of God is a restraint on the people:

> ¹⁸ Where there is no revelation, the **people cast off restraint**; but **happy is he who keeps the law**. *Proverbs 29:18*

Essentially, God's word restrains people from sinning which is a connection that is again made in Psalm 119:

> ⁹ How can a **young man cleanse** his way? By **taking heed** according to **Your word**...¹¹ **Your word** I have hidden in my heart, **that I might not sin** against You. *Psalm 119:9,11*

God's word residing in the heart of man is what restrains man from sinning against God. Without the word of God, people succumb to their inner desires and are unable to resist Satan:

> ¹⁴ ...I have written to you, young men, because you are strong, and the **word of God abides in you**, and **you have overcome the wicked one**. *1 John 2:14*

Without firm, stable rules in place, chaos and sin ensue. This is evidenced in our society today. As biblical rules and principles are gradually stripped away one by one, the fabric of society slowly, but surely unravels. With lawlessness abounding from a lack of God's word, sin prevails. Sin, in turn, grieves the Holy Spirit causing its presence to be diminished as people increasingly turn from God. When the Holy Spirit is absent, people lose their ability to discern right from wrong which then results in more sin. What follows from that point is nothing short of disaster. It is a vicious cycle that starts with the removal of God's word. Third, God's word is symbolically linked to a sharp two-edged sword, fire, and a hammer.

> ²⁹ "Is not **My word like a fire**?" says the LORD, "And **like a hammer that breaks** the rock in pieces?" *Jeremiah 23:29*

> ¹² For the **word of God** is living and powerful, and **sharper than any two-edged** sword... *Hebrews 4:12*

> ¹⁷ And take the helmet of salvation, and the **sword** of the Spirit, **which is the word of God**... *Ephesians 6:17*

All three items mentioned indicate a measure of force which is consistent with the concept of restraint. Fire, swords and hammers are all weapons used to compel something which matches the force requirement inherent in the definition of the word "restrain". Finally, during the end time period, there will be a famine of the word:

> [11] "Behold, the days are coming," says the Lord GOD, "That I will **send a famine** on the land, not a famine of bread, nor a thirst for water, but **of hearing the words of the LORD.**" *Amos 8:11*

A famine of the word indicates that the presence of the word of God has been removed from or greatly reduced on earth. Traces of this can already be observed as forces such as the ACLU push to remove Christian references from public places of government. When Chief Justice Roy Moore opposed the removal of the Ten Commandments from an Alabama judicial building, he was removed from his judicial position and charged with ethics violation despite the fact that 75% of the people polled at that time supported leaving the statue of the Ten Commandments in place. As the presence of the word of God diminishes in our world, it is consistent with a restraint that is being removed.

Primarily, the Restrainer is connected to a "falling away" (2 Thessalonians 2:3). A general falling away of the people from God and His word is one of the final signs that happens before the Tribulation period begins and the identity of the Antichrist is revealed. This phenomenon is known as "apostasy" and defined by *Webster's Dictionary* as:

> APOSTASY: 1. An act of refusing to continue to follow, obey or recognize a religious faith. 2. Abandonment of a previous loyalty.

Evidence of people falling away from God and His word can be seen in our society today. In statistics given by Thom S. Rainer in his book *The Bridger Generation*, the percentage of Bible-based Christians has been in a steady state of decline since 1927. Those born from 1927-1945 are called Builders and are comprised of 65% Bible-based believers. In Boomers, those born 1946-1964, Bible-based Christians make up 35% of their generation. Among Busters born 1965-1983, only 16% of that generation are Bible-based believers. Sadly, Millennials born 1984 or later boast only a paltry 4% of Bible-based believers. Little by little, it no longer becomes necessary to silence Christian voices because they no longer exist to be silenced. As God's word progressively disappears from the earth and greater numbers of people fall away from Him, the Restrainer is removed and society inches closer and closer to conditions that are ripe for the advent of the Tribulation.

Another verse which supports a connection between the word of God and the Restrainer is Daniel 8:12:

> [12]...**he** (the Antichrist) **cast truth down to the ground.** He did all this and prospered. *Daniel 8:12*

God's word is truth. The Antichrist rejects truth and embraces deceit to succeed:

> [25] Through his cunning **he** (the Antichrist) **shall cause deceit to prosper** under his rule... *Daniel 8:25*

Without deception, the Antichrist cannot prevail. In order to rule the world, first the Antichrist must eliminate God's word. When the truth, or God's word, is removed from the earth, then the Antichrist is free to deceive the world. But hope still exists. Jesus is the Word of God and He will one day return:

> [13] **He** (Jesus) was clothed with a robe dipped in blood, and His name **is called The Word of God**. *Revelation 19:13*

Knowing this, we can rest assured that the word of God will be back at the end of the Tribulation when we see Jesus. Bringing with Him law, order and righteousness, our world will once again be as it should be under God's control.

TALK IT OUT

1. Who or what do you think the Restrainer is that must be removed before the identity of the Antichrist can be revealed and the Tribulation can begin? Is it the church, word of God, Holy Spirit, Roman government, binding of Satan, providence of God, Jewish state, Michael the Archangel or something else?

2. Do you think God's word is already being removed from our society? Discuss examples of the disappearance of the word of God in our society.

3. Amos 8:11 refers to an end time "famine of the word". What do you think that means? Do you think a "famine of the word" has already begun?

4. How far do you think the "falling away" will progress before God will consider the verse to be fulfilled? What percentage of the population do you think will be Christian by the time the Tribulation begins? In which age groups? How far away from that point do you think we are right now?

5. When the Holy Spirit is grieved, it can leave a believer. Do you think the Holy Spirit is leaving believers now which in turn causes a lack of discernment, wisdom and understanding in the people? Discuss examples of wisdom or lack thereof in the general populace.

6. Does it feel to you like Christianity is declining in the US? What about in the world? Do you think Christianity can rebound in numbers from where it is right now or do you think the number of Christians can only go down from here? How quickly do you think that rise or decline will happen?

Ideas for the Week:

- ✓ Strike up a conversation with a non-Christian this week. Ask them about their views on Christianity and the church. Speak the truth, but do so in love.
- ✓ Share the website www.EveryStudent.com with a young Christian or a seeker.
- ✓ Buy a Bible, bookmark your favorite passage and leave it in a public place like a bench at the mall, by the sink in a public restroom or a coffee shop table for someone to find.
- ✓ As you go about your week, find small ways to insert short comments about prayer into your conversations with strangers as a way to open the door for someone to talk to you about your faith and your relationship with God. For example, if you are shopping for a sweater, pray about it as you shop. Then, when you are at the checkout counter, make a brief comment to the cashier such as "I'm so happy about the deal I got on this. I prayed that God would lead me to just the right sweater."

Closing Prayer

NOTE: Add names and individual personal prayer requests to the space provided below before closing in prayer.

Lord, we thank You for our time together today to grow deeper in our walk with You and fellowship with each other. As we close today, we lift up: _____

_____

_____

_____

_____

_____

Father, we exalt You above all else and faithfully cling to Your word. We know that without Your guidance, we would be lost. Reveal to us Your wisdom and fill us with Your Holy Spirit. Prevent us from grieving the Holy Spirit and show us how we can make our lives more pleasing to You. In Jesus' name we pray, Amen.

SUPPORTING SCRIPTURES

THE RESTRAINER

¹Now, brethren, concerning the coming of our Lord Jesus Christ and our gathering together to Him, we ask you, ²not to be soon shaken in mind or troubled, either by spirit or by word or by letter, as if from us, as though the day of Christ had come. ³Let no one deceive you by any means; for that Day will not come unless the falling away comes first, and the man of sin is revealed, the son of perdition, ⁴who opposes and exalts himself above all that is called God or that is worshiped, so that he sits as God in the temple of God, showing himself that he is God. ⁵Do you not remember that when I was still with you, I told you these things? ⁶And now you know what is restraining, that he may be revealed in his own time. ⁷For the mystery of lawlessness is already at work; only He who now restrains will do so until He is taken out of the way. ⁸And then the lawless one will be revealed, whom the Lord will consume with the breath of His mouth and destroy with the brightness of His coming. ⁹The coming of the lawless one is according to the working of Satan, with all power, signs, and lying wonders, ¹⁰and with all unrighteous deception among those who perish, because they did not receive the love of the truth, that they might be saved.   *2 Thessalonians 2:1-10*

THE HOLY SPIRIT

²⁶But the Helper, the Holy Spirit, whom the Father will send in My name, He will teach you all things, and bring to your remembrance all things that I said to you.   *John 14:26*

²⁶Likewise the Spirit also helps in our weaknesses. For we do not know what we should pray for as we ought, but the Spirit Himself makes intercession for us with groanings which cannot be uttered.   *Romans 8:26*

²The Spirit of the LORD shall rest upon Him, the Spirit of wisdom and understanding, the Spirit of counsel and might, the Spirit of knowledge and of the fear of the LORD.   *Isaiah 11:2*

²²But the fruit of the Spirit is love, joy, peace, longsuffering, kindness, goodness, faithfulness, ²³gentleness, self-control.   *Galatians 5:22-23*

³⁸Then Peter said to them, "Repent, and let every one of you be baptized in the name of Jesus Christ for the remission of sins; and you shall receive the gift of the Holy Spirit."   *Acts 2:38*

⁶And you became followers of us and of the Lord, having received the word in much affliction, with joy of the Holy Spirit…   *1 Thessalonians 1:6*

¹⁹ Or do you not know that your body is the temple of the Holy Spirit who is in you, whom you have from God, and you are not your own? *1 Corinthians 6:19*

¹⁶ Do you not know that you are the temple of God and that the Spirit of God dwells in you? *1 Corinthians 3:16*

¹⁵ If you love Me, keep My commandments. ¹⁶ And I will pray the Father, and He will give you another Helper, that He may abide with you forever— ¹⁷ the Spirit of truth, whom the world cannot receive, because it neither sees Him nor knows Him; but you know Him, for He dwells with you and will be in you. *John 14:15-17*

⁷ …but if I depart, I will send Him to you. ⁸ And when He has come, He will convict the world of sin, and of righteousness, and of judgment: ⁹ of sin, because they do not believe in Me; ¹⁰ of righteousness, because I go to My Father and you see Me no more; ¹¹ of judgment, because the ruler of this world is judged. *John 16:7-11*

¹³ However, when He, the Spirit of truth, has come, He will guide you into all truth; for He will not speak on His own authority, but whatever He hears He will speak; and He will tell you things to come. *John 16:13*

¹⁷ Now the Lord is the Spirit; and where the Spirit of the Lord is, there is liberty. *2 Corinthians 3:17*

¹¹ For what man knows the things of a man except the spirit of the man which is in him? Even so no one knows the things of God except the Spirit of God. *1 Corinthians 2:11*

⁴ And they were all filled with the Holy Spirit and began to speak with other tongues, as the Spirit gave them utterance. *Acts 2:4*

¹⁴ For as many as are led by the Spirit of God, these are sons of God. *Romans 8:14*

⁵¹ You stiff-necked and uncircumcised in heart and ears! You always resist the Holy Spirit; as your fathers did, so do you. *Acts 7:51*

³⁰ And do not grieve the Holy Spirit of God, by whom you were sealed for the day of redemption. *Ephesians 4:30*

²⁹ Of how much worse punishment, do you suppose, will he be thought worthy who has trampled the Son of God underfoot, counted the blood of the covenant by which he was sanctified a common thing, and insulted the Spirit of grace? *Hebrews 10:29*

¹⁴ But the Spirit of the LORD departed from Saul... *1 Samuel 16:14*

¹¹ Do not cast me away from Your presence, and do not take Your Holy Spirit from me. *Psalm 51:11*

⁶ For You have forsaken Your people, the house of Jacob, because they are filled with eastern ways; they are soothsayers like the Philistines, and they are pleased with the children of foreigners. ⁷ Their land is also full of silver and gold, and there is no end to their treasures; their land is also full of horses, and there is no end to their chariots. ⁸ Their land is also full of idols; they worship the work of their own hands, that which their own fingers have made. *Isaiah 2:6-8*

¹⁷ And the dragon (Satan) was enraged with the woman, and he went to make war with the rest of her offspring, who keep the commandments of God and have the testimony of Jesus Christ (Christians). *Revelation 12:17*

WAR ON THE SAINTS
²⁵ He shall speak pompous words against the Most High, shall persecute the saints of the Most High, and shall intend to change times and law. Then the saints shall be given into his hand for a time and times and half a time. *Daniel 7:25*

MICHAEL, THE ARCHANGEL
¹At that time Michael shall stand up, the great prince who stands watch over the sons of your people; and there shall be a time of trouble, such as never was since there was a nation, even to that time. *Daniel 12:1*

⁷ And war broke out in heaven: Michael and his angels fought with the dragon; and the dragon and his angels fought... *Revelation 12:7*

GOD'S WORD
¹In the beginning was the Word, and the Word was with God, and the Word was God. *John 1:1*

¹⁸ Where there is no revelation, the people cast off restraint; but happy is he who keeps the law. *Proverbs 29:18*

¹² For the word of God is living and powerful, and sharper than any two-edged sword, piercing even to the division of soul and spirit, and of joints and marrow, and is a discerner of the thoughts and intents of the heart. *Hebrews 4:12*

¹⁷ And take the helmet of salvation, and the sword of the Spirit, which is the word of God... *Ephesians 6:17*

[11] Your word I have hidden in my heart, that I might not sin against You. *Psalm 119:11*

[29] "Is not My word like a fire?" says the LORD, "And like a hammer that breaks the rock in pieces?" *Jeremiah 23:29*

[14] I have written to you, fathers, because you have known Him who is from the beginning. I have written to you, young men, because you are strong, and the word of God abides in you, and you have overcome the wicked one. *1 John 2:14*

[9] How can a young man cleanse his way? By taking heed according to Your word...[11] Your word I have hidden in my heart, that I might not sin against You. *Psalm 119:9,11*

[11] "Behold, the days are coming," says the Lord GOD, "That I will send a famine on the land, not a famine of bread, nor a thirst for water, but of hearing the words of the LORD." *Amos 8:11*

[13] He (Jesus) was clothed with a robe dipped in blood, and His name is called The Word of God. *Revelation 19:13*

[12] Because of transgression, an army was given over to the horn to oppose the daily sacrifices; and he (the Antichrist) cast truth down to the ground. He did all this and prospered. *Daniel 8:12*

[25] Through his cunning he (the Antichrist) shall cause deceit to prosper under his rule... *Daniel 8:25*

NOTES

"Aim a little higher than you think possible, and give a lot of thanks to God for health, family and friends." — Art Linkletter

WEEK 20: DANIEL'S 70TH WEEK

Opening Prayer: Lord, we ask that You send Your Holy Spirit to us to guide us in the teaching and understanding of Your word that we may obtain a better understanding of the prophetic events surrounding us now and waiting for us in the future. Bless our fellowship in Your word that it may be fruitful and draw us into a deeper relationship both with You and those around us. Use us as Your vessels that through us, we may reflect Your glory to all whom we encounter. Illuminate our hearts and minds so that we may boldly shine the brightness of Your light everywhere we go and that we may be beacons of Your hope in a darkened world. In Jesus name we pray, Amen.

Ice Breaker: Below is a stock chart. Using only the information provided in the graph, predict the overall direction you think the stock is headed. Does the stock look like it is going up or down? After everyone reaches a consensus, then turn the page for the answer.

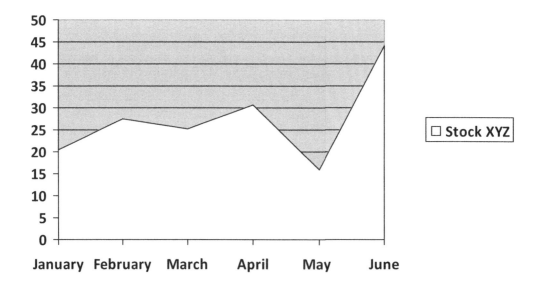

This stock appears to be going: _____

Focus: While we see only a portion of events, God, in His omniscience, always guides rightly because He sees the big picture.

Answer: From the data given over a period of six months, the stock appears to be going up. However, if the stock is viewed over a longer period of time, it can be seen that the upward spike is just an anomaly in an otherwise downward trend. Fragmented pieces can be misleading. To determine a true direction, it is important to examine all data that contributes to the overall big picture.

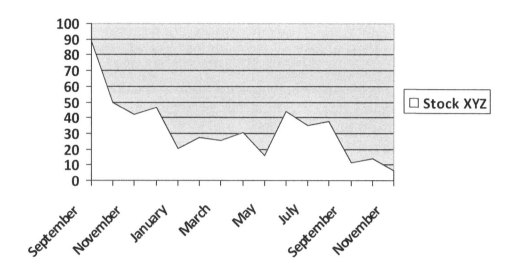

Word of the Week

> [19] You will say then, "Branches were broken off that I might be **grafted in**."
>
> *Romans 11:19*

GRAFTED IN: In the original Greek writings, the word for the process of being grafted in is "egkentrizo" (pronounced eng-ken-trid'-zo). Grafting is a horticultural process by which a main plant, called the rootstock, has a plant of another related variety manually attached to the main plant. Over time, the graft joint heals and the two plants become one plant. By combining different species as one plant, it becomes possible to trait select for desired characteristics making the final plant more desirable than either of the original two plants by themselves. During the Church Age, the Gentiles are grafted on to the root of Jesse so that when the Messiah returns, both Gentiles and Jews will be one body worshipping Jesus in perfect harmony.

Lesson: Discerning the big picture for the Tribulation involves pulling back for a perspective that begins far in advance of the immediate seven-year time period before Jesus returns. In the book of Daniel, a broad prophetic timeline is given using a symbolic terminology of weeks:

> [22] And he (Gabriel) informed me (Daniel), and talked with me...[24] "**Seventy weeks** are determined for your people and for your holy city, to finish the transgression, to make an end of sins, to make reconciliation for iniquity, to bring in everlasting righteousness, to seal up vision and prophecy, and to anoint the Most Holy. [25] ...**from the** going forth of the **command to restore and build Jerusalem until Messiah the Prince**, there shall be **seven weeks and sixty-two weeks**; the street shall be built again, and the wall, even in troublesome times. [26] And **after the sixty-two weeks Messiah shall be cut off**, but not for Himself; and the people of the prince who is to come **shall destroy the city and the sanctuary**. The end of it shall be with a flood, and till the end of the war desolations are determined. [27] Then he shall confirm a **covenant with many for one week**..." *Daniel 9:22,24-27*

Each week represents seven years using the day-for-a-year prophetic rule. Mathematically, seventy weeks represents a timespan of four hundred and ninety years, or seventy times seven. Within this period of time, there are three distinct periods. Initially, there is a period of seven weeks, or forty-nine years. For the initial period of forty-nine years, Daniel 9:25 sets a starting point for the countdown when King Artaxerxes of Persia issued the command to rebuild Jerusalem in 445 BC:

> [1] And it came to pass in the month of Nisan, **in the twentieth year of King Artaxerxes**, when wine was before him, that I (Nehemiah) took the wine and gave it to the king. Now I had never been sad in his presence before. [2] Therefore the king said to me, "Why is your face sad...What do you request?" So, I prayed to the God of heaven. [5] And I said to the king, "If it pleases the king...I ask that you **send me to Judah**, to the city of my fathers' tombs, **that I may rebuild it**." [6] ...So **it pleased the king to send me**; and I set him a time. *Nehemiah 2:1-6*

Following the seven weeks is a period of sixty-two weeks, or four hundred and thirty-four years initiated by Jesus' death. Combining the first and second periods creates a total of four hundred and eighty-three years. Using the Jewish calendar of three hundred and sixty days per year, four hundred and eighty-three years later puts the time at 30 AD which, coincidentally, is also the point when Jesus entered Jerusalem:

> ¹ Now when **they** (Jesus and His disciples) **drew near Jerusalem**... *Matthew 21:1*

Daniel 9:26 establishes the completion of the four hundred and eighty-three years with the crucifixion of Jesus. In fulfillment of this prophetic verse, Jesus was crucified approximately three years after He entered Jerusalem:

> ¹⁷ And He (Jesus), bearing His cross, went out to a place called the Place of a Skull, which is called in Hebrew, Golgotha, ¹⁸ where **they crucified Him**, and two others with Him, one on either side, and Jesus in the center. *John 19:17*

After the crucifixion of Jesus, Jerusalem was destroyed in 70 AD by the Romans which is the final fulfilment of Daniel 9:26. Lastly, there is a final period of one week, or seven years, which has yet to be fulfilled. After an unspecified gap in time, the final week of seven years represents the Tribulation time period. Specifically, the seventieth week begins with a peace agreement brokered by the Antichrist, progresses with the destruction of the third temple in Jerusalem and the cessation of daily sacrifices midway through the Tribulation, and ends with the return of Jesus.

Between the previously fulfilled two periods of four hundred and eighty-three years and the yet to be fulfilled final seven years is a gap known as our current Church Age. Beginning at the crucifixion of Christ and ending with the Tribulation, the Church Age is the span of time God uses to graft the Gentiles onto His family tree:

> ¹¹ ...But **through their (Israel's) fall**, to provoke them to jealousy, **salvation has come to the Gentiles**...¹⁶ For if the firstfruit is holy, the lump is also holy; **and if the root is holy, so are the branches**. ¹⁷ And if some of the branches were broken off, and **you, being a wild olive tree, were grafted in among them**, and with them became a partaker of the root and fatness of the olive tree, ¹⁸ do not boast against the branches. But if you do boast, remember that you do not support the root, but **the root supports you**. ¹⁹ You will say then, "**Branches were broken off that I might be grafted in**." ²⁰ Well said. Because of unbelief they were broken off, and you stand by faith. Do not be haughty, but fear. ²¹ For if God did not spare the natural branches, He may not spare

you either. ²² Therefore consider the goodness and severity of God: on those who fell, severity; but toward you, goodness, if you continue in His goodness. Otherwise you also will be cut off. ²³ And they also, if they do not continue in unbelief, will be grafted in, for God is able to graft them in again. ²⁴ **For if you were cut out of the olive tree which is wild by nature, and were grafted contrary to nature into a cultivated olive tree, how much more will these, who are natural branches, be grafted into their own olive tree?** ²⁵ For I do not desire, brethren, that you should be ignorant of this mystery, lest you should be wise in your own opinion, that blindness in part has happened to Israel until the fullness of the Gentiles has come in. *Romans 11:11,16-25*

¹ There shall come forth **a Rod from the stem of Jesse**, and a **Branch shall grow out of his roots**…¹⁰ And in that day there shall be **a Root of Jesse**, who shall stand as a banner to the people; for the Gentiles shall seek Him, and His resting place shall be glorious. *Isaiah 11:1, 10*

¹⁶ "I, **Jesus**, have sent My angel to testify to you these things in the churches. **I am the Root** and the Offspring of David, the Bright and Morning Star." *Revelation 22:16*

When the grafting process is complete at the end of the Church Age, Satan tries to kill the entire tree consisting of both Jews and Gentiles during the final week which is the seven-year Tribulation period.

Despite numerous references to the saints and those who have the testimony of Jesus being present during the Tribulation, there are those who claim the church is gone during the Tribulation. They contend that the church is not specifically mentioned by name in Revelation chapters four through twenty-two, therefore, they reason, the church must be gone by that time. Rationalizing the absence of the church even further, pre-Tributionists cite Revelation 4:1:

¹After these things **I** looked, and behold, a door standing open in heaven. And the first voice which **I** heard was like a trumpet speaking with **me**, saying, "**Come up here**, and I will show **you** things which must take place after this." *Revelation 4:1*

Proponents of the pre-Tribulation position present that this verse calls the church to come up to heaven thereby removing it from the earth. The plain text reading of the scripture simply refers to John, as an individual, being called up to heaven so that the vision can be revealed to him. Other scriptures do not equate John as representing the church and this verse cannot be interpreted with that substitution.

Pertinent to the discussion of the whereabouts of the church during the Tribulation is that the book of Revelation is not written chronologically. By comparing Revelation 6:15-17 with Revelation 13:7 it can be seen that the events given throughout the book of Revelation are presented out of order:

> [15] And the kings of the earth, the great men, the rich men, the commanders, the mighty men, every slave and every free man, hid themselves in the caves and in the rocks of the mountains, [16] and said to the mountains and rocks, "Fall on us and hide us from the face of Him who sits on the throne and from the wrath of the Lamb! [17] For the great day of His wrath has come, and who is able to stand?" ***Revelation 6:15-17*** (Day of the Lord, **End of Tribulation** event)

> [7] It was granted to him (the Antichrist) to make war with the saints and to overcome them. And authority was given him over every tribe, tongue, and nation. ***Revelation 13:7*** (Antichrist War on Christians, **Mid-Tribulation** event)

Revelation 6:15-17 comments on the Day of the Lord which happens at the end of the Tribulation while Revelation 13:7, a later chapter, addresses the Antichrist's power and success persecuting God's people which occurs at an earlier point during the Tribulation. Chapter thirteen comes after chapter six, but their respective events are reversed in order. Clearly, Jesus does not come back before the Antichrist attempts to wipe out Christians which suggests the book of Revelation cannot be read and interpreted as a chronological account of events.

Order and sequencing issues can be found again in Revelation chapters 8-11 as events are discussed out of chronological order. Chapters 8 and 9 list trumpets one through six which includes an Armageddon reference. Chapter 10 breaks away from trumpets to discuss John having a conversation with an angel. Then, chapter 11 begins with a discussion about the two witnesses prophesying, being killed and being resurrected at the end of the Tribulation. After that, scripture resumes with the seventh trumpet. The sixth and seventh trumpet represent end of Tribulation events, yet are separated by the witnesses prophesying which is an early Tribulation event.

Another example of a chronological failure can be found in Revelation 9 and Revelation 16:

> [13] Then the sixth angel sounded: And I heard a voice from the four

horns of the golden altar which is before God, ¹⁴ saying to the sixth angel who had the trumpet, "Release the four angels who are bound at the great **river Euphrates**." ¹⁵ So the four angels, who had been prepared for the hour and day and month and year, were released to kill a third of mankind. ¹⁶ Now the number of the **army of the horsemen was two hundred million**; I heard the number of them. ¹⁷ And thus I saw the horses in the vision: those who sat on them had breastplates of fiery red, hyacinth blue, and sulfur yellow; and the heads of the horses were like the heads of lions; and out of their mouths came fire, smoke, and brimstone. ¹⁸ By these three plagues a third of mankind was killed—by the fire and the smoke and the brimstone which came out of their mouths. ¹⁹ For their power is in their mouth and in their tails; for their tails are like serpents, having heads; and with them they do harm. *Revelation 9:13-18*

¹² Then the sixth angel poured out his bowl on the great **river Euphrates**, and its water was dried up, so that the way of the **kings from the east** might be prepared. ¹³ And I saw three unclean spirits like frogs coming out of the mouth of the dragon, out of the mouth of the beast, and out of the mouth of the false prophet. ¹⁴ For they are spirits of demons, performing signs, which go out to the kings of the earth and of the **whole world, to gather them to the battle** of that great day of God Almighty. ¹⁵ "Behold, I am coming as a thief. Blessed is he who watches, and keeps his garments, lest he walk naked and they see his shame." ¹⁶ And **they gathered them together** to the place called in Hebrew, **Armageddon**. *Revelation 16:12-16*

Both verses reference the battle of Armageddon. Since a strict, chronological interpretation does not allow for a discussion of Armageddon in Revelation 9 and then another discussion of Armageddon again in a later chapter, a problem exists in adopting a chronological view of Revelation. A thematic approach to reading Revelation is more likely. Since events are not given in chronological order, the statement that the church is not formally mentioned after chapter four cannot be used as a valid argument to explain the absence of any formal mention of the church because the verses do not present a linear account of events.

Another problem with the church being raptured away to be with Jesus before the Tribulation can be found in Revelation 19:7:

⁷ Let us be glad and rejoice and give Him glory, for the marriage of the Lamb has come, and **His wife** (the church) **has made herself**

ready. *Revelation 19:7*

Jesus, the Lamb, marries His bride, the church, after He returns. Revelation 19:7 states the Lambs wife, or the church, makes herself "ready". In Jewish wedding tradition, the bride "readies" herself before the wedding while the groom is away preparing a place for them to live after they are married. If the church is still "readying" herself to be with Jesus, then the church is not with Jesus and must still be on the earth.

Scripturally, there are a large number of saints present during the Tribulation:

> [9] After these things I looked, and behold, **a great multitude** which no one could number, of all nations, tribes, peoples, and tongues, standing before the throne and before the Lamb, clothed with white robes, with palm branches in their hands, [10] and crying out with a loud voice, saying, "Salvation belongs to our God who sits on the throne, and to the Lamb!"...[14] ..."These are the ones **who come out of the great tribulation**, and washed their robes and made them white in the blood of the Lamb. *Rev. 7:9-10, 13-14*

From this passage, it is clear that those who worship God and obey His laws are still present on earth at that time. Described as a "great multitude", a large quantity of Christians worship God during the Tribulation. Since the church is the body of Christ, if believers are present on earth, then God's church is present on earth. Essentially, earthly saints, which comprise the combined body of Christ, are the church. If saints are present, then the church is present since the church is the body of Christ. Without the body of Christ, or saints, there is no church:

> [12] For as the body is one and has many members, but all the members of that one body, being many, are one body, so also is Christ...[14] For in fact the body is not one member but many... [20] But now indeed there **are many members, yet one body**...[27] Now **you are the body of Christ**, and members individually. *1 Corinthians 12:12,14,27*

Although there are a large number of Christians on earth during the Tribulation, it is not necessary for a large number of saints to be together for there to be a church:

> [20] For where **two or three are gathered** together in My name, **I am there in the midst** of them. *Matthew 18:20*

The only requirement for a church is for two or three saints to be in communion with each other in Jesus' name. When two or three saints gather, the church is present. If there are even a few saints on earth, then there is a church on earth. It may be that formal church organizations will be outlawed by the Antichrist at some future point during the Tribulation or the church will become so corrupted that it no longer resembles what God meant it to be, but there will still be a faithful remnant of believers who hold true to their beliefs and convictions during that time as confirmed by the numerous references to the earthly saints who are present during the Tribulation.

Conversion to Christianity has been suggested as a way to explain saint references during the Tribulation. Some have posited that the numerous references to saints throughout the Tribulation necessarily means that a revival takes place where people repent of their sin, accept the gift of salvation and join the kingdom of God. Regarding the argument that there are new Christians who come to know the Lord during the Tribulation, this position is based on an assumptive interpretation of Revelation 7:9-14:

> [9] After these things I looked, and behold, **a great multitude** which no one could number, of all nations, tribes, peoples, and tongues, standing before the throne and before the Lamb, clothed with white robes, with palm branches in their hands, [10] and crying out with a loud voice, saying, "Salvation belongs to our God who sits on the throne, and to the Lamb!"... [13] Then one of the elders answered, saying to me, "**Who are these** arrayed in white robes, and where did they come from?" [14] And I said to him, "Sir, you know." So, he said to me, "**These are the ones who come out of the great tribulation, and washed their robes and made them white in the blood of the Lamb.** *Revelation 7:9-10, 13-14*

The plain text reading of the passage simply states that Christians are present during the Tribulation. If it is initially assumed that the church is gone during the Tribulation, then the assumption follows that the saints who emerge from the Tribulation must be new converts created during the Tribulation. However, taken at face value with no pre-existing assumptions, Revelation 7:9-15 simply means a large surviving remnant of the church stays true to their faith throughout the full seven years. The conversion argument is based on an absence of information. There are no other verses which plainly state there is a mass revival that takes place during the Tribulation causing people to come to know God and accept the gift of salvation. In the absence of plain text scripture validating the conversion argument, an assumption is required to reach that conclusion. On the contrary, what is clearly and unequivocally stated in scripture about conversion during the Tribulation is that in spite of the torments of the plagues, people refuse to repent of their sin, get angry with God and blaspheme Him:

> [18] By these three plagues a third of mankind was killed...[20] But the **rest of mankind**, who were not killed by these plagues, **did not repent** of the works of their hands...[21] And **they did not repent** of their murders or their sorceries or their sexual immorality or their thefts. *Revelation 9:18,20-21*
>
> [9] And **men were scorched** with great heat, and **they blasphemed the name of God** who has power over these plagues; and **they did not repent** and give Him glory. *Revelation 16:9*
>
> [10] ...and they gnawed their tongues because of the pain. [11] **They blasphemed the God of heaven** because of their pains and their sores, and **did not repent** of their deeds. *Revelation 16:10-11*

The Seals, Trumpets and Bowls judgments that God releases on the people do not have the effect of creating a mass revival involving repentance and conversion. Instead, scripture specifically states these events cause non-Christians to blaspheme and curse God. It does not say that men realize their errors, accept salvation and become new saints added to the kingdom during the Tribulation. Given the stated lack of conversion at that time, Revelation 7:9-15 can only refer to the church which goes through the Tribulation.

New Christians need to be nurtured and supported to grow in their faith. Without guidance and direction from more experienced and knowledgeable Christians, new converts would struggle in their walk much like new seedlings that are exposed to intense sunlight too early wither and die. If mature Christians are gone during the Tribulation, it would put new Christians at an extreme disadvantage. It is not in God's nature to set people up for failure. As long as there are people who are new to the faith, God will provide other, more mature Christians to help them grow. Scripture also states the church is present during the Tribulation as an opportunity to give testimony:

> [9] "But watch out for yourselves, for they will deliver you up to councils, and you will be beaten in the synagogues. **You will be brought before rulers and kings for My sake, for a testimony to them.** [10] And the gospel must first be preached to all the nations. [11] But **when they arrest you** and deliver you up, do not worry beforehand, or premeditate what you will speak. But **whatever is given you in that hour, speak that**; for it is not you who speak, but the Holy Spirit. *Mark 13:9-11*

There are those Christians within the church whose purpose it is to give testimony during the Tribulation. New Christians, who are early in their Christian walk, have a limited testimony to give. Mature Christians, who have experienced the faithfulness of God throughout their lives, are more prepared to provide examples of personal testimony as the Holy Spirit gives them utterance.

Also problematic for the church being gone before the Tribulation is that those who die for their faith during the Tribulation cannot enter into the temple until the last set of Tribulation plagues is finished:

> [8] The temple was filled with smoke from the glory of God and from His power, and **no one was able to enter the temple till the seven plagues** of the seven angels were **completed**. *Rev. 15:8*

If saints are not allowed into the temple until all of the plagues are finished at the end of the Tribulation, it presents a problem for the pre-Tribulation position. If, as pre-Tribulation advocates propose, saints are raptured and gone before the Tribulation, they would arrive at the temple too early and not be able to enter.

Another example of the church's presence on earth during the Tribulation is presented in Matthew 24:

> [21] For then **there will be great tribulation, such as has not been since the beginning of the world until this time**, no, nor ever shall be. [22] And unless those days were shortened, no flesh would be saved; but for the elect's sake those days will be shortened. [23] "**Then** if anyone says to you, 'Look, here is the Christ!' or 'There!' do not believe it. [24] For false Christs and **false prophets** will rise and show great signs and wonders to **deceive, if possible, even the elect**. *Matthew 24:21-24*

CAN YOU BELIEVE IT? It is estimated that 70 million Christians have been martyred for their faith since Jesus was crucified and the Church Age began.

The presence of false prophets during the Tribulation in an indication that the church still exists during the Tribulation. In order for false prophets to have anyone to deceive, the church must be present. In fact, the deception is so compelling, that even "the elect" within the church who represent the best of the best are at risk of being deceived.

Along with the influence of false religious leaders, the Sabbath still matters to God during the Tribulation:

> [20] And **pray that your flight may not be** in winter or **on the Sabbath**. *Matthew 24:20*

People are specifically told to ask God not to make them flee on the Sabbath. If there were no church, the Sabbath would not matter to God because there would be no one to keep it.

Further proof of the presence of God's church on earth during the Tribulation can be found in that Satan and the Antichrist are at war against Tribulation Christians which means Christians, also known as the body of Christ or the church, must be present on earth for this to happen.

> [7] It was **granted to him** (the Antichrist) **to make war with the saints** and to overcome them. And authority was given him over every tribe, tongue, and nation. *Revelation 13:7*

> [17] And the **dragon** (Satan) was enraged with the woman, and he **went to make war** with the rest of her offspring, **who keep the commandments of God and have the testimony of Jesus Christ** (Christians). *Revelation 12:17*

During the Tribulation, prayers of earthly saints are still being received in heaven by angels and elders where they deliver them to God on behalf of the saints on earth:

> [8] Now when He had taken the scroll, the four living creatures and the **twenty-four elders** fell down before the Lamb, **each having** a harp, and golden bowls full of incense, which are **the prayers of the saints**. *Revelation 5:8*

> [3] Then **another angel**, having a golden censer, came and stood at the altar. He was given much incense, that **he should offer it with the prayers of all the saints** upon the golden altar which was before the throne. [4] And the smoke of the incense, with **the prayers of the saints, ascended before God** from the angel's hand. *Revelation 8:3-4*

If all the saints were in heaven at this point, there would be no need for the angels to hand deliver their prayers to God. Eventually, when God's children are in heaven, they will have direct access to God as He dwells with them in person:

> ³And I heard a loud voice from **heaven** saying, "Behold, the **tabernacle of God is with men**, and **He will dwell with them**, and they shall be His people. **God Himself will be with them** and be their God." *Revelation 21:3*

If the saints were in heaven during the Tribulation, they would be able to communicate with God directly and have no need of angelic assistance.

Through it all, those in the church who faithfully press on through the Tribulation until Christ returns will experience persecution. Scripture speaks to the coordinated disdain for God's people:

> ¹Why do the nations rage, and the people plot a vain thing? ²The **kings of the earth** set themselves, and the **rulers take counsel together, against the LORD and against His Anointed**, saying, ³"Let us break their bonds in pieces and cast away their cords from us." *Psalm 2:1-3*

Tribulation Christians are specifically encouraged to "endure to the end":

> ¹³But he who **endures to the end** shall be saved. *Matthew 24:13*

> ¹³And you will be hated by all for My name's sake. But he who **endures to the end** shall be saved. *Mark 13:13*

If the church leaves before the Tribulation begins as some pre-Tribulation advocates assert, there would be no need to encourage believers to "endure to the end" as they would be gone from the earth and have nothing to endure. This warning indicates times will be rough and require a level of endurance from Christians as they progress through the Tribulation. Implied in these verses is that some Christians will not "endure to the end". Trials and tribulations have a way of refining Christians by trying their hearts and souls. God's servants will either become stronger through the struggles presented or fall away like chaff from wheat which flies away in the wind when it is threshed. For those who remain strong in the Lord, persecution will provide opportunities for testimony. During this final period in history before Christ returns, it is more important than ever for Christians to boldly proclaim God's word so that everyone has a fair chance to choose to follow the Living God. Unfortunately, some Christians will perish for their beliefs:

> ¹⁵He was granted power to give breath to the image of the beast, that the image of the beast should both speak and **cause as many as would not worship the image of the beast to be killed**. *Revelation 13:15*

Only Christians will reject worshipping the image of the beast, so it is Christians that this verse refers to as being killed. Ultimately, the Church Age ends with the persecution of the saints, or the church, throughout the Tribulation and the final return of God's son, Jesus the Christ.

Talk It Out

1. Do you think we are in the Tribulation period now or is it yet to happen? If you believe it is yet to happen, how far in the future do you think it will be? If you do not think we are in the Tribulation, do you think the birth pangs have begun which will ultimately lead us into the Tribulation?

2. Discuss the magnitude of Tribulation hardships by analyzing historical hardships (Spanish flu epidemic, Hitler, Stalin and WWII, Irish potato famine, Hiroshima and Nagasaki, the Great Depression, etc.) and comparing them to what might be experienced by humanity during the Tribulation. Since Mark 13:19 says there will be times like no one has ever experienced before, how do you think the Tribulation will change how people experience famine, disease, war and economic failure?

3. Do you think the Antichrist will outlaw churches during the Tribulation leaving individuals who worship God to meet in secret as in the early days of the church? If the Antichrist does allow churches to continue to formally exist and function, do you think he will regulate what they can and cannot say or do? Or will the church become so corrupted under the leadership of the False Prophet that it becomes a useful tool for the Antichrist to use to control the masses?

4. How would you compare the persecution of the early church as a whole to that of what the modern-day church experiences as a whole? How, specifically, are Christians persecuted today? What challenges does the modern-day church face?

5. Do you believe the church will be present during the Tribulation or gone before the Tribulation? Support your argument with verses.

6. If there are saints on earth during the Tribulation, do you believe that means the church is on earth during the Tribulation or that people are converted during the Tribulation? Define the relationship between saints and the church.

Ideas for the Week:

- ✓ Purchase a Jewish Calendar at https://www.perrystone.org/jewish-calendar/ to be aware of dates and feasts that may be of prophetic significance to God.
- ✓ Following the instructions given at https://www.wikihow.com/Graft-a-Tree to graft a branch of a lemon tree onto a lime tree or any other plant combination of your choosing.
- ✓ Offer to speak and share your personal testimony with local groups who regularly seek speakers (i.e. MOPS at www.mops.org, church events, senior citizen assisted living facilities, etc.)
- ✓ Maintain periodic contact with any new believers you know to help them grow in their walk with the Lord.

Closing Prayer

NOTE: Add names and individual personal prayer requests to the space provided below before closing in prayer.

Lord, we thank You for our time together today to grow deeper in our walk with You and fellowship with each other. As we close today, we lift up: _____

_____

_____

_____

_____

_____

_____

Father, all things happen in Your perfect timing. Give us patience to wait on the things You decree must linger and motivation to act on those things You call quickly. Let us always submit to Your pacing in our lives and grant us contentment that we may be satisfied with Your timing for that in our life which You order. In Jesus' name we pray, Amen.

SUPPORTING SCRIPTURES

THE SEVENTY WEEKS

[22] And he (Gabriel) informed me (Daniel), and talked with me, and said, "O Daniel, I have now come forth to give you skill to understand. [23] At the beginning of your supplications the command went out, and I have come to tell you, for you are greatly beloved; therefore consider the matter, and understand the vision: [24] "Seventy weeks are determined for your people and for your holy city, to finish the transgression, to make an end of sins, to make reconciliation for iniquity, to bring in everlasting righteousness, to seal up vision and prophecy, and to anoint the Most Holy. [25] Know therefore and understand, that from the going forth of the command to restore and build Jerusalem until Messiah the Prince, there shall be seven weeks and sixty-two weeks; the street shall be built again, and the wall, even in troublesome times. [26] And after the sixty-two weeks Messiah shall be cut off, but not for Himself; and the people of the prince who is to come shall destroy the city and the sanctuary. The end of it shall be with a flood, and till the end of the war desolations are determined. [27] Then he shall confirm a covenant with many for one week; but in the middle of the week he shall bring an end to sacrifice and offering. And on the wing of abominations shall be one who makes desolate, even until the consummation, which is determined, is poured out on the desolate." *Daniel 9:22-27*

COMMAND TO REBUILD JERUSALEM

[1] And it came to pass in the month of Nisan, in the twentieth year of King Artaxerxes, when wine was before him, that I (Nehemiah) took the wine and gave it to the king. Now I had never been sad in his presence before. [2] Therefore the king said to me, "Why is your face sad, since you are not sick? This is nothing but sorrow of heart." So, I became dreadfully afraid, [3] and said to the king, "May the king live forever! Why should my face not be sad, when the city, the place of my fathers' tombs, lies waste, and its gates are burned with fire?" [4] Then the king said to me, "What do you request?" So, I prayed to the God of heaven. [5] And I said to the king, "If it pleases the king, and if your servant has found favor in your sight, I ask that you send me to Judah, to the city of my fathers' tombs, that I may rebuild it." [6] Then the king said to me (the queen also sitting beside him), "How long will your journey be? And when will you return?" So, it pleased the king to send me; and I set him a time. *Nehemiah 2:1-6*

JESUS

[1] Now when they drew near Jerusalem, and came to Bethphage, at the Mount of Olives, then Jesus sent two disciples, [2] saying to them, "Go into the village opposite you, and immediately you will find a donkey tied, and a colt with her. Loose them and bring them to Me. [3] And if anyone says anything to you, you

shall say, 'The Lord has need of them,' and immediately he will send them."...[6] So the disciples went and did as Jesus commanded them. *Matthew 21:1-3,6*

[17] And He (Jesus), bearing His cross, went out to a place called the Place of a Skull, which is called in Hebrew, Golgotha, [18] where they crucified Him, and two others with Him, one on either side, and Jesus in the center. *John 19:17*

GENTILES AND THE CHURCH AGE
[11] ...But through their (Israel's) fall, to provoke them to jealousy, salvation has come to the Gentiles. [12] Now if their fall is riches for the world, and their failure riches for the Gentiles, how much more their fullness! [13] For I speak to you Gentiles; inasmuch as I am an apostle to the Gentiles, I magnify my ministry, [14] if by any means I may provoke to jealousy those who are my flesh and save some of them. [15] For if their being cast away is the reconciling of the world, what will their acceptance be but life from the dead? [16] For if the firstfruit is holy, the lump is also holy; and if the root is holy, so are the branches. [17] And if some of the branches were broken off, and you, being a wild olive tree, were grafted in among them, and with them became a partaker of the root and fatness of the olive tree, [18] do not boast against the branches. But if you do boast, remember that you do not support the root, but the root supports you. [19] You will say then, "Branches were broken off that I might be grafted in." [20] Well said. Because of unbelief they were broken off, and you stand by faith. Do not be haughty, but fear. [21] For if God did not spare the natural branches, He may not spare you either. [22] Therefore consider the goodness and severity of God: on those who fell, severity; but toward you, goodness, if you continue in His goodness. Otherwise you also will be cut off. [23] And they also, if they do not continue in unbelief, will be grafted in, for God is able to graft them in again. [24] For if you were cut out of the olive tree which is wild by nature, and were grafted contrary to nature into a cultivated olive tree, how much more will these, who are natural branches, be grafted into their own olive tree? [25] For I do not desire, brethren, that you should be ignorant of this mystery, lest you should be wise in your own opinion, that blindness in part has happened to Israel until the fullness of the Gentiles has come in. *Romans 11:11-25*

[1] There shall come forth a Rod from the stem of Jesse, and a Branch shall grow out of his roots...[10] And in that day there shall be a Root of Jesse, who shall stand as a banner to the people; for the Gentiles shall seek Him, and His resting place shall be glorious. *Isaiah 11:1,10*

¹⁶ "I, Jesus, have sent My angel to testify to you these things in the churches. I am the Root and the Offspring of David, the Bright and Morning Star." *Revelation 22:16*

THE TRIBULATION CHURCH
²² And He put all things under His feet, and gave Him (Christ) to be head over all things to the church, ²³ which is His body.... *Ephesians 1:22-23*

¹⁷ And the dragon was enraged with the woman, and he went to make war with the rest of her offspring, who keep the commandments of God and have the testimony of Jesus Christ. *Revelation 12:17*

¹² Here is the patience of the saints; here are those who keep the commandments of God and the faith of Jesus. *Revelation 14:12*

²⁰ For where two or three are gathered together in My name, I am there in the midst of them." *Matthew 18:20*

⁴Then I saw the souls of those who had been beheaded for their witness to Jesus and for the word of God, who had not worshiped the beast or his image, and had not received his mark on their foreheads or on their hands. *Revelation 20:4*

⁶ I saw the woman, drunk with the blood of the saints and with the blood of the martyrs of Jesus. And when I saw her, I marveled with great amazement. *Revelation 17:6*

¹⁰ And I fell at his feet to worship him. But he said to me, "See that you do not do that! I am your fellow servant, and of your brethren who have the testimony of Jesus. Worship God! For the testimony of Jesus is the spirit of prophecy." *Revelation 19:10*

¹⁹ For in those days there will be tribulation, such as has not been since the beginning of the creation which God created until this time, nor ever shall be. *Mark 13:19*

⁹ After these things I looked, and behold, a great multitude which no one could number, of all nations, tribes, peoples, and tongues, standing before the throne and before the Lamb, clothed with white robes, with palm branches in their hands, ¹⁰ and crying out with a loud voice, saying, "Salvation belongs to our God who sits on the throne, and to the Lamb!"...¹³ Then one of the elders answered, saying to me, "Who are these arrayed in white robes, and where did they come from?" ¹⁴ And I said to him, "Sir, you know." So, he said to me, "These are the ones who come out of the great tribulation, and washed their robes and made

them white in the blood of the Lamb. [15] Therefore they are before the throne of God, and serve Him day and night in His temple. And He who sits on the throne will dwell among them. *Revelation 7:9-10, 13-15*

[3] Then another angel, having a golden censer, came and stood at the altar. He was given much incense, that he should offer it with the prayers of all the saints upon the golden altar which was before the throne. [4] And the smoke of the incense, with the prayers of the saints, ascended before God from the angel's hand. *Revelation 8:3-4*

[8] Now when He had taken the scroll, the four living creatures and the twenty-four elders fell down before the Lamb, each having a harp, and golden bowls full of incense, which are the prayers of the saints. *Revelation 5:8*

[12] For as the body is one and has many members, but all the members of that one body, being many, are one body, so also is Christ...[14] For in fact the body is not one member but many... [20] But now indeed there are many members, yet one body...[27] Now you are the body of Christ, and members individually. *1 Corinthians 12:12,14,20,27*

[3] And I heard a loud voice from heaven saying, "Behold, the tabernacle of God is with men, and He will dwell with them, and they shall be His people. God Himself will be with them and be their God." *Revelation 21:3*

STIFFNECKED HUMANITY DURING TRIBULATION
[18] By these three plagues a third of mankind was killed... [20] But the rest of mankind, who were not killed by these plagues, did not repent of the works of their hands, that they should not worship demons, and idols of gold, silver, brass, stone, and wood, which can neither see nor hear nor walk. [21] And they did not repent of their murders or their sorceries or their sexual immorality or their thefts. *Revelation 9:18,20-21*

[9] And men were scorched with great heat, and they blasphemed the name of God who has power over these plagues; and they did not repent and give Him glory. [10] Then the fifth angel poured out his bowl on the throne of the beast, and his kingdom became full of darkness; and they gnawed their tongues because of the pain. [11] They blasphemed the God of heaven because of their pains and their sores, and did not repent of their deeds. *Revelation 16:9-11*

TRIBULATION SAINTS AND CHURCH PERSECUTED
[30] When you are in distress, and all these things come upon you in the latter days... *Deuteronomy 4:30*

[1] Why do the nations rage, and the people plot a vain thing? [2] The kings of the

earth set themselves, and the rulers take counsel together, against the LORD and against His Anointed, saying, ³ "Let us break their bonds in pieces and cast away their cords from us." *Psalm 2:1-3*

⁹ "Then they will deliver you up to tribulation and kill you, and you will be hated by all nations for My name's sake. ¹⁰ And then many will be offended, will betray one another, and will hate one another. ¹¹ Then many false prophets will rise up and deceive many. ¹² And because lawlessness will abound, the love of many will grow cold. ¹³ But he who endures to the end shall be saved...²⁰ And pray that your flight may not be in winter or on the Sabbath. ²¹ For then there will be great tribulation, such as has not been since the beginning of the world until this time, no, nor ever shall be. ²² And unless those days were shortened, no flesh would be saved; but for the elect's sake those days will be shortened. ²³ "Then if anyone says to you, 'Look, here is the Christ!' or 'There!' do not believe it. ²⁴ For false Christs and false prophets will rise and show great signs and wonders to deceive, if possible, even the elect. *Matthew 24:9-13,20-24*

⁷ It was granted to him (the Antichrist) to make war with the saints and to overcome them. And authority was given him over every tribe, tongue, and nation...¹⁵ He was granted power to give breath to the image of the beast, that the image of the beast should both speak and cause as many as would not worship the image of the beast to be killed. *Revelation 13:7,15*

⁹"But watch out for yourselves, for they will deliver you up to councils, and you will be beaten in the synagogues. You will be brought before rulers and kings for My sake, for a testimony to them. ¹⁰ And the gospel must first be preached to all the nations. ¹¹ But when they arrest you and deliver you up, do not worry beforehand, or premeditate what you will speak. But whatever is given you in that hour, speak that; for it is not you who speak, but the Holy Spirit. ¹² Now brother will betray brother to death, and a father his child; and children will rise up against parents and cause them to be put to death. ¹³ And you will be hated by all for My name's sake. But he who endures to the end shall be saved. *Mark 13:9-13*

¹⁷ And the dragon was enraged with the woman (Israel), and he went to make war with the rest of her offspring (Gentiles), who keep the commandments of God and have the testimony of Jesus Christ. *Revelation 12:13-17*

CHRONOLOGY
¹After these things I looked, and behold, a door standing open in heaven. And the first voice which I heard was like a trumpet speaking with me, saying, "Come up here, and I will show you things which must take place after this." *Revelation 4:1*

¹⁵ And the kings of the earth, the great men, the rich men, the commanders, the mighty men, every slave and every free man, hid themselves in the caves and in the rocks of the mountains, ¹⁶ and said to the mountains and rocks, "Fall on us and hide us from the face of Him who sits on the throne and from the wrath of the Lamb! ¹⁷ For the great day of His wrath has come, and who is able to stand?" *Revelation 6:15-17*

¹³ Then the sixth angel sounded: And I heard a voice from the four horns of the golden altar which is before God, ¹⁴ saying to the sixth angel who had the trumpet, "Release the four angels who are bound at the great river Euphrates." ¹⁵ So the four angels, who had been prepared for the hour and day and month and year, were released to kill a third of mankind. ¹⁶ Now the number of the army of the horsemen was two hundred million; I heard the number of them. ¹⁷ And thus I saw the horses in the vision: those who sat on them had breastplates of fiery red, hyacinth blue, and sulfur yellow; and the heads of the horses were like the heads of lions; and out of their mouths came fire, smoke, and brimstone. ¹⁸ By these three plagues a third of mankind was killed—by the fire and the smoke and the brimstone which came out of their mouths. ¹⁹ For their power is in their mouth and in their tails; for their tails are like serpents, having heads; and with them they do harm. *Revelation 9:13-18*

¹² Then the sixth angel poured out his bowl on the great river Euphrates, and its water was dried up, so that the way of the kings from the east might be prepared. ¹³ And I saw three unclean spirits like frogs coming out of the mouth of the dragon, out of the mouth of the beast, and out of the mouth of the false prophet. ¹⁴ For they are spirits of demons, performing signs, which go out to the kings of the earth and of the whole world, to gather them to the battle of that great day of God Almighty. ¹⁵ "Behold, I am coming as a thief. Blessed is he who watches, and keeps his garments, lest he walk naked and they see his shame." ¹⁶ And they gathered them together to the place called in Hebrew, Armageddon. *Revelation 16:12-16*

⁷ Let us be glad and rejoice and give Him glory, for the marriage of the Lamb has come, and His wife (the church) has made herself ready. *Revelation 19:7*

NOTES

"When God forgave me, I figured I'd better do it too."
— Johnny Cash

The Rapture and Return
WEEK 21: RESURRECTION OF THE DEAD

Opening Prayer: Lord, we ask that You send Your Holy Spirit to us to guide us in the teaching and understanding of Your word that we may obtain a better understanding of the prophetic events surrounding us now and waiting for us in the future. Bless our fellowship in Your word that it may be fruitful and draw us into a deeper relationship both with You and those around us. Use us as Your vessels that through us, we may reflect Your glory to all whom we encounter. Illuminate our hearts and minds so that we may boldly shine the brightness of Your light everywhere we go and that we may be beacons of Your hope in a darkened world. In Jesus name we pray, Amen.

Ice Breaker: No one is perfect, except for God. Imperfect Christians who are alive during the end times and who God deems righteous of heart will be raptured to be with Jesus when He returns at His second coming. If you had a time machine to go back in time and could only change one of your sins, what one mistake would you change to make your present-day self a little more "rapture ready" when the time is right?

If I could go back in time with the maturity I possess now, the one sin or mistake I would most like to correct is: _____

Focus: God is not forgetful and will never leave someone behind who is supposed to be with Him.

Imitation Resurrection

Satan, the great counterfeiter, imitates Jesus' resurrection in the fictitious story of the Egyptian god Osiris:

1. Jesus is eternal. Osiris was called the "Lord of Eternity".
2. Jesus is "King of Kings and Lord of Lords". Osiris was an earthly king.
3. Jesus came to fulfill the law. Osiris made laws.
4. Jesus traveled to Egypt. Osiris left Egypt to travel to Asia.
5. Jesus was crucified at the hands of those who hated Him. Osiris was murdered by his brother, Set, who hated him.
6. Jesus died on a wooden cross. Osiris' coffin became part of a tree.
7. Jesus was resurrected after His death. Osiris' wife, Isis, resurrected Osiris' body after his death.
8. Jesus judges mankind. Osiris, living and ruling in the underworld, is believed to have judged the dead in the Hall of Two Truths.

ARE WE THE TERMINAL GENERATION?

Word of the Week

> ⁵² ...For the trumpet will sound, and the dead will be **raised** incorruptible, and we shall be **changed**.
>
> *1 Corinthians 15:52*

RAISED and CHANGED: As it implies, the word "raised", from the Greek word "egeiro" (pronounced eg-i'-ro), means to wake something up as if from a state of sleep. As it applies to death and the resurrection, the dead will be woken up from a point of unconsciousness such as is experienced during sleep. After returning to active consciousness, Christians will receive new bodies. The Greek word "allasso" (pronounced al-las'-so) means to exchange one thing for another being transformed into something different. When Christians are raised to be with Jesus, they will exist in a different physical state than their earthly form.

Lesson: When Jesus returns, there is an event that will happen where believers will be caught up to meet Him in the air. This phenomenon is commonly referred to as the rapture. The term "rapture", like other words in the Christian vocabulary such as "trinity" and "Bible", is technically not found in scripture. Although distinctly missing from scripture, the word "rapture" is a commonly accepted term that refers to the gathering together of believers that occurs when they meet Jesus in the air at His return. Semantics aside, the rapture is still a real event that Christians in the Terminal Generation will experience as a part of prophetic end time events.

When the rapture occurs, it will happen at lightning speed "in the twinkling of an eye":

> ⁵¹ Behold, I tell you a mystery: We shall not all sleep, but **we shall all be changed**— ⁵² **in a moment, in the twinkling of an eye**, at the last trumpet. For the trumpet will sound, and the dead will be raised incorruptible, and **we shall be changed**. ⁵³ For this corruptible must put on incorruption, and this mortal must put on immortality. *I Corinthians 15:51-53*

Scientists define three different types of eye movements: the wink, the blink and the twink. A twink refers to the speed at which a particle of light is reflected off the eye which is equivalent to the speed of light, or 186,000 miles per hour. Given that a twink happens at the speed of light, the time it takes for a twinkle to happen is about a billionth of a second. When the rapture occurs, those who are caught up in the air will perceive it as being instantaneous. In addition to the transportation of consciousness from one place to another, those who are raptured will also receive new, transformed bodies as well:

> 20 For our citizenship is in heaven, from which we also eagerly wait for the Savior, the Lord Jesus Christ, 21 who will **transform our lowly body that it may be conformed to His glorious body...**" *Philippians 3:20-21*

FREAKY FACT: Biblically, winking is associated with sin.

Mirroring the likeness of Christ Himself, the immortal bodies believers receive will be fashioned like Jesus' resurrection body and suited to abide with Him throughout eternity:

> 2 Beloved, now we are children of God; and it has not yet been revealed what we shall be, but we know that when He is revealed, **we shall be like Him**, for we shall see Him as He is. *1 John 3:2*

Even in our new bodies, we will recognize others and others will recognize us:

> 12 For now we see in a mirror, dimly, but then face to face. Now I know in part, but then **I shall know just as I also am known**. *1 Corinthians 13:12*

Like the body of Christ, our new bodies will have the supernatural capability to be multiple places at once, yet still be able to appear solid at will to be able to enjoy earthly pleasures such as touching others and eating:

> 6 After that **He was seen by over five hundred brethren at once**... *1 Corinthians 15:6*

> 37 But they were terrified and frightened, and **supposed they had seen a spirit**. 38 And He said to them, "Why are you troubled? And why do doubts arise in your hearts? 39 Behold My hands and My feet, that it is I Myself. **Handle Me** and see, for a spirit does not have flesh and bones as you see I have."...41 But while they still did not believe for joy, and marveled, He said to them, "Have you any food here?" 42 So they gave Him a piece of a broiled fish and

some honeycomb. ⁴³ And **He took it and ate in their presence**. *Luke 24:36-39, 41-43*

When Jesus returns to redeem His people, it will be a noisy, easily observable event. Every eye will see Him:

> ⁷ Behold, He is coming with clouds, and **every eye will see Him**, even they who pierced Him. *Revelation 1:7*

No one will miss out on what is happening. Those who are not chosen to be raptured will respond with great fear and attempt to hide from the Lord in "the caves and rocks of the mountains":

> ¹⁵ And the **kings** of the earth, the **great men**, the **rich men**, the **commanders**, the mighty men, every **slave** and every **free man**, **hid themselves in the caves and in the rocks of the mountains**, ¹⁶ and said to the mountains and rocks, "Fall on us and hide us from the face of Him who sits on the throne and from the wrath of the Lamb! ¹⁷ For the great day of His wrath has come, and who is able to stand?" *Revelation 6:15-17*

> ...²⁶ **men's hearts failing them from fear** and the expectation of those things which are coming on the earth, for the powers of the heavens will be shaken. ²⁷ Then **they will see the Son of Man coming in a cloud with power and great glory**. *Luke 21:25-27*

It is not a far stretch of the imagination to envision world leaders fleeing to fortified underground cement bunkers and the US military futilely mounting a defense from deep within the Cheyanne Mountain Range complex in fulfillment of this verse.

A common issue of rapture and return debate is the concept of a secret, separate rapture. This concept stems from verses which equate Jesus' return to being like a "thief in the night" implying some sort of clandestine event. Clarification of the intent of that analogy is given in 2 Peter 3:10:

> ¹⁰ But the day of the Lord will come as a **thief in the night**, in which the heavens will pass away **with a great noise**, and the **elements will melt with fervent** heat; both the earth and the works that are in it will be burned up." *2 Peter 3:10*

Returning as a "thief in the night" on the Day of the Lord speaks to the element of surprise in not knowing when Jesus will return. This is consistent with Matthew 24:36 which states that no one knows the day or hour of Jesus' return:

³⁶ But of that day and hour **no one knows**... *Matthew 24:36*

Read together, both verses reference the element of surprise followed by much commotion; not a secret, hidden event. After the surprise is revealed, there is nothing quiet or subtle about His coming. Every moment after the big reveal is noisy, bright and full of witnesses. The rapture, which follows His return, is not a quiet, separate event either:

> ¹⁶ For the **Lord Himself will descend from heaven with <u>a shout</u>**, with the **<u>voice</u> of an archangel**, and with **the <u>trumpet</u> of God**. And the dead in Christ will rise first. ¹⁷ **Then we** who are alive and remain **shall be caught up together with them in the clouds** to meet the Lord in the air. And thus, we shall always be with the Lord." *1 Thessalonians 4:16-17*

Preceded by the sound of Jesus Himself giving a loud shout, the voice of an archangel and a heavenly trumpet, the rapture will be an event noticed by all followed by massive destruction on the earth. Neither the Lord's coming nor the rapture are quiet, secret events and life does not continue on as usual once they have occurred.

Many debate the timing of the rapture. Pre-Tribulationists assert that Christians will be raptured at the beginning of the Tribulation. Post-Tribulationists present that believers will be raptured at the end of the Tribulation. Scripture provides a clear answer to the question. According to John 6:44, those who are raised up are raised up on the "last day":

> ⁴⁴ No one can come to Me unless the Father who sent Me draws him; and **I will raise him up at the last day**. *John 6:44*

Timing for the raising of the dead in Christ is reiterated again in 1 Corinthians 15:22-24:

> ²² For as in Adam all die, even so **in Christ all shall be made alive**. ²³ But each one in his own order: Christ the firstfruits, **afterward those who are Christ's at His coming**. ²⁴ **Then comes the end**, when He delivers the kingdom to God the Father, when He puts an end to all rule and all authority and power. *I Corinthians 15:22-24*

Note the assigned order of events when Christ returns:

> ¹⁶ For the **Lord Himself will descend** from heaven with a shout, with the voice of an archangel, and with the trumpet of God. And

the **dead in Christ will rise <u>first</u>**. ¹⁷ **<u>Then</u> we who are alive and remain shall be caught up together with them** in the clouds to meet the Lord in the air. And thus, we shall always be with the Lord." *1 Thessalonians 4:16-17*

In proper order, first Jesus returns, then the dead in Christ are raised and finally, the living are raptured. If the dead in Christ, who must first be raised before the living can be raptured, cannot be raised until the last day, then it is impossible for living Christians to be raptured prior to the "last day". To hold that Christians are raptured at the beginning of the Tribulation allows them to be with Jesus before the end of the Tribulation when the dead are raised at Jesus' return and is therefore a violation of scripture. The raising of deceased Christians must precede the rapture of the living which is strictly defined as an end Tribulation event. Also supporting that the rapture occurs at the end of the Tribulation is Daniel 7:25:

> ²⁵ **He** (the Antichrist)...**shall persecute the saints** of the Most High...Then **the saints shall be given into his hand** for a time and times and half a time. *Daniel 7:25*

In order for the Antichrist to persecute the saints, they must be on the earth and subject to the Antichrist's rule during the Tribulation. If the saints are raptured away at the beginning of the Tribulation as some put forth, the Antichrist would not have any saints to persecute.

Regarding the resurrection of the dead, Christians and non-Christians alike will be resurrected, but at different times. Believers will be resurrected at the time of Christ's return. Unbelievers will not be resurrected until much later after Jesus returns:

> ⁴Then **I saw the souls of those who had been beheaded for their witness to Jesus** and for the word of God, who had not worshiped the beast or his image, and had not received his mark on their foreheads or on their hands. And **they lived** and reigned with Christ for a thousand years. ⁵ **But the rest of the dead did not live again until the thousand years were finished**. *Revelation 20:4-5*

Crucial to the heart of the rapture debate is where we go when we die. Rightly dividing God's word to determine where deceased Christians reside before this end time event is an important piece to decode the entire rapture mystery. Scripture assigns a specific order of events regarding the rapture. First, deceased Christians, or the "dead in Christ", will be raised to meet Jesus. After deceased Christians are resurrected, living Christians will follow in a rapture of the living. Note that the rapture of living Christians does not precede the raising of the dead in Christ—there is a specified sequence of events. This presents a theological conundrum for many Christians since it is a widely held popular belief that when a Christian passes, that person then goes up to heaven to be with the Lord which begs the question, "How can Christians be resurrected when Jesus returns if they are already with Him in heaven?" Two verses are typically cited to support the belief that deceased Christians immediately go to heaven. First, 2 Corinthians 5:8 is commonly misquoted as "to be absent from the body is to be present with the Lord." The fallacy of this interpretation is that the actual scriptural text for the verse across many translations of the Bible uses the word "and" instead of "is" which alters the meaning of the verse:

> [8] We are confident, yes, well pleased rather to be absent from the body **and** to be present with the Lord. *2 Corinthians 5:8*

Considered in the full context of the passage including the surrounding verses 1-7, Paul does not equate being out of the body as being equal to being with the Lord as the word "is" would suggest. They are not one and the same. Read in context in the entirety of the passage including verses 1-7 with the conjunction "and" instead of the verb "is", it becomes clear that Paul is referencing a preference for being with the Lord over residing in his earthly body.

Another commonly quoted passage to support the belief that the dead are currently in heaven with Christ is Luke 23:43:

> [43] And Jesus said to him, "Assuredly, I say to you, **today** you will be with Me in Paradise." *Luke 23:43*

Using this passage as proof that the dead are in heaven right now assumes that Jesus literally meant the criminal who accepted salvation in his final moments of life would go to heaven that specific day which was the day of his death. However, there is a problem with this interpretation. 1 Corinthians 15:4 clearly states that Jesus did not rise again until the third day:

> [4] and that He (Jesus) was buried, and that **He rose again the third day** according to the Scriptures... *1 Corinthians 15:4*

Ephesians 4:9-10 elaborates more on the whereabouts of Jesus before He went to heaven:

> [9] Now this, "He ascended"—what does it mean but that He (Jesus) also **first descended** into the lower parts of the earth? [10] He who

descended is also the One who ascended far above all the heavens, that He might fill all things. *Ephesians 4:9-10*

Commonly accepted as a statement of faith, many churches routinely recite the *Apostle's Creed* in their worship services reiterating the same concept:

> I believe in God the Father Almighty, Maker of heaven and earth. And in Jesus Christ his only Son our Lord; who was conceived by the Holy Ghost, born of the Virgin Mary, suffered under Pontius Pilate, was crucified, dead, and buried; **he descended into hell**; **the third day he rose again** from the dead; **he ascended into heaven**...

If Jesus first descended "into the lower parts of the earth" and did not ascend for three days, He could not have been in heaven on the first day of His death with the criminal who was crucified beside Him. To suppose that the criminal literally went directly to heaven at the moment of his death would put him in heaven before the arrival of Christ which cannot happen because Christ must arrive in heaven first being the "firstfruit":

> [23]...**Christ the firstfruits**, afterward those who are Christ's **at His coming**. *I Corinthians 15:23*

Therefore, using the term "today" from Luke 23:43 to confirm the timing that the thief was in heaven with Jesus on the exact day of his actual death is not a valid interpretation for the scripture reference. A more likely interpretation for Luke 23:43 that does not violate scriptural principles is that Jesus was referring to the decision the thief made that day to accept Jesus as God's son which would ultimately put him in heaven with Jesus at some point in the future. John 3:13 is even more direct about the matter when it states outright that no one except Jesus is in heaven:

> [13] **No one has ascended to heaven** but He who came down from heaven, that is, the **Son of Man** who **is in heaven**. *John 3:13*

In essence, concerning the resurrection of the Christian dead, if Christians went immediately to be with the Lord upon their death, there would be no need for Jesus to resurrect them at a later date. In fact, the concept of the dead presently residing in heaven with Jesus immediately after death presents a direct contradiction to resurrection scriptures. If the dead are in heaven with Jesus as is commonly taught in many modern churches, then they would not be in their graves ready to be resurrected later in the Tribulation timeframe making a future resurrection a literal impossibility since they would already be with Jesus in that scenario. In order to allow for the concept of a Christian resurrection of the dead when Jesus returns as is clearly stated in 1 Thessalonians 4:16-17, the dead must be waiting for Him in their graves.

Consistent with this interpretation are a number of other passages which refer to the dead as "sleeping":

> [30] For this reason many are weak and sick among you, and **many sleep**. *1 Corinthians 11:30*

> ...[10] who died for us, that **whether we wake or sleep**, we should live together with Him. *1 Thessalonians 5:10*

Jesus plainly explains in John 11:12-14 that when He talks about sleep, He means death:

> [12] Then His disciples said, "Lord, if **he sleeps** he will get well." [13] However, Jesus spoke of his death, but they thought that He was speaking about taking rest in sleep. [14] Then **Jesus said** to them plainly, "**Lazarus is dead.**" *John 11:12-14*

Contradicting the popular view that the dead are partying with Jesus in heaven, Ecclesiastes 9:5 specifically states that the unconscious sleeping dead "know nothing" indicating a general lack of awareness of anything which is similar to a state of sleep:

> [5] For the living know that they will die; but **the dead know nothing**... *Ecclesiastes 9:5*

Elaborating further is Isaiah 26:19 which states the sleeping dead wake up indicating a change in consciousness from unconscious to conscious:

> [19] Your dead shall live; together with my dead body they shall arise. **Awake** and sing, **you who dwell in dust**...and **the earth shall cast out the dead**. *Isaiah 26:19*

Those who are in a state of sleep do not recognize the passage of time. From the moment of death, their next conscious recognition is waking up to the presence of Jesus. Isaiah 26:19 then further states the dead leave their graves after waking. In agreement with this action is John 5:28-29 and Daniel 12:2 which both indicate that Christians and non-Christians alike wait for Jesus in their graves:

> [25] Most assuredly, I say to you, the hour is coming, and now is, when the dead will hear the voice of the Son of God; and those who hear will live...[28] Do not marvel at this; for the hour is coming

in which **all who are in the graves will hear His voice** ²⁹ **and come forth**—those who have done good, to the resurrection of life, and those who have done evil, to the resurrection of condemnation. *John 5:25, 28-29*

²And many of **those who sleep in the dust of the earth shall awake**, some to everlasting life, some to shame and everlasting contempt. *Daniel 12:2*

Ezekiel 37:13 references Christians being brought out of their graves by the Lord:

¹³Then you shall know that I am the LORD, **when I have opened your graves**, O My people, and **brought you up from your graves**. *Ezekiel 37:13*

Logically speaking, the dead must first be in their graves in order to leave them later. When His people come out of their graves, they emerge up from the earth, not down from heaven.

Consistent with the view of deceased souls sleeping in their graves is Psalm 115:17 which states the dead are silent and "do not praise the Lord.":

¹⁷The **dead do not praise the LORD**, nor any who **go down into silence**. *Psalm 115:17*

Agreeing with Isaiah 26:19 that the dead sing when they wake up, Revelation 19:5 also indicates when the dead are eventually with the Lord, they audibly praise God:

⁵Then a voice came from the throne, saying, "**Praise our God, all you His servants** and those who fear Him, both small and great!" *Revelation 19:5*

The dead cannot be in heaven if they are not joyfully worshipping before the throne. If deceased souls are currently in heaven with Jesus, they would not be silent and would definitely be praising God! Further substantiating that the dead are not currently with Jesus in heaven is John 14:2-3 when Jesus promises to prepare a house for His people in heaven and then return to retrieve them later:

² In My Father's house are many mansions; if it were not so, I would have told you. **I go to prepare a place for you**. ³ And if I go and prepare a place for you, **I will come again and receive you** to Myself; that where I am, there you may be also. *John 14:2-3*

No reference can be found anywhere in scripture of dead souls helping Jesus build the homes in heaven or watching Him as He builds homes for them. If deceased Christians are in heaven as is commonly taught, there would be no need for Jesus to come back and retrieve the dead to bring them back to their new homes as scripture specifically states He will do. Parallels can be drawn between Jesus building a mansion for His bride, the church, and a Jewish wedding ceremony. In ancient times, after a bride and groom were betrothed, the groom would leave to build a place for them to live after they were married. When the groom was finished, he would then return at a generally expected time at a surprise moment to retrieve his betrothed and take her to their new home. Like the Jewish wedding ceremony, when Jesus leaves to build a home for His bride, the church, the bride is not with Him at that time.

Another piece of evidence that deceased Christians are in an unconscious state is that the deceased souls of the martyrs wake up from under the altar and ask the Lord how much longer they are going to have to wait for His return to earth in Revelation 6:9-11:

> [9] When He opened the fifth seal, I saw **under the altar** the souls of those who had been slain for the word of God and for the testimony which they held. [10] And they cried with a loud voice, saying, "How long, O Lord, holy and true, until You judge and avenge our blood on those who dwell on the earth?" [11] Then a white robe was given to each of them; and it was said to them that they should **rest a little while longer**, until both the number of their fellow servants and their brethren, who would be killed as they were, was completed. *Revelation 6:9-11*

Jesus responds by telling them to be patient and go back to sleep. Much like a parent is there for a child who wakes in the middle of the night, Jesus watches over the souls of the sleeping deceased to tend to their needs should they wake up, but He is not keeping daily company and having regular interactions with deceased souls. Daniel is also told to "rest" and "arise" at a later date:

> [13] "But you (Daniel), go your way till the end; for you shall **rest**, and will **arise** to your inheritance **at the end of the days**." *Daniel 12:13*

Regarding the receipt of his inheritance, if Daniel was with Jesus, there would be no need for him to wait for his inheritance since he would already have it being in the presence of Jesus. Another example of a Christian soul waking up from the sleep of death can be found in 1 Samuel 28:14-15 when Saul consults a medium to call upon Samuel after he is deceased:

> ¹⁴ So he (Saul) said to her (the medium), "What is his form?" And she said, "An old man is coming up, and he is covered with a mantle." And Saul perceived that it was Samuel, and he stooped with his face to the ground and bowed down. ¹⁵ Now Samuel said to Saul, "Why have you **disturbed me by bringing me up**?" And Saul answered, "I am deeply distressed; for the Philistines make war against me, and God has departed from me and does not answer me anymore, neither by prophets nor by dreams. Therefore, I have called you, that you may reveal to me what I should do." *1 Samuel 28:14-15*

This passage indicates Samuel awoke and arose from a grave located someplace below and did not descend from above to get to earth. Either deceased souls are in their graves below waiting for Jesus to return and resurrect them at a later point in time or they are in heaven with Him until His return, but they are not simultaneously in two places at once. And if they are not in graves waiting to go up when Jesus calls, then it is not possible to resurrect them before the rapture.

A portrait of the future resurrection is provided in Matthew. After Jesus' resurrection, He resurrected a portion of the deceased saints of His day:

> ⁵⁰ And Jesus cried out again with a loud voice, and yielded up His spirit. ⁵¹ Then, behold, the veil of the temple was torn in two from top to bottom; and the earth quaked, and the rocks were split, ⁵² and the graves were opened; and **many bodies of the saints who had fallen asleep** were **raised**; ⁵³ and coming out of the graves **after His resurrection**, they **went into the holy city** and **appeared to many**. *Matthew 27:50-52*

Note the use of the word "many" as opposed to the concept of "all" indicating there were some saints who remained in their graves. When Jesus returns, only the righteous will be raised while the rest of mankind remains in their graves. When the Christian dead are resurrected, they will go with Jesus to the "holy city" which will be the rebuilt Jerusalem. Resurrected souls will be recognizable to those they know just as the resurrected souls in this passage were recognized by the living. It is not stated where the resurrected souls went after they were resurrected. Since John 3:13 states that no one is in heaven, it must be assumed that Jesus put the souls who were awakened back to sleep again much like He tells the souls who wake up in Revelation 6:9-11 to go back to sleep.

Sadly, not everyone who expects to be raptured will be raptured. When Jesus returns to rapture His people to be with Him at His return, approximately only fifty percent of the population are worthy of being taken.

> [39]...so also will the **coming of the Son of Man** be. [40] Then **two men** will be **in the field: one will be taken and the other left**. [41] **Two women** will be **grinding at the mill: one will be taken and the other left**. [42] Watch therefore, for you do not know what hour your Lord is coming. [43] But know this, that if the master of the house had known what hour the thief would come, he would have watched and not allowed his house to be broken into. [44] Therefore you also be ready, for the Son of Man is coming at an hour you do not expect. *Matthew 24:39-44*

The mathematical concept of fifty percent is reiterated again in Luke:

> [30] Even so will it be in the day **when the Son of Man is revealed**. [31] In that day, he who is on the housetop, and his goods are in the house, let him not come down to take them away. And likewise, the one who is in the field, let him not turn back. [32] Remember Lot's wife. [33] Whoever seeks to save his life will lose it, and whoever loses his life will preserve it. [34] I tell you, in that night there will be **two men in one bed: the one will be taken and the other will be left**. [35] **Two women will be grinding together: the one will be taken and the other left**. [36] **Two men will be in the field: the one will be taken and the other left**. *Luke 17:30-36*

Again, in the parable of the Ten Virgins, the fifty percent guideline is emphasized:

> [1]Then the kingdom of heaven shall be likened to **ten virgins** who took their lamps and went out to meet the bridegroom. [2] Now **five of them were wise, and five were foolish**. [3] Those who were foolish took their lamps and took no oil with them, [4] but the wise took oil in their vessels with their lamps. [5] But while the bridegroom was delayed, they all slumbered and slept. [6] And at midnight a cry was heard: "Behold, **the bridegroom is coming**; go out to meet him!" [7] Then all those virgins arose and trimmed their lamps. [8] And the foolish said to the wise, "Give us some of your oil, for our lamps are going out." [9] But the wise answered, saying, "No, lest there should not be enough for us and you; but go rather to those who sell, and buy for yourselves." [10] And while they went to buy, the bridegroom came, and **those who were ready went in with him to the wedding; and the door was shut**. [11] Afterward the other virgins came also, saying, "Lord, Lord, open to us!" [12] But **He answered** and said, "Assuredly, I say to you, **I do not know you**."

[13] "Watch therefore, for you know neither the day nor the hour in which the Son of Man is coming. *Matthew 25:1-13*

However, this parable adds more dimension to the discussion: only five out of ten *Christians* are raptured. All ten of the women in this parable expect to be able to go with Jesus. Clearly, all ten are initially comfortable in the knowledge that they belong with Jesus. However, only five are ready to leave with Him when He arrives and the other five get left behind. When the remaining five attempt to come back at a later point, they are sent away by Jesus and He claims not to know them. Another parable is given in Luke reiterating that there will be those who think they are going to be with Jesus, but they are tragically mistaken:

> [22] And He went through the cities and villages, teaching, and journeying toward Jerusalem. [23] Then one said to Him, "Lord, are there few who are saved?" And He said to them, [24] "Strive to enter through the narrow gate, for many, I say to you, will seek to enter and will not be able. [25] When once the Master of the house has risen up and shut the door, and you begin to stand outside and knock at the door, saying, '**Lord, Lord, open for us**,' and He will answer and say to you, '**I do not know you**, where you are from,' [26] then you will begin to say, '**We ate and drank in Your presence**, and You taught in our streets.' [27] But He will say, 'I tell you I do not know you, where you are from. Depart from Me, all you workers of iniquity.' [28] There will be weeping and gnashing of teeth, when you see Abraham and Isaac and Jacob and all the prophets in the kingdom of God, and **yourselves thrust out**." *Luke 13:22-28*

When compared to the greater populace as a whole, the picture presented is even more dismal:

> [14] "Return, O backsliding children," says the LORD; "for I am married to you. I will take you, **one from a city** and **two from a family**, and I will bring you to Zion. *Jeremiah 3:14*

Only one person in an entire city might be worthy of being taken. Even within families, only one or two people qualify as worthy. Highlighting the importance of being ready when Jesus arrives, these parables underscore just how serious the consequences are for those who take their faith too lightly, ignore their relationship with Jesus, slack off in their earthly responsibilities to support the church through tithes and volunteering and fail to actively demonstrate love for their fellow human beings. When the times comes, there are going to be a lot of Christians who are caught off guard. Don't be one of them.

Talk It Out

1. Do you find the fact the word "rapture" is not technically mentioned in scripture to be an obstacle in accepting the concept of believers being caught up in the air to meet Jesus when He returns?

2. What do you think our new bodies will be like when the rapture occurs?

3. Do you think the "thief in the night" analogy to Jesus' return refers to a quiet, secret happening or the element of surprise which catches people unprepared in the midst of an otherwise obvious event?

4. Where do you think deceased Christian souls spend their time awaiting Christ's return? Are they in heaven now or unconsciously sleeping in the earth until Jesus wakes them up?

5. Why do you think the deceased martyrs become impatient and pester Jesus about the timing of His return? What do you think of the response Jesus gives them to go back to sleep?

6. If Jesus came today would you be ready to go with Him, or would you be running to find oil like one of the other five virgins? What kind of "oil" do you think a Christian needs to be rapture-worthy?

7. REVIEW: Over the last few weeks, a number of points have been presented about the rapture and return. Discuss whether or not you agree or disagree with the following statements:

    A. Saints are on earth during the Tribulation
    B. Revelation is written out of chronological order and cannot be used as a valid argument that the church is not mentioned after chapter 4.
    C. The Restrainer who is removed is the word of God.
    D. There is an order of events that must occur with the rapture which states Jesus first descends with a shout and trumpet, next, the dead are resurrected, then living Christians are raptured.
    E. The dead are waiting in their graves for the return of Christ.

"We have a generation of people who think they can stand before the judgment seat of God despite their sins." — R.C. Sproul

Ideas for the Week:

- ✓ Shine a flashlight over water to see just how fast a shimmering twinkle can be.
- ✓ Watch the Tim LaHaye series *Left Behind* with a few friends. Have a discussion after the show about the biblical probability of a Pre-Tribulation rapture scenario and compare the story against scripture.
- ✓ Go to the store and stock up your home for long term independent living. If you believe in a Post-Tribulation rapture, you'll eventually need the supplies. If you believe in a Pre-Tribulation rapture scenario, then you'll be leaving provisions for those left behind. Either way, it's a good idea to be as self-sufficient as possible.
- ✓ Inventory the number of Bibles in your home. Make sure you have more than a few. If you believe in a post-Tribulation rapture, you may need to hold worship services in your home. If you believe in a pre-Tribulation rapture, those left behind may not be able to get Bibles and your stash will help spread the word during the darkness of the Tribulation.

Closing Prayer

NOTE: Add names and individual personal prayer requests to the space provided below before closing in prayer.

Lord, we thank You for our time together today to grow deeper in our walk with You and fellowship with each other. As we close today, we lift up:_____

_____

_____

_____

_____

_____

Father, whether alive or dead, we rest in the comfort of Your bosom, knowing we are safe in Your protective arms. Only You know how long our days are upon the earth. We ask You to bless us that all would be well with us while we are here and that our days may be full of service to You as we work to strengthen Your kingdom and spread the gospel. In Jesus' name we pray, Amen.

SUPPORTING SCRIPTURES

JESUS RETURNS

⁹...He (Jesus) was taken up, and a cloud received Him out of their sight. ¹⁰ And while they looked steadfastly toward heaven as He went up, behold, two men stood by them in white apparel, ¹¹ who also said, "...why do you stand gazing up into heaven? This same Jesus, who was taken up from you into heaven, will so come in like manner as you saw Him go into heaven." *Acts 1:9-11*

² In My Father's house are many mansions; if it were not so, I would have told you. I go to prepare a place for you. ³ And if I go and prepare a place for you, I will come again and receive you to Myself; that where I am, there you may be also. *John 14:2-3*

⁷ Behold, He is coming with clouds, and every eye will see Him, even they who pierced Him. *Revelation 1:7*

²² For as in Adam all die, even so in Christ all shall be made alive. ²³ But each one in his own order: Christ the firstfruits, afterward those who are Christ's at His coming. ²⁴ Then comes the end, when He delivers the kingdom to God the Father, when He puts an end to all rule and all authority and power. *I Corinthians 15:22-24*

...¹³ so that He may establish your hearts blameless in holiness before our God and Father at the coming of our Lord Jesus Christ with all His saints. *1 Thessalonians 3:13*

⁵...Thus the Lord my God will come, and all the saints with You. *Zechariah 14:5*

³¹ When the Son of Man comes...and all the holy angels with Him... *Matt. 25:31*

³⁶ But of that day and hour no one knows... *Matthew 24:36*

THE NOISE AND BRIGHTNESS OF HIS COMING

³ Our God shall come, and shall not keep silent; a fire shall devour before Him, and it shall be very tempestuous all around Him. *Psalm 50:3*

²⁵ And there will be signs in the sun, in the moon, and in the stars; and on the earth distress of nations, with perplexity, the sea and the waves roaring; ²⁶ men's hearts failing them from fear and the expectation of those things which are coming on the earth, for the powers of the heavens will be shaken. ²⁷ Then they will see the Son of Man coming in a cloud with power and great glory. *Luke 21:25-27*

¹⁵ And the kings of the earth, the great men, the rich men, the commanders, the

mighty men, every slave and every free man, hid themselves in the caves and in the rocks of the mountains, [16] and said to the mountains and rocks, "Fall on us and hide us from the face of Him who sits on the throne and from the wrath of the Lamb! [17] For the great day of His wrath has come, and who is able to stand?" *Revelation 6:15-17*

[10] But the day of the Lord will come as a thief in the night, in which the heavens will pass away with a great noise, and the elements will melt with fervent heat; both the earth and the works that are in it will be burned up. *2 Peter 3:10*

[8] And then the lawless one will be revealed, whom the Lord will consume with the breath of His mouth and destroy with the brightness of His coming. *2 Thessalonians 2:8*

[7] …when the Lord Jesus is revealed from heaven with His mighty angels, [8] in flaming fire taking vengeance on those who do not know God, and on those who do not obey the gospel of our Lord Jesus Christ. *2 Thessalonians 1:7-8*

RESURRECTION OF THE DEAD
[1]… and there shall be a time of trouble, such as never was since there was a nation, even to that time. And at that time your people shall be delivered, every one who is found written in the book. [2] And many of those who sleep in the dust of the earth shall awake, some to everlasting life, some to shame and everlasting contempt. *Daniel 12:1-2*

[32] If, in the manner of men, I have fought with beasts at Ephesus, what advantage is it to me? If the dead do not rise, "Let us eat and drink, for tomorrow we die!" *1 Corinthians 15:32*

[40] And this is the will of Him who sent Me, that everyone who sees the Son and believes in Him may have everlasting life; and I will raise him up at the last day. *John 6:40*

RAPTURE SPEED AND BODY
[35] But someone will say, "How are the dead raised up? And with what body do they come?" [36] Foolish one, what you sow is not made alive unless it dies. [37] And what you sow, you do not sow that body that shall be, but mere grain—perhaps wheat or some other grain. [38] But God gives it a body as He pleases, and to each seed its own body. [39] All flesh is not the same flesh, but there is one kind of flesh of men, another flesh of animals, another of fish, and another of birds. [40] There are also celestial bodies and terrestrial bodies; but the glory of the celestial is one, and the glory of the terrestrial is another. [41] There is one glory of the sun, another glory of the moon, and another glory of the stars; for one star differs from another star in glory. [42] So also is the resurrection of the dead. The body is sown

in corruption, it is raised in incorruption. [43] It is sown in dishonor; it is raised in glory. It is sown in weakness; it is raised in power. [44] It is sown a natural body; it is raised a spiritual body. There is a natural body, and there is a spiritual body. [45] And so it is written, "The first man Adam became a living being." The last Adam became a life-giving spirit. [46] However, the spiritual is not first, but the natural, and afterward the spiritual. [47] The first man was of the earth, made of dust; the second Man is the Lord from heaven. [48] As was the man of dust, so also are those who are made of dust; and as is the heavenly Man, so also are those who are heavenly. [49] And as we have borne the image of the man of dust, we shall also bear the image of the heavenly Man. [50] Now this I say, brethren, that flesh and blood cannot inherit the kingdom of God; nor does corruption inherit incorruption. [51] Behold, I tell you a mystery: We shall not all sleep, but we shall all be changed— [52] in a moment, in the twinkling of an eye, at the last trumpet. For the trumpet will sound, and the dead will be raised incorruptible, and we shall be changed. [53] For this corruptible must put on incorruption, and this mortal must put on immortality. [54] So when this corruptible has put on incorruption, and this mortal has put on immortality, then shall be brought to pass the saying that is written: "Death is swallowed up in victory. [55] O Death, where is your sting? O Hades, where is your victory?" *1 Corinthians 15:50-55*

[20] For our citizenship is in heaven, from which we also eagerly wait for the Savior, the Lord Jesus Christ, [21] who will transform our lowly body that it may be conformed to His glorious body..." *Philippians 3:20-21*

[12] For now we see in a mirror, dimly, but then face to face. Now I know in part, but then I shall know just as I also am known. *1 Corinthians 13:12*

[2] Beloved, now we are children of God; and it has not yet been revealed what we shall be, but we know that when He is revealed, we shall be like Him, for we shall see Him as He is. *1 John 3:2*

[6] After that He was seen by over five hundred brethren at once… *1 Cor. 15:6*

[36] Now as they said these things, Jesus Himself stood in the midst of them, and said to them, "Peace to you." [37] But they were terrified and frightened, and supposed they had seen a spirit. [38] And He said to them, "Why are you troubled? And why do doubts arise in your hearts? [39] Behold My hands and My feet, that it is I Myself. Handle Me and see, for a spirit does not have flesh and bones as you see I have."…[41] But while they still did not believe for joy, and marveled, He said to them, "Have you any food here?" [42] So they gave Him a piece of a broiled fish and some honeycomb. [43] And He took it and ate in their presence. *Luke 24:36-39, 41-43*

³⁰ For in the resurrection they neither marry nor are given in marriage, but are like angels of God in heaven. *Matthew 22:30*

RAPTURE ORDER

¹³ But I do not want you to be ignorant, brethren, concerning those who have fallen asleep, lest you sorrow as others who have no hope. ¹⁴ For if we believe that Jesus died and rose again, even so God will bring with Him those who sleep in Jesus. ¹⁵ For this we say to you by the word of the Lord, that we who are alive and remain until the coming of the Lord will by no means precede those who are asleep. ¹⁶ For the Lord Himself will descend from heaven with a shout, with the voice of an archangel, and with the trumpet of God. And the dead in Christ will rise first. ¹⁷ Then we who are alive and remain shall be caught up together with them in the clouds to meet the Lord in the air. And thus, we shall always be with the Lord. *1 Thessalonians 4:13-17*

⁴⁴ No one can come to Me unless the Father who sent Me draws him; and I will raise him up at the last day. *John 6:44*

²⁵ He (the Antichrist) shall speak pompous words against the Most High, shall persecute the saints of the Most High, and shall intend to change times and law. Then the saints shall be given into his hand for a time and times and half a time. *Daniel 7:25*

RAPTURE PERCENTAGE

¹Then the kingdom of heaven shall be likened to ten virgins who took their lamps and went out to meet the bridegroom. ² Now five of them were wise, and five were foolish. ³ Those who were foolish took their lamps and took no oil with them, ⁴ but the wise took oil in their vessels with their lamps. ⁵ But while the bridegroom was delayed, they all slumbered and slept. ⁶ And at midnight a cry was heard: "Behold, the bridegroom is coming; go out to meet him!" ⁷ Then all those virgins arose and trimmed their lamps. ⁸ And the foolish said to the wise, "Give us some of your oil, for our lamps are going out." ⁹ But the wise answered, saying, "No, lest there should not be enough for us and you; but go rather to those who sell, and buy for yourselves." ¹⁰ And while they went to buy, the bridegroom came, and those who were ready went in with him to the wedding; and the door was shut. ¹¹ Afterward the other virgins came also, saying, "Lord, Lord, open to us!" ¹² But he answered and said, "Assuredly, I say to you, I do not know you." ¹³ "Watch therefore, for you know neither the day nor the hour in which the Son of Man is coming. *Matthew 25:1-13*

²² And He went through the cities and villages, teaching, and journeying toward Jerusalem. ²³ Then one said to Him, "Lord, are there few who are saved?" And He said to them, ²⁴ "Strive to enter through the narrow gate, for many, I say to

you, will seek to enter and will not be able. ²⁵ When once the Master of the house has risen up and shut the door, and you begin to stand outside and knock at the door, saying, 'Lord, Lord, open for us,' and He will answer and say to you, 'I do not know you, where you are from,' ²⁶ then you will begin to say, 'We ate and drank in Your presence, and You taught in our streets.' ²⁷ But He will say, 'I tell you I do not know you, where you are from. Depart from Me, all you workers of iniquity.' ²⁸ There will be weeping and gnashing of teeth, when you see Abraham and Isaac and Jacob and all the prophets in the kingdom of God, and yourselves thrust out." *Luke 13:22-28*

³⁷ But as the days of Noah were, so also will the coming of the Son of Man be. ³⁸ For as in the days before the flood, they were eating and drinking, marrying and giving in marriage, until the day that Noah entered the ark, ³⁹ and did not know until the flood came and took them all away, so also will the coming of the Son of Man be. ⁴⁰ Then two men will be in the field: one will be taken and the other left. ⁴¹ Two women will be grinding at the mill: one will be taken and the other left. ⁴² Watch therefore, for you do not know what hour your Lord is coming. ⁴³ But know this, that if the master of the house had known what hour the thief would come, he would have watched and not allowed his house to be broken into. ⁴⁴ Therefore you also be ready, for the Son of Man is coming at an hour you do not expect. *Matthew 24:36-44*

³⁰ Even so will it be in the day when the Son of Man is revealed. ³¹ In that day, he who is on the housetop, and his goods are in the house, let him not come down to take them away. And likewise, the one who is in the field, let him not turn back. ³² Remember Lot's wife. ³³ Whoever seeks to save his life will lose it, and whoever loses his life will preserve it. ³⁴ I tell you, in that night there will be two men in one bed: the one will be taken and the other will be left. ³⁵ Two women will be grinding together: the one will be taken and the other left. ³⁶ Two men will be in the field: the one will be taken and the other left. *Luke 17:30-36*

¹⁴ "Return, O backsliding children," says the LORD; "for I am married to you. I will take you, one from a city and two from a family, and I will bring you to Zion. *Jeremiah 3:14*

THE DEAD
¹ For we know that if our earthly house, this tent, is destroyed, we have a building from God, a house not made with hands, eternal in the heavens. ² For in this we groan, earnestly desiring to be clothed with our habitation which is from heaven, ³ if indeed, having been clothed, we shall not be found naked. ⁴ For we who are in this tent groan, being burdened, not because we want to be unclothed, but further clothed, that mortality may be swallowed up by life. ⁵ Now He who has prepared us for this very thing is God, who also has given us the Spirit as a

guarantee. ⁶ So we are always confident, knowing that while we are at home in the body, we are absent from the Lord. ⁷ For we walk by faith, not by sight. ⁸ We are confident, yes, well pleased rather to be absent from the body and to be present with the Lord. *2 Corinthians 5:1-8*

⁴² Then he (the criminal crucified next to Jesus) said to Jesus, "Lord, remember me when You come into Your kingdom." ⁴³ And Jesus said to him, "Assuredly, I say to you, today you will be with Me in Paradise." *Luke 23:42-43*

⁴ and that He (Jesus) was buried, and that He rose again the third day according to the Scriptures… *1 Corinthians 15:4*

⁹ Now this, "He ascended"—what does it mean but that He (Jesus) also first descended into the lower parts of the earth? ¹⁰ He who descended is also the One who ascended far above all the heavens, that He might fill all things. *Ephesians 4:9-10*

²⁰ But now Christ is risen from the dead, and has become the firstfruits of those who have fallen asleep. *1 Corinthians 15:20*

¹³ No one has ascended to heaven but He who came down from heaven, that is, the Son of Man who is in heaven. *John 3:13*

¹³ Then you shall know that I am the LORD, when I have opened your graves, O My people, and brought you up from your graves. *Ezekiel 37:13*

¹² Then His disciples said, "Lord, if he sleeps, he will get well." ¹³ However, Jesus spoke of his death, but they thought that He was speaking about taking rest in sleep. ¹⁴ Then Jesus said to them plainly, "Lazarus is dead." *John 11:12-14*

⁹ When He opened the fifth seal, I saw under the altar the souls of those who had been slain for the word of God and for the testimony which they held. ¹⁰ And they cried with a loud voice, saying, "How long, O Lord, holy and true, until You judge and avenge our blood on those who dwell on the earth?" ¹¹ Then a white robe was given to each of them; and it was said to them that they should rest a little while longer, until both the number of their fellow servants and their brethren, who would be killed as they were, was completed. *Revelation 6:9-11*

²⁵ Most assuredly, I say to you, the hour is coming, and now is, when the dead will hear the voice of the Son of God; and those who hear will live…²⁸ Do not marvel at this; for the hour is coming in which all who are in the graves will hear His voice ²⁹ and come forth—those who have done good, to the resurrection of life, and those who have done evil, to the resurrection of condemnation. *John 5:25, 28-29*

³⁰ For this reason many are weak and sick among you, and many sleep. *1 Corinthians 11:30*

...¹⁰ who died for us, that whether we wake or sleep, we should live together with Him. *1 Thessalonians 5:10*

¹⁹ Your dead shall live; together with my dead body they shall arise. Awake and sing, you who dwell in dust...and the earth shall cast out the dead. *Isaiah 26:19*

⁵ For the living know that they will die; but the dead know nothing... *Ecc. 9:5*

¹⁷ The dead do not praise the LORD, nor any who go down into silence. *Psalm 115:17*

⁵ Then a voice came from the throne, saying, "Praise our God, all you His servants and those who fear Him, both small and great!" *Revelation 19:5*

¹³ "But you (Daniel), go your way till the end; for you shall rest, and will arise to your inheritance at the end of the days." *Daniel 12:13*

¹⁴ So he (Saul) said to her (the medium), "What is his form?" And she said, "An old man is coming up, and he is covered with a mantle." And Saul perceived that it was Samuel, and he stooped with his face to the ground and bowed down. ¹⁵ Now Samuel said to Saul, "Why have you disturbed me by bringing me up?" And Saul answered, "I am deeply distressed; for the Philistines make war against me, and God has departed from me and does not answer me anymore, neither by prophets nor by dreams. Therefore, I have called you, that you may reveal to me what I should do." *1 Samuel 28:14-15*

⁴ Then I saw the souls of those who had been beheaded for their witness to Jesus and for the word of God, who had not worshiped the beast or his image, and had not received his mark on their foreheads or on their hands. And they lived and reigned with Christ for a thousand years. ⁵ But the rest of the dead did not live again until the thousand years were finished. *Revelation 20:4-5*

⁵⁰ And Jesus cried out again with a loud voice, and yielded up His spirit. ⁵¹ Then, behold, the veil of the temple was torn in two from top to bottom; and the earth quaked, and the rocks were split, ⁵² and the graves were opened; and many bodies of the saints who had fallen asleep were raised; ⁵³ and coming out of the graves after His resurrection, they went into the holy city and appeared to many. *Matthew 27:50-52*

NOTES

"No circumstance, person or difficulty can stop the plans and the promises of God." — Dr. David Jeremiah

CHRISTINE TATE

WEEK 22: GOD'S WRATH

Opening Prayer: Lord, we ask that You send Your Holy Spirit to us to guide us in the teaching and understanding of Your word that we may obtain a better understanding of the prophetic events surrounding us now and waiting for us in the future. Bless our fellowship in Your word that it may be fruitful and draw us into a deeper relationship both with You and those around us. Use us as Your vessels that through us, we may reflect Your glory to all whom we encounter. Illuminate our hearts and minds so that we may boldly shine the brightness of Your light everywhere we go and that we may be beacons of Your hope in a darkened world. In Jesus name we pray, Amen.

Ice Breaker: When Jesus comes back to gather His people, He will separate the wicked and the righteous. Those who do not follow Him will no longer have access to God's people and will not be able to interact with them. Assuming you are with Jesus, finish the following sentence with one word:

I'm glad I won't have to deal with people who are _____ anymore.

Share your answer with the group.

   **Focus:** The righteous will not be destroyed with the wicked.

Nature or Nurture?

God considers homosexual behavior to be a sin. For decades, a debate has raged as to whether those given to same sex attraction are born that way or if they have in some way been adversely influenced by their environment. New research suggests that atrazine, an endocrine disrupting chemical and popular weed killer in the United States, may affect hormones in a way that negatively impacts both health and sexuality. Employees who work in an atrazine manufacturing plant in Louisiana have a nine times higher risk of developing prostate cancer. Atrazine is also known to drop testosterone levels and escalate estrogen levels in males. In experiments done on frogs, atrazine demonstrated widespread feminizing effects on male amphibians at $1/30^{th}$ the levels considered "safe" by the EPA for drinking water. In females, atrazine stops natural estrogen production. Atrazine contamination can be found in eighty-seven percent of our drinking water.

ARE WE THE TERMINAL GENERATION?

Word of the Week

> ² Then I saw another angel ascending from the east, having the seal of the living God...³ saying, "Do not harm the earth, the sea, or the trees till we have **sealed** the servants of our God on their foreheads."
>
> *Revelation 7:2-3*

SEALED: Before any harm may befall the earth during the Tribulation, an angel marks God's people with the seal of God. The word seal comes from the Greek word "sphragizo" (pronounced sfrag-id'-zo) and refers to the process by which something is marked for the purpose of both identifying the item as belonging to the owner of the seal and as a way to hide something. For example, when a letter is sealed with a wax insignia, the insignia on the seal identifies the sender of the letter while its contents are hidden from the view of any prying eyes who might want an unauthorized peek at the letter's contents. In the case of this verse, Christians are marked prior to the destruction unleashed during the Tribulation to not only mark them as belonging to God, but to hide them from the effects of the devastation about to be unleashed on the world.

Lesson: One of the most contested questions of our day regarding prophetic events is when the rapture will take place. The concept of a pre-Tribulation rapture is primarily a modern-day teaching. Up until the mid-1800's, most early theologians and church fathers such as Charles Spurgeon, Martin Luther, John Calvin, Irenaeus, Justin Martyr and John Chrysostom among others embraced the concept of a post-Tribulation rapture believing Jesus would gather His people to be with Him at the end of the Tribulation. Around the mid-1800's, a pre-Tribulation rapture theology espoused by John Nelson Darby of the Plymouth Brethren gained widespread popularity and is today the dominant teaching in many churches across America as well as taught by many well-known televangelists such as Jack Van Impe, Hal Lindsey, John Hagee, Grant Jeffrey, Billy Graham, Perry Stone and David Jeremiah.

Among arguments presented by modern church leaders against a post-Tribulation rapture is the issue of God's wrath. Pre-Tributationists cite 1 Thessalonians 5:9 as evidence that believers will be removed from the earth prior to the Tribulation:

> ⁹ For **God did not appoint us to wrath**, but to obtain salvation through our Lord Jesus Christ... *1 Thessalonians 5:9*

As such, they argue it logically follows that the rapture must occur before the seven-year Tribulation to spare the church from the wrath of God. Scripture clearly tells us that God's wrath is reserved for those who do not know God and for those who do know God, but refuse to obey His laws:

> ⁷ ...when the Lord Jesus is revealed from heaven with His mighty angels, ⁸ in flaming fire **taking vengeance on those who do not know God, and on those who do not obey the gospel** of our Lord Jesus Christ. *2 Thessalonians 1:7-8*

Righteous, God-fearing, law-abiding Christians have nothing to fear. While it is inarguably true from scripture that believers are not appointed to endure God's wrath, the interpretation and application of what that essentially means is open for debate. *Webster's Dictionary* defines "wrath" as:

> WRATH: 1. Strong vengeful anger or indignation or 2. Retributory punishment for an offense or crime.

God's wrath is linked to vengeance and retribution when Jesus comes back on the Day of the Lord:

> ⁷ ...**when the Lord Jesus is revealed** from heaven with His mighty angels, ⁸ in flaming fire **taking vengeance** on those who do not know God, and on those who do not obey the gospel of our Lord Jesus Christ. *2 Thessalonians 1:7-8*

During the Tribulation, the seven seals, trumpets and bowls are linked to punishments designed to encourage mankind to repent of their evil ways:

> ²¹ **And they did not repent** of their murders or their sorceries or their sexual immorality or their thefts. *Revelation 9:21* (Sixth Trumpet from Lesson Six)

> ⁹ And men were scorched with great heat, and they blasphemed the name of God who has power over these **plagues; and they did not repent and give Him glory**. *Revelation 16:9* (Fourth Bowl from Lesson Seven)

Note that Revelation 16:9 refers to the fourth bowl as a plague. Then, in Revelation 15:1, plagues are defined as a form of God's wrath:

> ¹Then I saw another sign in heaven, great and marvelous: seven angels having the **seven last plagues**, for **in them the wrath of God is complete**. *Revelation 15:1*

Essentially, there are two stages to God's wrath. Both the events on the Day of the Lord and the plagues of the seals, trumpets and bowls are distinctly burdensome to mankind, but they have different purposes. In the first stage of God's wrath, the plagues delivered during the Tribulation are both an expression of His anger and attempts by God to encourage mankind to repent and change their behavior so that they may ultimately be saved. Much like parents discipline a child in hopes of motivating the child to change his or her habits, God issues various plagues as forms of discipline during the Tribulation intending to motivate people to cease from their ungodly ways. As angry as God is with mankind during the Tribulation, His hope is still for a last call to repentance. After each plague befalls mankind, people still have the option to repent. Unfortunately, when the Day of the Lord arrives, stage two of God's wrath begins and the punishments are no longer corrective in nature, but retributory and full of vengeance. Destructive at its core and presented in full force on the Day of the Lord, the nature of God's wrath changes focusing only on destruction of the old to make way for the new rule and reign of Christ:

> ¹⁰ But the **day of the Lord** will come as a thief in the night, in which the heavens will pass away with a great noise, and the elements will melt with fervent heat; both **the earth and the works that are in it will be burned up**. *2 Peter 3:10*

In stage one representing Tribulation plagues, life may be miserable from the plagues, but life still continues on as usual until another plague is unleashed. Then, when all of the plagues are delivered and it is time for Jesus to return, God's wrath takes a destructive turn in stage two. From the Day of the Lord forward, the world as we know it ceases to exist. When Jesus returns, the time for change is over, repentance is no longer an option and all non-believers can do is hide from the wrath of God in utter fear and dread as God rains down destructive vengeance meant for those who dwell upon the earth.

An argument from Revelation 3:10 that pre-Tribulation advocates use to support their position that the church will be removed before the Tribulation begins revolves around the interpretation of the word "from":

> ¹⁰ Because you have kept My command to persevere, I also will keep you **from** the hour of trial which shall come upon the whole world, to test those who dwell on the earth. *Revelation 3:10*

The pre-Tribulation argument maintains the word "from" equates to the church being raptured up and away "from" the chaos on earth so as not to be caught in either stage of God's wrath. Pronounced "ek", the word "from" is translated from the original Greek as "out of" or "away from". Pre-Tribulation advocates prefer to use the "out of" option for this translation to support their position that the rapture will take the church "out of" the Tribulation period thereby saving Christians from the effects of Tribulation plagues. However, "away from" is equally viable as a translation option and leaves room to interpret the verse as simply protecting the church through the Tribulation. The word "ek" is used again in John 17:15:

> [15] **I do not pray** that You should **take them out of the world**, but that You should keep them **from** the evil one. *John 17:15*

In this more specific, alternate context, John clarifies that keeping God's children from their problems does not mean removing them from off the earth. For further clarification on what it means to be delivered from the Tribulation, Daniel 12:1 offers additional insight:

> [1] At that time Michael shall stand up, the great prince who stands watch over the sons of your people; and there shall be a time of trouble, such as never was since there was a nation, even to that time. And at that time your people shall be **delivered**, every one who is found written in the book. *Daniel 12:1*

In this context of delivering Christians from the Tribulation, the word "delivered", which is "malat" (pronounced maw-lat) in the original Hebrew, translates as "slip away, escape, save". "Malat" is also used in Genesis 19:20 when Lot flees from Sodom and Gomorrah:

> [20] See now, this city is near enough to flee to, and it is a little one; please let me **escape (malat)** there (is it not a little one?) and my soul shall live. *Genesis 19:20*

Lot escaped to a nearby area of safety while still remaining on the earth and his soul continued to live an earthly life. This application of physical protection is consistent with Luke 21:36 where believers are warned to pray they will "be counted worthy to escape" the events of the Tribulation. In the entire area of Sodom and Gomorrah, only Lot was counted worthy to escape to a nearby cave with a few of his family members. Bearing in mind that God never changes, it is likely that God might use the same approach to protect His children during the Tribulation:

> [6] For I am the LORD, **I do not change**... *Malachi 3:6*

Throughout the Bible, God's reliable and discernable pattern is to protect people through trouble, not take them out of trouble. God is more than able to protect His children from whatever may be coming in the future without physically removing them from the earth. In reference to the Tribulation period, God promises to protect obedient Tribulation believers in Deuteronomy 4:30-31:

> [30] When you are **in distress**, and all these things come upon you in the **latter days**, when you **turn to the LORD your God and obey** His voice [31] (for the LORD your God is a merciful God), **He will not forsake you nor destroy you,** nor forget the covenant of your fathers which He swore to them. *Deuteronomy 4:30-31*

Again, in Joel 3:16, God reiterates that Christians will be sheltered in the midst of the turmoil when Jesus returns:

> [16] The LORD also will roar from Zion, and utter His voice from Jerusalem; the heavens and earth will shake; but the **LORD will be a shelter for His people,** and the strength of the children of Israel. *Joel 3:16*

Numerous examples can be found throughout the Bible of God leaving His people in the midst of a disaster, yet protecting them through it. Noah was protected through the destruction of the earth while being kept away from the water, safely enclosed in an ark. Lot was the only person worth saving in all of Sodom and Gomorrah, so God removed him and his daughters to the safety of a cave before the destruction began so they would remain unharmed (Luke 17:26-30). Daniel was saved while still in the midst of the hungry lions when he was thrown into the lion's den. Shadrach, Meshach and Abednego remained in the midst of the furnace's fire without being harmed by the fire. God's people, the Hebrews, were protected from the plagues of Egypt while living in the midst of the plagues. Later, the Hebrews were saved from Pharaoh, their version of the Antichrist, when God kept them away from Egypt in the desert. Of note is that before the angel of death passed through Egypt to kill all the firstborn sons of the Egyptians, God marked the Hebrews so that they would not be affected by the last plague as it passed over them:

> [13] Now the **blood shall be a sign** for you **on the houses** where you are. And **when I see the blood, I will pass over you**; and the **plague shall not be on you** to destroy you when I strike the land of Egypt...[23] For the LORD will pass through to strike the Egyptians; and when He sees the blood on the lintel and on the two doorposts, **the LORD will pass over the door and not allow**

the destroyer to come into your houses to strike you. *Exodus 12:13,23*

Similarly, there is a marking and sealing process that occurs for God's followers during the Tribulation:

> [2] Then I saw another angel...[3] saying, "**Do not harm** the earth, the sea, or the trees **till we have sealed the servants of our God** on their foreheads." *Revelation 7:2-3*

> [4] ...and the LORD said to him, "Go through the midst of the city, through the midst of Jerusalem, and **put a mark on the foreheads of the men who sigh and cry over all the abominations** that are done within it. [5] To the others He said in my hearing, "Go after him through the city and kill; do not let your eye spare, nor have any pity. [6] Utterly slay old and young men, maidens and little children and women; but **do not come near anyone on whom is the mark**; and **begin at My sanctuary**." So, they began with the elders who were before the temple." *Ezekiel 9:4-6*

After Tribulation Christians are sealed, they are also instructed to shelter in place in their homes during the punishment plagues much like God commanded the Hebrews to do:

> [20] Come, **my people, enter your chambers**, and **shut your doors behind you**; hide yourself, as it were, for a little moment, **until the indignation is past**. [21] For behold, the **LORD comes out** of His place **to punish** the inhabitants of the earth for their iniquity; the earth will also disclose her blood, and will no more cover her slain. *Isaiah 26:20-21*

If God's people are meant to be raptured before the Tribulation punishments, there would be no need to mark God's people nor would they need to hide in their homes while the punishment passes. The fact that God's people need to be sealed at all before plagues can begin or are instructed to shelter in place is yet another confirmation that Christians will still be present on earth during the Tribulation while the plagues are released on mankind. Once marked as belonging to God, followers will be unaffected by the plagues of the seals, trumpets and bowls.

God has a longstanding practice of issuing rewards for meritorious behavior and punishments for errant behavior:

> ³ If you **walk in My statutes and keep My commandments**, and perform them,⁴ then **I will give you rain** in its season, the **land shall yield its produce**, and the **trees of the field shall yield their fruit**...¹⁴ But **if you do not obey Me**, and do not observe all these commandments, ¹⁵ and if you despise My statutes, or if your soul abhors My judgments, so that you do not perform all My commandments, but break My covenant, ¹⁶ I also will do this to you: I will even **appoint terror over you**, **wasting disease** and fever which shall consume the eyes and cause sorrow of heart. And you shall **sow your seed in vain**, for your enemies shall eat it. ¹⁷ I will set My face against you, and you shall be **defeated by your enemies**. Those who hate you shall reign over you, and you shall flee when no one pursues you. ¹⁸ And after all this, if you do not obey Me, then **I will punish you seven times more** for your sins. *Leviticus 26:3-4,14-18*

Only those who are obedient to God's law will receive the seal of God which protects them from the punishment of God's plagues:

> ¹⁶ Bind up the testimony, **seal the law** among **my disciples**. *Isaiah 8:16*

> ³⁰ And do not grieve the **Holy Spirit** of God, **by whom you were sealed** for the day of redemption. *Ephesians 4:30*

As only those who are obedient to God's law will be sealed, it is necessary, as stated in Luke 21:36, to pray that we be "counted worthy" so that we may receive God's seal. To be counted worthy, followers must follow the word of God and obey His laws. Those who are unworthy will not receive the seal necessary to protect them from the coming plagues. Having received the seal of God, Christians will be rendered immune from the plagues of the seals, trumpets and bowls about to be delivered. In danger of experiencing the full force of the plagues, however, are those who are not sealed by God:

> ⁴ They (locusts) were commanded not to **harm** the grass of the earth, or any green thing, or any tree, but **only** **those men who do not have the seal of God on their foreheads**. *Revelation 9:4*

With the system of seals in place, there is no need to rapture believers away from the punishments about to ensue from the plagues of the seals, trumpets and bowls since God does not give permission for His children to be harmed by those plagues. Matthew 24:9-12 reaffirms that Christians will still be present through the plagues of the Tribulation by stating that there will be those who endure to the end:

> ⁹ "Then they will deliver you up to tribulation and kill you, and you will be hated by all nations for My name's sake… ¹³ But **he who endures to the end** shall be saved. *Matthew 24:9, 13*

Logically speaking, if Christians were to be raptured before the Tribulation, there would be no need to "endure to the end".

Though the seal of God protects believers through the Tribulation to the end, God's followers cannot have both the seal of God and the mark of the beast. It must be one or the other:

> ⁹ Then a **third angel** followed them, saying with a loud voice, "**If anyone** worships the beast and his image, and **receives his (the beast's) mark** on his forehead or on his hand, ¹⁰ **he himself shall also drink of the wine of the wrath of God**… *Revelation 14:9-10*

STRANGE FACT: A company called *The After the Rapture Pet Care* promises to take care of Christian's pets who are left behind when their owners are raptured.

Satan, the great counterfeiter, with the assistance of the Antichrist and False Prophet, tries to mark as many people as he can so they cannot receive God's seal. Unfortunately, we can only receive one mark—God's mark or Satan's mark. Those unfortunate enough to choose Satan's mark will only experience punishment plagues during the Tribulation and then God's retributory wrath and vengeance when Jesus returns.

Also, of note from Revelation 14:9-10 is that the wrath of God does not happen until after people are given the choice to take the mark of the beast. From a timing perspective, that choice does not happen until after the Tribulation begins. Only after the Antichrist rises to power are people forced to make the choice to take the mark of the beast. Plagues may not begin until everyone is marked. Before the Tribulation, no one has had the opportunity to take the mark of the beast. That event must take place first before the wrath of God arrives which makes it impossible for Christians to be raptured for the entire Tribulation time period as pre-Tribulation advocates purport.

The key issue at stake is when God's wrath occurs. Towards that end, it is important to examine the purpose of the rapture and exactly what the rapture is saving people from. Pre-Tribulation proponents present that the entire Tribulation period encompasses God's wrath necessitating the removal of the church prior to the beginning of the Tribulation to save people from the horrendous events that will happen during the Tribulation. Post-Tribulation beliefs present that while times are difficult during the Tribulation, God's people are supernaturally protected from the plagues in stage one of God's wrath making it unnecessary to rapture anyone until the nature of God's wrath changes into something entirely different in stage two of God's wrath. At the later Tribulation point where God's wrath changes character and begins a permanently destructive path when Jesus returns on the Day of the Lord, it then becomes necessary to rapture Christians away from imminent harm.

Examining the various types of adversity yields insight into exactly what Christians need to be protected against. First, there is Christian persecution directed by Satan. Under the forces of the satanically backed Antichrist, things will unquestionably be difficult for Christians during the Tribulation. As Daniel 12:1 states, there will be "a time of trouble, such as never was". But hard times are not unique to the Tribulation nor are satanically backed attacks on Christians the same thing as God's wrath. Satan has been targeting and attacking Christians since the Garden of Eden. Job experienced undue hardship from Satan's meddling, the disciples experienced discrimination, torture and death for their beliefs and Jesus Himself was tempted in the wilderness directly by Satan. Nowhere does scripture indicate the purpose of the rapture is to protect Christians from Satan's warfare during the Tribulation. Next, there are the stage one plagues which are issued by God in the form of seals, trumpets and bowls. Throughout the Bible, God commonly uses corrective punishments to change people. Jonah was swallowed by a whale when he refused to obey God. As horrible as that must have been, it was a corrective punishment administered by God which successfully generated a change of heart in Jonah. Corrective punishment is administered for the purpose of changing a person's ways and does not affect Christians during the Tribulation since, as we have seen, Christians are sealed by God and protected from the plagues. Since Christians are protected from the plagues by God's seal, it cannot be the purpose of the rapture to save Christians from those plagues. Clearly, the rapture is not linked to providing a way for people to avoid God's discipline or avoid Satan's attacks. The purpose for the rapture is to save God's people from experiencing God's stage two wrath when Jesus returns on the Day of the Lord. Coming in a spirit of vengeance at the end of the Tribulation, that time period is one of massive destruction and retributory punishment from which believers will need to be physically removed so as not to experience God's final wrath. Remember to pray always that you be counted worthy to escape!

Talk It Out

1. The majority of early church fathers and theologians embraced a post-Tribulation rapture theology as compared to our modern era where the reverse is true with many church leaders endorsing a pre-Tribulation rapture theology. Why do you think mainstream rapture theology changed in the mid-1800's? Does it affect your view of pre-Tribulation rapture theology knowing that for much of church history, the post-Tribulation theory dominated religious thought?

2. How do you define "wrath"? Where does the element of vengeance fit into the picture? Is vengeance associated with punishment or wrath? Is there a distinction between the seven seals, trumpets, bowls and God's wrath or are they one and the same? Why do you think the seven seals, trumpets and bowls punishments fail to generate repentance in people?

3. In Revelation 3:10, do you think the word "from" means that God will keep His people out of the Tribulation by rapturing them off the earth or that He will keep His people through the Tribulation by protecting them in the midst of chaos and disaster?

4. What do you think God means when He warns us to pray always that we might be accounted worthy to escape? What type of an "escape" do you think God is offering us?

5. What do you think the seal of God is? Do you think having the seal of God will protect Christians from the seals, trumpets and bowl plagues delivered during the Tribulation or does it mean something else to you?

Ideas for the Week:

- ✓ Make a list of your current sins (i.e. anger, bitterness and unforgiveness). Take your list to God and ask God for His forgiveness.
- ✓ Make it a daily habit to ask God to count you worthy to escape whatever may be coming.
- ✓ As a symbol of your belonging to God, hang a cross over your front door or next to the doorbell in remembrance of what the Hebrews did on the night the angel of death passed over their homes.
- ✓ Invite friends over and host a Passover Seder dinner. Instructions can be found at https://www.dummies.com/education/holidays/the-haggadah-and-the-steps-of-a-seder/. Traditional Passover recipes can be found at http://dish.allrecipes.com/best-traditional-passover-recipes/ and instructions for a Seder plate can be found at https://www.rd.com/food/recipes-cooking/the-traditional-foods-of-passover/.

Closing Prayer

NOTE: Add names and individual personal prayer requests to the space provided below before closing in prayer.

Lord, we thank You for our time together today to grow deeper in our walk with You and fellowship with each other. As we close today, we lift up: _____

_____

_____

_____

_____

Father, we thank You that You have not appointed us to wrath and are grateful that we can rest in the safety and surety of Your protection in all circumstances. Praying that You may count us worthy to escape that which is coming upon the earth, we ask You to mark us with Your mark and seal us with Your seal that we may always be easily identified as belonging to Your kingdom eternally. In Jesus' name we pray, Amen.

SUPPORTING SCRIPTURES

GOD'S WRATH

⁹ For God did not appoint us to wrath, but to obtain salvation through our Lord Jesus Christ... *1 Thessalonians 5:9*

⁹ Much more then, having now been justified by His blood, we shall be saved from wrath through Him (Jesus). *Romans 5:9*

¹⁰ ...even Jesus who delivers us from the wrath to come. *1 Thessalonians 1:10*

¹ Then I saw another sign in heaven, great and marvelous: seven angels having the seven last plagues, for in them the wrath of God is complete. *Revelation 15:1*

¹⁷ I do not pray that You should take them out of the world, but that You should keep them from the evil one. *John 17:15*

³⁶ Watch therefore, and pray always that you may be counted worthy to escape all these things that will come to pass, and to stand before the Son of Man. *Luke 21:36*

⁷ ...when the Lord Jesus is revealed from heaven with His mighty angels, ⁸ in flaming fire taking vengeance on those who do not know God, and on those who do not obey the gospel of our Lord Jesus Christ. *2 Thessalonians 1:7-8*

¹⁷ I will execute great vengeance on them with furious rebukes; and they shall know that I am the LORD, when I lay My vengeance upon them. *Ezekiel 25:17*

¹⁹ Beloved, do not avenge yourselves, but rather give place to wrath; for it is written, "Vengeance is Mine, I will repay," says the Lord. *Romans 12:19*

...⁶ that no one should take advantage of and defraud his brother... because the Lord is the avenger of all such... *1 Thessalonians 4:6*

¹⁵ And the kings of the earth, the great men, the rich men, the commanders, the mighty men, every slave and every free man, hid themselves in the caves and in the rocks of the mountains, ¹⁶ and said to the mountains and rocks, "Fall on us and hide us from the face of Him who sits on the throne and from the wrath of the Lamb! ¹⁷ For the great day of His wrath has come, and who is able to stand?" *Revelation 6:15-17*

¹⁴ ...The noise of the day of the LORD is bitter; there the mighty men shall cry out. ¹⁵ That day is a day of wrath, a day of trouble and distress, a day of devastation and desolation, a day of darkness and gloominess, a day of clouds and thick

darkness... *Zephaniah 1:14-15*

¹⁰ But the day of the Lord will come as a thief in the night, in which the heavens will pass away with a great noise, and the elements will melt with fervent heat; both the earth and the works that are in it will be burned up. *2 Peter 3:10*

¹⁰ Because you have kept My command to persevere, I also will keep you from the hour of trial which shall come upon the whole world, to test those who dwell on the earth. *Revelation 3:10*

⁵ But in accordance with your hardness and your impenitent heart you are treasuring up for yourself wrath in the day of wrath and revelation of the righteous judgment of God... *Romans 2:5*

¹⁸ For the wrath of God is revealed from heaven against all ungodliness and unrighteousness of men, who suppress the truth in unrighteousness... *Romans 1:18*

² God is jealous, and the LORD avenges; the LORD avenges and is furious. The LORD will take vengeance on His adversaries, and He reserves wrath for His enemies; ³ the LORD is slow to anger and great in power, and will not at all acquit the wicked. *Nahum 1:2*

TRIBULATION HARDSHIP
¹ ...and there shall be a time of trouble, such as never was since there was a nation, even to that time. And at that time your people shall be delivered, every one who is found written in the book. *Daniel 12:1*

GOD'S TRIBULATION PROTECTION
²⁶ And as it was in the days of Noah, so it will be also in the days of the Son of Man: ²⁷ They ate, they drank, they married wives, they were given in marriage, until the day that Noah entered the ark, and the flood came and destroyed them all. ²⁸ Likewise as it was also in the days of Lot: They ate, they drank, they bought, they sold, they planted, they built; ²⁹ but on the day that Lot went out of Sodom it rained fire and brimstone from heaven and destroyed them all. ³⁰ Even so will it be in the day when the Son of Man is revealed. Luke 17:26-30

¹⁶ The LORD also will roar from Zion, and utter His voice from Jerusalem; the heavens and earth will shake; but the LORD will be a shelter for His people, and the strength of the children of Israel. *Joel 3:16*

...⁹ then the Lord knows how to deliver the godly out of temptations and to reserve the unjust under punishment for the day of judgment... *2 Peter 2:9*

⁸ And it shall come to pass in all the land," says the LORD, "That two-thirds in it

shall be cut off and die, but one-third shall be left in it: ⁹ I will bring the one-third through the fire, will refine them as silver is refined, and test them as gold is tested. They will call on My name, and I will answer them. I will say, "This is My people"; and each one will say, "The LORD is my God." *Zechariah 13:8-9*

³⁰ When you are in distress, and all these things come upon you in the latter days, when you turn to the LORD your God and obey His voice ³¹ (for the LORD your God is a merciful God), He will not forsake you nor destroy you, nor forget the covenant of your fathers which He swore to them. *Deuteronomy 4:30-31*

³ But the Lord is faithful, who will establish you and guard you from the evil one. *2 Thessalonians 3:3*

¹³ These are the ones who come out of the great tribulation…¹⁷ …And God will wipe away every tear from their eyes. *Revelation 7:13,17*

⁹ Then they will deliver you up to tribulation and kill you, and you will be hated by all nations for My name's sake…¹³ But he who endures to the end shall be saved. *Matthew 24:9, 13*

⁹ But watch out for yourselves, for they will deliver you up to councils, and you will be beaten in the synagogues. You will be brought before rulers and kings for My sake, for a testimony to them. ¹⁰ And the gospel must first be preached to all the nations. ¹¹ But when they arrest you and deliver you up, do not worry beforehand, or premeditate what you will speak. But whatever is given you in that hour, speak that; for it is not you who speak, but the Holy Spirit. ¹² Now brother will betray brother to death, and a father his child; and children will rise up against parents and cause them to be put to death. ¹³ And you will be hated by all for My name's sake. But he who endures to the end shall be saved. *Mark 13:9-13*

¹⁷ And you will be hated by all for My name's sake. ¹⁸ But not a hair of your head shall be lost. *Luke 21:17-18*

⁶ For I am the LORD, I do not change… *Malachi 3:6*

GOD'S SEAL
⁹ Then a third angel followed them, saying with a loud voice, "If anyone worships the beast and his image, and receives his mark on his forehead or on his hand, ¹⁰ he himself shall also drink of the wine of the wrath of God, which is poured out full strength into the cup of His indignation. *Revelation 14:9-10*

¹⁶ He (the False Prophet) causes all, both small and great, rich and poor, free and slave, to receive a mark on their right hand or on their foreheads… *Revelation 13:16*

² ...and those who have the victory over the beast...and over his mark...having harps of God. *Revelation 15:2*

⁴ ...Then I saw the souls of those...who had not worshiped the beast or his image, and had not received his mark on their foreheads or on their hands. And they lived and reigned with Christ for a thousand years. *Revelation 20:4*

² Then I saw another angel ascending from the east, having the seal of the living God...³ saying, "Do not harm the earth, the sea, or the trees till we have sealed the servants of our God on their foreheads." *Revelation 7:2-3*

⁴ They shall see His face, and His name shall be on their foreheads. *Revelation 22:4*

⁴ They were commanded not to harm the grass of the earth, or any green thing, or any tree, but only those men who do not have the seal of God on their foreheads. *Revelation 9:4*

¹⁶ Bind up the testimony, seal the law among my disciples. *Isaiah 8:16*

³⁸ "And because of all this, we make a sure covenant and write it; our leaders, our Levites, and our priests seal it." *Nehemiah 9:38*

...⁴ and the LORD said to him, "Go through the midst of the city, through the midst of Jerusalem, and put a mark on the foreheads of the men who sigh and cry over all the abominations that are done within it." ⁵ To the others He said in my hearing, "Go after him through the city and kill; do not let your eye spare, nor have any pity. ⁶ Utterly slay old and young men, maidens and little children and women; but do not come near anyone on whom is the mark; and begin at My sanctuary." So, they began with the elders who were before the temple. *Ezekiel 9:4-6*

¹⁹ Nevertheless the solid foundation of God stands, having this seal: "The Lord knows those who are His,"... *2 Timothy 2:19*

⁷ The LORD is good, a stronghold in the day of trouble; and He knows those who trust in Him. *Nahum 1:7*

...²² who also has sealed us and given us the Spirit in our hearts as a guarantee. *2 Corinthians 1:22*

¹³ In Him you also trusted, after you heard the word of truth, the gospel of your salvation; in whom also, having believed, you were sealed with the Holy Spirit of promise... *Ephesians 1:13*

[30] And do not grieve the Holy Spirit of God, by whom you were sealed for the day of redemption. *Ephesians 4:30*

[13] Now the blood shall be a sign for you on the houses where you are. And when I see the blood, I will pass over you; and the plague shall not be on you to destroy you when I strike the land of Egypt...[23] For the LORD will pass through to strike the Egyptians; and when He sees the blood on the lintel and on the two doorposts, the LORD will pass over the door and not allow the destroyer to come into your houses to strike you. *Exodus 12:13,23*

[20] Come, my people, enter your chambers, and shut your doors behind you; hide yourself, as it were, for a little moment, until the indignation is past. [21] For behold, the LORD comes out of His place to punish the inhabitants of the earth for their iniquity; the earth will also disclose her blood, and will no more cover her slain. *Isaiah 26:20-21*

[30] And do not grieve the Holy Spirit of God, by whom you were sealed for the day of redemption. *Ephesians 4:30*

[3] If you walk in My statutes and keep My commandments, and perform them,[4] then I will give you rain in its season, the land shall yield its produce, and the trees of the field shall yield their fruit...[14] But if you do not obey Me, and do not observe all these commandments, [15] and if you despise My statutes, or if your soul abhors My judgments, so that you do not perform all My commandments, but break My covenant, [16] I also will do this to you: I will even appoint terror over you, wasting disease and fever which shall consume the eyes and cause sorrow of heart. And you shall sow your seed in vain, for your enemies shall eat it. [17] I will set My face against you, and you shall be defeated by your enemies. Those who hate you shall reign over you, and you shall flee when no one pursues you. [18] And after all this, if you do not obey Me, then I will punish you seven times more for your sins. *Leviticus 26:3-4,14-18*

NOTES

"Stand up straight and realize who you are, that you tower over your circumstances. You are a child of God. Stand up straight." — Maya Angelou

WEEK 23: DAY OF THE LORD

Opening Prayer: Lord, we ask that You send Your Holy Spirit to us to guide us in the teaching and understanding of Your word that we may obtain a better understanding of the prophetic events surrounding us now and waiting for us in the future. Bless our fellowship in Your word that it may be fruitful and draw us into a deeper relationship both with You and those around us. Use us as Your vessels that through us, we may reflect Your glory to all whom we encounter. Illuminate our hearts and minds so that we may boldly shine the brightness of Your light everywhere we go and that we may be beacons of Your hope in a darkened world. In Jesus name we pray, Amen.

Ice Breaker: Most wedding ceremonies include a meal as part of a social gathering at the reception after the vows are exchanged. Think of a time when you attended a wedding. Maybe it was your own wedding. Or it could have been the marriage of a close friend or relative. What was the marriage supper like at the reception? Describe the meal and activities to your group. Where did it take place? Who was there? What was served? Were there any special toasts? Was a prayer given before the meal? Did anything unusual happen at the meal? Share your personal stories together as a group.

Focus: Man's judgment may error, but our God, who sees the inward thoughts and intents of man, will always execute perfect judgment.

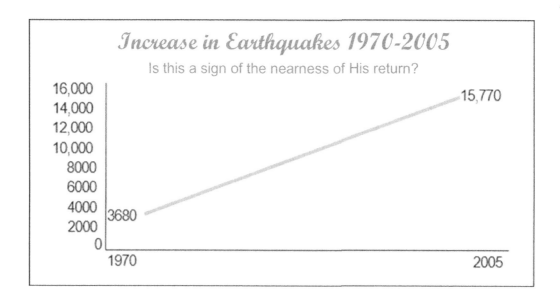

ARE WE THE TERMINAL GENERATION?

Word of the Week

> ^{2} "I will utterly **consume** everything from the face of the land," says the LORD; ^{3} "I will **consume** man and beast; I will **consume** the birds of the heavens, the fish of the sea, and the stumbling blocks along with the wicked. I will cut off man from the face of the land," says the LORD.
> *Zephaniah 1:2-3*

CONSUME: In Hebrew, the word for "consume" is "cuwph" (pronounced soof). To consume something means to make a complete end of it so that it no longer exists. In this passage, it can be seen that at Jesus' return, nothing is left on planet earth when Jesus is finished. All humans, animals, fish and fowl are removed from the face of the earth. No life exists anywhere on terra firma. As with any construction project, first the old must be destroyed before the new can begin. A better tomorrow awaits in the future, but first, Jesus must cleanse the dirt from the past so that there is a clean slate to build for the future.

Lesson: When Jesus returns, the event is referred to as the Day of the Lord. On the Day of the Lord, Jesus receives the earth and its inhabitants as a gift from His Father:

> ^{7}..."You are My Son, today I have begotten You. ^{8} Ask of Me, and **I will give You the nations for Your inheritance, and the ends of the earth for Your possession.** *Psalm 2:7-8*

Jesus' return occurs after the Tribulation:

> ^{29} **Immediately after the tribulation of those days**... ^{30} Then the sign of the **Son of Man will appear in heaven**... *Matthew 24:29-31*

Whenever scriptures reference the Day of the Lord, the time measurement used is that of a day:

> ^{14} The great **day of the LORD** is near; it is near and hastens quickly. The noise of the **day of the LORD** is bitter; there the mighty men shall cry out. ^{15} That **day is a day of wrath, a day of trouble and distress, a day of devastation and desolation,** a

day of darkness and gloominess, a day of clouds and thick darkness... *Zephaniah 1:14-15*

Within the Day of the Lord, there is a sub-timeframe called the "hour of trial" against which no one can withstand:

> [10] Because you have kept My command to persevere, I also will keep you from **the hour of trial** which shall come upon the whole world, to test those who dwell on the earth. *Revelation 3:10*

When the Day of the Lord unfolds, life as mankind knows it is over:

> [15]...the mighty men, every slave and every free man, **hid themselves in the caves**...For the **great day of His wrath has come**... *Revelation 6:15-17*

Using the typical day for a year principle of prophetic scripture interpretation and the Jewish calendar of 360 days, the scripturally defined period of a "day" for Jesus' return lasts for one year or 360 days. Consistent with a timeframe longer than a literal twenty-four-hour day is the use of the plural form of the word "day" referring to the entire period surrounding Armageddon, Jesus' return and the ensuring events:

> [1]...in those **days**...[2] I will also gather all nations, and bring them down to the Valley of Jehoshaphat... *Joel 3:1-2*

Narrowing that down even further, there are fifteen days, or an hour's worth, of that time which is particularly harsh. More evidence that the term "day" refers to a prophetic year as opposed to a literal twenty-four-hour day can be found in Ezekiel 7:19:

> [19] They will **throw their silver into the streets, and their gold will be like refuse**; their silver and their gold will not be able to deliver them **in the day** of the wrath **of the LORD**; they will not satisfy their souls, **nor fill their stomachs**, because it became their stumbling block of iniquity. *Ezekiel 7:19*

In this passage which happens on the Day of the Lord, people have time to become desperate enough to throw their valuables in the street which would likely take longer than a literal twenty-four-hour day. Having survived the plagues of the seals, trumpets and bowls still refusing to repent and cursing God, it is unlikely people will reach that level of desperation in just another twenty-four literal hours. Also mentioned is the fact that people go hungry. If the Day of the Lord is a literal twenty-four-hour day, that would not be a lengthy enough period of time to produce extreme hunger. Instructions are given in Joel 2:15-17 for God's people to do a fast, gather together in a special religious service and entreat God to spare them on the Day of the Lord:

> [15] Blow the trumpet in Zion, **consecrate a fast, call a sacred assembly**; [16] gather the people…[17] Let the priests…say, "**Spare** Your people, O LORD…" *Joel 2:15-17*

Those actions, especially the fast, take time to organize and accomplish. Typically, when people fast, they fast for days, not hours. Even hiding in bunkers as mentioned in Revelation 6:15-17 implies a timeframe greater than twenty-four literal hours as government quality bunkers are fortified and deep enough to hold out for longer than a literal twenty-four-hour day. Those without access to bunkers would hide in cement basements in their homes which also provides an extended level of protection longer than a literal day. In Joel 2:8, militaries around the world mount unsuccessful defenses against the invasion:

> [1] For the day of the LORD…is at hand [2]… A people come, great and strong, the like of whom has never been; nor will there ever be any such after them, even for many successive generations…**[5] Over mountaintops they leap**…[8] **Though they lunge between the weapons**, they are not cut down. *Joel 2:1-2, 5, 8*

This implies that countries have time to mount unsuccessful defenses and realize they cannot prevail against the Lord. Given the levels of modern human pride, it is likely the Lord will give them longer than twenty-four hours to arrive at that realization, stew in their situation and come to the full realization of what awaits them. After all, the Lord has waited two thousand years to fully deliver His wrath, what's a few extra earthly days to God?

Multiple events occur during the Day of the Lord necessitating a longer timeframe than just a literal twenty-four-hour day. In Zechariah 12:7, use of the word "first" implies that more than one event occurs and that the events occur in a specific order:

> [7] "The LORD will save the tents of Judah **first**…[9] It shall be in that day that I will seek to destroy all the nations that come against Jerusalem. *Zechariah 12:7, 9*

As seen from the above verse, Jesus gives priority to saving that which He wishes to save before He begins His final reign of destruction. The Day of the Lord is a complicated period of time with many events that must take place which might explain the necessity of Christ's return being a prophetic year of 360 days. Among the numerous events which happen during the Day of the Lord are:

PHASE 1: Aerial gathering from above.

1. **Jesus returns in the air.**

   When Jesus returns, life appears normal catching many by surprise:

   > [37] But **as the days of Noah** were, so also will the coming of the Son of Man be. [38] For as in the days before the flood, they were **eating and drinking, marrying and giving in marriage**, until the day that Noah entered the ark, [39] **and did not know** until the flood came and took them all away, so **also will the coming of the Son of Man** be. *Matthew 24:37-39*

   Speculation is that Christ will one day return on the Feast of Trumpets which occurs annually around the September/October timeframe. Traditionally, this Jewish feast involves the blowing of a trumpet which can be connected to the trumpet blown in Revelation 11:15 announcing the arrival of Christ:

   > [51] Behold, I tell you a mystery: We shall not all sleep, but we shall all be changed— [52] in a moment, in the twinkling of an eye, **at the last trumpet**. For **the trumpet will sound**, and the dead will be raised incorruptible, and we shall be changed. *Corinthians 15:51-52*

   With the sound of a trumpet, Jesus arrives unexpectedly at lightning speed coming from the east in a cloud of glory with His angels and other holy traveling companions to put an end to man's rule and establish God's kingdom. When Jesus returns, it will be in the air:

   > [9] ...**He (Jesus) was taken up**, and a cloud received Him out of their sight. [10] And while they looked steadfastly toward heaven as He went up, behold, two men stood by them in white apparel, [11] who also said, "Men of Galilee, why do you stand gazing up into heaven? This same Jesus, who was taken up from you into heaven, **will so come in like manner as you saw Him go into heaven**." *Acts 1:9-11*

   At His coming, everyone will see him including deceased Christians and non-Christians alike:

> ⁷ Behold, **He is coming with clouds**, and **every eye will see Him**, even they who pierced Him. *Revelation 1:7*

When He returns, Jesus is accompanied by a host of angels and other angelic creatures:

> ³¹ When the **Son of Man comes** in His glory, and **all the holy angels with Him**, then He will sit on the throne of His glory. *Matthew 25:31*

> …¹³ so that He may establish your hearts blameless in holiness before our God and Father at the **coming of our Lord Jesus Christ with all His saints**. *1 Thessalonians 3:13*

At His return, Jesus finishes gathering those who will be with Him to safety in the air of earth's atmosphere, then unleashes utter destruction:

> ⁶ Wail, for the **day of the LORD** is at hand! It will come as **destruction from the Almighty**. *Isaiah 13:6*

Though the nations of the earth strike at Him with their weaponry, their weapons are useless against Him (Joel 2:1-2, 5, 8) which terrifies even the mightiest of men (Revelation 6:15-17).

2. **The Elect are gathered.**

Jesus sends His angels on an errand to gather together a special group of people known as the Elect who have the seal of God on their forehead. Matthew 24:29 provides a time marker that the Elect are gathered to be with Jesus "immediately after the tribulation of those days" indicating it is one of the first tasks that Jesus accomplishes when He returns:

> ²⁹ **Immediately after the tribulation of those days** the sun will be darkened, and the moon will not give its light; the stars will fall from heaven, and the powers of the heavens will be shaken. ³⁰ Then the sign of the **Son of Man will appear in heaven**, and then all the tribes of the earth will mourn, and they will see the Son of Man coming on the clouds of heaven with power and great glory. ³¹ And He will **send His angels** with a great sound of a trumpet, and they will **gather together His elect** from the four

winds, from one end of heaven to the other... *Matthew 24:29-31*

Not to be confused with the Israeli remnant who survives the Antichrist's attack on Jerusalem and is supernaturally protected at Petra for the second half of the Tribulation or the Christian church which is raptured when Jesus returns, the Elect are a special group of holy men comprised of twelve thousand men from each of the twelve tribes of Israel for a total of one hundred forty-four thousand people:

> ⁴ And I heard the number of those who were sealed. **One hundred and forty-four thousand** of all the tribes of the **children of Israel were sealed**... *Revelation 7:4*

Musical in nature, this special group sings a special song that no one else can sing:

> ¹ Then I looked, and behold, a Lamb standing on Mount Zion, and **with Him one hundred and forty-four thousand**, having His Father's name written on their foreheads. ² ... And I heard the sound of **harpists playing their harps**. ³ **They sang** as it were a new song before the throne, before the four living creatures, and the elders; and no one could learn that song except the hundred and forty-four thousand who were redeemed from the earth. ⁴ These are the ones who **not defiled with women**, for they are **virgins**. These are the ones who **follow the Lamb wherever He goes**. These were redeemed from among men, being firstfruits to God and to the Lamb. ⁵ And in their mouth was found **no deceit**, for they **are without fault** before the throne of God. *Revelation 14:1-5*

Members of this group are male virgins who are scrupulously honest and faultless. Destined to be the personal traveling companions of Jesus in His new reign, they follow Jesus everywhere He goes after He returns.

3. **The Israeli remnant who have been supernaturally protected at Petra are gathered.**

After the Elect are gathered, Jesus gathers a second group of people who are Israeli survivors of the Antichrist's attack on Jerusalem:

> ¹² "I will surely assemble all of you, O Jacob, I will surely **gather the remnant of Israel**; I will put them together like

> sheep of the fold*, like a flock in the midst of their pasture; they shall make a loud noise because of so many people.
> *Micah 2:12*

Comprised of both men and women, this group has been supernaturally sustained at Petra waiting for Christ to come and rescue them when He returns.

4. **The two witnesses are resurrected.**

   After having been dead for the second half of the Tribulation, the two witnesses are resurrected and called up to be with Jesus:

   > [11] Now **after the three-and-a-half days the breath of life from God entered them** (the two witnesses), and they stood on their feet, and great fear fell on those who saw them. [12] And they heard a loud voice from heaven saying to them, "**Come up here.**" And **they ascended to heaven in a cloud**, and their enemies saw them. [13] In the same hour there was a great earthquake, and a tenth of the city fell.
   > *Revelation 11:11-13*

   The term used in Revelation 11:11-13 is "come here" implying they are gathered to be where Jesus is at that point which would be in the air above the earth. There are three heavens and nothing in Revelation 11:11-13 refers to the two witnesses being taken to a heaven that is anything other than the first heaven in the skies of earth's atmosphere. Scripture just states they "ascended to heaven". From there, it cannot automatically be assumed that they ascend to the third heaven where God dwells, only that they meet Jesus in the sky.

5. **Dead Christians are resurrected.**

   Having gathered His Elect and the surviving remnant of Israel, and resurrected His two witnesses, Jesus resurrects deceased Christians:

   > [16] For the **Lord Himself will descend from heaven** with a shout, with the voice of an archangel, and with the trumpet of God. And **the dead in Christ will rise first**. *1 Thessalonians 4:16*

6. **Christians who are alive are raptured to be with Jesus.**

   Following Jesus' return and the resurrection of the dead, in proper scriptural order is the rapture of living Christians to be with Jesus:

> ¹⁷ **Then** we who are alive and remain **shall be caught up** together with them **in the clouds** to meet the Lord **in the air**. And thus, we shall always be with the Lord." *1 Thessalonians 4:17*

In the original Greek, the word for "caught up" is "harpazo" which means to seize, snatch away or carry off by force. Inherent in the definition is the implication that a last-minute removal from imminent danger must happen immediately and with force or dire consequences will occur. When Jesus returns, the last trumpet blows signaling the end and believers are caught up in the air over the earth to be with Him. Note that verse seventeen says believers are caught up in the air, not up to heaven. They meet Jesus in the earth's atmosphere as evidenced by the reference to being "in the clouds" with Jesus and His angels. Those who are raptured do not leave the atmosphere of the earth. They are merely joined to Jesus while He is in the sky above the earth. Once safely in the presence of Jesus, Christians will never again be separated from Him. At this point in the process, all of His saints are safely with Him and the destruction of phase two commences.

PHASE 2: Aerial battle and victory.

7. Jesus stops the Battle of Armageddon.

Once all of those who are supposed to be with Jesus are safely with Him, Jesus supernaturally defends Israel and puts a stop to the Battle of Armageddon.

> ¹ Behold, the **day of the LORD** is coming, and your spoil will be divided in your midst. ² For I will **gather all the nations to battle against Jerusalem**; the city shall be taken, the houses rifled, and the women ravished. Half of the city shall go into captivity, but the remnant of the people shall not be cut off from the city. ³ Then **the LORD will go forth and fight against those nations**, as He fights in the day of battle. *Zechariah 14:1-3*

Having finished gathering all of His people back into His presence, both alive and deceased, they are with Him in the air over earth to witness the destructive power of His might as He fights for Israel and destroys all the nations who come against her. A description of the effects of the battle found in Zechariah indicates a possible EMP (electromagnetic pulse) is used against the nations who attack Jerusalem:

> ¹The burden of the word of the LORD against Israel. Thus, says the LORD, who stretches out the heavens, lays the foundation of the earth, and forms the spirit of man within him: ² "Behold, I will make Jerusalem a cup of drunkenness to all the surrounding peoples, **when they lay siege against Judah and Jerusalem**. ³ And it shall happen in that day that I will make Jerusalem a very heavy stone for all peoples; all who would heave it away will surely be cut in pieces, **though all nations of the earth are gathered against it**. ⁴ In that day," says the LORD, "**I will strike every horse with confusion**, and its rider with madness; I will open My eyes on the house of Judah, and **will strike every horse of the peoples with blindness**. *Zechariah 12:1-4*

Cars are modern day "horses". Headlights resemble eyes when viewed from the front. If the car loses power, the headlights go out and the car becomes "blind".

8. **The Antichrist and False Prophet are captured.**

As part of the Battle of Armageddon, Jesus successfully captures both the Antichrist and his sidekick, the False Prophet.

> …¹⁹ And I saw the beast, the kings of the earth, and their armies, gathered together to make war against Him who sat on the horse and against His army. ²⁰ Then **the beast was captured, and with him the false prophet** who worked signs in his presence, by which he deceived those who received the mark of the beast and those who worshiped his image. *Revelation 19:19-20*

PHASE 3: Judgment and Celebration on earth.

9. **Jesus physically arrives on earth.**

With the Battle of Armageddon won, the Antichrist and False Prophet out of the way, and the nations subdued, Jesus sets foot on earth on the Mount of Olives where He announces He is taking over control of the earth and establishing His reign:

> ⁴ And in that day **His feet will stand on the Mount of Olives**, which faces Jerusalem on the east. And the Mount of Olives shall be split in two, from east to west,

making a very large valley; half of the mountain shall move toward the north and half of it toward the south. ⁵ Then you shall flee through My mountain valley, for the mountain valley shall reach to Azal...Thus the LORD my God will come, and all the saints with You. ⁶ It shall come to pass in that day that there will be no light; the lights will diminish. ⁷ It shall be one day which is known to the LORD—neither day nor night. But at evening time it shall happen that it will be light...⁹ **And the LORD shall be King over all the earth**... *Zechariah 14:4-7, 9*

10. Judgement and sentencing of the Antichrist, False Prophet and nations occurs.

Next, Jesus gathers all nations together in the Valley of Jehoshaphat to render judgment against them for their transgressions against the Lord. Charges against them include the dividing up of Israeli land, dispersing the Israeli people, and robbing His temple of His treasures:

> ¹...in those days...² I will also gather all nations, and bring them down to the **Valley of Jehoshaphat**; and **I will enter into judgment with them** there on account of My people, My heritage **Israel, whom they have scattered** among the nations; they have also **divided up My land**...⁴ ...Swiftly and speedily I will return your retaliation upon your own head; ⁵ because you have **taken My silver and My gold**, and have carried into your temples My prized possessions...⁹ Proclaim this among the nations: "Prepare for war! Wake up the mighty men, let all the men of war draw near, let them come up..." ¹¹ Assemble and come, all you nations, and gather together all around. Cause Your mighty ones to go down there, O LORD. ¹² Let the nations be wakened, and come up to the Valley of Jehoshaphat; for there I will sit to judge all the surrounding nations...¹⁴ Multitudes, multitudes in the valley of decision! For the day of the LORD is near in the valley of decision. ¹⁵ The sun and moon will grow dark, and the stars will diminish their brightness. ¹⁶ The LORD also will roar from Zion, and utter His voice from Jerusalem; the heavens and earth will shake; but the LORD will be a shelter for His people, and the strength of the children of Israel. ¹⁷ So you shall know that I am the LORD your God, dwelling in Zion My holy mountain. Then Jerusalem shall be holy, and no

aliens shall ever pass through her again. *Joel 3:1-2, 4-5, 9, 11-12, 14-17*

The Antichrist and False Prophet are judged at that time too:

> [26] But **the court shall be seated**, and **they shall take away his** (the Antichrist) **dominion**, to consume and destroy it forever. [27] Then the kingdom and dominion, and the greatness of the kingdoms under the whole heaven, shall be given to the people, the saints of the Most High. *Daniel 7:26-27*

All those being judged are found guilty. After their sentences are rendered, the Antichrist and False Prophet are both immediately thrown into the lake of fire. Following that, the nations are killed:

> [20] ...**These two** (the Antichrist and False Prophet) **were cast alive into the lake of fire** burning with brimstone. [21] And the **rest were killed** with the sword which proceeded from the mouth of Him who sat on the horse. And all the birds were filled with their flesh. *Rev. 19:20*

After the punishment, the dead are not even permitted to be buried:

> [31] "A noise will come to the ends of the earth—For the LORD has a controversy with the nations; He will plead His case with all flesh. He will give those who are wicked to the sword," says the LORD. [32] Thus says the LORD of hosts: "Behold, disaster shall go forth from nation to nation, and a great whirlwind shall be raised up from the farthest parts of the earth. [33] And at that day **the slain of the LORD shall be from one end of the earth even to the other end** of the earth. They **shall not be** lamented, or gathered, or **buried**; they shall become refuse on the ground." *Jeremiah 25:31-33*

11. Mystery Babylon is judged and destroyed.

After the nations are judged, Mystery Babylon is found guilty and destroyed by Jesus in an act of retributory punishment for her sins too:

> [2] ...He (Jesus) has **judged the great harlot** who corrupted the earth with her fornication; and **He has avenged** on her the blood of His servants shed by her. *Revelation 19:2*

12. Marriage Supper of the Lamb.

With everything finally, properly in order, Christ now becomes engaged to His future bride, the church, and holds a celebratory feast in honor of the event which is known as the Marriage Supper of the Lamb:

> [7] Let us be glad and rejoice and give Him glory, for the **marriage of the Lamb** has come, and His **wife** has made herself ready. [8] And to her it was granted to be arrayed in fine linen, clean and bright, for the fine linen is the righteous acts of the saints. [9] Then he said to me, "Write: **'Blessed are those who are called to the marriage supper of the Lamb!'** " *Revelation 19:7-9*

The parable of the Wedding Feast is an allegory for this event and reveals additional information about the feast:

> [1] And Jesus answered and spoke to them again by parables and said: [2] "The kingdom of heaven is like a certain king who arranged a marriage for his son, [3] and sent out his servants to call those who were invited to the wedding; and they were not willing to come. [4] Again, he sent out other servants, saying, 'Tell those who are invited, "See, I have prepared my dinner; my oxen and fatted cattle are killed, and all things are ready. Come to the wedding." ' [5] But they made light of it and went their ways, one to his own farm, another to his business. [6] And the rest seized his servants, treated them spitefully, and killed them. [7] **But when the king heard about it, he was furious. And he sent out his armies, destroyed those murderers, and burned up their city.** [8] **Then he said to his servants, 'The wedding is ready, but those who were invited were not worthy.** [9] Therefore go into the highways, and as many as you find, invite to the wedding.' [10] So those servants went out into the highways and gathered together all whom they found, both **bad** and good. And the wedding hall was filled with guests. [11] But when the king came in to see the guests, he saw **a man there who did not have on a wedding garment**. [12] So he said to him, "Friend, how did you come in here **without a wedding garment**?" And he was speechless. [13] Then the king said to the servants, "Bind him hand and foot, take him away, and **cast him into outer darkness**; there will be weeping and gnashing

of teeth. ¹⁴ For many are called, but few are chosen." *Matthew 22:1-14*

From Matthew 22:7-8, it can be observed that the wedding feast happens after the Battle of Armageddon. Zephaniah also links the wedding supper to a timeline that immediately follows the judgment and punishments in the Valley of Jehoshaphat on the Day of the Lord:

> ⁷ Be silent in the presence of the Lord GOD; for **the day of the LORD is at hand, for the LORD has prepared a sacrifice; he has invited His guests**. ⁸ And it shall be, <u>**in the day of the LORD's sacrifice**</u>, **that I will punish the princes and the king's children, and all such as are clothed with foreign apparel.** ⁹ <u>**In the same day I will punish**</u> all those who leap over the threshold, who fill their masters' houses with violence and deceit. *Zeph. 1:7-9*

The uninvited man from Matthew 22:11 who gets thrown into outer darkness in Matthew 22:13 is the Antichrist which puts his expulsion before the celebration. The fact that the wedding hall was filled with "both bad and good" guests in Matthew 22:10 suggests that the location of the feast is here on earth as "bad" guests would have no access to the third heaven where God dwells. In addition, guests without garments would not be in heaven either.

Another parable which provides further insight into the Marriage Supper of the Lamb is the parable of the Ten Virgins:

> ¹Then the kingdom of heaven shall be likened to ten virgins who took their lamps and went out **to meet the bridegroom**. ² Now five of them were wise, and five were foolish. ³ Those who were foolish took their lamps and took no oil with them, ⁴ but the wise took oil in their vessels with their lamps. ⁵ But while the bridegroom was delayed, they all slumbered and slept. ⁶ And at midnight a cry was heard: "Behold, the bridegroom is coming; go out to meet him!" ⁷ Then all those virgins arose and trimmed their lamps. ⁸ And the foolish said to the wise, "Give us some of your oil, for our lamps are going out." ⁹ But the wise answered, saying, "No, lest there should not be enough for us and you; but go rather to those who sell, and buy for yourselves." ¹⁰ And while they went to buy, the bridegroom came, and those who were ready went in with him to the

wedding; and the door was shut. **¹¹ Afterward the other virgins came also, saying, "Lord, Lord, open to us!" ¹² But he answered and said, "Assuredly, I say to you, I do not know you."** ¹³ "Watch therefore, for you know neither the day nor the hour in which the Son of Man is coming. *Matthew 25:1-13*

In this parable, five of the ten virgins must go buy more oil before they can attend the wedding. When they return after presumably finding more oil, the door is shut and cannot be reopened for them. If the wedding occurs in heaven, the five who missed the opportunity to enter would have no way to go back and knock on the door. The implication in this parable is that the wedding takes place on earth. Theoretically, if the wedding supper occurs in heaven, then Jesus would need to return once for his church at the second coming, go back to heaven for the marriage supper and then come back again to rule and reign on earth. Commonly referred to as a U-Turn theory, it is implausible to consider because Jesus only comes to earth twice (birth and resurrection, then second coming), not three times:

> ²⁸ …Christ …will **appear a second time**, apart from sin, for salvation. *Hebrews 9:28*

Also confirming the wedding feast takes place on earth is Isaiah 25:9 referencing the feast is held on a mountain, presumably the Mount of Olives where Jesus returns:

> ⁴ And in that day **His feet will stand on the Mount of Olives**, which faces Jerusalem on the east. *Zechariah 14:4*

> ⁶ And **in this mountain** the LORD **of hosts will make** for all people **a feast** of choice pieces, a feast of wines on the lees, of fat things full of marrow, of well-refined wines on the lees. ⁷ And He will destroy on this mountain the surface of the covering cast over all people, and the veil that is spread over all nations. ⁸ He will swallow up death forever, and the Lord GOD will wipe away tears from all faces; the rebuke of His people He will take away from all the earth; for the LORD has spoken. ⁹ And it will be said in that day: "Behold, this is our God; we have waited for Him, and He will save us. This is the LORD; we have waited for Him; we will be glad and rejoice in His salvation." *Isaiah 25:6-9*

Seven Blessings
A Jewish Wedding Ritual

1. May the life you share together be as sweet as this wine you drink today. Blessed is the Source of Life, who created the fruit of the vine.

2. May your love for one another always be a source of inspiration and happiness. Blessed is the Source of Joy, who creates a wonderful, brilliant world.

3. May your journey together be blessed with generosity and forgiveness. May you enable each other to fulfill your dreams, and may you be committed to the paths of courage and hope. Blessed is the Source of Generosity who created such good, remarkable people…you two!

4. Wherever you travel, and wherever life takes you, may the love of your family and friends always echo in your hearts…even across great distances and times. Blessed is the Source of Love who supports the edifice of love.

5. With the strength of your relationship, may you help transform the world in big ways and small ways. May your love for each other be a source of warmth and inspiration for your community. Blessed is the Source of Healing who brings wellbeing to the world through Her children.

6. May you always find a refuge tucked within your love – a place to hide out, and a place to reflect. Blessed is the Source of Safety, who brings joy to the brides.

7. Blessed is the Source of Life, who creates wonder, pleasure, song, and delight! May the bride and groom be filled with gladness, and rejoicing, love, harmony, and companionship. And may they be blessed with lots and lots of peace! Blessed is the Source of Life, who is the Source of Peace.

Courtesy of Rabbi Josh Bolton via Sefaria

SHEVA BRACHOT: It is customary in a Jewish wedding for seven blessings to be recited over the newly married couple. This practice in Hebrew is known as Sheva Brachot (pronounced SHEH-vuh brah-CHOTE) which literally means "seven blessings".

Again, in Ezekiel 39:17, another reference is provided of the Lord throwing a sacrificial feast on the mountains of Israel:

> ¹⁷ …Assemble yourselves and come; gather together from all sides to My sacrificial meal which I am sacrificing for you, **a great sacrificial meal on the mountains of Israel**… *Ezekiel 39:17*

Speaking to the timing of the feast, in Matthew 26:29 Jesus specifically tells His disciples that the feast will not occur until His Father's kingdom is set up:

> ²⁶ And as they were eating, Jesus took bread, blessed and broke it, and gave it to the disciples and said, "Take, eat; this is My body." ²⁷ Then He took the cup, and gave thanks, and gave it to them, saying, "Drink from it, all of you. ²⁸ For this is My blood of the new covenant, which is shed for many for the remission of sins. ²⁹ But I say to you, **I will not drink of this fruit of the vine from now on until that day when I drink it new with you in My Father's kingdom.**" *Matthew 26:26-29*

Since the final delivery of His Father's kingdom is the last thing to happen in the order of events (1 Corinthians 15:24), the marriage feast must be a later event.

13. Jesus delivers the kingdom to His Father.

With everything in order and Jesus in full control of the earth, Jesus makes the final delivery of the kingdom to God thus officially ending the Day of the Lord and the Tribulation period:

> ²⁴ Then comes **the end, when He delivers the kingdom to God** the Father, when He puts an end to all rule and all authority and power. *1 Corinthians 15:24*

It is a touching reciprocal gesture of a gift returned. In Psalm 2:7-9, God gave the world to Jesus as a gift and now Jesus gives everything back to His Father.

One day Jesus will return and believers will be raptured to be with Him. Psychologically, the concept of a pre-Tribulation rapture is emotionally soothing and easier to accept than a post-Tribulation rapture position. After all, who wouldn't prefer a get-out-of-jail-free card over facing Satan's earthly wrath against Christians during the Tribulation? Unfortunately, according to 1 Thessalonians 4:16-17, the rapture cannot occur until Jesus returns. When Jesus returns it is to destroy the rule of man on earth and set up His new reign which makes a pre-Tribulation rapture with life continuing on for another seven years a virtual impossibility. Until Jesus returns, it is important for believers to be prepared for Christ's return at all times. He wants His followers to be watchful, living each day as though His return will be at any moment:

> [6] Therefore let us not sleep, as others do, but **let us watch** and be sober... *1 Thessalonians 5:6*

God never tells us to do something unless there is a reason for it. If He tells us to pay attention, it is because we need to pay attention. The message is simply, "Be Ready."

Talk It Out

1. Are you ready for Jesus' return? If not, why not? Does the concept of a rapture frighten you or give you comfort?

2. 1 Thessalonians 4:17 says we will be caught up "in the clouds" to meet Jesus "in the air". Do you think that refers to the atmosphere above earth or someplace else?

3. After examining the evidence, do you think scripture supports the concept of a pre-Tribulation rapture or a post-Tribulation rapture? Support your position with scriptural concepts.

4. Do you think the "Day" of the Lord refers to a literal twenty-four-hour day or one year with a length of 360 days as is common with prophetic interpretation?

5. Do you think it is fair that the Antichrist and False Prophet are thrown into the lake of fire? Is their punishment too severe, not severe enough, or just right?

6. Do you think the Marriage Supper of the Lamb is held on earth or in heaven?

7. What foods do you think Jesus will serve at the Marriage Supper of the Lamb? What are your favorite foods to eat at a feast?

Ideas for the Week:

- ✓ Do a search for "trumpets in the sky" on YouTube and watch/listen to the different videos uploaded from around the world or use this link https://www.youtube.com/watch?v=vul4SYL4QiQ.
- ✓ Listen to the sound of a shofar on YouTube at https://www.youtube.com/watch?v=Rnkb7M3dKTg. Compare the sound of the shofar to the sound in the videos from "trumpets in the sky".
- ✓ Visit the *World Hum* map and database at www.thehum.info to see where the sounds are occurring worldwide.
- ✓ Read about the Feast of Trumpets at https://jewsforjesus.org/publications/newsletter/newsletter-sep-2000/the-feast-of-trumpets/.

Closing Prayer

NOTE: *Add names and individual personal prayer requests to the space provided below before closing in prayer.*

Lord, we thank You for our time together today to grow deeper in our walk with You and fellowship with each other. As we close today, we lift up: _____

_____

_____

_____

_____

_____

_____

Father, we may not know the exact hour of Jesus' return, but we do know that it is at the very door. Heighten our awareness of the signs of the time so that we may be ready to meet Jesus in the air at His Return. Make us ever more ready to be with Him forever as the time drawers nearer and nearer. In Jesus' name we pray, Amen.

SUPPORTING SCRIPTURES

DAY OF THE LORD

[28] ...Christ ...will appear a second time, apart from sin, for salvation. *Hebrews 9:28*

[7] I will declare the decree: The LORD has said to Me, "You are My Son, today I have begotten You. [8] Ask of Me, and I will give You the nations for Your inheritance, and the ends of the earth for Your possession. [9] You shall break them with a rod of iron; You shall dash them to pieces like a potter's vessel." *Psalm 2:7-9*

[9] ...He (Jesus) was taken up, and a cloud received Him out of their sight. [10] And while they looked steadfastly toward heaven as He went up, behold, two men stood by them in white apparel, [11] who also said, "Men of Galilee, why do you stand gazing up into heaven? This same Jesus, who was taken up from you into heaven, will so come in like manner as you saw Him go into heaven." *Acts 1:9-11*

[6] Wail, for the day of the LORD is at hand! It will come as destruction from the Almighty. *Isaiah 13:6*

[10] Because you have kept My command to persevere, I also will keep you from the hour of trial which shall come upon the whole world, to test those who dwell on the earth. *Revelation 3:10*

[1] For the day of the LORD...is at hand [2] ... A people come, great and strong, the like of whom has never been; nor will there ever be any such after them, even for many successive generations...[5] Over mountaintops they leap...[8] Though they lunge between the weapons, they are not cut down. *Joel 2:1-2, 5, 8*

[2] "I will utterly consume everything from the face of the land," says the LORD; [3] "I will consume man and beast; I will consume the birds of the heavens, the fish of the sea, and the stumbling blocks along with the wicked. I will cut off man from the face of the land," says the LORD. *Zephaniah 1:2-3*

[15] And the kings of the earth, the great men, the rich men, the commanders, the mighty men, every slave and every free man, hid themselves in the caves and in the rocks of the mountains, [16] and said to the mountains and rocks, "Fall on us and hide us from the face of Him who sits on the throne and from the wrath of the Lamb!" *Revelation 6:15-16*

[19] They will throw their silver into the streets, and their gold will be like refuse; their silver and their gold will not be able to deliver them in the day of the wrath of

the LORD; they will not satisfy their souls, nor fill their stomachs, because it became their stumbling block of iniquity. *Ezekiel 7:19*

¹⁵ Blow the trumpet in Zion, consecrate a fast, call a sacred assembly; ¹⁶ gather the people...¹⁷ Let the priests...say, "Spare Your people, O LORD..." *Joel 2:15-17*

²⁷ For as the lightning comes from the east and flashes to the west, so also will the coming of the Son of Man be. *Matthew 24:27*

⁷ Behold, He is coming with clouds, and every eye will see Him, even they who pierced Him. *Revelation 1:7*

⁴⁰ Therefore you also be ready, for the Son of Man is coming at an hour you do not expect. *Luke 12:40*

⁷ The LORD will save the tents of Judah first...⁹ It shall be in that day that I will seek to destroy all the nations that come against Jerusalem. *Zechariah 12:7, 9*

TRUMPETS
⁵¹Behold, I tell you a mystery: We shall not all sleep, but we shall all be changed— ⁵² in a moment, in the twinkling of an eye, at the last trumpet. For the trumpet will sound, and the dead will be raised incorruptible, and we shall be changed. *Corinthians 15:51-52*

¹⁵ Then the seventh angel sounded (his trumpet): And there were loud voices in heaven, saying, "The kingdoms of this world have become the kingdoms of our Lord and of His Christ, and He shall reign forever and ever!" *Revelation 11:15*

JESUS RETURNS WITH ANGELS AND HOLY CREATURES
...¹¹ who also said, "Men of Galilee, why do you stand gazing up into heaven? This same Jesus, who was taken up from you into heaven, will so come in like manner as you saw Him go into heaven." *Acts 1:11*

¹⁴ ..."Behold, the Lord comes with ten thousands of His saints ¹⁵ to execute judgment on all, to convict all who are ungodly among them ... *Jude 1:14*

⁴ And in that day His feet will stand on the Mount of Olives, which faces Jerusalem on the east....Thus the Lord my God will come, and all the saints with You. *Zechariah 14:4-5*

...¹³ so that He may establish your hearts blameless in holiness before our God and Father at the coming of our Lord Jesus Christ with all His saints. *1 Thessalonians 3:13*

³¹ When the Son of Man comes in His glory, and all the holy angels with Him, then He will sit on the throne of His glory. *Matthew 25:31*

³⁸ For whoever is ashamed of Me and My words in this adulterous and sinful generation, of him the Son of Man also will be ashamed when He comes in the glory of His Father with the holy angels." *Mark 8:38*

³⁹ The enemy who sowed them is the devil, the harvest is the end of the age, and the reapers are the angels. *Matthew 13:39*

⁴¹ The Son of Man will send out His angels, and they will gather out of His kingdom all things that offend, and those who practice lawlessness… *Matthew 13:41*

⁴⁹ So it will be at the end of the age. The angels will come forth, separate the wicked from among the just… *Matthew 13:49*

²⁷ And then He will send His angels, and gather together His elect from the four winds, from the farthest part of earth to the farthest part of heaven. *Mark 13:27*

²⁶ For whoever is ashamed of Me and My words, of him the Son of Man will be ashamed when He comes in His own glory, and in His Father's, and of the holy angels. *Luke 9:26*

¹⁶ For the Lord Himself will descend from heaven with a shout, with the voice of an archangel, and with the trumpet of God. *1 Thessalonians 4:16*

…⁷ and to give you who are troubled rest with us when the Lord Jesus is revealed from heaven with His mighty angels… *2 Thessalonians 1:7*

THE ELECT
²⁹ Immediately after the tribulation of those days the sun will be darkened, and the moon will not give its light; the stars will fall from heaven, and the powers of the heavens will be shaken. ³⁰ Then the sign of the Son of Man will appear in heaven, and then all the tribes of the earth will mourn, and they will see the Son of Man coming on the clouds of heaven with power and great glory. ³¹ And He will send His angels with a great sound of a trumpet, and they will gather together His elect from the four winds, from one end of heaven to the other… *Matthew 24:29-31*

² Then I saw another angel ascending from the east, having the seal of the living God. And he cried with a loud voice to the four angels to whom it was granted to harm the earth and the sea, ³ saying, "Do not harm the earth, the sea, or the trees till we have sealed the servants of our God on their foreheads." ⁴ And I heard the number of those who were sealed. One hundred and forty-four

thousand of all the tribes of the children of Israel were sealed: ⁵ of the tribe of Judah twelve thousand were sealed; of the tribe of Reuben twelve thousand were sealed; of the tribe of Gad twelve thousand were sealed; ⁶ of the tribe of Asher twelve thousand were sealed; of the tribe of Naphtali twelve thousand were sealed; of the tribe of Manasseh twelve thousand were sealed; ⁷ of the tribe of Simeon twelve thousand were sealed; of the tribe of Levi twelve thousand were sealed; of the tribe of Issachar twelve thousand were sealed; ⁸ of the tribe of Zebulun twelve thousand were sealed; of the tribe of Joseph twelve thousand were sealed; of the tribe of Benjamin twelve thousand were sealed. *Revelation 7:2-8*

¹ Then I looked, and behold, a Lamb standing on Mount Zion, and with Him one hundred and forty-four thousand, having His Father's name written on their foreheads. ² ... And I heard the sound of harpists playing their harps. ³ They sang as it were a new song before the throne, before the four living creatures, and the elders; and no one could learn that song except the hundred and forty-four thousand who were redeemed from the earth. ⁴ These are the ones who were not defiled with women, for they are virgins. These are the ones who follow the Lamb wherever He goes. These were redeemed from among men, being firstfruits to God and to the Lamb. ⁵ And in their mouth was found no deceit, for they are without fault before the throne of God. *Revelation 14:1-5*

THE ISRAELI REMNANT

²⁰ But when you see Jerusalem surrounded by armies...²¹ Then let those who are in Judea flee to the mountains, let those who are in the midst of her depart, and let not those who are in the country enter her. ²³ But woe to those who are pregnant and to those who are nursing babies in those days! *Luke 21:20-21, 23*

¹ Who is this who comes from Edom, with dyed garments from Bozrah, this One who is glorious in His apparel, traveling in the greatness of His strength?—"I who speak in righteousness, mighty to save." *Isaiah 63:1*

¹² "I will surely assemble all of you, O Jacob, I will surely gather the remnant of Israel; I will put them together like sheep of the fold*, like a flock in the midst of their pasture; they shall make a loud noise because of so many people. *Micah 2:12*

NOTE: *The King James translation of Micah 2:12 translates "sheep of the fold" as the "sheep of Bozrah".

²⁰ And it shall come to pass in that day that the remnant of Israel, and such as have escaped of the house of Jacob, will never again depend on him who defeated them, but will depend on the LORD, the Holy One of Israel, in truth.

²¹ The remnant will return, the remnant of Jacob, to the Mighty God. ²² For though your people, O Israel, be as the sand of the sea, a remnant of them will return... *Isaiah 10:20-22*

THE TWO WITNESSES RESURRECTED
¹¹ Now after the three-and-a-half days the breath of life from God entered them (the two witnesses), and they stood on their feet, and great fear fell on those who saw them. ¹² And they heard a loud voice from heaven saying to them, "Come up here." And they ascended to heaven in a cloud, and their enemies saw them. ¹³ In the same hour there was a great earthquake, and a tenth of the city fell. *Revelation 11:11-13*

THE RESURRECTION AND RAPTURE
¹⁶ For the Lord Himself will descend from heaven with a shout, with the voice of an archangel, and with the trumpet of God. And the dead in Christ will rise first. ¹⁷ Then we who are alive and remain shall be caught up together with them in the clouds to meet the Lord in the air. And thus, we shall always be with the Lord. *1 Thessalonians 4:16-17*

...⁷ but in the days of the sounding of the seventh angel, when he is about to sound, the mystery of God would be finished, as He declared to His servants the prophets. *Revelation 10:7*

³⁷ But as the days of Noah were, so also will the coming of the Son of Man be. ³⁸ For as in the days before the flood, they were eating and drinking, marrying and giving in marriage, until the day that Noah entered the ark, ³⁹ and did not know until the flood came and took them all away, so also will the coming of the Son of Man be. ⁴⁰ Then two men will be in the field: one will be taken and the other left. ⁴¹ Two women will be grinding at the mill: one will be taken and the other left. ⁴² Watch therefore, for you do not know what hour your Lord is coming...⁴⁴ Therefore you also be ready, for the Son of Man is coming at an hour you do not expect. *Matthew 24:37-42, 44*

THE BATTLE OF ARMAGEDDON
¹ Behold, the day of the LORD is coming, and your spoil will be divided in your midst. ² For I will gather all the nations to battle against Jerusalem; the city shall be taken, the houses rifled, and the women ravished. Half of the city shall go into captivity, but the remnant of the people shall not be cut off from the city. ³ Then the LORD will go forth and fight against those nations, as He fights in the day of battle. *Zechariah 14:1-3*

¹⁶ The LORD also will roar from Zion, and utter His voice from Jerusalem; the heavens and earth will shake; but the LORD will be a shelter for His people, and

the strength of the children of Israel. *Joel 3:16*

¹The burden of the word of the LORD against Israel. Thus, says the LORD, who stretches out the heavens, lays the foundation of the earth, and forms the spirit of man within him: ² "Behold, I will make Jerusalem a cup of drunkenness to all the surrounding peoples, when they lay siege against Judah and Jerusalem. ³ And it shall happen in that day that I will make Jerusalem a very heavy stone for all peoples; all who would heave it away will surely be cut in pieces, though all nations of the earth are gathered against it. ⁴ In that day," says the LORD, "I will strike every horse with confusion, and its rider with madness; I will open My eyes on the house of Judah, and will strike every horse of the peoples with blindness. *Zechariah 12:1-4*

THE BEAST AND FALSE PROPHET CAPTURED
...¹⁹ And I saw the beast, the kings of the earth, and their armies, gathered together to make war against Him who sat on the horse and against His army. ²⁰ Then the beast was captured, and with him the false prophet who worked signs in his presence, by which he deceived those who received the mark of the beast and those who worshiped his image. These two were cast alive into the lake of fire burning with brimstone. ²¹ And the rest were killed with the sword which proceeded from the mouth of Him who sat on the horse. And all the birds were filled with their flesh. *Revelation 19:11-16, 19-21*

JESUS ARRIVES ON EARTH AFTER ARMAGEDDON
⁴ And in that day His feet will stand on the Mount of Olives, which faces Jerusalem on the east. And the Mount of Olives shall be split in two, from east to west, making a very large valley; half of the mountain shall move toward the north and half of it toward the south. ⁵ Then you shall flee through My mountain valley, for the mountain valley shall reach to Azal...Thus the LORD my God will come, and all the saints with You. ⁶ It shall come to pass in that day that there will be no light; the lights will diminish. ⁷ It shall be one day which is known to the LORD—neither day nor night. But at evening time it shall happen that it will be light...⁹ And the LORD shall be King over all the earth... *Zechariah 14:4-7, 9*

JUDGMENT OF THE NATIONS
¹...in those days...² I will also gather all nations, and bring them down to the Valley of Jehoshaphat; and I will enter into judgment with them there on account of My people, My heritage Israel, whom they have scattered among the nations; they have also divided up My land...⁴ ...Swiftly and speedily I will return your retaliation upon your own head; ⁵ because you have taken My silver and My gold, and have carried into your temples My prized possessions...⁹ Proclaim this among the nations: "Prepare for war! Wake up the mighty men, let all the men of war draw near, let them come up..." ¹¹ Assemble and come, all you nations,

and gather together all around. Cause Your mighty ones to go down there, O LORD. [12] Let the nations be wakened, and come up to the Valley of Jehoshaphat; for there I will sit to judge all the surrounding nations…[14] Multitudes, multitudes in the valley of decision! For the day of the LORD is near in the valley of decision. [15] The sun and moon will grow dark, and the stars will diminish their brightness. [16] The LORD also will roar from Zion, and utter His voice from Jerusalem; the heavens and earth will shake; but the LORD will be a shelter for His people, and the strength of the children of Israel. [17] So you shall know that I am the LORD your God, dwelling in Zion My holy mountain. Then Jerusalem shall be holy, and no aliens shall ever pass through her again." *Joel 3:1-2, 4-5, 9, 11-12, 14-17*

[31] "A noise will come to the ends of the earth—for the LORD has a controversy with the nations; He will plead His case with all flesh. He will give those who are wicked to the sword," says the LORD. [32] Thus says the LORD of hosts: "Behold, disaster shall go forth from nation to nation, and a great whirlwind shall be raised up from the farthest parts of the earth. [33] And at that day the slain of the LORD shall be from one end of the earth even to the other end of the earth. They shall not be lamented, or gathered, or buried; they shall become refuse on the ground." *Jeremiah 25:31-33*

[26] But the court shall be seated, and they shall take away his (the Antichrist) dominion, to consume and destroy it forever. [27] Then the kingdom and dominion, and the greatness of the kingdoms under the whole heaven, shall be given to the people, the saints of the Most High. His kingdom is an everlasting kingdom, and all dominions shall serve and obey Him. *Daniel 7:26-27*

MYSTERY BABYLON DESTROYED
[2] …He (Jesus) has judged the great harlot who corrupted the earth with her fornication; and He has avenged on her the blood of His servants shed by her. *Revelation 19:2*

MARRIAGE SUPPER OF THE LAMB
[7] Let us be glad and rejoice and give Him glory, for the marriage of the Lamb has come, and His wife has made herself ready. [8] And to her it was granted to be arrayed in fine linen, clean and bright, for the fine linen is the righteous acts of the saints. [9] Then he said to me, "Write: 'Blessed are those who are called to the marriage supper of the Lamb!' " *Revelation 19:7-9*

[7] Be silent in the presence of the Lord GOD; for the day of the LORD is at hand, for the LORD has prepared a sacrifice; he has invited His guests. [8] And it shall be, in the day of the LORD's sacrifice, that I will punish the princes and the king's children, and all such as are clothed with foreign apparel. [9] In the same day I will

punish all those who leap over the threshold, who fill their masters' houses with violence and deceit. *Zephaniah 1:7-9*

¹And Jesus answered and spoke to them again by parables and said: ² "The kingdom of heaven is like a certain king who arranged a marriage for his son, ³ and sent out his servants to call those who were invited to the wedding; and they were not willing to come. ⁴ Again, he sent out other servants, saying, 'Tell those who are invited, "See, I have prepared my dinner; my oxen and fatted cattle are killed, and all things are ready. Come to the wedding." ' ⁵ But they made light of it and went their ways, one to his own farm, another to his business. ⁶ And the rest seized his servants, treated them spitefully, and killed them. ⁷ But when the king heard about it, he was furious. And he sent out his armies, destroyed those murderers, and burned up their city. ⁸ Then he said to his servants, "The wedding is ready, but those who were invited were not worthy. ⁹ Therefore go into the highways, and as many as you find, invite to the wedding." ¹⁰ So those servants went out into the highways and gathered together all whom they found, both bad and good. And the wedding hall was filled with guests. ¹¹ But when the king came in to see the guests, he saw a man there who did not have on a wedding garment. ¹² So he said to him, "Friend, how did you come in here without a wedding garment?" And he was speechless. ¹³ Then the king said to the servants, "Bind him hand and foot, take him away, and cast him into outer darkness; there will be weeping and gnashing of teeth. ¹⁴ For many are called, but few are chosen." *Matthew 22:1-14*

¹Then the kingdom of heaven shall be likened to ten virgins who took their lamps and went out to meet the bridegroom. ² Now five of them were wise, and five were foolish. ³ Those who were foolish took their lamps and took no oil with them, ⁴ but the wise took oil in their vessels with their lamps. ⁵ But while the bridegroom was delayed, they all slumbered and slept. ⁶ And at midnight a cry was heard: "Behold, the bridegroom is coming; go out to meet him!" ⁷ Then all those virgins arose and trimmed their lamps. ⁸ And the foolish said to the wise, "Give us some of your oil, for our lamps are going out." ⁹ But the wise answered, saying, "No, lest there should not be enough for us and you; but go rather to those who sell, and buy for yourselves." ¹⁰ And while they went to buy, the bridegroom came, and those who were ready went in with him to the wedding; and the door was shut. ¹¹ Afterward the other virgins came also, saying, "Lord, Lord, open to us!" ¹² But he answered and said, "Assuredly, I say to you, I do not know you." ¹³ "Watch therefore, for you know neither the day nor the hour in which the Son of Man is coming. *Matthew 25:1-13*

⁶ And in this mountain the LORD of hosts will make for all people a feast of choice pieces, a feast of wines on the lees, of fat things full of marrow, of well-refined wines on the lees. ⁷ And He will destroy on this mountain the surface of the

covering cast over all people, and the veil that is spread over all nations. ⁸ He will swallow up death forever, and the Lord GOD will wipe away tears from all faces; the rebuke of His people He will take away from all the earth; for the LORD has spoken. ⁹ And it will be said in that day: "Behold, this is our God; we have waited for Him, and He will save us. This is the LORD; we have waited for Him; we will be glad and rejoice in His salvation." *Isaiah 25:6-9*

²⁶ And as they were eating, Jesus took bread, blessed and broke it, and gave it to the disciples and said, "Take, eat; this is My body." ²⁷ Then He took the cup, and gave thanks, and gave it to them, saying, "Drink from it, all of you. ²⁸ For this is My blood of the new covenant, which is shed for many for the remission of sins. ²⁹ But I say to you, I will not drink of this fruit of the vine from now on until that day when I drink it new with you in My Father's kingdom." *Matthew 26:26-29*

²⁴ Then comes the end, when He delivers the kingdom to God the Father, when He puts an end to all rule and all authority and power. *1 Corinthians 15:24*

¹⁷ …Assemble yourselves and come; gather together from all sides to My sacrificial meal which I am sacrificing for you, a great sacrificial meal on the mountains of Israel… *Ezekiel 39:17*

⁶ Therefore let us not sleep, as others do, but let us watch and be sober… *1 Thessalonians 5:6*

NOTES

"It doesn't matter if a million people tell you what you can't do, or if ten million tell you no. If you get one yes from God, that's all you need." — Tyler Perry

ARE WE THE TERMINAL GENERATION?

WEEK 24: THE MILLENNIAL REIGN AND BEYOND

Opening Prayer: Lord, we ask that You send Your Holy Spirit to us to guide us in the teaching and understanding of Your word that we may obtain a better understanding of the prophetic events surrounding us now and waiting for us in the future. Bless our fellowship in Your word that it may be fruitful and draw us into a deeper relationship both with You and those around us. Use us as Your vessels that through us, we may reflect Your glory to all whom we encounter. Illuminate our hearts and minds so that we may boldly shine the brightness of Your light everywhere we go and that we may be beacons of Your hope in a darkened world. In Jesus name we pray, Amen.

Ice Breaker: What does your dream home look like? Would you rather live in the mountains or the city? Do you want a home with traditional or contemporary architecture? What color scheme would you choose for the exterior? How big would your home be? Is your dream home on land or would you rather live in a houseboat? Share your vision of your dream home with the group.

 **Focus:** Those who remain faithful and true to Jesus and the word of God throughout the Tribulation will rule and reign with Him during the Millennial Reign.

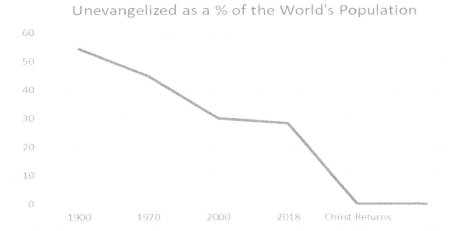

When Jesus returns, no one will be unevangelized!

Word of the Week

> ...⁶ they (resurrected and raptured Christians) shall be priests of God and of Christ, and shall **reign** with Him a thousand years.
>
> *Revelation 20:6*

REIGN: The word "reign" comes from the Greek word "basileuo" (pronounced bas-il-yoo'-o) and means to exercise authority, power and control. In God's perfect order, governments have structure. When Moses was in the desert with the Israelites, he appointed rulers of tens, rulers of fifties, rulers of hundreds and rulers of thousands (Deuteronomy 1:15). Society had a governing structure among the Hebrews with Moses as the primary leader. Even in heaven, Jesus answers to the Father while the angels are subject to Jesus' authority (Matthew 26:53, John 5:19). Order in the Millennial Reign will be no different. Those Christians who make it into the Millennial Reign through their faith in Jesus will be organized into a new society with varying levels of leadership authority. Just as in Moses' day, not everyone will have the same position or occupy the same position during the Millennial Reign. A serial killer who genuinely accepts the gift of salvation on his death bed may make it into the Millennial Reign through God's grace to all those who believe, but that does not mean that person will occupy the same level of leadership within Millennial Reign society as a lifelong believer such as Mother Teresa who spent all of her earthly years proving her unwavering servitude and devotion to Jesus.

Lesson: After Jesus arrives on earth, establishes control, gathers the elect as His traveling companions and announces His engagement to the church at a wedding feast, He establishes His formal kingdom on earth. Thus, begins a one-thousand-year time period where Jesus rules the earth in peace with His followers. Commonly referred to as the Millennial Reign, this period of time ushers in a peaceful new way of life in the presence of Jesus. Much like the term "rapture", the term "millennial reign" is technically not found in scripture, but is widely accepted as referring to the one-thousand-year time period after Jesus returns. A parallel can be drawn in scripture between the Millennial Reign and the forty days Jesus walked the earth between His resurrection and ascension. After Jesus' death, He returned to earth for a brief period of time:

> ...³ to whom He also **presented Himself alive after His suffering** by many infallible proofs, being **seen by them during forty days**... *Acts 1:3*
>
> ⁶ After that He was **seen by over five hundred brethren** at once... *1 Corinthians 15:6*

When that finite period ended, He continued on to heaven to be with His Father. In like manner during the Millennial Reign, Christians who have been resurrected or raptured off the earth then return to earth for a finite period of time with Jesus before continuing on to spend eternity in heaven with both God and Jesus.

Through the Tribulation, the standard practice for prophetic interpretation of using a day for a year applies. However, 2 Peter 3:8,10 changes the time exchange rate specifically for the Day of the Lord:

> ⁸ But, beloved, **do not forget this one thing**, that <u>**with the Lord one day is as a thousand years, and a thousand years as one day**</u>...¹⁰ But the **day of the Lord** will come as a thief in the night... *2 Peter 3:8,10*

Time does not change until we are in the presence of the Lord and with Him from that point forward. Since Jesus is not with people on earth during the Tribulation, the standard day-for-a-year practice is in effect. Once Jesus returns to change the world forever on the Day of the Lord, the time reference also changes. Essentially, the Day of the Lord is one thousand years long instead of one year in length which broadens it to encompass the entire Millennial Reign.

One of Jesus' first acts before entering the Millennial Reign is to punish Satan for his rebelliousness. Sentencing Satan to one thousand years in prison, the length of the entire Millennial Reign, Jesus has an angel bind Satan and cast him into the bottomless pit where he remains until the Millennial Reign ends:

> ¹ Then I saw **an angel** coming down from heaven, having the key to the bottomless pit and a great chain in his hand. ² He **laid hold of the dragon**, that serpent of old, who is the Devil and Satan, and **bound him for a thousand years**; ³ and **he cast him into the bottomless pit**, and shut him up, and set a seal on him, so that he should deceive the nations no more **till the thousand years were finished**. *Revelation 20:1-3*

Essentially, Jesus relegates Satan to house arrest. When the two witnesses completed their testimony, Satan emerged from his normal dwelling place, or his home, which is the bottomless pit:

> ³ And I will give power to my two witnesses, and they will prophesy one thousand two hundred and sixty days, clothed in sackcloth...⁷ When they finish their testimony, **the beast that ascends out of the bottomless pit** will make war against them, overcome them, and kill them... *Revelation 11:3, 7*

While confined to house arrest, Satan is rendered helpless. Powerless to deceive anyone and interfere with Jesus' plans, all Satan can do is bide his time in the bottomless pit until his sentence is complete.

Although the earth is in a state of deep distress after Jesus returns, He heals the earth to make it habitable once again for His people. Tribulation seal, trumpet and bowl judgments have left the earth in a state of total devastation. Rivers and oceans have been turned to blood, all marine life is dead, mountains are gone, severe damage from massive hailstones scars the face of the earth, mountains are moved and earthquakes rock the earth with such force that the earth is split open and wobbles on its axis in a pole shift. Even the heavens are affected as stars fall from the sky:

> ¹⁹ The **earth** is **violently broken**, the earth is **split open**, the earth is shaken exceedingly. ²⁰ The earth shall **reel to and fro** like a drunkard, and shall **totter like a hut**.... *Isaiah 24:19-20*

> ⁴ All the **host of heaven shall be dissolved**, and the heavens shall be rolled up like a scroll; all their **host shall fall down as the leaf falls from the vine**, and as fruit falling from a fig tree. *Is. 34:4*

During the destruction, God's people, who have been raptured off the earth, are safely protected with Jesus. The wicked who are left on earth are completely and utterly destroyed. But God promises that the world will never end and God is true to His word. Devoid of all human life, the extensively damaged earth still exists:

> ²³ I beheld **the earth**, and indeed it was **without form, and void**; and the heavens, they had **no light**. ²⁴ I beheld the **mountains**, and indeed they **trembled**, and all the **hills moved back and forth**. ²⁵ ...there was **no man**, and all **the birds of the heavens had fled**. ²⁶ I beheld, and indeed the fruitful land was a wilderness, and all its **cities were broken down** at the presence of the LORD, **by His fierce anger**. ²⁷ For thus says the LORD: "The whole land shall be desolate; yet <u>**I will not make a full end**</u>. *Jeremiah 4:23-27*

By this point, the extensively battered earth needs an extreme overhaul in order to be habitable again. To allow His children to once again inhabit the earth during the Millennial Reign, Jesus renovates the earth:

> [25] "**So I will restore to you** the years that the swarming locust has eaten, the crawling locust, the consuming locust, and the chewing locust, my great army which I sent among you. *Joel 2:25*

Again, in Malachi 4:1, reference is made to healing the earth. The bodies of the wicked dead are scattered on the earth, so it must be the earth that is healed because of the reference to "trampling the wicked" underfoot:

> [1] "For behold, the day is coming, burning like an oven, and all the proud, yes, **all who do wickedly will be stubble**. And the day which is coming shall burn them up," says the LORD of hosts, "That will leave them neither root nor branch. [2] But to you who fear My name **the Son of Righteousness shall arise with healing** in His wings; and you shall go out and grow fat like stall-fed calves. [3] **You shall trample the wicked, for they shall be ashes under the soles of your feet on the day that I do this**," says the LORD of hosts. *Malachi 4:1*

Restoration is a lengthy process. Darkness covers the earth after the Tribulation *(Jeremiah 4:23)*, but light returns "at evening time":

> [7] ...But **at evening time** it shall happen that **it will be light**... *Zechariah 14:7*

Symbolically, evening represents the halfway point in a twenty-four-hour day. Translating that to the Millennial Reign of one thousand years, light returning at evening time means light is restored about five hundred years later. Until that time, Christians wait patiently with Jesus for the earth to be renewed and functional again. Further indicating that renewal has occurred, Zechariah 14:8 states that living waters are flowing:

> [8] And in that day, it shall be that **living waters shall flow from Jerusalem**... *Zechariah 14:8*

Bringing life back to the formerly dead oceans, the living waters are a source of healing to restore life to the seas:

> [8] Then he said to me: "**This water** flows toward the eastern region, goes down into the valley, and **enters the sea. When it reaches**

> the sea, its waters are healed. ⁹ And it shall be that **every living thing that moves, wherever the rivers go, will live**. There will be a very great **multitude of fish**, because these waters go there; for **they will be healed**... *Ezekiel 47:8-9*

With the resurrection of the earth almost complete and the environment ready for habitation again, Jesus and His devoted followers, now serving as His priests, along with the Jewish Elect who accompany Jesus everywhere (*Revelation 14:1-5*), take up residency in Jerusalem where they rule and reign the world together in peace for the rest of the Millennial Reign:

> ⁵...This is the **first resurrection**...⁶ they shall be **priests of God** and of Christ, and shall **reign with Him a thousand years**. *Revelation 20:5-6*

> ² Now it shall come to pass in the latter days that the mountain of **the LORD's house** shall be established **on the top of the mountains**, and shall be exalted above the hills; and all nations shall flow to it. ³ Many people shall come and say, "Come, and let us go up to the mountain of the LORD, to the house of the God of Jacob; **he will teach us His ways, and we shall walk in His paths**." For out of Zion shall go forth the law, and the word of the LORD **from Jerusalem**. *Isaiah 2:2-3*

> ²⁷ Then you shall know that **I am in the midst of Israel**... *Joel 2:27*

It should be noted, however, that not everyone fulfills the role of a priest to Jesus in the Millennial Reign:

> ⁵ Now therefore, if you will indeed obey My voice and keep My covenant, then you shall be a special treasure to Me above all people; for all the earth is Mine. ⁶ And **you shall be to Me a kingdom of priests and a holy nation**. These are the words which you shall speak to the children of Israel. *Exodus 19:5-6*

While some of His children are priests of the Lord, others constitute the occupants of a holy nation. Just as Moses incorporated a hierarchical structure of government to rule the Hebrews, Jesus assigns different levels of participation to various individuals in His new kingdom. Regardless of social status in the kingdom, Israel finally recognizes Jesus as the true Messiah:

> [10] And I will pour on the house of David and on the inhabitants of Jerusalem the Spirit of grace and supplication; then **they will look on Me whom they pierced.** Yes, **they will mourn for Him** as one mourns for his only son, and grieve for Him as one grieves for a firstborn. *Zechariah 12:10*

In the current Church Age, the Jewish people do not recognize that the Messiah has already come and are waiting for their Messiah to arrive in the future. With the realization that Jesus was, is and always will be the true Messiah, they can finally worship Him as they should. Truly peace finally arrives in Jerusalem when Jesus takes up residency there.

Life during the Millennial Reign bears many striking similarities to the way mankind has existed for centuries. Farming will be part of the Millennial Reign. On the farms, people will build their own homes and plant their own crops:

> [21] They **shall build houses and inhabit them**; they **shall plant vineyards and eat their fruit.** [22] They shall not build and another inhabit; they shall not plant and another eat; for as the days of a tree, so shall be the days of My people, and My elect shall long enjoy the work of their hands. *Isaiah 65:21-22*

People will have pottery for cooking and cook the food they grow themselves:

> [21] Yes, **every pot in Jerusalem and Judah** shall be holiness to the LORD of hosts. Everyone who sacrifices shall come and take them **and cook in them.** *Zechariah 14:21*

An abundance of food will be available. After cooking the food that they have grown, people will eat with satisfaction that which was cooked:

> [26] You shall **eat in plenty and be satisfied**, and praise the name of the LORD your God, who has dealt wondrously with you; and My people shall never be put to shame. *Joel 2:26*

Harkening back to the age of Methuselah, Jesus significantly increases human lifespans during the Millennial Reign with people living to be extremely old and being blessed to know many of their descendants:

> [20] "No more shall an infant from there live but a few days, nor an old man who has not fulfilled his days; for the **child shall die one hundred years old**, but the sinner being one hundred years old shall be accursed. *Isaiah 65:20*

> ⁴ Thus says the LORD of hosts: "**Old men and old women** shall again sit in the streets of Jerusalem, **each one with his staff** in his hand because of **great age**. ⁵ The streets of **the city shall be full of boys and girls playing** in its streets." *Zechariah 8:5*

Requiring a staff with advancing years, the aging process is again associated with declining strength. Playing children are mentioned in Zechariah 8:5 and Isaiah 65:20. Through the centuries on our current earth, many children have died from miscarriages, abortions, childhood diseases and injuries. When the resurrection occurs at Jesus' return, those children of all ages will be raised to join everyone in the Millennial Reign:

> ²³ **They shall not** labor in vain, nor **bring forth children for trouble**; for they shall be the descendants of the blessed of the LORD, and their offspring with them. *Isaiah 65:23*

> ⁸ The **nursing child** shall play by the cobra's hole, and **the weaned child** shall put his hand in the viper's den. *Isaiah 11:8*

Various ages of children are mentioned implying that marriage still exists since God has never desired that families should be broken and we know that He does not change. Interestingly, traditional wedding vows which state "until death do us part" are not quoted from the Bible. Commonly recited wedding vows implying a separation at death date back to the Sarum Rite performed around the 11th century in Medieval England and can be found in *The Book of Common Prayer* from 1549. The Bible only states that two become one in marriage and that man does not have the right to separate them again.

> ³ And Pharisees came up to him and tested him by asking, "Is it lawful to divorce one's wife for any cause?" ⁴ He answered, "Have you not read that he who created them from the beginning made them male and female, ⁵ and said, 'Therefore a man shall leave his father and his mother and hold fast to his wife, and **the two shall become one flesh**'? ⁶ So they are **no longer two but one flesh**. What therefore God has joined together, **let not man separate**." ⁷ They said to him, "Why then did Moses command one to give a certificate of divorce and to send her away?" ⁸ He said to them, "Because of your hardness of heart Moses allowed you to divorce your wives, but from the beginning it was not so. ⁹ And I say to you: **whoever divorces his wife, except for sexual immorality, and marries another, commits adultery**." *Matthew 19:3-9*

Divorce is allowed, but remarriage is not. In certain, specific cases, remarriage is permitted in the case of adultery or the death of a spouse, but even then, nothing in the Bible indicates that flesh is ever separated again once it is joined. The fact that divorce annuls the joining of a marriage is an assumption that is made. A plain text reading of scripture simply says that divorce allows two people who were joined together to live apart for the rest of their lives. Also, the Bible does not specifically say that the marriage union ends with death leaving open the possibility that family structures remain intact through the Millennial Reign.

Further proof that marriage exists during the Millennial Reign can be found in the rules for Millennial Reign priests:

> [22] They (priests) shall not **take as wife** a widow or a divorced woman, but take **virgins of the descendants of the house of Israel, or widows of priests**... *Ezekiel 44:22*

During the Millennial Reign, Sabbaths will still be observed and people will worship the Lord in person:

> [23] And it shall come to pass that from one New Moon to another, and from one Sabbath to another, **all flesh shall come to worship** before Me," says the LORD. *Isaiah 66:22*

Jesus Himself will be personally attentive to everything we say and will respond without delay:

> [24] It shall come to pass that **before they call, I will answer**; and while they are still speaking, I will hear. *Isaiah 65:24*

Music and singing will be heard and beauty will abound in formerly desolate places:

> [2] And I heard a voice from heaven...And I heard the sound of harpists **playing their harps**. [3] **They sang** as it were a new song before the throne, before the four living creatures, and the elders; and no one could learn that song except the hundred and forty-four thousand who were redeemed from the earth. *Revelation 14:2-3*

> [1] The wilderness and the wasteland shall be glad for them, and the **desert shall rejoice and blossom** as the rose... *Isaiah 35:1*

There will be no violence or destruction anywhere. Even naturally predatory animals will live in peace with other animals in perfect tranquility:

> [25] The **wolf and the lamb shall feed together**, the lion shall eat straw like the ox, and dust shall be the serpent's food. They shall not hurt nor destroy in all My holy mountain," says the LORD. *Isaiah 65:20-25*

> [18] **Violence shall no longer be heard in your land**, neither wasting nor destruction within your borders; but you shall call your walls Salvation, and your gates Praise. *Isaiah 60:18*

Illness and congenital defects such as deafness and blindness will be a thing of the past as people enjoy robust health:

> [5] Then the **eyes of the blind shall be opened**, and the **ears of the deaf shall be unstopped**. [6] Then the **lame shall leap** like a deer, and the **tongue of the dumb sing**. *Isaiah 35:5-6*

> [24] And the **inhabitant will not say, "I am sick"**; the people who dwell in it will be forgiven their iniquity. *Isaiah 33:24*

Unfortunately, despite the idyllic conditions offered by Jesus in the renewed earth, sin still exists during the Millennial Reign. Even though only Christians entered the Millennial Reign with Christ, there are those who still cannot live up to the behavioral standards set by Jesus:

> [20] No more shall an infant from there live but a few days, nor an old man who has not fulfilled his days; for the child shall die one hundred years old, but **the sinner** being one hundred years old shall be accursed. *Isaiah 65:20*

During the Millennial Reign, it is still necessary for Jesus to rebuke people. If they were not sinning, it would not be necessary to rebuke them:

> [4] **He shall judge between the nations**, and **rebuke many people**... *Isaiah 2:4*

Punishments of drought are issued during the Millennial Reign for people who do not obey Jesus' instructions. Sin has not been wiped out yet because there are still some who are not obedient to what has been decreed:

> [16] And it shall come to pass that **everyone who is left of all the nations which came against Jerusalem** shall go up from year to year to worship the King, the LORD of hosts, and to keep the Feast of Tabernacles. [17] And it shall be that **whichever of the families** of the earth **do not come up to Jerusalem to worship**

the King, the LORD of hosts, **on them there will be no rain**. ¹⁸ If the family of Egypt will not come up and enter in, they shall have no rain; **they shall receive the plague with which the LORD strikes the nations who do not come up to keep the Feast of Tabernacles**. ¹⁹ This shall be **the punishment of Egypt** and **the punishment of all the nations** that do not come up to keep the Feast of Tabernacles. *Zechariah 14:16-19*

Further evidence of the growing presence of sin during the Millennial Reign can be found in events occurring at the end of the Millennial Reign. When the thousand years are finished, Satan receives a parole, albeit short-lived:

> ³...But **after** these things (the thousand years) **he** (Satan) **must be released** for a little while. *Revelation 20:3*

Never one to let an opportunity for chaos and revolt pass, Satan again chooses the wrong path and mounts another rebellion enticing the nations of the earth to attempt to take over Christ's kingdom yet again:

> ⁷ Now when the thousand years have expired, **Satan** will be released from his prison ⁸ and will go out to **deceive the nations** which are in the four corners of the earth, **Gog and Magog**, to **gather them together to battle, whose number is as the sand of the sea**. *Revelation 20:7-8*

Satan's rebellion is actually a testament to the successful repopulation of the earth. When Satan gathers Gog and Magog together to battle, Revelation 20:8 refers to them as "whose number is as the sand of the sea". Through man's propensity for a sinful nature, Satan has an army of willing participants who join him in his attempt to overtake Jerusalem. Only this time, things end quite differently than all of his previous attempts to thwart God's purposes. God will not allow Satan to continue his tireless campaign against God's kingdom:

FACTOID: In the United States, 76% of people believe there is active angelic and demonic activity in the world.

> ⁹ What do you conspire against the LORD? He will make an utter end of it. **Affliction will not rise up a second time**. *Nahum 1:9*

Satan's first mistake was when he tried to stage a coup d'état against God and was kicked out of heaven with one third of the angels. Satan rebelled again when he attempted to achieve world domination through the figurehead of the Antichrist and ended up locked in a bottomless pit for a thousand years. Satan's final rebellion is at the end of the Millennial Reign when he ultimately tries to use the nations of the world as a weapon in his unending quest to possess Jerusalem. Known as the second War of Gog and Magog, Satan again deceives the nations in an attempt to mount a revolution against Jesus and take over His kingdom. For the second time, Russia and her allies are led astray by the Devil. With Gog and Magog again in compliance with his will, Satan repeats history and leads another attack against Jerusalem, God's "beloved city":

> ⁹ They went up on the breadth of the earth and **surrounded the camp of the saints and the beloved city**. And **fire** came down **from God** out of heaven and **devoured them**. ¹⁰ The **devil**, who deceived them, was **cast into the lake of fire** and brimstone where the beast and the false prophet are. And they will be tormented day and night forever and ever. *Revelation 20:7-10*

God Himself crushes Satan's last futile attempt to rule over humanity by reigning down fire from heaven which devours the nations. For their part in matters, the Devil and his host of fallen angels are thrown permanently into the lake of fire with the Antichrist and False Prophet who are already there waiting for them:

> ⁶ And the **angels who did not keep their proper domain**, but left their own abode, He has reserved in everlasting chains under darkness for the judgment of the great day; ⁷ as Sodom and Gomorrah, and the cities around them in a similar manner to these, having given themselves over to sexual immorality and gone after strange flesh, are set forth as an example, **suffering the vengeance of eternal fire**. *Jude 1:6-7*

Hell is described as a place where the "worm does not die and the fire is not quenched":

> ⁴³ ... to go to hell, into the fire that shall never be quenched— ⁴⁴ where their **worm does not die** and the **fire is not quenched**. *Mark 9:43*

There they will remain throughout eternity where they are tormented day and night. Satan is finally overcome for good this time.

Another event that happens at the end of the Millennium is the rest of the dead are raised to judgment:

> [4] And I saw **thrones**, and they sat on them, and **judgment was committed** to them. Then I saw the **souls** of those who had been **beheaded** for their witness to Jesus and for the word of God, who had not worshiped the beast or his image, and had not received his mark on their foreheads or on their hands. And **they lived and reigned with Christ** for a thousand years. *Revelation 20:4*

Having been victimized by the wicked dead in this life, Jesus and His followers require justice in the end. As those who are allowed to judge and rule with Christ, it is only fair that Jesus consults those who also suffered with Him at the hands of the wicked. Judged by Christians who are ruling and reigning with Christ, the wicked dead, too, are thrown into the Lake of Fire to burn and be tormented for all of eternity with Satan, the Antichrist, the False Prophet and his demonic followers:

> [11] Then I saw a great white throne and Him who sat on it, from whose face the earth and the heaven fled away. And there was found no place for them. [12] And I saw the dead, small and great, standing before God, and books were opened. And another book was opened, which is **the Book of Life**. And the **dead were judged** according to their works, by the things which were written in the books. [13] The sea gave up the dead who were in it, and Death and Hades delivered up the dead who were in them. And they were judged, each one according to his works. [14] Then Death and Hades were cast into the lake of fire. This is the second death. [15] And anyone **not found written** in the Book of Life was **cast into the lake of fire**. *Revelation 20:11-15*

With all sin and wickedness finished and everything finally as it should be, the old, renovated earth and heavens are replaced with a new heaven and new earth:

> [33] **Heaven** and **earth** will **pass away**... *Luke 21:33*

> [17] For behold, **I create new heavens and a new earth**; and the **former shall not be remembered** or come to mind. *Isaiah 65:17*

Ultimately, the old earth is destroyed by fire after the judgment of the wicked:

> ⁷ But the **heavens and the earth** which are now preserved by the same word, are **reserved for fire** until the **day of judgment** and perdition of **ungodly men**...¹³ Nevertheless we, according to His promise, **look for new heavens and a new earth** in which righteousness dwells. *2 Peter 3:7,13*

A distinction exists between the Day of the Lord when Jesus comes back to renovate the earth to inhabit during the Millennial Reign and the Day of God when God, the Father, joins His Son, Jesus, on an entirely new earth:

> ¹⁰ But the **day of the Lord** will come as a thief in the night...¹² looking for and hastening the coming of the **day of God**... *2 Peter 3:10,12*

When the Day of God ushers in a brand-new earth, God also abandons the old covenant He had with Israel and establishes a brand-new covenant with His people:

> ¹⁰ For **this is the covenant that I will make** with the house of Israel **after those days**, says the LORD: I will put My laws in their mind and write them on their hearts; and I will be their God, and they shall be My people. ¹¹ None of them shall teach his neighbor, and none his brother, saying, 'Know the LORD,' for all shall know Me, from the least of them to the greatest of them. ¹² For I will be merciful to their unrighteousness, and their sins and their lawless deeds I will remember no more. ¹³ In that He says, "**A new covenant**," **He has made the first obsolete. Now what is becoming obsolete and growing old is ready to vanish away**. *Hebrews 8:10-13*

In establishing a new covenant, God gives Israel the right to be in His presence and have direct access to Him which is a far better promise than needing the intermediary of Jesus to represent them before the throne of God. Establishing a process for altering the contract, scripture gives God the right to change the covenant when day or night no longer exist. By creating the new heaven and earth without day or night, God fulfills the requirement of that rule to change the contract:

> ²⁰ Thus says the LORD: "If you can **break My covenant with the day and My covenant with the night**, so that there will not be day and night in their season, ²¹ **then My covenant may also be broken** with David My servant..." *Jeremiah 33:20-21*

Unique from its forgotten predecessor, the new earth created on the Day of God has distinctly different characteristics than the resurrected earth of the Millennial Reign. For example, the earth described in the Millennial Reign has seas while the New Earth does not have any oceans. Following is a comprehensive list of the differences between the renovated earth of the Millennial Reign and the New Earth inhabited after the Millennial Reign:

MILLENNIAL REIGN ON RENEWED EARTH	NEW HEAVEN AND EARTH WITH NEW JERUSALEM
1,000-year reign (*Revelation 20:5-6*)	Eternal Kingdom (*Daniel 2:44 and 7:18*)
Called the Day of the Lord (*2 Peter 3:10*)	Called the Day of God (*2 Peter 3:12*)
Jesus lives with humanity (*Isaiah 2:2-4*)	God and Jesus live with humanity (*Revelation 22:3*)
Jesus renovates the existing earth (*Zechariah 14:1, 4, 6-11*)	God creates a New Heaven and New Earth replacing the old, renovated earth (*Isaiah 65:17, Revelation 21:1*)
Jerusalem is a city on the earth (*Zechariah 14:1, 4, 6-11*)	New Jerusalem descends from the sky in the shape of a cube (*Revelation 21:2*)
Jerusalem has a temple where worship occurs (*Ezekiel 47:1*)	New Jerusalem does not have a temple (*Revelation 21:22*)
Millennial Temple has 6 gates: 3 outer gates and 3 inner gates (*Ezekiel 40:6, 20, 24, 28-37*)	New Jerusalem has twelve gates around the city (*Revelation 21:12-13*)
Earth has oceans and seas (*Zechariah 14:8, Isaiah 11:9, Ezekiel 47:8, Revelation 20:13*)	The New Earth does not have oceans and seas (*Revelation 21:1*)
The sun and moon exist (*Isaiah 66:22*)	The sun and moon do not exist (*Revelation 21:23, 22:5*)
Seasons exist (*Zechariah 14:8*)	Uncomfortable weather changes are gone (*Revelation 7:16*)
Physical side of transformed, resurrected body is needed for earth life (*Isaiah 65:20-24*)	Spiritual side of transformed, resurrected body is needed for heavenly life (*Ephesians 2:6, Matthew 22:30*)
Rebellion is still possible (*Revelation 20:7-10*)	There is no more rebellion (*Nahum 1:9*)
Satan is temporarily in the bottomless pit (*Revelation 20:1-3*)	Satan is permanently in the lake of fire (*Revelation 20:10*)

Day and night exist (*Isaiah 4:2-5*)	Day and night are no more (*Revelation 22:5*)
People live in houses they build (*Isaiah 65:21*)	People live in mansions God builds for them (*John 14:2-3*)
People farm for food to eat (*Isaiah 65:21*)	Hunger and thirst are gone (*Revelation 7:16*)
The wicked are slain by the Lord (*Isaiah 11:4*)	The wicked dead are judged by God and thrown in the lake of fire (*Revelation 20:11-15*)
Human lifespan is lengthened (*Isaiah 65:20, Zechariah 8:5*), but the aging process exists and death is still possible (*Isaiah 65:20*)	Death is no more and life is eternal (*Isaiah 25:8, Revelation 21:4, Daniel 7:18*)
Marriage and family structure exist; children grow up (*Ezekiel 44:21-22,25, Isaiah 11:8, Isaiah 65:23*)	No Marriage or Reproduction (*Matthew 22:30*)
Israel with the Gentiles grafted in is betrothed to Jesus. (*Revelation 19:7*)	Israel with the Gentiles grafted in is married to Jesus. (*Revelation 21:9-10*)
Many fruit-bearing trees (*Ezekiel 47:7*)	Tree of Life (*Revelation 22:2*)
Humans dwell on earth (*Zechariah 14:10-11*)	Humans explore heavenly places with Jesus (*Ephesians 2:4, 6-7*)
People will still sin (*Isaiah 65:20*)	Sin will be eradicated (*Jeremiah 3:16-17*)
Old Covenant in effect (*Zechariah 14:21*)	New Covenant in effect (*Hebrews 8:10-13*)

There is debate as to from where Jesus reigns during the Millennial Reign. Satan's rebellion proves the Millennial Reign occurs on the renovated earth as inhabitants must be on the earth in order to be destroyed by "fire from heaven". If the reign and satanic revolt happens in heaven, it is improbable that God would send fire from heaven to heaven to end the rebellion. Also, it is highly unlikely that God would reign down destructive fire on His brand-new earth which will accompany everyone into eternity. More evidence that the Millennial Reign occurs on the renovated earth is that the seas give up the wicked dead for judgment at the end of the Millennial Reign:

> [13] The **sea gave up the dead** who were in it, and Death and Hades delivered up the dead who were in them. **And they were judged**, each one according to his works. *Revelation 20:13*

First, the new earth does not have any seas:

> ¹ Now I saw a **new heaven** and a **new earth**, for the first heaven and the **first earth had passed away**. Also, there was **no more sea**. *Revelation 21:1*

Second, when the wicked dead died, they were on the old earth and as such must be raised from the original earth. Israel is specifically mentioned by name during the Millennial Reign:

> ² In that day the Branch of the LORD shall be beautiful and glorious; and the fruit of the earth shall be excellent and appealing for those of **Israel** who have escaped. *Isaiah 4:2*

Nowhere is the country of Israel mentioned in connection with the new earth.

Once the old earth is destroyed, and replaced with a new heaven and earth, a new Jerusalem is also revealed:

> ¹ Now I saw a new heaven and a new earth, for the first heaven and the first earth had passed away. Also, there was no more sea. ² Then I, John, saw the holy city, **New Jerusalem, coming down out of heaven from God**, prepared as a bride adorned for her husband. *Revelation 21:1-2*

In the new earth, the city of New Jerusalem descends from heaven and becomes the dwelling place of God.

> ³ And I heard a loud voice from heaven saying, "Behold, **the tabernacle of God is with men, and He will dwell with them**, and they shall be His people. God Himself will be with them and be their God. *Revelation 21:3*

No longer are we only in the presence of Jesus; mankind dwells for eternity with both the Father and the Son. When God joins the kingdom, He erases death, sorrow, and pain and wipes away every tear:

> ⁸ He will **swallow up death** forever, and the Lord GOD will **wipe away tears from all faces**; the rebuke of His people He will take away from all the earth; for the LORD has spoken. *Isaiah 25:8*

> ...¹⁷ for the Lamb who is in the midst of the throne will shepherd them and lead them to living fountains of waters. And God will **wipe away every tear** from their eyes." *Revelation 7:17*

> ¹ Now I saw a **new heaven and a new earth**, for the first heaven and the first earth had passed away. Also, there was no more sea. ² Then I, John, saw the holy city, **New Jerusalem**, coming down out of heaven from God, prepared as a bride adorned for her husband. ³ And I heard a loud voice from heaven saying, "Behold, the tabernacle of God is with men, and He will dwell with them, and they shall be His people. God Himself will be with them and be their God. ⁴ And God **will wipe away every tear** from their eyes; there shall be **no more death, nor sorrow, nor crying**. There shall be **no more pain**, for the former things have passed away." *Revelation 21:1-4*

Joy, gladness and singing fill the New Jerusalem. God Himself even sings to us:

> ¹⁷ The LORD your God in your midst, the Mighty One, will save; He will rejoice over you with gladness, He will quiet you with His love, **He will rejoice over you with singing.** *Zephaniah 3:17*

God's dwelling place is a magnificent sight to behold. Instead of us building our own home as in the Millennial Reign, God prepares a mansion for us in the New Jerusalem and has many other surprises lined up for us that are too magnificent for us to even imagine:

> ² In **My Father's house** are many mansions; if it were not so, I would have told you. **I go to prepare a place for you.** And if I go and prepare a place for you, I will come again and receive you to Myself; that where I am, there you may be also. *John 14:2-3*

> ⁹ But as it is written: "**Eye has not seen, nor ear heard**, nor have entered into the heart of man the **things which God has prepared** for those who love Him." *1 Corinthians 2:9*

Massive in size, the New Jerusalem has twelve gates and gleams with all kinds of brilliant stones. According to the *Amazing Facts* website, the New Jerusalem is large enough to accommodate all the people who have ever lived and still have room left over. Shaped like a cube, each side is 375 miles long. Surrounding the city is a wall that is 216 feet tall, or approximately twenty stories in height. Streets are made of gold so pure they appear transparent. There is no need of a temple in the New Jerusalem because God Himself dwells there. Illuminating the city with the brightness of God's glory, it is never night:

> ²¹ The twelve gates were twelve pearls: each individual gate was of one pearl. And the street of the city was **pure gold, like**

> **transparent glass**. ²² But I saw **no temple in it**, for the Lord God Almighty and the Lamb are its temple. ²³ The city had **no need of the sun or of the moon** to shine in it, for the **glory of God illuminated it. The Lamb is its light**. ²⁴ And the nations of those who are saved shall walk in its light, and the kings of the earth bring their glory and honor into it. ²⁵ Its gates shall not be shut at all by day (there shall be **no night there**). ²⁶ And they shall bring the glory and the honor of the nations into it. ²⁷ But there shall by no means enter it anything that defiles, or causes an abomination or a lie, but **only those who are written in the Lamb's Book of Life**. *Revelation 21:21-27*

The sun and moon are things of the past and not found on the new earth. Neither is there hunger, thirst or temperature extremes from the seasons anymore:

> ¹⁶ They shall **neither hunger anymore nor thirst anymore**; the **sun shall not strike them, nor any heat**... *Revelation 7:16*

Only those who are written in the Lamb's Book of Life may enter the New Jerusalem as nothing unclean may be a part of God's new earth.

It is at this time that the marriage ceremony of the Lamb occurs. The marriage feast announcing the betrothal of the Lamb happened at the beginning of the Millennial Reign on earth, but the actual marriage ceremony happens after the one-thousand-year engagement period in heaven. Jan Joyce, from the website *Rightly Dividing the Word of Truth*, points out that in Jewish culture, a woman who becomes engaged is referred to as a "wife". Even though she is not officially married to her future husband at that time, from the point of the wedding banquet announcing the engagement onward, she is referred to in that manner. Only after the wedding ceremony, which happens at a later point, is she referred to as a "bride". Relating that tradition to prophecy, the Marriage Supper of the Lamb, which happens at the end of the Tribulation and before the Millennial Reign, refers to Christ's betrothed as a "wife":

> ⁷ Let us be glad and rejoice and give Him glory, for the marriage of the Lamb has come, and His **wife** has made herself ready. *Revelation 19:7*

Through the Millennial Reign, the engagement lasts for a thousand years. At the end of the Millennial Reign, the marriage ceremony happens in heaven at which point Christ's betrothed is no longer referred to as a "wife", but a "bride":

> ⁹ Then one of the seven angels who had the seven bowls filled with the seven last plagues came to me and talked with me, saying, "Come, I will show you **the bride**, the Lamb's wife." ¹⁰ And he carried me away in the Spirit to a great and high mountain, and showed me the great city, **the holy Jerusalem, descending out of heaven from God**... *Revelation 21:9-10*

From that point forward when the marriage ceremony is finalized in heaven, marriage and reproduction will be a thing of the past:

> ³⁰ For in the resurrection **they neither marry nor are given in marriage**, but are like angels of God **in heaven**. *Matthew 22:30*

No more will marriage be a part of our existence when we are in heaven. When the church consisting of natural Jews and grafted Gentiles marries Christ and officially becomes the bride of the Lamb, Jesus becomes our permanent life partner. He will love us and take care of our needs as we faithfully love and respect Him in return. With Jesus as our eternal spouse, there is no need to marry others.

Once all sin has been destroyed and the new heaven, new earth and new Jerusalem are revealed, reward crowns are distributed in heaven:

> ¹⁵ Then the seventh angel sounded: And there were loud voices **in heaven**, saying, "The kingdoms of this world have become the kingdoms of our Lord and of His Christ, and He shall reign forever and ever!" ¹⁶ And the twenty-four elders who sat before God on their thrones fell on their faces and worshiped God, ¹⁷ saying: "We give You thanks, O Lord God Almighty, The One who is and who was and who is to come, Because You have taken Your great power and reigned. ¹⁸ The nations were angry, and Your wrath has come, and the time of the dead, that they should be judged, and that **You should reward Your servants** the prophets and the saints, and those who fear Your name, small and great, and should destroy those who destroy the earth." *Revelation 11:15-18*

> ¹² And behold, I am coming quickly, and **My reward is with Me, to give to every one according to his work**...¹⁴ Blessed are those who do His commandments, that they may have the right to the tree of life, and may enter through the gates into the city. *Revelation 22:12,4*

> ⁴ and **when the Chief Shepherd appears**, you will receive **the crown**... *1 Peter 5:4*

> ²³ Rejoice in that day and leap for joy! For indeed your **reward** is great **in heaven**... *Luke 6:23*

For noteworthy deeds done in the body on the first earth, five crowns are passed out to believers: the Crown of Righteousness, the Crown of Glory, the Crown of Life, the Crown of Rejoicing and the Incorruptible Crown:

> ⁸ Finally, there is laid up for me the **crown of righteousness**, which the Lord, the righteous Judge, will give to me on that Day, and not to me only but also to all who have loved His appearing. *2 Timothy 4:8* (Crown of Righteousness)

> ² Shepherd the flock of God which is among you, serving as overseers, not by compulsion but willingly, not for dishonest gain but eagerly; ³ nor as being lords over those entrusted to you, but being examples to the flock; ⁴ and when the Chief Shepherd appears, you will receive **the crown of glory** that does not fade away. *1 Peter 5:2-4* (Crown of Glory)

> ¹⁰ Do not fear any of those things which you are about to suffer. Indeed, the devil is about to throw some of you into prison, that you may be tested, and you will have tribulation ten days. Be faithful until death, and I will give you **the crown of life**. *Revelation 2:10* (Crown of Life)

> ²⁵ And everyone who competes for the prize is temperate in all things. Now they do it to obtain a perishable crown, but we for an **imperishable crown**. ²⁶ Therefore I run thus: not with uncertainty. Thus, I fight: not as one who beats the air. ²⁷ But I discipline my body and bring it into subjection, lest, when I have preached to others, I myself should become disqualified. *1 Corinthians 9:25-27* (Incorruptible Crown)

> ¹⁹ For what is our hope, or joy, or **crown of rejoicing**? Is it not even you in the presence of our Lord Jesus Christ at His coming? ²⁰ For you are our glory and joy. *1 Thessalonians 2:19-20* (Crown of Rejoicing)

Crowns are a coveted reward in heaven symbolizing a life well-lived for Jesus. God issues a warning to everyone though not to lose a crown through falling away while in this life and failing to finish running the race:

> [11] Behold, I am coming quickly! Hold fast what you have, **that no one may take your crown.** *Revelation 3:11*

> [8] Look to yourselves, that we **do not lose those things we worked for**, but that we may receive **a full reward**. *2 John 1:8*

Many of the early church fathers will be present to receive their crowns and we will spend eternity socializing with Christian and Jewish ancestors such as Abraham, Isaac, Jacob and Daniel among others:

> [11] And I say to you that many will come from east and west, **and sit down with Abraham, Isaac, and Jacob in the kingdom of heaven.** *Matthew 8:11*

> [13] "But **you (Daniel)**...shall rest, and will arise to your inheritance at the end of the days." *Daniel 12:13*

> [9] After these things I looked, and behold, a great multitude which no one could number, of **all nations, tribes, peoples, and tongues**, standing before the throne and before the Lamb, clothed with white robes, with palm branches in their hands... *Rev. 7:9*

From there, believers are free to enjoy eternity in the presence of the Living God in their eternal bodies fit for the eternal kingdom. Spiritual bodies are a necessity if we are to travel the heavens with Jesus:

> [4] But God...made us alive **together with Christ**...[6] and raised us up together, and made us **sit together in the heavenly places** in Christ Jesus... *Ephesians 2:4,6*

NASA reports that the negative effects of space travel on human bodies as we exist now include demineralization of bones, muscle loss, cardiovascular weakening, kidney stones, sleep disorders, cataracts, weakened immune systems, radiation sickness with possible cancer risks, depression and psychiatric disorders. With spiritual bodies, none of these issues will be a concern.

In essence, the Millennial Reign is a second winnowing. Eternally fair and just, our God is a God of second chances. But He does not give unending forgiveness and grace forever. After God saved His people out of Egypt, they spent forty years in the desert where sin reared its ugly head again. God then purged the evil out of the midst of the Hebrews before He let them into the promised land:

> [5] But I want to remind you, though you once knew this, that the Lord, **having saved the people** out of the land of Egypt, **afterward destroyed** those who did not believe. *Jude 1:5*

Much like the period of time the Israelites spent in the desert between the hardship of Egypt and the glory of the promised land, the Millennial Reign is also a second winnowing before God lets His people into heaven. Salvation through faith is enough to be allowed into the Millennial Reign, but those who refuse to obey Jesus in the desert of the Millennial Reign will never see the promised land of heaven. The parable of the fig tree is another apt analogy for the Millennial Reign:

> [6] ..."A certain man had a **fig tree** planted in his vineyard, and he came seeking fruit on it and found none. [7] Then he said to the keeper of his vineyard, 'Look, for three years **I have come seeking fruit on this fig tree and find none**. Cut it down...' [8] But he answered and said to him, 'Sir, let it alone this year also, until I dig around it and fertilize it. [9] And if it bears fruit, well. But if not, after that **you can cut it down**.'" *Luke 13:6-9*

Just as Jesus had no use for a fig tree that wouldn't provide figs in the parable of the fig tree, He has no use for Christians who do not bear fruit either. As such, those Christians who cannot bring themselves to obey Jesus after the rapture and before entry into heaven will not make it out of the Millennial Reign. But for those who are worthy to pass on to heaven, our new promised land, it will truly be an amazing experience for those who are able to successfully complete the race and be part of the New Earth and New Jerusalem.

Talk It Out

1. Does the concept of living during the Millennial Reign with Christ excite you or scare you? What appeals to you about life in the Millennial Reign? Is there anything that scares you about the Millennial Reign?

2. Since there will be no violence in the land during the Millennial Reign (Isaiah 60:18), yet people still eat (Joel 3:18), do you think everyone will be a vegetarian?

3. Do you think your name is written in the Lamb's Book of Life? Will you be admitted to the New Heaven, New Earth and New Jerusalem after the Millennial Reign? What about the people you know in your daily life (i.e. family, friends, co-workers, etc.)?

4. Compare the experience of the Hebrews in the desert between Egypt and the promised land with that of the experience of Christians in the Millennial Reign between leaving our current earth and entering heaven.

5. Who do you think will be with you during the Millennial Reign and in heaven? Will there be a difference between those who make it into the Millennial Reign and those who make it into the New Heaven, New Earth and New Jerusalem?

6. What do you think family relationships will be like in the Millennial Reign? Will people get along? Will marriage relationships carry over from our previous existence? Will you be raising children you have lost?

7. If a pole shift were to occur during the earth's renovation process, how do you think it would affect continental land masses? Which direction do you think the earth would shift? Would Israel's borders be affected so that it is different in geography during the Millennial Reign from what it is now or would the pole shift only affect other land masses on other parts of the globe leaving Israel's geography untouched?

8. Between Abraham, Isaac, Jacob and Daniel, who would be the first person you would want to talk to when you see them in the Millennial Reign? What do you want to ask him? What topics would you like to discuss with him?

9. If Jesus passed out reward crowns today, which crowns do you think you would receive? Are you in danger of losing any crowns?

Ideas for the Week:

- ✓ Take a class to learn Hebrew.
- ✓ Learn more about Jewish culture and history at www.myjewishlearning.com.
- ✓ Plan a vacation to the Holy Land where you can see the places Jesus loves so much in person.
- ✓ Build a mock version of the temple where Jesus will dwell during the Millennial Reign using popsicle sticks. Display it at your church or share it with a children's Sunday School class along with a brief explanation of its significance.

Closing Prayer

NOTE: Add names and individual personal prayer requests to the space provided below before closing in prayer.

Lord, we thank You for our time together today to grow deeper in our walk with You and fellowship with each other. As we close today, we lift up: _____

_____

_____

_____

_____

_____

_____

_____

_____

_____

Father, we look forward to the day when we can experience both Your presence and the company of Jesus in person. We eagerly await the joys and adventures You have planned for us. Eternity is still not long enough to be part of Your kingdom. Come quickly, Lord Jesus! In Jesus' name we pray, Amen.

SUPPORTING SCRIPTURES

WORLD WITHOUT END
[18] But the saints of the Most High shall receive the kingdom, and possess the kingdom forever, even forever and ever. *Daniel 7:18* (NOTE: Ephesians 3:21 and Isaiah 45:27 also reference a world without end.)

EARTH IN CHAOS
[3] ...the sea, and it became blood as of a dead man; and every living creature in the sea died. [4] ...the rivers and springs of water, and they became blood... [20] Then every island fled away, and the mountains were not found. [21] And great hail from heaven fell upon men, each...the weight of a talent. *Rev. 16:3-4, 20-21*

[19] The earth is violently broken, the earth is split open, the earth is shaken exceedingly. [20] The earth shall reel to and fro like a drunkard, and shall totter like a hut; its transgression shall be heavy upon it, and it will fall, and not rise again. *Isaiah 24:19-20*

[21] When He (Jesus) arises to shake the earth mightily. *Isaiah 2:21*

[4] All the host of heaven shall be dissolved, and the heavens shall be rolled up like a scroll; all their host shall fall down as the leaf falls from the vine, and as fruit falling from a fig tree. *Isaiah 34:4*

[5] The mountains melt like wax at the presence of the LORD, at the presence of the Lord of the whole earth. *Psalm 97:5*

[23] I beheld the earth, and indeed it was without form, and void; and the heavens, they had no light. [24] I beheld the mountains, and indeed they trembled, and all the hills moved back and forth. [25] I beheld, and indeed there was no man, and all the birds of the heavens had fled. [26] I beheld, and indeed the fruitful land was a wilderness, and all its cities were broken down at the presence of the LORD, by His fierce anger. [27] For thus says the LORD: "The whole land shall be desolate; yet I will not make a full end. *Jeremiah 4:23-27*

THE WICKED ARE DEAD
[15] For behold, the LORD will come with fire and with His chariots, like a whirlwind, to render His anger with fury, and His rebuke with flames of fire. [16] For by fire and by His sword the LORD will judge all flesh; and the slain of the LORD shall be many. *Isaiah 66:15-16*

...[7] and to give you who are troubled rest with us when the Lord Jesus is revealed from heaven with His mighty angels, [8] in flaming fire taking vengeance on those who do not know God, and on those who do not obey the gospel of our Lord

Jesus Christ. *2 Thessalonians 1:7-8*

⁴ ...He shall strike the earth with the rod of His mouth, and with the breath of His lips He shall slay the wicked. *Isaiah 11:4*

² As smoke is driven away, so drive them away; as wax melts before the fire, so let the wicked perish at the presence of God. *Psalm 68:2*

RENOVATION
¹ Behold, the day of the LORD is coming... ⁴ And in that day His feet will stand on the Mount of Olives, which faces Jerusalem on the east. And the Mount of Olives shall be split in two, from east to west, making a very large valley; half of the mountain shall move toward the north and half of it toward the south... ⁶ It shall come to pass in that day that there will be no light; the lights will diminish. ⁷ It shall be one day which is known to the LORD—neither day nor night. But at evening time it shall happen that it will be light. ⁸ And in that day, it shall be that living waters shall flow from Jerusalem, half of them toward the eastern sea and half of them toward the western sea; in both summer and winter it shall occur. ⁹ And the LORD shall be King over all the earth. In that day it shall be—"The LORD is one," and His name one. ¹⁰ All the land shall be turned into a plain from Geba to Rimmon south of Jerusalem. Jerusalem shall be raised up and inhabited in her place from Benjamin's Gate to the place of the First Gate and the Corner Gate, and from the Tower of Hananel to the king's winepresses. ¹¹ The people shall dwell in it; and no longer shall there be utter destruction, but Jerusalem shall be safely inhabited. ¹² And this shall be the plague with which the LORD will strike all the people who fought against Jerusalem: their flesh shall dissolve while they stand on their feet, their eyes shall dissolve in their sockets, and their tongues shall dissolve in their mouths. ¹⁶ And it shall come to pass that everyone of all the nations which came against Jerusalem shall go up from year to year to worship the King, the LORD of hosts, and to keep the Feast of Tabernacles. ¹⁷ And it shall be that whichever of the families of the earth do not come up to Jerusalem to worship the King, the LORD of hosts, on them there will be no rain. ¹⁸ If the family of Egypt will not come up and enter in, they shall have no rain; they shall receive the plague with which the LORD strikes the nations who do not come up to keep the Feast of Tabernacles. ¹⁹ This shall be the punishment of Egypt and the punishment of all the nations that do not come up to keep the Feast of Tabernacles. ²⁰ In that day "HOLINESS TO THE LORD" shall be engraved on the bells of the horses. The pots in the LORD's house shall be like the bowls before the altar. ²¹ Yes, every pot in Jerusalem and Judah shall be holiness to the LORD of hosts. Everyone who sacrifices shall come and take them and cook in them. In that day there shall no longer be a Canaanite in the house of the LORD of hosts. *Zechariah 14:1, 4, 6-12, 16-21*

¹ "For behold, the day is coming, burning like an oven, and all the proud, yes, all who do wickedly will be stubble. And the day which is coming shall burn them up," says the LORD of hosts, "That will leave them neither root nor branch. ² But to you who fear My name the Son of Righteousness shall arise with healing in His wings; and you shall go out and grow fat like stall-fed calves. ³ You shall trample the wicked, for they shall be ashes under the soles of your feet on the day that I do this," says the LORD of hosts. *Malachi 4:1*

¹⁸ Then the LORD will be zealous for His land, and pity His people. ¹⁹ The LORD will answer and say to His people, "Behold, I will send you grain and new wine and oil, and you will be satisfied by them; I will no longer make you a reproach among the nations...²² Do not be afraid, you beasts of the field; for the open pastures are springing up, and the tree bears its fruit; the fig tree and the vine yield their strength. ²³ Be glad then, you children of Zion, and rejoice in the LORD your God; for He has given you the former rain faithfully, and He will cause the rain to come down for you—the former rain, and the latter rain in the first month. ²⁴ The threshing floors shall be full of wheat, and the vats shall overflow with new wine and oil. ²⁵ "So I will restore to you the years that the swarming locust has eaten, the crawling locust, the consuming locust, and the chewing locust, my great army which I sent among you. ²⁶ You shall eat in plenty and be satisfied, and praise the name of the LORD your God, who has dealt wondrously with you; and My people shall never be put to shame. ²⁷ Then you shall know that I am in the midst of Israel: I am the LORD your God and there is no other. My people shall never be put to shame. *Joel 2:18-19, 22-27*

CHRIST RULES WITH HIS FOLLOWERS IN JERUSALEM
¹⁵ Now out of His mouth goes a sharp sword, that with it He (Jesus) should strike the nations. And He Himself will rule them with a rod of iron...¹⁶ And He has on His robe and on His thigh a name written: KING OF KINGS AND LORD OF LORDS. *Revelation 19:15-16*

⁵...This is the first resurrection...⁶ they shall be priests of God and of Christ, and shall reign with Him a thousand years. *Revelation 20:5-6*

¹² If we endure, we shall also reign with Him. *2 Timothy 2:12*

¹⁴ "Return, O backsliding children," says the LORD; "for I am married to you. I will take you, one from a city and two from a family, and I will bring you to Zion. *Jeremiah 3:14*

² Now it shall come to pass in the latter days that the mountain of the LORD's house shall be established on the top of the mountains, and shall be exalted above the hills; and all nations shall flow to it. ³ Many people shall come and say,

"Come, and let us go up to the mountain of the LORD, to the house of the God of Jacob; he will teach us His ways, and we shall walk in His paths." For out of Zion shall go forth the law, and the word of the LORD from Jerusalem. ^{4} He shall judge between the nations, and rebuke many people; they shall beat their swords into plowshares, and their spears into pruning hooks; nation shall not lift up sword against nation, neither shall they learn war anymore. *Isaiah 2:2-4*

^{10} And I will pour on the house of David and on the inhabitants of Jerusalem the Spirit of grace and supplication; then they will look on Me whom they pierced. Yes, they will mourn for Him as one mourns for his only son, and grieve for Him as one grieves for a firstborn. *Zechariah 12:10*

^{18} But the saints of the Most High shall receive the kingdom, and possess the kingdom forever, even forever and ever. *Daniel 7:18*

MILLENNIAL TEMPLE GATES

^{6} Then he went to the gateway which faced east; and he went up its stairs and measured the threshold of the gateway, which was one rod wide, and the other threshold was one rod wide...^{20} On the outer court was also a gateway facing north, and he measured its length and its width...^{24} After that he brought me toward the south, and there a gateway was facing south; and he measured its gateposts and archways according to these same measurements...^{28} Then he brought me to the inner court through the southern gateway; he measured the southern gateway according to these same measurements. ^{29} Also its gate chambers, its gateposts, and its archways were according to these same measurements; there were windows in it and in its archways all around; it was fifty cubits long and twenty-five cubits wide. ^{30} There were archways all around, twenty-five cubits long and five cubits wide. ^{31} Its archways faced the outer court, palm trees were on its gateposts, and going up to it were eight steps. ^{32} And he brought me into the inner court facing east; he measured the gateway according to these same measurements. ^{33} Also its gate chambers, its gateposts, and its archways were according to these same measurements; and there were windows in it and in its archways all around; it was fifty cubits long and twenty-five cubits wide. ^{34} Its archways faced the outer court, and palm trees were on its gateposts on this side and on that side; and going up to it were eight steps. ^{35} Then he brought me to the north gateway and measured it according to these same measurements— ^{36} also its gate chambers, its gateposts, and its archways. It had windows all around; its length was fifty cubits and its width twenty-five cubits. ^{37} Its gateposts faced the outer court, palm trees were on its gateposts on this side and on that side, and going up to it were eight steps. *Ezekiel 40:6,20,24,28-37*

GOD'S STRUCTURE OF GOVERNMENT

[15] So I took the heads of your tribes, wise and knowledgeable men, and made them heads over you, leaders of thousands, leaders of hundreds, leaders of fifties, leaders of tens, and officers for your tribes. *Deuteronomy 1:15*

[19] Then Jesus answered and said to them, "Most assuredly, I say to you, the Son can do nothing of Himself, but what He sees the Father do; for whatever He does, the Son also does in like manner." *John 5:19*

[53] Or do you think that I cannot now pray to My Father, and He will provide Me with more than twelve legions of angels? *Matthew 26:53*

SATAN BOUND IN BOTTOMLESS PIT

[1] Then I saw an angel coming down from heaven, having the key to the bottomless pit and a great chain in his hand. [2] He laid hold of the dragon, that serpent of old, who is the Devil and Satan, and bound him for a thousand years; [3] and he cast him into the bottomless pit, and shut him up, and set a seal on him, so that he should deceive the nations no more till the thousand years were finished. *Revelation 20:1-3*

[3] And I will give power to my two witnesses, and they will prophesy one thousand two hundred and sixty days, clothed in sackcloth...[7] When they finish their testimony, the beast that ascends out of the bottomless pit will make war against them, overcome them, and kill them... *Revelation 11:3, 7*

LIFE DURING THE MILLENNIAL REIGN

[1] Then I looked, and behold, a Lamb standing on Mount Zion, and with Him one hundred and forty-four thousand, having His Father's name written on their foreheads. [2] And I heard a voice from heaven, like the voice of many waters, and like the voice of loud thunder. And I heard the sound of harpists playing their harps. [3] They sang as it were a new song before the throne, before the four living creatures, and the elders; and no one could learn that song except the hundred and forty-four thousand who were redeemed from the earth. [4] These are the ones who were not defiled with women, for they are virgins. These are the ones who follow the Lamb wherever He goes. These were redeemed from among men, being firstfruits to God and to the Lamb. [5] And in their mouth was found no deceit, for they are without fault before the throne of God. *Revelation 14:1-5*

[20] "No more shall an infant from there live but a few days, nor an old man who has not fulfilled his days; for the child shall die one hundred years old, but the sinner being one hundred years old shall be accursed. [21] They shall build houses and inhabit them; they shall plant vineyards and eat their fruit. [22] They shall not build and another inhabit; they shall not plant and another eat; for as the days of

a tree, so shall be the days of My people, and My elect shall long enjoy the work of their hands. ²³ They shall not labor in vain, nor bring forth children for trouble; for they shall be the descendants of the blessed of the LORD, and their offspring with them. ²⁴ It shall come to pass that before they call, I will answer; and while they are still speaking, I will hear. ²⁵ The wolf and the lamb shall feed together, the lion shall eat straw like the ox, and dust shall be the serpent's food. They shall not hurt nor destroy in all My holy mountain," says the LORD. *Is. 65:20-25*

²¹ No priest shall drink wine when he enters the inner court. ²² They shall not take as wife a widow or a divorced woman, but take virgins of the descendants of the house of Israel, or widows of priests...²⁵ They shall not defile themselves by coming near a dead person. Only for father or mother, for son or daughter, for brother or unmarried sister may they defile themselves. *Ezekiel 44:21-22,25*

⁴ ...Old men and old women shall again sit in the streets of Jerusalem, each one with his staff in his hand because of great age. ⁵ The streets of the city shall be full of boys and girls playing in its streets. *Zechariah 8:5*

²³ And it shall come to pass that from one New Moon to another, and from one Sabbath to another, all flesh shall come to worship before Me," says the LORD. *Isaiah 66:22*

¹ The wilderness and the wasteland shall be glad for them, and the desert shall rejoice and blossom as the rose... *Isaiah 35:1*

⁵ Then the eyes of the blind shall be opened, and the ears of the deaf shall be unstopped. ⁶ Then the lame shall leap like a deer, and the tongue of the dumb sing. For waters shall burst forth in the wilderness, and streams in the desert. *Isaiah 35:5-6*

¹⁸ Violence shall no longer be heard in your land, neither wasting nor destruction within your borders; but you shall call your walls Salvation, and your gates Praise. *Isaiah 60:18*

⁶ The wolf also shall dwell with the lamb, the leopard shall lie down with the young goat, the calf and the young lion and the fatling together; and a little child shall lead them. ⁷ The cow and the bear shall graze; their young ones shall lie down together; and the lion shall eat straw like the ox. ⁸ The nursing child shall play by the cobra's hole, and the weaned child shall put his hand in the viper's den. ⁹ They shall not hurt nor destroy in all My holy mountain, for the earth shall be full of the knowledge of the LORD as the waters cover the sea. *Isaiah 11:6-9*

²⁴ And the inhabitant will not say, "I am sick"; the people who dwell in it will be forgiven their iniquity. *Isaiah 33:24*

² In that day the Branch of the LORD shall be beautiful and glorious; and the fruit of the earth shall be excellent and appealing for those of Israel who have escaped. ³ And it shall come to pass that he who is left in Zion and remains in Jerusalem will be called holy—everyone who is recorded among the living in Jerusalem. ⁴ When the Lord has washed away the filth of the daughters of Zion, and purged the blood of Jerusalem from her midst, by the spirit of judgment and by the spirit of burning, ⁵ then the LORD will create above every dwelling place of Mount Zion, and above her assemblies, a cloud and smoke by day and the shining of a flaming fire by night. For over all the glory there will be a covering. ⁶ And there will be a tabernacle for shade in the daytime from the heat, for a place of refuge, and for a shelter from storm and rain. *Isaiah 4:2-5*

¹⁸ And it will come to pass in that day that the mountains shall drip with new wine, the hills shall flow with milk, and all the brooks of Judah shall be flooded with water; a fountain shall flow from the house of the LORD and water the Valley of Acacias. ¹⁹ Egypt shall be a desolation, and Edom a desolate wilderness, because of violence against the people of Judah, for they have shed innocent blood in their land. ²⁰ But Judah shall abide forever, and Jerusalem from generation to generation. ²¹ For I will acquit them of the guilt of bloodshed, whom I had not acquitted; for the LORD dwells in Zion. *Joel 3:18-21*

¹ Then he brought me back to the door of the temple; and there was water, flowing from under the threshold of the temple toward the east, for the front of the temple faced east; the water was flowing from under the right side of the temple, south of the altar. ² He brought me out by way of the north gate, and led me around on the outside to the outer gateway that faces east; and there was water, running out on the right side. ³ And when the man went out to the east with the line in his hand, he measured one thousand cubits, and he brought me through the waters; the water came up to my ankles. ⁴ Again he measured one thousand and brought me through the waters; the water came up to my knees. Again, he measured one thousand and brought me through; the water came up to my waist. ⁵ Again he measured one thousand, and it was a river that I could not cross; for the water was too deep, water in which one must swim, a river that could not be crossed. ⁶ He said to me, "Son of man, have you seen this?" Then he brought me and returned me to the bank of the river. ⁷ When I returned, there, along the bank of the river, were very many trees on one side and the other. ⁸ Then he said to me: "This water flows toward the eastern region, goes down into the valley, and enters the sea. When it reaches the sea, its waters are healed. ⁹ And it shall be that every living thing that moves, wherever the rivers go, will live. There will be a very great multitude of fish, because these waters go there; for they will be healed, and everything will live wherever the river goes. ¹⁰ It shall be that fishermen will stand by it from En Gedi to En Eglaim; they will be places for

spreading their nets. Their fish will be of the same kinds as the fish of the Great Sea, exceedingly many. ¹¹But its swamps and marshes will not be healed; they will be given over to salt. ¹² Along the bank of the river, on this side and that, will grow all kinds of trees used for food; their leaves will not wither, and their fruit will not fail. They will bear fruit every month, because their water flows from the sanctuary. Their fruit will be for food, and their leaves for medicine." *Ezk. 47:1-12*

SATAN PAROLED
³…But after these things (the thousand years) he (Satan) must be released for a little while. *Revelation 20:3*

SATANIC REBELLION CRUSHED
⁹ What do you conspire against the LORD? He will make an utter end of it. Affliction will not rise up a second time. *Nahum 1:9*

⁷ Now when the thousand years have expired, Satan will be released from his prison ⁸ and will go out to deceive the nations which are in the four corners of the earth, Gog and Magog, to gather them together to battle, whose number is as the sand of the sea. ⁹ They went up on the breadth of the earth and surrounded the camp of the saints and the beloved city. And fire came down from God out of heaven and devoured them. ¹⁰ The devil, who deceived them, was cast into the lake of fire and brimstone where the beast and the false prophet are. And they will be tormented day and night forever and ever. *Revelation 20:7-10*

⁴³ … to go to hell, into the fire that shall never be quenched— ⁴⁴ where their worm does not die and the fire is not quenched. *Mark 9:43*

⁵ But I want to remind you, though you once knew this, that the Lord, having saved the people out of the land of Egypt, afterward destroyed those who did not believe. ⁶And the angels who did not keep their proper domain, but left their own abode, He has reserved in everlasting chains under darkness for the judgment of the great day; ⁷ as Sodom and Gomorrah, and the cities around them in a similar manner to these, having given themselves over to sexual immorality and gone after strange flesh, are set forth as an example, suffering the vengeance of eternal fire. *Jude 1:5-7*

RESURRECTION OF THE WICKED
⁵ But the rest of the dead did not live again until the thousand years were finished… *Revelation 20:5*

¹⁹ …and the earth shall cast out the dead. *Isaiah 26:19*

² And many of those who sleep in the dust of the earth shall awake, some to everlasting life, some to shame and everlasting contempt. *Daniel 12:2*

[28] ...the hour is coming in which all who are in the graves will hear His voice [29] and come forth—those who have done good, to the resurrection of life, and those who have done evil, to the resurrection of condemnation. *John 5:28-29*

[15] ...that there will be a resurrection of the dead, both of the just and the unjust. *Acts 24:15*

JUDGMENT OF THE WICKED
[27] ...it is appointed for men to die once, but after this the judgment... *Heb. 9:27*

[10] For we must all appear before the judgment seat of Christ, that each one may receive the things done in the body, according to what he has done, whether good or bad. *2 Corinthians 5:10*

[10] ...For we shall all stand before the judgment seat of Christ... [12] So then each of us shall give account of himself to God. *Romans 14:10,12*

[4] And I saw thrones, and they sat on them, and judgment was committed to them. Then I saw the souls of those who had been beheaded for their witness to Jesus and for the word of God, who had not worshiped the beast or his image, and had not received his mark on their foreheads or on their hands. And they lived and reigned with Christ for a thousand years. *Revelation 20:4*

[2] ...the saints will judge the world? And if the world will be judged by you, are you unworthy to judge the smallest matters? [3] Do you not know that we shall judge angels? How much more, things that pertain to this life? *1 Corinthians 6:2-3*

[11] Then I saw a great white throne and Him who sat on it, from whose face the earth and the heaven fled away. And there was found no place for them. [12] And I saw the dead, small and great, standing before God, and books were opened. And another book was opened, which is the Book of Life. And the dead were judged according to their works, by the things which were written in the books. [13] The sea gave up the dead who were in it, and Death and Hades delivered up the dead who were in them. And they were judged, each one according to his works. [14] Then Death and Hades were cast into the lake of fire. This is the second death. [15] And anyone not found written in the Book of Life was cast into the lake of fire. *Revelation 20:11-15*

[1] I charge you therefore before God and the Lord Jesus Christ, who will judge the living and the dead at His appearing and His kingdom: *2 Timothy 4:1*

NEW HEAVEN AND EARTH
[33] Heaven and earth will pass away... *Luke 21:33*

¹⁷ For behold, I create new heavens and a new earth; and the former shall not be remembered or come to mind. *Isaiah 65:17*

⁷ But the heavens and the earth which are now preserved by the same word, are reserved for fire until the day of judgment and perdition of ungodly men. ⁸ But, beloved, do not forget this one thing, that with the Lord one day is as a thousand years, and a thousand years as one day. ⁹ The Lord is not slack concerning His promise, as some count slackness, but is longsuffering toward us, not willing that any should perish but that all should come to repentance. ¹⁰ But the day of the Lord will come as a thief in the night, in which the heavens will pass away with a great noise, and the elements will melt with fervent heat; both the earth and the works that are in it will be burned up. ¹¹ Therefore, since all these things will be dissolved, what manner of persons ought you to be in holy conduct and godliness, ¹² looking for and hastening the coming of the day of God because of which the heavens will be dissolved, being on fire, and the elements will melt with fervent heat? ¹³ Nevertheless we, according to His promise, look for new heavens and a new earth in which righteousness dwells. *2 Peter 3:7-13*

⁴⁴ And in the days of these kings the God of heaven will set up a kingdom which shall never be destroyed; and the kingdom shall not be left to other people; it shall break in pieces and consume all these kingdoms, and it shall stand forever. *Daniel 2:44*

¹ Now I saw a new heaven and a new earth, for the first heaven and the first earth had passed away. Also, there was no more sea. ² Then I, John, saw the holy city, New Jerusalem, coming down out of heaven from God, prepared as a bride adorned for her husband. ³ And I heard a loud voice from heaven saying, "Behold, the tabernacle of God is with men, and He will dwell with them, and they shall be His people. God Himself will be with them and be their God. ⁴ And God will wipe away every tear from their eyes; there shall be no more death, nor sorrow, nor crying. There shall be no more pain, for the former things have passed away." ⁵ Then He who sat on the throne said, "Behold, I make all things new." And He said to me, "Write, for these words are true and faithful." ⁶ And He said to me, "It is done! I am the Alpha and the Omega, the Beginning and the End. I will give of the fountain of the water of life freely to him who thirsts. ⁷ He who overcomes shall inherit all things, and I will be his God and he shall be My son. ⁸ But the cowardly, unbelieving, abominable, murderers, sexually immoral, sorcerers, idolaters, and all liars shall have their part in the lake which burns with fire and brimstone, which is the second death." *Revelation 21:1-8*

⁴ But God...made us alive together with Christ...⁶ and raised us up together, and made us sit together in the heavenly places in Christ Jesus, ⁷ that in the ages to

come He might show the exceeding riches of His grace in His kindness toward us in Christ Jesus. *Ephesians 2:4, 6-7*

[11] You will show me the path of life; in Your presence is fullness of joy; at Your right hand are pleasures forevermore. *Psalm 16:11*

[8] He will swallow up death forever, and the Lord GOD will wipe away tears from all faces; the rebuke of His people He will take away from all the earth; for the LORD has spoken. *Isaiah 25:8*

[32] He will be great, and will be called the Son of the Highest; and the Lord God will give Him the throne of His father David. [33] And He will reign over the house of Jacob forever, and of His kingdom there will be no end." *Luke 1:32-33*

NEW COVENANT
[10] For this is the covenant that I will make with the house of Israel after those days, says the LORD: I will put My laws in their mind and write them on their hearts; and I will be their God, and they shall be My people. [11] None of them shall teach his neighbor, and none his brother, saying, "Know the LORD," for all shall know Me, from the least of them to the greatest of them. [12] For I will be merciful to their unrighteousness, and their sins and their lawless deeds I will remember no more. [13] In that He says, "A new covenant," He has made the first obsolete. Now what is becoming obsolete and growing old is ready to vanish away. *Hebrews 8:10-13*

[19] And the word of the LORD came to Jeremiah, saying, [20] "Thus says the LORD: 'If you can break My covenant with the day and My covenant with the night, so that there will not be day and night in their season, [21] then My covenant may also be broken with David My servant…' " *Jeremiah 33:19-21*

THE NEW JERUSALEM
[16] "Then it shall come to pass, when you are multiplied and increased in the land in those days," says the LORD, "that they will say no more, 'The ark of the covenant of the LORD.' It shall not come to mind, nor shall they remember it, nor shall they visit it, nor shall it be made anymore. [17] "At that time Jerusalem shall be called The Throne of the LORD, and all the nations shall be gathered to it, to the name of the LORD, to Jerusalem. No more shall they follow the dictates of their evil hearts. *Jeremiah 3:16-17*

[9] Then one of the seven angels who had the seven bowls filled with the seven last plagues came to me and talked with me, saying, "Come, I will show you the bride, the Lamb's wife." [10] And he carried me away in the Spirit to a great and high mountain, and showed me the great city, the holy Jerusalem, descending out of heaven from God, [11] having the glory of God. Her light was like a most

precious stone, like a jasper stone, clear as crystal. ¹² Also she had a great and high wall with twelve gates, and twelve angels at the gates, and names written on them, which are the names of the twelve tribes of the children of Israel: ¹³ three gates on the east, three gates on the north, three gates on the south, and three gates on the west. ¹⁴ Now the wall of the city had twelve foundations, and on them were the names of the twelve apostles of the Lamb. ¹⁵ And he who talked with me had a gold reed to measure the city, its gates, and its wall. ¹⁶ The city is laid out as a square; its length is as great as its breadth. And he measured the city with the reed: twelve thousand furlongs. Its length, breadth, and height are equal. ¹⁷ Then he measured its wall: one hundred and forty-four cubits, according to the measure of a man, that is, of an angel. ¹⁸ The construction of its wall was of jasper; and the city was pure gold, like clear glass. ¹⁹ The foundations of the wall of the city were adorned with all kinds of precious stones: the first foundation was jasper, the second sapphire, the third chalcedony, the fourth emerald, ²⁰ the fifth sardonyx, the sixth sardius, the seventh chrysolite, the eighth beryl, the ninth topaz, the tenth chrysoprase, the eleventh jacinth, and the twelfth amethyst. ²¹ The twelve gates were twelve pearls: each individual gate was of one pearl. And the street of the city was pure gold, like transparent glass. ²² But I saw no temple in it, for the Lord God Almighty and the Lamb are its temple. ²³ The city had no need of the sun or of the moon to shine in it, for the glory of God illuminated it. The Lamb is its light. ²⁴ And the nations of those who are saved shall walk in its light, and the kings of the earth bring their glory and honor into it. ²⁵ Its gates shall not be shut at all by day (there shall be no night there). ²⁶ And they shall bring the glory and the honor of the nations into it. ²⁷ But there shall by no means enter it anything that defiles, or causes an abomination or a lie, but only those who are written in the Lamb's Book of Life. *Revelation 21:9-27*

RIVER AND TREE OF LIFE
¹ And he showed me a pure river of water of life, clear as crystal, proceeding from the throne of God and of the Lamb. ² In the middle of its street, and on either side of the river, was the tree of life (see also Genesis 3:22 and Revelation 2:7), which bore twelve fruits, each tree yielding its fruit every month. The leaves of the tree were for the healing of the nations. ³ And there shall be no more curse, but the throne of God and of the Lamb shall be in it, and His servants shall serve Him. ⁴ They shall see His face, and His name shall be on their foreheads. ⁵ There shall be no night there: They need no lamp nor light of the sun, for the Lord God gives them light. And they shall reign forever and ever. *Revelation 22:1-5*

¹⁶ But now they desire a better, that is, a heavenly country. Therefore, God is not ashamed to be called their God, for He has prepared a city for them. *Heb. 11:16*

² And I saw something like a sea of glass mingled with fire, and those who have the victory over the beast, over his image and over his mark and over the number

of his name, standing on the sea of glass, having harps of God. *Revelation 15:2*

REWARDS

^{15}...And there were loud voices in heaven, saying, "The kingdoms of this world have become the kingdoms of our Lord and of His Christ, and He shall reign forever and ever!" ^{16} And the twenty-four elders who sat before God on their thrones fell on their faces and worshiped God, ^{17} saying: "We give You thanks, O Lord God Almighty, The One who is and who was and who is to come, because You have taken Your great power and reigned. ^{18} The nations were angry, and Your wrath has come, and the time of the dead, that they should be judged, and that You should reward Your servants the prophets and the saints, and those who fear Your name, small and great, and should destroy those who destroy the earth." ^{19} Then the temple of God was opened in heaven, and the ark of His covenant was seen in His temple. And there were lightnings, noises, thunderings, an earthquake, and great hail. *Revelation 11:15-19*

^{23} Rejoice in that day and leap for joy! For indeed your reward is great in heaven... *Luke 6:23*

^{12} And behold, I am coming quickly, and My reward is with Me, to give to every one according to his work...^{14} Blessed are those who do His commandments, that they may have the right to the tree of life, and may enter through the gates into the city. *Revelation 22:12, 14*

^{11} Behold, I am coming quickly! Hold fast what you have, that no one may take your crown. *Revelation 3:11*

^{8} Look to yourselves, that we do not lose those things we worked for, but that we may receive a full reward. *2 John 1:8*

^{8} Finally, there is laid up for me the crown of righteousness, which the Lord, the righteous Judge, will give to me on that Day, and not to me only but also to all who have loved His appearing. *2 Timothy 4:8* (Crown of Righteousness)

^{2} Shepherd the flock of God which is among you, serving as overseers, not by compulsion but willingly, not for dishonest gain but eagerly; ^{3} nor as being lords over those entrusted to you, but being examples to the flock; ^{4} and when the Chief Shepherd appears, you will receive the crown of glory that does not fade away. *1 Peter 5:2-4* (Crown of Glory)

^{10} Do not fear any of those things which you are about to suffer. Indeed, the devil is about to throw some of you into prison, that you may be tested, and you will have tribulation ten days. Be faithful until death, and I will give you the crown of life. *Revelation 2:10* (Crown of Life)

²⁵And everyone who competes for the prize is temperate in all things. Now they do it to obtain a perishable crown, but we for an imperishable crown. ²⁶Therefore I run thus: not with uncertainty. Thus, I fight: not as one who beats the air. ²⁷But I discipline my body and bring it into subjection, lest, when I have preached to others, I myself should become disqualified. *1 Cor. 9:25-27* (Incorruptible Crown)

¹⁹ For what is our hope, or joy, or crown of rejoicing? Is it not even you in the presence of our Lord Jesus Christ at His coming? ²⁰ For you are our glory and joy. *1 Thessalonians 2:19-20* (Crown of Rejoicing)

PHYSICAL FORM
³⁶ Now as they said these things, Jesus Himself stood in the midst of them, and said to them, "Peace to you." ³⁷ But they were terrified and frightened, and supposed they had seen a spirit. ³⁸ And He (Jesus) said to them, "Why are you troubled? And why do doubts arise in your hearts? ³⁹ Behold My hands and My feet, that it is I Myself. Handle Me and see, for a spirit does not have flesh and bones as you see I have."... ⁴¹ But while they still did not believe for joy, and marveled, He said to them, "Have you any food here?" ⁴² So they gave Him a piece of a broiled fish and some honeycomb. ⁴³ And He took it and ate in their presence. *Luke 24:36-39, 41-43*

²⁰ For our citizenship is in heaven, from which we also eagerly wait for the Savior, the Lord Jesus Christ, ²¹ who will transform our lowly body that it may be conformed to His glorious body..." *Philippians 3:20-21*

...³ to whom He also presented Himself alive after His suffering by many infallible proofs, being seen by them during forty days and speaking of the things pertaining to the kingdom of God. *Acts 1:3*

⁶...He was seen by over five hundred brethren at once... *1 Corinthians 15:6*

³⁵ But someone will say, "How are the dead raised up? And with what body do they come?" ³⁶ Foolish one, what you sow is not made alive unless it dies. ³⁷ And what you sow, you do not sow that body that shall be, but mere grain—perhaps wheat or some other grain. ³⁸ But God gives it a body as He pleases, and to each seed its own body. ³⁹ All flesh is not the same flesh, but there is one kind of flesh of men, another flesh of animals, another of fish, and another of birds. ⁴⁰ There are also celestial bodies and terrestrial bodies; but the glory of the celestial is one, and the glory of the terrestrial is another. ⁴¹ There is one glory of the sun, another glory of the moon, and another glory of the stars; for one star differs from another star in glory. ⁴² So also is the resurrection of the dead. The body is sown in corruption, it is raised in incorruption. ⁴³ It is sown in dishonor; it is raised in glory. It is sown in weakness; it is raised in power. ⁴⁴ It is sown a natural body; it

is raised a spiritual body. There is a natural body, and there is a spiritual body. [45] And so it is written, "The first man Adam became a living being." The last Adam became a life-giving spirit. [46] However, the spiritual is not first, but the natural, and afterward the spiritual. [47] The first man was of the earth, made of dust; the second Man is the Lord from heaven. [48] As was the man of dust, so also are those who are made of dust; and as is the heavenly Man, so also are those who are heavenly. [49] And as we have borne the image of the man of dust, we shall also bear the image of the heavenly Man. [50] Now this I say, brethren, that flesh and blood cannot inherit the kingdom of God; nor does corruption inherit incorruption. [51] Behold, I tell you a mystery: We shall not all sleep, but we shall all be changed— [52] in a moment, in the twinkling of an eye, at the last trumpet. For the trumpet will sound, and the dead will be raised incorruptible, and we shall be changed. [53] For this corruptible must put on incorruption, and this mortal must put on immortality. [54] So when this corruptible has put on incorruption, and this mortal has put on immortality, then shall be brought to pass the saying that is written: "Death is swallowed up in victory. [55] O Death, where is your sting? O Hades, where is your victory?" *1 Corinthians 15:35-55*

[12] For now we see in a mirror, dimly, but then face to face. Now I know in part, but then I shall know just as I also am known. *1 Corinthians 13:12*

[2] Beloved, now we are children of God; and it has not yet been revealed what we shall be, but we know that when He is revealed, we shall be like Him, for we shall see Him as He is. *1 John 3:2*

LIFE IN THE NEW EARTH, NEW HEAVEN AND NEW JERUSALEM
[9] After these things I looked, and behold, a great multitude which no one could number, of all nations, tribes, peoples, and tongues, standing before the throne and before the Lamb, clothed with white robes, with palm branches in their hands, [10] and crying out with a loud voice, saying, "Salvation belongs to our God who sits on the throne, and to the Lamb!" [11] All the angels stood around the throne and the elders and the four living creatures, and fell on their faces before the throne and worshiped God, [12] saying: "Amen! Blessing and glory and wisdom, thanksgiving and honor and power and might, be to our God forever and ever. Amen." [13] Then one of the elders answered, saying to me, "Who are these arrayed in white robes, and where did they come from?" [14] And I said to him, "Sir, you know." So, he said to me, "These are the ones who come out of the great tribulation, and washed their robes and made them white in the blood of the Lamb. [15] Therefore they are before the throne of God, and serve Him day and night in His temple. And He who sits on the throne will dwell among them. [16] They shall neither hunger anymore nor thirst anymore; the sun shall not strike them, nor any heat; [17] for the Lamb who is in the midst of the throne will shepherd them

and lead them to living fountains of waters. And God will wipe away every tear from their eyes." *Revelation 7:9-17*

[11] And I say to you that many will come from east and west, and sit down with Abraham, Isaac, and Jacob in the kingdom of heaven. *Matthew 8:11*

[13] "But you (Daniel), go your way till the end; for you shall rest, and will arise to your inheritance at the end of the days." *Daniel 12:13*

[10] And the ransomed of the LORD shall return, and come to Zion with singing, with everlasting joy on their heads. They shall obtain joy and gladness, and sorrow and sighing shall flee away. *Isaiah 35:10* (NOTE: Isaiah 51:11 is almost identical in wording to this verse)

[9] ...Eye has not seen, nor ear heard, nor have entered into the heart of man the things which God has prepared for those who love Him. *1 Corinthians 2:9*

[2] In My Father's house are many mansions; if it were not so, I would have told you. I go to prepare a place for you. And if I go and prepare a place for you, I will come again and receive you to Myself; that where I am, there you may be also. *John 14:2-3*

[30] For in the resurrection they neither marry nor are given in marriage, but are like angels of God in heaven. *Matthew 22:30*

[17] The LORD your God in your midst, the Mighty One, will save; He will rejoice over you with gladness, He will quiet you with His love, He will rejoice over you with singing. *Zephaniah 3:17*

[24] Then comes the end, when He delivers the kingdom to God the Father, when He puts an end to all rule and all authority and power. *1 Corinthians 15:24*

NOTES

"God loves each of us as if there were only one of us."
— Saint Augustine

ARE WE THE TERMINAL GENERATION?

THE TIMELINE

WEEK 25: PUTTING IT ALL TOGETHER

Opening Prayer: Lord, we ask that You send Your Holy Spirit to us to guide us in the teaching and understanding of Your word that we may obtain a better understanding of the prophetic events surrounding us now and waiting for us in the future. Bless our fellowship in Your word that it may be fruitful and draw us into a deeper relationship both with You and those around us. Use us as Your vessels that through us, we may reflect Your glory to all whom we encounter. Illuminate our hearts and minds so that we may boldly shine the brightness of Your light everywhere we go and that we may be beacons of Your hope in a darkened world. In Jesus name we pray, Amen.

Ice Breaker: What does the future hold for you? Do you have goals and plans? It's time to make some resolutions for the future! Since it can sometimes be easier to see what someone else needs instead of identifying your own needs, each group member will make 3 short-term, achievable resolutions for someone else based on what they have learned about the person during the course of this study. The resolutions should be things that the person can begin to work on immediately. With everyone sitting in a circle, make 3 resolutions for the person sitting 2 places to your left. When everyone is finished, go around the circle and share the resolutions you chose for the person and why with the rest of the group. Another variation of this activity is for the group as a whole to make 3 resolutions for each person in the group. The person receiving the resolutions should not offer ideas when it is their turn to receive resolutions. Remember to give suggestions for resolutions with a loving spirit and receive outside insights with a thankful and open heart.

RESOLUTIONS MY GROUP SUGGESTED FOR ME:

1.
2.
3.

Focus: Everything that happens is ordered by God and occurs on His timeline when He determines the time is right.

Word of the Week

> ¹⁷ As **iron** sharpens **iron**, so a man sharpens the countenance of his friend.
> *Proverbs 27:17*

IRON: The word "iron" in Proverbs 27:17 is from the Hebrew word "barzel" (pronounced bar-zel') which refers to a metal ore used in tools, utensils and other items. One of the most common elements on earth, iron is known to corrode quickly. Iron can also be easily magnetized. Commonly used during Roman times, iron is an appropriate analogy for man as humans are plentiful on the earth, susceptible to corruption and, by nature, magnetically drawn to be in relationship with others. As Christians, we are to magnify the glory of the Lord drawing others into the kingdom of God just like magnetized iron draws other iron particles to join with it.

Lesson: One of the most debated areas of any discussion involving end times prophecy is the order and timing of the prophetic events described by God in the Bible. Generally speaking, the first half of the Tribulation is the time when the Antichrist brokers a peace deal between Israel and her enemies followed by the appearance of two witnesses who unleash punishments on the earth while the third temple is being built in Jerusalem. Joining the punishments of the two witnesses are the forces of the Four Horsemen of the Apocalypse which are violently thrust on an unsuspecting world. Bringing with them war, famine, disease and death, life becomes exceptionally troublesome for mankind as more trumpet, seal and bowl judgments arrive. Under the leadership of the Antichrist and his assistant, the False Prophet, a new world order is created along with a one world religion. At some point, the Antichrist receives a deadly wound to his head and miraculously imitates a resurrection like that of Jesus. Those who do not know God are in awe of the "miracle" and willingly follow the Antichrist. The False Prophet, under the direction of the Antichrist, forces all people to take the Mark of the Beast rendering anyone without the Mark of the Beast unable to participate in commerce activities. Joining the chaos is also the War of Ezekiel. Likening the Tribulation to sorrows, or birth pains, the Tribulation ushers in a period of great suffering unlike anything the world has ever seen. Considering the magnitude of various hardships experienced throughout history, the comparison is staggering. Much like labor pains, the process of giving birth to

Jesus' second return intensifies as the Tribulation progresses. Events happen faster, closer together and with greater intensity until Jesus arrives.

Midway through the Tribulation, the third temple is completed and temple animal sacrifices resume once again. At that time, the Antichrist and his armies forcibly take control of Jerusalem while an Israeli remnant escapes to Petra where they are supernaturally sustained throughout the rest of the Tribulation. Then, the Antichrist walks into the rebuilt temple, sits down, declares himself to be God and ceases all temple sacrifices. This event is referred to in the Bible as the "Abomination of Desolation". After mounting a successful occupation of Jerusalem, the Antichrist begins a focused campaign to severely persecute God's people for three-and-a-half years in an event known as the treading of the Gentiles. From there, things disintegrate quickly. When the War in Heaven is over, Satan and his demonic army are cast down to the earth. The second half of the Tribulation, known as the Great Tribulation, is an especially intense time of Christian persecution.

At the end of the seven-year peace agreement, the Tribulation culminates with all the nations of the world coming against Israel in what is known at the Battle of Armageddon. Outnumbered and outgunned, Christ personally returns to defend Israel and defeat her enemies ushering in His kingdom. After gathering those whom Jesus wants to save, the nations are judged, the Antichrist and False Prophet are thrown into the Lake of Fire and Mystery Babylon is destroyed. With the chaos over, Jesus officially becomes engaged to his finally wife, the church, and delivers the kingdom to God, thus ending the Church Age.

FUN FACT: Sir Isaac Newton had a passion for end time prophecy and believed that Christ would return in the year 2060.

With the end of the Church Age, the Millennial Reign begins as Christ rules and reigns with His followers for 1000 years. Beginning with Satan being sentenced to 1000 years in the bottomless pit, the earth receives a renovation. Next, Jesus moves to Jerusalem to reign while the earth repopulates. At the end of the Millennial Reign, Satan is paroled and mounts yet another rebellion. After failing to take over Jerusalem again, Satan and his angels are remanded to the Lake of

Fire to burn for eternity. Then, the wicked dead are raised to judgment and join Satan in his hopeless fate. Finally, the Day of God ushers in a new heaven, earth and Jerusalem. Jesus completes the marriage ceremony to his new bride, the church, and reward crowns are issued to those who have excelled in special areas of service to God. Along with the new abode comes a new covenant as well. From that point on, everyone receives angelic bodies and spends eternity dwelling in perfect bliss with both God and Jesus.

At his *Overcomers* tour in Norfolk, Virginia on April 4, 2019, Dr. David Jeremiah stated that twenty-five percent of the bible is devoted to prophecy. Chapters such as Daniel, Isaiah, Jeremiah, Ezekiel and Revelation among others provide enormous amounts of information about the coming Tribulation time period and the return of Jesus. Being a just and fair God, God always warns His people of impending danger so they can prepare. Noah prepared. The Hebrews prepared. Lot left Sodom and Gomorrah. God never gives us extraneous information we do not need. If God has given us this information, it is because He feels we need to have the information. It is always a prudent idea to be prepared for possible unforeseen circumstances, and the Tribulation is no different. If pre-Tribulation advocates are correct, your preps will be left on earth to aid those left behind as a final act of love toward those who must face the coming hardships. The act of providing for others after you are gone will go towards earning a crown of righteousness in heaven yielding an eternal reward. However, if post-Tribulation advocates are correct that we will not see Jesus and be raptured to be with Him until we have gone through the Tribulation, then Christians need to be as physically prepared as possible to weather the coming storms. While it is true that God will mark His children to protect them from the Tribulation, it is also true that God expects us to do our part to the best of our ability:

> [6]**I planted, Apollos watered**, but God gave the increase. *1 Corinthians 3:6*

God only took over after Paul and Apollos planted and watered. For our part, preparing means to store up food and supplies, to have evacuation plans in place and to be as knowledgeable as possible on other survival matters such as first-aid and self-defense. Once we have done all that we can reasonably be expected to do, God will always step in and carry us the rest of the way.

Since prophecy is a discussion about future events which have not yet happened, it cannot be known with inarguable certainty which belief set represents the correct interpretation. Whether a renowned scholar, pastor, or layman, all anyone can do is carefully consider the verses presented, research what can be researched, then apply Spirit inspired wisdom blended with solid logic to generate a position:

> [18] "Come now, and **let us reason together**," says the LORD...
> *Isaiah 1:18*

God is a champion of intellectual reasoning as a way to determine truth. Notice the word "together" in Isaiah 1:18. Although reasoning can be a solitary experience, God encourages us to discuss a matter between ourselves.

> [17] As **iron sharpens iron**, so a man sharpens the countenance of his friend. *Proverbs 27:17*

Healthy discourse with other Christians challenges our preconceived notions and reveals potential holes in our reasoning. Without open discussion of scripture with others, there is a limit to how far our own intellectual abilities can take us. Discussions also cannot be moderated by socially defined lines of political correctness. Truth does not recognize political correctness. Whether the ideas presented are popular or not, everyone must be free to express all concepts as long as they are spoken in love and based in scripture.

Formal education is not essential to know truth. The Holy Spirit is the ultimate teacher and provider of truth:

> [26] But the Helper, **the Holy Spirit**, whom the Father will send in My name, He **will teach you all things**, and bring to your remembrance all things that I said to you. *John 14:26*

Notice that John 14:26 says the Holy Spirit will teach us "all" things which includes prophetic interpretation. Listen carefully to the prompting of the Holy Spirit within you to discern God's word and determine the truth of the matter. After careful study, research, debate and consideration, commit to a position and follow what you believe to be right:

> [5] One person esteems one day above another; another esteems every day alike. Let each **be fully convinced in his own mind**. *Romans 14:5*

One position that God abhors is that of a fence sitter. Decide a matter any way that you believe to be true, but make a firm decision one way or the other:

> [15] "I know your works, that you are neither cold nor hot. I could wish you were cold or hot. [16] So then, **because you are lukewarm**, and neither cold nor hot, I will **vomit you out of My mouth**. *Revelation 13:15-16*

Revelation 13:15-16 makes it clear that God would rather have us believe something that is wrong rather than fail to take a position on something at all. It makes sense that God would rather have us believe something errantly than to refuse to take a position. If we truly believe something, yet are wrong about it, God can then work to correct the places where our reasoning and understanding go askew. If we choose to remain in a place of ignorance or apathy, not advocating for any specific position, there is no starting point for God to begin His work of correction within us.

Once each person is "fully convinced in his own mind", it is important not to judge others who may have reached a different conclusion. Only God can judge:

> [12] ...**Who are you to judge** another? *James 4:12*

God's judgments are based on the intent of the heart. Being right is not as imperative as the intent to be righteous. From God's divine perspective, only He knows what a person thinks or intends in the deepest regions of their heart:

> [7] ...For the LORD does not see as man sees; for man looks at the outward appearance, but **the LORD looks at the heart**. *1 Samuel 16:7*

Regardless how we interpret prophetic events, the most important thing any of us can do is to be in right standing with God. Life is but a vapor and then it is gone, but eternity lasts forever. Just as heaven endures through the ages, so, too, does hell. Hell is not merely a fictitious metaphor or a symbol for an esoteric concept. Hell is just as real as heaven is real. It is a place where fire that never goes out torments those who are there day and night for eternity:

> [10] And they will be **tormented** (in hell) **day and night forever** and ever. *Revelation 20:10*

A reference to a worm that never dies indicates an additional form of torment for those unfortunate enough to end up in hell:

> [43] ... to go to **hell**, into the fire that shall never be quenched—
> [44] where their **worm does not die** and the **fire is not quenched**. *Mark 9:43*

Eternity is a long time to exist in a place as miserable as hell. Sin never pays. If there is sin in your life, ask God for forgiveness and then change the path you are on so that you are sinning no more. Forgiveness is God's glory to grant us, but first we have to repent and change our ways.

ARE WE THE TERMINAL GENERATION?

There is a special blessing for those who consider prophecy carefully:

> [3] **Blessed is he who reads and those who hear the words of this prophecy**, and keep those things which are written in it; for the time is near. *Revelation 1:3*

Until God reveals the exact order of events as they happen, prophetic debates will continue with different people arguing for different theories. Romans 14:5 sums it up best when it advises each of us to be convinced in our own minds. Whatever position you take on the various issues surrounding prophetic events, be convinced within yourself that you are discerning the word of God correctly and continue discussing prophecy with other believers, always watching for Jesus' return:

> [28] Now when these things begin to happen, **look up** and lift up your heads, because **your redemption draws near**. *Luke 21:28*

So, are we the Terminal Generation? Will we see the return of Christ in our lifetime? Is the rapture to be part of our experience or is it yet for another generation? Is it a coincidence that those now dubbed the "Millennial Generation" may see the Millennial Reign? In due time, prophecy will turn into history, all will be revealed, and the only thing that will truly matter is the eternal life we will spend with God and Jesus. Until then, do everything you can to be righteous in God's eyes, continue watching as prophetic events unfold in our world and be blessed!

Talk It Out

FINAL QUESTION 1: What order do you believe end time events will occur? A proposed timeline of end time events is provided on pages 465-466. Do you agree with the order of events given in the timeline? Discuss why you agree or disagree with this proposed outline of events. Be sure to back up your position with scripture-based reasoning. Refer back to the weekly lessons if necessary. If you disagree with the order of events, use the Elements of the Timeline list on pages 467-468 to shuffle the numbers and reorganize the events the way you believe they will occur.

FINAL QUESTION 2: What did you learn as you advanced through this study? Did your beliefs change in any area? What did you find most interesting as you progressed through the course of this study?

Ideas for the Week:

- ✓ Go back through this book and re-read the weekly lessons to refresh your memory and help you pull everything together.
- ✓ Practice doing Hebrew and Greek word studies using the instructions given on page 486.
- ✓ Sign up to be on the email list to be notified when Independence *in the Suburbs* by Christine Tate is released at www.christinetate.webstarts.com. *Independence in the Suburbs* is a companion manual to this book which gives practical advice about how to be self-sufficient while still living in a suburban environment. It is a great way for anyone expecting to live through the Tribulation to take concrete steps towards self-sufficiency while living within the restrictions imposed by suburban life. The anticipated release date for *Independence in the Suburbs* is late 2020.
- ✓ As headlines break, track how our world is progressing towards Jesus' return on God's prophetic timeline by updating the chart on pages 479-480 in the Bonus Material section as they happen.

Closing Prayer

NOTE: Add names and individual personal prayer requests to the space provided below before closing in prayer.

Lord, we thank You for our time together today to grow deeper in our walk with You and fellowship with each other. As we close today, we lift up: _____

_____

_____

_____

_____

Father, we know that Your definition of time is so very different than our definition of time. What seems so far in the future to us is but a breath away for You. You know the right timing for everything that happens to us. Let everything in our lives be done in Your perfect timing as You see fit to move our lives forward. Guide us in truth that we may always correctly discern Your word and Your ways. In Jesus' name we pray, Amen.

ARE WE THE TERMINAL GENERATION?

Daniel's 70ᵗʰ Week and Beyond

1. Spread of the gospel to all the world is completed.
2. Restrainer (God's Word) is removed prompting a Falling Away (Decline of the Church)

Tribulation Begins (God's Wrath Stage I)

First Half of the Tribulation

3. God's people are sealed
4. War of Ezekiel
5. Damascus Destroyed
6. Antichrist brokers a Peace Agreement with Israel
7. Identity of the Antichrist revealed by brokering peace treaty
8. New World Order/One World Religion begins
9. Mark of the Beast and control of commerce
10. Two witnesses arrive
11. Two witnesses testify and confirm the location for the third temple
12. Seals, trumpets and bowl plagues begin (Four Horsemen)
13. Two witnesses prophesy and perform signs.
14. Construction of Third Temple completed and animal sacrifices resume

Tribulation Midpoint (3 ½ Year point)

Second Half of the Tribulation

15. God's wrath intensifies against unbelievers as plagues continue
16. War in Heaven
17. Satan and demons cast down to earth
18. Antichrist healed from deadly wound in apparent resurrection
19. Satan and Antichrist intensify persecution of Christians
20. Jerusalem attacked and armies of Antichrist take over Jerusalem
21. Two witnesses are killed and not buried
22. Israeli remnant flees to Petra
23. Temple sacrifices stopped
24. Abomination of Desolation
25. Satan focuses primarily on persecution of Christians

Tribulation Ends (7-year point)

Day of the Lord (God's Wrath Stage II)	26. Christ returns in the air on Day of the Lord
	Phase I: *Saving that which needs saved*
	  27. Dead in Christ raised from the dead and gathered to be with Jesus
	  28. Two Witnesses gathered (resurrected and ascend to heaven)
	  29. Rapture of living believers gathered to be with Jesus in translated bodies
	  30. Elect gathered
	  31. Israeli remnant gathered
	Phase II: *Destruction*
	  32. Jesus stops the Battle of Armageddon
	  33. Antichrist and False Prophet are captured
	  34. Jesus sets foot on earth
	  35. Judgment and sentencing of the Antichrist, False Prophet and nations
	  36. Mystery Babylon judged and destroyed
	Phase III: *Victory and Celebration*
	  37. Marriage Supper of the Lamb
	  38. Kingdom delivered to God
	  39. Church Age Ends

Millennial Reign (1000) Years)	40. Jesus Rules and Reigns with Believers for 1000 years in the Millennial Reign 41. Satan sentenced to 1000 years in bottomless pit 42. Earth Renovated 43. Earth inhabited again with Jesus living in Jerusalem 44. Satan paroled 45. Satan mounts final rebellion (2nd War of Gog and Magog) 46. Satan and his angels thrown into lake of fire 47. Resurrection of the wicked 48. Judgment of the wicked 49. Wicked thrown into Lake of Fire
Day of God	49. Old Earth Destroyed 50. New Heaven, Earth and Jerusalem are created 51. Marriage Ceremony of the Lamb 52. Reward crowns handed out 53. New Covenant established 54. Eternity with God and Jesus together

ARE WE THE TERMINAL GENERATION?

ELEMENTS OF THE TIMELINE

1.	Spread of the gospel to all the world is completed
2.	Restrainer (God's Word) is removed prompting a Falling Away (Decline of the Church)
3.	God's people are sealed
4.	War of Ezekiel
5.	Damascus Destroyed
6.	Antichrist brokers a Peace Agreement with Israel
7.	Identity of the Antichrist revealed by brokering peace treaty
8.	New World Order/One World Religion begins
9.	Mark of the Beast and control of commerce
10.	Two witnesses arrive
11.	Two witnesses testify and confirm the location for the third temple
12.	Seals, trumpets and bowl plagues begin (Four Horsemen)
13.	Two witnesses prophesy and perform signs
14.	Construction of Third Temple completed and animal sacrifices resume
15.	God's wrath intensifies against unbelievers as plagues continue
16.	War in Heaven
17.	Satan and demons cast down to earth
18.	Antichrist healed from deadly wound in apparent resurrection
19.	Satan and Antichrist intensify persecution of Christians
20.	Jerusalem attacked and armies of Antichrist take over Jerusalem
21.	Two witnesses are killed and not buried.
22.	Israeli remnant flees to Petra
23.	Temple sacrifices stopped
24.	Abomination of Desolation
25.	Satan focuses primarily on persecution of Christians
26.	Christ returns in the air on Day of the Lord
27.	Dead in Christ raised from the dead and gathered to be with Jesus
28.	Two Witnesses gathered (resurrected and ascend to heaven)
29.	Rapture of living believers gathered to be with Jesus in translated bodies
30.	Elect gathered
31.	Israeli remnant gathered
32.	Jesus stops the Battle of Armageddon

	33. Antichrist and False Prophet are captured
	34. Jesus sets foot on earth
	35. Judgment and sentencing of the Antichrist, False Prophet and nations
	36. Mystery Babylon judged and destroyed
	37. Marriage Supper of the Lamb
	38. Kingdom delivered to God
	39. Church Age Ends
	40. Jesus Rules and Reigns with Believers for 1000 years in the Millennial Reign
	41. Satan sentenced to 1000 years in bottomless pit
	42. Earth Renovated
	43. Earth inhabited again with Jesus living in Jerusalem
	44. Satan paroled
	45. Satan mounts final rebellion (2nd War of Gog and Magog)
	46. Satan and his angels thrown into lake of fire
	47. Resurrection of the wicked
	48. Judgment of the wicked
	49. Old Earth Destroyed
	50. New Heaven, New Earth and New Jerusalem are created
	51. Marriage Ceremony of the Lamb
	52. Reward crowns handed out
	53. New Covenant established
	54. Eternity with God and Jesus together

"While I have no problem with the church adapting to the culture, we must ensure that we remain painstakingly true to the Gospel of Jesus Christ and that we remain obedient servants to His truths."

— Dr. Jerry Falwell

SUPPORTING SCRIPTURES

KNOWLEDGE

¹⁸ "Come now, and let us reason together," says the LORD… *Isaiah 1:18*

²⁶ But the Helper, the Holy Spirit, whom the Father will send in My name, He will teach you all things, and bring to your remembrance all things that I said to you. *John 14:26*

¹¹ For what man knows the things of a man except the spirit of the man which is in him? Even so no one knows the things of God except the Spirit of God. *1 Corinthians 2:11*

¹⁷ As iron sharpens iron, so a man sharpens the countenance of his friend. *Proverbs 27:17*

⁵ One person esteems one day above another; another esteems every day alike. Let each be fully convinced in his own mind. *Romans 14:5*

¹⁵ I know your works, that you are neither cold nor hot. I could wish you were cold or hot. ¹⁶ So then, because you are lukewarm, and neither cold nor hot, I will vomit you out of My mouth. *Revelation 13:15-16*

³⁰ He who is not with Me is against Me, and he who does not gather with Me scatters abroad. *Matthew 12:30*

⁶ I planted, Apollos watered, but God gave the increase. *1 Corinthians 3:6*

²⁸ Now when these things begin to happen, look up and lift up your heads, because your redemption draws near. *Luke 21:28*

³ Blessed is he who reads and those who hear the words of this prophecy, and keep those things which are written in it; for the time is near. *Revelation 1:3*

INTENT

¹² …Who are you to judge another? *James 4:12*

⁸ So God, who knows the heart… *Acts 15:8*

⁷ …For the LORD does not see as man sees; for man looks at the outward appearance, but the LORD looks at the heart. *1 Samuel 16:7*

⁵ Then the LORD saw that the wickedness of man was great in the earth, and that every intent of the thoughts of his heart was only evil continually. *Genesis 6:5*

[19] As in water face reflects face, so a man's heart reveals the man. *Proverbs 27:19*

HELL
[10] And they will be tormented (in hell) day and night forever and ever. *Revelation 20:10*

[43] ... to go to hell, into the fire that shall never be quenched— [44] where their worm does not die and the fire is not quenched. *Mark 9:43*

BEGINNING OF THE TRIBULATION
[14] And this gospel of the kingdom will be preached in all the world as a witness to all the nations, and then the end will come. *Matthew 24:14*

[8] All these are the beginning of sorrows. *Matthew 24:8*

[3] ...for that Day will not come unless the falling away comes first, and the man of sin is revealed... *2 Thessalonians 2:3*

[8] And then the lawless one will be revealed... *2 Thessalonians 2:8*

PEACE TREATY
[27] Then he (the Antichrist) shall confirm a covenant with many for one week... *Daniel 9:27*

NEW WORLD ORDER / ONE WORLD RELIGION
[4] So they worshiped the dragon (Satan) who gave authority to the beast; and they worshiped the beast (the Antichrist)... *Revelation 13:4*

[12] "The ten horns which you saw are ten kings who have received no kingdom as yet, but they receive authority for one hour as kings with the beast. [13] These are of one mind, and they will give their power and authority to the beast. *Revelation 17:12-13*

WAR OF EZEKIEL
[1] Now the word of the LORD came to me, saying, [2] "Son of man, set your face against Gog, of the land of Magog, the prince of Rosh, Meshech, and Tubal, and prophesy against him, [3] and say, 'Thus says the Lord GOD: "Behold, I am against you, O Gog, the prince of Rosh, Meshech, and Tubal. [4] I will turn you around, put hooks into your jaws, and lead you out, with all your army, horses, and horsemen, all splendidly clothed, a great company with bucklers and shields, all of them handling swords. [5] Persia, Ethiopia, and Libya are with them, all of them with shield and helmet; [6] Gomer and all its troops; the house of Togarmah from the far north and all its troops—many people are with you. *Ezekiel 38:1-6*

TWO WITNESSES

³ And I will give power to my two witnesses, and they will prophesy one thousand two hundred and sixty days, clothed in sackcloth...⁷ When they finish their testimony, the beast that ascends out of the bottomless pit will make war against them, overcome them, and kill them... ¹¹ Now after the three-and-a-half days the breath of life from God entered them, and they stood on their feet, and great fear fell on those who saw them. *Revelation 11:3, 7 and 11*

GOD'S PEOPLE SEALED

² Then I saw another angel...³ saying, "Do not harm the earth, the sea, or the trees till we have sealed the servants of our God on their foreheads." *Revelation 7:2-3*

⁴ And the LORD said to him, "Go through the midst of the city, through the midst of Jerusalem, and put a mark on the foreheads of the men who sigh and cry over all the abominations that are done within it." ⁵ To the others He said in my hearing, "Go after him through the city and kill; do not let your eye spare, nor have any pity. ⁶ Utterly slay old and young men, maidens and little children and women; but do not come near anyone on whom is the mark; and begin at My sanctuary." So, they began with the elders who were before the temple. *Ezekiel 9:4-6*

PLAGUES

² And I looked, and behold, a white horse. He who sat on it had a bow; and a crown was given to him, and he went out conquering and to conquer. ³ When He opened the second seal, I heard the second living creature saying, "Come and see." ⁴ Another horse, fiery red, went out. And it was granted to the one who sat on it to take peace from the earth, and that people should kill one another; and there was given to him a great sword. ⁵ When He opened the third seal, I heard the third living creature say, "Come and see." So, I looked, and behold, a black horse, and he who sat on it had a pair of scales in his hand. ⁶ And I heard a voice in the midst of the four living creatures saying, "A quart of wheat for a denarius, and three quarts of barley for a denarius; and do not harm the oil and the wine." ⁷ When He opened the fourth seal, I heard the voice of the fourth living creature saying, "Come and see." ⁸ So I looked, and behold, a pale horse. And the name of him who sat on it was Death, and Hades followed with him. And power was given to them over a fourth of the earth, to kill with sword, with hunger, with death, and by the beasts of the earth. *Revelation 6:2-8*

WAR IN HEAVEN

¹At that time Michael shall stand up, the great prince who stands watch over the sons of your people; and there shall be a time of trouble, such as never was since there was a nation... *Daniel 12:1*

⁷ And war broke out in heaven: Michael and his angels fought with the dragon; and the dragon and his angels fought, ⁸ but they did not prevail, nor was a place found for them in heaven any longer. ⁹ So the great dragon was cast out, that serpent of old, called the Devil and Satan, who deceives the whole world; he was cast to the earth, and his angels were cast out with him. *Revelation 12:7-9*

ANTICHRIST RESURRECTED
³ And I saw one of his heads as if it had been mortally wounded, and his deadly wound was healed. And all the world marveled and followed the beast. *Revelation 13:3*

CHRISTIANS PERSECUTED
¹⁷ And the dragon was enraged with the woman, and he went to make war with the rest of her offspring, who keep the commandments of God and have the testimony of Jesus Christ. *Revelation 12:17*

²⁵ He (the Antichrist) shall speak pompous words against the Most High, shall persecute the saints of the Most High, and shall intend to change times and law. Then the saints shall be given into his hand for a time and times and half a time. *Daniel 7:25*

ABOMINATION OF DESOLATION
²⁷ But in the middle of the week He (the Antichrist) shall bring an end to sacrifice and offering. And on the wing of abominations shall be one who makes desolate, even until the consummation, which is determined, is poured out on the desolate." *Daniel 9:27*

...⁴ who opposes and exalts himself (the Antichrist) above all that is called God or that is worshiped, so that he sits as God in the temple of God, showing himself that he is God. *2 Thessalonians 2:4*

¹⁵ Therefore when you see the 'abomination of desolation,' spoken of by Daniel the prophet, standing in the holy place (whoever reads, let him understand), ¹⁶ then let those who are in Judea flee to the mountains. ¹⁷ Let him who is on the housetop not go down to take anything out of his house. ¹⁸ And let him who is in the field not go back to get his clothes. ¹⁹ But woe to those who are pregnant and to those who are nursing babies in those days! ²⁰ And pray that your flight may not be in winter or on the Sabbath. ²¹ For then there will be great tribulation, such as has not been since the beginning of the world until this time, no, nor ever shall be. ²² And unless those days were shortened, no flesh would be saved; but for the elect's sake those days will be shortened. *Matthew 24:15-21*

¹¹ And from the time that the daily sacrifice is taken away, and the abomination of desolation is set up, there shall be one thousand two hundred and ninety days.

¹² Blessed is he who waits, and comes to the one thousand three hundred and thirty-five days. *Daniel 12:11-12*

¹¹ He even exalted himself as high as the Prince of the host; and by him the daily sacrifices were taken away, and the place of His sanctuary was cast down. ¹² Because of transgression, an army was given over to the horn to oppose the daily sacrifices; and he cast truth down to the ground. He did all this and prospered. *Daniel 8:11-12*

²⁰ But when you see Jerusalem surrounded by armies, then know that its desolation is near. ²¹ Then let those who are in Judea flee to the mountains, let those who are in the midst of her depart, and let not those who are in the country enter her. ²² For these are the days of vengeance, that all things which are written may be fulfilled. ²³ But woe to those who are pregnant and to those who are nursing babies in those days! For there will be great distress in the land and wrath upon this people. ²⁴ And they will fall by the edge of the sword, and be led away captive into all nations. And Jerusalem will be trampled by Gentiles until the times of the Gentiles are fulfilled. *Luke 21:20-24*

² But leave out the court which is outside the temple, and do not measure it, for it has been given to the Gentiles. And they will tread the holy city underfoot for forty-two months. *Revelation 11:2-3*

MARK OF THE BEAST
¹⁶ He (the false prophet) causes all, both small and great, rich and poor, free and slave, to receive a mark on their right hand or on their foreheads, ¹⁷ and that no one may buy or sell except one who has the mark or the name of the beast, or the number of his name. ¹;⁸ Here is wisdom. Let him who has understanding calculate the number of the beast, for it is the number of a man: His number is 666. *Revelation 13:16-18*

ARMAGEDDON
¹² Then the sixth angel poured out his bowl on the great river Euphrates, and its water was dried up, so that the way of the kings from the east might be prepared. ¹³ And I saw three unclean spirits like frogs coming out of the mouth of the dragon, out of the mouth of the beast, and out of the mouth of the false prophet. ¹⁴ For they are spirits of demons, performing signs, which go out to the kings of the earth and of the whole world, to gather them to the battle of that great day of God Almighty. ¹⁵ "Behold, I am coming as a thief. Blessed is he who watches, and keeps his garments, lest he walk naked and they see his shame." ¹⁶ And they gathered them together to the place called in Hebrew, Armageddon. *Revelation 16:12-16*

[19] And I saw the beast, the kings of the earth, and their armies, gathered together to make war against Him who sat on the horse and against His army. [20] Then the beast was captured, and with him the false prophet who worked signs in his presence, by which he deceived those who received the mark of the beast and those who worshiped his image. These two were cast alive into the lake of fire burning with brimstone. [21] And the rest were killed with the sword which proceeded from the mouth of Him who sat on the horse. And all the birds were filled with their flesh. *Revelation 19:19-21*

DAY OF THE LORD
[4] And in that day His feet will stand on the Mount of Olives, which faces Jerusalem on the east. *Zechariah 14:4*

[31] And He will send His angels with a great sound of a trumpet, and they will gather together His elect from the four winds, from one end of heaven to the other… *Matthew 24:31*

[12] "I will surely assemble all of you, O Jacob, I will surely gather the remnant of Israel; I will put them together like sheep of the fold*, Like a flock in the midst of their pasture; They shall make a loud noise because of so many people. *Micah 2:12*

[16] For the Lord Himself will descend from heaven with a shout, with the voice of an archangel, and with the trumpet of God. And the dead in Christ will rise first. [17] Then we who are alive and remain shall be caught up together with them in the clouds to meet the Lord in the air. And thus, we shall always be with the Lord." *1 Thessalonians 4:16-17*

JUDGMENT OF THE NATIONS
[1] …in those days…[2] I will also gather all nations, and bring them down to the Valley of Jehoshaphat; and I will enter into judgment with them there on account of My people, My heritage Israel, whom they have scattered among the nations; they have also divided up My land…*Joel 3:1-2*

[31] "A noise will come to the ends of the earth—For the LORD has a controversy with the nations; He will plead His case with all flesh. He will give those who are wicked to the sword," says the LORD." [32] Thus says the LORD of hosts: "Behold, disaster shall go forth from nation to nation, and a great whirlwind shall be raised up from the farthest parts of the earth. [33] And at that day the slain of the LORD shall be from one end of the earth even to the other end of the earth. They shall not be lamented, or gathered, or buried; they shall become refuse on the ground." *Jeremiah 25:31-33*

[26] But the court shall be seated, and they shall take away his (the Antichrist)

dominion, to consume and destroy it forever. ²⁷ Then the kingdom and dominion, and the greatness of the kingdoms under the whole heaven, shall be given to the people, the saints of the Most High. His kingdom is an everlasting kingdom, and all dominions shall serve and obey Him. *Daniel 7:26-27*

MYSTERY BABYLON DESTROYED
² …He (Jesus) has judged the great harlot who corrupted the earth with her fornication; and He has avenged on her the blood of His servants shed by her. *Revelation 19:2*

MARRIAGE AND MARRIAGE SUPPER OF THE LAMB
⁷ Let us be glad and rejoice and give Him glory, for the marriage of the Lamb has come, and His wife has made herself ready. *Revelation 19:7*

⁹ Then one of the seven angels who had the seven bowls filled with the seven last plagues came to me and talked with me, saying, "Come, I will show you the bride, the Lamb's wife." ¹⁰ And he carried me away in the Spirit to a great and high mountain, and showed me the great city, the holy Jerusalem, descending out of heaven from God… *Revelation 21:9-10*

⁶ And in this mountain the LORD of hosts will make for all people a feast of choice pieces, a feast of wines on the lees, of fat things full of marrow, of well-refined wines on the lees. *Isaiah 25:6*

MILLENNIAL REIGN
⁴⁴ And in the days of these kings the God of heaven will set up a kingdom which shall never be destroyed; and the kingdom shall not be left to other people; it shall break in pieces and consume all these kingdoms, and it shall stand forever. *Daniel 2:44*

²⁴ Then comes the end, when He delivers the kingdom to God the Father, when He puts an end to all rule and all authority and power. *1 Corinthians 15:24*

⁵ …This is the first resurrection… ⁶ they shall be priests of God and of Christ, and shall reign with Him a thousand years. *Revelation 20:5-6*

SATAN SENTENCED TO BOTTOMLESS PIT
¹Then I saw an angel coming down from heaven, having the key to the bottomless pit and a great chain in his hand. ² He laid hold of the dragon, that serpent of old, who is the Devil and Satan, and bound him for a thousand years; ³ and he cast him into the bottomless pit, and shut him up, and set a seal on him, so that he should deceive the nations no more till the thousand years were finished. *Revelation 20:1-3*

EARTH HEALED AND INHABITED

⁸ Then he said to me: "This water flows toward the eastern region, goes down into the valley, and enters the sea. When it reaches the sea, its waters are healed. ⁹ And it shall be that every living thing that moves, wherever the rivers go, will live. There will be a very great multitude of fish, because these waters go there; for they will be healed... *Ezekiel 47:8-9*

² In that day the Branch of the LORD shall be beautiful and glorious; and the fruit of the earth shall be excellent and appealing for those of Israel who have escaped. ³ And it shall come to pass that he who is left in Zion and remains in Jerusalem will be called holy—everyone who is recorded among the living in Jerusalem. ⁴ When the Lord has washed away the filth of the daughters of Zion, and purged the blood of Jerusalem from her midst, by the spirit of judgment and by the spirit of burning, ⁵ then the LORD will create above every dwelling place of Mount Zion, and above her assemblies, a cloud and smoke by day and the shining of a flaming fire by night. For over all the glory there will be a covering. ⁶ And there will be a tabernacle for shade in the daytime from the heat, for a place of refuge, and for a shelter from storm and rain. *Isaiah 4:2-5*

SATAN PAROLED, REBELS AND IS CAST INTO LAKE OF FIRE

⁷ Now when the thousand years have expired, Satan will be released from his prison ⁸ and will go out to deceive the nations which are in the four corners of the earth, Gog and Magog, to gather them together to battle, whose number is as the sand of the sea. ⁹ They went up on the breadth of the earth and surrounded the camp of the saints and the beloved city. And fire came down from God out of heaven and devoured them. ¹⁰ The devil, who deceived them, was cast into the lake of fire and brimstone where the beast and the false prophet are. And they will be tormented day and night forever and ever. *Revelation 20:7-10*

RESURRECTION AND JUDGMENT OF THE WICKED

⁵ But the rest of the dead did not live again until the thousand years were finished... *Revelation 20:5*

¹¹ Then I saw a great white throne and Him who sat on it, from whose face the earth and the heaven fled away. And there was found no place for them. ¹² And I saw the dead, small and great, standing before God, and books were opened. And another book was opened, which is the Book of Life. And the dead were judged according to their works, by the things which were written in the books. ¹³ The sea gave up the dead who were in it, and Death and Hades delivered up the dead who were in them. And they were judged, each one according to his works. ¹⁴ Then Death and Hades were cast into the lake of fire. This is the second death. ¹⁵ And anyone not found written in the Book of Life was cast into the lake of fire. *Revelation 20:11-15*

NEW HEAVEN, EARTH AND JERUSALEM
[33] Heaven and earth will pass away... *Luke 21:33*

[17] For behold, I create new heavens and a new earth; and the former shall not be remembered or come to mind. *Isaiah 65:17*

[10] And he carried me away in the Spirit to a great and high mountain, and showed me the great city, the holy Jerusalem, descending out of heaven from God, [11] having the glory of God. *Revelation 21:10*

NEW COVENANT AND BODIES
[13] In that He says, "A new covenant," He has made the first obsolete. Now what is becoming obsolete and growing old is ready to vanish away. *Hebrews 8:10-13*

[49] And as we have borne the image of the man of dust, we shall also bear the image of the heavenly Man. *1 Corinthians 15:49*

REWARDS AND ETERNITY WITH GOD
[12] And behold, I am coming quickly, and My reward is with Me, to give to every one according to his work...[14] Blessed are those who do His commandments, that they may have the right to the tree of life, and may enter through the gates into the city. *Revelation 22:12, 14*

[9] But as it is written: "Eye has not seen, nor ear heard, nor have entered into the heart of man the things which God has prepared for those who love Him." *1 Corinthians 2:9*

NOTES

"Sometimes it's best if we don't know what God has planned for us in the future. It would spoil the surprise!"

— Christine Tate

Bonus Material

CHECKLIST FOR OUR WORLD

As reality catches up to the predictions of prophecy, use the list of events below to check off the boxes as they occur.

- [ ] Spread of the gospel to all the world is completed.
- [ ] Restrainer (God's Word) is removed prompting a Falling Away (Decline of the Church)
- [ ] God's people are sealed
- [ ] War of Ezekiel
- [ ] Damascus Destroyed
- [ ] Antichrist brokers a Peace Agreement with Israel
- [ ] Identity of the Antichrist revealed by brokering peace treaty
- [ ] New World Order/One World Religion begins
- [ ] Mark of the Beast and control of commerce
- [ ] Two witnesses arrive
- [ ] Two witnesses testify and confirm the location for the third temple
- [ ] Seals, trumpets and bowl plagues begin (Four Horsemen)
- [ ] Two witnesses prophesy and perform signs
- [ ] Construction of Third Temple completed and animal sacrifices resume
- [ ] God's wrath intensifies against unbelievers as plagues continue
- [ ] War in Heaven
- [ ] Satan and demons cast down to earth
- [ ] Antichrist healed from deadly wound in apparent resurrection
- [ ] Satan and Antichrist intensify persecution of Christians
- [ ] Jerusalem attacked and armies of Antichrist take over Jerusalem
- [ ] Two witnesses are killed and not buried.
- [ ] Israeli remnant flees to Petra
- [ ] Temple sacrifices stopped
- [ ] Abomination of Desolation
- [ ] Satan focuses primarily on persecution of Christians
- [ ] Christ returns in the air on Day of the Lord

- [ ] Dead in Christ raised from the dead and gathered to be with Jesus
- [ ] Two Witnesses gathered (resurrected and ascend to heaven)
- [ ] Rapture of living believers gathered to be with Jesus in translated bodies
- [ ] Elect gathered
- [ ] Israeli remnant gathered
- [ ] Jesus stops Battle of Armageddon
- [ ] Antichrist and False Prophet are captured
- [ ] Jesus sets foot on earth
- [ ] Judgment and sentencing of the Antichrist, False Prophet and nations
- [ ] Mystery Babylon destroyed
- [ ] Marriage Supper of the lamb
- [ ] Kingdom delivered to God
- [ ] Church Age Ends
- [ ] Jesus Rules and Reigns with Believers for 1000 years in the Millennial Reign
- [ ] Satan sentenced to 1000 years in bottomless pit
- [ ] Earth Renovated
- [ ] Earth inhabited again with Jesus living in Jerusalem
- [ ] Satan paroled
- [ ] Satan mounts final rebellion (2nd War of God and Magog)
- [ ] Satan and his angels thrown into lake of fire
- [ ] Resurrection of the wicked
- [ ] Judgment of the wicked
- [ ] Old Earth Destroyed
- [ ] New Heaven, New Earth and New Jerusalem are created
- [ ] Marriage Ceremony of the Lamb
- [ ] Reward crowns handed out
- [ ] New Covenant established
- [ ] Eternity with God and Jesus together

AUTHOR'S INTERPRETATION OF END TIME EVENTS

The challenge of decoding prophecy has been a passion of mine for almost three decades now. When I first set out to explore what the Bible had to say about the future, it seemed overwhelmingly cryptic. With tenacity and perseverance through the years, little by little, God helped me piece together what is today my interpretation of what I believe scripture has to say about the return of Christ and the future beyond. This book is the culmination of those many years of study. What follows is my theory about how events might unfold.

I believe we are the Terminal Generation and are in the final countdown to the beginning of the Tribulation. Our world becomes more violent and less godly with each passing day. Thanks to technology, we are closer than ever to the fulfillment of the gospel going out to the whole world. As the final call to repentance is being issued, the Restrainer, also known as the word of God, is beginning to be removed. With older, more God-fearing generations passing away, we are left with an increasingly atheistic or agnostic society at best. Churches across the country are struggling to survive due to declining attendance as older generations pass away and new generations fail to replace them. In many congregations, the youth are conspicuously absent or dishearteningly diminished. Without the younger generation in the churches, youth programs are falling by the wayside in many houses of worship. As a military family who has lived in many places and visited a vast number of churches across America, I can attest to this personally. Outside of church, a societal push to remove Christianity from anything public or governmental is weakening our country and threatening our way of life. Our country is only strong because our foundations are rooted in His kingdom and we have been blessed by God. If we reject God, the blessing will be removed.

Eventually, I believe we will hit the boiling point where God says, "No more!" and the Tribulation will begin with a bang. Literally. Kicking off the beginning of the final, seven-year countdown, I believe we will face nuclear war in the Middle East from the War of Ezekiel. One morning, we'll wake up and the big news story of the day will be that a confederacy of nations from the Arab League attacked Israel with the aim of taking over Israel's oil reserves forcing Israel to defend herself with nuclear weapons. In the process, Israel's response utterly destroys Damascus and renders it uninhabitable. Since it is known that the USA is a mighty nation and Israel's strongest ally, a pre-emptive strike may also be launched against the United States (Mystery Babylon) by Iran (Medes) or allies of Iran rendering us unable to come to her defense. Iran famously calls the United States the "great Satan" and Israel the "little Satan", so it would be no surprise if we were somehow included in their war plans. In all, I believe one-third of the earth will be involved in the nuclear war.

With the USA shattered and unable to do anything except attempt to manage the mayhem within our own borders, the Antichrist is poised to step onto the world scene. A chaotic and broken world demands a solution. With this opening of opportunity at hand, the Antichrist has what he needs to gain political control of the world. Motivated to end the war, Israel allows the Antichrist to successfully broker a peace agreement between her and her Muslim neighbors in the Middle East. A peace deal is signed for seven years between Israel and the Arab League. One special term of the peace agreement is that Israel is allowed to build the third temple on the temple mount. Construction begins immediately and the two witnesses appear, seemingly from out of nowhere, to validate the correct location of the temple. As the temple is built, the witnesses continue to be a source of media amusement prophesying to the world via satellite on global television.

Meanwhile, the aftermath of the nuclear war cannot be contained to just the Middle East or the United States. Fear grips the globe. Violence erupts as the earth is in chaos. People riot, loot and kill each other for the smallest of items. With the globe in various stages of destruction around the world and countries unable to function, the Antichrist steps in and reorganizes the world into ten world regions. Incidentally, I believe it is a possibility that Donald Trump may be our last traditional US President. His successor, potentially our first female President, might be the leader who reorganizes our country into one region of the global government under the leadership of the Antichrist.

Food and resources will be scarce, so under the authority of his new world government, the Antichrist rations the supplies that are available by instituting the mark of the beast economic system. Without the mark, no one can buy or sell anything. Desperate for food, people are willing to do anything just to be fed. Those who do not have the mark do not get fed. The mark of the beast, an RFID implant, causes a sore where it is injected, but people are willing to endure it if it means feeding themselves and their families.

In an effort to control the masses, the Antichrist institutes a new world religion under the guise of uniting humanity for the greater good. Led by the False Prophet, I believe the new world religion will combine elements of both Islam and Christianity with the Antichrist at the center. Recognizing the danger of what is happening, a resistance movement attempts to assassinate the Antichrist. He is shot in the head and comes back to life in an act of demonic possession further cementing his power and authority with the uninformed masses.

Resources continue to dwindle and it becomes harder to feed a hungry global population. Seas are poisoned from the nuclear blasts. Eventually, all marine life is lost. Freshwater sources are unusable to water crops. Out of the one-third of the world that participated in the nuclear war, the soot and ash from the blast blocks out sunlight causing more crop failure. In other parts of the world, the ozone is damaged from radiological drift. In those parts of the globe, the sun scorches men and burns up crops before they can produce their yield. Eventually, upper atmosphere air currents cause the soot and ash to drift around the globe further causing growing conditions to decline. Prices soar as food scarcity increases. As nature dies from the aftereffects of the nuclear war, animals lose their food sources too and begin to roam into cities looking for food. Desperate larger animals attack people and attempt to eat small children. Upper atmosphere currents cause the toxic soot and ash to engulf the world. Air quality disintegrates everywhere and darkness spreads around the globe as the sun is gradually blocked out until it reaches a point of total darkness. Radioactive fallout causes painful injuries to people of varying degrees.

I believe there will be a resistance movement that mounts a sustained attack against the Antichrist's kingdom for five months. Part of their battle plan involves launching a cyberattack against the RFID chips which adds further torment to those who took the mark. Angered by the coordinated attacks from the resistance, three-and-a-half-years after the peace agreement is signed, the Antichrist gathers a confederacy of Arab nations to break the peace treaty and attack Israel. Motivated by hunger, the need for oil and a responsibility to feed those who have pledged their allegiance to the Antichrist, the Arab confederacy all too willingly cooperates with the Antichrist's invasion plan. Israel is a rich source of food of many kinds and has underground oil reserves that can be tapped to fuel the Antichrist's military. The Antichrist and his league take over Jerusalem killing many of the people. A surviving remnant successfully flees to Petra where they are supernaturally sustained for the duration of the Tribulation. During the attack, the Antichrist kills the two witnesses and leaves their bodies to rot in the street. Then, he stops the daily temple sacrifices, places a profane object in the sanctuary, sits down and declares himself to be God. The object, possibly a statue of himself as God, may contain a hidden suitcase nuclear device that can be detonated at any point on the Antichrist's command. In full control of Jerusalem, the Antichrist reaches the peak of his evil nature and no longer pretends to be a man of peace out to help the people.

Spending the next three-and-a-half years persecuting Christians to the full extent of his ability and unable to squelch the resistance movement, the Antichrist arranges his final act of vengeance by mobilizing all ten of his world regions to attack Jerusalem. At that time, Jesus returns to defend Israel and prevents the Antichrist and allied forces from succeeding. Before he begins His destructive assault on the Antichrist and assisting nations, He resurrects the Christian dead including the two witnesses who were left to rot in the street at the mid-Tribulation point. Then, with the assistance of His angels and accompanying Living Creatures, He gathers all of His living, earthly people to safety in a mass rapture including the Israeli remnant at Petra, the Elect, and the Gentiles who have been grafted onto the Israeli tree. With everyone safely in His protective care in the atmosphere above the earth, Jesus destroys the Antichrist and his forces. Capturing the Antichrist and False Prophet alive, Jesus descends to the earth to convene a court and pass judgment on his captives. All are found guilty. For their role in matters, the Antichrist and False Prophet are thrown into the lake of fire. Sentencing is carried out on the nations who colluded with the Antichrist and they are put to death. Mystery Babylon is sentenced for her crimes and is destroyed too. Lastly, Satan is sentenced to one thousand years of house arrest and thrown into the bottomless pit, his regular abode, where he cannot leave.

With the earth now under kingdom control, Jesus notifies God that the kingdom belongs to Him. Thus begins the Millennial Reign. Then, Jesus initiates the engagement phase of the marriage process and throws a feast on the mountains of Israel for His future bride. After throwing the wedding feast, Jesus renovates earth and moves into the rebuilt temple in Jerusalem. For the next one thousand years, Jesus spends His time living amongst His people on earth and making trips to heaven where He builds permanent homes for His people in the New Jerusalem.

During the Millennial Reign on earth, society has a government and structure. Those who are most worthy serve in the temple as priests. Some live around the temple in Jerusalem and function as governors. Others live on farms all over the world where life resembles the old pioneer days. People build their own homes, grow their own food, cook their own meals and raise resurrected children who never had a chance to be a part of a family or grow up in the previous earth. There is no sickness or disability. Lifespans during the Millennial Reign are re-set back to the age of Methuselah. Although people do age, it is an extremely slow process that only results in a mild decline of strength or balance.

Unfortunately, death and sin do still exist during the Millennial Reign. Inhabitants of earth are required to fulfill certain worship practices and obligations, but there are still some people who refuse to obey the law. When they refuse to make the trip to Jerusalem to worship and visit with the Lord, the punishment is drought. As citizens of the Millennial Reign prove themselves disobedient and unworthy to continue on into the new promised land, heaven, they experience death and are added to the numbers of the wicked dead. Only this time, there will be no rapture or resurrection for them until the end of the Millennial Reign when they are raised with the rest of the wicked dead for their final judgment. At the end of the

Millennial Reign, when Satan is paroled, the Devil goes to those sinners still alive who refuse to obey the Lord's commands and convinces them to attack Jerusalem, a request with which they foolishly comply. When they attack Jerusalem, God destroys them with fire and throws the Devil into the lake of fire where he is permanently powerless to ever cause trouble again.

Once Satan and sin have been destroyed forever, God delivers the new heaven, earth and Jerusalem to mankind. From there everyone who has obediently obeyed Jesus during the Millennial Reign is allowed to move on to heaven where the marriage ceremony occurs forever officially making the combined Hebrew and Gentile church the bride of Christ. Sin and death are forever gone. We all then spend eternity with both God and Jesus enjoying the heavens and their delights with them. There is no day or night or heat or cold, the streets are golden and all is well for the rest of eternity.

Is my interpretation correct? Only time will tell as the future becomes the present and God sequentially reveals the mysteries of the ages to us all. Until then, my beloved brothers and sisters in Christ, my sincere hope is that this study provides you with some interesting food for thought and prompts you to do your own analysis of prophetic scriptures as they relate to end time events. May you all have amazingly fascinating discussions as you are led by the Holy Spirit. We are one family in Christ and I'm looking forward to the new adventures we will all experience together in the Millennial Reign and beyond.

                                              Your Sister in Christ,

                                              Christine Tate

STUDY TOOLS

Prophetic symbols

Fig Tree = Israel
Dragon = Satan
First Beast = The Antichrist
Second Beast = The False Prophet
Magog = Central Asia through Northern part of Russia
Medes/Persia = Iran/Iraq/Afghanistan
Bozrah, Ammon, Moab and Edom = Jordan
Cush = Sudan
Rosh = Russia
Babylon = Iraq
Sheba and Dedan = Saudi Arabia
Put = Libya
Tyre = Lebanon
Togarmah = Turkey
Gomer = Eastern Europe
Tarshish/Young Lions of Tarshish = Great Britain, Canada, Australia, New Zealand, South Africa and the United States

Researching Hebrew and Greek Words

Commentaries, seminars and lectures are useful starting points for studying the Bible, but it is always important to read the Bible for yourself, listen to what the Holy Spirit tells you and do your own research to back it up. An easy way to perform your own word studies is to use an online concordance. Follow the instructions below to brush up on your ancient Hebrew and Greek in no time:

1. Strong's Exhaustive Online Concordance can be found at:
https://www.biblestudytools.com/concordances/strongs-exhaustive-concordance/
2. Select either the King James Version or the New American Standard Bible. It must be one or the other.
3. Using the chapter and verse selection chart, choose the chapter and verse for the word you intend to study.
4. Above the scripture text is a tool bar. The last icon on the right is a gear symbol. Click the gear symbol.
5. A pop-up box titled "Scripture Formatting" will appear. Select "Strong's Numbers" in the box. Then click "Close". The box will disappear and the scripture text will turn blue.
6. Click on any blue word within the text for the original translation and related information.

ARE WE THE TERMINAL GENERATION?

Sources

WEEK 1:
1. https://www.biblestudytools.com/lexicons/greek/kjv/chalepos.html
2. https://www.coolsmarty.com/2019/05/12/fact-of-the-day-344/
3. https://www.coolsmarty.com/2019/06/16/fact-of-the-day-379/
4. https://www.huffingtonpost.com/2013/04/01/christ-second-coming-survey_n_2993218.html
5. https://www.shrm.org/about-shrm/press-room/press-releases/Pages/2019-Workplace-Violence-Research-Report.aspx
6. https://domesticviolencestatistics.org/domestic-violence-statistics/
7. https://www.christianpost.com/news/almost-42-million-abortions-performed-in-2018-more-deaths-than-from-cancer-aids-traffic-accidents.html
8. https://www.azquotes.com/author/11775-Alexander_Pope
9. https://www.davidjeremiah.org/magazine/daily-devotional?date=2019-06-20&goto=recommended-reading&tid=email_edevo
10. Feather Quill Pen Image, ID 17351588 © Annatv81, Dreamstime.com
11. Rabbit with Clock Image, ID 110975573 © Tigatelu, Dreamstime.com
12. Light Bulb Image, ID 17648518 © Yael Weiss, Dreamstime.com
13. Dove and Cross Image, Public Domain, https://www.publicdomainpictures.net/en/view-image.php?image=70702&picture=cross-and-dove-symbol
14. Cross and World Image, Public Domain, https://www.publicdomainpictures.net/en/view-image.php?image=74374&picture=christian-cross-clipart
15. Open Book Image, Public Domain, http://www.freestockphotos.biz/stockphoto/14376

WEEK 2:
1. http://www.general-intelligence.com/library/hr.pdf
2. https://www.civicsandcitizenship.edu.au/cce/pl_early_laws,9534.html
3. https://listverse.com/2018/09/14/10-kinky-sexual-practices-of-ancient-babylon/
4. https://www.biblestudytools.com/lexicons/greek/kjv/porne.html
5. https://www.thoughtco.com/christianity-statistics-700533
6. http://ian.macky.net/pat/map/world/world_countries_blue_names.gif
7. http://protocolhistory.webs.com/columbus1492.htm
8. https://www.aoc.gov/capitol-hill/architecture-styles/neoclassical-architecture-

capitol-hill
9. http://www.state.gov/s/srgia/166853.htm
10. https://chrisspivey.org/the-idols-of-america-the-statue-of-liberty/
11. https://www.telegraph.co.uk/travel/destinations/north-america/united-states/new-york/articles/statue-of-liberty-fascinating-facts/
12. https://www.independent.co.uk/life-style/horoscopes-millennials-why-do-so-many-believe-zodiac-star-signs-a7531806.html
13. https://www.josh.org/millennials-bible-3-surprising-insights/
14. https://commonsensehome.com/electromagnetic-pulse-emp/
15. https://www.azquotes.com/author/4399-Albert_Einstein
16. Feather Quill Pen Image, ID 17351588 © Annatv81, Dreamstime.com
17. Eagle with Flag Image, ID 123696176 © Tigatelu, Dreamstime.com
18. Light Bulb Image, ID 17648518 © Yael Weiss, Dreamstime.com
19. Dove and Cross Image, Public Domain, https://www.publicdomainpictures.net/en/view-image.php?image=70702&picture=cross-and-dove-symbol
20. Cross and World Image, Public Domain, https://www.publicdomainpictures.net/en/view-image.php?image=74374&picture=christian-cross-clipart
21. Open Book Image, Public Domain, http://www.freestockphotos.biz/stockphoto/14376

WEEK 3:
1. https://inricristo.org/who-is-inri-cristo/
2. https://www.biblestudytools.com/lexicons/hebrew/kjv/pasha.html
3. https://www.christianpost.com/news/brazilian-inri-cristo-who-claims-to-be-jesus-christ-prepares-for-comedy-theater-show-64224/
4. https://www.biblestudytools.com/lexicons/hebrew/kjv/reem.html
5. https://www.biblestudytools.com/lexicons/hebrew/kjv/rechem.html
6. https://www.azquotes.com/author/781-Pearl_Bailey
7. *New Scofield Reference Edition Bible*. Edited by C.I. Scofield, D.D. Oxford University Press, Inc., 1967.
8. *King James Version Bible*. Broadman & Holman Publishers, 1996.
9. Poster Background Image, Creative Commons Public Domain, http://orig01.deviantart.net/2ab6/f/2014/095/f/3/parchment_blank_by_omegaman91-d7d4eg4.png
10. Feather Quill Pen Image, ID 17351588 © Annatv81, Dreamstime.com
11. Group of Animals Holding Sign Image, ID 55848227 © Tigatelu, Dreamstime.com
12. Light Bulb Image, ID 17648518 © Yael Weiss, Dreamstime.com
13. Dove and Cross Image, Public Domain, https://www.publicdomainpictures.net/en/view-

image.php?image=70702&picture=cross-and-dove-symbol
14. Cross and World Image, Public Domain, https://www.publicdomainpictures.net/en/view-image.php?image=74374&picture=christian-cross-clipart
15. Open Book Image, Public Domain, http://www.freestockphotos.biz/stockphoto/14376

WEEK 4:
1. https://govtrackinsider.com/it-costs-2-to-make-a-penny-and-7-to-make-a-nickel-but-cents-act-could-bring-those-costs-down-aa6aabfc9a8b
2. https://www.biblestudytools.com/lexicons/hebrew/kjv/towphaphah.html
3. https://www.merriam-webster.com/dictionary/phylactery
4. https://www.homeagain.com/what-is-a-microchip.html
5. https://www.creditdonkey.com/tattoo-statistics.html
6. https://en.wikipedia.org/wiki/UV_tattoo
7. https://www.usatoday.com/story/tech/nation-now/2017/07/24/wisconsin-company-install-rice-sized-microchips-employees/503867001/
8. https://www.cnet.com/news/implanted-id-chip-finds-way-into-ers-bars/
9. http://www.nbcnews.com/id/5439055/ns/technology_and_science-tech_and_gadgets/t/microchips-implanted-mexican-officials/#.W-nKt_ZFyUk
10. https://www.cnbc.com/2017/09/13/how-much-americans-at-have-in-their-savings-accounts.html
11. https://www.azquotes.com/author/4992-Henry_Ford
12. Feather Quill Pen Image, ID 17351588 © Annatv81, Dreamstime.com
13. Hand Illustration Image, ID 130416120 © Nina Sitkevich, Dreamstime.com
14. Duck Holding Egg Image, ID 45710019 © Tigatelu, Dreamstime.com
15. Light Bulb Image, ID 17648518 © Yael Weiss, Dreamstime.com
16. Dove and Cross Image, Public Domain, https://www.publicdomainpictures.net/en/view-image.php?image=70702&picture=cross-and-dove-symbol
17. Cross and World Image, Public Domain, https://www.publicdomainpictures.net/en/view-image.php?image=74374&picture=christian-cross-clipart
18. Open Book Image, Public Domain, http://www.freestockphotos.biz/stockphoto/14376
19. Recycling Image, Public Domain, http://1.bp.blogspot.com/--cDFsgYG72s/UUZD9hqpHPI/AAAAAAAAAjE/Di1QA10ud7Q/s1600/natwest.jpg

WEEK 5:
1. https://www.worldvision.org/hunger-news-stories/east-africa-hunger-famine-facts
2. https://www.biblestudytools.com/lexicons/greek/kjv/eirene.html

3. https://top5ofanything.com/list/6fd77eae/Countries-that-Produce-the-most-Food-
4. https://www.worldatlas.com/articles/leading-olive-producing-countries.html
5. https://www.definitions.net/definition/denarius
6. https://www.dol.gov/general/topic/wages/minimumwage
7. https://www.reference.com/food/average-cost-loaf-bread-f32af82c91411d2
8. https://www.epa.gov/pollinator-protection/colony-collapse-disorder
9. https://www.nbc12.com/2019/06/17/virginia-residents-can-get-free-beehives/
10. https://www.ssa.gov/OACT/COLA/AWI.html
11. https://www.myjewishlearning.com/the-nosher/23-recipes-that-use-zaatar-the-israeli-spice-you-need-to-know/
12. https://www.azquotes.com/author/14750-Aiden_Wilson_Tozer
13. Feather Quill Pen Image, ID 17351588 © Annatv81, Dreamstime.com
14. Snail Eating Leaf Image, ID 138406539 © Tigatelu, Dreamstime.com
15. Light Bulb Image, ID 17648518 © Yael Weiss, Dreamstime.com
16. Dove and Cross Image, Public Domain, https://www.publicdomainpictures.net/en/view-image.php?image=70702&picture=cross-and-dove-symbol
17. Cross and World Image, Public Domain, https://www.publicdomainpictures.net/en/view-image.php?image=74374&picture=christian-cross-clipart
18. Open Book Image, Public Domain, http://www.freestockphotos.biz/stockphoto/14376

WEEK 6:
1. https://www.biblestudytools.com/lexicons/greek/kjv/pharmakeia.html
2. https://www.etymonline.com/word/pharmacy
3. https://www.theguardian.com/world/2015/oct/29/china-abandons-one-child-policy
4. https://www.quora.com/Does-China-have-mandatory-military-service
5. http://worldpopulationreview.com/countries/china-population/
6. https://www.coolsmarty.com/2019/05/16/fact-of-the-day-348/
7. https://en.wikipedia.org/wiki/China–Mongolia_relations
8. https://www.britannica.com/place/Mongolia
9. https://www.merriam-webster.com/dictionary/breastplate
10. https://www.worldometers.info/world-population/
11. https://www.azquotes.com/author/13978-Charles_Spurgeon
12. Feather Quill Pen Image, ID 17351588 © Annatv81, Dreamstime.com
13. Handstand Panda Image, ID 34606509 © Tigatelu, Dreamstime.com
14. Light Bulb Image, ID 17648518 © Yael Weiss, Dreamstime.com
15. Dove and Cross Image, Public Domain, https://www.publicdomainpictures.net/en/view-

image.php?image=70702&picture=cross-and-dove-symbol
16. Cross and World Image, Public Domain, https://www.publicdomainpictures.net/en/view-image.php?image=74374&picture=christian-cross-clipart
17. Open Book Image, Public Domain, http://www.freestockphotos.biz/stockphoto/14376
18. Photos of Helicopters, o0o0xmods0o0o at https://morguefile.com/photos/morguefile/2/military%20helicopter/pop
19. Mongolian Soldiers Image, www.shutterstock.com, Image ID 1410641291 by Nomad 1988
20. Map of Mongolia, www.shutterstock.com, Image ID 684819643 by Peter Hermes Furian

WEEK 7:
1. https://www.thoughtco.com/what-is-a-talent-700699
2. https://www.thetrumpet.com/11828-turkey-dries-up-the-euphrates
3. https://sdf-press.com/en/2018/02/turkey-cuts-water-supply-in-the-euphrates-river-to-syria/
4. https://www.britannica.com/topic/Ataturk-Dam
5. https://www.biblestudytools.com/lexicons/greek/kjv/toxon.html
6. https://www.wordnik.com/words/toxon
7. https://www.care2.com/greenliving/10-things-you-didnt-know-came-from-the-ocean.html
8. https://unveilingtheapocalypse.blogspot.com/2012/01/wormwood-chernobyl-and-hrushiv.html
9. http://laromkarnvapen.se/en/consequences-nuclear-weapons/climate-environment/
10. https://www.cdc.gov/nceh/radiation/emergencies/ars.htm?CDC_AA_refVal=https%3A%2F%2Femergency.cdc.gov%2Fradiation%2Fars.asp
11. https://www.merriam-webster.com/dictionary/blasphemy
12. https://www.azquotes.com/author/16182-Zig_Ziglar
13. Feather Quill Pen Image, ID 17351588 © Annatv81, Dreamstime.com
14. Two Bunnies Behind Sign Image, ID 85874611 © Tigatelu, Dreamstime.com
15. Light Bulb Image, ID 17648518 © Yael Weiss, Dreamstime.com
16. Dove and Cross Image, Public Domain, https://www.publicdomainpictures.net/en/view-image.php?image=70702&picture=cross-and-dove-symbol
17. Cross and World Image, Public Domain, https://www.publicdomainpictures.net/en/view-image.php?image=74374&picture=christian-cross-clipart
18. Open Book Image, Public Domain, http://www.freestockphotos.biz/stockphoto/14376

WEEK 8:
1. https://www.thoughtco.com/balfour-declaration-1778163
2. https://www.jpost.com/Israel-News/Study-13-percent-of-Israelis-identify-as-Reform-or-Conservative-569456
3. https://www.biblestudytools.com/lexicons/greek/kjv/genea.html
4. https://en.wikipedia.org/wiki/Agriculture_in_Israel
5. https://www.merriam-webster.com/dictionary/generation
6. https://www.azquotes.com/author/8805-C_S_Lewis
7. Feather Quill Pen Image, ID 17351588 © Annatv81, Dreamstime.com
8. Raccoon Hanging Image, ID 147670011 © Tigatelu, Dreamstime.com
9. Light Bulb Image, ID 17648518 © Yael Weiss, Dreamstime.com
10. Dove and Cross Image, Public Domain, https://www.publicdomainpictures.net/en/view-image.php?image=70702&picture=cross-and-dove-symbol
11. Cross and World Image, Public Domain, https://www.publicdomainpictures.net/en/view-image.php?image=74374&picture=christian-cross-clipart
12. Open Book Image, Public Domain, http://www.freestockphotos.biz/stockphoto/14376

WEEK 9:
1. http://www.aboutmissions.org/statistics.html
2. https://www.biblestudytools.com/lexicons/greek/kjv/elaia.html
3. https://www.organicfacts.net/olives.html
4. https://www.haaretz.com/jewish/.premium-history-of-the-temple-in-jerusalem-1.5256337
5. https://www.gatestoneinstitute.org/1496/mosques-on-sacred-sites-of-defeated-enemies
6. https://www.smithsonianmag.com/travel/keepers-of-the-lost-ark-179998820/
7. https://en.wikipedia.org/wiki/Church_of_Our_Lady_Mary_of_Zion
8. https://www.ancient-code.com/the-mystery-of-the-ark-of-the-covenant/
9. https://www.springfieldspringfield.co.uk/view_episode_scripts.php?tv-show=ancient-aliens&episode=s06e10
10. https://www.myjewishlearning.com/article/hallel/?utm_source=mjl_maropost&utm_campaign=MJL&utm_medium=email&mpweb=1161-11494-265184
11. https://www.chaostrophic.com/10-crazy-theories-ark-covenant/
12. https://www.bible-history.com/interestingfacts/arkofthecovenant/2-thecherubim.html
13. https://www.azquotes.com/author/14530-Mother_Teresa
14. Feather Quill Pen Image, ID 17351588 © Annatv81, Dreamstime.com
15. Lion with Sign Image, ID 45744072 © Tigatelu, Dreamstime.com
16. Light Bulb Image, ID 17648518 © Yael Weiss, Dreamstime.com

17. Dove and Cross Image, Public Domain, https://www.publicdomainpictures.net/en/view-image.php?image=70702&picture=cross-and-dove-symbol
18. Cross and World Image, Public Domain, https://www.publicdomainpictures.net/en/view-image.php?image=74374&picture=christian-cross-clipart
19. Open Book Image, Public Domain, http://www.freestockphotos.biz/stockphoto/14376

WEEK 10:
1. https://www.azquotes.com/quotes/topics/church.html
2. https://www.biblestudytools.com/lexicons/hebrew/kjv/pishteh.html
3. https://www.ehow.com/list_7397295_characteristics-linen-fabric.html
4. https://www.jewishvirtuallibrary.org/the-sanhedrin
5. http://christinprophecy.org/articles/the-rebirth-of-the-sanhedrin/
6. https://www.haaretz.com/1.4808340
7. http://www.khouse.org/articles/1997/15/
8. https://www.gatestoneinstitute.org/1496/mosques-on-sacred-sites-of-defeated-enemies
9. http://www.israelnationalnews.com/Articles/Article.aspx/996
10. https://www.thekingiscoming.com/blog/2018/9/19/red-heifer-born-in-israel
11. https://www.templeinstitute.org/vessels_gallery.htm
12. https://www.nytimes.com/2017/12/06/world/middleeast/trump-jerusalem-israel-capital.html
13. https://www.breakingisraelnews.com/118441/miracle-dedication-altar-third-temple/
14. https://www.breakingisraelnews.com/112628/davids-harp-heralding-third-temple/
15. https://www.breakingisraelnews.com/97947/sanhedrin-prepares-oil-temple-menorah-fulfilling-amos-prophecy-jewish-land/
16. http://www.israelnationalnews.com/News/News.aspx/76624
17. http://www.prophecynewswatch.com/article.cfm?recent_news_id=66
18. https://www.breakingisraelnews.com/64632/third-temple-closer-than-ever-search-begins-eligible-jewish-priests-jewish-world/
19. https://www.breakingisraelnews.com/tag/rebuilding-the-third-temple/
20. http://christinprophecy.org/articles/the-rebirth-of-the-sanhedrin/
21. http://prophecyupdate.blogspot.com/2018/01/rebuilding-third-temple-very-soon-this.html
22. http://www.bible.ca/archeology/bible-archeology-jerusalem-temple-mount-dome-of-rock.htm
23. http://www.gojerusalem.com/article/186/The-Temple-Mount/
24. https://www.azquotes.com/author/1659-Corrie_Ten_Boom

25. Feather Quill Pen Image, ID 17351588 © Annatv81, Dreamstime.com
26. Penguin Sitting on Money Image, ID 76875516 © Bolid2000, Dreamstime.com
27. Light Bulb Image, ID 17648518 © Yael Weiss, Dreamstime.com
28. Dove and Cross Image, Public Domain, https://www.publicdomainpictures.net/en/view-image.php?image=70702&picture=cross-and-dove-symbol
29. Cross and World Image, Public Domain, https://www.publicdomainpictures.net/en/view-image.php?image=74374&picture=christian-cross-clipart
30. Open Book Image, Public Domain, http://www.freestockphotos.biz/stockphoto/14376
31. https://www.breakingisraelnews.com/102784/sanhedrin-temple-movement-issue-silver-half-shekel-images-trump-cyrus/
32. https://www.ou.org/torah/halacha/hashoneh-halachos-2-mishneh-torah/1217-when-the-half-shekel-donation-was-required/
33. https://www.toptruisms.com/quote/53575?token=000wo8537l2ptlq&pk_medium=email&pk_campaign=multiquote

WEEK 11:
1. https://www.biblestudytools.com/lexicons/greek/kjv/martus.html
2. http://www.prophecynewswatch.com/article.cfm?recent_news_id=66#pgcUTdGZbuSfjoME.99
3. https://www.myjewishlearning.com/article/shofar-history-and-tradition/
4. http://biblecharts.org/oldtestament/interestingfactsaboutsolomonstemple.pdf
5. https://www.azquotes.com/author/8880-Abraham_Lincoln
6. Feather Quill Pen Image, ID 17351588 © Annatv81, Dreamstime.com
7. Musical Grasshopper Image, ID 98485868 © Tigatelu, Dreamstime.com
8. Light Bulb Image, ID 17648518 © Yael Weiss, Dreamstime.com
9. Dove and Cross Image, Public Domain, https://www.publicdomainpictures.net/en/view-image.php?image=70702&picture=cross-and-dove-symbol
10. Cross and World Image, Public Domain, https://www.publicdomainpictures.net/en/view-image.php?image=74374&picture=christian-cross-clipart
11. Open Book Image, Public Domain, http://www.freestockphotos.biz/stockphoto/14376

WEEK 12:
1. https://www.military.com/veteran-jobs/career-advice/military-transition/medal-honor-recipients-3-secrets-success.html?spMailingID=3806673&spUserID=Mjk4MDU3NDgwNjUS1&spJobl

D=821211282&spReportId=ODIxMjExMjgyS0
2. https://www.biblestudytools.com/lexicons/hebrew/kjv/shalowm.html
3. https://en.wikipedia.org/wiki/Great_Tribulation
4. https://www.worlddata.info/alliances/arab-league.php
5. https://samuelwhitefield.com/wp-content/uploads/2014/01/When-do-the-Times-of-the-Gentiles-End-Luke-21.pdf
6. http://historylink101.com/2/Rome/roman-farming.htm
7. https://www.preceptaustin.org/tribulation-thlipsis_greek_word_study
8. Burnham, Jim & Chacon, Father Frank. (2007). *Beginning Apologetics 9: How to Answer Muslims.* San Juan Catholic Seminars. (PO Box 5253 Farmington NM 87499-5253. ISBN: 978-1-930084-22-3. Ph: 505-327-5343, CatholicApologetics.com, catholic@catholicapologetics.com)
9. *The Koran: Translated with notes by N.J. Dawood.* Trans. N.J. Dawood. England: Penguin Books, 1997.
10. https://sites.google.com/site/muslimdeception/taqiyya
11. https://www.biblestudytools.com/lexicons/hebrew/kjv/gabar.html
12. https://www.gatestoneinstitute.org/1496/mosques-on-sacred-sites-of-defeated-enemies
13. http://www.jcpa.org/text/ahmadinejad2-words.pdf
14. https://www.algemeiner.com/2018/09/26/report-palestinian-textbooks-claim-entirety-of-israel-as-arab-land-call-jews-sinful-and-liars/
15. https://www.cfr.org/backgrounder/arab-league
16. http://www.prophecynewswatch.com/article.cfm?recent_news_id=471
17. https://www.biblestudytools.com/lexicons/hebrew/kjv/gabar.html
18. https://www.jpost.com/Arab-Israeli-Conflict/Abbas-has-decided-to-sign-peace-deal-with-Israel-490530
https://www.biblestudytools.com/lexicons/hebrew/kjv/beriyth.html
19. https://www.biblestudytools.com/lexicons/hebrew/kjv/azab.html
20. https://www.coolsmarty.com/2019/05/02/fact-of-the-day-334/
21. https://www.azquotes.com/author/5776-Billy_Graham
22. https://www.biblegateway.com/
23. Feather Quill Pen Image, ID 17351588 © Annatv81, Dreamstime.com
24. Dove with Olive Branch Image, ID 138406579 © Tigatelu, Dreamstime.com
25. Talking Dove Image, ID 138406560 © Tigatelu, Dreamstime.com
26. Light Bulb Image, ID 17648518 © Yael Weiss, Dreamstime.com
27. Dove and Cross Image, Public Domain, https://www.publicdomainpictures.net/en/view-image.php?image=70702&picture=cross-and-dove-symbol
28. Cross and World Image, Public Domain, https://www.publicdomainpictures.net/en/view-image.php?image=74374&picture=christian-cross-clipart
29. Open Book Image, Public Domain,

http://www.freestockphotos.biz/stockphoto/14376

WEEK 13:
1. https://www.census.gov/newsroom/pdf/women_workforce_slides.pdf
2. http://2.bp.blogspot.com/_SqhhJb_P3Kk/TKODvOt150I/AAAAAAAAM58/v6RMb1Dv2jc/w1200-h630-p-k-no-nu/marriage+rates.png
3. https://www.biblestudytools.com/lexicons/greek/kjv/exousia.html
4. https://sustainabledevelopment.un.org/post2015/transformingourworld
5. http://mdgs.un.org/unsd/mdg/Resources/Static/Products/Progress2015/English2015.pdf
6. http://transcripts.cnn.com/TRANSCRIPTS/0804/25/gb.01.html
7. https://www.cement.org/cement-concrete-applications/how-cement-is-made
8. https://dailycaller.com/2014/01/15/un-climate-chief-communism-is-best-to-fight-global-warming/
9. http://frankbroughton.us/blog/archives/121
10. https://sustainabledevelopment.un.org/outcomedocuments/agenda21
11. https://www.coolsmarty.com/2019/06/05/fact-of-the-day-368/
12. https://www.azquotes.com/author/12140-Ronald_Reagan
13. Regional Map, United Nations website for Millennium Development Goals Indicator. *The Millennium Development Goals Report 2015,* page 71, http://mdgs.un.org/unsd/mdg/Resources/Static/Products/Progress2015/English2015.pdf.
14. Feather Quill Pen Image, ID 17351588 © Annatv81, Dreamstime.com
15. Pickle Image, ID 51245352 © Tigatelu, Dreamstime.com
16. Light Bulb Image, ID 17648518 © Yael Weiss, Dreamstime.com
17. Dove and Cross Image, Public Domain, https://www.publicdomainpictures.net/en/view-image.php?image=70702&picture=cross-and-dove-symbol
18. Cross and World Image, Public Domain, https://www.publicdomainpictures.net/en/view-image.php?image=74374&picture=christian-cross-clipart
19. Open Book Image, Public Domain, http://www.freestockphotos.biz/stockphoto/14376

WEEK 14:
1. https://www.azquotes.com/author/157-Mahmoud_Ahmadinejad
2. https://www.biblestudytools.com/lexicons/hebrew/kjv/behalah.html
3. http://www.israelnationalnews.com/Articles/Article.aspx/16556
4. http://www.acommonword.com/the-acw-document/
5. http://faith.yale.edu/common-word/common-word-christian-response
6. http://news.yahoo.com/father-son-ousted-trinity-bible-translations-003300519.html

7. https://www.thereligionofpeace.com/pages/quran/violence.aspx
8. https://www.answering-islam.org/Books/Hughes/j.htm
9. https://www.washingtontimes.com/news/2016/jun/13/ugly-truth-about-sharia-law/
10. https://www.thereligionofpeace.com/pages/quran/homosexuality.aspx
11. http://www.christiancrafters.com/games_icebreakers.html
12. https://en.wikipedia.org/wiki/Twelver#Calendar
13. https://myblessedhope.com/tag/twelvers/
14. https://liberapedia.wikia.org/wiki/Problems_with_Muslim_Sharia_Law
15. https://stepfeed.com/10-fascinating-facts-about-the-middle-east-you-didn-t-know-1597
16. https://en.wikipedia.org/wiki/Great_Satan
17. https://www.acommonword.com/the-acw-document/
18. https://www.vaticannews.va/en/pope/news/2019-01/pope-francis-morocco-visit-logo-hope-interreligious-dialogue.html
19. http://www.joelrosenberg.com/files/2013/09/STUDY-Damascus-prophecies-R.pdf
20. https://www.pbs.org/newshour/politics/middle_east-july-dec06-syria-terror_09-14
21. https://www.christianitytoday.com/news/2018/march/bill-hybels-misconduct-willow-creek-john-nancy-ortberg.html
22. http://www.billionbibles.org/sharia/sharia-law.html.
23. https://www.oikoumene.org/en/resources/documents/other-ecumenical-bodies/kairos-palestine-document
24. https://en.wikipedia.org/wiki/Robert_Schuller
25. https://en.wikipedia.org/wiki/Bill_Hybels
26. https://www.militarytimes.com/flashpoints/2018/02/02/us-says-syria-making-new-chemical-weapons-despite-2013-deal/
27. http://godreports.com/2015/09/how-islam-takes-over-countries/
28. https://www.cnbc.com/2017/04/06/islam-to-become-the-worlds-largest-religion-as-muslim-births-increase.html
29. https://www.coolsmarty.com/?s=boeing+727
30. https://www.azquotes.com/author/37403-Christine_Caine
31. Feather Quill Pen Image, ID 17351588 © Annatv81, Dreamstime.com
32. Bandit Rat Image, ID 136771630 © Tigatelu, Dreamstime.com
33. Light Bulb Image, ID 17648518 © Yael Weiss, Dreamstime.com
34. Dove and Cross Image, Public Domain, https://www.publicdomainpictures.net/en/view-image.php?image=70702&picture=cross-and-dove-symbol
35. Cross and World Image, Public Domain, https://www.publicdomainpictures.net/en/view-image.php?image=74374&picture=christian-cross-clipart

36. Open Book Image, Public Domain, http://www.freestockphotos.biz/stockphoto/14376
37. Coffee Cup Image, Public Domain, Creative Commons, https://upload.wikimedia.org/wikipedia/commons/thumb/1/1a/Applications-ristretto.svg/120px-Applications-ristretto.svg.png
38. Saw Image, Public Domain, https://www.publicdomainpictures.net/pictures/80000/nahled/hand-saw-clipart.jpg
39. Rug Image, Public Domain, https://clubpenguinmemories.com/files/2014/08/212px-ice_rug_icon.png

WEEK 15:
1. http://www.sporcle.com/games/Phonglehorn/SameName
2. http://www.merriam-webster.com/dictionary/allah
3. https://www.pewresearch.org/fact-tank/2017/04/05/christians-remain-worlds-largest-religious-group-but-they-are-declining-in-europe/
4. http://www.billionbibles.org/sharia/allah-moon-god.html
5. https://endtimesprophecyreport.com/2013/06/26/one-world-religion-25-quotes-about-the-coming-nwo-one-world-religion/
6. https://www.azquotes.com/author/37751-Brock_Chisholm
7. https://www.azquotes.com/author/22648-David_Spangler
8. https://www.azquotes.com/author/28927-Peter_Hoagland
9. https://www.azquotes.com/quote/604915
10. https://www.washingtonpost.com/arts-entertainment/2019/01/18/pence-says-criticism-wifes-job-anti-lgbt-christian-school-is-deeply-offensive-us/?utm_term=.09eead2502e2
11. https://nypost.com/2019/01/25/exposing-the-times-anti-christian-bias/
12. https://www.infowars.com/jesus-denied-shoutout-during-valedictorians-graduation-speech/
13. https://www.myjewishlearning.com/article/how-to-treat-holy-jewish-books/?utm_source=mjl_maropost&utm_campaign=MJL&utm_medium=email&mpweb=1161-10970-265184
14. https://www.azquotes.com/author/11166-Joel_Osteen
15. Feather Quill Pen Image, ID 17351588 © Annatv81, Dreamstime.com
16. Reading Rabbits Image, ID 141049901 © Tigatelu, Dreamstime.com
17. Light Bulb Image, ID 17648518 © Yael Weiss, Dreamstime.com
18. Dove and Cross Image, Public Domain, https://www.publicdomainpictures.net/en/view-image.php?image=70702&picture=cross-and-dove-symbol
19. Cross and World Image, Public Domain, https://www.publicdomainpictures.net/en/view-image.php?image=74374&picture=christian-cross-clipart
20. Open Book Image, Public Domain,

ARE WE THE TERMINAL GENERATION?

http://www.freestockphotos.biz/stockphoto/14376

WEEK 16:
1. https://www.azquotes.com/author/8805-C_S_Lewis/tag/war
2. https://www.biblestudytools.com/lexicons/hebrew/kjv/tehowm.html
3. https://www.thepropheticyears.com/wordpress/the-gogmagog-war-of-ezekiel-and-armageddon-are-different-wars.html
4. https://bibleprophecyfortoday.com/2015/05/15/is-this-sheba-dedan-and-the-merchants-of-tarsishs-last-dance/
5. https://www.britannica.com/place/Russia/Religion
6. https://www.usgs.gov/faqs/can-nuclear-explosions-cause-earthquakes?qt-news_science_products=0#qt-news_science_products
7. https://www.livescience.com/30970-rock-fractures-amplify-earthquake-shaking.html
8. https://gracethrufaith.com/end-times-prophecy/the-end-times-according-to-isaiah-part-2/
9. http://www.israelnationalnews.com/News/News.aspx/156476
10. https://www.rushlimbaugh.com/daily/2015/10/09/could_oil_in_israel_change_the_middle_east/
11. https://www.myjewishlearning.com/article/the-centrality-of-kvod-ha-met-honoring-the-dead/
12. https://globalnews.ca/news/818947/how-do-you-destroy-chemical-weapons/
13. https://www.forbes.com/sites/jamesconca/2013/04/23/destroying-nuclear-weapons-takes-a-little-moxie/#72d8bbfa1fcc
14. https://www.azquotes.com/author/7392-Thomas_Jefferson
15. Dog Photo, Bushko at https://morguefile.com/photos/morguefile/1/cat/pop
16. Cat Photo, Bryan Hanson at https://morguefile.com/photos/morguefile/2/dog/pop
17. Missile Photo, Kenn W. Kiser a.k.a. "click" at https://morguefile.com/photos/morguefile/1/nuclear%20bomb/pop
18. Arrow Photo, earl53 at https://morguefile.com/photos/morguefile/1/bow%20and%20arrow/pop
19. Map, https://www.zionoil.com/
20. Feather Quill Pen Image, ID 17351588 © Annatv81, Dreamstime.com
21. Skunk Image, ID 67685039 © Tigatelu, Dreamstime.com
22. Light Bulb Image, ID 17648518 © Yael Weiss, Dreamstime.com
23. Dove and Cross Image, Public Domain, https://www.publicdomainpictures.net/en/view-image.php?image=70702&picture=cross-and-dove-symbol
24. Cross and World Image, Public Domain, https://www.publicdomainpictures.net/en/view-image.php?image=74374&picture=christian-cross-clipart

25. Open Book Image, Public Domain, http://www.freestockphotos.biz/stockphoto/14376

WEEK 17:
1. https://www.brainyquote.com/topics/war
2. https://www.biblestudytools.com/lexicons/greek/kjv/antidikos.html
3. https://gracethrufaith.com/ask-a-bible-teacher/why-petra/
4. https://www.jerusalem-insiders-guide.com/weather-in-jerusalem.html
5. http://ldolphin.org/kingdom/ch11.html
6. https://www.bible-knowledge.com/war-in-heaven/
7. https://www.myjewishlearning.com/article/electricity-on-shabbat/
8. https://www.azquotes.com/author/13978-Charles_Spurgeon
9. https://www.azquotes.com/author/4490-Ralph_Waldo_Emerson
10. *Photo of Petra courtesy of mandit1990 at https://morguefile.com/creative/mandit1990/1/all.*
11. Feather Quill Pen Image, ID 17351588 © Annatv81, Dreamstime.com
12. Gopher with Sign Image, ID 100093905 © Tigatelu, Dreamstime.com
13. Light Bulb Image, ID 17648518 © Yael Weiss, Dreamstime.com
14. Dove and Cross Image, Public Domain, https://www.publicdomainpictures.net/en/view-image.php?image=70702&picture=cross-and-dove-symbol
15. Cross and World Image, Public Domain, https://www.publicdomainpictures.net/en/view-image.php?image=74374&picture=christian-cross-clipart
16. Open Book Image, Public Domain, http://www.freestockphotos.biz/stockphoto/14376

WEEK 18:
1. https://www.biblestudytools.com/lexicons/hebrew/kjv/naqam-2.html
2. https://www.livescience.com/64579-doomsday-clock-2019-announcement.html
3. https://www.britannica.com/place/Armageddon
4. https://www.gotquestions.org/Petra.html
5. http://inaweofeverything.blogspot.com/2012/01/fun-calculations-from-bible.html
6. https://www.opendoorsusa.org/
7. https://www.myjewishlearning.com/article/the-israel-defense-forces/?utm_source=mjl_maropost&utm_campaign=MJL&utm_medium=email&mpweb=1161-10659-265184
8. https://straitandnarrowministry.com/2019/06/20/the-sound-of-gods-angels/
9. https://www.biblestudytools.com/lexicons/hebrew/kjv/qadowsh.html
10. https://www.biblestudytools.com/lexicons/greek/kjv/hagios.html

11. https://www.azquotes.com/author/20607-Eleanor_Powell
12. Feather Quill Pen Image, ID 17351588 © Annatv81, Dreamstime.com
13. Bear with Sign Image, ID 45856478 © Tigatelu, Dreamstime.com
14. Light Bulb Image, ID 17648518 © Yael Weiss, Dreamstime.com
15. Dove and Cross Image, Public Domain, https://www.publicdomainpictures.net/en/view-image.php?image=70702&picture=cross-and-dove-symbol
16. Cross and World Image, Public Domain, https://www.publicdomainpictures.net/en/view-image.php?image=74374&picture=christian-cross-clipart
17. Open Book Image, Public Domain, http://www.freestockphotos.biz/stockphoto/14376

WEEK 19:
1. https://www.biblestudytools.com/lexicons/greek/kjv/apostasia.html
2. https://www.gotquestions.org/restrainer.html
3. https://www.merriam-webster.com/dictionary/restrainer
4. http://www.cc.org/blog/god_being_expelled_america
5. https://www.merriam-webster.com/dictionary/apostasy
6. Thom S. Rainer, *The Bridger Generation: America's Second Largest Generation, What They Believe, How to Reach Them* (Nashville, TN: Broadman & Holman Publishers, 1997).
7. https://www.coolsmarty.com/2019/01/21/fact-of-the-day-233/
8. https://www.azquotes.com/author/8914-Art_Linkletter
9. Feather Quill Pen Image, ID 17351588 © Annatv81, Dreamstime.com
10. Elephant Measuring Stick Image, ID 50763427 © Tigatelu, Dreamstime.com
11. Light Bulb Image, ID 17648518 © Yael Weiss, Dreamstime.com
12. Dove and Cross Image, Public Domain, https://www.publicdomainpictures.net/en/view-image.php?image=70702&picture=cross-and-dove-symbol
13. Cross and World Image, Public Domain, https://www.publicdomainpictures.net/en/view-image.php?image=74374&picture=christian-cross-clipart
14. Open Book Image, Public Domain, http://www.freestockphotos.biz/stockphoto/14376

WEEK 20:
1. https://www.biblestudytools.com/lexicons/greek/kjv/egkentrizo.html
2. https://www.gotquestions.org/seventy-weeks.html
3. https://www.christiantoday.com/article/70-million-christians-martyred-faith-since-jesus-walked-earth/38403.htm
4. http://www.solagroup.org/articles/faqs/faq_0027.html

5. https://www.azquotes.com/author/2597-Johnny_Cash
6. Feather Quill Pen Image, ID 17351588 © Annatv81, Dreamstime.com
7. Construction Worker Beaver Image, ID 30567990 © Tigatelu, Dreamstime.com
8. Light Bulb Image, ID 17648518 © Yael Weiss, Dreamstime.com
9. Dove and Cross Image, Public Domain, https://www.publicdomainpictures.net/en/view-image.php?image=70702&picture=cross-and-dove-symbol
10. Cross and World Image, Public Domain, https://www.publicdomainpictures.net/en/view-image.php?image=74374&picture=christian-cross-clipart
11. Open Book Image, Public Domain, http://www.freestockphotos.biz/stockphoto/14376

WEEK 21:
1. https://www.shorthistory.org/ancient-civilizations/ancient-egypt/osiris-the-god-of-egyptian-resurrection/
2. https://www.gordonconwell.edu/ockenga/research/documents/StatusofGlobalChristianity2018.pdf
3. https://www.biblestudytools.com/lexicons/greek/kjv/egeiro.html
4. https://www.biblestudytools.com/lexicons/greek/kjv/allasso.html
5. https://www.discoveryworld.us/science/a-wink-a-blink-and-a-twink/
6. https://www.biblestudytools.com/dictionary/wink/
7. https://www.learnreligions.com/the-apostles-creed-p2-700364
8. http://www.messianicfellowship.50webs.com/wedding.html
9. https://www.azquotes.com/author/17405-R_C_Sproul
10. https://www.azquotes.com/author/7419-David_Jeremiah
11. Feather Quill Pen Image, ID 17351588 © Annatv81, Dreamstime.com
12. Winking Sun Image, ID 98485757 © Tigatelu, Dreamstime.com
13. Light Bulb Image, ID 17648518 © Yael Weiss, Dreamstime.com
14. Dove and Cross Image, Public Domain, https://www.publicdomainpictures.net/en/view-image.php?image=70702&picture=cross-and-dove-symbol
15. Cross and World Image, Public Domain, https://www.publicdomainpictures.net/en/view-image.php?image=74374&picture=christian-cross-clipart
16. Open Book Image, Public Domain, http://www.freestockphotos.biz/stockphoto/14376

WEEK 22:
1. http://discovermagazine.com/2003/feb/featfrogs/
2. https://healthiertalk.com/atrazine-tap-water-low-testosterone/

3. https://www.biblestudytools.com/lexicons/greek/kjv/sphragizo.html
4. http://archive.spurgeon.org/eschat.php#ans-sum
5. https://en.wikipedia.org/wiki/John_Nelson_Darby
6. https://www.theopedia.com/rapture
7. https://www.biblestudytools.com/lexicons/greek/kjv/ek.html
8. https://www.biblestudytools.com/lexicons/hebrew/kjv/malat.html
9. https://www.merriam-webster.com/dictionary/wrath
10. https://www.coolsmarty.com/2019/05/04/fact-of-the-day-336/
11. https://www.azquotes.com/author/440-Maya_Angelou
12. Feather Quill Pen Image, ID 17351588 © Annatv81, Dreamstime.com
13. Cat and Dog Image, ID 61673583 © Tigatelu, Dreamstime.com
14. Light Bulb Image, ID 17648518 © Yael Weiss, Dreamstime.com
15. Dove and Cross Image, Public Domain, https://www.publicdomainpictures.net/en/view-image.php?image=70702&picture=cross-and-dove-symbol
16. Cross and World Image, Public Domain, https://www.publicdomainpictures.net/en/view-image.php?image=74374&picture=christian-cross-clipart
17. Open Book Image, Public Domain, http://www.freestockphotos.biz/stockphoto/14376

WEEK 23:
1. http://prophecy.landmarkbiblebaptist.net/quake-chart_files/quake-chart.html
2. https://www.biblestudytools.com/lexicons/hebrew/kjv/cuwph.html
3. https://www.biblestudytools.com/lexicons/greek/kjv/harpazo.html
4. https://www.beliefnet.com/faiths/why-should-christians-celebrate-the-feast-of-trumpets.aspx
5. https://www.logosapostolic.org/bible_study/RP355-5JesusComesWithSaints.htm
6. https://www.biblestudytools.com/lexicons/greek/kjv/hagios.html
7. https://www.biblestudytools.com/lexicons/hebrew/kjv/qadowsh.html
8. https://www.myjewishlearning.com/article/the-sheva-berakhot/?utm_source=mjl_maropost&utm_campaign=MJL&utm_medium=email&mpweb=1161-11115-265184
9. https://www.azquotes.com/author/11559-Tyler_Perry
10. Feather Quill Pen Image, ID 17351588 © Annatv81, Dreamstime.com
11. Wedding Frogs Image, ID 34605892 © Tigatelu, Dreamstime.com
12. Heart Border Image, ID 83469647 © Tigatelu, Dreamstime.com
13. Light Bulb Image, ID 17648518 © Yael Weiss, Dreamstime.com
14. Dove and Cross Image, Public Domain, https://www.publicdomainpictures.net/en/view-image.php?image=70702&picture=cross-and-dove-symbol

15. Cross and World Image, Public Domain, https://www.publicdomainpictures.net/en/view-image.php?image=74374&picture=christian-cross-clipart
16. Open Book Image, Public Domain, http://www.freestockphotos.biz/stockphoto/14376

WEEK 24:
1. https://www.biblestudytools.com/lexicons/greek/kjv/basileuo.html
2. https://www.atheoryofus.net/christianity-statistics/
3. https://www.pyneshouse.co.uk/history-of-traditional-wedding-vows/
4. https://en.wikipedia.org/wiki/Use_of_Sarum
5. https://rightwordtruth.com/when-will-the-marriage-of-the-lamb-take-place/
6. https://www.amazingfacts.org/media-library/study-guide/e/4981/t/a-colossal-city-in-space
7. http://www.khouse.org/articles/2014/1213
8. https://www.nasa.gov/hrp/bodyinspace
9. https://truthnet.org/Ezekiel/11/Ezekiel-40-Messiah-Millennium-Temple.htm
10. https://www.azquotes.com/author/663-Saint_Augustine
11. Feather Quill Pen Image, ID 17351588 © Annatv81, Dreamstime.com
12. Wolf and Rabbit Image, ID 142663266 © Tigatelu, Dreamstime.com
13. Light Bulb Image, ID 17648518 © Yael Weiss, Dreamstime.com
14. Dove and Cross Image, Public Domain, https://www.publicdomainpictures.net/en/view-image.php?image=70702&picture=cross-and-dove-symbol
15. Cross and World Image, Public Domain, https://www.publicdomainpictures.net/en/view-image.php?image=74374&picture=christian-cross-clipart
16. Open Book Image, Public Domain, http://www.freestockphotos.biz/stockphoto/14376

WEEK 25:
1. https://www.azquotes.com/author/4652-Jerry_Falwell
2. https://www.biblestudytools.com/lexicons/hebrew/kjv/barzel.html
3. https://en.wikipedia.org/wiki/Iron
4. https://www.chemicool.com/elements/iron.html
5. https://www.lookchem.com/Periodic-Table/Iron/
6. https://isaac-newton.org/statement-on-the-date-2060/
7. Feather Quill Pen Image, ID 17351588 © Annatv81, Dreamstime.com
8. Thinking Monkey Image, ID 35167196 © Anna Velichkovsky, Dreamstime.com
9. Light Bulb Image, ID 17648518 © Yael Weiss, Dreamstime.com
10. Dove and Cross Image, Public Domain,

https://www.publicdomainpictures.net/en/view-image.php?image=70702&picture=cross-and-dove-symbol

11. Cross and World Image, Public Domain, https://www.publicdomainpictures.net/en/view-image.php?image=74374&picture=christian-cross-clipart

12. Open Book Image, Public Domain, http://www.freestockphotos.biz/stockphoto/14376

Made in the USA
Monee, IL
26 February 2023